Praise
from a
Future Generation

*The Warren Commission's Hearings Before the President's
Commission on the Assassination of President Kennedy.*

Praise
from a
Future Generation

The Assassination of
John F. Kennedy
and the
First Generation Critics
of the Warren Report

John Kelin

Foreword by H. C. Nash

Wings Press
San Antonio, Texas
2007

Praise from a Future Generation: The Assassination of John F. Kennedy and the First Generation Critics of the Warren Report © 2007 by Wings Press for John Kelin

Foreword © 2007 by Wings Press for H. C. Nash

Photographs used by permission as indicated.

First Wings Press Edition, 2007

ISBN-10: 0-916727-32-7
ISBN-13: 978-0-916727-32-1
(trade hardcover edition)

Wings Press
627 E. Guenther
San Antonio, Texas 78210
Phone/fax: (210) 271-7805
On-line catalogue and ordering: www.wingspress.com
All Wings Press titles are distributed to the trade by
the Independent Publishers Group
www.ipgbook.com

Library of Congress Cataloging-in-Publication data:

Kelin, John. 1956-
   Praise from a future generation : the assassination of John F. Kennedy and the first gener-
ation critics of the Warren report / John Kelin ; foreword by H.C. Nash. -- First Wings
Press ed.
        p. cm.
   Includes bibliographical references and index.
   ISBN-13: 978-0-916727-32-1 (trade hardcover ed. : alk. paper)
   ISBN-10: 0-916727-32-7 (trade hardcover ed. : alk. paper)
   1. Kennedy, John F. (John Fitzgerald), 1917-1963--Assassination. 2. United States.
Warren Commission. Report of the President's Commission on the Assassination of
President John F. Kennedy. I. Title.

   E842.9.K45 2007
   973.922092--dc22
                                            2006100159

To Cindy, for countless reasons;
And to Marshall and Dana, the best of us both.

And to all of the critics.

Contents

Foreword

H.C. Nash

A people indifferent to the meaning of the historical past is a people devoid of tools for dealing with the present, never mind the future. John Kelin's extensive study of the first generation of Warren Commission critics, a labor of love if ever there was one, offers all its readers this object lesson.

Praise from a Future Generation pays tribute to a small group of tenacious men and women who refused to buckle under to the most subversive lies ever told the American people, but it is not merely a tribute, and it is by no means sentimental. It is a complex narrative of witness and loss that provides more of the underlying meaning of Dallas than William Manchester's blockbuster *The Death of a President* or the conventionally craven historical accounts of academics, for whom the term "conspiracy" is an *a priori* no-no of unspoken consensus.

This is an ambitious and moving account. We are given a synthesis of the issues of evidence, the struggles of the critics to be heard, the obtuseness of the defenders of the Warren Report (most conspicuously the young assistant counsel Arlen Specter of Philadelphia, patriarch of the "single bullet" theory), the chronology of major turning points in the investigative history (most colorfully, Jim Garrison's saga), beautifully telling anecdotes – overall, a mosaic of protest, interaction, conflict, irresolution, and partial redemption more compelling, and more disturbing, than anything else in our national history.

The Warren Commission went out of business in September 1964, but there is no statute of limitation on murder. Even though the assassination of John F. Kennedy was not a federal crime (today it would be), the U.S. government could, by executive order of the president or an act of Congress, reexamine once again "the crime of the century." Suppose that at some point another official reinvestigation of JFK's devastating death were conducted and that those responsible for the conspiratorial events of November 22, 1963, were named. Would the investigative work of Mark Lane, author of *Rush to Judgment*, play a significant role in such proceedings? Very likely. Vincent Salandria, who, with his brother-in-law

Harold Feldman, befriended Marguerite Oswald and began publishing early in 1964? Very likely. Sylvia Meagher, who took it upon herself to index the Warren Commission's twenty-six volumes of supporting material, since the government was too cavalier to do so? Very likely. The work of Harold Weisberg, author of the *Whitewash* series of critical books and another on Lee Harvey Oswald's intelligence connections? Very likely. The work of Ray Marcus concerning photographic evidence of a shooter or shooters on the grassy knoll? Very likely. The work of Shirley Martin, Mary Ferrell, Joachim Joesten, Maggie Field, Penn Jones, Jr., Lillian Castellano, Léo Sauvage, and other researchers chronicled here, whether they published or not? Very likely.

John Kelin has undertaken to chronicle the labors of these alert men and women – most of whom suspected, intuited, knew in their heart of hearts that John Kennedy had been brutally murdered on the streets of Dallas because 1) certain hate-filled individuals had conspired to kill him, and 2) certain powerful people and institutions, some of them secretive and antidemocratic in the broadest sense, would profit from his death. Did they have a great deal to go on in the beginning? Well, they were quite amazed that the authorities in Dallas could have come up with a solitary suspect so very soon, and convict him in a chaotic press conference before he even benefited from the services of an attorney. (He never did so benefit.) They wondered how so much background information could have been developed on such a suspect with such dispatch. Within 48 hours they saw the alleged assassin shot to death in the custody of the Dallas cops by a nightclub owner of dubious reputation. Furthermore, it might be said, many of them were too savvy and skeptical beforehand to trust information handed down by the Dallas cops, the Federal Bureau of Investigation, the Central Intelligence Agency, or any special commission appointed by Lyndon B. Johnson, "the accidental president," who just happened to be . . . a Texan. (Never mind that LBJ was also a fawning, red-blooded supporter of FBI Director J. Edgar Hoover, whose bureau would submit a lone-assassin "preliminary" report to the White House within weeks of the event itself.)

The author has done eloquent justice to these determined patriots. He has traced their steps by way of indefatigable research, providing a cross-referential backdrop of conversational exchanges, letters, magazine articles, films, books, and public events. Character(s) and personality clash and coalesce, align and realign, but the issues that moved these people form the matrix of their acting out. (Imagine the documentary record one might find today had e-mail been at their disposal!)

This work is overdue. Kelin, who spent five years on the research and the writing, has made his own distinguished contribution in repaying the debt of his "future generation" to the Warren Commission's initial critics, and, in the process, to the imperatives of historical justice, the moral "uses of the past."

Who will read this book, and what will they take from it? A whole new generation of researchers, many of them energized for the first time by 9/11 and the Bush cohort's protofascist methods of governance, are consulting newly declassified material in the National Archives, made available by the Assassination Records Review Board (prodded into existence, ironically enough, by Oliver Stone's *JFK*). Until the 1990's it would have been difficult to find formal academic interest in the case, but today there are undergraduate credit courses and graduate seminars on this controversial case in dozens of colleges and universities. Hood College, the University of Massachusetts at Dartmouth, Baylor University, and many other institutions of higher learning have developed invaluable archives on the assassinations of the 1960's. And the Web? Isn't it clear that JFK and 9/11 bloggers are populist forces to be reckoned with in the political culture at large?

All Americans who one way or the other have come to understand the calamitous meaning of John F. Kennedy's political murder will discover new insights in John Kelin's book. Those too young or too complacent to have pondered such meaning previously would do well to venture with deep breathing into the dark waters reflected here.

And let us take this vow, o Americans:
Get those people
who killed John Kennedy
Get them, haul them
away from wherever they are,
away from their ambassadorships,
from their commodities markets
or beet cartels,
or wherever they are
and yank their hematoidal cover stories
and groans of national security
into the harsh & purest light

o women o men
of America
let them see
the searing light

get them! get them! get them!

– Ed Sanders
from "Elegy for John F. Kennedy"

Note: Used by permission of the author. Ed Sander's long poem, "Elegy for John F. Kennedy," was written for the "November 22 Coalition" rally in Boston, Mass., 1975, and was first published in *The Drummer*. It appeared subsequently in Tom Miller's *The Assassination Please Almanac.*

Introduction

The assassination of President John F. Kennedy is my earliest clear memory in life. I was seven years old and in second grade at Columbia Elementary School in Peoria, Illinois. I had been aware that Kennedy was President and enjoyed the fact that we both had the same first name, but the import of his sudden death was lost on me. My parents spent that weekend in front of the TV set, but what I most remember is that on Saturday morning, all of my favorite cartoons were pre-empted.

I had no real sense of Warren Commission criticism until the mid-1970s. For some reason there was a copy of Thomas G. Buchanan's *Who Killed Kennedy?* lying around the house, but I hadn't read it. Then in the fall of 1976 I attended a lecture by Mark Lane on the campus of Eastern Michigan University, where I was a second-year student with an undeclared major. I don't remember Lane's showing the film version of *Rush to Judgment* that night, but he must have at least shown excerpts, because I clearly recall seeing filmed interviews with S.M. Holland, Acquilla Clemons, and other important witnesses. As arresting as those clips were, even more stunning was the Zapruder film. Its graphic depiction of JFK's head exploding was easily the lecture's high point. Using slow motion and freeze frame, Lane made sure that all of us sitting in that hot, poorly ventilated auditorium understood that Kennedy's head and shoulders were slammed backward and to the left, and that Lee Harvey Oswald's alleged shooting position was behind the presidential limousine.

In a way, that lecture was the genesis of this book. I went home and read Buchanan, which was useful in spite of its 1964 publication date. I read Lane's book, and followed developments with the House Select Committee on Assassinations, then just beginning its work. I was impressed when the Committee later concluded there had been a conspiracy. Yet during the 1980s my interest in the case began to wane, as it seemed to me that the Kennedy assassination, while indisputably the result of a criminal conspiracy, was an unsolvable mystery.

Then came the spring and summer of 1991. Oliver Stone's movie *JFK* was in production and not due in theaters until late in the year, but the media frenzy surrounding it was already intense. How could that fail to get my attention? My interest in the case blossomed anew. I revisited Buchanan and Lane and found a larger body of early criticism at the public library near my home in Sunnyvale, California, all the while anticipating the release of Stone's film.

But the point of departure for *Praise from a Future Generation* did not arrive until November 1998, when I happened to meet Vincent J. Salandria at the national conference of the Coalition on Political Assassinations in Dallas. I was there in the self-appointed role of chronicler of what has come to be known as the JFK research community, which I suppose is the descendant of the subjects of this book. The material I gathered was published in *Fair Play*, a web site "e-zine" I had co-founded with a like-minded individual four years earlier.

Vince's reputation preceded him. An attorney in private practice, he had written a series of incisive articles that appeared in small publications in the years immediately after the Warren Commission completed its work. Later he served in an advisory capacity to Jim Garrison in the latter's controversial assassination investigation. I was delighted to meet him that November evening in 1998. We exchanged business cards and Vince graciously gave me a copy of the speech he delivered that night, and permission to put it on the web site.

In the months that followed he and I got to know each other by telephone and e-mail. That spring we collaborated on an anthology of his assassination writings entitled *False Mystery*. Then in late 1999 he astonished me by offering me his assassination-related correspondence. "My wife will just burn it all as soon as I'm dead," he told me, only half-joking. Did I want it? I did, and a week or so later the material arrived on my doorstep in four large boxes.

The contents of those boxes became a window into something that increasingly I found as fascinating as the assassination itself: the lives and work of those who have come to be known as first-generation Warren Commission critics. Like Salandria, these were private citizens who, on their own initiative, began to critically examine the government's case against Lee Harvey Oswald – and find it wanting. Vince had corresponded with everyone who mattered during those early years, and now, without even trying, I was in possession of this remarkable raw material. It took about a month to read it, and even then I only skimmed much of it. But I could see the broad outlines of a story I was very interested in telling. There were gaps in this material – some very significant gaps – but no obstacles that were insurmountable.

And so I spent the next five years performing the necessary research. Gradually I contacted and interviewed all of the surviving critics, and the relatives of some of those who had died. In several cases, these people shared material from their personal archives with me. More than once I was struck by the fact that the spirit of sharing that was evident when they were actively researching the case remained intact, and all these years later was being extended to me.

There is one critic who, in spite of my efforts, is under-represented in this narrative, and that is the late Mary Ferrell. I regret that this is so. I spoke with Mrs. Ferrell by telephone a number of times, but our formal interviews were limited to two meetings in Dallas on two successive evenings, November 17 and 18, 2000.

Compared to some of the other critics there is very little about Mary Ferrell on the public record. She told me that she deliberately kept a low profile in the early years, which, she added, was probably how she escaped the notice of Richard Warren Lewis and Lawrence Schiller in their triple threat, *The Scavengers and Critics of the Warren Report.*

Although Mrs. Ferrell's memory was very sharp and unaided by notes, our interviews were not conducive to thoughtful reflection. Both took place late at night, after long days at the "November in Dallas" conference, held annually by JFK Lancer Productions and Publications. While Mrs. Ferrell recalled her activities over the assassination weekend in some detail, she seemed more interested in discussing Jim Garrison, whose investigation she had been opposed to. She described meeting with Garrison in New Orleans in 1967, and saying at that time, "He's the most charming man I've ever met. But, poor dear, he's let this assassination drive him crazy!"

If, late in life, Mrs. Ferrell was having a change of heart about Garrison, she said nothing about it to me. But this may have been so: in an interview conducted by Garrison biographer Joan Mellen a little over a year after my own, Mrs. Ferrell had a much mellower attitude, allowing that Garrison "was so close."

At the time we met, I had already described to Mrs. Ferrell my objectives in writing about the first-generation Warren Report critics. "I'm inclined to help you all I can with whatever you want," she told me. But it was not to be. After our discussions that weekend, I followed up with a number of phone calls and e-mails, but we never did connect in a meaningful way. This work is the poorer for it. Mary Ferrell died in Dallas on February 20, 2004.

Inevitably, some sections of this book are stronger than others, and while I am confidant in its overall accuracy, some areas are better documented than others. For example, in researching the background of Harold Weisberg, who was 86 when we first spoke, documenting his activities as a younger man was sometimes difficult. At times I felt like Ralph Fielding Snell, the fictitious interviewer of Jack Crabb, protagonist of Thomas Berger's 1964 novel *Little Big Man*. "Snell" informed his readers that, having elicited a fantastic story of the Old West from a wizened centenarian in a nursing home, he agonized over how much of the story was true.

I have never doubted Harold Weisberg's veracity, but as a matter of principle attempted to confirm everything he told me, as indeed I tried to confirm everything else in this book. But this was not always possible. During his days as a magazine writer, for example, Harold told me he was obliged to use a pseudonymous, "non-Jewish" byline on his articles. So when, after much searching, I located one such article in a now-defunct magazine – an article he had previously described to me in considerable detail – I did not have the satisfaction of seeing his name in print. Yet the article I held in my hands matched the description Harold had provided. I have no doubt that the "Jefferson Hale" credited with writing it was in fact Harold Weisberg. But not unlike Ralph Fielding Snell, the lack of absolute confirmation has on occasion nagged at me.

The literature on the Kennedy assassination is vast, and ranges from scholarly analyses to junk scarcely worth the paper that it is printed on. Little, however, has been written about the Warren Commission critics and their work. *Praise from a Future Generation* seeks to fill that void.

I would like to express my deepest gratitude to all of the many people who assisted me in ways large and small over the five years this book was researched and written. Some of these people also granted interviews, and these are cited elsewhere. It is a cliché to apologize in advance for inadvertently omitting someone, but since I fear such an omission, I extend that apology in all sincerity.

My thanks go to Robert Chapman for putting me in touch with Mary Ferrell; to Chris Courtwright for a copy of a document supporting Roger Craig, which Chris discovered in the National Archives; and to Milicent Cranor for encouragement, for obtaining several documents for me in New York, and for reading an early draft. Thanks go to my old chum Bill Dickerson for sharing newspapers from November 1963, which his family had kept for years; to James W. Douglass for reading a draft; to independent filmmaker Gwen Field for feeding me and letting me see her late mother's panoplies; to Immie Feldman for sharing materials; and to Fred Feldman for helping me understand some of his father's attitudes.

My thanks also go to writer Gaeton Fonzi, who supplied me with a transcript of his historic 1966 interview with Arlen Specter; to Floyd Ingram of the *Midlothian Mirror*; to Michael Jones, for a copy of *The Windmill Fighter*; to Paul Krassner; to Joseph Lobenthal, who shared his private papers from his New School course; to Raymond Marcus, who shared material with me even as much of it was being transferred to a permanent archive; to Tony Marzani, for answering so many questions and giving me a copy of his late father's film *Deadline for Action* and a number of books, including the European edition of *Who Killed Kennedy?*; to Ivan Meek, who read an early draft; to Dr. Gerald McKnight for feeding and encouraging me, and providing me with a copy of Harold Weisberg's "Senator Russell Dissents;" and to Dr. Joan Mellen, author of the Jim Garrison biography *A Farewell to Justice* and many other books, for encouragement when I really needed it – especially during the period that this project lacked focus.

H.C. Nash read and critiqued drafts, early and late; in the 1970s he wrote what turned out to be an indispensable Penn Jones biography called *Citizen's Arrest*, probably the first such book on one of the critics. Clay Ogilvie provided me with a copy of Harold Weisberg's testimony before the New Orleans Grand Jury and helped me navigate portions of the Weisberg archive, which he has been organizing and digitizing for a number of years. Jan Samet O'Leary, Director of the Beneficial-Hodson Library at Hood College, was unfailing in helping me obtain documents from Hood's Sylvia Meagher archive. My thanks also go to Joe Martin of Seattle, and to Steven M. Martin of Colorado, who shared important memories and impressed upon me that his mother Shirley's principal interest was not so much who killed JFK, but who *didn't*. Wallis Osterholz at New School University sent me a 1964 syllabus describing the school's Warren Report class. Chris Pike shared his extensive Penn Jones data and a print of the picture appearing in the photo section. Vincent J. Salandria lent support far beyond what I might have antici-pated. My thanks go to the noted filmmaker Pierre Sauvage for allowing me access to his late father's private papers, and for providing me with audio tapes of several of his father's radio interviews. My thanks go also to Gary Schoener and Christopher Sharrett, Ph.D. Beth Sanders is a thoroughly professional photographer who kindly photographed the twenty-six volumes for me free of charge. David Starks conducted videotaped interviews with several of the early critics that were extremely useful. Dr. Cyril H. Wecht, M.D., LL.B., provided me with a copy of his 1966 article, "A Critique of the Medical Aspects of the Investigation into the Assasination of President Kennedy," and other background material. Sheri Southern read and critiqued a late draft. She also wondered how Sylvia Meagher pronounced her last name. It was "Marr." Sheri, as have many others, read the name as "May-grr." I'll bet Sylvia heard that once or twice during her life.

The staff at the Texas/Dallas History and Archives at the Dallas Public Library helped me sort through their assassination collection. My thanks goes to the Assassination Archives and Research Center in Washington, D.C., for data on public opinion polls. And my thanks also goes to members of the Louisville (CO) Public Library's Thursday night writer's group, who listened to and commented on countless out-of-context excerpts from the developing manuscript. A special thanks goes to Bryce Milligan of Wings Press, who put a lot of work into this project – probably much more than I know – and to Robert Bonazzi, both for his encouragement and insights after reading an early draft and for his labors in helping to bring the book to press.

Finally, words cannot possibly express the debt of gratitude I feel for my magnificent wife, Cindy Swearingen, whose unwavering support made this all possible.

The sources for this book are the interviews I conducted; the private papers of my critic-subjects, some of which have been transferred to college archives; the work, both published and unpublished, of these critics; contemporaneous material from print and electronic media; and documents obtained from the National Archives.

It must seem a paradox that my principal source of information on the assassination itself is the Warren Report and the twenty-six volume *Hearings Before the President's Commission on the Assassination of President Kennedy*. To the best of my ability, this book is an accurate account of an untold story from recent American history. It should go without saying that none of those who helped me along the way are responsible for the content of this narrative. Many people held the pieces, but I am the one who assembled the puzzle.

Praise from a
Future Generation

There are in our midst exceptional people . . . journalists and writers, amateur and professional, who have been making no less than heroic efforts to unravel the answers to how, why and what-for John F. Kennedy was felled . . . to them belongs the praise of future generations.

– M.S. Arnoni
The Minority of One, 1966

PART ONE

You might ask, why bother? Hasn't the Warren Commission done its job?

– Sylvan Fox, from the introduction to
The Unanswered Questions about President Kennedy's Assassination

Chapter 1

Air Force One

During its flight from Dallas to Washington, D.C., on November 22, 1963, the occupants of Air Force One were informed that there was no conspiracy in the shooting death of John F. Kennedy, whose body was also on the plane. It was no more than four hours since the President had been pronounced dead at Parkland Hospital in Dallas. Lee Harvey Oswald was under arrest but would not be charged with Kennedy's murder for another eight and a half hours. Yet the presidential jet's passengers were told he was the sole, unaided assassin.[1]

The Cabinet plane, flying from Hawaii to Japan for an economic summit, received the same no conspiracy, lone assassin message as Air Force One, and at about the same time. The common denominator was the source of each announcement: the White House Situation Room.[2]

"That," wrote Philadelphia attorney Vincent J. Salandria, "is conclusive evidence of high-level U.S. governmental guilt. The first announcement of Oswald as the lone assassin, before there was any evidence against him, and while there was overwhelmingly convincing evidence of conspiracy, had come from the White House Situation Room. Only the assassins could have made that premature declaration that Oswald was the assassin."[3]

Salandria wrote those words in 1998, in one of his strongest, most direct public statements on the matter. Yet he had come to this conclusion many years before. Salandria was among the earliest researchers of the Kennedy assassination – one of a small group of private citizens at first working independently of, and largely in isolation from, one another. Although the suspicions of most of them were aroused and acted upon on the very day President Kennedy was slain, the initial efforts of this small group – by one estimate, there were fewer than twenty – went mostly unnoticed by the general public. In some cases these critics preferred it that way. In others, the writings they produced were not easily published – were deemed unpopular and perhaps dangerous – and could find their way to print only in limited-circulation magazines or self-published books that did not enjoy the benefit of a major publisher's distribution power.[4]

And yet these early researchers – usually called first-generation critics – were not deterred, for if they shared one trait, it was a dedication to the truth. And the truth, they were convinced, had not been served by the nation's media, or by those government bodies charged with investigating the brutal murder, in broad daylight before hundreds of eyewitnesses, on the streets of a modern American city, of its chief executive.

"By the evening of November 22, 1963," recalled Ray Marcus, another of the first-generation critics, "I found myself being drawn into the case. The government was saying there was only one assassin; that there was no conspiracy. It was obvious that even if this subsequently turned out to be true, it could not have been *known* to be true at that time."[5]

Dallas legal secretary Mary Ferrell was, at the moment of the assassination, about ten blocks from Dealey Plaza, where Kennedy was slain. She was struck by the remarkable speed with which Lee Harvey Oswald was arrested. "The Dallas Police were not gifted with ESP," she said. Mrs. Ferrell heard the description of the suspect, broadcast some twenty minutes after the assassination; it was so general it would have fit countless men in the greater Dallas-Forth Worth metroplex. "I went home, turned on the television, I'm glued to it. And one hour and one minute later, at 1:51 pm, the Dallas Police arrested a man seated in a darkened theater, across town in Oak Cliff, and I'm thinking, 'Oh, this is remarkable!'"[6]

On his farm in Maryland two days later, Harold Weisberg was watching TV coverage of the assassination. The arrested man was about to be transferred from the Dallas jail to a more secure lockup when Weisberg looked at his wife and said: "You know, honey, this poor son-of-a-bitch is going to get killed."

"What are you talking about?"

"Oswald. Everything that is happening is making it impossible to try him. Somebody wants to close his mouth." A few minutes later, a national television audience first became acquainted with Jack Ruby.[7]

The early critics were in general agreement that there was no real case against Oswald, and an examination of police reports filed the day of the assassination supports that view. From the beginning, the evidence indicated the likelihood of more than one gunman in Dealey Plaza. Some eyewitnesses observed activity in the Texas School Book Depository that was at odds with what authorities claimed happened there. The attention of many others – one count placed the number as high as fifty-one – was drawn to a grassy, tree-lined slope on the north side of Elm Street, soon to gain infamy as the "grassy knoll." Attention was also drawn to an adjacent concrete pergola, referred to variously as a "monument," "arcade," or "brick structure." Still others reported activity in the surrounding area suggestive of a radio-coordinated ambush in the making. Once the fusillade was over, a Dallas police officer who had run toward the knoll encountered a woman who cried out, "They're shooting the President from the bushes!"[8]

Even if every last one of these and other witnesses were wrong, some of the early critics observed, the official pronouncement of Oswald's sole guilt was too early and too final. It was not what one would expect from an impartial, preliminary investigation.

"Dealey Plaza," Vince Salandria said, "reeked of conspiracy."[9]

Exactly one week after Kennedy's assassination, new President Lyndon Johnson announced the appointment of a Special Commission "to study and report upon all facts and circumstances relating to the assassination of the late President, John F. Kennedy, and the subsequent violent death of the man charged with the assassination." This Commission was composed of some of the most prominent and respected public servants of the day. A White House press release issued at the time stated the Commission would "have before it all evidence uncovered by the Federal Bureau of Investigation" and pertinent data from any other government agency. It also had the power to "conduct any further investigation that it deems desirable." The Commission was instructed "to satisfy itself that the truth is known as far as it can be discovered, and to report its findings and conclusions to [President Johnson], to the American people, and to the world."[10]

The press release noted that a Texas inquiry into President Kennedy's assassination had been announced by Waggoner Carr, the Texas Attorney General, and that Carr was now pledging to cooperate with the Federal probe. By early December the Texas inquiry had been postponed. This decision was announced after Carr met with Justice Department officials in Washington, and with Chief Justice Earl Warren, who was chairing the Special Commission.[11]

Preparations were underway for a separate investigation by the Senate Judiciary Committee; the House Judiciary Committee and the House Committee on Un-American Activities were also considering probes. One purpose of the presidential Commission, said *The New York*

Times, was to stop the competing investigations, "and give the public a single report that would command the nation's full confidence."12

The special panel quickly became known as the Warren Commission after its chairman. There were six other members: Senator Richard Russell of Georgia, Senator John Sherman Cooper of Kentucky, Representative Hale Boggs of Louisiana, Representative Gerald Ford of Michigan, former CIA Director Allen Dulles, and John J. McCloy, who had served as a disarmament adviser to President Kennedy, and was the former president of the World Bank.13

The bulk of the Commission's work, however, would fall on members of its staff, which took most of the witness depositions. "Of the 489 witnesses who gave testimony, less than one-fourth appeared before the Commission itself," first-generation critic Sylvia Meagher wrote, in a trenchant analysis of the Warren panel's work. "Even in those cases, the seven members of the full Commission were never present as a body or throughout an entire session."14

The Warren Commission was in existence for about ten months. Its findings appeared first in the fall of 1964, in a single-volume summary. Two months later the Government Printing Office published a twenty-six-volume set of hearings and exhibits from which the summary was ostensibly derived. The single-volume summary, known popularly as the Warren Report, saturated the public mind: it was published simultaneously by five commercial publishers at what industry observers said was record speed. The first copy of the mass market paperback edition was sold precisely one minute after the report was officially released. The Government Printing Office published a sixth, official version, and the complete text was also published in *The New York Times*. By early November, 1964, nearly three million copies of the Warren Report were in print. Major media outlets, almost without exception, lauded the Report as a superlative piece of investigation and reportage.15

The Commission listed twelve main conclusions. Of those, the most important was that a total of three shots had been fired at the presidential motorcade, all of them by Lee Harvey Oswald. Oswald had no help from anyone. He had fired from a southeast corner window on the sixth floor of the Texas School Book Depository building. One bullet had wounded President Kennedy in the neck. This same bullet went on to cause multiple wounds to Governor John Connally. A short time after the assassination, Oswald also shot and killed Dallas Police Officer J.D. Tippit.16

But long before the Commission published a word – before it even heard its first witness – the first-generation critics, American citizens who were convinced that something was not right in the story that came out of Dallas in November 1963, were trying to sort out the confusing mass of data and answer some questions for themselves.

The people who would come to be known as Warren Report critics were a varied group. They included a poultry farmer with a background in journalism and government work; several lawyers, one of them a former state legislator; the operator of a small business; three housewives; an educator; a researcher for the World Health Organization; a French journalist; and the publisher of a smalltown newspaper.

At the time of the assassination, most of the critics were unaware of each other, although most assumed that other private citizens had also been drawn into the case. Curious about this, Ray Marcus reckoned that one out of every one thousand adult Americans must be as interested and active as he was; he estimated a figure of about 120,000 people. He was astonished to later determine the actual number was nearer to twelve.[17]

There was a great deal of confusion in the days and weeks immediately following the assassination. It was still unclear how many shots had even been fired on the motorcade, and from where those shots originated. Emergency room doctors said Kennedy's throat wound was one of entrance. But Kennedy's limousine had already passed the building Oswald allegedly fired from – so how could he have wounded Kennedy in the front? A major magazine duly reported that JFK had turned in his seat at the moment he was shot, thus explaining the contradiction, but photographs published by the same magazine showed, incontrovertibly, the President had *not* turned. Moreover, accounts of the location of the President's head wound – was it in the back of the skull, the right rear of the skull, the right temple? – varied greatly. Something was amiss.

One of the autopsy surgeons said he had been forbidden to talk. This same doctor admitted to having burned some of his autopsy notes. The published autopsy seemed to raise as many questions as it answered; one doctor called it "a grossly incomplete record."[18]

The confusion was so great that journalist Léo Sauvage – an exception among the first critics in that he was neither a private citizen nor an American – wired his home office at *Le Figaro*, a leading Paris daily newspaper, that one of the few certainties in Dallas was that President Kennedy was dead. There was little concrete to go on.[19]

For most of the critics, it was simply the suspicion that something was rotten – in the city of Dallas and the state of the union. And so, with intense curiosity but limited resources, they scoured newspapers, clipped articles and tried to sort the fact from the fiction.

Strictly speaking, once the Warren Commission was established and taking testimony from witnesses, it acted openly. The hearings were private, in that the public and press were barred from the proceedings, but witnesses were free to repeat their testimony once it was taken. In practice, however, the Commission acted covertly. Some of the critics wondered – if the facts of the assassination were as simple as the official government pronouncements made them out to be – why the proceedings were held behind closed doors. "I became disturbed by the secret and therefore undemocratic hearings of the Warren Commission," Vince Salandria told an acquaintance. On his farm in Maryland, Harold Weisberg felt much the same way. "With the Commission working in secret, there were no new leads for an inquiring press to follow." Later he added: "I have always felt, very strongly, that the most important thing in this country is for the people to be fully and accurately informed. That goes back to the first days of this country – people risked their lives for that."[20]

The official judgment, issued in September 1964 but virtually a foregone conclusion by the end of the day of the assassination, was that President Kennedy was killed by a lone, unassisted, and probably demented gunman. In spite of the confidence with which this presumed truth was stated, Federal authorities deemed it prudent to keep a watchful eye on those who publicly declared their doubts about the Warren Commission findings. The FBI, which had supplied the Commission with the bulk of its investigatory data, emerged as its principle guardian following publication of its Report, noting and filing from the very start what few articles critical of the Commission's work appeared in the nation's press, and keeping track of those public utterances that ran counter to the lone assassin story. In 1965 one critic told his colleagues that FBI recordings of another critic's lectures would fill half a room. In January 1967, a Central Intelligence Agency memorandum was prepared offering strategies for "discrediting the claims of the conspiracy theorists."[21]

Senator Joe McCarthy was dishonored and dead, but the United States was not far removed from the anti-Communist hysteria of the immediate post-World War II years. The FBI was thus careful to note, during its clandestine monitoring, whether a subject had any hint of Communism in his or her background. While many of the early critics were politically of the Left, not all of them were; in any case personal politics, in a land of presumed freedom of choice and diversity, should be irrelevant to the questions of who, if not Lee Harvey Oswald, killed

President Kennedy and why. Regardless of their place on the political spectrum, many of the early critics were motivated by their sense of patriotism; all were in pursuit of the truth.

FBI memos dating to the earliest period following the JFK killing show that virtually every active critic of the Commission was monitored to some degree. In a nation fond of proclaiming its constitutionally guaranteed freedoms, such monitoring cannot be considered benign. One of the earliest articles on the case was characterized in an FBI memo as "another bitter attack upon the Bureau." The article was based primarily on readily available newspaper accounts, and simply raised the question of whether Lee Harvey Oswald had any covert intelligence connections.[22]

Most of the early critics were simply doing what they felt they had to do, regardless of how the authorities viewed their activities. "I did the research with the expectation that they were following my work, if they had an interest in it," Vince Salandria later said. He acknowledged there was an element of personal risk involved, and later attributed several Internal Revenue Service audits to his work. But the consequences appear to have been greater for some witnesses to events related to November 22, 1963: it was gradually learned that some of these witnesses were intimidated with threats, or worse. Before long critic Penn Jones, Jr., was compiling a list of what he referred to as the "strange deaths" of some assassination witnesses.[23]

The more prominent the critic, it seems, the more paper was generated within the Bureau, and in some instances the more mean-spirited it was. A memo from William Branigan to William Sullivan, for example, noted one prominent critic's supposed affiliation with "Communist Party front groups" in the years preceding the assassination. The memo also carried the intelligence that this critic had once been investigated for allegedly violating laws defining permissible sexual activity. Since this FBI memo says nothing about prosecution resulting from the allegations, the investigation apparently came up empty. But records were kept – the memo had copies of the evidence attached – and one cannot discount the possibility that this material was used against the critic to deter his activities or blunt his message.

And it is entirely possible that the information in the memorandum was false, or deliberately misleading. "They're masters of distortion," Harold Weisberg once said of the FBI, after he'd reviewed a 1966 Bureau memorandum on himself. The memo ostensibly detailed his dismissal, in 1939, from a Senate subcommittee job, and in 1947 from a position with the State Department. Weisberg declared that the FBI memorandum took a series of truths and half-truths, and cleverly assembled them to give an entirely inaccurate and false impression. "You just can't believe them on anything. It's awful, it's simply awful that in a country like this, the major police organization can't be trusted."[24]

The Federal Government, it now seems, was absolutely determined that the Warren Commission's explanation of the assassination be accepted by the public at large. "That's the crucial thing, they don't care about a few people," said Ray Marcus. A willing media worked hand in hand with the government in a publicity blitz that asked few questions, and pounded home the message that in spite of any evidence to the contrary, one lone individual was responsible for the murder of President Kennedy.[25]

In the 1970s, it would emerge that segments of the major media had been penetrated by CIA "assets" who, working in key positions, provided the government with desirable spin control, and in some cases spread false information on a host of issues. That was not common knowledge when the Warren Commission was active. A CIA bulletin dated September 22, 1964 – two days before the Warren Report was delivered to President Johnson – stated that around the world, there was wide-spread suspicion that Kennedy was assassinated as the result of a political plot. "Covert assets should explain the tragedy wherever it is genuinely misunderstood and counter all efforts to misconstrue it intentionally . . . communists and other extremists always attempt to prove a political conspiracy behind violence."[26]

Some of the critics concluded that their ranks, too, had been pene-trated by people posing as assassination researchers, but who in fact had ulterior motives. "My sense of the critical community is that it was from the beginning heavily infiltrated by the intelligence community," Vince Salandria wrote long afterward. "Powerful persons and forces which consummate a successful coup would not be satisfied to surrender to honest critics the task of analyzing the implications of the cover story."[27]

Ray Marcus came to view this as a simple matter of fact. "It's unten-able to believe in a major coverup without believing that misinformation, agents of misinformation, misinformation in the critics' community was utilized," he said. "If it wasn't, it would probably be the first time in even pre-recorded history that somebody didn't infiltrate somebody into the opposing camp."[28]

As the first-generation researchers proceeded in their work, and became aware not only of each other, but of how few others were engaged in the same pursuit, there were developments that were perhaps inevitable. Alliances were formed based on geography, areas of interest, and personal temperament. Some of these alliances were intermittent and uneasy, while others blossomed into lasting friendships. Some were later split by deep suspicion. The awesome implications of the critics' work did much to foster profound distrust.

But loose though many of them were, the alliances forged early on endured through the first years of the ongoing, unofficial investigations. Then came the electrifying news that a formal investigation had been launched by the New Orleans District Attorney's office – the first time, as one critic put it, that "a public official armed with subpoena power" was solidly in the anti-Warren Commission camp. This development at first excited the critical community, then began tearing it apart, in some cases severing long-standing relationships beyond repair. The investigation elicited strong responses and there was no middle ground.[29]

What didn't change was the dedication to the truth that from the start had motivated each of the first-generation critics. The controversial investigation in New Orleans could not alter that. And while for better or worse that investigation failed, and some of the early critics withdrew from active involvement, as a group their immediate understanding that a conspiracy – an obvious conspiracy – had resulted in the assassination of President Kennedy remained intact. Only the details seemed to divide them.

"History teaches us that significant changes are often accomplished by small numbers of people, facing large odds," Mary Ferrell said in 1992, at a conference of assassination researchers in Dallas. By this time the first-generation critics had been replaced by a second, a third, a fourth; a congressional committee had concluded that President Kennedy had been the victim of a probable conspiracy that it did not define. The significant changes Mrs. Ferrell spoke of included those wrought by America's Founding Fathers; so it can be, she said, with that tiny minority still interested in the Kennedy assassination. She continued: public opinion polls have consistently revealed the widespread view "that a conspiracy and government-sponsored cover-up blotted out the rights of our citizens and sanctity of the rule of law."[30]

Harold Weisberg once tried to summarize why the assassination of John F. Kennedy remained a vital issue four decades after the event. "People are troubled by it," he said. "I hear from a lot of young people who tell me they were not born at the time Kennedy died, and express their love for the man, and their unease about the whole thing. I hear from many of those who say 'I was eight, ten years old,' as well as many who were older, who are mature citizens. And the one thing that crosses all political lines is unease and dissatisfaction. And worry."[31]

Chapter 2

The Beplumed Knight

Mark Lane was not the first assassination critic. No one can truly make that claim, for the simple reason that the first-generation critics began researching the case independent of one another, on November 22, 1963.

But as a practicing criminal attorney and a former member of the New York State Assembly, Mark Lane had the stature and clout to get his views into print, and a personality suited to the task. Suspicious that Lee Harvey Oswald might have been framed, he wrote a legal brief in his defense that, within a month of the assassination, appeared as an article in a national newspaper. An item about that article appeared in *The New York Times* and spurred several critics or would-be critics to act on their suspicions, the implications of which had perhaps until then seemed too enormously daunting.

Before its publication, Lane sent a copy of the brief to Earl Warren, who had just agreed to head the presidential commission investigating the assassination. "It would be appropriate," Lane wrote in a cover letter, "that Mr. Oswald, from whom every legal right was stripped, be accorded counsel who may participate with the single purpose of representing the rights of the accused." Lane received an undated reply on December 30, written by the Commission's General Counsel J. Lee Rankin. "The views contained in your letter will be given appropriate consideration by the Commission prior to the preparation of any final report."[1]

Lane's "Defense Brief for Oswald" was published in *The National Guardian* on December 19, 1963. "That was extremely important," Ray Marcus said of the brief. "And I'm sure it was to other critics, or potential critics, around the country. Because some of the things – some of the things – that were troubling me, he was addressing directly."[2]

Marcus sat down at his typewriter on January 8, 1964, and wrote a letter to Lane. He told him the *Guardian* article was "an amazing document, and quite possibly, an historic one." Others, including several journalists, were also inspired by the article. Yet Lane would later write that "the most important person to read the brief was a housewife in Hominy, Oklahoma." Her name was Shirley Martin, and she would provide a critical link in a chain of events that would deepen Lane's involvement in the case.[3]

The "Defense Brief for Oswald" countered, point-by-point, a list of allegations and issues raised by Dallas District Attorney Henry Wade in a press conference just after Lee Oswald's death. Wade had claimed there was no doubt that Oswald was the assassin. He said that witnesses saw Oswald at the "sniper's nest" window; that he could prove Oswald had recently fired a gun; that after the assassination, Oswald had shot and killed a Dallas police officer. Lane studied Wade's charges when they were published in *The New York Times*. "Perused lightly, the list seems impressive," he said. "But in capital cases evidence is not perused lightly."[4]

Lane's article began: "In all likelihood there does not exist a single American community where reside 12 men or women, good and true, who presume that Lee Harvey Oswald did not assassinate President Kennedy. No more savage comment can be made in reference to the breakdown of the Anglo-Saxon system of jurisprudence." Lane asked his readers "only for a temporary suspension of certainty. . . . Let those who would deny a fair consideration of the evidence to Oswald because of a rage inspired, they say, by their devotion to the late President, ponder this thought: If Oswald is innocent . . . then the assassin of President Kennedy remains at large."[5]

Lane wrote that there was really only one witness placing Oswald at the window of the sixth floor of the Texas School Book Depository. This witness was quoted in the press as follows: "I can't identify him, but if I see a man who looks like him, I'll point him out." Such an identification was "at best speculative and would not be permitted in that form at trial."[6]

Wade said that paraffin tests proved Oswald had recently fired a gun. Conceding that tests on his hands were positive, Lane countered that Wade "neglected to state the additional facts that tests had been conducted on Oswald's face and that the tests revealed that there were no traces of gunpowder on Oswald's face," where one would expect to find them if he had fired a rifle.[7]

The charge that Oswald had murdered Officer J.D. Tippit, Lane said, was very weak. Dallas authorities first said Tippit was shot in a movie theater. This was later changed to his having been shot on a street – as indeed he was – then changed again, to a different street. Lane said the lack of certainty was suspicious.[8]

Lane blasted the press for its uncritical reporting of the arrest and detention of Oswald. "Very likely no prospective defendant in the history of civilization has been tried and condemned through the utilization of the media as thoroughly as was Oswald." There were additional reasons to question the case against Oswald, including Oswald's denials of guilt; initial reports that the President's throat wound was one of entrance when Oswald was allegedly firing from behind; and whether Oswald was a capable enough marksman to have even done the shooting.[9]

Lane's defense brief concluded that the case assembled by the authorities proved only that the assassination could not have happened the way they said it had. Inevitably, this would lead to a twisting of the truth. "The facts as presented to date by the FBI and the Dallas district attorney (soon to be rewritten no doubt) have overcome the presumption of guilt manufactured when the case was initiated."[10]

Lane's article was provocative and highly unusual for this early period. When *The New York Times* ran a piece about it the same day it appeared in the *Guardian*, Shirley Martin, who had subscribed to the *Times* immediately after the assassination, recognized it as the news she had been waiting for. "Mark Lane's article in *The National Guardian* gave us hope that what we believed – something fishy in Dallas – was true," she recalled many years later.[11]

The *Times* item began: "A former New York Assemblyman has urged Chief Justice Earl Warren's investigating commission to appoint a defense counsel for Lee H. Oswald in its inquiry into the assassination of President Kennedy." Mrs. Martin clipped it and sent it to Marguerite Oswald, the mother of the accused assassin. Later she got the full *Guardian* article and sent her that, too.[12]

Later still, Mrs. Martin telephoned Mrs. Oswald to talk about Lane. "We were both excited. Here was Richard Coeur de Lion riding to the rescue in the form of a stouthearted New York lawyer. Marguerite took it from there."[13]

Marguerite Oswald contacted Lane and asked him to represent her dead son before the Warren Commission. "That I was interested was obvious," Lane said later. "Yet there were problems which appeared insurmountable." Principal among these was money. Much of Lane's legal work during this period consisted of the pro bono defense of poor people; what made this work possible was Lane's sole corporate client. This corporate client was already embarrassed by the *Guardian* article. "Any future similar activity would result in the reluctant, but certain, termination of my services."[14]

Lane had told *The New York Times* in December that he was not offering to defend Lee Oswald, but that he would be willing to do so if asked. So when he seemed to hesitate, Mrs. Oswald challenged him. "He's being tried by the Warren Commission," she said. "He has no lawyer. Will you represent his interests or didn't you mean what you wrote?"[15]

Lane agreed to do what he could.

After he said he would take the case, Lane sent a telegram to the Commission informing it of his intentions. He also sent copies of statements that Marguerite had sworn to. But Earl Warren wouldn't hear of it. In a Warren Commission meeting on January 21, 1964, the Chief Justice told his colleagues, "We are dealing with the mother of Oswald and this lawyer by the name of Lane in New York. He wants to come right into our councils here and sit with us, and attend all of our meetings and defend Oswald, and of course that can't be done."[16]

Lane's was not the only voice then urging that Lee Oswald be defended before the Commission. On December 29 Percy Foreman, then-president of the National Association of Defense Attorneys, said on national television that Oswald should be represented. "There's no other way, in my opinion, that the evidence in this case can be properly evaluated," he told CBS. But he added that this should be done more for the American public's benefit than Oswald's.[17]

By this time – January 1964 – Lane had traveled to Dallas for some preliminary investigating, and had begun speaking publicly on the assassination in New York City. About five hundred people attended a speech at the Henry Hudson Hotel on January 24. Lane told them there was not sufficient evidence to have convicted Oswald at trial.[18]

Lane was then just short of his 37th birthday. A native of New York City, he had been admitted to the New York State Bar in 1951 and had been in private practice in East Harlem ever since. Much of his work was as defense counsel in criminal cases. "My clients were, far more often than not, African-American or Puerto Rican, and impoverished," he recalled. In high-profile cases, his experience had taught him, the victims were almost always white. "It was clear that the right to a fair trial was diminished in many instances by prejudicial pretrial publicity. The source of the information often was the office of the prosecuting attorney or the police department." This general truth applied to the JFK case and would be a major factor in Lane's involvement in the assassination investigation.[19]

A friend once observed that Lane "sees himself as a beplumed knight on a white charger whenever he undertakes a cause." In a 1961 profile, *The New York Times* described him as being of medium height and soft-spoken in ordinary conversation – but that he "seems to reach towering heights when he speaks from a platform or in a courtroom. His eyes flash through his horn-rimmed glasses and his voice swells to fortissimo."[20]

As the 1950s progressed, Lane was increasingly involved in city and state politics. He was a key worker in the campaign that elected Alfred E. Santangelo to Congress; he was subsequently named the Congressman's executive assistant and ran his New York congressional office for three years. In 1959 Lane became active in the New York Committee for Democratic Voters, a Democratic reform group challenging Tammany Hall, Manhattan's established Democratic machine. Also in the committee were Eleanor Roosevelt, the former first lady and one of its co-founders, and Francis W. H. Adams, a former police commissioner who would later serve as counsel to the Warren Commission.[21]

That same year Lane worked as New York organizer for John F. Kennedy's presidential campaign. Soon Lane was himself running for office, vying for a seat on the New York State Assembly. His district included many Puerto Ricans who were Americans by birth, but whose first language was Spanish. Lane and his campaign team believed that literacy tests, given only in English, unfairly excluded these constituents from the democratic process.[22]

"I passed out the answers to the literacy tests and encouraged the people to become voters," Lane wrote later. As a direct result of these efforts hundreds of people were registered. At Lane's invitation, members of the U.S. Attorney's Office and the media were able to see first hand this challenge to the literacy-test laws. No charges were filed and the law permitting literacy tests was later invalidated.[23]

According to Lane, Tammany Hall considered his candidacy a serious threat to its continued power. Consequently, although Lane was the official Democratic candidate, Tammany Democrats endorsed his Republican opponent in the general election. Pressure was intense; at one point Lane asked for and received police protection for himself and three campaign workers because of threats they had received. On August 29, 1961, as Lane drove through East Harlem in an open convertible on his way to a political rally, someone threw an unopened beer can from the roof of a building. The can struck a glancing blow to Lane's head, opening a wound that required four stitches.[24]

Later during the campaign, Lane had an opportunity to meet presidential nominee John F. Kennedy, who was meeting with state and local Democratic candidates to give their campaigns a boost. Each was photographed with Kennedy, but there was a technical problem with the picture of JFK and Lane. Bobby Kennedy, JFK's campaign manager, heard about it and stepped in. "That's our campaign they're screwing up," he told Lane. "John wants you to be elected." Bobby arranged for a private photo session with Lane and the presidential candidate. Lane always felt the pictures, and Kennedy's support, were key factors in his being elected to the State Assembly. Like JFK's own victory that November, Lane was elected by a narrow margin.[25]

At the time President Kennedy was killed, Lane was having lunch at a Chinese restaurant in New York. He had by this time completed his term on the State Assembly and had not sought re-election.[26]

As he completed his midday repast of dim sum and chrysanthemum tea, he was unaware of the Dallas tragedy, thinking only of the case he was arguing that day. He was due back in court within the hour, but as he made his way there he saw groups of people clustered about transistor radios. "The scene was immediately reminiscent of newsreels taken in European capitals when news of war was broadcast," he said later. He asked someone what had happened – then sprinted back to the courthouse.[27]

In the courthouse press room, reporters, lawyers, and others were hearing the same conflicting accounts the rest of the nation was getting. The uncertainty was considerable. Finally a *New York Times* reporter snarled, "I'll find out what the fuck's going on," found a phone, and called the *Times* newsroom. He returned a few minutes later with tears in his eyes, and told Lane: "He's dead."[28]

Stunned, Lane proceeded to court fully expecting the judge to cancel proceedings and set a new trial date. But postponing the case, the judge said, would accomplish nothing. "Let's move along with this trial."[29]

Several hours later the jury acquitted Lane's client. Lane left the court feeling like one of the least informed people in the country. As he rushed down the steps of the Criminal Court Building he met up with a trial judge of his acquaintance, also on his way out. "Well, Lane," the judge asked, "do you think he did it alone?"[30]

"Who, sir? Did what?"

"Do you think this Oswald killed the President?"

"I'm afraid that I don't know anything about it," Lane replied, explaining he'd been in court for the last few hours.

"He couldn't very well shoot him from the back and cause an entrance wound in his throat, could he?" the judge asked. "The doctors said the throat wound was an entrance wound. It'll be an interesting trial. I want to see how they answer that question."[31]

Several years later, Lane wrote: "It seems that the judge's question remains without satisfactory answer. And there was no trial."[32]

Like Shirley Martin, Marguerite Oswald initially viewed Mark Lane as Richard the Lion Heart. In early January, 1964, she announced that she had hired Lane to represent her dead son Lee before the Warren Commission. He would receive no fee. In announcing that Lane had been retained, Marguerite vowed to "fight to my last breath" to prove her son was innocent of the assassination of President Kennedy. She had taken a post office box in Fort Worth, where she lived, and urged anyone with information helpful to her cause to write her there.[33]

Marguerite was herself due to appear before the Commission, but Lane would not be representing her. The agreement by which he represented Lee Harvey Oswald stipulated he would not also represent Marguerite. The agreement also stated that if, from his own investigations, Lane concluded that Lee Oswald had indeed been the presidential assassin, he could say so publicly, "a condition that would be quite improper were he still alive."[34]

Lane continued his investigations in Dallas, which involved tracking down as many witnesses as he could. Shirley Martin, who had also been contacting witnesses, was able to put him in touch with several people. Lane also embarked on an ambitious speaking tour to promote Lee Oswald's case and to raise money. In January he had begun delivering speeches in New York City almost daily. By February he had spoken on the West Coast in San Francisco and Los Angeles, the Midwest in Detroit, then back to New York State in Buffalo. In March he was in Czechoslovakia, and in early April, after a quick trip back to the United States, in Hungary.[35]

Lane's speech in Buffalo, delivered at a Unitarian-Universalist Church, was co-sponsored by a student group and a Socialist organization. During the speech demonstrators outside the building carried signs reading "Our Churches Are For God, Not For Communism."[36]

During each of these appearances, Lane hammered at the same basic anomalies he had written about in his defense brief. How could Oswald wound Kennedy in the throat when firing from behind? What about the witnesses who reported gunfire coming from the grassy knoll, and heard more than three shots? Why was the alleged assassination weapon first described as a German Mauser, but later identified as an Italian Mannlicher-Carcano?[37]

On February 18, 1964, Lane spoke at New York City's Town Hall at a public meeting sponsored by *The National Guardian*. Marguerite Oswald was on the speaker's platform with Lane.[38]

The Town Hall engagement was sold out. About 1,500 people were in attendance. A jittery Town Hall management insisted on a $25,000 deposit to cover possible damage to the premises, on the grounds that Marguerite's appearance there "could be incendiary." *The Guardian*'s James Aronson, while calling it a disgrace to free speech, reluctantly paid the deposit after insisting that the usual $600 rate had already been confirmed in writing.[39]

Lane spoke first. After recounting some of the inconsistencies and problems he had been publicizing all along, he revealed something new: a tape recording of a telephone conversation he had with assassination eyewitness Jean Hill. Mrs. Hill had told Lane she heard at least four shots fired on the presidential motorcade, and perhaps up to six shots, and that they came from the direction of the railroad overpass just ahead of Kennedy's limousine. And that, Lane said, meant the fatal shots did not necessarily come from the Texas School Book Depository Building, where Oswald allegedly was at the time of the shooting.[40]

When Marguerite stood before the audience she described how hard she had worked to raise Lee and her other sons, and how proud she was of her sons John Edward Pic, an Air Force staff sergeant, and Robert, who then worked for a brick company in Texas. She tried playing on the crowd's emotions: "Everybody has sympathy for Mrs. Kennedy," she said. "Doesn't anybody feel sorry for me? I've had enough misery."[41]

Marguerite described some of the events following Lee Oswald's arrest on November 22, when neither she nor Lee's wife Marina was allowed to see him. "Why would Jack Ruby be allowed within a few feet of a prisoner – of *any* prisoner – when I could not see my own son?" she asked. She insisted that the evening before Lee was gunned down, an FBI agent showed her a photograph of a man and asked if she could identify him. She could not. But after her son was murdered she said she recognized the man in the picture as Jack Ruby. The FBI insisted that Marguerite was mistaken.[42]

It was at this Town Hall meeting that Lane first made public an explosive allegation: that eight days before the President's assassination, a secret meeting had been held in Dallas involving Officer J.D. Tippit, Bernard Weissman, whose name was attached to a bitter anti-Kennedy advertisement published the morning of the assassination, and a third man.[43]

Lane did not then reveal the name of the third man. But he did say that the meeting was held at the Carousel Club, the nightclub owned by Jack Ruby.[44]

Lane would soon be telling the Warren Commission about this in person. Although he had no first-hand knowledge of the assassination, due to his investigations in Dallas the Commission called him to testify in Washington on March 4, 1964.[45]

Lane had already been before the Commission, appearing briefly with Marguerite Oswald on February 11, her second of three days giving testimony. Lane asked Chief Justice Warren if he might sit in for an hour or two, a request that Marguerite's lawyer, John F. Doyle, objected to. Warren didn't like it either, telling Marguerite: "Either he represents you or he does not." Marguerite said that he did not, and Warren replied, "Then we will excuse Mr. Lane."[46]

Lane's March testimony began at 2:30 in the afternoon. Chief Justice Earl Warren, Senator John Sherman Cooper, and Representative Gerald Ford were the only Commission members present. General Counsel J. Lee Rankin and his assistant Norman Redlich were there too, along with two assistants to Walter E. Craig, president of the American Bar Association. Although Lane's request to represent Oswald had been denied, the Commission had reconsidered its position and on February 25, 1964, appointed Craig to the job – "in fairness to the alleged assassin." According to a later analysis by Sylvia Meagher, participation by Craig or his representatives was minimal, none of it coming until after several key witnesses had testified. It was, she said, a "sorry arrangement [that] was a mockery that further compromised the Commission's claim to impartiality."[47]

Chief Justice Warren began: "The Commission proposes to question Mr. Lane on all matters of which he has knowledge concerning the assassination of President Kennedy and the subsequent killing of Lee Harvey Oswald." He asked Lane to stand and swear to tell the truth, the whole truth, and nothing but the truth, and Lane obliged.[48]

Then, after some preliminary questions to establish Lane's professional standing, the witness said: "I would like to request that this portion of the hearing, in any event, be opened to the public. I think that there are matters here of grave concern to all the people of our country, and that it would, therefore, be fruitful and constructive for the sessions to be conducted in a public fashion, open to the public and to the press."49

Warren was amenable, and the meeting was briefly adjourned so that everyone could move to an adjoining auditorium. When they resumed, Warren re-stated Lane's request for an open hearing, commenting: "I explained to him that that was thoroughly agreeable to the Commission. The Commission does not operate in a secret way. Any witness who desires to have his – give his testimony in public may do so.

"We have done it in the quiet of our rooms," Warren continued, "for the convenience of witnesses, and in order to accelerate the program." This was the first public Commission session. As it developed, there would be only one more.50

Finally, Lane's testimony got underway. Immediately he brought up the subject of a controversial photograph "allegedly showing Lee Harvey Oswald holding in his hand a rifle which has been described in at least one publication, *Life* magazine, as the weapon with which he assassinated President Kennedy." Lane proposed to demonstrate to the Commission that more than one version of the picture existed, and that the image had therefore been "doctored and forged." He offered into evidence a copy of the February 21, 1964, issue of *Life*, which was marked Commission Exhibit 334.51

Although Lane may not have been aware of it, Lee Oswald, on the day before he was shot dead, had also declared the photograph a forgery. In a report on Oswald's Saturday, November 23 interrogation, Dallas Police Captain J.W. Fritz said that Oswald "said the picture was not his, that the face was his face, but that this picture had been made by someone superimposing his face, the other part of the picture was not him at all. . . ." According to Fritz, Oswald added that he had a good understanding of photography, and that in time he would be able to show that the picture had been made by someone else.52

Lane submitted other copies of the photograph. One of them had been obtained from *The New York Times*, which the Commission labeled Exhibit 335, and another from *Newsweek* magazine. He also gave the Commission an enlarged detail from the *Times* version of the picture, and still other versions of the same picture.53

Lane first showed the *Life* version of the photo, and then the second copy from the *Times*. "I suggest that is the identical picture with the one published on the cover of *Life* magazine, Exhibit 334, in every respect, including the creases in the trousers, the background, with the exception of the rifle in the hands of Oswald, which appears to have no telescopic scope in Exhibit 335." There were other discrepancies, he said – certain details around Oswald's head and in the background were present in one version, but not the other. Details from the other versions of the picture revealed similar irregularities.[54]

There were other photographs of the purported murder weapon that on close examination seemed to be of different rifles. "I wonder," Lane said, "if I might ask the Commission if it might produce the rifle now, so that we might compare the actual rifle with the pictures."

"We will do that in due course," Warren replied. "But we don't have the rifle here now, Mr. Lane. We will make the proper comparisons, you may be sure, with experts."[55]

From there, Lane introduced as evidence several newspaper articles. One was suggestive of witness intimidation. Others demonstrated Lane's argument about changing facts: how investigators had initially declared Kennedy's first wound an entrance wound to the neck, but over time had offered differing accounts about when and where he was shot. Lane showed the Commission newspaper photos with "superimposed dotted lines showing the trajectory of the three bullets, showing that the first bullet was fired while the presidential car was still on Houston Street, still approaching the Book Depository Building." But some of the eyewitnesses, including Governor and Mrs. Connally, who were in the presidential limousine, said the car had already turned from Houston onto Elm, and was past the Book Depository when the shooting began. How could Oswald wound Kennedy in the front if he had been firing from behind? The plot thickened when Lane described how *Life* magazine published an article stating that the limo had indeed gone past the Book Depository, but that JFK had turned in his seat and was facing the building when first hit.[56]

This seemed to get everyone's attention. "Do you have the date of that article?" Rankin asked.

"That was the December 6 *Life* magazine," Lane replied. "The full page article was entitled 'End to Nagging Rumors, the Six Critical Seconds.' The problem – "

"May I ask a question there – just to clarify?" asked Senator Cooper. "Did you say that in this article that *Life* said that the late President had turned around and was facing the Book Depository Building when the shot was fired?"

"Yes, Senator," Lane replied, explaining that there was a problem with this. In its own previous issue, he said, *Life* had published photographs showing beyond question that Kennedy had *not* turned at the critical moment.[57]

Lane moved on. He told the Commission about eyewitness Jean Hill, who heard four to six gunshots and said they had come from the grassy knoll; about *Dallas Morning News* reporter Mary Woodward, who not only thought she heard shots from the knoll or the railroad overpass area, but had written about it in the next day's *Morning News*; about the Book Depository's vice-president and its building manager, both of whom thought shots came from the direction of the grassy knoll; about police constable Seymour Weitzman, who ran toward the knoll area after the shots were fired. Weitzman was one of several officers credited with discovering the alleged murder weapon on the Book Depository's sixth floor. At the time he identified it as a 7.65 Mauser of German manufacture, as did Deputy Sheriff Eugene Boone and Police Captain Will Fritz. Dallas prosecutor Henry Wade later repeated that identification. Not until the following day, November 23, was the weapon publicly identified as an Italian rifle, a 6.5 Mannlicher-Carcano.[58]

"If I were permitted to cross-examine Mr. Wade," Lane told the Commission, "which evidently you have decided that I shall not be permitted to do, and Officer Weitzman, I would seek to find out how about the most important single element in probably this case or any other murder case, physical evidence, the murder weapon, in a case which I am sure is Mr. Wade's most important case – how he could be so completely in error about this."[59]

Finally, after delving into other areas of the case that his investigation had touched upon, Lane told those present about the alleged meeting at the Carousel Club involving J.D. Tippit, Bernard Weissman, and a third man. "I will be pleased to give you the name of the third person as given to me, but not in the presence of the press. I would rather do that in executive session – that one piece of testimony."

"That is satisfactory to do that, if you wish," Warren said.[60]

So the meeting was adjourned, and reconvened in Executive Session, where it had begun three hours earlier. "The third name that I was informed," Lane began, "the person that I was informed was there, the third person, is named Jack Ruby. It was my feeling, of course, while his case was pending it would not be proper to comment on that in the presence of the press."

"You mean the third person in the group apparently conferring?" J. Lee Rankin asked.

"Yes," Lane said, "Tippit, Weissman, and Ruby."

"Have you made any public statement of this kind before on this subject – about this meeting?" Warren asked.

"Not about Ruby – about a meeting between Weissman and Tippit, yes."

"But you have never named Ruby publicly?"

"No," Lane replied, "I have not. I shall not."[61]

The Commission was interested in where Lane had heard the story. Lane said he was not then at liberty to reveal his informant's name, but said he would try to get permission to do so. "I hope he will be willing to come forward and testify as to what took place."[62]

But the informant was not willing. Lane had first heard about the meeting from Thayer Waldo, a reporter on the *Fort Worth Star Telegram*, but Waldo was apparently not the source of the information. Waldo was later questioned by the Commission – but not asked about the meeting.[63]

Of the three men whom Lane named as attending the meeting at the Carousel Club, one, Dallas Police Officer J.D. Tippit, was dead. Another, Jack Ruby, was standing trial for murdering Lee Harvey Oswald. But the third man, Bernard Weissman, was alive and well, and free. *The New York Times* contacted him after Lane gave his name to the Warren Commission: "Mr. Weissman repeated earlier denials of any such meeting, any acquaintance with Mr. Tippit, Ruby or Oswald and ever having been in the Carousel," the paper reported.[64]

The earlier denials had come after Lane discussed the alleged meeting on a radio talk show. Weissman told the *Times* that since that show, "he twice by telephone challenged Mr. Lane to confront him publicly with any alleged witnesses so that he could deny the story to their faces 'and mark Mr. Lane as just a headline-hunter.'"[65]

Weissman's name was linked to the assassination by a notorious full-page newspaper ad that had appeared in *The Dallas Morning News* on the morning of November 22, 1963. The ad cost about $1,500 to place; it was paid for in part by Nelson Bunker Hunt, son of Dallas oil billionaire and arch-conservative H.L. Hunt. Although Weissman's politics were also right-wing, it appears that he was maneuvered into placing the ad by forces he did not entirely understand.[66]

"Welcome Mr. Kennedy," the ad said in large type. "We free-thinking and America-thinking citizens of Dallas still have, through a Constitution largely ignored by you, the right to address our grievances, to question you, to disagree with you, and to criticize you."[67]

There followed a series of loaded questions: Why is Latin America turning either anti-American or Communistic? Why did Kennedy say there was a wall of freedom around Cuba when Cuba itself was not free? Why did the head of the Communist Party USA praise most of Kennedy's policies? Why did Kennedy "scrap the Monroe Doctrine in favor of the 'Spirit of Moscow'?" The ad closed: "We DEMAND answers to these questions, and we want them NOW."[68]

Weissman's name, identifying him as Chairman of the "American Fact-Finding Committee," appeared at the bottom of the ad, and was the only name attached to it. Weissman later conceded that while the ad's authors were serious, the Committee itself was ad hoc. Its name, "American Fact-Finding Committee," was not even chosen until the morning Weissman placed the ad's original proof.[69]

President Kennedy had apparently seen the advertisement that morning as he sipped coffee in his Forth Worth hotel room. He is reported to have commented to his wife Jacqueline, "We're really in nut country now."[70]

Lane had discussed the alleged Weissman-Tippit-Ruby meeting on a radio call-in show the evening of February 18, soon after he had first mentioned it at the Town Hall gathering. As he had promised the Warren Commission, he did not mention Jack Ruby by name. Weissman, who left Dallas just after the assassination, was one of the callers to the show, phoning the radio station from his home in Mt. Vernon, New York, a little after midnight.[71]

"Hello, is Mr. Lane present?" he began. "This is Bernie Weissman."

"Yes," said the show's host, Murray Burnett. "Bernard Weissman of Dallas?"

"Yes. That's right."

"Yes," Lane interjected. "Hello."

"Mr. Lane?"

"Yes. I saw your ad down there. Very impressed by it."

"Yeah, so I understand," Weissman said. "You know that there has been several statements you've made this evening, as a matter of fact the newspapers have been bothering me somewhat also about them."[72]

The ensuing conversation didn't accomplish much. Weissman denied the meeting took place, and said he had never been in the Carousel Club.

"Never?" Lane challenged him. "In your *life*?"

"And I don't know Oswald, or Ruby, or anybody else involved in this thing."

Burnett suggested that Weissman call the station back when the program was over to further discuss matters with Lane. He agreed to do so. "Do you have anything else you want to say on the air?" Burnett asked.

"Frankly, no. That's all."

"Thank you for calling."[73]

On April 1, 1964, Marguerite Oswald announced that Mark Lane was no longer representing the interests of her murdered son. This news came on the same day Lane's new organization, the Citizens' Committee of Inquiry, was formally announced. Lane, the new group said in a press release, would function as the chairman of the new Committee, whose initiating members included actor Sterling Hayden and author Jessica Mitford.[74]

Marguerite Oswald told reporters that she was pleased with the work Lane had done on her behalf. But it appears that privately, she was upset with him. Shirley Martin was by this time getting to know Marguerite, and she later shared with Lane some of her insights: "I must tell you finally she is very angry with you. Her expression in this regard is: 'If I were a man I would wipe the floor up with him (you)!' My opinion is that this reaction is piqued by female vanity. Perhaps Mrs. Oswald in her terrible loneliness after the assassination (and the shock was terrible) may have formed a small attachment for you (as a patient can for his analyst); the realization that you couldn't give her much of your time (nor wanted to) may have brought on this reaction."[75]

In its press material, the Citizens' Committee of Inquiry described itself as an independent organization that would conduct its own investigation into the circumstances of JFK's assassination. It noted that Lane's "work as Lee Oswald's attorney was completed and that his future association with the case would not be in an attorney-client capacity but rather through the independent Citizens' Committee." Its first objective was sending experienced investigators to Dallas "to check out the more than 200 different leads that have already come to our attention."[76]

Vince Salandria was among a number of first-generation researchers in contact with Lane during the first months of 1964. On March 18, he wrote to Lane about "an idea which we request you pass on." His brother-in-law Harold Feldman, Salandria explained, was interested in writing an article about Lee Harvey Oswald. Both men believed the key to under-standing his character was held by his mother. And so Salandria offered to pay Marguerite Oswald's way to Philadelphia, where he and Feldman lived, and provide her with room and board. In this way they hoped that Feldman, a lay psychologist and frequent contributor to psychoanalytic journals, might have an opportunity to conduct protracted interviews with Mrs. Oswald and maybe even produce a biography. "Any business possibilities that may grow out of these transactions," Salandria told Lane, "we are confidant you can arrange."[77]

But a few weeks later Salandria wrote again. "I read in today's *Times* where you and Mrs. Marguerite Oswald have parted company. So much for my proposal of March 18."[78]

Nevertheless, in a few months' time Feldman and Salandria would be traveling to Dallas, where they would meet with Marguerite. The plan for an Oswald biography may have stalled, but Feldman would undertake a magazine article profiling Marguerite, whom he came to view with great empathy. He was rankled by the common press charac-terization of her as at best a flake, and impressed by her strength of character. "If she is unstable," he later wrote, "then Mount Rushmore is putty."[79]

Chapter 3

Oswald and the FBI

When the Imperial Japanese Navy attacked the United States naval installation at Pearl Harbor on December 7, 1941, Vincent J. Salandria was thirteen years old and in eighth grade at Vare Junior High School in Philadelphia. The attack, called a surprise by President Franklin Roosevelt, had a calamitous effect on the American military, but provided justification for the U.S. entrance into World War II.

Even at that age Salandria had a keen interest in world affairs, and came to a rapid conclusion about Pearl Harbor. When on December 8 his math teacher suggested the class discuss what had happened – no one was talking about anything else – Salandria did not hesitate to share his views.

"I went to the front of the classroom and informed my classmates that I could not accept as plausible President Roosevelt's assertion that the attack on Pearl Harbor was a surprise, sneak attack," he said long afterward. "I pointed out that all of us had known for months about the tension between the U.S. and Japan. I asked how, in light of those months of crisis and tautly strained relations between the two countries, could the battleships at Pearl Harbor have been lined up so closely together, presenting perfect targets for the Japanese? How could the planes I saw in the newspapers burning on our airfields have been positioned wing-tip to wing-tip?

"I reminded the class that President Roosevelt had promised that he would not send our troops into a foreign war. I then offered my conclusion that inviting the Pearl Harbor attack was President Roosevelt's duplicitous device to eliminate the powerful neutralist sentiment in our country while thrusting us into the war."[1]

In the aftermath of Pearl Harbor, a presidential commission headed by Owen J. Roberts, an associate justice of the U.S. Supreme Court, investigated the tragedy. President Roosevelt was much lauded for creating the prestigious commission, in particular for getting Justice Roberts to lead it. As the Roberts Commission began, a common view was that "the whole truth concerning the unhappy eventualities of December 7th will be revealed in an irrefutable and satisfactory manner." The Roberts Commission would ultimately assign sole blame for the vastating attack on two military men, Admiral Husband E. Kimmel and General Walter C. Short.[2]

The Roberts Commission was a model for the Warren Commission, created two decades later to investigate the Kennedy assassination. The conclusions of neither body would withstand the test of time.[3]

In the fall of 1963, Vince Salandria was teaching social studies at Philadelphia's John Bartram High School in the mornings, and practicing law in the afternoon and evenings. In addition to his private practice, he had for twelve years been a volunteer lawyer for the American Civil Liberties Union.[4]

As with the attack on Pearl Harbor twenty-two years before, Salandria's reaction to the killing of JFK, and the almost instantaneous proclamation of Lee Harvey Oswald's lone guilt, was immediate skepticism. "I'm particularly sensitive to the possibilities of governments [sic] not being as diligent as they should in situations of this sort," he once said. "Why am I particularly sensitive? I guess it comes from my Italian peasant background which always disputes governmental action and is inherently skeptical."[5]

Salandria had not been a Kennedy supporter, viewing the President as a rich and privileged Cold Warrior. "I thought he acted irresponsibly in the Bay of Pigs and in the Cuban Missile Crisis." But Salandria's views on Kennedy had softened, due in part to the 1963 Nuclear Test Ban Treaty, which the President had pushed for in spite of opposition by the Joint Chiefs of Staff. John F. Kennedy, it appeared to Salandria, was moving toward peace.[6]

On Monday, November 25, he went to school after a long weekend of watching assassination coverage on television, reading about it in the paper, and discussing it with his brother-in-law, Harold Feldman. "I waited for others to see what had happened and what had not happened on November 22," he said. "When nobody saw or was willing to say he saw, then I made it the subject of discussion in the building. I terrified the faculty."[7]

The media had reported Lee Harvey Oswald's complicated connections to a variety of mostly left-leaning political groups, and for Salandria that was a tip-off. The former Marine's defection to the Soviet Union, his one-man chapter of the Fair Play for Cuba Committee in New Orleans, his letters to the Communist Party USA, his membership in the ACLU, his study of Russian while in the Marine

Corps – all suggested to Salandria that Oswald was not a genuine leftist. "It was apparent to me that no legitimate leftist straddles so many diverse political fences in a fractionalized American left," he said. A more probable explanation for all those connections, Salandria came to believe, was that Oswald was a U.S. intelligence agent.[8]

Although his colleagues balked, Salandria's students were interested in what he had to say. He told them that the CIA may have killed President Kennedy. Along with the regular curriculum the assassination became a daily topic in Salandria's class. He helped some of the students get inexpensive copies of the Warren Report, and several decided to write term papers on the assassination.[9]

What Salandria was saying was controversial stuff. "The faculty attacked me at every opportunity," he recalled. "The sponsor of the school newspaper allowed a student to attack me in the newspaper for my analysis of the assassination."[10]

But Salandria insisted that as a simple matter of academic freedom, he had a right to teach his analysis. The school principal, John Welsh, began sitting in on his class to observe what he was teaching, and as December 7, 1963 approached, Salandria took advantage of the calendar. "I lectured on Franklin D. Roosevelt's setting up Pearl Harbor as a means of getting us into the war through the back door." Salandria meant to challenge Welsh, but Welsh wound up recommending that Bartram's other Social Studies teachers familiarize themselves with this alternate point of view.[11]

Salandria was at this time 35 years old. He had been born in an Italian ghetto in Philadelphia in 1928. As a boy he was nicknamed "Hank" for his admiration of Hank Greenberg, the great Detroit Tigers slugger. Salandria's father was a tailor who took great pride in the custom-fitted suits and overcoats he produced in his shop, where he worked long hours each day. His mother worked alongside her husband as a seamstress, and also raised their eight children. As with so much of the country, the depression years were hard on the Salandria family. "When we were kids," he once recalled, "we went to a barber school where we got haircuts for 15¢."[12]

Both his parents had immigrated to the United States from Italy not long after the turn of the century. They expected Vince, their fourth child but first son, to become a doctor or a lawyer. "Since I can't deal with blood, there was truly no alternative for me other than the law."[13]

He studied law at the University of Pennsylvania, where he had already graduated Phi Beta Kappa. The dean of the Penn law school was

Owen J. Roberts, the by-then-retired Supreme Court justice who had presided over the Commission investigating the Pearl Harbor attack. In spite of his early convictions, Salandria did not confront Roberts with what he was certain was the truth about Pearl Harbor. "I did not want to harm any career I might have in the law," he admitted. Moreover he did not feel that Roberts, although a man of integrity, could ever concede that Kimmel and Short did not, in fact, bear full responsibility for the Pearl Harbor disaster.[14]

But Salandria's political perspective had been deeply influenced by the government's handling of Pearl Harbor, and was a major factor in his thinking after President Kennedy was assassinated. Historians in virtually all American universities, he came to believe, "show no interest in revealing how through Pearl Harbor President Roosevelt secretly manipulated and controlled our foreign policy. Instead we learn that the Central Intelligence Agency's creation was a necessity in order that we should not be again surprised as we were at Pearl Harbor. In failing to confront the truth we got the CIA. By our unwillingness to embrace hard truth about how power works in our nation, we pay a horrible price in the loss of democracy."[15]

Salandria was driving from Bartram High to his law office when news of President Kennedy's assassination came over the radio. "My first thoughts were that the admirals were involved in it. Don't ask why admirals, rather than generals or CIA. But that is the first thought that occurred to me."[16]

On Saturday morning, November 23, Salandria discussed the case with his brother-in-law Harold Feldman, who told him: "Look, Oswald will probably be killed." It would happen sooner rather than later, Feldman continued, and added: "And they'll get a Jew to do it, because they always involve a Jew in these things."[17]

Harold Feldman was a freelance writer, and a translator proficient in a wide range of languages, including Albanian and Tagalog. As a lay psychoanalyst he had published extensively in psychoanalytic journals. In 1954 he published an article examining the psychology of assassins. After the JFK assassination he determined that Lee Harvey Oswald did not fit the historic profile of a lone assassin. "He denied his guilt consistently, which no other lone assassin in history had ever done," Feldman said. "They usually brag about it."[18]

Like Salandria, Feldman was interested in world affairs. Also like his brother-in-law, he was not a supporter of President Kennedy. He once criticized the Kennedy family in general for what he believed was a lack of moral courage: "Not an ounce in a carload of Kennedys, at least as far as I've ever seen."[19]

Feldman and Salandria met that Saturday to review what was then known about the Dallas events. They agreed it was important to keep their minds open as to whether Lee Oswald, whose name was dominating television and radio broadcasts, was guilty and was not part of a conspiracy. But that open mind would have to close, they felt, if Oswald was killed.[20]

Picking up on Harold's reasoning, Salandria said: "If Oswald is killed this weekend by a Jew, then we must look for a WASP conspiracy." Feldman's assertion that "they'll get a Jew to do it" was probably an intuitive response to a developing situation, but Feldman and Salandria agreed that a Jewish killer would frighten the Left, and dampen the interests of normally left-leaning Jews in thinking critically about the assassination. Moreover, they both felt that the assassination could not be honestly probed by the government. "The investigation of it would have to be undertaken by private individuals . . . perhaps we would, on this matter, do work ourselves."[21]

On Sunday, November 24, Salandria was watching the assassination coverage in his home with a psychiatrist friend, who was Jewish. Jack Ruby, née Rubenstein, leaped forward from a crowd of reporters and police and shot Oswald down.

"That's the Jew," Salandria blurted out.

The psychiatrist left hurriedly in confusion, never to return.[22]

Over the following weeks, the work Salandria had spoken of began in earnest. He and Feldman clipped and collated the multitude of articles on the assassination that were appearing in the nation's press. They gave special attention to those articles they felt indicated Oswald might have some kind of connection to U.S. Intelligence. The result of this early work was an article researched by both men but written by Harold called "Oswald and the FBI," which appeared in *The Nation* on January 27, 1964.[23]

"The Warren Commission should, if possible, tell us how President Kennedy was killed, who killed him, and why," the article optimistically began.

> But beyond that, it *must* tell us if the FBI or any other government intelligence agency was in any way connected with the alleged assassin,

Lee Harvey Oswald. At this moment, the possibility of such associations in the young man's life is intolerably a subject for speculation.[24]

Rumors about Oswald's possible intelligence connections were
circulating well before Harold Feldman's article was published. Three
weeks before the Warren Commission first discussed the question, reporter
Lonnie Hudkins ran a story in *The Houston Post* outlining what Hudkins
characterized as a "fantastic rumor." And *Philadelphia Inquirer* reporter Joe
Goulden, in an article published on December 8, 1963, alleged that "the
Federal Bureau of Investigation tried to recruit Oswald as an undercover
informant in Castro groups" two months before the assassination.[25]

Harold Feldman's article, which drew together these whispers and
hints, appears to have caused the Warren Commission a great deal of
consternation. As Commission member Gerald Ford wrote,

> Mr. Feldman had laid down four pages of hard-to-answer questions
> in his article, "Oswald and the FBI," in the January 27, 1964 issue [of
> *The Nation*]. Fortunately, the public did not know how serious the
> matter appeared to be at the moment. Although the speculations in
> Feldman's article were enough to arouse a good deal of public inter-
> est, the theories had no official basis and they did not create the panic
> they might have if it had been known that even the Attorney General
> of Texas was afraid that some of them might have a basis in fact.[26]

Also on January 27, General Counsel J. Lee Rankin, during a secret
Executive Session, told the Commission that he had invited the Texas
officials from whom the story came to come to Washington. "And they
did on Friday," he said. "At that time they were – they said that the rumors
were constant there, that Oswald was an undercover agent, but they
extended it also to the CIA, saying that they had a number for him
assigned to him in connection with the CIA and gave that to him, and
none of them had any original information of their own." The source for
their information was Lonnie Hudkins. After his article appeared,
Hudkins was interviewed informally by Leon Jaworski, who reported
back to the Commission that Hudkins had invented the story – a most
serious charge against a journalist. But when he was interviewed by the
Secret Service in December, Hudkins had said his source was Allan
Sweatt, the head of the criminal division of the Dallas Sheriff's
Office.[27]

"We do have a dirty rumor," Rankin conceded, "that is very bad for
the Commission."[28]

The FBI and CIA both promised thorough investigations to determine whether there had been any relationship between Oswald and their respective agencies. And publicly, at least, the Warren Commission was content that the ensuing self-investigations were honest. In its Report, published some nine months later, the Commission stated:

> The Directors of the CIA and the FBI have testified before the Commission that Oswald was never in the employ of their agencies in any capacity. The Commission has concluded on the basis of its own investigations of the files of Federal agencies that Oswald was not and had never been an agent of any agency of the U.S. Government (aside from his service in the Marines) and was not and had never been used by any U.S. Government agency for any purpose.[29]

Commission member Gerald Ford, however, was more forthcoming in his account of this period. "Harold Feldman set forth a formidable sequence of circumstantial evidence pointing to the same things the Attorney General and Mr. Wade had brought up in telephone conversations with Lee Rankin. His speculations were elaborate."[30]

But even though the Commission had Feldman's "speculations" in hand, they failed to notice an error in "Oswald and the FBI." In 1965, Harold admitted privately, "You know that we made one mistake the Warren Report never picked up on." He referred to a section of the article which contrasted letters Oswald had written – some to his mother, and another to the Fair Play for Cuba Committee in New York City, both of which were published in *The New York Times*. Feldman had written in his article that "Whoever wrote the letters to New York was coherent, commanded a good vocabulary, rarely misspelled a word, and punctuated decently. Oswald himself wrote English that a sixth grader would blush to acknowledge . . . until the authorship of the letters to the FPCC is settled, I think it reasonable to suppose that Oswald did not compose them, at least not without help."[31]

But many months after his article appeared, Oswald's letters were published in the Warren Commission's Hearings and Exhibits, and Feldman conceded the mistake:

> We made a big porridge of the contrast in spelling between O's letters to mother O and his letters to the Fair Play for Cuba Committee. The only versions we had were the ones that appeared in the *NY Times*. From the copies in the Exhibits, it

is almost certain that the *Times* corrected the spellings in one set of letters and not in the other set. But the Commission never mentions this and leaves my thesis on the letters practically uncontested, just the lame excuse that O wrote and rewrote his "business" mail.[32]

The Warren Commission may have missed or overlooked Feldman's mistake, but the Federal Bureau of Investigation did not. Charging this particular section of Feldman's article was "ridiculous," William Branigan said that Oswald, in his letters to the Fair Play for Cuba Committee, was attempting to impress the FPCC's main office with his organizational skills, and that "we obtained a copy of letter in question through an anonymous source and there are numerous misspellings in the letter not shown in Feldman's article."[33]

The FBI, it seems, viewed "Oswald and the FBI" as an institutional affront. When it appeared, a number of memoranda were written and sent within the Bureau. Branigan wrote to Assistant Director William Sullivan that Bureau records showed the FBI conducted a "Loyalty of Government Employees" investigation of Harold Feldman in 1949. This unearthed the fact the Feldman's brother Abraham was once affiliated with the Revolutionary Communist Vanguard, "which followed the teachings of Lenin and Marx and which believed in the overthrow of the U.S. Government by means of propaganda, demonstrations and mass action." The memo noted that the organization had disbanded in 1940, but that Harold had attended some of its meetings during the 1930s.[34]

Of the article itself, Branigan called it "another bitter attack upon the Bureau. Using utter falsehoods, rumors, gossip and newspaper reports taken out of context, the author leaves the impression that Oswald was an informant of the FBI. This is the line being taken by the Communist Party (CP) and other groups who are bitter in their opposition of the Bureau and is another attempt to discredit the Bureau. Oswald, of course, never was approached by us to become a Bureau informant."[35]

At the conclusion of Branigan's ten-page memo, which itemized Feldman's various assertions, there was a recommendation for action – which in this instance was that none be taken.

Few doubts about the lone-assassin scenario were being publicly expressed in late 1963 and early 1964. Almost without exception, the major organs of the media, print and electronic, seemed unwilling to give the lone-assassin story a critical review. Harold Weisberg was told by his literary agent that "nobody in New York was considering anything other than what the government was saying."[36]

As a publication of the Left, one might expect that *The Nation*, for one, would have immediately been asking questions about the government's lone-gunman theory. It did not. The issues published just after the assassination called JFK "A Most Unstuffy Man," carried tributes from a variety of dignitaries, and lauded Kennedy for his "sense of social urgency." In particular he was commended for his moves toward disarmament and peace, which *The Nation* called "the President's finest achievement." But insofar as the investigation of the assassination was concerned, *The Nation* at this early juncture seemed to be taking a wait-and-see approach.[37]

The Nation had originally rejected "Oswald and the FBI." Editor Carey McWilliams responded favorably to a description of the article in December, promising to give the piece "a prompt reading." But in early January he told Feldman, "I have decided – most reluctantly, I must confess – not to use your piece. It is certainly a well-done job, and I was sorely tempted, but it seems to me that on balance and for a variety of reasons we should not use it at this time."[38]

Fred J. Cook, a New Jersey-based investigative reporter, was also having some difficulties with *The Nation*, to which he was a regular contributor. Cook's suspicions about the Kennedy killing were aroused as he watched television coverage over the assassination weekend. Instinctively, he wanted to investigate things in Dallas for himself. "But I had no organization behind me to finance such a trip; the task was far beyond the resources of *The Nation*, even if it had been willing, so I sat and watched like millions of others as the drama unfolded."[39]

Cook did what digging he could, and learned that the Mannlicher Carcano – the alleged assassination weapon – was as a rule a grossly inferior rifle. And he began thinking about an article.

"Carey McWilliams was not enthusiastic about the trend of my researches," Cook wrote long afterward. McWilliams professed complete faith in the integrity of the Warren Commission, which at that time had just been formed and was more than a month from hearing any witnesses. And so Cook felt he had no choice but to suspend his assassination work, and resume what he had underway when the assassination had interrupted everything else.[40]

In his memoirs, McWilliams acknowledged the criticism he received for at first resisting work that questioned the official story. But he insisted he had been "quite willing to test the findings of the Warren Report," provided it was responsible, and indeed *The Nation* was by no means in complete lockstep with the mainstream media. On January 14, 1964 – barely a week after first rejecting Harold Feldman's article – McWilliams accepted it. A few revisions were made, although the substance of "Oswald and the FBI" was unchanged. "We have made some cuts," he told Feldman, "but I think they are all to the good."[41]

And so the article appeared in the January 27 issue. Around that same time, J. Lee Rankin was appointed general counsel to the Warren Commission, and Norman Redlich named his personal assistant. Editors of *The Nation*, in the same January 27 issue, used this and the selection of other staff counsel to reaffirm its confidence in the Commission. "These are excellent lawyers, men of the highest integrity," the magazine stated. In that same editorial *The Nation* seemed to distance itself from Feldman's article, commenting that it "is published not to make a charge but to raise a question that, in fairness to the FBI and to the public, requires a specific finding."[42]

Whatever negative feedback to Feldman's article *The Nation* may have had was not represented by any letter to the editor. The only reaction the magazine published came from a New Jersey reader who said he was "delighted to see . . . the article by Harold Feldman, 'Oswald and the FBI.'" He included a few lines of verse:

> *Lines Anent an Inquiry*
>
> A loner in the Lone Star State
> Where he was resident
>
> A loner in the Lone Star State
> He shot our President?
>
> A loner in the Lone Star State
> We know of his defections
>
> But who is likely to relate
> Just what were his connections?[43]

In December 1963 Carey McWilliams had also rejected Mark Lane's "Defense Brief for Oswald." *The Nation* was the first publication

Lane had offered it to, but at that time, according to Lane, McWilliams was adamant that the magazine would not be questioning the official story. Lane had phoned McWilliams and told him he did not believe Oswald's guilt had been proven, and that his "Brief" would urge a careful, dispassionate evaluation of the evidence. But McWilliams' almost immediate response had been, "We cannot take it. We don't want it. I am sorry but we have decided not to touch that subject." McWilliams had insisted that Lane not even send him the article.[44]

By his own account, Lane made his "Defense Brief for Oswald" available to "almost every periodical in the United States," but there were no takers. "No one was willing to read it, let alone consider publishing it," he said. Then the editor of *The National Guardian*, having heard of the piece, contacted Lane. He read it and gave it an enthusiastic reception. But because *The National Guardian* was a small, left-leaning weekly, it was a reluctant Lane who agreed to let them publish it. "My choice," he later wrote, "seemed to be between *The National Guardian* and my file drawer."[45]

One of the magazines to reject Lane's article was *The New Republic*, but this magazine was on firmer ground in doing so, since it was then considering a similar article. "Seeds of Doubt," by Jack Minnis and Staughton Lynd, appeared in its December 21, 1963, edition. Minnis was the research director for the Student Nonviolent Coordinating Committee, while Lynd was a history professor at Spelman College; the latter would play a role in publishing a Salandria article nearly a year later. Both men were in Atlanta, Georgia, and began collaborating on the article after noting discrepancies in news reports about the President's wounds. Some of their questions were also puzzling a few reporters and the early critics, including "(1) How Lee Oswald, from a position behind and slightly to the right of President Kennedy, fired a shot which entered the President's neck just below the Adam's apple," and "(2) how Oswald, using a bolt-action rifle, fired three shots with deadly accuracy in five and one-half seconds at a target 75 – 100 yards away moving about 25 miles an hour."[46]

But articles like "Seeds of Doubt," Mark Lane's defense brief, and Harold Feldman's "Oswald and the FBI" were exceptions to the rule during this early period. Endorsement of the lone-assassin scenario would, for several more years, be the rule for virtually all print and electronic media, making dissemination of honest appraisals of the Warren Commission's published work a grinding, uphill battle.

One early critic resolved the problem by taking matters into his own hands.

At the time of the assassination, Harold Weisberg was fifty years old, and dissolving what had been a successful poultry farm in Maryland. As a younger man Weisberg had been a journalist, an investigator for the United States Senate, and during World War II an intelligence analyst with the Office of Strategic Services. He didn't know it yet, but the skills he had developed in this earlier part of his career were about to be called upon.

Though his business was undergoing liquidation, Weisberg still spent his days doing farm-related chores, often listening to a radio as he worked. His favorite station was WQQW. The station once held a contest which asked the question, What's the most unusual place you listen to us? Entrants were required to answer in twenty-five words or fewer. Weisberg won the contest with four: "In the hen house." His prize was a small transistor radio, and he was back in the hen house listening to it on November 22, 1963, when regular programming was interrupted by news of the assassination. He rushed to his TV set and watched, horrified, as the events of that weekend began playing out.[47]

Among the developments was the almost instantaneous proclamation of Lee Harvey Oswald's lone guilt. Law enforcement officials in Texas were quoted as saying they had amassed enough evidence to easily convict him. Some newspapers openly referred to Oswald as the assassin.[48]

"All the things were happening that shouldn't happen," Weisberg told an interviewer in 1997. "They couldn't try Oswald. All of this evidence was contaminated. How are you going to get an impartial jury? None of this should have happened."[49]

By Sunday, Weisberg was trying to get back to a semblance of his routine. He did some chores around the farm, and in late morning returned to the main house from the hen house for a cup of coffee. The television remained on.

In Dallas, police were about to transfer Lee Oswald from their downtown lockup to the county jail.

By this time Harold Weisberg, like Harold Feldman one hundred miles away in Philadelphia, was convinced that Oswald would be eliminated. "My thinking was simple," he said. "All that was being done was making it impossible to try him; someone wanted to close his mouth, and the only way to really do that was to close it permanently – to kill him."[50]

Chapter 4

Promises To Keep

The woods are lovely, dark and deep,
But I have promises to keep,
and miles to go before I sleep,
and miles to go before I sleep.

Harold Weisberg had a deep appreciation for these concluding lines of Robert Frost's "Stopping by Woods on a Snowy Evening." They gave meaning to his American citizenship – something he viewed as a priceless accident of birth. His parents had come to the United States from Ukraine, in eastern Europe, early in the 20th century. Harold was born in Philadelphia, Pennsylvania, on April 8, 1913, the first member of his family born in their adopted homeland. "Born into freedom, is the way I like to think of it. And it gives me promises to keep, in Frost's words."[1]

The promises Weisberg meant to keep related to a deeply felt sense of duty to country. Conducting an independent, unofficial investigation into President Kennedy's assassination, following an unsatisfactory official one, was part of that duty, a promise to keep before his eternal sleep. He knew from the start that the assassination of JFK had to have been a conspiracy. It was also plainly one of the major events in the history of the United States. "It cannot be consigned to history with the dubious epitaph of these never-intended-to-be-honest official investigations. The assassination of President Kennedy turned the world around. That kind of thing cannot be ignored."[2]

Weisberg felt well equipped to analyze the Warren Commission's work on its own merits. His early career, first as a journalist and later writing and editing government reports for the U.S. Senate, gave him a unique perspective with which to evaluate the Commission's performance. "To begin with," he once said, "the question was, had they really investigated the crime?"[3]

Weisberg was convinced they had not. He would further conclude not only that the Warren Commission had gone about its work improperly, and had deliberately avoided the truth; he was equally convinced that by late on the evening of November 24, 1963 – after Lee Oswald had been shot to death in the basement of the Dallas police jail, guaranteeing there would be no trial – high-ranking government officials had resolved to prevent an honest investigation.[4]

Most incredibly, Weisberg determined, they had left a paper trail.

When Harold was in the fifth grade, the Weisberg family moved from Philadelphia to Wilmington, Delaware, where he grew up. By the time he was in high school he was set on becoming a writer; before long he was editing his high school newspaper, *The Wilmington High School News*.[5]

By the early 1930s he was attending the University of Delaware and simultaneously writing for *The Wilmington Morning News*. His salary was a mere pittance. When his father died unexpectedly, Weisberg dropped out of college and moved to Washington where he could make more money. "I sent a third of my wages home every week, on payday."[6]

It was while at *The Wilmington Morning News* that Weisberg began to more clearly recognize class disparity in the United States. Aided by President Roosevelt's New Deal, efforts nationwide to organize labor unions and establish collective bargaining had reached a crescendo. Resistance to unions by big business was fierce and often violent, and the violence was answered in kind. The savagery of the era is recalled in the names by which key events are remembered: San Francisco's "Bloody Thursday" in July 1934; "The Memorial Day Massacre" in South Chicago, 1937; and that same year, "The Battle of the Overpass" at the Ford Motor Company's plant in River Rouge, Michigan.

In July 1935 FDR signed the National Labor Relations Act, known as the Wagner Act after its main sponsor, New York Democratic Senator Robert F. Wagner. In effect, the Wagner Act replaced an earlier New Deal statute, the National Industrial Recovery Act of 1933, which the Supreme Court had declared unconstitutional. The Wagner Act reaffirmed that portion of NIRA that guaranteed workers the right to organize and bargain collectively through representatives. It also defined unfair labor practices by employers, and established the National Labor Relations Board to carry out the terms of the new law.[7]

Momentum from the Wagner Act led to the creation of the Committee on Education and Labor in 1936. A subcommittee to investigate anti-union activities on the part of organized business was soon formed. Known as the Senate Civil Liberties Committee, it was more informally referred to as the La Follette Committee after its chairman, Wisconsin Senator Robert M. La Follette, Jr.[8]

A family friend had helped Weisberg land his first Washington job – a file clerk position with the Agriculture Department. Once there, he began trying for a job in its Public Information Department, but before that materialized, he applied to and was hired by La Follette's new committee.[9]

Resistance to the Committee was almost immediate. Witnesses dodged subpoenas, and Committee targets tried to sanitize their records. One of Weisberg's first jobs was scotch-taping ripped up pieces of paper back together, the mutilated documents a shrewd investigator had recovered from a trash bin. Weisberg and his colleagues were able to reassemble a number of them and use them in preparing for the Committee's first hearings, which began on September 22, 1936, and investigated the steel and automotive industries.[10]

For the first time, the ugly reality of corporate America's anti-labor tactics came under close public scrutiny. These tactics included espionage, which the La Follette Committee would conclude was "a common, almost universal, practice" by which corporations disrupted worker attempts to unionize. When espionage proved ineffective, organized business sometimes resorted to brute force.[11]

In 1937, the La Follette Committee turned its attention to Harlan, Kentucky, where years of conflict between coal operators and the men who worked the mines had earned it the sobriquet Bloody Harlan. Coal operators used every tactic at their disposal to prevent miners from organizing. "We can't do business if they have unions," one operator said.[12]

Harlan County had the reputation of being the toughest place in the United States to unionize. Any miner sympathetic to the union cause was vulnerable to a charge of criminal syndicalism. During an attempt to organize in the 1920s, spies had infiltrated United Mine Workers locals and identified the leaders; the organizing was crushed.[13]

Over the years other committees and investigators, including a group led by novelist Theodore Dreiser, had preceded La Follette to Bloody Harlan. Dreiser's committee inspected mines and miners' living conditions in 1931; what it learned was even worse than expected. Deeply moved, committee member John Dos Passos wrote, "I'd never understood the meaning of the word 'depression' until I began to poke around in those mountains. Miners were living in the most abject misery."[14]

In May of 1938, following the La Follette Committee investigation, a conspiracy trial began in London, Kentucky, against a group of men charged with violations of the Wagner Act. Harold Weisberg was among those in town for the trial. "It was, altogether, sixty-some indictments all in one," he remembered. "And it was coal operators and their deputized thugs. They could get a thug and make a sheriff out of him, he could do any goddam thing he wanted. And mostly it was intimidating people not to join unions."[15]

Weisberg's role was assisting Justice Department lawyers in preparing subpoenas for witnesses, and sharing information he had developed working with La Follette. "I had knowledge that they didn't have," he recalled. The trial lasted deep into the summer before at last going to the jury. After ten hours of deliberation, the foreman reported they were hopelessly deadlocked, with seven jurors favoring acquittal. And so the proceeding came to an end.[16]

But according to Weisberg, the reason for the stalemate involved jury tampering. He learned of it as he was out walking late one night, as was his custom. The clerk of the court knew Weisberg enjoyed late-night walks and was waiting for him in the shadows of a large tree. "And he walked with me a while and told me the story."[17]

The coal companies, Weisberg was told as they walked the darkened streets, had rigged the jury. They had bought the mortgages to the homes of those jurors who had them. "So [they] knew damned well that they didn't vote to convict, or they'd lose their houses," Weisberg said, "in addition to any other possible things."[18]

Weisberg was shocked by what the clerk had to say. He went straight to prosecutor Brien McMahon and told him what had happened. "He didn't believe it," Weisberg recalled. "He was so convinced, as I had been, that nobody would dare try and fix a federal jury, that he didn't believe it." Although at that time the trial was not yet over, Weisberg saw no point in staying. He made arrangements to get back to Washington.[19]

Weisberg had spent four months in the Harlan coal region. Long afterward, he still recalled the harshness of life there. "It's an awful tough place."[20]

A year and a half later, in October of 1939, Weisberg was abruptly fired from the La Follette Committee. The stated reason for his dismissal was that he had leaked confidential information to the press. According to a report in FBI files, Senator La Follette "was quite certain the newspaper involved was *The Daily Worker*."[21]

"All of that's false," Weisberg said years later, after reviewing the FBI data. What he had done, he insisted, was to give a pre-publication, typeset draft of Committee proceedings to a reporter. Nothing in it, he maintained, was confidential; distributing such information was routine. "I never leaked a thing. I didn't have anything to leak! Everything we had was public record."[22]

The real reason he was dismissed, Weisberg said, was that he had fallen into disfavor with Senator La Follette. The Senator by then felt he had reaped all the political benefit he would get from the probe, and wanted to end it. He was also under pressure from the Senate to wrap up the Committee; in 1938 he obtained funding only after pledging to complete the investigations within eight months. But there was also pressure for the Committee to continue, some of it coming from FDR himself. Weisberg participated in some behind-the-scenes maneuvering that resulted in a final appropriation of fifty thousand dollars, extending the Committee's life in order to investigate the plight of migrant farm workers in California. "La Follette wanted to get me for that, and of course he did."[23]

Weisberg was ready to try something new, and for the next few years earned his living as a freelance writer. His most important stories exposed illegal business arrangements between American and German corporations – what were called Nazi cartels. Much of his work during this period was published in *Click*, a then-popular magazine similar to *Life*. To Weisberg's great irritation, most of his articles appeared uncredited because the magazine's owner did not want to use Jewish-sounding names, and Weisberg refused to use a pen name.[24]

On at least one occasion the magazine's editor assigned Weisberg a pen name without first consulting him. An article appearing in late 1941 and attributed to "Jefferson Hale" was really Weisberg's. "Japan's *Mein Kampf*" analyzed Japanese foreign policy and began: "America is next on Japan's list of victims!" *Click* published the article in its November issue, about a month before the Japanese attack on Pearl Harbor.[25]

After the United States entered World War II, Weisberg joined the Army. That he chose to serve was a little unusual. An avowed pacifist, he had resisted compulsory military training in college, and could have had an exemption from military service during the war. But he didn't take it. "I figured we had to beat that son-of-a-bitch Hitler, and whatever I could do to do it, I would do."[26]

And so he was inducted shortly before Christmas, 1942. During this hitch, a case of the mumps landed him in Walter Reed Hospital. As he convalesced, Weisberg requested a review of his service record, which resulted in his re-assignment to the Office of Strategic Services, or

OSS. "I was not a spook," he said in 1993. After World War Two, President Harry Truman disbanded the OSS, and distributed its divisions to other government agencies. In this manner Weisberg found himself working for the State Department.[27]

The postwar years marked the resurgence of an anti-Communist Red Scare in the United States. A Special Committee on Un-American Activities had been established in 1938. Its chairman, Texas Democrat Martin Dies, declared that the federal government was riddled with "hundreds of left-wingers and radicals who do not believe in our system of private enterprise." One of his objectives as committee chairman was to "paralyze the left wing element of the Roosevelt Administration."[28]

Its critics said the Dies Committee, as it was known, was a loose cannon – a dangerous panel that abused its power. In his weekly newsletter *In Fact*, George Seldes wrote:

> Power to investigate is the power to destroy.
> The La Follette Committee investigated the attacks on civil liberties, notably the attack on labor. It aimed to destroy the prevailing system of industrial espionage, vigilantism, violence, frequently murder.
> The Dies Committee on the other hand aims to destroy every liberal, labor, pro-labor and progressive movement in the U.S. by branding it "Red."[29]

The wartime alliance between the United States and Soviet Union had ended with the war, and anti-communist sentiment gained momentum on both the foreign and domestic fronts. The Truman Doctrine, ostensibly addressed to disputes in Greece and Turkey, was more generally aimed at containing communist expansion. At home, President Truman signed into law the Federal Employees Loyalty Program, which authorized investigations into the backgrounds of all federal employees.[30]

By 1947 the Dies Committee had become the House Committee on Un-American Activities, known as HUAC, the first permanent committee established to investigate subversive activity. The first government agency to come under scrutiny was the State Department, which became one of HUAC's principal concerns. In June 1947 Harold Weisberg was one of ten employees fired under sweeping powers granted to the secretary of state the previous year in a special rider to its appropriation bill. Known as the McCarran rider after its author, Senator Pat McCarran, the new authority enabled the secretary of state to dismiss any employee "in his absolute discretion . . . whenever he shall deem such termination necessary or advisable in the interests of the United States." A few years later, McCarran would help develop the Internal Security Act of 1950, which would also bear his name.[31]

The chief counsel to the American Communist Party called the McCarran Act "nothing less than a blueprint for American fascism. I say this without hyperbole." John J. Abt was a New Dealer who had been with the Public Works Administration, and in the late 1930s served as chief counsel to the La Follette Committee. Although he would never represent him, Abt was the lawyer requested by Lee Harvey Oswald after his arrest for the assassination of President Kennedy.[32]

The only thing resembling an explanation for the dismissals was that Weisberg and the other nine were potential security risks. "There were no charges filed against me. I was given no hearing," Weisberg said later. "There's nothing much more anti-American than that." But a State Department internal investigator scoffed at such a notion: "Hearings . . . what the hell for? That was a waste of time!"[33]

Weisberg said that nine of the ten fired employees were Jewish, and he always suspected that anti-Semitism was the real reason for their dismissal. But Secretary of State George C. Marshall said the ten were fired because of indirect associations with representatives of foreign powers.[34]

Three of the fired employees, following a review of the case by the State Department's Personnel Security Board, were allowed to resign without prejudice. The remaining seven, including Harold Weisberg, retained the prestigious law firm of Arnold, Fortas and Porter for their defense. The firm's sole objective was to allow the fired men to resign without prejudice, simply to remove the stigma of being dismissed as potential security risks. Each of the seven signed a written statement specifically denying "any association, directly or indirectly, with any one known or suspected by them of being a representative of a foreign power."[35]

The firm was able to interest *The New York Herald Tribune* in the story, which on November 2, 1947, began a series of articles about the dismissals "in all its grim detail." None of the ten were ever publicly identified. The stories were a sensation and the reporter, Bert Andrews, developed the material into a book, *Washington Witch Hunt*, for which he won a Pulitzer Prize in 1948.[36]

Ultimately, Weisberg and the others were allowed to resign without prejudice. With considerable pride, he once recalled: "I beat the sons of bitches."[37]

Not long after this tumultuous episode came to an end, Weisberg and his wife Lillian bought a parcel of land, and on it built a farm which they hoped would give them a measure of independence. With no background in agriculture, the Weisbergs made unlikely farmers. The plan was to establish a poultry business. "The peaceful clucking of contented chickens is what I looked forward to," Harold wrote.[38]

He found the property, a fourteen-acre tract of abandoned farmland, in the rolling hills of Montgomery County, Maryland. The land had lain fallow for decades, and much of it was a tangle of tree, brush, and weed. Weisberg cleared the land himself, using only hand tools. Late in his life, he credited this hard physical labor as one reason he lived as long as he did, in spite of the health problems that accompanied his old age.[39]

Over time, the farm prospered. At their peak the Weisbergs were raising chickens, Rock-Cornish game hens, waterfowl, and selling the birds and their eggs. The farm was later dubbed Coq d' Or, after the opera by Russian composer Nikolai Rimsky-Korsakov, *Le Coq d' Or*, or *The Golden Cockerel*. Weisberg, a classical music lover, was listening to it one day when one of his customers came by. "And she said, 'That's the name that you should have for your farm. You do have a golden bird.'"[40]

The Weisbergs operated Coq d' Or farm for a dozen years, during which time they earned a reputation for excellence. Lillian Weisberg became the national chicken-cooking champion in 1956, and Harold won a national barbecuing championship three years later. They also won awards for the chickens they raised. Then, in the early 1960s, everything changed. Helicopters from a nearby military base flew regular maneuvers over Coq d'Or, and in spite of complaints from Weisberg continued to do so. The sound of the helicopters, he maintained, ruined his flock. "The chickens couldn't stand the noise," he remembered. "They equated the sound with the beating wings of a hawk."[41]

Weisberg sued, and won a small settlement. He took the money but was left with no choice but to shut down operations. The suit did, he said years later, help set a new legal precedent. "I established the property owner's ownership of the air space, to the point where he needs it to enjoy his property."[42]

Weisberg was fascinated by the Kennedy assassination when it happened. He was a lifelong Democrat but reluctant Kennedy supporter; he voted for JFK only because he considered the alternative, Richard Nixon, so bad. The post-assassination media coverage was so heavily biased against Lee Harvey Oswald that it was plain that selecting an impartial jury was a virtual impossibility. Weisberg said he was not surprised when Oswald was killed, although the manner of his death – on television and in police headquarters – shocked him.[43]

Weisberg had already decided to resume his writing career and was developing a book about the dangers of excessive noise. About a week after the assassination, he sent a proposal for a magazine article about the assassination to his agent New York. The response, he always recalled with astonishment, was that the agent severed her relationship with him. She told him in no uncertain terms that nobody would consider publishing anything other than what the government said. "Can you understand how shocking that was to me? With my back-ground? And my beliefs about the functions of information in a country like ours?"[44]

At that, he said, he decided to take what the government said about the assassination and analyze it, much as he had done professionally in the OSS. But in late November 1963, there was not a lot he could do: the Warren Commission had barely formed, and its findings would not be available until some still-unknown point in the future. And so, while one of his principal activities in the months to come would remain the liquidation of his farm, he shelved the book about noise and began tracking the Kennedy case in the newspapers and broadcast media.

On the evening of November 24, 1963, when Lee Oswald had only been dead a matter of hours, Deputy Attorney General Nicholas Katzenbach picked up a pen and a yellow legal pad and wrote a memo-randum that began: "It is important that all of the facts surrounding President Kennedy's assassination be made public in a way which will satisfy people in the United States and abroad that all the facts have been told and that a statement to this effect be made now."[45]

Harold Weisberg came across this handwritten memorandum years later through one of the many Freedom of Information requests he filed, in search of unpublished Warren Commission records. "It doesn't say, 'we won't investigate the crime,'" Weisberg said of the memo. "That would be a horrible thing. But through all the polish, what they are saying is, 'We'll put the hat on Oswald.'"[46]

The memo was written after a series of phone calls between Katzenbach, Lyndon Johnson, LBJ aide Bill Moyers, and J. Edgar Hoover. Composed in longhand on Sunday night, and typed by

Katzenbach's secretary the next morning, it contains several significant statements appearing to suggest that more emphasis be placed on convincing the public of what the government said than on ascertaining the truth. "The public must be satisfied that Oswald was the assassin; that he did not have confederates who are still at large; and that the evidence was such that he would have been convicted at trial," Katzenbach wrote. "The only other step would be the appointment of a presidential Commission of unimpeachable personnel to review and examine the evidence and announce its conclusions. . . . We need something to head off public speculation or Congressional hearings of the wrong sort."[47]

To Weisberg, this memorandum was a smoking gun, a paper trail – proof that the government sought to prevent an honest investigation of the assassination. How could such a highly-placed government official write such a memo just two days after Kennedy's death, he wondered, when the investigation had hardly begun? "They're talking about what they're doing and not doing. So, there was a de facto conspiracy not to investigate the crime itself."[48]

If Weisberg was correct, it begs the question: Why would the government conspire to prevent an honest investigation? The conclusion that the government had something to hide is but a small step, yet Weisberg, although he maintained that assassination was by definition a political crime, could see no evidence of a government conspiracy before the fact. And in the years to come, he steadfastly refused to speculate in his published works about who the true assassins were. "I think that anybody who undertakes to write on a subject like this owes it to his intended reader to have what is proven or provable, and not theoretical," he said. "Even if the government killed the president, or if people in the government killed the president, it is irresponsible to say that without proof."[49]

Still, Weisberg could imagine what might have happened. "You want to know what they killed him for, you can certainly say that to get different policies in the White House was a possibility," he once told an interviewer. "We don't know these things, because the crime was never investigated. But you can't ignore it."[50]

Chapter 5

"I Guess You're On Your Own"

In the early 1960s, the American south was a hazardous place for anyone attempting to effect social change. One could be beaten senseless merely for entering a greasy spoon restaurant and taking a seat.

The toughest and most reactionary state in all the south was Mississippi. In June 1963 NAACP field secretary Medgar Evers was shot to death in front of his home in Jackson, one of an untold number of violent acts committed against progressives that year. The following summer, at least eighty civil rights workers there were beaten, and many more arrested on trumped-up charges, in blatant acts of intimidation.[1]

"There's no state with a record that approaches that of Mississippi in inhumanity, murder, brutality, and racial hatred," said NAACP Executive Director Roy Wilkins. "It is absolutely at the bottom of the list."[2]

The summer of 1964 – designated "Freedom Summer," a direct challenge to Mississippi's institutionalized racism – was the season that civil rights workers Andrew Goodman, Michael Schwerner, and James Chaney were abducted and murdered, an act that shocked the movement and focused national attention on Mississippi. Even before any activists arrived for the summer's struggle there had been a sharp increase in racial tension. In the spring of 1964, one commentator later observed, Mississippi was primed for violence.[3]

Like much of the south, white Mississippi was resisting federal laws that reached to the very core of what life there had been for generations. Local custom took precedence over Supreme Court rulings against segregation in public schools and public facilities. These rulings, in particular the landmark *Brown v. Board of Education* in 1954, helped spawn citizens' councils across the south, which formalized white resistance and put the authority of the Federal government on a collision course with rights of individual states. The Supreme Court, in particular Chief Justice Earl Warren, became a nemesis for those who would perpetuate the status quo.[4]

What the white south could not ignore was the resolve of those opposed to its racist way of life. At the grassroots level, and at considerable personal risk, these opponents were determined to make American democracy live up to its promise. Beginning in the 1950s, nonviolent activism in the form of boycotts and sit-ins began forcing the issue, placing civil rights on the national agenda and propelling leaders like Dr. Martin Luther King, Jr. to national prominence.

The oppression of blacks from the era of slavery through the 1960s was a crime against humanity – a tragic and shameful saga littered with untold stories of the brutality with which this American apartheid was enforced. Only occasionally would the circumstances of racial violence generate widespread attention, as in the case of Emmett Till, a fourteen-year-old Chicago boy who was abducted and murdered while visiting relatives in Mississippi in 1955. Two white men were charged in the case, but in spite of strong evidence of their guilt they were acquitted.[5]

In 1961, activists began testing a Supreme Court ruling that outlawed segregation of interstate facilities, particularly those in bus stations and airports. Freedom Riders, as they came to be known, rode buses across state lines throughout the south and attempted to use illegally segregated restaurants, waiting rooms, and restrooms along the way. Their actions were deliberately provocative. "We felt that we could then count upon the racists of the South to create a crisis, so that the federal government would be compelled to enforce federal law," said James Farmer of the Congress of Racial Equality, or CORE. "That was the rationale for the Freedom Ride.[6]

It was a good strategy. The Freedom Rides began in Washington, D.C., and in their early stages were fairly peaceful. But the riders, all of them volunteers, knew that as they got into the Deep South there would be trouble. Many whites found the defiance of local custom intolerable. One rider later contended that everyone on his bus was prepared to die. In Alabama on Sunday, May 14, buses were firebombed and Freedom Riders savagely beaten by white mobs. There was no police protection for the riders and none of the attackers were arrested. It would emerge that local authorities had promised Ku Klux Klansmen fifteen minutes to attack the riders unimpeded. An FBI informant had alerted his superiors to this conspiracy, but J. Edgar Hoover failed to tell Attorney General Robert Kennedy.[7]

The Kennedy administration would not openly support the Freedom Riders; neither could they stop them. Hoping to prevent further violence, the administration cut a deal with Mississippi officials. Senator James Eastland promised the riders safe passage to Jackson. In return, the Kennedys pledged not to interfere in the arrest of the riders on their arrival, thus capitulating to Mississippi's racist power structure. Yet the

Freedom Rides continued. By summer's end some three hundred had been arrested. In June Mark Lane, then a member of the New York State Assembly, was among eleven people arrested after attempting to use a segregated restroom at the Jackson airport. "The Negroes in this state are going to move forward," Lane told reporters. "There's nothing in the world that can stop that." The charges against him were later dismissed. In September, the Interstate Commerce Commission issued its own ban on segregation in interstate travel.[8]

The most explosive situation in the Magnolia State developed in the fall of 1962, when a black Air Force veteran named James Meredith sued for the right to attend the University of Mississippi. No blacks had ever attended "Ole Miss" before, and white reaction was predictably hostile. State judges upheld the university's right to deny Meredith entrance, but in late September a federal court ordered that Meredith be allowed to register. State officials defied the order; on September 25, Governor Ross Barnett personally blocked Meredith from entering the school's admissions office on its campus in Oxford.[9]

From his home in Dallas, retired General Edwin Walker viewed the attempts to register Meredith with scorn. He began issuing statements urging civilians to defy the "anti-Christ Supreme Court" and march in support of Governor Barnett by resisting efforts to integrate the University. "Ten thousand strong from every state in the Union, rally to the cause of freedom . . . bring your flag, your tent, and your skillet," he was quoted as saying. Five years earlier Walker had commanded troops that enforced public school integration in Little Rock, but he said that had been a mistake. "This time," Walker said, "I am out of uniform and I am on the right side."[10]

The standoff between Governor Barnett and the Kennedy administration was considered the most serious threat to federal authority since the time of the Civil War. The inevitable explosion came on September 30 after Meredith, escorted by federal marshals, was finally admitted to the campus. An angry crowd gathered outside Meredith's dorm, and before long rioting broke out. President Kennedy was forced to send five thousand Army troops to the campus to quell the riot, which lasted through the night. By the time it was over, two people were dead and many more were injured. Former General Walker had flown to the campus and was among 200 people arrested. He faced four charges, including insurrection. Unable to post bail, he was flown to the U.S. Medical Center for Federal Prisoners in Springfield, Missouri. According to some published reports, Walker was released a week later only after agreeing to undergo a psychiatric examination in Dallas.[11]

Meredith, a transfer student, remained under the protection of U.S. Marshals until he graduated from Ole Miss a year later.[12]

In the spring of 1964, Matt and Jeannine Herron were living in Mississippi and preparing for the coming summer. "The crisis appears to be ahead," Jeannine wrote in a letter to Vince Salandria, dated March 14. "We are fine – greatly sobered by the human behavior we have witnessed here, but more alive and passionate than we have ever been."[13]

The Herrons had long been active in peace and social issues. During this period, Matt was one of a team of photographers and journalists attempting to document the lives of blacks and whites living in the Deep South – "it was undergoing rapid change," he recalled. Inevitably their work came to include the civil rights movement. Jeannine was co-founder and program director of the Child Development Group of Mississippi, the largest Head Start program in the south. Earlier in the year she had attended the first trial of Byron de la Beckwith, charged in the Medgar Evers murder, and had written about it for *The Nation*.[14]

As soon as he heard about the Kennedy assassination, Matt grabbed his camera gear and took the first available flight to Dallas. He did not have an assignment but was confidant the demand for photographs would be great. He remembered viewing the events there "with Mississippi eyes" that were, he felt, more suspicious of authority than most. "Mostly the police lied to you," he said, "so I viewed the bulletins from the Dallas Police Department with a good deal more skepticism than did most of my fellow journalists."[15]

He was quickly convinced that something was amiss. "In my brief encounters with Oswald and his one press conference, he did not seem like a guy who had just assassinated a President. I kept an open mind on that one."[16]

There was a tremendous amount of confusion that weekend; it was especially high that first day. "There were so many stories bouncing around that when the 'official' version emerged a day later, I was more than skeptical." Herron outlined his suspicions to an editor at *Look* magazine, concluding, "If I'm right it's the biggest story of the twentieth century, and I want to do it for *Look*." It didn't work out that way; the magazine assigned more seasoned staff members to the story.[17]

The Herrons knew Vince Salandria from their mutual involvement in the peace movement in Philadelphia. That spring of 1964, Jeannine was attempting to lure Salandria down to Mississippi for the summer's struggle. Up to one thousand volunteers, mostly from the north and mostly students but also groups of lawyers and other professionals, were preparing to come south to participate in voter registration drives and community-building projects.

"The offer to come to Mississippi tempts me," Salandria said in April.[18]

"You would never forget it," Jeannine told him. "I guarantee you would not return home the same."

Freedom Summer, or the Summer Project as it was really known, was set to begin in mid-June under the general direction of the Council of Federated Organizations (COFO), a coalition of civil rights groups founded in 1961. While a broad objective was to register black voters, there was a more specific goal of establishing the Mississippi Freedom Democratic Party to serve the state's disenfranchised black citizens. The mostly white volunteers would also operate "Freedom Schools" and other social programs. Before heading to Mississippi they were required to attend a week-long orientation on the campus of Western College for Women in Oxford, Ohio.[19]

Fierce resistance from white Mississippians, the volunteers were told, could be taken for granted. They would be viewed as outside agitators, troublemakers – and targets. "This is a serious operation that you are involved in," cautioned John Doar of the Justice Department's Civil Rights division, when he addressed the volunteers during orientation. "There is no possible way that anyone can be completely protected from violence." Staughton Lynd, then a history professor at Spelman College, reminded them that the President had the authority to send federal troops into a state during a crisis situation. "The question is," he said, "is the situation in Mississippi a crisis? What we are trying to communicate is that it is."[20]

Michael Schwerner, a twenty-four-year-old native New Yorker, had been in Meridian, Mississippi, since early in the year, where he headed a branch office of CORE. Twenty-one-year-old James Chaney was a native Mississippian and also a CORE volunteer working in Meridian. Both young men were in Ohio participating in the orientation, offering their experience to the uninitiated.[21]

They returned to Mississippi with Andrew Goodman, a 21-year-old Summer Project volunteer. Goodman was a student at Queens College and, like Schwerner, a native New Yorker. Together the three drove to Meridian, in Lauderdale County, arriving on Saturday, June 20. The next morning they left to investigate the burning of Mt. Zion Church, a black church near Philadelphia, Mississippi, in Neshoba County, some 35 miles away. Schwerner and Chaney had been to the church a few weeks before, and had persuaded its leaders to host a Freedom School.[22]

The trip was a risky one: Neshoba County was a Ku Klux Klan stronghold, and while the young volunteers could not have known it, the Klan had targeted Schwerner for elimination. The three young men must have been alarmed but not terribly surprised when, on their return to Meridian that afternoon, they were pulled over by a Neshoba County deputy sheriff for allegedly exceeding the speed limit. The deputy arrested Chaney, who had been driving, and held Schwerner and Goodman "for investigation," as the deputy later described it.[23]

The deputy, Cecil Price, held them in jail until about 10:30 that night and released them after Chaney paid a $20 fine. Price said later that after telling the three to get out of Neshoba County, he escorted their station wagon a short distance and observed as the vehicle turned south on Highway 19, heading back toward Meridian.[24]

They never made it. Schwerner had left word at the Meridian office that if they hadn't returned by 4 p.m. that Sunday, an emergency plan was to go immediately into effect. Co-workers began calling every city and county jail, every police and sheriff's office, and every hospital between Meridian and Neshoba County. The Philadelphia jail where the trio were still held was among those called, but the caller was told they were not there. Summer Project organizer Bob Moses was still in Ohio when informed of Schwerner, Chaney, and Goodman's disappearance. He later said he knew immediately the three were dead.[25]

The disappearance drew immediate national publicity. In Washington the Justice Department announced that it had ordered the FBI to make a full inquiry into the case, but in Philadelphia many residents scoffed at all the attention. CBS News anchor Walter Cronkite angered many with a reference to "Bloody Neshoba," an appellation historically associated not with Neshoba, but neighboring Kemper County. Some residents offered the opinion that the disappearance was really just a publicity stunt. This continued even after the station wagon that Schwerner, Chaney, and Goodman had been driving was discovered on Tuesday, having been burned and dumped in a swamp north of Philadelphia – not south, the direction Cecil Price had said they were going when last seen. There were no bodies in the car. The next day Lyndon Johnson dispatched Allen Dulles, who still sat on the Warren Commission, to Mississippi to meet with its governor, Paul Johnson.[26]

Before this meeting took place, Dulles agreed to speak with several Summer Project volunteers and other black leaders, including Bob Moses and Lawrence Guyot. Guyot said the appearance of Dulles was the only time he opposed the role of the federal government in Mississippi. He recalled that Dulles had said, "Look, I'm going to meet with the Governor in an hour, and we want this mess cleaned up."

Aaron Henry, president of the state NAACP, stood up and said, "What do you mean?"

"These civil rights demonstrations are causing this kind of friction," Dulles replied, "and we're just not gonna have it, even if we have to bring troops in here."

"You're talking to the wrong people," Henry had shot back. "Everything we're trying to do is constitutionally protected and we oughta be having more help from the federal government rather than you, as an agent of the federal government, come and tell us to be quiet."[27]

Dulles also met with Rita Schwerner, Michael Schwerner's wife, who had already told the press that if the missing men had all been black their disappearance would have gone unpublicized. Dulles kept her waiting for 45 minutes. When he finally saw her their meeting did not last long. After five minutes Dulles extended his hand. "I want to offer you my deepest sympathy," he said, "but I'm sorry, I have an appointment now." He headed for the door.

"I don't want sympathy," she called after him. "I want my husband back."[28]

It didn't happen. In August, forty-four days after they disappeared, the bodies of the three missing men were discovered buried in an earthen dam not far from the Neshoba County fairgrounds. There, the county coroner made a preliminary examination of the remains before sending them to the University of Mississippi Medical Center in Jackson, seventy miles away. Press accounts said each victim had been shot – Schwerner and Goodman once each, and Chaney three times – but that there was no other evidence of bodily harm to the three young men.[29]

A few days after the autopsies COFO arranged for an independent examination of one of the bodies – that of James Chaney, the only black victim – that offered appalling clues concealed by the first autopsy. Pathologist David M. Spain was stunned by the differences he found between the nationally reported first exam and the body that lay before him. Chaney had been savagely beaten, probably with a chain or a pipe; numerous bones had been smashed into pulp. The beating alone, Dr. Spain later wrote, was enough to kill him, though he had indeed been shot. "I could barely believe the destruction to these frail young bones," the horrified doctor recalled. "In my twenty-five years as a pathologist and medical examiner, I have never seen bones so severely shattered, except in tremendously high speed accidents or airplane crashes."[30]

On June 11, 1963 – the same day that Medgar Evers was fatally shot from ambush in Mississippi – President Kennedy called on Congress to enact sweeping civil rights legislation that would speed school desegregation and open up public facilities to all Americans. The United States, he told a national television audience, was facing nothing less than a moral crisis as a nation and as a people.[31]

Just over one year later, and some seven months after Kennedy's death, President Johnson signed the Civil Rights Act of 1964. In August, members of the Mississippi Freedom Democratic Party traveled to the Democratic National Convention in Atlantic City where they hoped to be seated as delegates. State party regulars opposed them. In spite of compelling personal testimony, some of it broadcast on national TV, and in spite of vacancies after an angry walkout by Mississippi's regular Democrats, the MFDP delegates were not allowed to cast votes at the convention.[32]

The JFK assassination remained a current event, and for private researchers there were many fresh trails to follow. Vince Salandria was being courted by Mark Lane for investigative work in Dallas, and this, finally, is how he elected to spend the summer of 1964. "I consider the assassination matter the big item," he had written Jeannine Herron in the spring:

> The civil rights fight is crucial and ultimately it will determine whether our society can undergo the life-giving revolution it needs. But I don't think the Civil Rights movement will win this summer. . . .

> If JFK, the great plutocrat who wore a crown, can be gunned down and out of this world, and murder will not out, then the killers of the good Medgar Evers, William L. Moore, and their successors and assigns, will enjoy immunity from prosecution. More martyrs will fall, and our lids will be too heavy with the past deception for our eyes to open and for our voices to cry out in outraged fury.[33]

Salandria and Mark Lane had met earlier that year in Philadelphia, Pennsylvania, when Lane was on an early speaking tour. Both men were invited to dinner at the home of Spencer Coxe, executive director of the Philadelphia office of the ACLU.[34]

As Salandria recalled it, Lane that evening sho⸱
in the question of whether Lee Oswald had beer
agent. That had been the clear implication of Haro'
The Nation in January and was in the fore of his ar
Lane conceded it was a possibility, according to Salaɪɪᴅ.
opinion beyond that.

Several years later Lane wrote: "[Marguerite] Oswald told me that
she believed that it was not unlikely that her son had been an intelligence
agent of the United States and that she intended to make her feelings
on that subject known. I saw no evidence at that time to support her
assertion, and I expected that she would suffer considerable public
ridicule if she made that unsupported charge. She did so, and the personal
attacks upon her mounted. . . . I was reluctant to be associated with what
I considered to be a possibly unfounded and certainly an unprovable and
inflammatory charge."[35]

That evening in Spencer Coxe's home, Lane suggested that
Salandria head up a Philadelphia office of the Citizens' Committee of
Inquiry, an offer Salandria declined, citing a deep-seated aversion to
committees.[36]

It was then that Lane suggested that Salandria do some investigative work in Dallas on CCI's behalf. The offer was not accepted
immediately. On April 1, Lane reiterated the offer in a letter: "If it is
possible for you to spend a week in Dallas, you could, I am certain, make
a major contribution to the development of the facts in this case."[37]

The school year not yet over, Salandria was unable to leave as soon
as Lane had hoped. But Salandria was definitely interested. He wrote
back immediately: "The itch to know thrusts me in the direction of fair
Dallas . . . from June 26 and for ten weeks thereafter, I can and will accept
such an assignment from you should it be forthcoming."[38]

Salandria had a very favorable impression of Lane, but it appears
that, as of mid-April, he was not certain Lane still needed him. "My initial
reaction to him is that he has a good mind, a feeling for facts, and considerable courage," Salandria told a friend. "If there is still more to get out
of Dallas this summer, and if he still wants my help, I will dig in for him."[39]

Salandria left Philadelphia for Dallas by automobile several days
earlier than he had indicated to Lane he'd be ready to go. He was
accompanied by his brother-in-law Harold Feldman, and by Feldman's
wife Irma, whom everyone knew as Immie.

"Mississippi is mighty close to Texas," he wrote Jeannine Herron. ᴐw he was trying to lure her to his all-consuming interest. "There will ᴗe lots to do, since we will be armed with important leads. You and Matt are invited." Although Matt would soon decide that "it seemed like a good time to get Jeannine and the kids out of Mississippi," they declined Salandria's offer, electing to stay in the Magnolia State, which Jeannine was referring to as "the bowels of fascism."[40]

The "important leads" came from Mark Lane's New York office. On June 23, Deirdre Griswold, the Citizens' Committee of Inquiry's executive director, sent six pages of questions, copies of affidavits, and other data to get Salandria started. A card file included names that, Griswold said, had only rarely appeared in the public record. "I'm sure you'll think of many more questions to be asked the different individuals involved," she wrote in a cover letter. She urged them to let her know how they could be reached in Dallas. "I guess you're on your own from here on in."[41]

A few weeks earlier, Griswold had written to Salandria. "A couple doing graduate work in sociology at Columbia . . . are also going to Dallas at the end of the month, and we'll discuss a division of labor so that there is no duplication of effort." The couple were George and Pat Nash, and they would be leaving for Dallas just a few days after Salandria and the Feldmans. In spite of Griswold's division of labor, the Nashes wound up interviewing some of the same people Salandria and Feldman talked to. In at least one instance they had markedly different impressions of their subjects.[42]

Salandria and the Nashes had met prior to their separate departures for Dallas, when they all had dinner together in the Salandria home. "Pat and I were impressed with all of you and heartened about not being there alone," George Nash had written to Vince. "Let's get together via phone before you leave."[43]

The school year for teachers had ended at Bartram High on Tuesday. Early Wednesday, June 24, Salandria and the Feldmans hit the road. Salandria was cautioning friends to keep word of their investigative trip in confidence, and in particular, not to mention it to anyone connected to the government.[44]

Harold and Vince took turns driving and napping in the back seat while Immie navigated. Stopping only to eat and gas up Salandria's 1955 Buick sedan, they had covered the nearly 1,500 miles to eastern Oklahoma by the evening of Thursday the 25th. There, they hoped to meet with another assassination researcher. Deirdre Griswold had told Salandria about "Mrs. M," whom she described as "a woman in

Oklahoma who has sent us a lot of stuff." She meant Shirley Martin, who after her initial contacts with Lane and Marguerite Oswald had traveled to Dallas several times for the express purpose of interviewing witnesses. Salandria and Feldman hoped to visit with her and her family at the Martin farm in rural Hominy.[45]

But their visit was unannounced, and when they reached the farm no one was home. "Where do families go," Salandria wondered that evening, "with no neighbors in sight and oil storage tanks in the field to the right of the home, an airplane in a field across the road?"[46]

Over the next few years a solid bond developed between Salandria, the Feldmans, and the Martin family. But their first meeting would have to wait. The three travelers pressed on to Dallas, still some 200 miles distant.

Chapter 6

"We All Loved Kennedy"

Looking back to the period of her life when she was actively investigating the assassination of JFK, Shirley Martin once remarked, "What in the world did we think we were doing?"[1]

After putting Marguerite Oswald in touch with Mark Lane, Mrs. Martin began traveling to Dallas in order to locate assassination witnesses and interview them. Not in an official capacity, of course: she was motivated by curiosity, and the feeling that something was not quite right. Her proximity to Dallas proved an irresistible lure. Yet the climate of fear in Dallas during this period was strong – so much so that some people felt anyone traveling there to ask questions about the killing was taking a reckless, unnecessary risk. Even before the assassination the city's national image had suffered: on October 24, after delivering a speech at the Dallas Municipal Auditorium, Ambassador Adlai Stevenson was attacked and spat upon by an anti-United Nations mob. The city was home to many associated with ultra-conservative politics, including former Army General Edwin Walker, the prominent, unabashed right-winger who in 1962 had publicly opposed the admission of James Meredith to Ole Miss.[2]

But for Mrs. Martin, an unwavering conviction that something was "very, very wrong" with the official version of President Kennedy's assassination compelled her to insert herself into the case. "I started early and was interviewing witnesses before the Commission began taking testimony in February, 1964, finally making seven trips to Dallas for this purpose," she once wrote. She piled four children and a dog into her car for the drive from Oklahoma. Mrs. Martin was home-schooling her children and viewed the trip as part of their education. The risk factor, she believed, was minimal; asked about it long afterward, she said that she would never have taken her kids there if there was any real concern for their safety.[3]

And yet she looked back on it all with a measure of disbelief. Although it was not the principal reason she got involved in the assassination case, President Kennedy meant a great deal to Shirley Martin. "We all loved Kennedy at our house," she recalled. "The revelations of the later years didn't change a thing."[4]

At the time of Mrs. Martin's early visits, Dallas civic leaders were going to some lengths to improve the city's image, first bruised by the Stevenson incident and then battered by the assassination. Mayor Earle Cabell insisted that his was an average American city. "We knew," he wrote in a national magazine, "that Dallas had no monopoly on the Far Right any more than it does on hate or bigotry or violence or lack of respect for authority."[5]

It took the Martin family, minus Mr. Martin, about half a day to drive to Dallas. It was February 1964. This was Shirley's first time there; if they had lived much farther away they probably wouldn't have made the trip. Mr. Martin was not enthusiastic about his wife's interest but did not stand in her way. He came with the rest of the family on later trips, and even talked building manager Roy Truly into giving him a tour of the Book Depository. On this first trip Shirley, who in addition to *The New York Times* had immediately subscribed to *The Dallas Morning News*, wanted to talk to some of the witnesses whose names had appeared in the paper. She also wanted to re-trace the routes that, according to published reports, Lee Oswald had taken – on foot, by bus, and by taxi – in the early afternoon of November 22, 1963.[6]

By car, they followed the route that Oswald was alleged to have taken from the Texas School Book Depository to his Beckley Street rooming house several miles away in Oak Cliff, a section of Dallas across the Trinity River. They did this not so much to time his movements, though time them they did, but to get a better feel for events. At the rooming house they knocked on the door and asked to come in and look around. At first they were denied entrance, but the manager there changed his mind after he was offered ten dollars.[7]

The owner, a man named Johnson, showed them Lee Oswald's old room. Not that there was much still there from when Oswald occupied it three months earlier. "The police took everything that wasn't nailed down," Johnson told them.

"Did Oswald keep a gun in the room?" Shirley asked.

"No rifle, that's for sure," Johnson replied.

"What about a revolver?"

"Well, maybe." The police, Johnson said, had found a holster among Oswald's effects.

There wasn't much else to see. Their brief tour of these dismal quarters was about over when Shirley asked a final question: "Did you like Oswald?"

"Well," Johnson said carefully, "I didn't *dis*like him. He was one of the best roomers we ever had. He was real clean." Sometimes, Johnson added, Oswald made phone calls and would speak in a foreign language. But mostly he kept to himself.[8]

In November of 1963 Mrs. Martin was living with her family on a farm near Hominy, Oklahoma, a small town not far from Tulsa. But she had spent just a portion of her life in the continental United States. She was born and raised in Intramuros, the city within a city in Manila, the Philippines. She was raised there by her grandparents after her parents' divorce. Her mother returned to her native Australia and her father, Olympic bronze medalist Bill Harris, was traveling the world as a goodwill ambassador for the United States.[9]

When she was fifteen years old, Shirley was sent to live with her mother in Australia. Soon after she left, her grandfather, a wealthy American industrialist, was captured by the Japanese army and sent to the dreaded Santa Tomas concentration camp, where he later died. An aunt and uncle were also captured. They were sent to the Los Baños concentration camp but survived their ordeal.[10]

In 1943 Shirley joined her father in Hawaii, where she spent the next seventeen years. It was there she met and married Air Force pilot Mark Martin. By the time they left Hawaii, it was on the brink of statehood and the Martins had three children: Victoria, Teresa and Steven.[11]

A job offer brought the Martin family to Hominy in 1960, where Mr. Martin would manage a large wheat-storage facility. As striking a change from Hawaii as life in rural Oklahoma must have been, Shirley grew to love the Sooner State and appreciate its splendor. "It's a terrific day," she once began a letter. "When Oklahoma puts on her spring clothes, she is divine. From here, I can see green, green, green."[12]

The Martin home was adjacent to the wheat-storage facility, on property with enough room to raise prized quarter horses. Mrs. Martin also took in every stray dog that came by: in late 1963 there were thirteen. The Martins added another child in Oklahoma, too. Mike Jacoway was a full-blooded Choctaw Indian who had been living in a Catholic orphanage in Oklahoma City. He was never formally adopted, but from the age of six lived with the Martin family. "We took him home for the summer and then decided we wanted him to stay for as long as he liked. He stayed until college."[13]

When the Martins arrived in Oklahoma, Senator John F. Kennedy was just appearing to be a viable presidential candidate. "I began researching him and liked what I read," Shirley remembered. The 1960 election was the very first in which she took part. Her participation was not limited to merely learning about the issues and candidates. Shirley and her oldest daughter Victoria, then fifteen, operated a small Democratic headquarters in Hominy. They had to drive to Tulsa for supplies, such as campaign buttons and stickers. "We were not popular as the Baptist churches in Hominy were noisily anti-Kennedy." Because she was so actively involved, there was a sense of elation, even synchronicity, on election night 1960, when victory was finally within JFK's grasp. In a letter written in 1964 she recalled a magazine article "that described the President-Elect as leaping into the air at news of winning Connecticut (the first state conceded) and the memory that coincidentally I had leaped into the air at this same instant."[14]

Almost immediately upon JFK's election Mrs. Martin had written to his press secretary Pierre Salinger; she was concerned that the election's outcome might be reversed by a recount. "Pierre was sweet. Don't worry, he said, indicating that it would all come out right." The Kennedy White House, she remembered, was extraordinarily good at answering letters.[15]

Few parents consciously favor one child over another. Yet some children exhibit traits that inevitably garner them extra attention, and this appears to have been the case with Victoria. "What strange alchemy of fate picked me out as the mother of this nearly perfect girl?" Shirley once mused. "She has qualities of strength and devotion that should be used in some way in this struggling world."[16]

It was a friend of Vickie's who notified the Martins of the assassination. They had just finished watching the soap opera *As The World Turns* and were making lunch when the friend telephoned.

"Turn on the TV! Turn on the TV!" he cried excitedly. "Kennedy has been shot!"[17]

What followed was the experience shared by millions of Americans – the Martins were riveted to the TV, engulfed by the dizzying flow of information from Dallas. Shirley was struck by the news footage of Lee Harvey Oswald in the police station corridors, in particular his declaration that "I didn't shoot anybody, sir!"[18]

Something, she quickly concluded, was not right. "My hackles went up over the apparently sweeping statements the police were making . . . my suspicions did not take long surfacing thanks to the Keystone Kops in Dallas."[19]

Mrs. Martin never did believe the official story. But as much as President Kennedy had meant to her, and as disturbed as she was by his sudden, violent death, there was an even greater sense that the man accused of destroying Kennedy was innocent, and the fall guy for an unknown and undefined conspiracy.

One of the first assassination eyewitnesses Shirley Martin contacted was Jean Hill, a Dallas schoolteacher who, coincidentally, hailed from Oklahoma. At the time of the assassination Mrs. Hill was standing along Elm Street with her friend Mary Moorman, who took an important and widely distributed photograph of the President just as he was hit. When Shirley spoke to her, Mrs. Hill had not yet testified to the Warren Commission. But she had told authorities on the day of the assassination that she had heard as many as six gunshots in Dealey Plaza, and after the shooting stopped had seen a man running from the Texas School Book Depository area west toward the railroad bridge.[20]

Shirley telephoned Jean Hill from Hominy on Friday, January 25, 1964. She could not have been prepared for some of the things Mrs. Hill told her; they were, in all likelihood, her first indications of the fear that remained in Dallas. According to Mrs. Hill, Miss Moorman had taken another photograph that day, this one just before her more famous one, which showed the Texas School Book Depository, and Oswald's alleged "sniper's nest," in the background. Jean Hill said she had seen this picture, and "there was no sign of anyone in the window at that time." Furthermore, Mrs. Hill had disturbing news about Warren Reynolds, a witness who may have seen Lee Oswald flee the scene of the Tippit shooting. Reynolds had not been interviewed by the FBI until January 21 – four days before Shirley called Jean Hill – and at that time did not positively identify Oswald as the man he had seen shortly after Tippit was shot. Mrs. Hill told Shirley that just the night before, Reynolds had been shot in the head by an unknown assailant.[21]

"Mrs. Hill told me," Shirley later wrote, "that she and Miss Moorman had received many threatening phone calls urging them to 'keep quiet' and when they reported these to the Dallas police, they received an official brush-off. Mrs. Hill said Miss Moorman would not talk to me as she was much more frightened and upset over the whole thing than Mrs. Hill was." Mrs. Hill also said that the man she saw running in the direction of the railroad bridge just after the assassination may have been Jack Ruby, an opinion she repeated to the Warren Commission two months later.[22]

During her visit to Dallas in February, Shirley telephoned the home of Ruth and Michael Paine, who lived in the Dallas suburb of Irving. She asked Ruth whether she could come to visit her, and Ruth said yes.[23]

The Paines had befriended the Oswalds in early 1963. In October of that year Ruth helped Oswald get a job at the Texas School Book Depository. At the time of the assassination the Paines were separated, as were the Oswalds. Marina was staying with Ruth at the Paine home in Irving, while Lee was staying in the Beckley rooming house. When police searched the Paine residence on the afternoon of November 22, 1963, Ruth had greeted the officers by saying, "I've been expecting you all." She led them to the garage, where much incriminating evidence against Lee Oswald was discovered. After his arrest, Oswald called Mrs. Paine from jail and asked her to contact attorney John Abt on his behalf. Mrs. Paine, who said later she was appalled that Oswald thought he could ask anything of her, tried without success to reach Abt, but never told Oswald she hadn't reached him.[24]

The Martins arrived at the Paine home soon after telephoning, and Ruth let them in. Shirley's daughter Teresa later recalled her surprise at how small the house was. Mrs. Paine allowed them to look around, and showed them the place in the garage where the alleged assassination rifle was supposedly stored. During the course of the visit, which lasted about two hours, Michael Paine arrived, and Ruth warmed him a TV dinner. Shirley and Teresa both recalled Michael's nervousness as he watched them and ate.[25]

When she testified to the Warren Commission the following March, Ruth told Commission members about this visit, but said she didn't remember exactly what Shirley had asked her about, only that "she was not satisfied with the evidence that led to a public conclusion that [Oswald] was guilty." Ruth told Shirley that in her opinion, Oswald did in fact kill President Kennedy.[26]

Mrs. Paine also notified the FBI about the visit. Special Agents Bardwell D. Odum and James P. Hosty interviewed Ruth Paine about it in her home on Saturday, February 29, 1964. At this time Mrs. Paine's memory would have been much fresher than when she testified before the

Commission. The agents' report on their interview with Mrs. Paine reads in part:

> Mrs. Martin stated she felt the evidence was not fully incriminating as far as Lee Harvey Oswald was concerned and she wanted to satisfy herself as to the facts. She indicated she had spent most of her time in Dallas retracing the route of Oswald following the shooting of President Kennedy and had timed the alleged escape route of Oswald following the shooting.
>
> Mrs. Martin stated she did not believe the gun photographed at the police department was the same gun which was being held by Oswald in a picture released to the press later. She referred to a photograph taken sometime prior to the assassination showing Oswald holding a rifle.
>
> Since the date of her contact with Mrs. Paine, Mrs. Martin has called on the telephone from her home in Hominy, Oklahoma, many times and has written almost daily letters to Mrs. Paine all along the same line, looking for inconsistencies in the case and seeking to find out why Oswald shot President Kennedy if such was the case.[27]

Before the agents left, Mrs. Paine offered them her opinion of Mrs. Martin. Shirley was, Ruth said, a "bright nut" with an excellent mind – up to a point. But she was coming to conclusions about Lee Oswald and the assassination that did not follow from the evidence.[28]

In subsequent memoranda FBI Director Hoover wrote, without citing Mrs. Paine as a source, that Shirley Martin was considered a "bright nut" and a "possible mental case." It seems curious that Hoover apparently relied on and repeated the opinions of an ordinary citizen. In view of their close ties to the Oswalds, and some of Ruth's behavior over the assassination weekend, some of the critics were already beginning to view Michael and Ruth Paine with suspicion.[29]

A Warren Commission document declassified in 1976 only heightened suspicions. Page 66 of this document, an FBI report, described a telephone call intercepted in Dallas on November 23, 1966, the day after the assassination. A "male voice was heard to say that he felt sure Lee Harvey Oswald had killed the President but did not feel Oswald was responsible, and further stated, 'We both know who is responsible.'" The document did not say it, but the call was placed between Michael Paine's office and Ruth Paine's house.[30]

For her part, something about Ruth Paine made Shirley uneasy. She had a feeling – and it was only a feeling – that there were microphones hidden in the Paine home tape-recording their conversations. "I felt from the very beginning, the first time I ever walked into her house, and that was with my three children and Michael Jacoway, and my little dog – I felt from that very moment that she was *on*," Shirley recalled long afterward. "You know what I mean?"[31]

Chapter 7

Mrs. Oswald and Mrs. Markham

In 1965, author Jean Stafford published an article in *McCall's* magazine entitled "The Strange World of Marguerite Oswald." Within a year the article had been expanded to a short book called *A Mother in History.* Ostensibly an objective profile of the mother of the alleged assassin, the book and article read as attacks on a woman who dared to speak out in support of her murdered son, whose name was forever linked to the most notorious crime of the era.[1]

For Stafford, the timing was fortuitous: when she received the assignment, her literary career needed a boost. She had just completed a year on the faculty at Wesleyan University. Few demands had been made on her there; she boasted to one friend that she was "being paid vast sums of money for doing absolutely nothing."[2]

It's difficult to figure what was in Stafford's head when she conducted her interviews with Marguerite Oswald. On one hand, she was a writer. She was paid $2,500 by a prominent, if mainstream, magazine to research and write what must have been considered a plum assignment. Yet Stafford's biographers record that she dreaded going to Texas for the interviews. More astonishing, she confided to one friend that she was writing the piece "for a magazine whose name I am ashamed to write down."[3]

A writer interested in truth – and what else does any artist have? – might have explored some of the allegations Mrs. Oswald made. Her most compelling statement was probably the unsupported charge that had concerned Mark Lane – that her son was a low-level intelligence agent.

"He never did tell me why he went to Russia," Marguerite told Stafford. "I have my own opinion. He spoke Russian, he wrote Russian, and he read Russian. Why? Because my boy was being trained as an agent, that's why."[4]

This statement cries out for a followup question. Even the Warren Report says the "evidence is inconclusive" as to why Oswald went to the Soviet Union. But if Stafford asked a followup, she did not include it in her finished piece. Her next recorded question was, What would Lee have done with his life if he had not been killed?[5]

Undeterred, Marguerite answered this question at length, concluding: "I think he was doing with his life what he wanted to do. And I'm gonna say he was working for his country as an agent. I think that at age sixteen, he became involved, that at age sixteen Lee Harvey Oswald was being trained as a government agent."[6]

This segued into the subject of Marina Oswald, which seems to have pleased Stafford immensely: "I knew that there was bad blood between the two women."[7]

By her own admission, Stafford considered herself merely a "court stenographer" during her three days with Marguerite. Presumably she transcribed the tape recordings of their conversations verbatim, adding only descriptive details to her article and book. Stafford later used the tapes for entertainment purposes. Biographer David Roberts wrote that she "held parties at which she played the Oswald tapes for her friends."[8]

There is no denying that Marguerite Oswald said some bizarre things to Stafford. "President Kennedy was a dying man," Stafford quoted her. "So I say it is possible that my son was chosen to shoot him in a mercy killing for the security of the country."[9]

But any writer can influence a reader's perception by selecting how material is presented, and Stafford seems to have relished leading readers to the most negative impressions possible. Her prose reveals an utter contempt for Mrs. Oswald; her dislike is palpable. Even one of Stafford's biographers seemed uneasy with her subject's poison pen. Ann Hulbert called *A Mother in History* "profoundly unsympathetic" and noted Stafford's "obvious loathing of a woman with whom she had nothing in common." The book was, Hulbert concluded, "a cruel portrait, executed pitilessly."[10]

Yet Hulbert and David Roberts both endorse the lone-nut scenario, as well as Stafford's negative portrait of Marguerite. Hulbert used phrases like "the assassin's peculiar mother" who engaged in a "long, addled monologue in defense of her son." Roberts referred to Mrs. Oswald as "this pathetic creature" who was "an unsophisticated, delusional woman."

A third biographer, Mary Ellen Williams Walsh, inserted an obligatory "alleged assassin" into her text – but still resorted to some sidewalk psychology. "The fatherless orphan [sic] sought his revenge by killing the most powerful representative figure of the father that he could approach."[11]

A much different portrait of Marguerite Oswald emerged in an article seen by far fewer people. "The Unsinkable Marguerite Oswald" was written by Harold Feldman a year before Stafford's article, and based on material he gathered in Dallas with his wife Immie and Vincent Salandria. It was published in the September 1964 issue of *The Realist*.[12]

The Feldmans and Salandria arrived in Dallas late Thursday night, June 25, 1964. On Friday Salandria called the local ACLU office and advised it of their presence and intentions. He said he'd be calling them if they ran into any trouble, and was told that the Dallas police would probably not give them any problems.[13]

The first person they looked up – the first of the "important leads" Salandria had mentioned to Jeannine Herron – was Marguerite Oswald. Harold telephoned her and she offered to give them a tour of Oak Cliff, the section of Dallas where Officer J.D. Tippit was shot to death less than an hour after Kennedy's assassination.[14]

Marguerite Oswald was then 56 years old. In his *Realist* article, Harold Feldman described his surprise at first speaking with her on the phone. Media accounts had led him to expect a sour, uncooperative person. "What I heard instead was a pleasant ladylike welcome – not a trace of cautious ambiguity, not a second of hesitation in the warm courtesy that carried within it only a faint suggestion of loneliness." This from a woman thrust into the international spotlight under nightmarishly horrendous circumstances.

Marguerite took the three amateur investigators to some of the sites related to the assassination weekend. They visited the apartment on Neely Street, where Lee and Marina Oswald lived for a time. They were admitted to the apartment "with sympathetic deference," and Marguerite guided her guests through the place.

This was the apartment in which Marina is said to have locked her husband in a bathroom, thus preventing him from stalking and perhaps assassinating Richard Nixon. But as they moved about the apartment, Marguerite pointed out that none of the doors had ever had locks on them.

From Neely Street, they went to the intersection of 10th and Patton where Officer Tippit was slain. According to the Warren Commission's Report – at this time, still several months from publication – at least a dozen witnesses saw an armed man in the vicinity of the Tippit crime scene around the time of the shooting. Only two of these witnesses, however, said they saw the actual shooting. A third witness was within a hundred feet of the shooting, but his view of events was blocked by shrubbery.

Of the two witnesses who said they saw the actual shooting, one told police he didn't think he could identify the gunman and did not view a lineup. This forced the role of star witness onto Helen Markham, a waitress in downtown Dallas who was about to cross 10th on her way to a bus stop when Tippit was killed. In its Report, the Warren Commission used ironclad language to describe her performance with Dallas Police, and in her testimony before the Commission: "She identified Lee Harvey Oswald as the man who shot the policeman."[15]

Yet as her Warren Commission testimony would later show, Mrs. Markham was not nearly so decisive. Three weeks before she gave this testimony, Mark Lane interviewed her by telephone. It appears Lane tried to guide Mrs. Markham to a description of Tippit's assailant that did not resemble Lee Oswald. He was "on the heavy side," Lane suggested, but Mrs. Markham would only say that "he wasn't didn't [sic] look too heavy, uh-uh." Lane had more success in getting her to concede that the gunman's hair was "just a little bit bushy, uh-huh." She also told Lane that the man she saw, whom she consistently referred to as Oswald, was short and wearing dark trousers and a light gray jacket.

In any case, Lane's office wanted a follow-up interview. And so it was to her home that Salandria, the Feldmans, and Marguerite Oswald went next. She lived just a few blocks from the Tippit killing scene, in an apartment located over a barber shop.

They found Mrs. Markham at home, cradling her infant grand-daughter in her arms and pacing back and forth. She declined to talk to them because, she said, she had to care for the baby. She would not let them pay for a babysitter, but did finally agree to let them return later in the day. As they spoke, Mrs. Markham allowed Marguerite Oswald to briefly hold the baby.[16]

Helen Markham, Feldman observed in his article, was still young, even though she was a grandmother – "but shabby, beaten, and spiritless."

Salandria, the Feldmans, and Mrs. Oswald returned later that afternoon. As they approached the apartment, two Dallas police cars which had been parked right outside pulled away.

What happened next, Feldman wrote, was "the most pitiful spectacle in our experience." The foursome knocked on the Markham apartment door. Mr. Markham was now home, and he stood barring the door as his wife cowered to one side.[17]

"I've never seen that kind of terror," Salandria recalled years later.

"Their teeth were actually chattering. And we could get little from them because of their terror."[18]

"Please go away," Mr. Markham had groaned. "Please go away, and don't come back."

Marguerite broke in. "You've been threatened, haven't you?"

"Yes," Mr. Markham replied. "Please, go away!"

Shocked, they did as they were asked. As they got back out to the street and headed toward Mrs. Oswald's car, Marguerite fought back tears. "That poor man!" she said. "He was frightened to death. What right do they have to threaten him? This is still America, by God."

Before they could drive away, however, the Markhams' twenty-year-old son caught up with them, and said that while his parents might be afraid to talk, he wasn't. He told them to meet him at the public library a few blocks away. This encounter, however, proved equally futile. Harold Feldman wrote that Bill Markham revealed an "unutterable contempt for his parents" in every word he spoke. He asked for money in exchange for his information about the Tippit killing, but Salandria cautioned that could leave them all open to a charge of bribing a witness.[19]

Pressed, Bill Markham admitted to having a police record; above all else he wanted money. "I need it, ma'am," he told Mrs. Oswald. He did advise them, free of charge, that the Secret Service had told his parents there would be trouble for them if they talked to outsiders. "But I'm not afraid, ma'am. I need money and if I don't get some one way, I'll get it another."

Mrs. Oswald urged the young man to move to another state and get a fresh start. This he was unwilling to do.

Marguerite was distraught. "Oh Lord," she said, "poor people are so helpless."

Harold and Immie Feldman were checked into a motel. Salandria, however, spent several nights as Marguerite Oswald's houseguest. Marguerite at this time lived in a modest three room house in Fort Worth, which she rented for thirty dollars a month.[20]

To Salandria's surprise, Marguerite exhibited little overt grief for her son, who had been dead for less than eight months. "Rather I detected pride in her son as a patriot," he recalled years later. "She was a very bright woman and most determined to demonstrate that Lee was a patriot and a hero." Marguerite was also, he felt, proud to be an American.[21]

Mrs. Oswald was at this time without a job. What little money she did have came almost entirely from selling personal documents. *Esquire* magazine, for example, paid $4,000 for sixteen letters Lee had written her from Russia. This was in sharp contrast to the support Lee's widow was getting from the government and public contributions. Harold Feldman reported that by summer 1964, Marina Oswald had received $75,000.

Feldman also reported that the Fort Worth Council of Churches established a fund for the Oswalds, but stipulated that none of the money raised would be made available to Marguerite. "The reason," he wrote, "is obvious enough. Marina cooperates."[22]

By Christmas 1963, one month after the assassination, the family of Patrolman Tippit had received $312,250, mostly from contributions from American citizens around the country.[23]

Ostensibly, Salandria stayed with Marguerite for protection, although the role of bodyguard struck him as an unlikely one. "I was, and still am, a pacifist. But she was anxious, and we thought that my presence would make her less anxious." Salandria believed that with strangers from out of town conducting unofficial investigations, Mrs. Oswald felt a heightened sense of danger.[24]

There was reason to believe they were being watched. Although they secured their motel room when they left each day, when the Feldmans returned at night the room was usually unlocked. Salandria later described the unlocked doors rather casually. "We chalked that up to a little game being played and did not suffer any anxiety."[25]

If Marguerite's grief was not overt, it did manifest itself in other ways. Almost every day, she would visit Lee Harvey's grave in Rosehill Cemetery. She cared for it tenderly, with the attention of the practical nurse that she had been prior to the assassination. She pulled weeds and left fresh flowers, and even carried a length of garden hose in the trunk of her car to water the grave, attaching it to a spigot by her son's plot.[26]

It was also manifested in her fighting spirit, and her determination to clear her son's name. She was "deeply concerned about the place of her family in the historical record," Feldman wrote in *The Realist*. Toward that end she made herself readily available to the media. The previous March, one week after Jack Ruby was convicted and condemned to die for her son's murder, she issued a press release which said in part:

> My son, Lee Harvey Oswald, the accused assassin of President John F. Kennedy, is in my opinion, innocent of the charge against him. I have more circumstantial evidence to substantiate this fact than the Dallas police have that he was the murderer of President Kennedy.

This is what motivates me to continue my fight for J[
and our "AMERICAN WAY OF LIFE" – namely, a man is '
CENT UNTIL PROVEN GUILTY."[27]

That summer of 1964, Marguerite repeated to Salandria what she
had already told Mark Lane and the Warren Commission, and would tell
Jean Stafford a year later: that her son was an intelligence agent, or an
agent-in-training. "She always considered that Lee's 'defection' to the
Soviet Union was in the capacity of an agent for our government,"
Salandria remembered. "She spoke of going to Washington after the
defection and getting red carpet treatment at the State Department. She
was given assurances that Lee was safe in the Soviet Union. They treated
her, she told me, with great respect."[28]

Around this time, during a speaking tour of Europe, Mark Lane was
contacted by Warren Commission General Counsel J. Lee Rankin and
asked to appear once again before the Commission, preferably by July 1.[29]

Lane had exchanged a series of letters with Rankin since his first
testimony in March, most of them about his allegation that there had
been a secret meeting among Jack Ruby, Officer J.D. Tippit, and Bernard
Weissman eight days before the assassination. The Commission, Rankin
said, wanted to know the source of this information. But as he had
during his original testimony, Lane insisted he was not at liberty to reveal
the source's name.[30]

Nevertheless he flew back to the United States as Rankin had asked.
But there was a snag: after landing in New York, Immigration officials
briefly stopped him and took away his passport. His name, he learned,
appeared on their "lookout" list. After a few minutes the passport was
returned and Lane was allowed to continue on his way.

Immediately, he linked this to another unusual incident from a few
months before, when he was accosted by two FBI agents as he left his
home in New York. "We have confidential information that you have
illegally obtained FBI reports," one of them said. Lane replied he didn't
know what they were talking about, and the men made no effort to stop
him when he nudged them aside and hailed a taxi. Angrily denouncing
the agents, Lane said the incident "smacked of police state tactics" and
wrote a letter of complaint to Commission counsel Rankin. Now, as he
arrived in Washington for his second appearance before the
Commission, he was convinced that this and the passport incident

were related, and had something to do with his private assassination investigation.[31]

Lane's testimony began at 2 p.m. on July 2. The session appears to have been rather hostile. He was questioned principally by General Counsel Rankin who, though interested in the source of the Ruby-Tippit-Weissman meeting allegation, was also keen to learn more about the telephone interview Lane conducted with Tippit murder witness Helen Markham on March 2.

Lane had briefly mentioned this interview during his first Commission appearance. And in subsequent lectures, Lane talked about it even more, telling audiences that the description Mrs. Markham gave him of J.D. Tippit's killer did not match Lee Harvey Oswald. Lane had tape recorded the interview and played the relevant portions during these lectures. But matters were greatly complicated when Mrs. Markham testified to the Commission on March 26, and swore that she had never spoken to Mark Lane.[32]

Rankin got right to the point. "Do you have any writing from Mrs. Markham in connection with the interview that you referred to in your [previous] testimony?"

"Any document which Mrs. Markham wrote? Is that the question?"

"Either that or anything that she signed which purports to be her statement or affidavit or other recording."[33]

Lane explained that there was a tape recording of the interview but that he did not have it with him. The Commission almost certainly knew about the tape, since Lane's lectures were routinely monitored by FBI informants. The Commission also knew that it was being lied to, by either Mark Lane or Helen Markham. This could prove to be a serious problem. Mrs. Markham's credibility was paramount, since she was the only witness to testify that she saw Lee Harvey Oswald gun down Officer Tippit.[34]

Lane's testimony about the recording was carefully phrased: taping and divulging the phone call was probably illegal. To the Commission, he insisted that keeping the tape confidential was a matter of attorney-client privilege. It was among his working papers, he said, from the investigation he conducted for Marguerite Oswald.[35]

Rankin was determined to get Lane to say more about the tape. "Mr. Lane," he tried again, "could you tell us whether there was anyone else present at this interview with Helen Markham that you recorded?"

"I don't believe that I said I recorded it. I believe I said it was recorded."

"Was it recorded by someone else?"

"I decline to answer any questions, because the questions you are asking clearly are not for the purpose for which this Commission has been established. And I tell you that I am amazed, quite frankly, Mr. Rankin, that the kind of harassment to which I have been subjected since I became involved in this case continues here in this room – I am amazed by that."[36]

Seizing the moment, Lane briefly described the incident outside his home: how two FBI agents stopped him and demanded he turn over documents they said he had.

"Did you do that?" Rankin asked.

"I did not give them those documents; no."

"Why not?"

"Does your tone and your question indicate you think I *should* have given those documents to agents of the FBI?"

"I would like to have you answer the question, if you would," Rankin said.

"You decline to answer my question?"

"Yes; *I* am examining *you*."

"Of course," Lane replied. "I did not give them any documents in my possession."[37]

When Rankin asked again about the Markham tape recording, Lane bristled. "I would like to make this quite clear to you, Mr. Rankin," he said. "I am not going to discuss any working papers in my possession. Those papers came into my possession as a result of an attorney-client relationship. The Supreme Court has written decisions regarding the sanctity of those documents."

"Did you know about the tape recording being made?" Gerald Ford asked.

"I beg your pardon?"

"Did you know," Ford repeated, "about the tape recording being made?"

"I decline to answer that question. Am I a defendant before this Commission, or is the Commission trying to find out who assassinated the President?"

"We are trying to find out information about a witness before this Commission – "

"Well, then," Lane told Ford, "call the witness before the Commission and ask the witness questions. And if the Commission – if the witness has testified contrary to what I say the witness has said, then I would suggest you do what I invited the Commission to do when this matter arose. Submit my testimony and Mrs. Markham's testimony to the U.S. attorney's office, and bring an action against both of us for perjury. And then at that trial I will present documents in my possession, and we will see who is convicted."

Rankin asked him again to reveal the source of his information that Jack Ruby had met with J.D. Tippit and Bernard Weissman at Ruby's Carousel Club eight days before the assassination.

"I will not do so, Mr. Rankin," Lane said.

"Do you realize," Rankin told him, "that the information you gave in closed session could have an unfavorable effect upon your country's interests in connection with this assassination, and your failure to disclose the name of your informant would do further injury?"

"Mr. Rankin," Lane countered, "I am astonished to hear that statement from you. There are 180 million Americans in this country. I am perhaps the only one who is a private citizen who has taken off the last six months to devote all of his efforts to securing whatever information can be found, and to making that known to this Commission, and publicly to the people of this country, at great personal cost . . . to hear you say that I am not cooperating with the Commission, and I am going to do harm to the country by not making information available to you, astonishes me.

"You have hundreds of agents of the FBI running all over the Dallas area – agents of the Secret Service, Dallas policemen. Are you telling me that in one trip to Dallas where I spent something like two days, I uncovered information which the whole police force of this nation has not yet in six months been able to secure? I cannot believe that is a valid assessment of this situation. I cannot, Mr. Rankin."

Earl Warren broke in. "Mr. Lane, may I say to you that until you give us the corroboration that you say you have, namely, that someone told you that that was a fact, we have every reason to doubt the truthfulness of what you have heretofore told us. And your refusal to answer at this time lends further strength to that belief."[38]

Shortly after this Lane had a chance to describe the incident at the airport. "I am deeply concerned about the fact that since I have become involved in this matter, and since I testified before this Commission, the U.S. Department of Immigration has placed my name in their immigration book, on the proscribed list, and that when I returned to this country, in response to your invitation to come here and testify before this Commission, I was halted by the immigration authorities because my name appeared in that proscribed list."

"And I told you at that time on the telephone, didn't I, that the Commission had nothing to do with that?" Rankin answered. "Is that right?"

"You did tell me that, and I ask you if you would be good enough to find out, since I did not accuse the Commission of having my name listed there, of course, to find out if my name was listed in relationship to the inquiry which I have conducted, and the testimony that I have given to this Commission."

"Were you prevented from entering the United States?" Warren asked.

"No," Lane replied. "I am here now, Mr. Chief Justice. But I was stopped."39

After a protracted exchange about the nuances of attorney-client privilege and whether it applied to Lane's withholding the Markham tape, Chief Justice Warren said, "Mr. Lane, you have manifested a great interest in Lee Harvey Oswald and his relationship to this entire affair. According to you, Mrs. Markham made a statement that would bear upon the probability of his guilt or innocence in connection with the assassination. Mrs. Markham has definitely contradicted what you have said, and do you not believe that it is in your own interest and in the interests of this country for you to give whatever corroboration you have to this Commission so that we may determine whether you or she is telling the truth?"

"I have given you all the information that I am permitted to give to you and to members of the Commission," Lane replied.

Before this session ended, Lane was able to inspect the alleged assassination rifle. But beyond that his second testimony seems not to have accomplished much. By July 16, Lane had sent the Commission a copy of the Markham tape. It was duly transcribed, and the transcription was published in the twenty-six volumes. Lane sent a letter with the tape, asking Earl Warren to acknowledge that the tape showed Lane had been telling the truth. But Warren never answered it.40

On July 24, 1964, nearly a month after Salandria, the Feldmans, and Marguerite Oswald attempted to interview a fearful Helen Markham, Mrs. Markham was interviewed by the FBI.41

Mrs. Markham described her June 27 contacts with Mrs. Oswald and the amateur investigators, whom she mistook for reporters. "She stated she was frightened and did not desire to talk with Mrs. Oswald and the two alleged reporters since she regarded Mrs. Oswald as a 'mean person,'" the FBI special agents wrote.

"reporters" misidentification seems to have been Mrs. 's error. "We never identified ourselves as reporters," Salandria y years later. "We identified ourselves for what we were, investigators of the Kennedy assassination."[42]

Except for decidedly negative spin control, Mrs. Markham's account to the FBI is similar to that which Feldman wrote about in *The Realist*. Salandria and Feldman, she told the agents, were "unkempt" and "wicked" in appearance. They carried cameras and a tape recorder with them but went away when Mrs. Markham refused to talk to them. One of the men returned soon afterward, however – Markham did not say which one – with a "highly agitated" Marguerite. She said she still did not want to talk to them and was caring for her infant granddaughter. No mention was made of Marguerite's holding the baby, or of Mr. Markham's being present. Mrs. Markham did tell the agents that her visitors offered to pay for a babysitter, "but she refused to take the money. Mrs. Oswald and the man then left." She also acknowledged that her son William had followed the investigators and spoken to them.[43]

Bill Markham also talked to the FBI; his interview took place on July 28. He admitted to talking to the foursome a month earlier. That interview took place in a car, and Salandria, identified in this part of the FBI report as "the man who claimed to be an attorney," had done most of the talking. The conversation was recorded. Markham told Salandria that his mother had witnessed the Tippit slaying and that her account of Oswald's shooting the officer was correct. But when asked whether his mother ever lied, the FBI report states, Markham told Salandria and the others "that she had lied on many occasions, even to members of her immediate family." He could not remember any other questions he had been asked.[44]

By this time, Salandria and the Feldmans were back in Philadelphia. One of Salandria's first moves was to give attention to his law practice, which he had been neglecting. Harold Feldman was reviewing notes and tape recordings from their interviews, and preparing his article on Marguerite.

Salandria was cautiously excited about what they had learned in Dallas. "It is my firm opinion which approximates certainty in my mind that Oswald was framed in the killing of Kennedy and may have been framed in the killing of J.D. Tippit," he wrote a friend. He added: "We spent a week with Marguerite Oswald. This is an amazing woman."[45]

Chapter 8

Mrs. Markham and Mrs. Clemons

Pinning the murder of J.D. Tippit on Lee Harvey Oswald was a critical component of the Warren Commission's case. If it could be convincingly shown that Oswald killed Officer Tippit, it would demonstrate a capacity for violence and the need to avoid capture. And most of the early critics believed the Commission was on very weak ground when it came to the question of the Tippit murder.

Although the exact time of Officer Tippit's killing remains a matter of some debate – and five minutes either way could exonerate or weigh heavily against Oswald – it is certain that he was shot to death less than an hour after the assassination of President Kennedy. The Warren Report placed the time of death at about 1:16 pm, or 46 minutes after the assassination. But there are indicators that it had to have happened earlier.[1]

Officially, Oswald left the Texas School Book Depository building at approximately 12:33 pm, just minutes after he shot and killed President Kennedy. He walked east on Elm Street for seven blocks and caught a bus at Elm and Murphy Streets. The bus took him back in the direction he had just come from, toward the TSBD. The bus was bogged down in heavy traffic; after a block and a half, the Commission said, Oswald apparently changed his mind about the bus and got off. He'd been on board for about four minutes. The Warren Commission put his time of exit at 12:44 pm.[2]

From the point where he got off the bus, the Commission said Oswald walked a few blocks to a nearby Greyhound bus station, where he got into a cab driven by William Whaley. Before they could leave, an elderly woman appeared and Oswald offered her the cab, but she said that the driver could call her one. Then, Whaley told the Commission, "I asked him where he wanted to go. And he said, '500 North Beckley.'" Police cars, their sirens screaming, were everywhere, and Whaley wondered aloud what was going on. Oswald, he recalled later, did not reply.[3]

Whaley dropped Oswald off a few blocks from the rooming house where he lived at 1026 North Beckley. The elapsed time between Oswald's getting in the cab and his arrival at the rooming house, according to the Commission, was about eleven minutes.[4]

The housekeeper at the rooming house, Earlene Roberts, testified that she was watching television coverage of Kennedy's assassination when Oswald, whom she knew by the alias "O.H. Lee," came into the house around 1 p.m., in unusual haste. He went straight to his room without speaking, she said, emerging three or four minutes later, zipping up a jacket as he left the house. Through a window, Mrs. Roberts saw Oswald standing near a bus stop in front of the house on the east side of Beckley.[5]

Oswald was next seen, according to the Warren Commission, at the corner of 10th Street and Patton, about nine-tenths of a mile from the rooming house. Exactly how he arrived there is not known. The Commission determined that he got there on foot: "If Oswald left his roominghouse shortly after 1 pm and walked at a brisk pace, he would have reached 10th and Patton shortly after 1:15 pm," the Commission said. But they offered no evidence to support the assertion that Oswald walked.[6]

The Commission did not mention it in its Report, but when Oswald was still in his room back at the Beckley house, Mrs. Roberts observed a police car pull up in front of the house and sound its horn. Mrs. Roberts was friendly with several policemen she had once worked for, and they would sometimes stop by, but looking out the window she could see it wasn't anyone she knew.[7]

"And who was in the car?" Commission lawyer Joseph Ball asked, in an exchange recorded in Volume 6 of the Hearings and Exhibits.

"I don't know," Mrs. Roberts answered. "I didn't pay any attention to it after I noticed it wasn't them – I didn't." It was never determined who was in that police car.[8]

In any event, Oswald was seen, according to the Commission, at 10th and Patton talking to Officer J.D. Tippit through the passenger side front or vent window of Tippit's squad car. After a few moments Tippit got out of the car and started to walk around the front of the vehicle when, the Commission said, Oswald suddenly pulled out a revolver and began shooting. Tippit was hit as many as four times and killed instantly. Oswald then started back toward Patton, ejecting bullet shells and reloading as he went.[9]

At least twelve people saw an armed man in the vicinity of the Tippit shooting; eleven of them, according to the Warren Commission, identified the man as Oswald. The twelfth witness "did not think that he could identify the man who fired the shots" although he was closest to Tippit and the gunman.[10]

Domingo Benavides, the witness closest to the shooting, was driving his pickup truck west on 10th Street when the shooting began.

He pulled over to the curb and ducked down. He told the Warren Commission that when he looked up over the dashboard, he saw the gunman empty his revolver and throw the bullet shells into some bushes as he ran off. Only then did Benavides get out of his truck and, using Tippit's car radio, report the shooting. The time, according to the Warren Report, was 1:16 pm.[11]

A man named T.F. Bowley gave evidence that the time was earlier, but he was neither called before the Commission as a witness nor mentioned anywhere in the Report. A sworn police statement included in the twenty-six volumes is the only record of what Bowley saw. On November 22 he was on his way to pick up his wife at work when he came to 10th and Patton. When he saw Officer Tippit on the ground he pulled over and got out of his car. "I looked at my watch and it said 1:10," he said in the statement made ten days later. Bowley checked Officer Tippit but he appeared to be dead. "A man was trying to use the radio in the squad car," Bowley said, "but stated he didn't know how to operate it. I knew how and took the radio from him." He gave the police dispatcher the location and, he said, an ambulance arrived "a few minutes later."[12]

Taxi driver William Scoggins was eating his lunch in his parked cab at the corner of 10th and Patton. He noticed a police car drive through the intersection, then pull alongside a man on the sidewalk. Scoggins saw the man approach the police car, but some bushes obscured most of what happened. He did see Tippit get out of the car, heard three or four shots, and saw the officer fall to the pavement. As the gunman fled, Scoggins, who had jumped from the cab and cowered behind it, heard him say either "Poor dumb cop" or "poor damn cop."[13]

Two young women heard gunfire and Mrs. Markham's screams. Barbara Davis and Virginia Davis ran out from their apartment house on the southeast corner of 10th and Patton in time to see a man run across their lawn and around the house; he appeared to be emptying a revolver as he ran, and indeed they later recovered a spent shell.[14]

A block south of the murder scene, two men in a used-car lot heard gunshots and saw a man running south on Patton, holding a revolver high in his right hand. One of the men, Ted Callaway, called out: "Hey, man, what the hell is going on?" The running man stopped, said something, then continued on his way, reaching Jefferson Boulevard, where he turned west. Callaway and the other man, Sam Guinyard, ran toward the sound of the gunshots and came upon the murder scene. Callaway and Scoggins both jumped into the latter's taxi and tried to find the fleeing man, but without success.[15]

After the man turned onto Jefferson he was followed on foot by two other men from the used-car lot. Warren Reynolds and Pat Patterson gave chase for about a block before the man ran behind a gas station, and his pursuers lost him.[16]

The only witness who saw the actual shooting was Helen Markham, the Dallas waitress who was on her way to catch a bus to work when it occurred. When Mark Lane interviewed her in March, Mrs. Markham told him that local and federal authorities warned her not to talk about what she saw. In June 1964 her ex-husband told Feldman and Salandria that they had been threatened.[17]

Mrs. Markham testified to the Warren Commission that she saw Tippit's police car pull up alongside Oswald, who was walking along 10th Street. She testified to seeing the car stop, Oswald walking over to it and chatting, Tippit emerging – and Oswald shooting him down. Oswald, Mrs. Markham said, fled down Patton "in kind of a little trot." Screaming, she approached Officer Tippit and saw him lying in a pool of blood.[18]

Lee Harvey Oswald was arrested in the Texas Theater by Dallas Police at about 1:50 that afternoon. Johnny Brewer, the manager of a shoestore a few doors east of the theater, heard police sirens, looked out of the store, and saw a man try to hide as the sirens grew louder. After a police car made a U-turn and drove off, the man continued down the sidewalk. Julia Postal, working in the theater's box office, saw the man as he ducked into the theater's outer lobby. She came out of her booth to the sidewalk, where Brewer came up to her and asked whether the man had bought a ticket. She said he had not. Her suspicions aroused, she said, "I don't know if this is the man they want . . . but he is running from them for some reason." She told Brewer to follow the man into the theater while she called the police. At least fifteen officers responded to the call. Patrolman M.N. McDonald was credited with making the arrest.[19]

Helen Markham, who had fainted but was revived with amonia, was asked to view a police lineup around 4:30 that afternoon. The Warren Report stated that she picked Oswald out of the lineup, and that later, in her Commission testimony, she "confirmed her positive identification of Lee Harvey Oswald as the man she saw kill Officer Tippit." But in her published testimony, what she really said about viewing Oswald in the lineup was "When I saw this man I wasn't sure, but I had cold chills just run all over me."[20]

➢◉◈

A few weeks before the Warren Report was published, staff counsel Wesley Liebeler spent a weekend reviewing its fourth chapter, "The Assassin." He did not like what he read. In a memorandum reviewing its weaknesses, Liebeler warned that the selective use of evidence could undermine the entire Report. Of the depiction of Officer J.D. Tippit's murder he said: "Some question might be raised when the public discovers that there was only one eyewitness to the Tippit killing, i.e., one person who saw Oswald kill him. All the rest only saw subsequent events. Mrs. Markham is nicely buried there, but I predict not for long."[21]

This comment reflected legitimate concern about Mrs. Markham's reliability. Some Commission attorneys had argued against using her as a principal witness, and one of them dismissed her statements as "totally unreliable." Liebeler had personally caught Mrs. Markham in an outright lie, and concluded that her testimony was contradictory and worthless.[22]

It was Liebeler who had examined Mrs. Markham when she testified a second time, on July 23. This testimony was taken in Dallas less than a month after she had been visited by Marguerite Oswald, the Feldmans, and Vince Salandria. It was about three weeks after Mark Lane's additional testimony, and the question of whether she had been interviewed by Lane, which she had previously denied, was now a critical issue.[23]

Liebeler got right to the point. "Have you ever talked to Mark Lane?" he asked.

"No; I haven't – I haven't never seen the man in my life."

"Have you ever talked to Mark Lane on the telephone?"

"No."

"And you remember," Liebeler continued, "that Congressman Ford specifically, and Mr. Dulles, asked you whether or not you had talked to Mark Lane on the telephone and you told them at that time that you had not talked to Mark Lane?"

"No, sir; I have never seen the man. If he was to come in here I wouldn't know who he was."

"Now, aside from the fact you have never seen the man, you also told the Commission when you were in Washington that you had never talked to him over the telephone?"

"Right."

"Have you talked to Mark Lane over the telephone since you were in Washington, before today?

"No, sir."

"You have never talked to Mark Lane over the telephone?"

"No, sir; no, sir," Markham said. But she seemed to confuse the Lane interview with the Feldmans, Salandria, and Marguerite Oswald. "Now, the old lady – and they told me they were reporters – came to my house."

"Right, but you have no recollection of ever talking yourself?"

"I never even talked to her even."

At that point Liebeler revealed what he knew. "Well, now, I'll tell you very frankly, that we have a tape recording of a conversation that purports to be a conversation between you and Mark Lane on the telephone . . . would you like to hear the tape, so you can tell us whether or not that is your voice?"

"Yes, sure," Mrs. Markham replied.

The proceeding was recessed while a tape recorder was brought into the room. When the tape was started, the voices of Mark Lane and Helen Markham filled the air.

Almost immediately, Liebeler asked that the tape be stopped. "You are shaking your head, as you listen to this tape recorder, Mrs. Markham . . . what do you mean to indicate by that?"

"I never talked to that man."

"Is that not your voice on the tape?"

"I can't tell about my voice, but that man – I never talked to no woman or no man like that."

"Well, we will play the recording some more, and are you following it along, Mrs. Markham?"

"Yes; I am right here."

The playback resumed. It was clearly a conversation between Mark Lane and Helen Markham. Mrs. Markham conceded that it was her voice, but tried to backpedal. Yes, she remembered the conversation, but the man who called said he was from the police department. More than once, she raised her right hand and swore she was telling the truth.

She began repeating herself: "He told me he was from the police department and this lady never talked to me."

"Which lady is that?"

"On this tape."

"Which lady on the tape?"

"It was a woman talking."

"The lady's voice that was talking on the tape here?"

"Yes."

"I thought that was *your* voice?"

In its Report, the Warren Commission would write that Mrs. Markham "subsequently admitted the existence of the conversation and offered an explanation for her denial. Addressing itself solely to the probative value of Mrs. Markham's contemporaneous description of the gunman and her positive identification of Oswald at a police lineup, the Commission considers her testimony reliable."[24]

George and Patricia Nash were graduate students at Columbia University in New York when they went to Dallas in the summer of 1964. July can be brutal in the Lone Star State: "Hot but otherwise OK," they wrote in a post card to Salandria soon after arriving, adding that they were staying at a "luxury $20.00 a week motel." They located some key witnesses and interviewed them – witnesses already contacted by others, in spite of Deirdre Griswold's efforts at a "division of labor." They also interviewed some important witnesses the Commission had inexplicably over-looked.[25]

They came away from their interview with Mrs. Markham feeling that any testimony she gave to the Warren Commission was of dubious value. Since she was such an important witness they quoted her at length in their article, "The Other Witnesses," published in the September 1964 issue of *The New Leader*. They had asked her if the Kennedy assassination and related events affected her personally.

"It sure has," she replied. "I've had a nervous breakdown. I'm the witness. I'm the one he was talking to when he died. I know what it's like when someone dies. I was with my father when he died. He [my father] said 'Well, I don't know.' And then he was dead. I couldn't understand what Tippit said. I guess he wanted me to call on the car radio and get some help. I was there with Tippit when they put him on the stretcher. He was dying."[26]

"Was it long until the ambulance came?" the Nashes asked.

"No."

"About how long?"

"I was there hollering and screaming, trying to get help. Wouldn't nobody come help me. I would guess that it was about 20 minutes before the ambulance came – 20, 25 minutes I was there alone until the ambulance came and then another five minutes until the police came . . . the police treated me like a queen. Me and the cab driver, I guess we're the only witnesses. When the police got there, I fainted. I fainted three or four times."[27]

Mrs. Markham's claim that she was alone with and talking to Officer Tippit is problematic, the Nashes pointed out, because the

Warren Commission said Tippit was killed instantly. Furthermore an ambulance is reliably reported to have arrived within minutes, not the twenty to twenty-five minutes Mrs. Markham said. The Nashes concluded that "it appears quite possible that Mrs. Markham came on the scene only after hearing the shots; and without Mrs. Markham, there is no one to say precisely what happened between Tippit and Oswald."[28]

The Nashes also located Mr. and Mrs. Frank Wright, who lived in a ground floor apartment on 10th Street about half a block from the murder scene. They were watching the unfolding news coverage of President Kennedy's assassination when they heard three sharp reports. Mr. Wright immediately recognized the sounds as gunshots. He jumped up and ran out the door, and looked down the street just as Officer Tippit was hitting the ground. "I saw him turn over and he didn't move any more," Wright told the Nashes.[29]

At the sound of gunfire Mrs. Wright jumped up, too. As her husband ran out the door she looked out the window and saw Tippit lying in the street. "I ran to the telephone, picked it up and dialed 'O.' I said, 'Call the police, a man's been shot!' After that I went outside to join my husband."[30]

Outside Mr. Wright, who said he was the first person in the street after the shots were fired, saw something no other witness described and that went unreported by the Warren Commission. "I saw a man standing right in front of the car," he told the Nashes, meaning Tippit's squad car. "He was looking toward the man on the ground. He stood there for a while and looked at the man. I couldn't tell who the man was on the ground. The man who was standing in front of him was about medium height. He had on a long coat. It ended just above his hands. I didn't see any gun."[31]

The man, Mr. Wright said, ran around the police car as fast as he could and got into his own car. "His car was a grey, little old coupe. It was about a 1950-1951, maybe a Plymouth. It was a grey car, parked on the same side of the street as the police car but beyond it from me. It was heading away from me. He got in that car and he drove away as quick as you could see."[32]

Mr. Wright turned his attention back to Officer Tippit. A woman had come out of her house at about the same time as Wright. As the man in the grey car drove off, the woman cried out: "Oh, he's been shot!" She threw up her hands and ran back toward her house.[33]

Very quickly, an ambulance arrived, and soon after that the police. The street began filling up with people. "I tried to tell two or three people what I saw," Mr. Wright said. "They didn't pay any attention. I've seen what came out on television and in the papers but I know that's not what happened. I knew a man drove off in a grey car. Nothing in the world's going to change my opinion. I saw that man drive off in a grey coupe just as clear as I was born. I know what I saw."[34]

The ambulance was dispatched from the Dudley M. Hughes Funeral Home, just two blocks away from the murder scene. The dispatcher recorded the time of the call from Mrs. Wright at 1:18; the ambulance driver radioed his arrival within a minute of his departure. They loaded Tippit into the ambulance and took him to the hospital; their arrival there was recorded at 1:26.[35]

Neither Mr. nor Mrs. Wright was ever questioned by the police or by anyone representing the Warren Commission. Mrs. Wright did tell the Nashes that about two months later, a man came by the house and talked to her for a few minutes. But he took no notes, did not talk to Mr. Wright, and did not even identify himself.[36]

Likewise, neither the ambulance driver, his assistant, the ambulance dispatcher, nor the managers of several apartment houses facing the murder site were questioned. All of these potential witnesses, the Nashes wrote in their article, were in agreement on the time between the shooting and the ambulance's quick arrival. And that was in sharp contrast with Mrs. Markham's statement that she was alone with Tippit for twenty to twenty-five minutes.[37]

Acquilla Clemons did not see Lee Harvey Oswald or anyone else gun down Dallas Police Officer J.D. Tippit on November 22, 1963. But she was near the scene of the shooting and witnessed its aftermath, and may have seen the killer flee the area. Like Frank Wright, what she had to say was at odds with Helen Markham's sworn testimony.

The first unofficial investigators to interview Mrs. Clemons in person, it appears, were Vince Salandria and Harold Feldman, during their investigative trip to Dallas in late June and early July. No record of their conversation appears to exist, but Salandria recalled, "I thought she was entirely credible."[38]

George and Pat Nash spoke to Mrs. Clemons at about the same time as Salandria and Feldman. They were unimpressed with her, but just by finding and interviewing her demonstrated that the Warren Commission was less than forthright in saying that "the only woman among the witnesses to the slaying of Tippit known to the Commission is

Helen Markham." The Nashes wrote that Mrs. Clemons' version of the Tippit shooting "was rather vague, and she may have based her story on second-hand accounts of others at the scene." Unfortunately they did not say what led them to this suspicion. Neither did they quote any of her comments, although they acknowledge having interviewed her.[39]

Not long after Salandria, Feldman and the Nashes spoke to her, Shirley Martin, accompanied by her children, interviewed Acquilla Clemons. Mrs. Martin was not at all confident that she would be granted the interview, so her daughter Vickie carried a tape recorder hidden in her purse. Vickie later transcribed the surreptitious recording of their conversation with Mrs. Clemons, and the tape was passed on to Mark Lane.[40]

As they prepared for the interview, the Martins did not yet know that, like Helen Markham, Acquilla Clemons had been visited by menacing authorities who advised her not to talk about what she had seen.

Mrs. Clemons cared for an elderly man in an Oak Cliff home near 10th and Patton, where Tippit was shot to death. That is where she was when Shirley and Vickie knocked on the door and waited for her to open it.

"Hello," said Shirley. "Are you Mrs. Clemons?"

"Yes."

"You are? May I speak to you a moment?"

"Yes, you can," Mrs. Clemons replied, and came out onto the front porch.

Before they began a neighbor walked by. "Hello, Miss Jane!" Mrs. Clemons called out.

The three of them settled into seats. "We'd like to talk to you about what you saw on Friday, November 22."

"I can't," Mrs. Clemons said. "It's been too long."

"What do you mean?"

"It's been too long, I can't remember."

"Oh," Shirley replied. "Well, some friends of ours said they talked to you about it, oh, about three weeks ago."

"Sure," Mrs. Clemons said, adding that it seemed longer than three weeks to her – perhaps a couple of months.

"Well," Shirley went on, "has anyone talked to you and told you not to talk to anyone?"

"Yes, they have."

"Is that the Dallas police?"

"Some of them."

"Well, I'm a private citizen," Shirley said. "I'm not representing any group." To explain Vickie's sitting close by, she added, "My daughter is trying to write a . . . children's book."

"They don't allow me to say anything," Mrs. Clemons said. "I'm not allowed to say anything."

"Who's that? You mean the Dallas police?"

"Some of them," Mrs. Clemons replied. "I don't know. I don't know one of them from the other." She said again that she did not know who the men were who told her not to talk, and added that her employer also did not want her involved in the case in any way.

Undaunted, Shirley continued. "This friend of mine was here . . . I don't know if you remember. Mr. Nash? Mr. Salandria? They talked to you?"

"Someone came by my house about two months ago," Mrs. Clemons recalled, adding that they had promised to send her a picture of Lee Oswald, but never did.

They began talking about what she had seen – two men in the vicinity of the Tippit shooting, after the shots were fired. The Warren Commission was soon to report that other than the known witnesses, there had been just one in the area – Lee Harvey Oswald.

"There was supposed to be two men, weren't there?"

"Well, it was two men. I don't know, I wouldn't know them if I was to see them."

"No, of course not," Shirley said. "I wouldn't expect you to do that. They were both on the same corner?"

Again, Mrs. Clemons would not commit herself. One man, she said, seemed to be talking to a second man, who was tall and wore yellow khaki pants and a white shirt. This tall man was on the other side of the street from the first man. But she didn't know if they were together, and she didn't know how the first man was dressed. He was the one with the gun, and Mrs. Clemons had been trying to hide from him.

Shirley continued: "And Mrs. Markham was coming down this way, wasn't she?"

"Who is Mrs. Markham?"

"She lives up on the corner up here."

"Well," Mrs. Clemons said, "me and her. . . . I guess she was the same lady that was telling me that the police shoot – boy shoot the police. I had to come back in the house. I don't know. Been too long."

Shirley asked Mrs. Clemons to describe the man with the gun: "Was he a short, kind of heavy-set man?"

"Yes, he was short. Heavy."

"He was kind of heavy?"

"Yeah, he was kind of stocky-built," Mrs. Clemons replied. "Stocky-build. Whatever you call it."

She didn't notice what his hair was like, nor did she recall his saying anything, because she was hurrying to get out of the man's sight. "I didn't want him to be shooting me."

It wasn't long after the shooting, Mrs. Clemons recalled to Shirley, that the street began filling with people – some from the neighborhood, and soon, more police. "There was so many policemen you couldn't walk out there. But I don't know. I don't know."

There were some things Mrs. Clemons had seen but was unable to explain, like the unidentified woman who drove up in a big fancy car soon after Tippit was shot. "She stayed there until everything was cleared. I don't know who she was."

"Beautiful red car?"

"No, it was gray."

"Nice one . . ."

"Yes, it was nice." Mrs. Clemons continued: "I don't know who she was. After they cleared everything, she went on. I don't know who she was."

Then Shirley asked about the shooting itself. "You heard three shots?"

"Yes, I heard three shots. I thought it was firecrackers. I wasn't paying any attention."

"And you think the policeman died right away?"

"He did," Mrs. Clemons answered. "He died before I got there."

Mrs. Clemons acknowledged having known Officer Tippit by sight, saying he was "a pretty nice guy." Then she reiterated that while the killer was "kind of heavy," she really couldn't describe him beyond that, because she had been trying to get out of the way. "I'm just not allowed to tell you. I can't tell you nothing. I don't know nothing."

"And have you been to the Warren Commission?" Shirley asked. "In Washington?"

"No, ma'am."

"No?" Shirley repeated. "Did they come and take a statement from you or anything?"

"No," Mrs. Clemons said, saying again that her employer did not want her involved.

Next, Shirley tried to get Mrs. Clemons to estimate the time of the Tippit shooting. But on the question of timing, Mrs. Clemons seemed thoroughly confused. By all accounts, the shooting happened after 1 p.m.; the Warren Commission placed it at about 1:15. But Mrs. Clemons insisted the shooting happened in the morning, before she had lunch, which she usually ate around 11:30. Moreover, she was certain that President Kennedy, who was shot around 12:30, was already dead.[41]

At this, Mrs. Martin may have had enough; or perhaps she felt she and Vickie were wearing out their welcome. Whichever, she said, "Well, I'd better not keep you any longer. I know you're busy. Let me give you this and thank you." She handed Mrs. Clemons a small sum of money. She and Vickie rose to leave. "We'll see you . . ."[42]

"Okay."

"Take care of yourself."

"I wish I could tell you something."

"Well, it's all history," Mrs. Martin said. "It's interesting . . ."

Then she and Vickie turned and began walking away. But before they got far, Mrs. Clemons called them back. "Do you know his wife?" she asked.

"Beg your pardon?"

"Do you know his wife?" Mrs. Clemons repeated.

"Policeman Tippit's?"

"No, Oswald's wife."

"I've seen her pictures. Why?"

"Well, I just wouldn't want you to mention anything I've said. The lady I work for here . . . things would go hard for me with her."

"Oh, you mean . . . does she know Oswald's wife?"

"No, she doesn't," Mrs. Clemons said, then said yet again that she could get in trouble if it became known she was talking to them.

"Oh, well, we don't know Oswald's wife," Shirley said.

"Only on television," Vickie added.

"She's not allowed to talk to anyone, you know," Shirley went on, meaning Marina Oswald.

"Well, I'm not allowed to talk to anybody but I just wanted to tell you that don't be mentioning me because this lady here, I'd probably lose my job."

Again, Mrs. Martin assured Mrs. Clemons that they would not mention having talked to her.

And again, Mrs. Clemons said she was not allowed to talk about what she had seen. A police officer had visited her and told her not to talk.

"Oh, I see," Mrs. Martin said. "So the police said you'd get a lot of publicity and you'd better not do it?"

Mrs. Clemons made it very plain. "Yeah, I'd better not," she said. "Might get killed on the way to work. See, I live over there," and she pointed in the general direction of her home.

Mrs. Martin was shocked. "Is that what the policeman said?"

"Yes. See, they'll kill people that know something about that. There's liable to be a whole lot of them."

"Who?"

"There might be a whole lot of Oswalds and things. You know, you don't know who you talk to, you just don't know."

"You scare me . . ."

"You have to be careful," Mrs. Clemons said. "You get killed."

"That's what the police said, too?"

"Sure. They told me that I had to be careful."

"Oh, for heaven's sake."

"See, they might be a routine. They may kill people that know something about it."

"Okay. I'm glad you warned me . . ."

"Sure," Mrs. Clemons said, adding something that was not intelligible when the tape recording was played back.

"Okay," Shirley said, as she and Vickie turned to leave for the last time. "Thank you."

Before November 22, 1963, was over, witnesses were viewing the captive Lee Oswald in a series of police lineups. Helen Markham would emerge as one of the most important witness for the Warren Commission. But of course there were others: Virginia Davis and Barbara Davis both identified Oswald as the man they saw flee the Tippit murder scene. William Scoggins did too, although not until the following day, by which time he had seen Oswald's photograph in the paper. Ted Callaway and Sam Guinyard both identified Oswald on Friday evening.[43]

Mr. and Mrs. Frank Wright were inexplicably ignored by all official investigators, although having called the ambulance, Mrs. Wright should have been easy to find – and obvious. Likewise Acquilla Clemons was not interviewed by local or federal authorities.

Warren Reynolds and Pat Patterson initially wavered, but later identified Oswald as the man they had seen. Reynolds was not interviewed by anyone until January 21, 1964, almost two months to the day after the events he had witnessed. On that day Reynolds sat down with FBI agents and was shown photographs of Oswald, whose image had long since saturated the public conscience. Reynolds said there was a resemblance to the man he had seen, but did not make a positive identification. Two days later Reynolds was shot in the head by an unknown assailant. A suspect was arrested in the Reynolds shooting, but on February 5, a woman named Betty Mooney MacDonald provided the suspect with an alibi, and he was released. MacDonald also told police that she had once worked as a stripper at Jack Ruby's nightclub. Barely one week later, MacDonald was arrested for disturbing the peace. After being put in jail, she hanged herself.[44]

Miraculously, Reynolds recovered from his wounds, and testified before the Warren Commission in July. He was certain, Reynolds told Wesley Liebeler, that there was a connection between his witnessing the fleeing man and the attempt on his life. Reynolds also said that a few weeks after he got out of the hospital a stranger tried without success to lure his ten-year-old daughter into a car.[45]

Liebeler showed Reynolds a photograph of Oswald again, and this time, he positively identified him as the man he saw running from the Tippit murder scene.[46]

On November 22, Domingo Benavides told Dallas police that he did not think he could identify the man who had fired the shots; as a result, the Warren Commission wrote, the police "did not take him to the police station." Mark Lane was incredulous. "The purpose of a lineup," he later wrote, "is precisely to resolve such doubts."[47]

In February 1964, Benavides' brother Edward was shot in the head during a barroom brawl. Unlike Warren Reynolds, he did not survive. But Domingo Benavides later identified Oswald as the man he saw, although in this case Benavides did not so testify to the Warren Commission but rather to CBS News, when he appeared on one of its broadcasts in June of 1967.[48]

Although the Reynolds and Benavides shootings both occurred during the life of the Warren Commission, this blue-ribbon panel showed no particular interest in them. In Midlothian, Texas, however, one man did: Penn Jones, Jr., a virtual one-man band as the owner, editor, publisher, and reporter of the small-town *Midlothian Mirror*. The more he examined these and similar events, the more convinced he became that there was a string of unsolved, suspicious deaths related to the assassination. "With the mounting list of these deaths," Jones once declared, "the likelihood grows that these people have been systematically and skillfully eliminated."[49]

Chapter 9

Texas

At lunchtime on November 22, 1963, William Penn Jones, Jr., sat in the Dallas Trade Mart waiting to see President Kennedy, a man he greatly admired. The President was due at a 1 p.m. luncheon to deliver a speech, and Jones was covering the event for the *Midlothian Mirror*, a small, weekly Texas newspaper he owned and operated.[1]

Jones had driven into Dallas from nearby Midlothian that morning accompanied by two colleagues, both of them editors of other small-town papers. The three reached the city in late morning, and by chance had driven through Dealey Plaza. "I thought to myself then, 'This would be a good place to see him,'" Jones said. "But that would've meant missin' lunch at the Trade Mart."[2]

Jones, who was about a month past his forty-ninth birthday, was just digging into a salad when news of Kennedy's assassination came over a small transistor radio carried by a man seated near him. "I rushed over to where these other fellows were sittin' and I said, 'He's been shot,' and everybody looked at me scornfully, as if Ain't I crazy," Jones remembered.[3]

But the other fellows believed him soon enough. They all jumped into Penn's car and drove to Parkland Hospital, where Kennedy's motorcade had sped after the Dealey Plaza ambush. Jones had a camera and began taking pictures: of the presidential limousine, of those members of the motorcade milling about, of the growing crowd outside Parkland. Before long they got word of the President's death. When the President's body was finally brought from the hospital, Jones, a World War II veteran, stood at attention and saluted his dead commander-in-chief, tears welling in his eyes.[4]

After the hearse had driven away the newspapermen headed to Dealey Plaza, where Jones took still more photographs, and then turned toward Love Field, where Kennedy had arrived a few hours earlier, and where Air Force One waited to take his body back to Washington. Traffic was very heavy and the plane took off before Jones arrived. "Man, I was not functioning by then," he told a journalist a decade later. "I took the other fellows home, and went home, and stayed by the radio and television." He was back at the *Mirror* office on Sunday morning, preparing an "Extra" edition of the paper, when Jack Ruby shot Oswald. With that, further work seemed pointless. "I just shut off the press and went home."[5]

But Jones later returned and was able to get out a special edition of *The Mirror* on Monday – the "Day of The President's Burial," he noted in the paper's masthead. In a banner headline, he had written "The Disgrace of Dallas," beneath which he placed a large photograph of JFK. "We think the disgrace of Dallas may well hang on its conscience for many years," he wrote. "This is truly a dark day for the world, for America, for Texas, and especially Dallas."[6]

Jones had once met JFK. It was during the 1956 presidential campaign, when the then-senator from Massachusetts stopped in Dallas to campaign for Adlai Stevenson. Kennedy obliged Jones by signing a copy of Kennedy's *Profiles in Courage*, which Jones had brought with him. From that time on, Jones held Kennedy in high regard. "After the assassination," he later wrote, "we recalled the words of Albert Camus about his friend and fellow underground worker, Rene Leynaud, who was murdered by the Germans. Camus wrote: '. . . His exceptionally proud heart, protected by his faith and his sense of honor, would have found the words needed. But his is now forever silent. . . .'"[7]

Penn Jones had purchased the *Midlothian Mirror* in 1945 for four thousand dollars. He was just back from military service in World War II and bursting with idealistic fervor: "I thought that with proper leadership and guidance we could be a real force for good in the world," he said. "That's the reason I wanted to be an editor."[8]

The Mirror at this time was once described as "a tuckered-out little weekly." It remained a weekly newspaper under the stewardship of Jones, and retained its small-town flavor, but Jones injected it with new vitality. He was not only its owner, but its publisher, editor and reporter as well. He was assisted by his wife, the former Louise Angove, whom he had nicknamed "L.A." L.A. became so central to the functioning of the *Mirror* that Penn always used the plural pronoun "we" in his editorials.[9]

Deciding to buy the *Mirror* was in part pragmatic: Midlothian, with a population of about 1,500 people, was located roughly between L.A.'s parents in Bowie and Penn's in Annona. Midlothian was even closer to Dallas. The paper was also within the Jones's limited means: "*The Mirror* was for sale cheaper than any of the others we looked into," Penn once recalled.[10]

The first issue of the *Midlothian Mirror* under Jones appeared on Friday, November 30, 1945. It was a day late: inexperience caused him to miss his Thursday deadline. In spite of his enthusiasm for his newly chosen profession, he once said he had no business buying a newspaper; he recalled that first issue as a "pitiful effort." Yet he was determined to improve, and had a clear vision of the editor's role in his community. In one of his first editorials, he promised thorough coverage of local news with an occasional comment on the national scene. And he stated what in view of subsequent events can be considered a warning shot: "We intend to insult those people who fail or refuse to fulfill the obligations or responsibilities they have inherited along with their citizenship in the greatest country on earth."[11]

But before he could publish those words, he had to learn the day-to-day operations of putting out a newspaper. "I had to get a guy from Fort Worth to show me how to turn on the Linotype," he once said, referring to the vintage 1919 Model 8 typesetting machine he had acquired along with the paper. It took time to learn everything and the first few years were rough. But he insisted: "I enjoyed every day of it up to the assassination."[12]

Penn Jones grew up on a forty-acre farm in a small town called Lane's Chapel, a few miles outside of Annona in East Texas. He was one of eight children, three of whom died in infancy. The family was poor; their house was an unpainted shack heated by a single fireplace. "When I was growing up in my home," he wrote, "we got few things above the essentials, but my mother and father were doing the best they could."[13]

He said his father, Penn Jones, Sr., had the reputation of being the hardest-working man in Red River County. It was a characteristic the younger Penn inherited. "Penn was an old bulldog," said a schoolmate. "Never quit on anything. He was determined to be first in whatever he did."[14]

Although Jones grew to just five feet three inches tall, he excelled in sports in high school, particularly football and track. After graduating in 1932 he got the urge to travel the country, hitchhiking and riding freight trains through the West and Midwest. Along the way he worked odd jobs, including picking cotton for thirty-five cents a day. Sometimes he sent money back home, and sometimes he returned home to work for short periods. That fall he entered Magnolia A&M Junior College in

Magnolia, Arkansas. He was there for less than two years, but in his second year was elected class president.[15]

In 1935 Penn transferred to the University of Texas. One of his biggest influences there was an economics instructor; Penn credited this man with making him a liberal. In 1936 he began taking law classes and his classmates included John B. Connally and Henry Wade. The former would go on to be the governor of Texas, and would be wounded in the same ambush that killed President Kennedy in 1963. The latter would at that time be the district attorney of Dallas.[16]

But Jones was evidently not cut out for the study of law. He left UT in June of 1940 before completing his course work. "I wasn't making it," he later conceded. He had joined the National Guard in 1933, and in October of 1940 was called to active duty as a lieutenant in the 36th Infantry Division. He was surprised to be initially stationed in Austin, at the Selective Service headquarters. But in 1943, not long after he and L.A. had married, he was sent overseas. He participated in two Allied invasions, in Salerno, Italy, and in southern France. By war's end, Penn Jones had received the Bronze Star and eight battle stars, and held the rank of captain.[17]

At the height of the war, an aunt wrote Jones a letter that said she was praying for him. Penn wrote back that she should pray for a safer world. "How can we have lasting peace?" he asked. "Unless every man has a definite answer to that question, he ought to be trying his best to find an answer . . . I promised the body of my best friend. I have promised bodies with no heads, bodies with no faces. I have promised every dead soldier that I'd do my best to see that their death was not in vain. Don't waste time praying for me." The aunt was so impressed with this reply that she sent a copy to her local newspaper, which published it and sent her a $25 savings bond. She sent the bond along to Penn, but he never cashed it.[18]

Penn Jones, liberal populist, had warned predominantly conservative Midlothian that he would insult those he felt were not living up to their obligations – their obligations as private citizens and public servants. He was as good as his word.

As early as 1947, Penn crossed swords with Midlothian's mayor when he criticized city government for paving the streets in Midlothian's black neighborhoods with scrap iron from a local foundry. Jones personally inspected the streets after some residents complained, and estimated that the slag included a thousand pounds of nails, wire, and other waste metal. Jones pulled some of it – about fifty pounds worth – from the streets and put it on display in the *Mirror* office. Then he wrote an editorial about it. The mayor, he was certain, never forgave him for that bad publicity.[19]

In August 1956 he joined with a friend, the writer John Howard Griffin, in desegregation efforts in Griffin's town of Mansfield, some twelve miles west of Midlothian. In many ways the events in Mansfield foreshadowed the crisis in Little Rock, Arkansas a year later. Mansfield was the first Texas school district ordered by a Federal court to allow blacks to attend its public schools. The school board was prepared to obey the court order, but the town's white racists put up immediate resistance. The Ku Klux Klan protested with several cross burnings, and angry crowds of up to 400 people surrounded Mansfield's high school over several days to prevent African American enrollment.[20]

"First time I ever saw a mob," Penn Jones recalled. Midlothian School Superintendent Lemuel Mills asked Jones to help him get a crowd together to go to Mansfield to join the white protests. Jones refused. Most of the town's white citizens, he believed, would accept black students in the school. "Mansfield, the people, were afraid of the bullies and also ashamed of the publicity they were making," he said. Texas Governor Alan Shivers declared that the three black teenagers attempting to enroll constituted a threat to public safety, and sent Texas Rangers to keep the black kids out. His efforts succeeded, and Mansfield public schools remained segregated until 1965.[21]

These and similar causes undertaken by Jones earned him designations considered highly insulting by the people of Midlothian. He was a communist, they said, or a Catholic, or a Jew – depending, apparently, on which intended epithet best fit the occasion.[22]

Jones made other enemies by editorializing against the town's conservative elements. But he considered it his duty to oppose those things he believed were wrong. He had a favorite expression: "You have to fight a little bit for democracy every day." Democracy, Jones believed, was a tender flower requiring much care. "If everyone were working at democracy, wouldn't the flower have beautiful blooms?" he said. "But so many people won't vote, won't participate, won't argue, won't lift a finger to keep freedom of their forefathers alive right here in America."[23]

And so Jones fought a little every day. His most celebrated battles took place with the Midlothian school board. "The school board was always the major problem," he once said. Things got off to a bad start the same year Jones took over *The Mirror*, when he discovered the Board held closed meetings. The decisions of a public school board were legitimate news stories, Jones believed, and he had a right to cover its meetings. But try as he might he was not allowed to attend. "They said, in effect, 'If you'll just print what we want you to print, we'll let you stay,'" he recalled. Jones was subsequently a leader in a drive to consolidate the area's nine school districts. "We raised taxes, and this earned me the undyin' hatred of landowners."[24]

Critical mass came in 1962 after the Midlothian school district allowed a speaker from the conservative John Birch Society to address the students at Midlothian High School. Attendance was compulsory. Penn's oldest son, a high school senior, told his father that the speaker, Edgar W. Seay, used the occasion to attack Franklin Roosevelt, Harry Truman, and the United Nations.[25]

This was too much for Jones. He headed straight to the office of school board president Lemuel Mills, and in effect demanded equal time. He even suggested the district get, as a liberal counterpoint to Edgar Seay, Federal district court judge Sarah T. Hughes, the jurist later called on to give the oath of office to Lyndon Johnson after President Kennedy's assassination.[26]

Mills called in the high school's principal, Roy Irvin, and Jones repeated his demand. Irvin said that the matter was none of Jones's business.[27]

"The hell it isn't!" Jones shot back.

There was a moment of silence. Then Irvin reportedly snarled, "You son of a bitch!" and began beating on the diminutive Jones.[28]

"He put some pretty good knots on my head," Jones remembered. But only a few: Jones began hitting Irvin right back, and according to his account knocked Irvin off his feet in thirty seconds.[29]

But the scuffle in Mills' office proved to be just a prelude. Soon thereafter Jones asked Seay to come to his office at the *Mirror*. After offering him a seat, Jones told him he wanted no more lectures to captive audiences of high school students. He added that if Seay ran for Congress, as he had said he would, Jones would publicly expose his homosexuality. Seay had declined to sit down and didn't want to listen to Penn's speech; instead he demanded to know whether Jones considered himself a loyal American. Jones replied with a question of his own – "How long have you been a homosexual?" – and the fists began to fly.[30]

Jones managed to push the much larger Seay through the *Mirror*'s glass door and into the street. Who got the better of the fight cannot now be said with certainty. Jones was later quoted as saying he was "whipped" in both fights, but also told another journalist, "I damn near choked him – he was turnin' purple." A police officer broke it up, reportedly telling Jones that Seay had had enough. "I will admit," Jones said, "that I lost my temper."[31]

Three days later, at 2:30 a.m. on April 30, 1962, an alarm sounded at the *Midlothian Mirror*. Its office was on fire. The office was deserted at that hour, but a family living over an adjacent store barely escaped the flames. Penn himself rushed to the scene and helped fight the blaze. He tried getting into the office from both the front and back, but the heat was too intense. "My lungs got full of smoke in a hurry, and I ran out vomiting," he once recalled. Firefighters were able to save the building, and the *Mirror*'s equipment was salvaged. But the office itself was ruined; the walls and ceiling were blackened by acrid smoke. Jones found a man to guard the building for the rest of the night; the watchman stayed on duty armed with Penn's shotgun.[32]

The space had to be completely remodeled. Penn placed the fire damage at eight-thousand dollars, only a portion of which was covered by insurance. Investigators concluded an incendiary device had been thrown through the front-door window. Penn was convinced it was the work of right-wing extremists, and almost certainly related to the events of preceding days. He offered a two thousand dollar reward for information leading to the arrest and conviction of the arsonist.[33]

Edgar Seay insisted he had nothing to do with the firebombing and submitted to a polygraph test, which he passed. Eventually a young retarded boy with a history of setting small fires was charged in the case. But neither Penn nor L.A. believed he was responsible or that his confession was genuine. "There were too many inconsistencies," L.A. said. Although the reward offer appeared in the *Mirror* for at least a year, it was never claimed.[34]

The firebombing made national news, but generated little sympathy for Penn Jones on the part of Midlothian's townfolk. One woman is reported to have sneered, "Some mighty bad things have happened to Mr. Jones, and he deserved every one of them." And as Penn, with the help of his sons and a few friends, began cleaning up the mess the next day, a crowd gathered and one man jeered: "Gonna get out a paper this week, Jones?"[35]

"Why, hell yes, man," Jones replied. Not only did he get the paper out, he revealed an ironic sense of humor with the headline: "Fight Shatters Glass in the *Mirror* Door; Fixed in Time to Accommodate Arsonist."[36]

In July of the following year, as a direct result of these events, Penn was awarded the Elijah Parish Lovejoy Award for Courage in Journalism, presented annually by the Journalism Department of Southern Illinois University. The award was named for an abolitionist newspaper editor who had been murdered by a mob in 1837 while literally defending his newspaper press. After Jones got the award he received congratulatory messages from several politicians, including President Kennedy.[37]

Penn and L.A. flew to Illinois knowing only that Penn was one of five finalists for the award. Perhaps superstitiously, he did not prepare any remarks for the occasion. "He made a very good speech off the cuff," L.A. said later. "He's awfully good on his feet."[38]

After she heard about the assassination, Dallas legal secretary Mary Ferrell dispatched her sons on a mission to collect every edition of every local newspaper they could possibly find.[39]

She had just had lunch at the Chaparral Club in the city's Southland Center when the shooting occurred. Mrs. Ferrell was a lifelong Republican and not a JFK supporter: "I didn't even care enough to go down on Elm Street to watch the motorcade," she said years later. Yet she emerged to Elm Street some ten blocks from Dealey Plaza to find a cluster of people huddled about a small transistor radio. "And I heard the first description of the alleged assailant. This was broadcast at ten minutes til one – twenty minutes after the shots. And they said the alleged assailant, they believed, was a white male, approximately thirty years of age, approximately six feet tall, approximately 165 pounds, wearing a white shirt and khaki pants."[40]

The description could have matched countless men in the Oak Cliff area alone, and yet Lee Oswald was apprehended within an hour. This was remarkably fast – all the more so because Oswald did not fit the broadcast description. "He was *not* wearing a white shirt and khaki pants," Mrs. Ferrell remembered. "He was wearing a dark reddish-brown – I've held it in my hands, in the Archives . . . it had a slight – a reddish thread, and a gold thread, kind of a plaid – but it was very dark. And he wasn't wearing khaki trousers, he was wearing brown wool trousers."[41]

Mary Ferrell had a reputation for being feisty, and late in her life, even in casual conversation, she was still able to get worked up about this immediate inconsistency. "Now, *nothing* fits the descriptions. So, how in the *hell* did the – oh, I'm sorry – how did the Dallas police capture this man?"[42]

It just didn't fit. "And I said, 'Something is wrong.' And I just, I thought, 'I'm going to find out what everybody said.' And I started with these newspapers."[43]

Methodically, with the help of her husband and sons, she got copies of each edition of the two Dallas dailies. She began by sending a son to the loading dock of each paper. Her husband Buck and a third son relieved the first two so they could sleep and get a bite to eat. This continued for four tumultuous days. "And we got every issue of every paper."[44]

The assassination was, of course, the only story getting attention at that time. Many newspapers, such as *The Dallas Morning News*, convicted Oswald, or at least promoted the idea that a single rifleman had committed the assassination – "Assassin Crouched and Took Deadly Aim," a *Morning News* headline said the on November 23. The day after Oswald was shot to death by Jack Ruby, *The Dallas Times Herald* ran a page one story headlined, "Tip to FBI Warned of Oswald Death." But this story, it seems, was published only in early editions of the *Times Herald*. "There were very few copies of that, that got loose," Mrs. Ferrell recalled. With her husband and sons strategically placed, she got one.[45]

Mrs. Ferrell began sorting out the articles and the information they contained, initially on slips of paper and soon on 3x5 index cards. She once described these early efforts. "I took every column of every newspaper and if I saw, 'John Doe said he was standing at Elm and Houston, and he saw, he heard, he thought the shots came from . . .' I put that down, who he was, what he said, what he heard. And then I went to City Directory and looked up who this man was, where he lived, what his wife's name was, what his work was, and I recorded all of that on these cards. And in many cases, the names were spelled wrong, and I had to determine who the person was they were talking about."[46]

About a month after President Kennedy's assassination, John Howard Griffin was interviewed by Philippe Labro, a journalist from French National Television. Trailed by a camera crew, the two men walked about Griffin's property in Mansfield, Texas. At Griffin's invitation, Penn Jones stood by observing.[47]

Griffin and Jones were old friends, having met in 1947. At that time Griffin was an unpublished author, although two novels appeared in the early 1950s. But Griffin's greatest acclaim came following the 1961 publication of an extraordinary book called *Black Like Me*, a true account of what the author termed an "experiment." Griffin had chemically darkened his skin and then traveled the Deep South for six weeks living as a black man.[48]

Labro wanted Griffin's opinion about the assassination. "I searched for answers and gave him little satisfaction," Griffin wrote of the encounter. "What did I know? What did anyone know at that time? Rumors, suspicions and speculations already suffocated the issue. I did not want to add to them."[49]

But, Griffin continued, "We felt certain about one thing: the story being presented to the world was so grossly pat as to be untrue. They said one troubled man had murdered the President of the United States. If it were as simple as that, why then had authorities been so determined to close the case almost before it had opened?"

In the aftermath of the assassination, Griffin said, there were those who were promoting obsessive theories about what really happened to JFK, and trying to make the known facts fit those theories. Griffin dismissed such people outright. But there were others who were possessed by a need for truth, and these people really counted for something. Penn Jones, Griffin went on, was so possessed. Since the day of the assassination he had dedicated himself to finding the truth, which in this instance might turn out to be unspeakably ugly.

"Is it wise to do this?" Griffin wondered. "Is it wise to lift the lid from a mystery and risk releasing a stench such as the world has never known, a stench that might well damage the world?"[50]

For Penn Jones there was simply no choice. "I am trying to do an honest job of investigating this thing, as I think all journalists should," he once said. "I'm not sure I'm giving you the truth all the time, but I'm trying to give you an honest job, and that's really all the public deserves. And they didn't get that from the Warren Commission."[51]

Jones conducted a few interviews in the months leading up to publication of the Warren Report, but later said his real investigating didn't begin until he had seen the official evidence. His first task was to get a handle on the Report and the twenty-six volumes. "We didn't see him for a month when the Warren Report came out," recalled a *Mirror* associate. "He just pored over it. From the very first day." Jones purchased no fewer than fifteen sets of the Hearings and Exhibits. Some he sent to friends; some he loaned out to interested people. At home there was an upstairs set and a downstairs set; another set was kept at the *Mirror* office. He studied the twenty-six volumes for several hours each day and continued his own investigation.[52]

An early trail Jones followed was that of Earlene Roberts, the housekeeper who told the Warren Commission that a police car had pulled in front of the rooming house and sounded its horn while Lee Oswald was in his room. This was after the assassination but before J.D. Tippit was slain. Jones was astounded by Roberts' testimony; he was determined to find her and interview her for himself. By his own reckoning he spent the better part of two years, on and off, trying to locate her. He once traveled to a small town near Dallas where he heard she had relocated. "We found 'Earlene Roberts,'" he remembered, "but it was the wrong one." Then time ran out. On January 9, 1966, Mrs. Roberts died in Dallas at the age of 60, reportedly from a heart attack.[53]

Earlene Roberts suffered from diabetes, and so her death, while unfortunate, appeared to lack any element of mystery. Yet she seemed to have been frightened by her experiences relating to the assassination; she told the Warren Commission she had been "put through the third degree" over her witnessing of the police car. Mrs. Roberts had some interesting coincidences in her background. She was the housekeeper at Lee Oswald's last address. Her sister was a Dallas real estate agent named Bertha Cheek. Mrs. Cheek was acquainted with Jack Ruby, who had once offered her a half-interest in his Carousel Club, an opportunity she passed up.[54]

This was quite a set of circumstances, and Jones began to wonder whether there was more to Mrs. Roberts' death than anyone knew. But even more startling was his discovery of a meeting held at Jack Ruby's apartment on the evening of November 24, 1963. By that time Ruby was in jail for murdering Oswald earlier that same day. But his roommate, George Senator, was in the apartment having a drink with Ruby's first lawyer Tom Howard when four more men showed up, including reporters Bill Hunter of the *Long Beach Press Telegram*, and Jim Koethe of the *Dallas Times Herald*. In less than one year Hunter and Koethe were both dead – Hunter shot to death in a police press room, and Koethe from a blow to the neck, sustained in his Dallas apartment. By March of 1965, Tom Howard was also dead, reportedly from a heart attack.[55]

"What went on in that meeting?" Penn Jones asked in the June 3, 1965, *Mirror*, in his first article reviewing the evidence. "Few are left to tell."[56]

In that same issue, Jones called for a re-opening of the assassination investigation. He also wrote: "The march of events has made us rush this assassination story into print. Other stories will be published on the subject as we get them in shape. We have not finished reading the twenty-six volumes of Warren Report testimony, and personal contact with many witnesses is time consuming, often difficult, and sometimes impossible."[57]

In early 1966 Jones caught up to Carroll Jarnagin, a Dallas attorney who less than two weeks after the assassination filed an astonishing report with the FBI. Jarnagin claimed that on October 4, 1963, while sitting in Jack Ruby's Carousel Club, he had overheard Ruby and Lee Harvey Oswald discussing plans to assassinate Texas Governor John Connally. He insisted to Penn Jones that the story was true. Jarnagin acknowleged that he was drunk when the alleged conversation took place, and that he had a drinking problem. And while Jones appears to have been skeptical of the story, he was adamant that Jarnigan should at least have testified before the Warren Commission.[58]

After many months checking leads and sifting the official evidence, Jones was not really sure what to think. But there was no doubt in his mind that something was seriously wrong. "We are so grateful for the many answers in the twenty six volumes of testimony," he wrote after the Commission published its evidence. "The answers are there for those who are willing to dig. . . .[59]

"After spending several thousand hours knocking on doors, asking questions, meanwhile reading the Report, we believe audacious actions were taken by the Commission lawyers and the chairman obfuscating the evidence left after President Kennedy, Tippit, and Oswald were killed."[60]

Chapter 10

Loyalty

The Red Scale that was still taking shape in 1947, when Harold Weisberg and nine others were fired from the State Department under the McCarran rider, had gained momentum by the summer of 1949. Suspicion was by then turning to the United Nations, and once again Nevada Senator Pat McCarran was involved, this time with the Senate Judiciary Committee, which he chaired, alleging that the international peacekeeping body was infiltrated by Communists, virtually from top to bottom. The UN was at this time just four years old, but it had been a favorite target of rightwingers almost from the beginning. American isolationists, anti-New Dealers, and other UN opponents were convinced that the agency's New York headquarters was a haven for Communist spies posing as diplomats.[1]

These allegations were the first rumblings of an eventual purge of American employees of the United Nations. The earliest charges came anonymously and behind closed doors from a man identified only as "Witness No. 8." This witness told a Senate judiciary subcommittee that the UN Secretariat was "terrorized" by communist agents who forced employees to do the bidding of the Soviet Union. He urged that Secretary-General Trygvie Lie be replaced. When word of this witness's charges became known, the UN's eighteen-member staff committee immediately adopted a resolution denouncing them as unsubstantiated, and meant solely to "cause damage to the United Nations in general and the Secretariat in particular." Byron Price, speaking on behalf of Lie, said the charges were the "nuttiest" he had heard. "I am sure that no fair-minded person will attach significance to the statement of a mysterious so-called 'official' who attempts wholesale character assassination of his colleagues but refuses to give his name."[2]

The controversy touched off by these events dragged on for several years, with fresh charges, new hearings, and behind-the-scenes tussling. As it dragged on the Red Scare became a red hysteria. Senator McCarran, flexing his considerable political muscle, led the passage of two major pieces of anti-communist legislation during this period. The Immigration and Nationality Act of 1952 made it easier to denaturalize and deport any naturalized citizen deemed subversive; it also restricted immigration from non-white countries. The Internal Security Act of 1950, popularly known as the McCarran Act, codified the belief in a communist conspiracy aimed at a global totalitarian dictatorship. The act set up the Subversive Activities Control Board, which monitored and regulated communist organizations, and authorized the use of concentration camps in times of crisis.[3]

In late 1952 outgoing President Harry Truman signed Executive Order 10422, establishing a mechanism to screen Americans seeking employment in the United Nations to ensure they were not engaged in espionage or subversive activities against the United States. The Executive Order also set up a loyalty board, but like virtually every other loyalty board of this era, judicial due process was shunted aside. Charges against some of those brought before the board were often vague, and those accused were denied the right to face their accusers, or even know who they were.[4]

Trygvie Lie, an anti-communist Norwegian, subsequently maintained that the idea of spies in the UN was ridiculous. "There was nothing to spy on in the United Nations," he insisted, arguing that member nations did not give it information they wanted to keep secret. Yet he appears to have done little if anything to oppose EO 10422. While Lie publicly protested, he secretly permitted American UN officials to ask for derogatory information from the FBI on American applicants to the Secretariat. He also allowed the FBI to question and fingerprint American UN employees, and even allowed a branch FBI office to be set up within the Secretariat to facilitate interrogations. He eventually reached an agreement with the State Department that allowed the screening of all American personnel, both applicants and those already employed.[5]

In 1952 Pat McCarran's Senate Subcommittee on Internal Security (SSIS) kicked its loyalty campaign into high gear. Thirty American employees of the United Nations were hauled before the SSIS that year. Forty-seven others were summoned to appear before a New York grand jury. The majority of those called before the two bodies invoked their Fifth Amendment right against self-incrimination on the question of past or present membership in the Communist Party, and in some cases on the question of espionage. Using the Fifth Amendment was a matter of some debate among left-wing lawyers during this time. Some believed it carried with it an admission of guilt; surely no innocent person would use it. But John Abt, the former La Follette Committee counsel and a leading opponent of the McCarran Act, was among those who argued otherwise. "From the Inquisition to the Salem witch trials, coerced testimony was a favored device by oppressors to condemn their opponents," he wrote. "So the Fifth Amendment's origins were not as protection for criminals accused of illegal acts but for precisely the sort of proceedings in which the House and Senate inquisitors were engaged. Taking the Fifth to defend against the McCarthyite inquisition was to honor our own political traditions."[6]

Yet not all of those called before loyalty boards honored those traditions. Ruth Elizabeth Crawford, who for five years had worked as a press officer in the United Nations International Children's Emergency Fund, was ordered to appear before McCarran's subcommittee on October 15, 1952. Inevitably she was asked: Are you now, or have you ever been, a member of the Communist Party?[7]

"I know that I might have invoked the Fifth Amendment," she said later. "I think those who do so are protecting a great principle: the Fifth Amendment, I learned in my need, is the only barrier between you and the invasion of your constitutional rights. Perhaps I was tired, tired of being asked a question which I thought no one had the right to ask me in the first place. For as an American did I not have the right to belong to any legally constituted party I chose?"[8]

And so she told her inquisitor Yes. Yes, in the mid-1930s she had been, for about a year, a member of the Communist Party. Moreover she was at present a member of the Progressive Party, which at that time was, rightly or wrongly, associated in the public mind with communism. "I never felt so American," she told a friend later, "as I did answering those questions." Nevertheless, her loyalty now in doubt, she was fired from the UN the following January. She appealed her dismissal on the grounds that she was being victimized for her political views. "What I did as an employee of the United Nations is an open record," she said at the time, "but no one now thinks to ask how well I did my work." In her defense she cited Article 19 of the United Nations' Universal Declaration of Human Rights: "Everyone has the right to freedom of opinion and expression. This right includes freedom to hold opinions without interference and to seek, receive, and impart information and ideas through any media and regardless of frontiers."[9]

Friends and colleagues rallied around Crawford, and in September 1953 were elated when the UN's Administrative Tribunal ruled that Crawford and ten others had been fired illegally. The tribunal ordered that four of those, including Crawford, be reinstated to their jobs. The

Washington Post editorialized that the ruling in Crawford's favor was "in keeping with American standards of justice and fair play." But elation over her apparent victory was short-lived. Dag Hammarskjöld, who since the firings had replaced Trygvie Lie as UN Secretary General, announced the next day that he would not reinstate the four, calling it "inadvisable from points of view which it is my duty to take into consideration." He did not elaborate. Crawford, though, said later she was certain that the decision was made "to stave off the wrath of the Congressional committees."[10]

Ultimately Crawford received a measure of vindication. She and the other ten who had been fired illegally were awarded payments by the International Court of Justice, which gave a decisive 9 to 3 ruling in their favor.[11]

In October 1953, Ruth Crawford sent out a form letter to a group of friends and former colleagues who were supporting her in the aftermath of her dismissal. She wrote that it was her hope that in the future, the UN would make its personnel policies "so clear as to bring about the defeat of those in our country who are seeking to discredit the United Nations through these baseless attacks on the loyalty of American citizens in its employ."[12]

Among the recipients of this letter was Sylvia Meagher, then a 32-year-old liaison officer with the World Health Organization, an agency of the UN. "I am so glad you called," Crawford told her in a handwritten postscript. "You are to be congratulated for your stand. If all had done so we would all be safer and happier now."[13]

In spite of Crawford's use of the past tense, Meagher's own ordeal with the loyalty board was far from over. It had begun early in 1953 when she received a communication labeled "Information Circular No. 8" from Dr. Brock Chisolm, director-general of the World Health Organization. This communication formally notified all WHO staff members, "particularly those who are United States nationals," of the probability they would have to comply with Executive Order 10422.[14]

Meagher's response was immediate, and reveals an essential toughness and dedication to principle that would guide her later work as a Warren Commission critic. "I have received Information Circular No. 8," she wrote Dr. Chisolm on February 5, "and should be grateful if you would clarify certain questions regarding my personal status. . . ."

She posed three questions to Dr. Chisolm: Why, after six years with the WHO, was it necessary to obtain information about her "to supplement the information I submitted as a condition to my initial appointment?" Why was this information being requested only about American employees? And finally – a question which Meagher said was the most urgent – what would happen to a staff member who refused to comply?[15]

Dr. Chisolm wrote back that the World Health Organization was not telling its American staff members to comply with EO 10422. Then the pressure was turned up a notch: Meagher received another communication, this one from the US Mission to the UN, requesting that she fill out a questionnaire and allow herself to be fingerprinted. Meagher replied that she was convinced no member state – in this case, the United States – had a right to determine her qualifications for employment in an international agency.[16]

And so she declined to supply the requested information. On April 16, 1953, she wrote to Albert F. Bender, special assistant to the Secretary-General, about the information requested in accordance with Executive Order 10422. "I have read this Executive Order carefully," Meagher wrote, "and find no provisions in it which give any official of the United States Mission the authority to make such a request . . . therefore, I feel that your request has no legitimate basis and represents an unwarranted invasion of my privacy. In consequence, as a matter of principle, I find myself unable to comply with your request." Should she be called before any committee or board, she continued, she would be willing to appear, and would not take the Fifth. "There is nothing in my private or professional life which I fear to expose to scrutiny."[17]

Then, on February 10, 1954, she received a letter from the chairman of the International Organizations Employees Loyalty Board, Pierce J. Gerety, which at last got to the heart of the matter. Gerety said that background reports "contain certain unevaluated information of a derogatory nature which, if true, might create a doubt concerning your loyalty to the Government of the United States." Attached was an eight-page document consisting of ten sections which Meagher was requested to complete "in writing and under oath." She had ten days to respond. "Your cooperation in this matter will be appreciated."[18]

Some of the questions in the document were perfunctory and innocuous – name and address, time and date of birth. But three questions in particular asked Meagher about her association with several individuals, and whether she was "aware of any Communist activities or sympathies" on their part. It also asked whether Meagher herself had "ever participated in, aided or acquiesced in any activities that would tend to further the cause of Communism."[19]

Harold Weisberg once observed that "when Sylvia was angry, she was the most articulate person in the world." This is evident in her reply sent by registered mail one week later. She told Gerety that her views as stated to Albert F. Bender nearly a year earlier – that this represented an unwarranted invasion of her privacy – were unchanged. Moreover, she said, "The Interrogatory does not contain one iota of information which in any way challenges my qualifications as an international civil servant . . . thus, no information has been given about me in this Interrogatory which can be considered 'derogatory' by any rational standards." She would not answer any of the questions. The investigations of her were groundless. "It would be a very grave and a most regrettable matter indeed if any body of responsible officials saw fit to attach even the slightest suspicion to my integrity or conduct because of my respect for principle or on the basis of the trivial, if not frivolous information which has been presented to me as 'derogatory' . . . I wish to assert most earnestly that I have never departed in letter or in spirit from the obligations of the Oath I took when I became an international civil servant more than seven years ago." For good measure, she attached the text of this oath.[20]

Ultimately, however, she was compelled to appear before the International Organizations Employees Loyalty Board on April 1, 1954, to whose members she read a prepared statement. The true depth of her anger is difficult to calculate by simply reading her typewritten words. Yet the sense of outrage at having her character and loyalty assailed is unmistakable.

"I do not consider it incumbent upon me to undertake, in effect, additional vows of loyalty," she said, "nor to protest my innocence of any wrongdoing, nor to prove my suitability for employment on the staff of the World Health Organization, in the absence of any consequential evidence or charges suggesting any culpability on my part . . . I am unable to see any justification for enquiries by anybody of authority into my private life or my private relationships with other persons, when these relationships have been completely non-political and in no way conspiratorial . . . I have the most solemn personal dedication to principle of justice and of human freedom and dignity . . . it is this dedication to principle which has been the basis of all my actions and of this statement." For Sylvia Meagher, principle and integrity were paramount.[21]

Just before Christmas that year, Pierce Gerety resigned as Chairman of the IOELB. In submitting his resignation he said that the IOELB was "successfully eliminating undesirable Americans from the employment rolls" of international groups, a fact for which the board took considerable pride. Gerety said that 3,939 United States citizens had been investigated over a 16 month period. He did not say whether any of those had been fired as a result. But Trygvie Lie dismissed at least forty-five UN employees in 1952 alone, most of them American, and the crisis is believed to have contributed to the suicide of an American legal counsel to the UN who was deeply troubled by firing employees who had merely invoked a constitutional right.[22]

Sylvia Meagher was not among those dismissed. The previous summer Gerety had signed a letter to the Secretary of State "for transmission to the Director General of the World Health Organization" stating that Meagher had been the subject of a full field investigation. "It has been determined that, on all the evidence, there is no reasonable doubt as to the loyalty of this person to the Government of the United States."[23]

This was the outcome Mrs. Meagher had anticipated. She was now free to continue her career with the WHO in the direction it had been headed when the loyalty issue arose two years earlier; she would in the years to come remain a valued and highly respected employee of the organization. Vindication arrived late, but it did come within her lifetime. In April 1986, the US District Court for the Eastern District of Pennsylvania declared Executive Order 10422 unconstitutional in that it violated the First Amendment rights of American citizens.[24]

Although she had been cleared, and her professional record remained unstained, Sylvia Meagher must have drawn some hard lessons from her experience – if nothing else, a better understanding of what large bureaucracies, in this instance her own government, were capable of, particularly in times of great stress.

Chapter 11

Friends in L.A.

Where were the experts? This question perplexed Ray Marcus from the very beginning of his research into the Kennedy assassination. He was asking it in 1964 when the case was still fresh. He was asking it in 1967, when the Jim Garrison investigation in New Orleans had given it a new dimension. And he was still asking it in the year 2000 – by which time the question was largely moot. Where were the experts – and why was he doing some of their work, in spite of his lack of *bona fides*? "I wish others more qualified had jumped into the field and I could have watched like most others," he once lamented.[1]

Wherever the experts were, Marcus could see no sign they were asking the questions and examining the evidence he believed should be addressed. He was unable to simply watch and wait for answers that might not come. There were three things he was particularly interested in, in the assassination's aftermath: the bullet officially designated Commission Exhibit 399, but often called the "magic" bullet; a Polaroid photograph of the assassination taken by a spectator in Dealey Plaza; and an 8 mm film of the assassination taken by another spectator. [2]

"We are talking about photographic evidence, and I am not a photographer," Marcus once said. "And I am talking about ballistics and a study I did in bullets and I am not a ballistician. And I am not a criminologist." To support his own admittedly amateur work, he frequently sought out experts and solicited their opinions. He got some of these opinions, but wasn't always able to use them. "I was told, 'Well, don't use my name,' 'I will not give you this in writing,' so this has been a problem." But some of the experts he talked to did allow him to use their names, and did offer their opinions in writing. And in the years to come, Marcus would spend a great deal of effort trying to publicize what he was convinced could be a breakthrough piece of photographic evidence – but with very little result. [3]

It was perhaps inevitable that Marcus would be drawn to the assassination. He had always been interested in political events, and the Kennedy assassination, regardless of its true perpetrators, had political consequences. On November 22, 1963, Marcus had just left his Los

Angeles apartment to run some errands when news of the shooting in Dallas came over his car radio. He rushed back home and turned on the TV. Within a few hours the arrest of Lee Harvey Oswald was announced. "When the government put out the word the same evening that there was no conspiracy and the assassin was safely in jail, I knew they couldn't possibly know that, and my involvement began."[4]

In common with most other critics, he started compiling news accounts of the assassination. A key observation came early, within just a few days of the assassination, when *Life* magazine published an extraordinary series of photographs documenting the entire shooting sequence. These were frames from an 8 mm home movie taken by an assassination eyewitness named Abraham Zapruder. *Life*, which purchased rights to Zapruder's film, used thirty-one frames in its November 29, 1963, issue. Although the film was in color, it was first published in black and white due to technical limitations imposed by press deadlines.[5]

Marcus bought two copies of the issue and began studying the grainy images closely. Before long, he noticed something unusual. "In one of those pictures, a picture of Connally immediately after he was hit, I saw something which led me to believe that at least that shot could not have come from the Book Depository Building," he said. It was still November 1963, and the only story getting any real media play was that a lone gunman had shot President Kennedy from above and behind. "I wasn't sure of it, as there weren't enough other photographs available. But the direction in which the shoulders slumped presented a picture of the man just as he was hit, and it indicated to me that the shot could have come from the front."[6]

Another discrepancy emerged. In some of the images *Life* published, the limousine has come from behind a street sign that had momentarily obstructed Zapruder's view. JFK's hands have come up and, still facing forward, he appears to be grasping his throat. But a week later, in its December 6 issue, *Life* stated:

> . . . the 8 mm film shows the President turning his body far around to the right as he waves to someone in the crowd. His throat is exposed – toward the sniper's nest – just before he clutches it.[7]

Even a cursory glance at the pictures *Life* had already published showed that Kennedy never turned around as the magazine described. This couldn't be just a mistake. But if he wasn't facing the sniper's nest, how was he wounded in the throat? It was obvious, Marcus was increasingly certain, that something was wrong. "From that time on," he said, "I began to believe that there might be a way to show that the official version was false from photographic evidence."[8]

It would be a dozen years before the Zapruder film was widely seen by the American public, and half-a-dozen years before bootleg copies began proliferating. No one outside the government would see the Zapruder film in motion until 1965. Those who did would be obliged to travel to the National Archives, where it was placed after the Warren Commission disbanded. But in late 1963 the frames published in *Life* were a starting point. Marcus began assembling them, placing them in sequence, and trying to grasp the story they told. In time he would develop a series of hypotheses about the assassination, all drawn from the Zapruder film; he would emerge as an authority on what have been called the six most intensely studied seconds of American history.

Raymond Jesse Marcus was born in Los Angeles in 1927, and grew up in its largely working-class Jewish section of Boyle Heights. "Our neighborhood," he recalled, "was a smaller – population wise – version of New York's lower east side, with much intellectual and political ferment."[9]

It was there that his lifelong interest in politics, especially those events with far-reaching implications, was fostered. The first political meeting he remembered attending was during the Spanish Civil War, called by a socialist youth group to urge President Roosevelt to lift an arms embargo against the Spanish government's loyalist forces. Marcus was ten years old. Around this time he also became aware of the rise of German Naziism: "I remember listening to Hitler's hysterical-sounding, Jew-hating speeches with my family on short-wave radio."[10]

After graduating from high school in 1945, Marcus volunteered for military service with the intention of becoming an Army Air Corps pilot. But World War II was in its waning stages, and while he was still in basic training came to a sudden and dramatic end when the United States dropped atomic bombs on Hiroshima and Nagasaki. Marcus was reassigned to a specialized weather unit that trained in Illinois. From there he went to Kwajalein Island in the Bikini Atoll, where the United States was conducting tests of the atomic bomb. When bomb-laden planes took off from Kwajalein, the island was first evacuated of all but essential personnel. "And I was chosen, with some of my other weather guys – we had to give the last-minute readings on these radio instruments . . . which was kind of exciting."[11]

Marcus served two years with the Army Air Corps and was mustered out in 1947. Back in L.A. he attended business school and entered the workforce after graduation. But his interest in politics remained strong. He began contacting public figures whose views, he felt, might help sway public opinion if they were widely promoted. In 1951, with the horror of Hiroshima and Nagasaki in his thoughts, he wrote to Albert Einstein, urging the great physicist and humanitarian to speak out against the war in Korea, which Marcus had heard Einstein opposed. He received a prompt reply, although not quite what he had hoped for. "As long as the war-hysteria in this country was not so developed as it is today," Einstein told him, "I have on several occasions publicly expressed my conviction and my warning against that trend which will lead to disastrous consequences for the U.S. and for the world. Today the passions and emotions are so strong that no preaching of reason can be effective."[12]

On December 29, 1963, not long after he had noticed the anomalies of the two issues of *Life* magazine, Ray Marcus wrote a letter to Earl Warren, who had recently been named to head the presidential commission investigating the assassination.

> Dear Sir:
> I write as a citizen who, like most other Americans, has still not recovered from the shocking and tragic events of that terrible weekend of November 22.
> The shock and grief have been augmented by anger and bewilderment at the amazing mass of contradictory statements which have come from the Dallas police and, reportedly, from the FBI, which are continuing up to the present time.[13]

Marcus told Chairman Warren that he fully supported the suggestion that Lee Harvey Oswald be represented by an attorney during the Commission's hearings, which had not yet begun, and continued: "I join the overwhelming majority of other Americans in extending to you and to your committee my heartfelt support in the arduous and trying task that history has laid before you." He never got a reply.

Looking back to this early period, Marcus once said, "I hoped that this was going to be an honest effort on the part of the Commission. And there was no question in my mind that they would have the ability, if they wanted to, to clear up the questions. But each day, it was clear that that wasn't going to be the case."[14]

About a week before writing to Earl Warren, Marcus had seen Mark Lane's defense brief for Oswald in *The National Guardian*. He was enormously impressed. Soon after writing Warren he wrote Lane, too, noting Lane's forecast that there would be changes in the official story. "Just as you predicted," Marcus wrote him, "the 'facts' are being re-written."[15]

Given a choice, Maggie Field would probably have spent most, or certainly more, of her life in France. As it was, she spent a significant amount of time there. But as events transpired she lived much of her adult life in Los Angeles, where she raised a family, and where, in the years after November 22, 1963, she became an authority on the JFK assassination and the published work of the Warren Commission. Living in Los Angeles also meant she had the good fortune to become a close friend and colleague to Ray Marcus.

From the very moment Mrs. Field heard of the assassination, she was certain that there had to have been a conspiracy. "My first words," she once told a friend, "were: 'Well, they really got him, just as if he were a sitting duck!' and I have never changed my opinion!"[16]

Her instinctive reaction on hearing the news was to gather her family around her. When Kennedy was pronounced dead in Dallas, it was about 11a.m. in LA. Although Mrs. Field hated to drive, she got into her car and drove to her daughter's school to bring her home. "We used to get out early on Fridays," Gwen Field recalled. Usually she took a bus home. But on that day she was surprised to see her mother arriving in the family car to pick her up. Mrs. Field was very distraught; Gwen remembered her mother driving home erratically.[17]

They spent the next few days in front of the television. To Maggie, none of it seemed right – the speed with which Oswald was arrested, the rapidity of the announcement of his guilt – she just didn't buy it. "I saw Oswald on TV, being paraded through the station back and forth like an animal," she once recalled, "and they asked him why he killed the President and he said, 'I didn't kill anyone.' I believed him. I really didn't have anything to go on then, but I was convinced that it was a political conspiracy and I was convinced that Oswald was not the assassin." She began collecting every written word on the case she could find; the details, as best she could determine, were not adding up.[18]

As it had with Ray Marcus, Mark Lane's "Defense Brief" published in *The National Guardian* in December 1963 meant a lot to Maggie Field.

It was her first indication that she was not alone in her doubt. Within a few months a seamstress who regularly came to the Field home was enlisted to help sort out the growing collection of newspaper and magazine clippings. Each day she and Mrs. Field would spread the clippings all over the master bedroom. Maggie would examine them and move them around like pieces on a game board. Eventually she mounted the different articles on large poster boards; she found juxtaposing various pieces of information in this manner useful. When the Warren Commission issued its Report in September 1964, Maggie bought a copy and read it carefully. Two months later, when its twenty-six volumes of supporting evidence were published, she bought three sets.[19]

Maggie Field was born on Long Island, in New York, in 1913. Her parents had emigrated to the United States, both as children, and separately, around the turn of the century – Bessie Kessler from Latvia, and Max Cohen from Lithuania. Bessie is remembered as a very strong woman. She arrived in New York with her mother and brother only to learn that her father, who preceded them, had died of tuberculosis. It was a precarious start in their adopted homeland, and for a time Bessie was the family's sole means of support. But within a few years Bessie and Max met and married. "They made this marriage that was not necessarily love based," Gwen Field said. "It was more business based." But together they excelled. By the time Maggie was born they were not just financially secure, but wealthy.[20]

Their business was clothing – the *shmate* industry, Yiddish for the self-deprecating term sometimes used by its practitioners, the rag trade. According to family lore, Max and Bessie were the first to copy French fashions and reproduce them commercially in the United States. They traveled to Paris several times a year. Bessie would sketch the clothing shown by top designers, and Max would manufacture them. "So my mother was raised in that context," Gwen Field said. "She was raised taking all these trips to Europe on luxury liners, and being in France a lot as a child, in this whole sort of luxury fashion industry. And they had mansions, and servants, and all of the above, and somehow even survived the depression without any damage, basically. I mean they did not have huge problems during that period."[21]

But Maggie was a sickly child; by the time she was twelve years old she had undergone five mastoidectomies. Indeed throughout her entire life her general state of health was never particularly good. Because of poor health she would often miss school, and so was something of an outsider among her schoolmates. But Maggie had something that set her apart: she could sing. With training she developed into a talented opera singer; at age fourteen her teacher arranged a tour that might have taken her all over the world. Max and Bessie, however, wouldn't hear of it. "They just thought that was nuts," Gwen Field said. Whether they suspected the male teacher's intentions or thought Maggie was simply too young for so ambitious an undertaking is not known. What is certain is that Max and Bessie would not allow it.[22]

A few years later she entered Smith College, a small liberal arts college for women in Northampton, Massachusetts. As a junior she majored in French, which allowed her to spend a year in France. She was there in 1933, when Adolf Hitler was elected chancellor of Germany, and witnessed the almost immediate influx of German Jews to France.[23]

Maggie quit college before graduation, got married, and lived in New York until she was in her late twenties. By that time World War II had begun. After her husband went into the service she decided the marriage was not a good one; she went to Reno, Nevada, where at that time so-called "quickie" divorces were relatively easy to obtain. From Nevada she went on to California – for a short stay, she thought. But fate intervened: in Los Angeles, Maggie met Joseph Field, the son of a family friend, and they fell in love. Four weekends after they met, Maggie and Joe were married, and nine days after that Joe shipped out to the Pacific theater for an expected two-year tour. Maggie briefly considered following her new husband as a USO singer, but this plan never materialized.[24]

In 1945 the war finally ended, and Maggie and Joe were at last able to begin their life together. Like Maggie, Joe was originally from the East Coast. But they decided to stay in Southern California, where they bought and for a time lived on an orange grove. As it developed, rural life was not for them and they relocated to Beverly Hills. Joe found work as a stock broker, which suited him well. Within a few years they started a family. Maggie had not been back to France since before the war – "Which was a huge thing for her, not to be able to be in France," her daughter Gwen recalled – instead staying home to raise her children. Life settled down to a comfortable routine. Joe adapted well to the outdoorsy, southern California lifestyle, for a time riding a bicycle to work every day. He remained with the same investment firm for many years.[25]

By the end of the 1950s Maggie had become involved in California politics. She had supported Adlai Stevenson's presidential bid in 1960 but threw her support to JFK after Stevenson dropped out of the race. She admired the new President, in part because of Jackie Kennedy's connections to France. She once took her daughter to see the president in downtown Los Angeles; as JFK left his hotel, they both got a chance to shake his hand. [26]

About a year after the president was murdered, Maggie met Ray Marcus for the first time. The occasion was a meeting to scrutinize the Warren Commission's published evidence. The assassination gave them instant common ground, and Ray and Maggie hit it off immediately. After many months of working in isolation, trying to extract the provable truth from what they were certain was not the truth, each found a comrade – someone who lived nearby, with whom each could share information and experiences and rely on for support. "For Maggie as for me," Marcus remembered long afterward, "we simply could not *not* get involved. Our own sense of logic, justice, historical truth, and common sense told us that something was very wrong, that something important and evil had happened and was happening to our country; that the official story was a lie of monumental and historic proportions; and that we could not sit passively on the sidelines, clucking our disapproval and not do anything."[27]

Chapter 12

The Report Goes Public

The Report of the *President's Commission on the Assassination of President John F. Kennedy* was given to Lyndon Johnson on Thursday, September 24, 1964, some ten months after JFK's assassination. It was not officially released until the following Sunday. The Report was delivered ceremonially, with all seven Commission members in attendance, along with General Counsel J. Lee Rankin.[1]

In a letter of thanks to the Commission, President Johnson wrote, "The Commission, I know, has been guided throughout by a determination to find and tell the whole truth of these terrible events. This is our obligation to the good name of the United States of America and to all men everywhere who respect our nation – and above all to the memory of President Kennedy."[2]

The New York Times said that President Johnson's words "reflected one major hope – that the Warren Commission report would minimize, if not end, the belief that is widespread in foreign countries that the full truth of the assassination has been withheld." The *Times* added that the President was expected to "dip deeply" into the report that weekend, at the LBJ Ranch in Johnson City, Texas.[3]

As Chief Justice Earl Warren handed the thick volume to the President, Mr. Johnson was overheard to say, "It's pretty heavy" – the only words reporters could clearly hear.[4]

The specifics of the report were not generally known, although it was taken for granted that it would name Lee Harvey Oswald as the sole gunman who killed JFK, wounded Texas Governor John B. Connally and bystander James Tague, and also killed Dallas Police Officer J.D. Tippit. That had been the consistent message since the day of the assassination.

Governor Connally was a White House guest when the Report was handed over to LBJ. He told reporters, "I don't think there will be any surprises . . . it's a hard question to answer. I don't know what you expect; there may be some surprises – we'll have to wait and see."[5]

The Governor added that he was mostly recovered from his wounds, and felt "wonderful." He also told the reporters that "I have always felt that there was a second shot that hit me."[6]

as in serious conflict with the Commission's single-bullet
to be made public. But the Warren Commission would not
answer questions about its work. That same afternoon, Chief
arren was asked if that day's presentation ended the
Commiss on's job. "He answered," the *Times* reported, "with an emphatic
'yes.'"7

It was the only word any Commission member said to the press that
day.8

The early critics were all eagerly awaiting the release of the Warren
Commission's report. Anticipation was even higher for the raw material
from which it was ostensibly derived – the Hearings and Exhibits, due to
be released in a twenty-six volume set about two months later.

But while most of these early critics were eager to see the report,
there was a sense that, as John Connally had said, there would be no
surprises – mainly because so much had already been reported by the
press. "The Warren Report was largely an anti-climax since their
principal conclusions had been leaked from the beginning," Ray Marcus
remembered. "It confirmed my suspicions of a major conspiracy and
coverup. The big surprise was how much evidence was included in the
volumes – and even the Report itself – which undermined the official
bullshit."9

Vince Salandria's immediate response was nearly identical. "The
Report confirmed for me that the cover story was totally unbelievable,"
he said. "Reading it convinced me that the Warren Commission and
its staff, being much brighter than I was, had to have realized that
the Report was a fabric of transparent lies that could never withstand
disinterested analysis."10

Harold Weisberg's reaction to the Commission's Report was visceral.
"I was sick," he said long afterward. "These were brilliant men, among the
best minds in the country. And they were whoring with our history."11

Penn Jones put it in the simplest terms: "I really believe that the only
way you can believe the Warren Report is not to read it."12

And yet the Report was treated with great respect when it first
appeared. "The evidence of Oswald's single-handed guilt is overwhelming," Harrison Salisbury wrote in the introduction to the Report's
New York Times paperback edition. *Time* magazine called the Report
"amazing in its detail, remarkable in its judicious caution and restraint, yet
utterly convincing."13

There were several key issues that were the initial focus of the early critics. These included the timing of the shots on the motorcade and the so-called "magic bullet;" the murder of Patrolman Tippit; and a number of eyewitness accounts that strongly suggested other conspirators in the Dealey Plaza vicinity and gunshots fired from the front of the President.[14]

These were among the most obvious areas of interest – as Marcus put it, the "stuff that leaped off the pages when you compared evidence and testimony of the volumes to the Report." But there was much more, and Salandria advised his fellow critics to be prepared for hard work. "Pace yourself for a long, back-breaking excavation job, into the layers of waste material under which the answers in this case lie."[15]

Shirley Martin was ready, but wondering if there was any more she could contribute. "I keep the Warren Report with me and read it over and again," she wrote. "I am making notes, writing to a few people, but mostly realizing that, except for a few more investigations, our part is nearly played. We wait now for Mr. Lane and for some of the influential people of the world to see what terrible mistakes have been made and to do something about them."[16]

With remarkable foresight, Salandria noted shortly before the release of the twenty six volumes that "the case seems to have a future."[17]

While Salandria was cautioning his fellow critics to be ready for long, back-breaking work, he preferred living his life at a more leisurely pace. He was an avid tennis player, and in a letter to Shirley Martin used his love of the game to draw an analogy to the unseen forces behind the JFK assassination.

"I would prefer to choose my competition to measure up more evenly," he told Shirley Martin. "I prefer to hit a tennis ball against a reasonably equipped opponent than to slug at hidden facets in a game where the other side of the court is manned by big-name pros who have the put-away shots, own the referees, make their own rules, keep changing the court size and base lines, rig the score, and control a variable wind which can alter the speed and trajectory of balls to suit their whims. To enjoy such a game at such odds is to be guilty of masochism. But, quit I won't! If you, Mark Lane, Joesten, Feldman, Marguerite, Lynd and a few others have done so many great things, I will try to do some lesser things by virtue of my being less than you."[18]

Another thing he was attempting to accomplish during this time was to re-fashion, along with Harold Feldman, the latter's article that had appeared in *The Nation* eight months earlier. "I have gone over with Harold the shot evidence in the Report," he told Shirley Martin. "He is in the process of shaping another article. We also have culled the agency evidence from the Report. We feel now that his 'Oswald and the FBI' can be updated to include the stuff which the Commission released indicating CIA connections."[19]

Oswald's presumed intelligence connections would remain a consistent theme in much of Salandria and Feldman's writings. But before any further work in this area was done, certain events triggered an altogether new article, this one focusing on the dynamics – Salandria would eventually label it "microanalysis" – of the Dealey Plaza execution.

Arlen Specter and William Coleman were both fresh from their work as Warren Commission attorneys when they were invited to speak before the Philadelphia Bar Association on October 22, 1964.[20]

The Warren Report had been out for about a month. Salandria had immediately ordered a copy from the Government Printing Office. "The Report was a happy anti-climax," he wrote of its lack of revelations. "I have read it with a sense of excitement." Salandria was eager to not only hear Specter and Coleman, but to put questions to them – Specter in particular. "They are smooth and intelligent chaps and quite likely will be artful dodgers," he said at the time. "But we will try."[21]

Salandria was, in fact, able to put some questions to Specter at that meeting, questions dealing with the shots fired at the motorcade, as described in the Warren Report; the trajectories of those shots; and the wounds inflicted on JFK and John Connally. "I merely took from the Report the evidence that was offered to us of a multiple assassin ambush and asked him how that could be comported with the conclusions of the Commission."[22]

Nothing even remotely confrontational was expected by the organizers of the meeting, held in Philadelphia's City Hall, and Salandria's questions caught Specter off guard. "It surprised me to see how quickly he became undone," Salandria wrote soon afterward. "Some of the lawyers present suggested I write up my ideas." He did so that very evening, and the result was one of the first published articles, and perhaps the first, analyzing some of the data set forth in the Warren Report. It bore the rather cumbersome title, "The Warren Report Analysis of Shots, Trajectories and Wounds: A Lawyer's Dissenting View," and appeared in the November 2, 1964, issue of *The Legal Intelligencer*, Philadelphia law journal.[23]

Salandria would always maintain that his article wrote itself. "It took about three hours to write and simply leaped out from the Warren Report into my lap." For Salandria, the contradictions in the Report were that glaring.[24]

The initial draft of the article was rather sarcastic in places, referring to "the illustrious Mr. Specter." Theodore Vorhees, chancellor of the Philadelphia Bar, agreed the article should be published, but asked Salandria to tone it down. "I volunteered to a second draft in a lower key," Salandria told a friend. "Specter will be the next D.A. in Philadelphia. His father just died. He seems to be an all right guy. I didn't want to hurt him, just the government case."[25]

At the Bar Association meeting, Specter had said: "The people are going to have to rely on the conclusions and the stature of the men on the Commission." Salandria seized on this:

> We know that Mr. Specter did not mean by the above statement that the Warren Commission was ever meant to be construed as a "ministry of truth." Nor would the members of the Commission, as public servants in a democracy, ever consider that their "stature" insulated their interpretations and findings from public criticism. Since we are all agreed on this score, we can now proceed to disagree.[26]

The Commission, Salandria wrote, was not necessarily wrong that three shots came from the Texas School Book Depository. "On the contrary, I am willing to concede for the purposes of this presentation that three shots did come from the Book Depository Building. But I will endeavor to prove that all the evidence of the Commission's Report points up that another shot or shots came from a source other than the Depository Building."[27]

Citing the Warren Report almost exclusively, Salandria noted that five eyewitnesses had indicated that shots had come from somewhere else. (Five months later Harold Feldman, using the Commission's twenty-six volumes of Hearings and Exhibits as his source, concluded that no fewer than fifty-one Dealey Plaza witnesses placed the source of shots in the grassy knoll area.) Salandria also recorded that Specter, at the Bar Association meeting, had dismissed the statements of Texas Senator Ralph Yarborough, who had been in the presidential motorcade and said he smelled gunpowder at the time JFK was shot. At the same time, Specter conceded that a Dallas police officer was reported to have also smelled gunpowder. "If the smell of gunpowder was detectable at street level immediately after the assassination, then this would indicate a source of shots other than the sixth floor of the Book Depository Building."[28]

Further evidence of shots from somewhere other than the Book Depository, Salandria wrote, was the wounding of spectator James Tague, who was grazed in the cheek by a bullet or bullet fragment. "Please take careful note that Tague was not on Elm Street, not on Main Street, but between Main and Commerce Streets 'near the Triple Underpass.' From my view of the pictures, maps and exhibits of the Commission Report (let us except my personal inspection of the situs in Dallas) I conclude that the South curb of Main Street near the Triple Underpass was not in the line of fire with the presidential limousine traveling on Elm Street."[29]

There was an apparent bullet mark on the south curb of Main Street, but FBI tests on the mark indicated the bullet that made them was a different type from the ammunition believed to have been used in the alleged assassination rifle. This, Salandria charged, revealed a serious flaw in the Warren Report. "The obvious deduction that this was a bullet fired from the north side of Elm Street, and that it came from a rifle which was different from the Carcano that the Commission described as the assassination weapon, is scrupulously avoided."[30]

The Commission maintained that three shots were fired on the motorcade. It also concluded that one of the shots "probably" missed its target. The recollections of Secret Service Agent Glen A. Bennett, Salandria wrote, indicated it was the first shot that missed, further noting that the Report stated that "substantial weight may be given Bennett's observations" because he wrote them down on the day of the assassination. Bennett had reported hearing a missed first shot and seeing a second shot hit Kennedy "about four inches down from the right shoulder."[31]

Governor Connally was also certain that he was not struck by the first shot, and scrutiny of the 8 mm home movie of the assassination, taken by Abraham Zapruder, supported that contention. "The Governor's body did not react immediately after the President's body reacted. Therefore, he was not hit by the same bullet that hit the President."[32]

On the number of shots, Salandria concluded: "If Governor Connally was not hit by the same first bullet to hit the President, then the Government's case is destroyed." This would demonstrate at least four shots: the first hit on Kennedy, a separate hit on Connally, the missed shot, and the shot that hit JFK in the head.

The article continued with a brief examination of the wounds, and the trajectories of the bullets that made them. Rea reminded that Secret Service Agent Bennett had seen a shot President "about four inches down from the right shoulder." The FBI's examination of Kennedy's jacket revealed a bullet hole "5 3/8 inches below the top of the collar and 1 3/4 inches to the right of the center back seam." A hole in his shirt lined up almost exactly, "5 3/4 inches below the top of the collar and 1 1/8 inches to the right of the middle of the back." And his necktie, cut off by emergency room personnel at Parkland hospital, had a nick on the side of the knot.[33]

> The Commission would have us believe that a trajectory of a bullet from the sixth story downward would hit the President four inches from the right shoulder, or 5 3/4 inches from the top of his shirt collar, and ranging upward emerge from his necktie knot without having hit any bones. This proposed trajectory of down and then up fails to comport with a sixth-floor shot, and if possible at all, must have been fired from a lower level.[34]

At the Philadelphia Bar Association meeting of October 22, Salandria told Arlen Specter that the Warren Commission should have successfully reenacted the shooting performance it attributed to Lee Oswald. "He asked whether I would have them kill a man," Salandria wrote. "The joke fell upon ears which detect no humor in murder."

> Having read the Report, I conclude that the evidence offered by the Commission indicates there was more than one rifleman firing on November 22, 1963. There were more than three shots. If Oswald was one of the gunmen, then with that gun, from that vantage point, in that timespan, suggested by the Commission, he could not have been alone in the performance of the terrible work that destroyed our President and wounded two other men.

Salandria sent a copy of *The Legal Intelligencer* with his article to Shirley Martin, who knew it was being published and was eagerly awaiting its arrival. "How we liked your dissent," she wrote back. "I was just about to write angrily to find out if it had been printed when the paper came. Please, Vince, write more to other sources. Stay in print and be heard."[35]

Mrs. Martin was aware of Salandria's streak of modesty. "You have such a good, clean, analytical approach, so removed from passion and wild-eyed theories. If you don't recognize your own value, you will just have to take my word for it. What would any of us do without you?"[36]

Within days of its publication, a photocopy of Salandria's article was sent to FBI Director J. Edgar Hoover. An accompanying memo provided what background on Salandria there was available. Salandria "was the addressee of a mailing of approximately 1,000 letters sent out by the Citizens Against Rearming Germany in March 1952," Hoover was informed. "This was a temporary propaganda organization substantially infiltrated by the CP."[37]

Additionally, the memo said that in April 1963 an informant had turned over a list of names used in connection with fundraising sponsored by the Independent Citizens Committee for Political Action, "a political action group comprising many innocent non-Communists but having substantial Communist direction from the top." Salandria's name appeared on the list.

The subject line of the memorandum was "The President's Commission on the Assassination of President Kennedy." Other than that, there was no indication of what Salandria's article was even about.

Two days after "The Warren Report Analysis of Shots, Trajectories and Wounds: A Lawyer's Dissenting View" was published, Salandria sent a copy to Earl Warren. "I invite your comment," he said in an accompanying note. There was no reply.[38]

Three weeks after the article was published, a letter by Salandria appeared in *The Legal Intelligencer*'s "Advise and Dissent" column. "Perhaps the reader recalls my view that at least some of the assassination shots originated from a point other than the Book Depository Building (where Oswald allegedly was). Further proof of this contention is provided by two different versions of the same issue of *Life* magazine."[39]

The letter went on to describe a seeming anomaly in the magazine's October 2, 1964, issue. This issue heralded the arrival of the Warren Report, although its coverage was anything but impartial, as the article appeared under the byline of former Warren Commission member Gerald Ford.

What caught Salandria's attention was not Ford's article, but certain photographs that accompanied it. Eight frames from the Zapruder film were published, numbered by the magazine 1 through 8. "In one of the copies, number 6 shows the President, with what appears to be a gaping wound in the right parietal region, falling towards his wife," Salandria wrote.

"In my other copy of the same issue, number 6 is an entirely different picture. This frame clearly shows beyond any question that an assassin's bullet has struck and is blasting away the right front of the President's head. In this photograph we clearly see that the bullet could not have struck the President from the rear." Salandria would later discover a third version of the October 2, 1964, issue of *Life* magazine; in time, he would ask a *Life* editor how three versions of a single issue came to be.[40]

As 1964 drew to a close, Salandria began re-working his *Legal Intelligencer* article. Just before Christmas he learned the new version would be published in *Liberation* magazine. "My mind is presently clogged up with an orgy of 'shots, trajectories and wounds,'" he told Shirley Martin. "How dreadful that I don't have a sense of humor, for there must be something enormously funny in my getting trapped in all this gore. That a simple Babbitt such as I should be sloshing along, knee deep in guts, has to be ludicrously quixotic, and I have to be failing to get the joke."[41]

Liberation agreed to publish the new article, which Salandria said wasn't much different from *The Legal Intelligencer* article, only after considerable arguing among its editorial board. "Staughton Lynd of Yale, about whom we have spoken, made the final decision. Dave Dellinger was the brave soul who made the fight for our side. There was a policy fight because of the fear that this would 'open up Pandora's box.'"[42]

PART TWO

A Government Printing Office spokesman said today that 1,442 sets of the published hearing testimony, at $76 a set, have been sold – mostly to ordinary citizens.

– The Associated Press, March 25, 1965

Chapter 13

The First Anniversary

The approach of Thanksgiving 1964 found Shirley Martin readying her family for another trip to Dallas. It was nearly one year since President Kennedy had been shot to death there, and Shirley wanted to be in Dealey Plaza to observe the first anniversary.

"Will be thinking of you at 12:30 Sunday," she wrote to Vince Salandria.[1]

Salandria had by this time become one of her favorites in her widening circle of critic-friends. "Vincent Salandria as you know is about the best man I've heard about since Mr. Kennedy died," she wrote enthusiastically to a contact in Mark Lane's office. But she tempered her enthusiasm: "He did not care for Mr. Kennedy and that makes me want to pull his nose sometimes."[2]

The Warren Report had been available for nearly two months, and the Hearings and Exhibits were about to be published. Like all of the early critics, Shirley was eager to read the twenty-six volumes. "Got a card from the government printing office this morning saying I could have my toys if I'd send $76 immediately. Mark lifted it out of my hand and said: 'I'll mail the check before noon . . . you have gone too far to back out now.'"[3]

Just before they left, Shirley received an urgent message from Salandria: "It is my fervent hope that this will beat your departure for Dallas," he began. "Presently I am doing some work which can turn out to be important on the shots. A good Catholic family can be of immense help. Here's how . . ."[4]

Salandria reminded her of some published comments by Father Oscar L. Huber, the pastor of Holy Trinity Catholic Church in Dallas, who had administered the last rites to President Kennedy. "He said he wet his right thumb with holy oil and anointed a Cross over the President's forehead," *The Philadelphia Evening Bulletin* had reported, "noticing, as he did so, a 'terrible wound' over his left eye."[5]

It was this account of a "terrible wound" that so interested Salandria. Like the President's throat and back wounds, the location of the wound to his head was a matter of dispute. Citing one of the emergency surgeons, the Warren Report described a large, gaping wound on the right rear portion of Kennedy's skull. Salandria's own research, including the seemingly indisputable Zapruder film frames published in the October 2, 1964, issue of *Life* magazine, supported a hit to the right side. But almost nothing at this early stage was certain; indeed, another of the emergency surgeons reported a wound on the *left* of JFK's skull. "If Father Huber recalled correctly," he wrote Shirley on November 19, "and if he was quoted correctly, then Dr. McClelland's statement on pages 526 and 527 [of the Warren Report] to the effect that 'cause of death was due to massive head and brain injury from a gunshot wound of the left temple,' is an accurate representation of what happened.

"Can you see Father Huber?" Salandria asked. "Can you check his recollection? Can you determine whether the government agents explored the wounds with him?"[6]

Mrs. Martin said that she would try.

November 22, 1964, fell on a Sunday. Houses of worship through-out Dallas experienced higher-than-usual turnouts as worshipers came to remember President Kennedy. A multi-denominational service at the Cathedral of the Sacred Heart, dedicated to JFK, was hailed as a mile-stone – "an historic moment in the religious life of the city," according to the executive director of the Greater Dallas Council of Churches.[7]

In Dealey Plaza, where the assassination had taken place, an estimated 200 people gathered to commemorate the first anniversary of President Kennedy's death. Floral tributes crowded the colonnade area of the concrete pergola along the top of the grassy knoll; one of these recalled the words JFK had spoken at his inauguration four years earlier: "Ask not what your country can do for you; ask what you can do for your country."[8]

The crowd watched the large clock on top of the Texas School Book Depository tick off the minutes to 12:30 p.m., the approximate time of the fusillade. And at 1 p.m., the time that Kennedy was pronounced dead a year earlier, automobiles in the plaza area slowed to a halt; heads were bowed and prayers whispered; tears slid down faces.[9]

"No need to tell you it was hard to be on Elm at 12:30," Shirley Martin said afterward. "Teresa cried hard."[10]

The Martins arrived back in Hominy late Monday night. Thanksgiving was just a few days away, and a busy week was made busier by the installation of new carpeting scheduled for the Martin home. But on Tuesday, November 24, Shirley found time to write Salandria about the matter he had so fervently written her of less than one week earlier.

"Saw Father Huber on Sunday," she began. "Went to mass there. Yes, your story is accurate although Father Huber makes gentle disclaimers against it. He says when he entered Emergency Room #1, he pulled the sheet just to the edge of the President's nose and then he saw what he assumed to be a bullet entry hole above the President's left eye. He says he spoke to Mrs. Kennedy, left Parkland, returned to his parish (which ironically is only a few doors from General Walker's), where he told his fellow priests that the President had been killed by a bullet into the left temple area.

"Father Huber says he *never* told this to the press. However, he supposes that someone to whom he spoke may have relayed it to the newsmen. The next day, Father Huber says he learned that the assassin had stood behind the President, therefore negating the possibility that what he saw had been an entry bullet wound. At once, Father Huber realized that what he had seen was only a 'blood clot.'

"He has brainwashed himself. The FBI have never spoken with him, nor did the Warren Commission approach him for a statement of any kind."[11]

Salandria had already written about Father Huber's originally published statements in his *Legal-Intelligencer* article published a few weeks earlier. In spite of his "gentle disclaimers," Father Huber seemed to confirm his original story to Shirley. And so his observations were repeated in a later article, written after Salandria had seen the twenty-six volumes, with the added comment that "Father Huber was not called as a witness. Nor was Dr. McClelland asked for an explanation of his designation of a wound in the left temple as the cause of death."[12]

On the day of the first anniversary of the Kennedy assassination, the front page of the *Dallas Times-Herald* featured a poignant political cartoon: the dark-clad figure of JFK, bent forward into a stiff wind, trudges through snow as he heads toward a darkening forest. The cartoonist put these words at JFK's side: "The Humanitarian Spirit of John Kennedy" – while the top of the panel bore the words of Robert Frost: "The woods are lovely, dark and deep/But I have promises to keep/And miles to go before I sleep. . . ."[13]

In Maryland, thirteen hundred miles from Dallas, Harold Weisberg was keeping a promise of his own. When the single-volume Warren Report went on sale at the Government Printing Office retail store in September, he bought three copies, and in November purchased two sets of the Commission's just-published twenty-six volumes of Hearings and Exhibits. He wanted one set of these twenty-seven books as working copies, and another to preserve; in 1992, the second set of Hearings and Exhibits was donated to a small college near his home, still sealed in its original carton.[14]

Weisberg began his analysis of the Report immediately. His later recollections of this early period conjured a rather folksy image: "I had a Concord voice-activated tape recorder," he said. "And I had an old-fashion platform rocker that I sat on near a stove with a lamp over my right shoulder, and dictated my first notes. And my wife re-typed them." The notes were hundreds of pages in length. A comprehensive index to the Warren Commission data did not then exist, so Weisberg began marking up his working copies of the Report and volumes. Ultimately his notes were not very useful, but when the time came for him to write, he was ready. He started around the first of the year, having landed a contract obliging him to deliver a manuscript in February. Years later he recalled working almost around the clock on the book, sometimes getting by on only a few hours' sleep. He called the finished work *The Report on the Warren Report*. Originally he subtitled it "The Six Wise Men of Industan," thus likening the Warren Commission to the fable of six blind men whose individual experiences with an elephant led each to a strikingly different conclusion. But Weisberg dropped that subtitle and re-christened the book. After his intensive review of the official evidence, the most appropriate title he could think of, and the best single-word description of the Warren Report, was *Whitewash*.[15]

By December 1964 most of the critics had purchased a set of the twenty-six volumes and were delving into them. Volume 15 contained a name index covering the first fifteen volumes, but the remaining eleven were uncharted. Shirley Martin must have had this in mind when she wrote to Harold Feldman: "The reading now is the important part. Whatever you and Vince can share with me of your ideas, etc., will be appreciated. Could you each keep a notebook and write down page number, volumes, as you read?"[16]

This was no small request. The combined twenty-six volumes contain some 20,000 pages and an estimated ten million words. The first fifteen of the blue-bound volumes consist of transcripts of witness depositions and testimony, while the balance are comprised of Commission exhibits and documents – mostly police and FBI reports, photographs, and other pertinent records. In some instances, though, there is material the inclusion of which is difficult to understand – like the copies of the dental records of Jack Ruby's mother, which dated to 1938. Those would not be relevant, Mark Lane once quipped, even if Ruby had bitten Oswald to death.[17]

In the beginning one approach to the case was to compare statements presented as fact in the Warren Report to their source in the twenty-six volumes. But the lack of a subject index was a serious obstacle for anyone trying to navigate this official record. Before long it was generally agreed among the critics that the Hearings and Exhibits, while providing a wealth of information undermining the official story, were nevertheless a disorderly jumble. Harold Weisberg called it organized chaos. Sylvia Meagher, whose career at the World Health Organization in New York was flourishing, put it thusly: "It would be tantamount to a search for information in the *Encyclopedia Britannica* if the contents were untitled, unalphabetized, and in random sequence." And so she set for herself the task of creating a subject index for the entire twenty-six volumes.[18]

In about one year's time she had nearly finished the job. "I have been putting aside everything that draws me, in an attempt to complete the subject index," she wrote in September 1965. "Happily, it is very, very near completion."[19]

Meagher once said she was surprised she had the drive to pursue her assassination work with the vigor she did. In the two years before the assassination, her sister, mother, and only brother had died in quick succession; this was followed by the death of her closest friend. Her sister-in-law died shortly after the assassination. "I was so saturated with death and deaths that I should not have expected to experience any emotion on that Friday – yet, I felt an immense surge of rage that has not yet subsided," she said. "Never for one moment could I believe LHO guilty; and every shifting version of events only reinforced my conviction that we had not had the truth."[20]

Meagher had always been concerned about injustice in American society and in the world at large. She was deeply disturbed by atrocities committed by white racists in the American south: the abduction and murder of fourteen-year-old Emmett Till in 1955, the assassination of Medgar Evers, the church bombing that killed four young girls in Alabama in 1963, and the murders of civil rights workers James Chaney, Michael Schwerner, and Andrew Goodman in Mississippi the following year. Yet she knew those crimes were merely the tip of the iceberg – the most publicized acts in a long and bloody saga. "I have become part savage from the exigencies of this ultra-civilized society in which we live," she told a friend, "fundamentally outraged almost to the brink of dementia by the depravity, the injustice, the indecency, and the decay that advertises itself in such lofty pious arch-hypocritical hyperbole . . . those who remain sane and undisturbed are the really sick ones – we who are crumbling before the utter horror at least have that much of sanity."[21]

On the day of the assassination she had sat stunned in her office at the United Nations as news of the tragedy filtered in. Meagher and her colleagues well remembered how UN Ambassador Adlai Stevenson had been assaulted in Dallas less than one month before. Confirmation of Kennedy's death was broadcast in New York around 2:30 that afternoon. "I said with irony that a leftist or pro-Castro assassin would undoubtedly be found," Meagher recalled, "and only an hour or so later heard with disbelief [that] a man named Oswald had been arrested for the crime."[22]

The story from Dallas, Meagher said, just didn't sound right – in particular the rapidity with which the authorities announced their evidence against Lee Oswald. Like all of the early critics, Meagher began reading everything on the case she could find, clipping and saving newspaper and magazine articles. Within a week of the assassination she had catalogued her thoughts in an inchoate document called "Bitter Thoughts After the 22nd of November." A few weeks later she wrote of her concerns in a letter to Earl Warren: "I have no doubt whatever that you personally will do everything humanly possible to determine the truth." She attended Mark Lane's early lectures in New York, including the Town Hall event at which Marguerite Oswald appeared, and contributed both money and insights to Lane's Citizens' Committee of Inquiry. During a trip to Europe that August she satisfied herself that few people outside of the United States believed that Oswald acted alone. Yet in spite of her suspicions, she later said she withheld judgment pending the release of the Warren Commission's material.[23]

Meagher immediately bought a copy of the Warren Report when it was published in September 1964. "One of the things I have learned not to trust," she told an interviewer a few years later, "is the sentence you have to read several times to get its meaning. One of the personalities of the United Nations had an established pattern of making statements that were couched in such obfuscation. He managed to skirt issues so cleverly, and I found the Commission did this a very great deal."[24]

Within two months of the Report's publication she had finished a 15,000-word article entitled "The Warren Commission Report: A

Critique." Perhaps reflecting her concern that a public stance against the Warren Commission might have a negative impact on an American employed by an international agency, she initially obscured her identity by blending her name with that of a friend, crediting her critique to "Isabel Meagher Davis."[25]

Like Harold Weisberg, Meagher brought to her analysis her years of experience working within a large bureaucracy. Unlike Weisberg, she also brought a no-nonsense prose style that wasted few words. Her critique began by scolding certain luminaries of the press for praising the Report before they could possibly have had time to read it and give it a reasoned, objective analysis. One theme common to the glowing reviews, Meagher wrote, was the implication that opposing views were unjustified and perhaps unpatriotic. Another was that anyone postulating a political conspiracy was guilty of irrational thinking – was, in a word, nuts. "These gentlemen do not seem to consider the possibility that ordinary individuals, innocent of either political extreme, are deeply troubled by a case and now a Warren report which abound with misrepresentation, lacunae, implausibilities, and simple absurdity. They are neither unscrupulous nor sick, unless passion for justice has fallen into disrepute and warrants such slanderous epithets." The critics, she said, were raising legitimate questions about the evidence against Lee Harvey Oswald.[26]

Meagher's critique covered some of the same ground as the early articles by Mark Lane and Vincent J. Salandria. She examined the shots allegedly fired in Dealey Plaza, and their trajectories, and the witnesses whose statements, at a glance, seemed so damning to Lee Harvey Oswald. In the years ahead, as some of her critic-colleagues occasionally bickered over who had first reached a particular insight or conclusion, she would comment on "parallel development," the notion that incisive minds working independently but from the same data would reach the same verdict.[27]

Based on the Warren Report, Meagher wrote, it was impossible to say whether Oswald was part of a conspiracy, was a fall-guy set up to take the blame, was completely innocent, or as the Warren Commission claimed, was the sole perpetrator of the deed. "There *is* evidence that incriminates Oswald," Meagher acknowledged, "although considerably less than the Warren Report claims." It seemed conclusive that he purchased the alleged assassination rifle and the alleged Tippit murder weapon by mail, and that both weapons were in the possession of the authorities soon after the two slayings. But it was not certain, she continued, that the fatal shots came from those weapons or that it was

Oswald who had pulled the trigger. Oswald lacked any apparent motive and had consistently denied any guilt. He also had dubious abilities as a marksman. The witnesses against him were all vulnerable. Moreover, there was a complete failure by responsible agencies to ever consider any possibility other than Oswald as lone gunman.

> Instead of objective criticism of the Warren Report and recognition of its defects, we have heard a gusher of extravagant praise and facile concurrence with its findings.
>
> Those who cannot believe that it is possible for justice to be perverted in this country, even at the highest levels, should bear in mind that the murderers of Emmett Till, Medgar Evers, the Birmingham children, James Chaney, Andrew Goodman, and Michael Schwerner, among others, are still at large. Conversely, there is ample literature on the shocking number of convicted "murderers" who turned out to be innocent, after many years of imprisonment and in some cases after eleventh-hour reprieve from execution. Nor should we forget that, to our national shame, police authorities themselves have been implicated in many crimes and criminal conspiracies, and not only in the Deep South.
>
> The Warren Report gives us no justification for declaring that the case is closed. Conscience demands that the search for the whole truth must continue.[28]

At the time of the assassination Sylvia Meagher lived in New York City, where she was born on July 22, 1921. Her only live-in companion was a cat. She had been divorced more than a decade but appears to have been uninterested in any new romance. "Some years ago, I suddenly began to feel that all my curiosity was satisfied – and life has been far less agonizing since my 'retirement,' or at least the agonies are new and different."[29]

She grew up Sylvia Orenstein in Brooklyn in what she once described as a rigidly Orthodox Jewish home, "with this angry God and always mournful or solemn atmosphere." It seemed incredible to her that life should be so joyless and fearful. As a consequence, she claimed that by the age of four she had already begun to dislike anything devoutly religious; as she grew older she defined herself as an atheist. "But it was already too late – I had become susceptible to guilt feelings before I got smart enough to rebel against the irrationality of all the preoccupation with the non-listening non-existent God; and the morality was already so imbued that now if I want to be relatively comfortable, emotionally, I have to do-unto-others and all the rest, even if I don't have to endure the incessant rituals and endless prayers."[30]

Details of her marriage are sketchy. While taking night classes at Brooklyn College she developed an infatuation for her English instructor. This was around the same time she began working at the World Health Organization. The demands of her job coupled with this infatuation led her to drop out of college in 1946; she never did obtain her degree.[31]

A relationship with the English instructor, James P. Meagher, did develop and evolve over a number of years. It appears they were married sometime in 1951. According to a document filled out by Sylvia in 1953, the couple briefly lived together in a home on New York Avenue from September to December of 1951. Yet in the same document Sylvia stated that she had lived at 299 West 12 St. since December 1948. While Sylvia cared very deeply for James Meagher, a prolonged relationship with him was apparently impossible for her to sustain due to his alcoholism, which ultimately forced her to leave him. The disease lead to James Meagher's early death, which years later Sylvia recalled as "a tragedy, as he was a most talented and admirable person in every way, and a poet, but could not resist the addiction and finally stopped trying."[32]

On November 23, 1964, the Warren Commission's Hearings and Exhibits were made public. Two days later a set arrived at Sylvia Meagher's 12th Street apartment. "I was wildly excited," she recalled. "I opened the box. There were the twenty-six volumes, everything I'd been looking forward to studying for a long time."[33]

Once she received the full set, she took her original Warren Report critique, which had been submitted to several periodicals, out of circulation. She'd had no success placing it: *The New Leader* and *The New Yorker* had both rejected it by mid-November, and *Ramparts*, among others, quickly followed suit.[34]

Each day, she took one of the volumes to work with her. She would read it on the way there and on the way back, and during her lunch hour. She also carried with her a large clipboard, on which she made constant notes and annotations. The Warren Commission's material was becoming familiar terrain indeed. But as Meagher began comparing the single-volume Report to the twenty-six volumes from which it was ostensibly derived, she reached an unavoidable conclusion. "It was appalling to find how many of the Commission's statements were unsupportable or even completely contradicted by the testimony and/or exhibits," she said that spring. "I began to list what is now a long series of deliberate misrepresentations, omissions, distortions, and other defects demonstrating not only extreme bias, incompetence, and carelessness but irrefutable instances of dishonesty." She hoped to develop her discoveries, she added, into a book.[35]

If she had been hooked before, it seems that by January 1965 she was thinking of almost nothing but the assassination and the official evidence. "I am trying to exclude everything in the way of social life," she confided to a friend – adding it was simply not possible to do that without alienating people she cared about. She bought a magnifying glass equipped with a built-in light so she could more easily scrutinize those exhibits that the Warren Commission had published in often blurred and tiny reproductions. "I just couldn't bear it any more," she said, "because I thought I was wasting valuable time."[36]

Then, in February, she heard about a Warren Report class being offered locally at the New School for Social Research. It was held once a week in the early evening and taught by a New York attorney. The school catalog promised:

> A close reading of the full text and selected biographical appendices studied primarily as a historical document. Portions of the report are illustrative of both passive social and active political responses to the assassination of President Kennedy. Comment is made on the legal sufficiency of the evidence . . . Commission membership, organization and study methods are reviewed in relation to the structure and findings of the report.[37]

Sylvia immediately registered for the course. She also convinced a close friend to come with her: Isabel Davis, who lived nearby, and who had loaned her name to Sylvia's Warren Report critique.

Most of the class was not nearly as familiar with the Warren Commission material as Meagher. "We had the rest of the group, including the instructor, at something of a disadvantage," she said at the time. "Nevertheless, the exchange of information on all sides has been most useful."[38]

The instructor, Joseph S. Lobenthal Jr., had been practicing law since 1961; the class was his inspiration. "I suspected I'd get fanatics and buffs, and I did," he recalled. When he read the Report and the twenty-six volumes just after their publication, he had been dissatisfied with its conclusions. It occurred to him that comparing the Commission's conclusions to the evidence in its Hearings and Exhibits might be useful, but it was too big a job for him to undertake by himself. Lobenthal had already taught some law courses at The New School, so he approached a dean with the idea of a class. "And he said, you know, go for it."[39]

The previous summer Lobenthal had spent several weeks in Mississippi, where the civil rights movement was in the midst of its Summer Project. He was there defending civil rights workers as a volunteer with the Lawyer's Constitutional Defense Committee. The volunteer lawyers would drive all over the state, wherever representation was needed. Lobenthal was there in August when the bodies of Goodman, Chaney, and Schwerner were discovered, but in spite of the hazards he never felt personally in danger. "I was never threatened," Lobenthal said. "Instead of being threatened, for the most part we were sandbagged. That was it. They wouldn't find papers, or would adjourn things out from under us after we'd made the trip without advising us. Things that were basically legal dirty tricks."[40]

When summer ended, Lobenthal returned to New York with a greater sense of purpose than he'd had before. "The Mississippi experience was a very exhilarating one . . . and I think that I just got, really, caught up in some public events, and the assassination was just . . . the idea of teaching it just came to me."[41]

While Lobenthal was nominally the instructor of the Warren Report course, he was also there to learn; he remembered the class as "almost a seminar of equals." Aside from Isabel Davis, others in the class would be associated with Meagher and other critics in the years to come. These included Thomas Stamm, William Crehan, Lobenthal, and Stewart Galanor, who was among those volunteers doing work for Mark Lane's Citizens' Committee of Inquiry.[42]

The uniqueness of the class, probably the first of its kind, earned it what must have been one of the shortest articles in the entire history of *Newsweek* magazine. In its February 1, 1965 issue, under the heading "Instant History," the magazine carried a single-paragraph, three-sentence story:

> It usually takes years and sometimes decades for courses in history to catch up with events in history. But the New School for Social Research, an adult education college in New York City, has narrowed the gap considerably. Beginning Feb. 1, The New School will offer a fifteen-week course on the Warren Commission report.[43]

Lobenthal lectured during the first and last class meetings, but otherwise, after some introductory remarks, a typical session was turned over to the students for discussion of difficult aspects of the case. "The 'approach' was to present hypotheses and to examine them in light of the available evidence," Lobenthal said at the time. Class members each pursued individual areas of interest, and when those areas were covered during class discussion, would present their findings.[44]

There were several guest lecturers. Dwight Macdonald, the editor and critic whose own analysis of the Warren Report was published that March in *Esquire* magazine, spoke to one session. Macdonald had briefly considered forming a private committee of his own to investigate the assassination, before electing to wait on the Warren Commission. Another guest was Léo Sauvage, the U.S. correspondent for *Le Figaro*, a leading Paris daily. Sauvage had already written critically of the assassination in articles published in *The Reporter* and *Commentary* magazines, as well as *Le Figaro*. He was also the author of *L'Affaire Oswald*, the first critical book based on the official evidence, at the time available only in French. Sauvage, too, would develop a close working relationship with Sylvia Meagher.[45]

The consensus of the class was seldom, if ever, unanimous on any given point. But there was general agreement that the Warren Commission's Report was not convincing, and that its conclusions were not supported by its own evidence. When the course ended in May, most of the students felt it was important that they continue their research and that they keep in touch. Lobenthal drew up a list of names, phone numbers and addresses and distributed it among the class.[46]

By this time – the late spring and early summer of 1965 – Meagher was hard at work on her subject index. And soon she would go directly to the source, writing a series of letters to former Warren Commission members and attorneys, in an attempt to hold them accountable for the official record of the assassination of President Kennedy.

She was also, during early and mid-1965, beginning to make contact with critics beyond the confines of the Warren Report class. One of these was Maggie Field, who had written to Joe Lobenthal about the Warren Report class, possibly after seeing the *Newsweek* item. Meagher and Field quickly developed a close bond. "Of all the people I have met or been in touch with since November 22, 1963," Sylvia told her, "you have the viewpoint and approach which seems the closest to my own; naturally, this is very gratifying and reassuring . . . I know that we are going to be good friends and colleagues."[47]

Chapter 14

A Middle-aged Lochinvar

 arly in the life of the Warren Commission, at a time when it had just
 begun taking testimony from witnesses, Earl Warren alarmed many
Americans by stating that for national security reasons not all of the
evidence the Commission gathered would be made public in the foreseeable future. "There will come a time," he told a reporter. "But it might
not be in your lifetime." Indeed the twenty-six volumes, while full of raw
material, represented but a portion of the collected data; after the
Commission finished its work, some 357 cubic feet of evidence was stored
in the National Archives under a 75-year seal. Chief Justice Warren
declined to discuss the Report publicly. He once claimed that as a
prosecutor he could have won a conviction against Lee Harvey Oswald in
two days, and is said to have derided the Report's critics as "charlatans."
But this opinion was privately expressed.[1]

Warren's example of silence was for the most part followed by the
other former Commission members. There was a notable, if inadvert,
exception to this in late 1965, when Allen Dulles was confronted by
David Lifton during an informal address to students at the University of
California in Los Angeles. Lifton was a UCLA graduate student whose
interest in the Kennedy assassination began after he heard Mark Lane
speak in 1964. That night he tried to show Dulles evidence that the
Zapruder film did not support the lone-gunman thesis. Dulles first grew
angry, then condescending, and finally said that if there were going to be any
more questions about the Warren Commission he'd just as soon go to bed.[2]

About a year before that, then-Congressman and future President
Gerald R. Ford wrote of the Commission's work in an article for the
October 2, 1964, issue of *Life* magazine. Ford's work was general in nature
and for the most part merely restated the Commission's case. But Ford
did make at least one point that would be disputed. Many critics had
wondered why, if the alleged murder rifle was an Italian-made
Mannlicher Carcano, it was originally identified by authorities as a
German-made Mauser. Mark Lane had forced the Commission to
confront this question during his Warren Commission testimony in
March 1964. Representative Ford wrote that just after the weapon was

discovered on November 22 a reporter "facing an immediate deadline, asked an officer standing nearby what make the rifle might be. He said he thought it might be a Mauser. The reporter filed his story" with that supposed misidentification.[3]

The appearance of the Warren Report in September 1964 had not curtailed Mark Lane's assassination-related activities; he was easily the most visible critic of this early period. In addition to his many speaking dates, he published at least two articles that fall, though neither got the attention his defense brief had in late 1963. In October "The Doubts Remain" appeared in *The National Guardian*, the same paper that had run his brief. This article was in part an attack on the makeup and procedures of the Commission. Lane argued that it was not the impartial body it claimed to be. "Were Oswald permitted to live to face trial, not a single member of the Commission would be permitted to serve as a juror on that trial," he wrote. "Defense counsel would have had reason for removing each of them." All seven members were associated with the government, which was also the prosecuting agency. That suggestion of bias was compounded, Lane said, by the Commission's decision to deny Lee Oswald's family the opportunity to select counsel to represent his interests.[4]

A second Lane article was published in the November 1964 issue of *The Minority of One*, a small New Jersey-based magazine. *The Minority of One* was an exception to the rule of the American media during this period, publishing editorials critical of the official explanation from the beginning. The magazine's basic philosophy was suggested by its name and summarized in its masthead: "Dedicated to the eradication of all restrictions on thought." Referred to privately as *TMO*, the magazine played a small but important role in assassination criticism during the 1960s, and its editor, M.S. Arnoni, enjoyed close relationships with several leading critics.[5]

Arnoni was a writer and political activist, a Polish Jew who had survived several Nazi concentration camps during World War II. Like all survivors his body still bore death-camp tattoos. He was known to sometimes wear a prisoner uniform at speaking engagements. Sylvia Meagher was greatly impressed by Arnoni's vitality. "It is hard to believe that a human being could possibly survive and recover from such unbelievable horrors," she remarked, "much less come out with such an uncompromising fighting spirit."[6]

In his January 1964 issue, published when the Warren Commission had formed but barely begun its work, Arnoni ran a front-page editorial that raised the specter of a government-sponsored plot in Kennedy's death. One of the difficulties critics faced, he said, was the inability of the American public to accept that such a thing could happen. "The popular view of the American body politic as a free and democratic set-up responsive to the spontaneous wishes of the majority lulls many people into rejecting without examination any theory predicated on sinister schemes within the power structure."[7]

A few months later Arnoni wrote an open letter to Earl Warren that appeared first as a paid advertisement in the March 20, 1964, issue of *The New York Times* and then as a *TMO* editorial. "Could it be," Arnoni wrote, "that there was a criminal plot not only against the person of John F. Kennedy but also against his attempts to bring the Cold War to an end? History teaches us that whenever a head of state is assassinated there is a strong likelihood of a political plot behind the act. It also teaches us that at times the plotters hold such positions of power as enable them to divert suspicions from themselves, or to intimidate into silence those who suspect them." He addressed Warren's comments that evidence relating to national security might not be made public "in your lifetime." Arnoni countered: "We think your primary duty to be to discover the truth, whatever it is, about a tragic national event and to tell this truth to *this* generation . . . it is no longer possible to be sure that yours will be the final truth about the assassination of President Kennedy . . . we believe we are speaking for many Americans, and not only Americans, when we respectfully call on you, Mr. Chief Justice, to tender your resignation as the Chairman of the presidential Commission."[8]

Arnoni published a sampling of reaction to the Open Letter in the April 1964 issue of *The Minority of One*. Some readers called him courageous, with views in accord with millions of others. Others said his views were asinine – and crazy.[9]

In its September 1964 issue, *The Minority of One* published an article entitled "16 Questions on the Assassination," credited to Lord Bertrand Russell, the renowned philosopher and humanitarian. The article raised serious questions that were not getting much, if any, play in the American media. Lord Russell, who was ninety-one years old at the time of the assassination, later said that because of the press coverage out of Dallas, he was suspicious almost immediately "that there had been an appalling miscarriage of justice and that possibly something very nasty was being covered up." He soon founded the Who Killed Kennedy?

committee in London. Its director was Ralph Schoenman, a young American living in England who had served as Lord Russell's secretary for several years. The committee's membership included historians Arnold Toynbee and Professor Hugh Trevor-Roper, theatre critic Kenneth Tynan, and French philosopher Jean-Paul Sartre.[10]

As with Lord Russell, the rapidity of events in Dallas, culminating with the murder of Lee Oswald while handcuffed to two police officers, was highly suspicious to Schoenman. "You didn't need a road map to see the hand of the authorities in this event," he said. The Who Killed Kennedy? committee was thus formed to examine the assassination's underlying elements. Not long after Mark Lane published his defense brief in *The National Guardian* in December 1963, Schoenman contacted him; before long the Who Killed Kennedy? committee and Lane's Citizens' Committee of Inquiry were closely allied.[11]

Bertrand Russell's stature lent the "16 Questions" article a measure of urgency it might not otherwise have received. But though it was credited to him, it was in fact a collaborative effort reflecting not only Russell's views, but those of Schoenman, the Who Killed Kennedy? committee, and Mark Lane. Years later Schoenman acknowledged that he was instrumental in drafting the document but maintained the question of credit was not important. "Do the questions that we pose about the official fiction stand up to the evidence or not?" he asked. "That's the only issue of any significance."[12]

The questions, presented here without the substantive commentary accompanying the original, were:

1. Why were all the members of the Warren Commission closely associated with the U.S. Government?

2. If, as we are told, Oswald was the lone assassin, where is the issue of national security?

3. If the government is so certain of its case, why has it conducted all its inquiries in the strictest secrecy?

4. Why did the Warren Commission not establish a panel to deal with the question of Who Killed Kennedy?

5. Why have so many liberals abandoned their own responsibility to a Commission whose circumstances they refuse to examine?

6. Why did the authorities follow many persons as potential assassins and fail to observe Oswald's entry into the book depository

building while allegedly carrying a rifle over three feet long?

7.   Why was the President's route changed at the last minute to take him past Oswald's place of work?

8.   Why has the medical evidence concerning the President's death been altered out of recognition?

9.   What is the evidence to substantiate the allegation that the President was shot from behind?

10.   Why has the FBI refused to publish what could be the most reliable evidence in the whole case?

11.   How is it that millions of people have been misled by complete forgeries in the press? [i.e. photographs]

12.   Why was the result of the paraffin test altered before being announced by the authorities?

13.   Why was the only description of Tippit's killer deliberately omitted by the police from the affidavit of the sole eyewitness?

14.   Why was Oswald's description in connection with the murder of Patrolman Tippit broadcast over Dallas police radio at 12:43 pm on November 22, when Tippit was not shot until 1:06 pm?

15.   How was it possible for Earl Warren to forecast that Marina Oswald's evidence would be exactly the reverse of what she had previously believed?

16.   How does a District Attorney of Wade's great experience account for all the extraordinary changes in evidence and testimony which he has announced during the Oswald case?

. . . These are only a few of the questions raised by the official versions of the assassination and by the way in which the entire case against Oswald has been conducted. Sixteen questions are no substitute for a full examination of all the factors in this case, but I hope that they indicate the importance of such an investigation. . . .

We view the problem with the utmost seriousness. U.S. Embassies have long ago reported to Washington world-wide disbelief in the official charges against Oswald, but this has scarcely been reflected by the American press. No U.S. television program or mass circulation newspaper has challenged the permanent basis of all the allegations – that Oswald was the assassin, and that he acted alone. It is a task which is left to the American people.[13]

Through most of 1964, Mark Lane's public appearances were in the form of lectures. Most were in the United States, but Lane also scheduled speaking dates in Europe, including Communist countries behind the Iron Curtain. In Los Angeles Ray Marcus had come to admire Lane's courage and considered him the "point man" for the critics, but he nevertheless told Lane that any Eastern European engagements would be a mistake. "Since the obvious purpose of your work in the case is to inform the world – but most particularly, the American public – of the facts regarding 'the crime of the century,' I feel strongly it would be a serious error on your part to speak in Hungary or any other Communist-led country at this time. . . . I urge you to re-consider your visit to Hungary." Four days later, Lane spoke to an enthusiastic audience in Budapest and granted several media interviews, in which he said the American press had cooperated in suppressing the truth about the assassination, and denied him the opportunity to make his case to the public.[14]

Back in the States, Lane was closely monitored by federal authorities. Lane was not unaware of the monitoring. In the fall of 1964 alone, no fewer than thirty informants attended his lectures in New York and reported back to the local FBI office. Earlier that summer Lane appeared regularly at the Gramercy Arts Theater, but in August the lectures were moved to a larger facility. An advertisement announcing the venue change appeared in the August 24 *New York Times*; the ad featured a quote from Bertrand Russell: "I urge all Americans to hear Mark Lane."[15]

In a confidential memo, the FBI noted the *Times* ad and stated: ". . . by means of a suitable pretext by a Special Agent of the Federal Bureau of Investigation, (FBI), it was determined Mark Lane would present his lectures 'Who Killed Kennedy' at the Jan Hus Theatre, New York City, on a nightly basis until September 28, 1964." An addition to the memo noted that the lectures had been extended through October 3. The "suitable pretext" referred to "telephone calls on 9/9/64 and 9/28/64 . . . by SA Ronald E. Young to the Citizens' Committee of Inquiry, 156 Fifth Avenue, NYC, under the guise of a person interested in LANE's defense of LEE HARVEY OSWALD." The lectures, if one can judge by this and similar FBI documents, were well attended and well received.[16]

Informants advised the FBI that admission to Lane's lectures was $2.00 for adults and $.99 for students. Lane said that all the funds raised by the lectures were used to pay operating expenses for the Citizens' Committee of Inquiry and to fund his personal investigation into the case. Another informant, this one an assistant secretary to an officer at the Chemical Bank New York Trust Company, told the FBI that the CCI had $11,042.05 in its bank account.[17]

Lane's speaking style was "in the manner of a college professor with little or no emotion" and he would offer no conclusion on many of the points he made; he "left any conclusion to be drawn by the audience based on his remarks and the 'evidence' presented.'" But he would imply, the informant said, that "some type of governmental conspiracy or plot was attempting, at whatever cost, to pin the assassination on Oswald and Oswald alone."[18]

At each lecture Lane used several aids, including a large map of Dealey Plaza, tape recordings of interviews with witnesses, and a slide projector to display news clippings and other documents. He did not use any prepared remarks. The basic anomalies he'd been presenting all year were discussed, and as time went by some new ones were added: Why was the murder rifle originally described as a Mauser? Why had the notorious photo of Oswald armed with the alleged murder weapons been retouched? Why did the witness to the murder of Officer Tippit describe a killer whose appearance did not match Oswald's? Why have some of the witnesses been menaced by authorities?[19]

The *New York World Telegram* sent a reporter to one lecture and on September 3 carried a story headlined "Oswald Is Innocent Nightly on 74th Street." Though its tone was somewhat incredulous, the article was nevertheless a departure for the mainstream media. It referred to Lane as "a dragonslayer in horn-rimmed glasses. The audience . . . came to be persuaded. Lane does not disappoint them."

> Each night in the air-conditioned darkness of a theater on the Upper East Side, John F. Kennedy dies again.
>
> Each night, Mark Lane, lecturing on "Who Killed Kennedy?," takes his audience into a never-never land gone mad, where the American dream of justice and fair play is destroyed.
>
> Lane, former New York Assemblyman who once served as unpaid defense counsel for Lee Harvey Oswald, the President's accused assassin, testified before the Warren Commission in July.
>
> What he tells audiences in the 300-seat Jan Hus Theater on E. 74th St. is virtually a replay of what he told the commission, which investigated the President's assassination.
>
> Lane's three-hour lecture is a fantastic adventure and it is all his adventure. He is the fellow who sets the course, steers the ship. This is Lane pleading for truth, Lane searching for truth, Lane finding truth.
>
> Then it is Lane pulverizing the arguments of the Dallas police, the Federal Bureau of Investigation, the Secret Service, and the

Warren Commission. It doesn't matter to Lane that they can supply evidence that Oswald was the killer. They have their truth, and he has his.[20]

The article concluded by quoting an audience member who had recently returned from a trip to Europe. "Everywhere I went, people asked me who killed Kennedy?" he said. "And when I told them Oswald, they laughed at me."[21]

On September 28, an FBI informant reported that Lane said the Warren Report, released just a few days before, "confirmed his long-held belief that the report would be a complete 'whitewash' and 'cover up' of the 'true facts' surrounding the death of President John F. Kennedy." The Report merely supported the basic government premise that Oswald had acted alone, Lane told his listeners; its sole purpose was to prove that there was no conspiracy.[22]

A few days later, as he completed another of his presentations at the Jan Hus Theater, Lane announced it was the last of his regular lectures. But he added that he would carry on his personal investigation into the death of President Kennedy. It was his intention, he said, to prove that the Warren Report's conclusions were false. At least three informants attended this lecture on October 3, 1964. They left no record of whether he mentioned it, but Lane was about to go head-to-head with the Report's defenders.[23]

Six days later and on the other side of the continent, Lane took part in the first of three debates on the question of who assassinated President Kennedy. The last of these debates was easily the most important, since it involved a former Commission attorney. The first two were against Melvin Belli, a flamboyant San Francisco-based attorney who earlier that year had, along with Dallas attorney Joe Tonahill, unsuccessfully defended Jack Ruby for murdering Lee Oswald. Belli accepted the Warren Report as a valid, honest document.[24]

Lane would later write that the debates with Belli were the suggestion of an actress associated with the CCI, and were an attempt to publicize the critics' dissenting point of view. But in some respects the public confrontation between Lane and Belli had an air of inevitability, since both men were the highest-profile attorneys outside of the government associated with opposing views on the case.[25]

On July 1, 1964, Belli had written to Earl Warren, warning him that the "rumors, innuendos and gossip" that there was a conspiracy in the

Kennedy assassination were very damaging to American prestige abroad.

> Mr. Mark Lane, though a single, humble voice, has added immeasurably to the calumnies about the events by "proving" the innocence of Oswald and inferring the existence of sinister forces that the American people have not been told about. . . .
>
> I respectfully suggest that it was most unfortunate that you were quoted as saying that some of the facts that might come from the Commission are so sinister that we would not hear them in our lifetime. I respectfully suggest that this gave much basis for the report of "conspiracy," "unseen government," etc. in the foreign press. . . .
>
> The fact that men of the caliber of those selected for the Warren Commission are the ultimate investigators for the people in this country should be comfort to those of us who do know of the greatness of our democracy and the sovereignty of we, the people.
>
> Yours respectfully,
>
> MELVIN M. BELLI [26]

Around the time of this letter, a profile of Belli was appearing in the July-August issue of *Fact* magazine. In it Belli was much less circumspect in discussing Warren's "not in your lifetime" remark. "That was a horse's ass thing for Justice Warren to say," Belli told the *Fact* reporter. He stated flatly that Jack Ruby was mentally unbalanced and that his trial in Dallas was "a mockery and a kangaroo court." More ominous was Belli's allegation that the night before Ruby shot Oswald, a Dallas police officer and his girlfriend talked to Ruby and tried to get him to "approve" the idea that Oswald should be killed. "They picked on Ruby because they knew what a weak-minded guy he was," Belli said. "The cop and his girl just disappeared, and I could never locate them, so I didn't mention them at the trial."[27]

Lane saw the article and immediately fired off a telegram to the Warren Commission, urging that Belli be called before them and questioned about this allegation. Belli never was called. The police officer, however, was. His name was Harry N. Olsen. Although he had quit the force shortly after the assassination and moved to Los Angeles, the Warren Commission located him without much difficulty, and he was questioned by Arlen Specter in his new hometown on August 6, 1964.[28]

Olsen's memory proved very spotty. But it was established that after the assassination he had married Kay Coleman, who in November 1963 was employed at Jack Ruby's Carousel Club. Around midnight on the day of the assassination Olsen and Coleman stopped by a downtown Dallas parking garage, where he knew an attendant. Jack Ruby was also there. They all talked for two to three hours, Olsen said, "about the President's assassination, and we were just talking about how we hated it, that it was a tragedy." Ruby, Olsen testified, had called Oswald a son-of-a-bitch.[29]

Two months before Olsen's testimony, when he had spoken to Earl Warren, Gerald Ford, Joe Tonahill, and others in the Dallas County Jail, Jack Ruby also talked about this late-night meeting, but included a detail that Olsen had left out. According to Ruby, who by then was facing a death sentence for murdering Oswald, Olsen said "they should cut [Oswald] inch by inch into ribbons." Kay Coleman, who was born in London, had added that "if he was in England, they would drag him through the streets and would have hung him." Coleman later denied making this remark and Olsen said he couldn't remember making the statement Ruby attributed to him.[30]

Olsen had quit the Dallas Police Department about a month after the assassination. When Arlen Specter asked him why he quit, Olsen first said it was because he wanted to move to California. Pressed, he conceded that Police Chief Jesse Curry asked him to resign because Olsen used so much sick time.

"Was there any other reason?" Specter asked.

There was a long pause before Olsen replied, "I don't remember exactly what was said."[31]

Years later Joe Tonahill said that like Belli, he believed there was a sinister element to the meeting between Ruby and the Olsens, and the subsequent murder of Lee Oswald. "It wouldn't have been any problem to reach in and get Ruby to do something like this, through the power of suggestion, through innuendo, without Ruby even realizing it," he told journalist Seth Kantor in 1976. "The conversation with Olsen and Kay could have been the beginning of it. It could have been a lot stronger. We don't know who all he talked with."[32]

Mark Lane and Melvin Belli agreed to a series of three debates, and within the Citizens' Committee of Inquiry at least, these were viewed as a breakthrough. The first one took place in San Francisco, Belli's hometown, on October 9, 1964, at the Masonic Memorial Auditorium. It was moderated by Jake Ehrlich, a prominent attorney and Belli's friend of many years standing. According to an FBI informant, at least four thousand people were in attendance, paying $1.50 to $5.00 admission.

As Lane recalled it, Belli insisted that both participants and the moderator wear tuxedos, a condition to which Lane readily agreed.[33]

Belli spoke first. "Let me first welcome you to our great and tolerant city," he said to Lane, "before I start tearing you to pieces." He professed absolute faith in the integrity of Earl Warren, the Commission he had chaired, and the United States government. The Report was a tribute to American democracy: no other country, Belli said, would have allowed an investigation such as the Warren Commission's. Moreover, thanks to America's free press, the public was fully and accurately informed. He criticized Lane for the work he had been doing. "Mark," Belli said, "I say to you that I think you have done a complete disservice to us, and I say this openly, by saying abroad that there was a conspiracy. Because I think it has done more to damage our image in the world today than any other thing that has happened to this generation."[34]

Who was the American public to rely on, Belli asked, if not the authorities legally empowered to investigate the crime? Lee Harvey Oswald was a psychotic who acted alone. "If ever there was a case that was proved beyond a reasonable doubt and to a moral certainty, here you have it by fingerprints, you have it by fibers, you have it by ballistics, you have eleven out of twelve people identifying him after the Tippit shooting, you have this Brennan at the window identifying him, and there is not one word of evidence that shows any conspiracy with anyone – CIA, FBI, Mr. Hunt or Mr. Johnson." These last were references to Texas billionaire H.L. Hunt and to President Lyndon Johnson.

Lane began his portion of the debate by telling the audience that it was the only jury Lee Harvey Oswald would ever have. Neither he nor Bertrand Russell had ever said they believed there was a conspiracy, nor had they speculated about President Johnson, the FBI, the CIA, or any-one else. "And it is unfortunate that the excellent press relations that Mr. Belli spoke of a little while ago have so completely distorted our positions that Mr. Belli believes in all sincerity that we have said things which we, of course, have never said." They had merely said that in a free and open democratic society, it should not be criminal or subversive to say there still existed a presumption of innocence in the United States. All they wanted, Lane continued, was a dialogue on what really did take place when President Kennedy was slain in Dallas.

He decried the secrecy in which the Warren Commission had conducted most of its work. "Since when do we have Top Secret trials in America? . . . Who are we supposed to rely on, Mr. Belli asks? I say the jury system . . . we rely on no Congressional elite."

Gerald Ford's explanation in *Life* magazine, at the time still on the newsstands, that the mis-identification of the alleged murder weapon was caused by a reporter facing a deadline, was "an absolutely false statement," Lane charged. To prove it he held up a copy of Seymour Weitzman's affidavit dated the day after the assassination. Ford had written that Weitzman "thought it might be a Mauser." Yet the affidavit was unambiguous: "This rifle was a 7.65 Mauser bolt action equipped with a 4/13 scope, a thick leather brownish-black sling on it. The rifle was between some boxes. . . ."[35]

The example of the rifle was typical of the Warren Commission's case. "Every single area of this case – every single one – disappears when it is examined," Lane said. Howard Brennan's identification of Oswald as the gunman was not credible. The Commission admitted the gunman had to have been seated or kneeling because the window was only partly open, but Brennan swore he was standing, and even gave police his height. Later that evening Brennan picked Oswald out of a police lineup, Lane quoted the Warren Report, as the man bearing the closest resemblance to the man he had seen in the window. But Brennan said he was unable to make a positive identification. "This was after he'd seen Oswald's picture on television."[36]

Oswald was interrogated on and off for some twelve hours, Lane said, but incredibly there were no tape recordings, notes, or stenographic records of this questioning made by the local or federal authorities involved, according to the Warren Report. "Those who have ever tried a criminal case know that in an important case that does not ever happen. And this is the most important case that any of those agencies have ever handled." Those statements attributed to Oswald, Lane said, were based solely on the memories of the Dallas police.[37]

Lane reminded his listeners of Chief Justice Earl Warren's statement that the American public might never get all of the facts of the assassination. Based on his unofficial investigation, Lane said it was just as true that the Warren Commission, relying on those whose duty it had been to investigate the assassination, never got all the facts during its lifetime.

Ten days later Lane and Belli debated again, this time at the Manhattan Center in New York City. At least three FBI informants were among those in the sold out house. William Kunstler served as moderator.[38]

Kunstler had an interesting connection to the assassination. After his arrest Lee Oswald had requested that John Abt represent him, but Abt was never formally approached by Oswald or anyone acting on his behalf. The ACLU's legal director asked Kunstler if he would take the case. "I agreed to represent Oswald and immediately headed for the airport," Kunstler recalled. "I wanted to get to him fast to let him know someone was willing to defend him and stop the authorities from interrogating him further." But Oswald was shot by Jack Ruby before Kunstler ever reached Dallas; he died without having had any legal representation. Several years later Kunstler was on a team of lawyers handling Ruby's appeal. His original conviction had been overturned in 1966, but Ruby died before his second trial took place.[39]

That night in New York, Kunstler stood with another of Oswald's would-be lawyers on one side of him, and the lawyer for the man who killed Oswald on the other. Mark Lane spoke first; otherwise there were few differences from the first encounter. According to one FBI report on the evening, Lane gave "a brief resume of his usual talk." As in San Francisco, he told the audience they were the only jury Lee Oswald would ever have. Also as before, he said that the American public should not simply have faith in the Warren Report. This time he cited Bertrand Russell, who once defined faith as the firm belief in something for which there was no evidence.[40]

Melvin Belli, for his part, seemed to imply that such faith was a necessity. "I hope it will never come to pass that we cannot believe in the integrity of our law enforcement officials," he said. A reporter for *The Village Voice* wrote that Belli was "like a fading Shakespearean – immortal in the provinces but impossible in the big city." Lane, meanwhile, seemed to have the crowd in the palm of his hand. The *Voice* reporter concluded that "it was not Belli's night."[41]

Neither Belli nor Lane, in New York or San Francisco, brought up the subject of Harry and Kay Olsen's after-hours meeting with Jack Ruby over the weekend of the assassination. Belli did, however, bring up Lane's allegation that there had been a meeting that included Ruby, Bernard Weissman, and J.D. Tippit in Ruby's Carousel Club eight days before the assassination. Belli said his former client did not know Weissman, and knew a different Tippit, not the officer slain on November 22.[42]

Nevertheless, Belli must have been stung by how things went for him that evening. Recalling this second debate, he acknowledged that Lane "was bright and he had an almost encyclopedic knowledge of the facts." He also said that "a disorderly crowd of New York liberals hissed and booed me and applauded Lane. *The Village Voice* reported that 'a middle-aged Lochinvar came out of the West and walked into an ambush.' I guess I did." When it was all over, Belli announced he was cancelling the third engagement, adding that he regretted ever getting involved in them in the first place.[43]

Chapter 15

The Oswald Affair

Over his long life, Carl Marzani had a varied career that was touched directly or indirectly by some of the major events of his time. He was born in Italy in 1913 and as a boy witnessed the rise of fascism in his native country. His father fled Italy after Mussolini instituted a loyalty oath, winding up in the United States in 1923. Young Carl arrived with the rest of his family a year later. He grew up in a coal-mining district in Pennsylvania, graduated from Williams College and Oxford University, served briefly with the International Brigade during the Spanish Civil War, and was with the Office of Strategic Services during World War II. Like Harold Weisberg, Marzani was transferred to the State Department when the OSS was dissolved after the war. After government service he became an independent filmmaker and produced a controversial pro-union film called *Deadline for Action*.[1]

Marzani is believed to have been the first federal employee persecuted during the Red Scare. From 1949 to 1951 he served time in federal prison following his conviction on fraud charges for having denied, during OSS security-clearance questioning, his past Communist Party membership. Marzani always maintained that OSS leadership considered him an excellent prospect – probably because he was a former American communist fluent in Italian – and by tacit agreement simply did not ask about his political affiliations. They accepted him, he said, based on his prior record with Naval Intelligence and Army Intelligence. In the early 1940s Major General William "Wild Bill" Donovan, head of the OSS, was looking for people skilled in foreign languages who could work effectively with foreign resistance movements, some of which were led by communists. "He went out and got people he knew were Communists to do certain jobs," recalled Harold Weisberg. "And yet, he was as conservative Republican as you could get."[2]

Marzani was certain that his documentary *Deadline for Action*, made in 1946, was the real reason for his incarceration. The film took an unapologetic pro-union stance, and spelled out in plain terms how big business was controlled by a handful of private financial groups – "the bedrock reality of the monopoly structure of the American economy," he said.[3]

At his trial, the principal witness against Marzani was a police spy and agent provocateur. The Supreme Court of the United States twice deadlocked on the case. Yet he was convicted for concealing his Communist Party membership and served nearly all of his three-year sentence in spite of pleas for parole by General Donovan, Albert Einstein, Thomas Mann, and others.[4]

During the trial, I.F. Stone wrote in *The Nation:*

> The nature of the indictment – not for Communist activities but for false statements to government investigators – made possible rulings which fatally handicapped the defense when Marzani came to trial. The prosecution could lug in inflammatory matter to show how Marzani served the Communists, but the defense was limited to character witnesses and Marzani's denials. Marzani's defense never really got into the record.[5]

After his release from prison Marzani joined a small publishing firm that he reorganized into Marzani and Munsell. The firm specialized in books, he said, that upset the status quo. When JFK was shot, Marzani had taken note of some of the discrepancies in news reports out of Dallas. Could Lee Oswald have fired from the sixth floor of the Texas School Book Depository and then made it to the building's second floor, where he was seen some ninety seconds later? That question "kept me running up and down our office building stairs, stopwatch in hand, to the great amusement of my staff," Marzani recalled. "Thoughts and suppositions about the case filled my mind for some long while."[6]

Marzani and Munsell quickly issued several booklets relating to the assassination, including *The Mood of the Nation,* a cross section of newspaper articles and editorials appearing in the nation's press, and *Critical Reactions to the Warren Report,* a collection of previously published articles examining the case. Included in this anthology were George and Pat Nash's "The Other Witnesses" and Mark Lane's "The Doubts Remain." Several items in support of the Government's position were also in the collection, like "Case for the Prosecution," by Murray Kempton, reprinted from *The New Republic,* and "A Measure of the Achievement," by Herbert L. Packer, reprinted from *The Nation.*

But the most important assassination title in the Marzani and Munsell catalog was probably *Oswald: Assassin or Fall Guy?* by Joachim Joesten. This was one of three books on the subject to appear in 1964, the others being *Who Killed Kennedy?* by Thomas G. Buchanan and *Red Roses from Texas* by Nerin E. Gun, both of them first published in Great Britain. The Joesten and Buchanan books were published before the Warren Commission had even issued its Report. But the Commission, reported *Time* magazine, "would spike each of the overseas theses."[7]

Marzani read Joesten's manuscript and considered it speculative in places, but nevertheless worthwhile. After deciding to publish it, Joesten recalled that Marzani "put his whole heart and soul" into the book, which he published within five weeks of receiving the manuscript.[8]

Joachim Joesten, a freelance writer, had traveled to Dallas a few weeks after the assassination and spent four days there, interviewing witnesses and examining key locations. He came to the conclusion that Lee Harvey Oswald was innocent, though he made an important distinction. "I wish to make it absolutely clear that I believe Oswald innocent only as charged, but that he was involved with the conspirators in some way. This is what 'fall guy' implies."[9]

In March 1964, Joesten was in Hamburg, Germany completing his book when he received a letter from the Warren Commission. General Counsel J. Lee Rankin politely requested both German and English copies of Joesten's book manuscript. On the same day he got Rankin's letter, Joesten also received a letter from the United States Embassy in Bonn. It wanted to discuss "an important official matter." Joesten telephoned the embassy and was told that if he was agreeable, they would dispatch one of their men by plane to meet with him the next day. Joesten said he was agreeable.[10]

All copies of Joesten's book manuscript were with either publishers or literary agents, so he was unable to comply with Rankin's request. But he did sit down with the embassy man, whom he identified only as Mr. Morris, and whom he took to be "every inch the career diplomat as well as [a] trained lawyer." They met at the American Consulate in Hamburg on March 21, 1964. A report on that meeting was forwarded to the Warren Commission, labeled Commission Exhibit No. 2709, and eventually published in volume twenty-six of the Commission's Hearings and Exhibits.[11]

The two men talked for about four hours, during which time Joesten told Morris everything he had learned – why he believed Oswald was innocent of killing President Kennedy and Officer Tippit, and who he thought was really responsible. Morris, Joesten believed, was impressed by what he showed him, although he seemed "particularly concerned with the fact that I believed Oswald had been connected with both the Central Intelligence Agency and with the Federal Bureau of Investigation."[12]

Later Joesten learned that a few weeks before his meeting with Morris, FBI agents had gone to his home in New York and interviewed his wife. They told her the Warren Commission was trying to locate her husband. "Since I had been located," Joesten said, "I couldn't help wondering if the FBI had simply used that excuse to enter my home, talk to my wife and, to put it plainly, snoop around." The FBI report on this visit also found its way into the twenty-six volumes, as Exhibit 2708. In this unflattering report Joachim Joesten is portrayed as mentally unstable. The FBI authors wrote that Mrs. Joesten said her husband had returned from Dallas convinced Oswald was innocent. "He kept rambling on all day about this fact," the agents wrote, "and also kept it up through the evening. . . . Mrs. Joesten advised that she definitely feels that her husband is on the verge of a nervous breakdown."[13]

Joesten, on that March day in Hamburg, told Morris that it appeared to him that "the assassination of the President was a military-type operation with firing from both front and rear." He alleged that former General Edwin Walker organized the assassination itself, and that Bernard Weissman was somehow involved. Weissman was the young man active in conservative politics who had placed the black-bordered "Welcome Mr. Kennedy" ad in *The Dallas Morning News* of November 22. In the early 1960s Weissman had served in the Army in Germany, and Joesten thought it probable that he knew General Walker. On June 23, 1964 – a few months after Joesten's interview with Morris – Weissman appeared before the Warren Commission. He was not asked whether he knew the general, but he was asked if Walker was the commander of American troops in Germany when Weissman was stationed there. Weissman said no, by that time Walker had been relieved of his command.[14]

Joachim Joesten was born in Cologne, Germany in 1907. As a young man he studied at universities in Germany, France, and Spain and became a journalist. A member of the Communist Party of Germany, he fled his native land after Hitler came to power. There followed periods in Denmark and Sweden, where he married in 1940. He and his wife reached New York in 1941, where he began working for *Newsweek* magazine. By 1944, still in New York, he was a full-time freelance writer.[15]

The Warren Commission obtained certain detailed background information on Joesten. Mark Lane made this public in 1967, when he told an audience that federal authorities had gathered data on most of the critics. "One of the files in the National Archives," he said, "is a document submitted to the Warren Commission by the CIA, listed as a 'basic source material' relied upon by the Warren Commission. What is it? A Gestapo file. The Gestapo prepared a file on Mr. Joesten back in 1937. Can you imagine the Chief Justice poring over the Gestapo file [concerning] the political reliability of one of the Commission's critics?"[16]

Whether Warren personally reviewed the document is not known. But in the fall of 1964 a set of the Gestapo papers was sent to J. Lee Rankin from then-CIA Deputy Director for Plans Richard Helms. "The documents concern Joachim Joesten, author of *Oswald: Assassin or Fall Guy?*, Marzani & Munsell Publishers, Inc., 1964," Helms wrote in a cover letter. The documents were captured, he continued, at the end of World War II, and held in England by the State Department and British authorities. Later they were microfilmed and returned to the West German government.[17]

One of these Gestapo documents, translated by the CIA, was a memorandum dated November 8, 1937, which spelled out reasons why Joesten's German citizenship should be revoked. Joesten, the memo said, arrived in Berlin in 1928 and established a lending library of books "primarily of Marxist tendency ... he joined the KPD (Communist Party of Germany) in 12 May 1932. ..." While living in Copenhagen in 1937, the Gestapo document continued, Joesten published an article in a French newspaper warning of Germany's military threat to Denmark. "Joachim Joesten, a notorious Marxist well-poisoner," the memo concluded, "has seriously transgressed against his duty to remain faithful to his (the German) people and state by his anti-German conduct in foreign countries."[18]

Oswald: Assassin or Fall Guy? was published in the summer of 1964, and bears the distinction of being the first critical book on the assassination to appear in the United States. Other books relating to the case also appeared in the U.S. that year. One was *The Wounded Land* by another German, Hans Habe, which was more a study of the social and political climate in which the assassination occurred. Another was *Kennedy Without Tears*, by Tom Wicker of *The New York Times*, an affectionate memoir of the late president. *Kennedy Without Tears,* which appeared first in the June 1964 issue of *Esquire*, was Wicker's attempt to present JFK "as he really was," deflating the romanticized image which had, inevitably, grown since his death. The book was a favorite of Shirley Martin's. "I'm grateful to Wicker for getting it down so right," she told Vince Salandria. "This nonsense-worship, this god-pattern, is ridiculous. Kennedy was all-human."[19]

Also appearing were a spate of titles recreating the assassination weekend through press photographs and minute-by-minute accounts of events as they developed. United Press International put out *Four Days*, the Associated Press published *The Torch Is Passed*, and Random House offered *There Was a President*. A Los Angeles outfit called Special Publications put out a book called *Four Dark Days in History*, which was occasionally confused with the UPI book. Each of these titles, in one way or another, contributed to the cause of the critics.

Reviewing *Oswald: Assassin or Fall Guy?* in *New Times*, Victor Perlo noted that Joesten's book had been rejected by several publishers before Marzani and Munsell accepted it. "This firm deserves credit for publishing and promoting the book, so that thousands of copies were sold in a short time, despite a blackout by commercial reviewers," he wrote. "Publisher-editor Carl Marzani edited the manuscript brilliantly."[20]

The evidence presented in the book, Perlo said, was skillfully assembled and presented, and had the unexpected effect of changing his mind. "This reviewer approached the Joesten book with skepticism. Despite my low opinion of the Dallas police and the FBI, I've had enough experience to know that utterly senseless things do happen in America. . . . But the Joesten book erased most of my skepticism. . . ."[21]

Wholly unmoved by the Joesten book, however, was Hugh Aynesworth, a veteran reporter for *The Dallas Morning News* who had covered the assassination from the beginning. Aynesworth wrote a harsh and derisive review that appeared in the trade magazine *Editor and Publisher*. "This account of the 'real' happenings of last November would be highly amusing if it were not for the tragic realm into which this 'free lance' author delves," he began.

> If you would listen to this one, he would have you thinking that Lee Harvey Oswald was a polite little misunderstood youth who just got mixed up in the wrong company. . . .
> Oh how terrible, says Joesten (an ex-German who became a U.S. citizen in 1948 and must wonder why), poor little Lee Harvey was the victim of a ruthless plot headed by Dallas police leaders, Dist. Atty. Henry Wade and his staff and a few "bad guys" from the FBI.

Joesten further states that Oswald was an agent of both the FBI and the CIA (how's that for a 24-year-old who couldn't spell "wrist"?).

It's the same old tripe with some new flavoring. . . .

The tip-off is the foreword, wherein Joesten dedicates his book to "Mark Lane . . . the brilliant and courageous New York attorney. . . ."

Lane is the troublemaker who spent two days in Dallas in January on his "investigation" and now pretends to be an expert on all aspects of the weird tragedy.[22]

Joesten's was the first critical book on the assassination published in the United States. After publication of the Warren Report, Marzani and Munsell put out a follow-up analysis that was included in a second edition of *Oswald: Assassin or Fall Guy?* It was attributed to Joesten, but Carl Marzani wrote at least some of it. The analysis appeared first as a pamphlet entitled *The Gaps in the Warren Report*.[23]

But the first book anywhere was *Who Killed Kennedy?* by Thomas G. Buchanan, a former *Washington Star* reporter then living in Paris. His work began as a series of articles published in *l'Express* in early 1964. This got the attention of the Warren Commission. Richard Helms sent CIA Director John McCone a memo stating in part:

> 1.   A competent American observer learned, in Paris on 10 April 1964, that Secker and Warburg Ltd., in London, will publish as a book the Thomas Gittings Buchanan articles which have appeared in Paris in l'Express. The publishing firm is also approaching publishers in the United States and the firm is rushing its edition, hoping to have it on sale by 15 May 1964.
>
> 2.   Buchanan's thesis is that the assassination of President Kennedy was the product of a rightist plot in the United States. He alleges in his articles that the slain Dallas policeman Tippett [sic] was part of the plot against President Kennedy. . . .[24]

Who Killed Kennedy? was indeed published first in England in the spring of 1964, and in the United States later that year. The mainstream media made much of the fact that Buchanan had been fired from the *Washington Star* in 1948 for membership in the Communist Party. But in a review of the book published in *The Minority of One*, Cedric Belfrage said it was irrelevant whether Buchanan was a former communist or a former Zen Buddhist; what was important was his "common sense of the assassination and the American crisis it symbolizes."[25]

The immediate reaction of most of the world, Buchanan asserted, was "to assume a link between the Kennedy assassination and the recent violence by Southerners against the Negro." This violence included the assassination of Medgar Evers and the bombing of the Sixteenth Street Baptist Church in Birmingham, Alabama, in which four young girls were killed. It also included the slaying of William Moore, a white mail carrier shot down during a quixotic march to Jackson, Mississippi, in April 1963.[26]

Oswald was probably not a genuine communist, Buchanan wrote; surely a government agency like the FBI or CIA had an interest in him. How else, for example, could a former defector to the Soviet Union have applied for a passport to return there and not only received it, but received it within twenty four hours? If nothing else, under terms of the McCarran Act, a real communist would first have been thoroughly investigated.[27]

The true perpetrators of the assassination, Buchanan concluded, were Texas oil millionaires motivated by President Kennedy's decision to eliminate an oil-depletion allowance that would have cost them millions of dollars.[28]

Who Killed Kennedy? was weakened in places by Buchanan's speculations. But it was quite effective in a section that reviewed the three previous presidential assassinations in American history: those of Abraham Lincoln, James Garfield, and William McKinley. The assassins John Wilkes Booth, Charles A. Guitteau, and Leon Czolgosz were uniformly portrayed in the media as loners and psychopaths. Buchanan reminded his readers that Lincoln's assassination was a conspiracy for which four people were hanged and others imprisoned, and that Garfield's assassination too had elements of a plot. And he showed that none of these assassins were insane by the usual definition of the term. The same was probably true of Lee Harvey Oswald. "If Lee Harvey Oswald were alive today," Buchanan wrote, "the same people who are now insisting he was crazy would have been the first . . . to demand that he be punished as a sane man for premeditated murder." Moreover none of the earlier assassins denied their deed – rather they were proud of it. Lee Oswald, on the other hand, insisted that he had not killed anyone.[29]

The American media indulged in a good deal of self-congratulatory hyperbole in the aftermath of the Kennedy assassination. In considering only the weekend of the actual killings, much of it was well-deserved.

This is particularly true of television news. It has become a truism that, given the complexity of its unprecedented live television coverage, the medium came of age between November 22, when JFK was shot, and November 25, when he was buried. But one reviewer noted a paradox. Television's finest hours came when its principal content – entertainment and advertising – were temporarily suspended. "Of necessity there must be mixed feelings when one's great moments are made possible only by repudiation of one's everyday values."[30]

In getting beyond the assassination weekend, the nation's press and television as a group relinquished its role as watchdog and quickly convicted Lee Harvey Oswald as the sole assassin. Small publications like *The Minority of One* and *The National Guardian* published important critical articles in late 1963, and a few national journals, such as *The Nation* and *The New Republic*, also published early articles. But as a rule, the media reported what the government told it with very few questions asked.

There was hardly anyone in the country with access to the media who did not weigh in with a comment on the assassination. Martin Dies, former chairman of the Special Committee on Un-American Activities in the 1930s – when it was known as the Dies Committee – wrote a long article entitled "Assassination and its Aftermath" that appeared in the March and April issues of the conservative *American Opinion*, the magazine of the John Birch Society. Dies made much of Lee Oswald's alleged communism and hinted at a Russian conspiracy. "I hope to discuss the circumstances linking the Soviet Union with Oswald's murder of the President. Naturally such evidence must be circumstantial and based upon the dogmatic pattern of Communist behavior. The Communists are too clever to leave any trace of connection with Oswald. . . ."[31]

A month earlier the same magazine offered, also in two parts, the views of the arch-conservative and palindromic Revilo P. Oliver, a professor of classics at the University of Illinois, Urbana. Professor Oliver, incorporating a pun in his title "Marxmanship in Dallas," stated more bluntly than did Martin Dies that Kennedy was killed by a communist conspiracy. "We all know what happened in Dallas on the twenty-second of November," he began. "It is imperative that we understand it. Lee Harvey Oswald was a young punk who defected to the Soviet, taking with him the operational codes of the Marine Corps and such other secrets as a fledgling traitor had been able to steal while in military service. . . ."

Oliver further stated:

> The assassination of Kennedy, quite apart from the considera-
> tion of the office that he held, was an act of violence both deplorable
> and ominous—as ominous as the violence excited by the infamous
> Martin Luther King and other criminals engaged in inciting race
> war with the approval and even, it is said, the active co-operation of
> the White House. It was as deplorable and ominous as the violence
> of the uniformed goons (protected by reluctant and ashamed sol-
> diers) whom Kennedy, in open violation of the American
> Constitution, sent into Oxford, Mississippi, to kick into submission
> American citizens, whom the late Mr. Kennedy had come to regard
> as his subjects. . . .
>
> I have mentioned but a few of the hundred reasons why we
> shall never forget John F. Kennedy. So long as there are Americans,
> his memory will be cherished with distaste.[32]

Professor Oliver called the Warren Commission "an illegal and
unconstitutional 'special commission' . . . improvised with the obvious
hope that it could be turned into a Soviet-style Kangaroo court."[33]

The Warren Commission was sufficiently intrigued to summon
Professor Oliver to appear before it, which he did on September 9, 1964.
When asked for the source of his allegation on the purpose of the
Commission, Professor Oliver declined to answer. His attorney said tartly:
"Let me say for the record that despite the hurt feelings of the members
of the Commission, I don't believe they have a proper right to inquire into
attacks that were made upon them. I can't see any relevancy at all to that."

Commission attorney Albert Jenner replied: "I do wish to say for the
record that the Commission, no member of the Commission, has any
hurt feelings whatsoever with respect to this article."[34]

In January 1964, at the same time Harold Feldman's "Oswald and
the FBI" appeared in *The Nation*, *Commentary* magazine ran a lead
editorial by its editor Norman Podhoretz noting that the Warren
Commission had just held its first meeting – the editorial was written in
early December – and that it was relying heavily on a report prepared by
the FBI. Would the Commission launch its own investigation? Would
there be public hearings? An evaluation of the performance of the Secret
Service, the Dallas Police, and indeed the FBI? Most importantly, the
editorial asked:

Is the possibility of a treasonous political conspiracy to be ruled out? Not the least fantastic aspect of this whole fantastic nightmare is the ease with which respectable opinion in America has arrived at the conclusion that such a possibility is absurd; in most other countries, what is regarded as absurd is the idea that the assassination could have been anything but a political murder.[35]

The way to confront this awesome question, Podhoretz said, was not to simply review what the FBI had to say about the case, but to conduct a scrupulous and painstaking independent investigation "with microscopic thoroughness and according to the highest standards of judicial impartiality."[36]

In late winter, *Commentary* ran a piece entitled "The Oswald Affair," by Léo Sauvage. Sauvage was the New York correspondent for *Le Figaro*, the leading Paris newspaper, who because of the *Commentary* article would soon speak to Joe Lobenthal's Warren Report class at the New School. He had not been with the press corps traveling with Kennedy to Dallas, but was immediately assigned the story; he filed many reports on the assassination. His first work on the assassination published in the United States appeared in the January 2, 1964, issue of *The Reporter*. His *Commentary* article summarized what he had learned to that point, written with the perspective of several months. "My father just became riveted by the story, and he just kept covering it, massively," Pierre Sauvage recalled long afterward. Léo Sauvage, he said, "had an obsessive compulsion toward truth."[37]

In January, his *Reporter* article had been skeptical of the official story. By the time of the *Commentary* piece Sauvage was certain that Lee Harvey Oswald was innocent. He wrote that "to the unbiased, critical mind, the case against him is a tissue of improbabilities, contradictions, and outright falsifications." But he wondered: Was his certainty of Oswald's innocence a hasty judgment? And he picked up the theme introduced by Norman Podhoretz in his January editorial: Might not the Warren Commission, at the time just beginning its work, turn up new evidence? Sauvage did not see how, for the Warren Commission was relying almost exclusively on the investigation conducted by the FBI. As early as December 3, 1963, citing unidentified sources, the major media reported the Bureau would "probably" determine that Oswald had acted alone. Yet the source for this story, Sauvage wrote, was the FBI itself. After its report was delivered to the Commission on December 9, and its lone-gunman conclusion universally publicized, how could the Commission decide otherwise?[38]

After the FBI report, opposing views had very little voice, and this, finally, is what prompted *Le Figaro's* New York correspondent, the man with the obsessive compulsion for truth, to concentrate for the next several years on the Kennedy assassination. "Before publication of the Warren Report," Sauvage later wrote, "there was the irresistible reaction against the audacity of those who loudly proclaimed the dead man's guilt but asked those who had doubts to keep silent. After the Report, there was something even more irresistible: the feeling that, in this case, silence would give consent to injustice."[39]

Léo Sauvage was born in Mannheim, Germany in 1913, but raised in Lorraine in eastern France. He was a gifted student who at age fifteen took the rigorous exams required of French students aspiring to secondary studies. This was a year before the usual age and required special permission. After successfully completing these exams, he attended the Sorbonne and Paris Law School, receiving degrees from both institutions.[40]

In the 1930s he worked as a freelance journalist in Paris. But with the fall of France to the Nazis in 1942 Sauvage, like all Jews, was in ever-greater danger. In spite of this he contributed material to several Resistance newspapers, and even founded a theater company that produced a play that had been banned by the collaborationist Vichy authorities. But his most urgent need was to support and protect his pregnant wife. As a Polish Jew Barbara Sauvage was especially vulnerable to deportation to the death camps. And so in 1943 the young couple fled Paris for the port city of Marseilles hoping to get out of France. Exit visas were nearly impossible to obtain, but attempting to leave France without one was perilous. Thus for countless refugees the situation seemed all but hopeless. Clandestine efforts to save French Jews were underway, and Sauvage petitioned an American organization called the Emergency Rescue Committee for help. A relief worker associated with the committee was among the relative few attempting to alert the world to the evil that was the Nazi regime:[41]

> There are some things so horrible that decent men and women find them impossible to believe, so monstrous that the civilized world recoils incredulous before them. The recent reports of the systematic extermination of the Jews in Nazi Europe are of this order.[42]

But the committee's principal objective was rescuing France's leading Jewish intellectuals and artists; it was unable to help Sauvage. With the Nazi threat closing in, Sauvage needed a miracle, and he got one: he learned of a village in the mountains of south-central France called Le Chambon, a singular community of French Huguenots quietly defying state orders to turn over Jews to the authorities. Sauvage and his wife went into hiding in Le Chambon in the fall of 1943 and stayed for nearly a year. During the entire period this village operated as a refuge, not a single Jew was ever turned away or betrayed. The Sauvages' first child was born there in 1944.[43]

After the liberation of France and the end of World War II, Léo Sauvage worked at several newspapers, eventually making his way back to Paris. From this base he published a weekly newspaper for several years called *La Rue,* a cultural paper that during its brief existence featured the work of France's most prominent intellectuals, including Albert Camus, Jean-Paul Sartre, and the poet Jacques Prévert.[44]

But postwar Europe faced a long period of rebuilding, and the ambitious journalist with a young family was looking for new opportunities. In 1948 Sauvage brought his family to the United States and for a time worked for Agence France-Presse, the French news agency. In 1950 he was hired by *Le Figaro*, where he would remain for the next quarter century. As the paper's New York correspondent he covered the United Nations and other political areas. But he also had great latitude to write about what interested him; consequently he gave a lot of attention to New York theater and to Latin America. In 1959 he became the first European correspondent to cover the fall of the Batista dictatorship. Later he wrote a highly acclaimed analysis of the Cuban revolution called *Che Guevara: Failure of a Revolutionary.*[45]

In his March 1964 *Commentary* article, Léo Sauvage raised a series of questions that, he declared, Oswald's accusers should be forced to answer. Did Oswald have an alibi? Was the President's throat wound one of entrance or of exit? Was Oswald a good enough rifleman to do what the authorities said he did? How many shots were fired? Why were no fingerprints found on the alleged assassination rifle? How come none of the theatre patrons who witnessed Oswald's arrest came forward with impartial accounts of how he was taken into custody?

Sauvage also noted that it was the amateur investigators, not official police agencies, who had exposed the weaknesses in the case against

Oswald. "In the face of so systematically prejudiced an investigation as has so far been made into the President's assassination," he wrote, "how else will the truth ever be arrived at if 'amateurs' fail to ask the questions that the professionals have obfuscated or left unanswered?"[46]

While he was in Dallas, Sauvage had interviewed Roy Truly, the manager of the School Book Depository. Truly was one of two witnesses who came closest to providing Oswald with an alibi: perhaps ninety seconds after the assassination he and a Dallas motorcycle cop, having run into the building together, had seen Oswald in the Book Depository's second-floor lunchroom. Sauvage wrote: "When I asked him whether it had taken a long time for him and the motorcycle policeman to reach the lunchroom, he answered (apparently not realizing what I was driving at): 'Oh, no! It was as soon as the last shot was fired when I saw the officer come running . . . I couldn't tell you exactly how much time it took, all this, but it wasn't long.'"[47]

Could Oswald have made it from the sixth floor to the lunchroom in that short timespan? When Truly and the officer saw Oswald he was not breathing heavily, in spite of his alleged sprint down the stairs; moreover he had taken time to buy a vending machine soft drink, which he was sipping when confronted by Truly and the officer. Did the FBI establish how much time it would take to run from the sixth to the second floor? And just as important, how much time elapsed between the final shot at the motorcade and the time Truly and the officer saw Oswald in the lunchroom? The press was barred from the building during official reenactments, but "none of the many reporters and photographers who for days kept a close watch on the Texas School Book Depository, writing and taking pictures of the various re-enactments of the assassination staged on Elm Street, ever saw a motorcycle policeman running into the building under the eyes of detectives with stopwatches in their hands."[48]

> I believe that the most important consequence of Oswald's death was not to close his mouth but to close his trial. For if Lee Harvey Oswald had ever had his day in court, with a good defense lawyer answering District Attorney Wade, cross-examining the Dallas police officers, and raking their witnesses over the coals, what might not have emerged?[49]

On March 11, 1964, even as his article appeared in *Commentary*, Léo Sauvage signed a contract with Random House to develop his ideas on the assassination into a full-length book. He would use the same title:

The Oswald Affair. The facts of the case, as presented by the Warren Commission, would receive a dispassionate analysis by a prominent journalist whose impartiality would not be compromised by any sense of patriotism. As the September release of the Warren Report drew near, Sauvage recalled, "I had not only finished writing the story of the Dallas investigation, but also had described the FBI leaks and the disturbing circumstances under which the Warren Commission had started its work: more leaks; more reckless statements, including some by the Chairman of the Commission . . . in short, I had already expressed a number of misgivings about the Warren Commission, and after reading its Report, I found that things were even worse than I had imagined."[50]

A book critical of the government's conclusions, written by an eminent journalist dedicated to the truth and published by one of the country's most prominent houses – was this not America's treasured freedom of the press functioning at its very best?

Ray Marcus was a charter subscriber to *I.F. Stone's Weekly*, which first appeared in January of 1953. In its inaugural issue I.F. Stone wrote that the *Weekly* was "an attempt to keep alive through a difficult period the kind of independent radical journalism" represented by such by then-defunct papers as *PM, The New York Star,* and *The New York Daily Compass,* each of which had once employed him. The "difficult period" was, of course, the anti-communist hysteria of the early 1950s. Stone modeled his new *Weekly* on *In Fact*, the newsletter published by George Seldes, which had folded a few years earlier. Ray Marcus, who had also been an *In Fact* subscriber, said he considered Stone's new paper a worthy successor.[51]

I.F. Stone's Weekly was virtually a one-man operation, with its journalist-founder serving as publisher, editor, reporter, proofreader, and layout man. His wife Esther served as his secretary and managed the paper's business operations. The *Weekly* was launched with some five thousand charter subscribers but in time reached 70,000. Stone promised his readers "politically uninhibited commentary and let-the-chips-fall-where-they-may reporting." Overall, he lived up to that pledge. "I had fought the loyalty purge, the FBI, the House Un-American Activities Committee, and McCarran as well as McCarthy," Stone once said. "There was nothing to the left of me but *The Daily Worker*."[52]

In the fall of 1964 Ray Marcus was eagerly awaiting Stone's analysis of the Warren Commission. "With his long demonstrated ability to demolish official falsehoods, I had little reason to doubt he would make mincemeat of the just-released Warren Report," he remembered. While Stone had initially cautioned against jumping to conclusions about the Kennedy murder, his first issue after the assassination had adopted some lone-nut rhetoric: "It is always dangerous to draw rational inferences from the behavior of a psychopath like Oswald." Nevertheless it was with great shock that Marcus read the *Weekly* of October 5, 1964. "It was a paean of praise for the Warren Commission and its conclusions."[53]

Stone had written:

> All my adult life as a newspaperman I have been fighting, in defense of the Left and of a sane politics, against conspiracy theories of history, character assassination, guilt by association and demonology. Now I see elements of the Left using these same tactics in the controversy over the Kennedy assassination and the Warren Commission Report. I believe the Commission has done a first-rate job, on a level that does our country proud and is worthy of so tragic an event. I regard the case against Lee Harvey Oswald as the lone killer of the President as conclusive. By the nature of the case, absolute certainty will never be attained, and those still convinced of Oswald's innocence have a right to pursue the search for evidence which might exculpate him. But I want to suggest that this search be carried on in a sober manner and with full awareness of what is involved.[54]

At the time of this issue of the *Weekly*, the Warren Report had just been published and the twenty-six volumes of supporting evidence and testimony were still not available. Surely, Marcus thought, Stone could not by this time have given the Report a careful reading. Yet the main body of his article attacked those who attacked the official story. "I want to start with my dear and revered friend, Bertrand Russell," Stone wrote. Lord Russell's criticisms of the Warren Report were irresponsible. He criticized Russell's association with Mark Lane and was particularly irritated with the comparison of Lane to Emile Zola, the French novelist who had written in defense of Alfred Dreyfus, a French Army Captain wrongly convicted of espionage in 1896. Stone implied that Russell didn't even read the Report, but Russell's then-executive secretary later said the Who Killed Kennedy? committee had an advance copy of the Warren Report a week before its official release date.[55]

Stone saved some of his harshest criticisms for *Oswald: Assassin or Fall Guy?* and *Who Killed Kennedy?*

The Joesten book is rubbish, and Carl Marzani – whom I defended against loose charges in the worst days of the witch hunt – ought to have had more sense of public responsibility than to publish it. Thomas G. Buchanan, another victim of witch hunt days, has gone in for similar rubbish in his book, *Who Killed Kennedy?* You couldn't convict a chicken thief on the flimsy slap-together of surmise, half-fact and whole untruth in either book.[56]

Would the Warren Commission and the FBI, CIA, and Secret Service really conspire to keep a plot against Kennedy secret? "People who believe such things," Stone wrote, "belong in the booby-hatch."[57]

Marcus was appalled by what he read. "What was totally lacking in I.F. Stone's comments was any evidence of the kind of critical analysis he normally employed in assessing official statements," he wrote long afterward. And so on October 8, 1964, he sat down at his typewriter and wrote Stone a long letter outlining the flaws in his Warren Report issue.[58]

"I read, first with disbelief, then with growing shock and anger, your diatribe against freedom of thought and expression . . . on what meat does this our I.F. feed that he has apparently been stricken so blind and arrogant . . . ?"

Marcus said that in order to accept the Warren Commission's lone-gunman scenario, one must accept fifteen points as true, including:

1. Oswald was not an agent; but while in the Marine Corps, he received letters from the Cuban Embassy, made himself obnoxious by attempting to preach Marxism to his barracks buddies; kept a copy of *Das Kapital* in his barracks; and regularly received a (White) Russian-language newspaper to help with his study of Russian – all this without attracting the attention of his superiors.

2. Oswald was not an agent; but the U.S. Govt., after helping him financially and in other ways to return to the U.S., did not even consider prosecuting him for spilling radar secrets to the Russians, the suspicion of which had caused us to change our codes; or for seditious statements he made in Russia.

3. Oswald was not an agent; but despite a background as a notorious defector and pro-Castro agitator, he received within 24 hours a passport to travel to many foreign countries, Communist included.

4. Oswald was not an agent; but despite a fat FBI file on him, and a number of known FBI contacts, and all the above points, he was able to get and keep a job at the Texas School Book Depository Building – with the knowledge of the FBI.

5. Oswald was not an agent, but despite all the above, he was not considered a risk and was not kept under surveillance during President Kennedy's trip; due to the fact that the FBI failed to inform the Secret Service and the Dallas Police; due to the fact that it took an "overly restrictive" view of its responsibility. (Many a liberal and progressive can testify as to the "overly restrictive view" the FBI normally takes of its responsibilities.)[59]

His letter to I.F. Stone ran seven and one-half pages. "If you have read this far," Marcus wrote near the end, "I admire your patience and thank you for your attention. Further I would take it as a hopeful sign that this letter may have some positive effect." In spite of his feelings about the October 5 issue, he wished Stone well and hoped the *Weekly* would continue for many years to come.[60]

He put the letter into an envelope and sealed it, affixed a stamp, and put it in his mailbox. He never received a reply.[61]

Chapter 16

Dueling Attorneys

While the former Warren Commission members were averse to publicly discussing their findings, some of the attorneys who had worked for them were not – especially as the Warren Report was increasingly called into question. Mark Lane had an idea why these staff attorneys were more willing than the former commissioners to discuss their work. "Unlike the majority of Commission members, who were engaged in active politics and therefore quite used to having their integrity called into question, some of the lawyers became enraged," he once wrote. "Thus they desired to respond."[1]

One of the first was Joseph Ball, a Long Beach, California, attorney who with fellow Commission attorney David Belin had investigated and written the first draft of the Warren Report's Chapter Four, which built the case against Oswald. Ball agreed to appear with Lane in suburban Los Angeles in December of 1964. The date was arranged jointly by a public affairs organization called Discussions Unlimited and by Ray Marcus, who had been in regular communication with Lane's Citizens' Committee of Inquiry since early in the year. Marcus had arranged other speaking dates for Lane throughout Southern California around this time. "These lectures were very well attended by large and receptive audiences," Marcus recalled. "The highlight of his scheduled appearances was to be [the] debate with Joseph Ball."[2]

But by the time Mark Lane and Joseph Ball were ready to appear on the same public platform, the rules for the event had changed. According to Lane, the original proposal was for the two men to square off in a one-on-one debate. When Ball said no to that, Discussions Unlimited asked what format would best suit him, and Ball replied that he would appear if Lane spoke and he were allowed to question him. "Ball specifically precluded the possibility that I might ask him any questions," Lane recalled. "I agreed." After a little more haggling, Lane said, the agreed-upon format was that Lane would speak and then submit to questioning by Ball and two other lawyers. Each would also have the opportunity to address the audience.[3]

In the days leading up to the debate, several critics and critics' friends met at the home of Maggie Field in Beverly Hills to review the Report and the twenty-six volumes of Hearings and Exhibits, which had just been published. Like Ray Marcus and others, Maggie had been corresponding with Lane. With the Joseph Ball debate being held so near to her, she got some names – probably from Lane's office – and invited several interested parties to her home with the aim of helping Lane prepare for the confrontation. "I didn't know the others at Maggie Fields' – even Maggie herself, until she phoned me," Ray Marcus remembered.[4]

In all, there were about fifteen people at the Field home, including Marcus, a Los Angeles accountant named Lillian Castellano, and Maggie's close friend Ronnie Solomon. They met over several days, dividing into groups and subgroups and pouring over the twenty-six volumes. It can be difficult, so many years later, to appreciate the newness of what they were engaged in. This was the first time most of them were getting a good look at the official published evidence in its unedited entirety – not just media accounts which were sometimes in conflict with one another. It was also one of the first times this evidence was given close scrutiny by skeptical and knowledgeable readers.

"The topics we were looking at included all the early questions," Ray Marcus said. These included medical evidence; Commission Exhibit 399 – the so-called "magic bullet," which was becoming one of Marcus's main interests; the statements of assassination eyewitnesses; the murder of Officer Tippit; and of course the roles of Lee Harvey Oswald and Jack Ruby. With their group approach they were able to cover a lot of ground in a relatively short period of time. Lane was present for some of the meetings, and was briefed on what was being discovered.[5]

Years later, Marcus said he was amazed by how much evidence in the Warren Commission's twenty-six volumes contradicted its conclusions. "That was a surprise," he recalled. "You'd have mixed feelings. You'd say, 'How the hell could they – here's their own evidence, how could they *do* this?' And on the other hand, we'd say, 'Gee, we're sure glad they put that stuff in there.'"[6]

The debate between Lane and Joseph Ball was scheduled for the evening of December 4, 1964, at Beverly Hills High School. Technically it was not a debate; it was, in fact, billed as a cross-examination of Mark Lane by a "panel of prominent attorneys." The panel was comprised of former Warren Commission attorney Ball; Herman Selvin, the former president of the Los Angeles County Bar Association; and A.L. Wirin, an eminent civil liberties attorney.[7]

Earlier that same day Lane had addressed the student body at Pitzer College, about forty miles east of Beverly Hills. Ray Marcus, who had arranged the engagement, had also driven him to it. As they drove, Marcus continued briefing Lane on what had been learned at Maggie Field's home. Lane had been very busy during his trip to Southern California, having also spoken at UCLA and UC-Santa Barbara. Marcus was concerned that by the time of the Beverly Hills event – easily the most important Lane had had anywhere up until then – he would be so fatigued he would fare poorly. He thought Lane might like to have a short nap on the ride back to Beverly Hills, and had even placed a mattress in back of his station wagon for that purpose. But Lane declined, insisting it wasn't necessary; he was alert and ready.[8]

The Beverly Hills High auditorium seated about two thousand people. It was filled early, and another thousand or so people were unable to get in. The atmosphere was charged with expectation. As things finally began, the moderator outlined the format to be followed that night. Lane would be allotted forty-five minutes and speak first, and the other three attorneys would cross-examine him. Was this three-against-one arrangement fair? "I do not think it ought to be considered in that light," the moderator said. "The only thing we are concerned with here is to ascertain as much of the truth as is possible to ascertain in one night. . . ."[9]

A few days before the debate Lane, having been briefed by those who met at Maggie Field's, fanned the flames in a CCI press release: "The Commission Report," he said, "is filled with distortions, statements taken out of context, and is in summation, a fraud." In his opening remarks, after beginning with by-now-familiar rhetoric – the audience, and by extension the American public, was the only jury that Lee Harvey Oswald would ever have – Lane said he had just repeated the fraud charge to a TV reporter. The comment had upset Joseph Ball, but Lane implied it was fully justified: "I had never made that statement prior to the time that the twenty-six volumes upon which it is allegedly based were released and we had an opportunity to read some of the important testimony."[10]

Where had the shots come from? Lane wondered. In their original statements on radio, TV and in newspapers, the surgeons who had attended the wounded president – Drs. Kemp Clark, Malcolm Perry, and Robert N. McClelland – were in agreement that the president's throat wound was one of entrance. Consequently, Lane said, "the first position taken by the FBI and the Dallas police was that the car was there on

Houston Street approaching the Book Depository Building when Oswald fired down." After the car turned onto Elm Street, this first position held, Oswald shifted his rifle and fired the shots that struck Kennedy in the head and wounded Governor Connally.

"There was a problem with that story, in addition to the fact that it was totally untrue," Lane said. "And that is that every single witness to the scene, including Governor Connally, Jacqueline Kennedy, Mrs. Connally and the films, showed that the car was there on Elm Street before the first shot was fired." And this made for a dilemma: How did Oswald shoot the president in the front if he was positioned behind him, as he would have been once the limousine turned onto Elm?

The FBI had performed repeated simulations of the shooting, Lane said, and suggested that the president had turned to wave at the crowd, thus exposing his throat to the building behind him. But widely-published photographs of the assassination showed indisputably that JFK was facing forward when he was shot. Lane himself had brought this to the Warren Commission's attention when he first testified nine months earlier.[11]

Dr. James Humes of the Naval Medical Center in Bethesda, Maryland, who led the autopsy team, told the press that he was forbidden to talk about it. "And so we waited for the Warren Commission Report to be released," Lane said, "and it came out, and there were no preliminary notes from Dr. Humes, the Marine Corps commander who was the expert. But then the twenty-six volumes came out, and we rushed to open up to this most important area to find out what those preliminary notes by Dr. Humes said. And I'll read it to you.[12]

"Volume 17. Commission Exhibit 397. Page 48. On the stationary of the United States Medical School, National Naval Medical Center, Bethesda Maryland, 24th of November 1963. 'Certificate. I, James J. Humes, certify that I have destroyed by burning certain preliminary draft notes' related to the autopsy he performed on President Kennedy."

But surely Dr. Humes had been asked, during his testimony before the Warren Commission on March 16, 1964, why he had burned his notes – "which did not belong to him, but belonged to the people of the United States," Lane said. "Perhaps he would volunteer the information; he did not. Well perhaps one of the attorneys questioning – the inquisitive attorneys questioning for the Warren Commission were going to ask him. And they did not! Never asked him why he burned the notes. And so that remains one of the dark secrets." And the neck wound, described by so many in a position to know as one of entry, became an exit wound in the Warren Report.

As he had during previous lectures, Lane discussed the original identification of the alleged assassination rifle, and Helen Markham, the Commission's sole eyewitness to the Tippit murder – "the only one who actually saw the shots fired and could say, 'I saw Lee Harvey Oswald fire the shots.'" Unlike during the debates with Belli, Lane now had her testimony from the just-released twenty-six volumes. The questioning had been conducted by Joseph Ball. Lane read from the Commission's third volume, with Mrs. Markham's testimony about the police lineup when she identified Oswald.

Oswald had been the number two man in the lineup. According to the Warren Report, Mrs. Markham identified him as Tippit's killer on November 22, and confirmed her identification when she testified before the Commission on March 26, 1964.[13]

Lane's reading gave a distinctly different impression. "Did you identify anybody in these four people?" he read, quoting Joseph Ball.

"I didn't know nobody," Lane read Markham's reply.

"I know you didn't know anybody," Lane quoted Ball, "but did anybody in that lineup look like anybody you had seen before?"

"No. I had never seen none of them, none of these men."

"Not one of the four?"

"Not one of them."

"Not one of all four?" The Beverly Hills audience began to laugh.

"No, sir."

Lane prefaced the next line in his own voice. "And now, ladies and gentlemen, the magic question. 'Was there a number two man in there?'

"Mrs. Markham: 'Number two is the man I picked.'"

"And shortly thereafter, Mr. Ball asked Mrs. Markham if she'd recognize him from his appearance, and she said, 'I asked – I looked at him. When I saw this man I wasn't sure, but I had cold chills run all over me.'"

"A rather mystic identification, I would suggest," Lane observed, and the Beverly Hills audience laughed some more.

"What's the Warren Commission's conclusion?" Lane continued. "The Warren Commission concludes that Mrs. Markham, in terms of the probative value of her testimony identifying Lee Harvey Oswald, is – quote – 'a reliable witness.'"

Lane went on to discuss the other questions: Oswald's marksmanship; the inferior weapon he was alleged to have used; tests on that weapon conducted by the FBI; Howard Brennan and his identification of Oswald; and how Oswald, according to the Commission, smuggled the rifle into the Texas School Book Depository on the morning of November 22.

He recounted how he became involved in the assassination work: he had written an article stating that due to pretrial publicity, Oswald, if he had lived, could not possibly have had a fair trial anywhere in the United States. But as he massed his evidence and mastered the available data, Lane said, it became clear to him that there were numerous unanswered questions; his article said that as well. Shirley Martin saw the article and sent it to Marguerite Oswald, and Marguerite contacted him – and he was drawn further into the case.

As he continued, his voice began to swell to the fortissimo described by *The New York Times* three years before. "Had I known at the outset, when I wrote that article, that I was going to be so involved that I would close my law practice, abandon my work, abandon my political career, be attacked by the very newspapers in New York City which used to hail my election to the state legislature; had I known that – had I known that I was going to be placed in the lookout books, so that when I come back into the country, I'm stopped by the immigration authorities – only in America, but no other country in the world – that my phones would be tapped, that not only would the FBI follow me around at lecture engagements, but present to the Warren Commission extracts of what I said at various lectures – I am not sure, if I knew all that, that I ever would have written that article in the first place.

"But I assure you of this: having come this far, and now knowing what is at stake – when the establishment seeks to suppress the facts, and knowing what is at stake in this country in reference to this case, no matter what the difficulties, and no matter what the obstacles, and no matter what the liberal establishment says, or any other establishment says, we are going to remain with this matter until such time as the American people secure that to which we are all entitled in a free, open, and democratic society. And that is some intelligible answers to the thus far unanswered questions of Dallas on November 22."

Lane was finished: he thanked the audience and returned to his seat to a thunderous round of applause.

The first lawyer to answer Lane was Herman Selvin, a past president of the Los Angeles County Bar Association. He was ill-prepared to discuss the assassination. Ray Marcus recalled that Selvin's remarks "clearly indicated he knew virtually nothing about the actual evidence in the case under discussion."[14]

Selvin accused Lane of taking bits of evidence out of context and disregarding everything else in the record in order to make his case. Lane resorted to an old lawyer's trick, Selvin charged: "When the law is against you, argue the facts. When the facts are against you, argue the law. When the law and the facts are against you, abuse the other attorney. The Warren Commission, in this case, is Mr. Lane's other attorney. He had practically nothing to say, except to accuse the Warren Commission of fraud, of deliberate suppression of evidence. And why?"

He wanted to put a few questions to Lane, Selvin said. "Do you admit that in Dallas, Texas, on the 22nd of November in 1963, John Fitzgerald Kennedy – then President of the United States – was shot and killed?"

"I would like to have a serious debate, Mr. Selvin," Lane replied without hesitation. "I hope we can get to that shortly."

There followed a moment's pause. A few snickers were heard from the audience, and then applause – for Lane. Selvin began to speak again but was virtually drowned out by clapping. Lane raised his voice over the crowd noise: "Because, Mr. Selvin, when you will not argue the facts, and you will not argue the evidence, you will not abuse the other side; you will tell anecdotes. Let's get down to the facts."

Most of Selvin's allotted time continued in much this vein. But as he neared the end he made the point that physical evidence was far more reliable than was eyewitness testimony. And the physical evidence, he said – in this case the autopsy performed in Bethesda, Maryland – showed that the wound on the back of President Kennedy's neck was consistent with an entrance wound. The wound in back of the President's head was also consistent with an entrance wound. "There is no way that the wound as located, examined and described by the autopsy surgeon could have been made by a shot entering from the front."

All of the physical evidence recovered from the Texas School Book Depository, Selvin said in conclusion, pointed to Lee Harvey Oswald alone as the assassin. "In the face of that, who is it – who is it that's indulging in speculation? The Warren Commission that heard, analyzed, and collated the evidence? Or Mr. Lane – who simply says, 'T'ain't so! T'ain't so!'"

Lane was allowed a five-minute rebuttal. So many issues had been raised, he said, and with the three-against-one format, five minutes was not enough. "Because we wanted to have a debate on this question. We had asked if any of the persons who want to support the Commission report would come here tonight and to debate it, and everyone said no, they would not, but they were willing to cross-examine me. And that's the way it was going to be."

As he had with Melvin Belli, Lane invoked the words of Bertrand Russell: "We are only asked to have faith about those matters for which there is no evidence . . . let's discuss the facts and forget about faith. Let's have faith in ourselves, in an open, democratic society, to look at the facts and to reach rational conclusions ourselves."

The autopsy that Selvin was placing faith in could not be relied upon, Lane said. The Warren Commission never did see the X-rays and photographs taken during the procedure. Instead it relied on drawings based not on the actual photos, but of a description of the wounds provided to an artist by Commander James Humes. The ballistics evidence was equally troublesome, Lane continued. Ballistics reports were always open to interpretation, he said, with prosecutors interpreting it in a way best supporting their case, and defense counsel interpreting it so that it supported theirs.

And where was Oswald's defense before the Commission? "There was no defense. I was retained to represent his interests by his mother, and the Commission said 'No, he's not entitled to counsel.'" Later the Commission reconsidered its position and appointed Walter Craig to defend Oswald, Lane said. But Craig had done an abysmal job. "Read the record. See if you can find some place where Mr. Craig was sitting in – see if you can find one question asked by Mr. Craig . . . he did not represent and he did not defend the interests" of Lee Harvey Oswald.

At that point the moderator told Lane he was out of time. Lane quickly added that he was willing to debate Joseph Ball or anyone else associated with the Commission at any time and at any place, under rules that would allow both parties to freely exchange ideas and cross-examine each other. "Wherever I am, I will go to that place. Hopefully it will be here in Beverly Hills one day, and we'll really have a debate." Again, Lane sat down to a supportive round of applause.

The moderator invited former Warren Commission attorney Joseph Ball to begin. Ball, a partner in the firm Ball, Hunt and Hart, started by saying that he was not part of any Establishment. "I'm a country lawyer from Long Beach," he insisted, as derisive groans swelled from the audience. He was asked to go to Washington to be part of the Commission's staff, and he did so. "And let me tell you something. I never received one bit of instruction or order from any member of the Commission, including the Chief Justice. I never received an order from Lee Rankin, the counsel. I was given a certain area to investigate and report on, and I did it the same as I do every other lawsuit that I handled in my practice."15

Ball said he didn't know whether Mark Lane was assaulting his honesty or integrity when he called the Warren Report a fraud. But many of the witnesses Lane had referred to were his responsibility. "It didn't make any difference to me whether I discovered Oswald was the assassin or that someone else was. . . . It would have been fine if I could have discovered something else, because I'd have probably got my name in *Time* magazine!"

He worked independently, he insisted – there was never any assistance from the FBI and he never asked for it or wanted it. He and the group he worked with were as impartial as possible.

"Mr. Lane has picked out two or three people," Ball continued, "like a Mrs. Markham, who is an utter screwball – and he's picked her out and shown the difficulties with her testimony. And I can assure you that there were twelve people who have identified Oswald, in one way or another, in connection with the murder of Tippit."

Lane jumped in. "Is that a question, sir? Because I have a yes or no answer to that – *that's not true.* There were two persons who said they saw the shots fired. Domingo Benavides, who said he could not identify the person, and Mrs. Helen Louise Markham, the only witness produced by the Commission who said she actually saw the shots fired, who said she could identify Oswald – "

"I must ask for more time, if Mr. Lane makes a speech," Ball said blandly. "What he has just said is not true. Now – "

"Give us the name of one witness who saw the shots fired besides Mrs. Markham," Lane demanded.

"What about Scoggins, the taxi driver – "

"He said he did not see the shots fired, sir."

"He saw – he saw – " Ball began, but then seemed to give up. "Well, anyway . . ."

"You know that!" Lane cried. At this point Lane may have felt he was as close to arguing Oswald's case with a Commission lawyer as he would ever get; Ball was losing the exchange.

"Mr. Lane makes a technical distinction," Ball continued. "This man saw Oswald on the sidewalk. He saw him walk to the car, he heard the shots, he saw Oswald flee toward his car, and he identified him. But that doesn't make – there were twelve people that identified him. But let's – "

"Identified him not as shooting – as being a block away, two blocks away, a half a block away – isn't that the twelve people you're talking about?"

"Let me ask some questions," Ball said, trying to regain a measure of control. "Do you – just answer this – do you believe the evidence is sufficient to prove that Oswald bought this Mannlicher carbine from a mail order house in Chicago?"

"Klein's store," Lane continued for Ball, "which advertised it in the February 1963 issue of *The American Rifleman.* Is that the rest of the question?"

"This rifle," Ball said, meaning the alleged assassination weapon.

"Absolutely not!" Lane cried. "This is the February 1963 issue of *The American Rifleman*," he continued, holding the magazine aloft. There was only one advertisement in that issue, from Klein's Sporting Goods, Lane said, and it was for a rifle other than the Mannlicher-Carcano.

The two went back and forth over the order from Klein's, and each man managed to call the other a liar. Finally Ball seemed to have had enough: examining Mark Lane, he declared, would only result "in a cat and dog fight."

"Well that's all right," Lane said. "It's about time we had a dialog in America on this question."

Ball tried to continue, staying with the issue of the Klein's Sporting Goods order allegedly filled out by Lee Oswald. But Lane would have none of it. "Is this just one long summation, sir?" he cut in. "You're here to cross-examine me."

"Mr. Lane, *please*," the moderator broke in. "You had a forty-five minute opening. You've had questions, which you've answered. Mr. Ball has a right to either examine you or make an observation. Now, you will have time – more time than anyone else – "

"There are three of them!" Lane protested.

"You were not interrupted, sir, for any of the forty-five minutes. And we are not here for one side or the other, and both sides have to be heard."

With Lane thus admonished, Ball continued. Oswald went under the name "Hidell," and that was the name he rented the postal box to which the rifle was delivered. The rifle was found on the sixth floor of the Texas School Book Depository, Ball said, and so were the shells from bullets traced to that weapon to the exclusion of all others. A whole bullet and two bullet fragments were found, and also traced to that rifle. Oswald fled the scene and was later arrested with a pistol shown to have been used to kill Officer Tippit. "I came to the conclusion," Ball said at last, "that I had never seen a case that was so conclusively proven by evidence under oath."

As Ball took his seat, someone in the audience shouted out that the evening's program stated "these three well-known attorneys will cross-examine Mr. Lane." Apparently the man felt there had not been enough of that. But the moderator replied, "I will be accountable for any changes to the format . . . this is a dialog between Joe Ball and Mr.

Lane. It has proven to be aborted. We will now turn to Mr. Wirin, and see whether we can – "

Sounding astonished, Lane interrupted. "You're surely not going to say that I'm not permitted to answer the questions that were raised – you're not saying that, sir?" The moderator was not saying that, and Lane was allowed five minutes to respond.

"First of all," he said, "Mr. Ball takes the position that Mrs. Markham is some kind of a nut. He may be right.

"What does the Commission say? Page 168: 'Addressing itself solely to the probative value of Mrs. Markham's contemporaneous description of the gunman, and her positive identification of Oswald at the police lineup – ' remember that? 'How about the number two man' – that was the positive identification they were making reference to – the Commission considers her testimony reliable. Sure they do. She's a nut to Mr. Ball, but she's a reliable nut. She said Oswald did it!"

Addressing the whole bullet Joseph Ball referred to, Lane said: "Now, is that whole bullet the bullet which crashed through the President's head, and shattered into pieces? Is that whole bullet the bullet which went through the Governor, smashed his ribs, and ended up in his thigh? A fragment of it? Or is that whole bullet the bullet which struck the curb, and smashed into smithereens? Or is that an additional bullet? It's a whole bullet. It's an additional bullet, obviously. So four shots were fired – and the Commission concedes that weapon is not capable of firing four shots in the six seconds."

The postal box where Oswald allegedly received the assassination rifle under the name "A. Hidell" was in fact maintained under his own name, Lane said, citing postal inspector Harry Holmes. It was possible that several innocent mistakes were made along the way, Lane said, resulting in a rifle different from the one advertised being delivered to the wrong postal box. "Somewhat unlikely – but certainly it is possible. But these are questions – are we not entitled to the answers?"

Lane concluded with a shot at Joseph Ball. "He's willing to stand on his questioning of Mrs. Markham. Why, after she said 'no, no, no, no, no, I did not see him there,' did he say, 'Was there a number two man there?' He's willing to stand on that questioning. I know he teaches procedure at law school – University of Southern California – I'd like to have a procedural lesson on why those questions are proper."

Finally, it was time for A.L. Wirin to address the crowd. From the audience, Ray Marcus paid close attention: this was the speaker for whom, after Lane, he was most looking forward to. As a leading advocate of civil liberties Wirin was a well-respected figure, even revered, in liberal and progressive circles. The ACLU had not performed well on behalf of Lee Oswald. "It was my hope," Marcus recalled, "and that of a significant part of the audience, that A.L. Wirin by now had taken a careful look at the circumstances of the case, and was prepared to subject official behavior and the Warren Commission's conclusions to sharp scrutiny. Disillusion was not long in coming."[16]

Wirin said he would forgo putting questions to Mark Lane, because he did not think such an approach would be very fruitful. Instead, he would make a short statement and allow Lane to reply however he wished.

"I want to address myself to Mr. Lane's statement," Wirin said, "which he repeated more than once tonight, that the report of the Commission is a fraud, and that the Commission, in its report, has indulged in a deception of the American public. I do not agree with that conclusion. I do not agree with that opinion. That is an opinion which Mr. Lane gave, and I disagree with it."

He always tried to make up his own mind on important issues, Wirin said, but there were times that he found he must rely on the opinions of others as he sought to form his own. "I consider Carey McWilliams and *The Nation*, as an individual and a newspaper, respectively, whose judgment I respect. I do not consider Carey McWilliams or *The Nation*, a person or a newspaper, which would participate in a fraud, or would condone it." *The Nation* ran an article in support of the Report shortly after the Report was published, Wirin continued. "Now, that carries a lot of weight with me."[17]

He was also impressed by I.F. Stone. "Now Mr. Stone, who has defended the rights of the Left, of Communists and others to fair treatment and freedom throughout his life – who is no apologist for any Rightists – said, 'I believe the Commission has done a first-rate job.' Very rarely does Mr. Stone ever commend a governmental agency. Very rarely. As very rarely do I."[18]

Wirin said he wanted to tell the audience what someone else had said about the Warren Commission. Reading a quote from the *Los Angeles Times*, Wirin said: "'The Warren Commission Report,' according to this quote on Mr. Kennedy's murder, 'does a remarkable job . . . of crime analysis. But when it comes to telling us why, and who is responsible, then I feel that it does not fulfill its function.'

"Indeed, this is a more conservative criticism of the Warren Commission than we heard from Mr. Lane tonight. This is the criticism of Herbert Philbrick – a stool pigeon and a rightist. And that's what the *rightists* are saying about the Warren Commission!"

This statement, after a stunned moment, brought gasps from the audience. "Now, just a minute!" Wirin said, his voice rising defensively as cries of protest were heard. "Now just a minute . . . "

"Ladies and gentlemen!" the moderator broke in. "Please let Mr. Wirin finish."

Wirin continued over the buzz of the crowd. Portions of the Report were honorable, he said, and had done a great service to the American public. Its criticisms of Dallas law enforcement were correct. More important, Wirin said, in stating that neither the Soviet Union nor Cuba had anything to do with the assassination, the Warren Commission went a long way toward exonerating American leftists. "Had the Commission not given this clearance, as it were, to many against whom the Rightists were pointing a finger, we might have had, following the assassination of President Kennedy, a real unleashing of terror against persons on the Left. So from my point of view, the Commission – instead of perpetrating a fraud on the American people – has rendered a service of major importance to the American people, particularly by protecting the rights, from hysteria and hostility, the rights of Americans who are, as I say, in the Left, or are left of center."

Joseph Ball and Herman Selvin both made very brief closing statements which added little to the content of the evening. Mark Lane was then allowed the final word. He must have been as stunned as anyone in the room by Wirin's "Philbrick" remark. Herbert Philbrick was an informant for the FBI who in the early 1940s had infiltrated American Communist groups and reported back on them to the Bureau. In the late forties he was a surprise witness at a trial of ten Communist Party leaders; his appearance on the witness stand stunned the defense. Depending on one's point of view Philbrick was either a hero or, as Wirin had characterized him, a stool pigeon. During the height of the Red Scare, in keeping with the tenor of the times, Philbrick was an establishment hero – so much so that he published an autobiography, *I Led Three Lives,* which became the basis for a popular television show during the early 1950s – one of Lee Harvey Oswald's favorites.[19]

As Lane began his concluding remarks for the evening, he said that, having never heard of Herman Selvin prior to the debate, he could not say he was surprised by Selvin's personal attacks on him. "The same disclaimer cannot be said for Mr. Wirin, who is known to us in New York, and known throughout the nation. And I had never thought the day would come when I would share a platform with Mr. Wirin, and hear him read a statement from Herbert Philbrick, and say 'If Mr. Philbrick said that, and Mr. Lane said that, what does that make Mr. Lane?'" That, Lane said, echoed the guilt-by-association tactics of the House Un-American Committee.

"I know that it is only because of the extreme pressure of this establishment which Mr. Wirin so well emphasized in quoting Carey McWilliams, or I.F. Stone, that this unusual statement was made by Mr. Wirin. I know that he would not make it ordinarily, and I know that it does not reflect his thinking generally." And he said he remained confident that the day would come when the United States government would have "the courage and honor to state that it was wrong" about Lee Harvey Oswald, just as the government of France, many years before, had admitted it was wrong in convicting Alfred Dreyfus of espionage twelve years after it had found him guilty.

The declaration, on the very day of the assassination, that Lee Harvey Oswald was the lone assassin was preposterous, Lane said. Who ever heard of an experienced investigator declaring a suspect acted alone on the very first day of his investigation? "Lone assassin? The first day? That was a reflection upon the FBI and the Dallas police – not upon Lee Harvey Oswald."

If Lee Harvey Oswald, after his death, was being condemned as the murderer just so the country might breathe easier, Lane said, so that there might be no unleashing of the terror that Wirin had suggested, it was a strategy that simply would not work. "For when justice is denied to one, be those of us here this evening be left, right, or center [sic], justice is denied to each of us – to every one of us."

Lane concluded with a touch of irony. "The Chief Justice said, when he was first questioning witnesses . . . you may never get the facts in your lifetime. And then they issued the Warren Commission Report, which tended to prove that his estimate was an accurate one."

The debate was tape-recorded by KPFK, a Pacifica radio station based in Los Angeles. As soon as it was over, a reporter from the station mingled with audience members and asked them what they thought of the exchange they had just witnessed. The first person he stopped thought for a moment before offering: "It was like, a shocking drama."[20]

The next person echoed that. "It was very shocking and frustrating."

"Why was it shocking?" the reporter asked.

"Because it seemed to me that Mark Lane really studied the issues very carefully, and had a lot of points to make that couldn't be refuted. But the people he was speaking to would not address themselves to the points he raised."

"Are you aware of the stature of the men that he was addressing?"

"I am," the man replied. "That's what makes it all the more frustrating."

Another man said, "I was very much disappointed in all three of those who questioned Mr. Lane. I think that they really should be ashamed of themselves, for the shabbiness of their thinking."

The next man said he once had great respect for Joseph Ball, but no more. Ball should at least have listened to what Lane had to say but did not seem willing. He added, "I don't think Mr. Lane should call things 'fraud.' I'm not of that opinion."

Several people said they were troubled by A.L. Wirin's "Herbert Philbrick" comment. "The fact that a scared liberal such as A.L. Wirin can compare [Mark Lane], who has gone through so much personal loss, to a man who informed, and just sold his life out to the FBI, such as Herbert Philbrick, is truly a shame, and I'm very sad that this day could occur."

Another added, "Mr. Wirin should be very much ashamed of himself for his statements tonight."

"I think Mr. Lane was brilliant," one woman told the reporter, "and I think that Mr. Wirin is a disappointment. He's on the decline."

"I don't think that Mark Lane set out to primarily prove the innocence of Lee Harvey Oswald," said one of the last audience members questioned. "Certainly, this was an important thing. But the byproduct of his defense of Oswald is to show that there has been, no matter what the motivation on the part of the Warren Commission, and many areas of government, an attempt to cover up. To use his term, defraud. I don't like the term. Because I don't think their motivations were as vicious as that."

The next day, the reporter sat down with Lane for a one-on-one interview. He began by conceding that he had the reputation at KPFK of being too sympathetic with his interview subjects. "I'm not really a reporter," he added. "I'm a high school English teacher."[21]

But for once, he said, he was not going to be sympathetic. What was Lane's opinion of the previous night's encounter with Wirin, Ball and Selvin?

Lane, sounding tired, answered at length. "I was surprised with Mr. Wirin's statements, which were, of course, totally unrelated to the Warren

Commission report." It appeared that Wirin was willing to sacrifice one person so that everyone else might feel safe.

Joseph Ball, meanwhile, didn't really answer any of the questions that were put to him, Lane said. But he did make one significant statement. "Mr. Ball said that Mrs. Markham is a screwball, and he threw up his hands in resignation as he said it." Lane reminded the reporter that Mrs. Markham, who gave conflicting statements to the Commission and was caught in at least one outright lie, was the sole identifying eyewitness to the Tippit killing, and that the Commission had concluded that Mrs. Markham's testimony was reliable. "If Mr. Ball is right, then there is no case at all, even according to the rather loose standards of the Commission, against Oswald for the murder of Officer Tippit."

At the New York office of the Citizens' Committee of Inquiry, there was a great deal of enthusiasm following the Beverly Hills event. The feeling was that Lane had scored a significant victory. Momentum was such that a Los Angeles branch of the CCI was soon formed.[22]

In Los Angeles, Ray Marcus collected CCI's profits from the evening and sent a check to Deirdre Griswold. "I have a very good tape (broadcast quality) of the Ball meeting," he told her. "As a possible source of funds as well as making available to more people an historic meeting, you might wish to consider the following: the tape would just about fit three 12-inch long-playing records." Lane had recorded his Warren Commission testimony and it was commercially available on the Folkways label. Marketing a debate record, even on a small scale through the CCI, Marcus suggested, could be a good source of much-needed funds.[23]

Griswold also saw the possibilities. "We are getting a tape from L.A. in a couple of days," she wrote to Vince Salandria. "I got the decided impression from our intelligence network that Mark clobbered 'em." Perhaps Salandria might arrange a party to play the tape and have those attending "kick in a few bucks," with proceeds to going to the CCI?[24]

"The idea is indeed terrific, but not for Philadelphia," Salandria wrote back. "We have tried this sort of fund-raising for other causes and have had no success." Nevertheless, he assured her, his support for CCI and his dedication to the assassination case were undiminished.[25]

Salandria evaluated the Commission's Hearings and Exhibits, finding much useful material. But he confided to Griswold that something troubled him about what he had read. "They make such easy pickings, that I keep worrying whether we were meant to dine on them."[26]

Chapter 17

Some Contacts

Thirty-one years after President Kennedy's death, the 8 mm home movie of his assassination was placed on the National Film Registry of the Library of Congress. By that time the legendary film taken by Dallas dress manufacturer Abraham Zapruder had become part of American pop culture; a Library of Congress official called it "probably the most famous amateur film of all time." Countless millions had seen the twenty-six-second Zapruder film in bootleg copies shown on college campuses, on television, or as part of a theatrical film. Placement on the National Film Registry meant the best available copy would be preserved for its historical significance, stored in optimal conditions in a climate controlled vault.[1]

Things were very different in 1963. Immediately after the assassination representatives from *Life* magazine purchased first the print rights, and then all rights to the film from Zapruder. The original film – the "camera original" – thus belonged to the magazine, while those studied by the FBI and published by the Warren Commission were later-generation copies. That a private corporation should control principal evidence of a stupendous crime went uncommented on by the government. While many of its most critical frames were published by *Life*, and nearly all of its frames published by the Commission, the film could not be seen in motion unless one received permission to see it, and traveled to the National Archives in Washington for that purpose. Yet most of the critics were quick to understand that analyzing the Zapruder film one frame at a time yielded the keenest insights. "In motion, the dramatic thing, of course, is his head being slammed back," Ray Marcus said. "The study is really in the stills."[2]

The Warren Commission had concluded that President Kennedy was probably first hit between Zapruder frames 210 and 225. This bullet exited his neck, the Commission said, at a velocity of about 1,772 feet per second, and went on to cause all of Governor Connally's wounds. Another shot missed the car and its occupants entirely. President Kennedy received his fatal head wound at Zapruder frame 313 – or "Z-313," in the shorthand some of the critics were beginning to adopt.

ıt shot originated from behind the President or from in front
ɔoth, quickly became a matter of intense debate.[3]

frames published by the Commission in Volume 18 lacked the
the original film. Moreover four frames, Z-208 through Z-211,
were ːexplicably missing from the 171 frames published by the
Commission, although 210 did appear as part of an exhibit included in
the Report. The next frame in sequence, Z-212, was also problematic; it
was obviously two different frames spliced together. The top portion of
the image was not in alignment with the lower portion. This led Harold
Weisberg to exclaim, "It has so amateurish a splice through it that a
single tree in the upper section is a full quarter of the frame to the left in
the lower section!"[4]

Nevertheless the Zapruder frames published in Volume 18 of the
Hearings and Exhibits were one of the best sources then available to work
from, if only for their near-completeness. Zapruder's camera had exposed
18.3 frames per second, according to FBI re-enactments. The FBI also
determined that it took a minimum of 2.3 seconds to cycle a new bullet
into the alleged assassination weapon's chamber after a shot was fired,
which meant that some 42 Zapruder frames would have to elapse
between shots. With such precise data on the shooting, the Zapruder film
came to be seen as a "clock" of the assassination. A number of the early
critics determined to study the images according to these numbers and
see what secrets might be revealed. Ray Marcus, Vincent Salandria,
Harold Weisberg, Sylvia Meagher, and Thomas Stamm, whom Meagher
had met in the New School course – all were among those interested in
studying the Zapruder film.[5]

The first article incorporating an analysis of the Zapruder film
appeared in *Liberation* magazine's January 1965 issue. This was the
article the magazine's editorial board feared would "open up Pandora's
box," and that Vince Salandria said "isn't too much different from *The
Legal Intelligencer* article" he had published a few months earlier.
Entitled "A Philadelphia Lawyer Analyzes the Shots, Trajectories,
and Wounds," Salandria reminded readers that the Warren Commission
had stated in its report that three shots, and three shots only, were fired
from the southeast-corner window of the sixth floor of the Texas School
Book Depository building, and that two of these shots probably caused all
of Kennedy's and Connally's wounds. The last shot fired had caused the
President's fatal head wound. One shot missed. And so the first shot to
hit Kennedy had to have been the same one to hit Connally. And this,
Salandria wrote, was a problem for the Commission.

> The Zapruder films indicate a definite reaction of the President to a hit in the neck region at frame 225. Governor Connally's body shows no reaction to any hit at this frame. The Governor has repeatedly stated in the Report and for the press and television, that he was not hit by the first shot that hit the President. Mrs. Connally corroborates her husband's testimony. . . .[6]

The Commission had suggested that Connally had a delayed reaction to being wounded – hence his lack of expression while JFK clearly reacts to his neck wound. But elementary physics, Salandria said, instructs that every action must have an equal and opposite reaction. "The thrust of this bullet through the body of the Governor was not recorded by the Zapruder films. The pictures are excellent evidence that the first bullet to hit the President did not hit the Governor."[7]

Salandria next pointed out that the Commission's version of events suggested the bullet that hit both Kennedy and Connally had to have changed direction several times – once in mid-air – in order to inflict the wounds it was credited with. The Commission had said the assassin fired from the Book Depository sixth floor at about a 20-degree downward angle. This bullet reportedly struck no bone, so one would expect, Salandria wrote, for it to continue downward at roughly the same angle. "Instead, this remarkable bullet turned upward" and exited through the President's necktie knot. Then "the Commission turned this bullet downward into the back of the Governor."[8]

The alignment of the wounds, Salandria said, indicated conclusively that the same bullet could not have hit both men; indeed, all of the evidence he had considered "spell out at least one separate shot hitting the Governor after the President had been hit by a different bullet. To conclude otherwise would be to grasp at not only the improbable but what photography, all the eyewitness testimony, logic, the laws of physics, and geometry tell us is impossible." And if a separate shot hit Connally, "we are confronted with an extra bullet, which puts the Commission theory of just three bullets from one gun into the limbo of historical myth."[9]

In Los Angeles, three thousand miles from this Philadelphia lawyer, the thinking of Ray Marcus was very much along these same lines. By early 1964 Marcus felt that the Zapruder film and related photographic evidence were enough to demonstrate that the official version of the assassination was false. A close review of the Zapruder frames published in *Life* magazine's November 29, 1963, issue had convinced him, in and of itself, that the position of Governor Connally's body as he sat in the presidential limousine was of a man who had been wounded by shots fired from the front.[10]

Before the year was out Marcus had his set of the Warren Commission volumes. By early 1965 he had read the relevant testimony and begun studying the Zapruder frames in painstaking detail. To increase his understanding, Marcus used a razor blade to slice out key portions of certain frames. He had these professionally reproduced and enlarged, some to several times their original size, some much larger; these were mounted on display boards in their proper sequence. "You begin to look for small differences of motion," Marcus recalled. "You could see them in the stills, things that you would not see in motion, unless it's way slowed down."[11]

Simultaneously he began drawing a series of inferences from what he had seen and read. The Commission had asserted that "it is not necessary to any essential findings of the Commission to determine just which shot hit Gov. Connally." Ray Marcus took exception to this: he believed that it *was* necessary to the Commission's findings. This became the first argument in a series of seven, which he cautiously referred to not as conclusions but hypotheses. These were set forth in a thirteen-page study completed in March 1965, entitled "Hypotheses re: the Zapruder Film."[12]

It was necessary to the Commission's findings, Marcus argued, because if Connally was not hit by the first bullet to hit Kennedy, and if Kennedy was first hit by a bullet fired from Oswald's rifle, then the first bullet to hit Connally could not have been fired by that weapon. This was because of the time required to load another round into the rifle's chamber after a shot had been fired. According to the FBI, Kennedy was hit no earlier than Z-210; he was visibly reacting to a shot, Marcus wrote, by Z-226. Connally was not reacting yet, but he was reacting by Z-244 – he was "slumping, and his mouth has opened. His right shoulder is sharply depressed." But this was too soon, by the Commission's own numbers. If JFK was hit at Z-210, and it took 2.3 seconds – or 42 frames – before another shot could be fired, then Connally couldn't have been hit before Z-252. Therefore it was necessary to the Commission's findings to determine which shot hit Governor Connally.[13]

Perhaps the most important hypothesis was the second one, which followed from the first. This stated that Governor Connally was not hit by the same bullet that first hit JFK. Marcus wrote that he accepted the Commission's view that Connally's wounds were all caused by one bullet.

This shot entered his back, exited just below his right nipple, went through his right wrist, and finally lodged in his right thigh. Zapruder frame 232 showed JFK clearly reacting to a wound while Connally was not reacting. But Connally's right hand can be seen resting on a limousine hand-hold. If he had been shot by this time, and sustained the wounds the Warren Commission said he had sustained, his hand would have been knocked away. "Since hand is clearly visible on top of hold-bar," Marcus wrote in a markedly clipped style, "he has not yet been struck."[14]

Marcus never attempted to publish his "Hypotheses." Rather he viewed it as a working paper, something to be shared with and commented on, and perhaps improved, by other critics. He showed his original, written in longhand, to Maggie Field, who by this time had become a good friend. Maggie was so impressed that she typed it for him, and sent a copy, without naming its author, to Sylvia Meagher, with whom she was now corresponding on a regular basis. Marcus sent a copy to Mark Lane.[15]

Mrs. Meagher replied with a four-page commentary. She included the observation that "the suppression of Zapruder frames 208, 209, 210, and 211 . . . has not been explained in the Warren Report or in testimony." These frames coincided with a possible first hit of President Kennedy. "It is legitimate to ask whether those frames might not have shown some action, movement, or other feature inimical to the official conclusions."[16]

Meagher was in agreement with most of Marcus's hypotheses. In Hypothesis D, Marcus stated that JFK was first hit at Zapruder frame 189, "and therefore, beyond reasonable doubt, that shot could not have come from TSBD building, since car was obscured from window by tree from frame 166-210 . . . except for $1/18$ -second opening at frame 185. . . ." While Meagher agreed that the reasoning for this hypothesis was sound, and that Kennedy was hit before frame 210, "I am not sure that there is sufficient evidence to determine exactly which frame corresponds with the first bullet that struck him."[17]

In Hypotheses E and F, Marcus tried to pinpoint the moments in which JFK received other wounds, including a wound to his head fired from the left rear. Meagher thought the evidence did not support these hypotheses. But she was in complete agreement with Hypothesis G, that the head wound Kennedy suffered in Zapruder frame 313 was fired from the right front. That would be from the area of the so-called "grassy knoll." At the time Ray Marcus completed his seven hypotheses, there was no photographic evidence to support the idea of a gunman at that location. But within a few months, this photographic evidence – not conclusive, but very powerful – would emerge.[18]

Two weeks after her response to the Ray Marcus hypotheses, Sylvia Meagher visited the National Archives in Washington, D.C., in order to view large color slides made from the frames of the Zapruder film. She arrived promptly at 9 o'clock on the morning of Thursday, July 22, 1965.[19]

Upon arrival she met briefly with archivist James B. Rhoads and a second man, probably archivist Marion Johnson, who carried with him several boxes of slides. Johnson led her to a projection room where another man was waiting for them. This man, introduced as Mr. Swanson, served as projectionist and stayed with Meagher for the entirety of her visit, except for a short lunch break. Sylvia found him very cooperative and patient. When Swanson went to lunch she was left by herself and allowed to examine the slides with a magnifying glass she had brought with her. But for most of the day it was just the two of them in the projection room, although Johnson came in several times in order to observe.[20]

Johnson happened to be there when Meagher and Swanson reached Z-207. As with this same sequence in Volume 18 of the Hearings and Exhibits, frames 208 through 211 were missing from the color slides. Seizing the moment, Meagher asked Johnson and Swanson why this was so. "They seemed not to be aware that these frames were missing nor could they give any explanation," Meagher recalled. They had her telephone James Rhoads. He too was not aware that the frames were missing, but did offer to look up an answer in the Commission testimony. Sylvia said not to bother. "I told Mr. Rhoads that I was familiar with that testimony and that the absence of the four frames was neither acknowledged nor explained."[21]

Meagher suggested that a call to Lyndal Shaneyfelt, the FBI photo expert who testified about the Zapruder film, might be in order. Rhoads agreed, and said he would get Shaneyfelt's number, but that Meagher should make the call since she was more familiar with the material.[22]

Shaneyfelt took the call himself. "I explained that I was viewing the Zapruder color slides at the Archives and asked him to clarify the reasons for the absence of frames 208 through 211," Meagher wrote.

Mr. Shaneyfelt explained that the original Zapruder film was copied when it was first processed; the frames were numbered from the copy; *Life* made up the color slides as a courtesy (but never made available the original film, which Mr. Shaneyfelt said jocularly was locked in a vault in New York) but frames 208 through 211 were missing, presumably because the original film was broken or damaged.

I pointed out to Mr. Shaneyfelt that there was a frame 210 (Warren Report page 102), for which his explanation failed to account. At this point he became vague and said, more or less, that he would have to look that up, or something equivalent. He added that those frames 208-211 were included in the copy of the Zapruder film and had been viewed as a motion picture, by the Commission and the investigators.[23]

The following November, Meagher telephoned *Life* and spoke to Herbert Orth, who had made the color slides for the Commission. She asked him whether there had been any interruption in the sequence of frames he had used in making these slides, and he replied, "No, there was not."[24]

Several years later Meagher would report that a spokesman for *Life* told her that the four frames in question were "accidentally torn" in the excitement of examining the film immediately after the magazine had obtained it in 1963. The missing frames were included in copies of the film made before the original was damaged.[25]

On that July day in 1965, Meagher continued her frame-by-frame examination of the film. She was especially horrified by frame 313, where the President is hit in the head: "Familiar as this frame is, I became dizzy and ill," she wrote. "There is a spray from the explosion in front of and above the President's right ear, with a thick strand spraying up and to the left side, slightly forward of the explosion."[26]

(a) I conclude from Mrs. Kennedy's sharp turn to her right in frames 203-204 that a shot has hit the President earlier than those frames and while the car was not visible from the sixth-floor window because of the tree.

(b) I am unable to judge when the Governor was shot. I would think that he was hit in about frame 227, by a pristine bullet which penetrated his back, wrist (then out of sight) and leg; except for the position and movement of his hand in subsequent frames. Once the hand becomes visible, it is never in position to take a shot that produced the known wounds.

(c) I believe the President was shot in the head in frame 313 from the right front (grassy knoll), because that was my strong impression as a Gestalt.[27]

Earlier that same summer, Meagher had begun writing a series of letters which she impishly, though privately, referred to as her "harassment file." But there was nothing lighthearted in her objective: she wanted a Warren Commission member, or one of its staff, to give some answers for the record on certain points of evidence. She informed several recipients, though not all, that she was working on a comparative study of the conclusions in the Warren Report, and the evidence as presented in the twenty-six volumes of Hearings and Exhibits. One day she would write: "One of the most reprehensible actions of the Warren Commission is that it disbanded the moment it handed over its Report, leaving no individual or corporate entity to answer legitimate questions arising from demonstrable misstatements of fact in the Report."[28]

One of her first letters was to former Commission chairman Earl Warren, whom she approached with great respect. "I beg you to excuse me for taking the liberty of addressing you personally with a request for information which I have not been able to obtain elsewhere," she wrote. It is not known whether Warren ever saw this letter, but he did not answer it. His executive secretary offered a token response: "I regret that we are unable to supply you with the information which you request." Meagher also wrote to Gerald Ford, and the former Commissioner did reply – but simply referred her to J. Lee Rankin, the Commission's chief counsel. A letter to Rankin went unanswered. So did a letter to assistant counsel Albert Jenner.[29]

Her letter to Joseph Ball, which referred to a tape recording of Ball's encounter with Mark Lane, elicited a curious response. "I do not recall ever having debated with Mark Lane in Beverly Hills, or in any other place, on any subject," Ball replied. Of course, this was merely semantics. Technically the December 1964 event between Lane, Ball, and two others was not a debate, but a "cross-examination" of Mark Lane by "a panel of prominent attorneys." Ball did concede to having heard Lane speak and asking him a few questions. He would be very pleased, he said, to discuss the case with Meagher. He did not, however, answer any of several direct questions she put to him about the Warren Commission evidence.[30]

Sylvia wrote back promptly. "I wouldn't call it a debate either but that is how the tape-recording was labelled," she began. Once again she asked that Ball address her questions. This time she suggested he telephone her, collect, if he preferred it. She never heard from him again.[31]

A letter to former Commission assistant counsel Melvin Eisenberg was by far the most successful endeavor in her harassment campaign, although it got off to a slow start. She first wrote to Eisenberg on June 8, 1965, and asked two specific questions. The first was a request for documentation for the Commission's assertion that the ammunition used in the alleged assassination rifle was "recently made by the Western Cartridge Co., which manufactures such ammunition currently." Her second question asked about Commission Exhibit 2560. This was a telephone message addressed to Eisenberg indicating that a gunsmith examining the rifle had determined that its scope was mounted "as if for a left-handed man." This statement was not supplemented by any testimony or document. Was Oswald, Meagher asked Eisenberg, left-handed or ambidextrous? Or did the apparent left-handed scope mounting not make a difference to a right-handed shooter?[32]

"I have taken the liberty of addressing these queries to you since I am not aware that the Warren Commission, before it dissolved, assigned any residual responsibility for providing clarification requested by members of the public or students of the case," she wrote him.[33]

Ten days later, not having received a reply, Sylvia telephoned Eisenberg, who like Meagher lived in New York City. He said he would respond to her letter by the end of the next week. When no such reply was forthcoming, she wrote him again. "I have been surprised and disappointed to hear nothing from you," she told him. "Perhaps my request appears to be an imposition on a private person that should have been addressed elsewhere." But surely he would agree, she continued, that there was a moral obligation to clarify legitimate questions posed in good faith.[34]

On the evening of Thursday, July 1, Sylvia was at home with a guest, William Crehan, whom she had come to know in the New School's Warren Report class. Though she initially suspected Crehan of being an FBI plant, she had come to trust him. Around 10 p.m. the telephone rang and Sylvia answered it. It was Eisenberg.[35]

"Mrs. Meagher signalled me at once to listen to the conversation on the telephone extension in the kitchen," Crehan said a few days later. "I did so, making notes, during the entire conversation."[36]

Eisenberg got right to the point. The statement that Oswald's ammunition had been recently made by the Western Cartridge Co., and was still being manufactured, was probably "inaccurate," he conceded. He could not recall any documents on this. The assertion had been in a Warren Report appendix called "Speculations and Rumors," one of the last things prepared. Commission historian Alfred Goldberg had put that section together; Meagher said she would direct her question to him.[37]

As for the left-handed scope, Eisenberg said he had not followed up on that part of the phone message he'd received. But he and several other Bureau agents had used the rifle without any difficulty. All of them, save one, were right-handed. Meagher thought Eisenberg sounded rather defensive about not following up on the phone message. He had commented, "If every single lead had been pursued, the report would never have been completed."[38]

Meagher brought up the matter of the ad for Klein's Sporting Goods, which appeared in the February 1963 issue of *The American Rifleman*. Mark Lane and Joseph Ball had clashed over this point during their encounter in Beverly Hills the previous December. The weapon allegedly ordered by Oswald under an assumed name was not the same model the Commission put forth as the assassination rifle. "Eisenberg was not aware that Klein's ad featured a different rifle," Sylvia wrote in her notes. "He would like to see a copy of the ad." The Commission had not reproduced the ad in its published evidence, but Sylvia had obtained a copy. She promised to send him one.[39]

Eisenberg said that most of the criticism of the Warren Report that he had read was "frankly, out of its mind." He specifically mentioned Dwight Macdonald, who had written a critique of the Report for *Esquire* magazine. Sylvia mentioned that Macdonald had appeared one evening at the New School class. She, too, dismissed his *Esquire* article which, while criticizing the Commission, accepted its conclusions. She suspected Macdonald had not even read the Warren Report. He was not, she said, a competent Commission critic.[40]

At one point during their conversation, Sylvia referred to an assertion in the Report – her notes did not record which one – and Eisenberg had replied that he was not familiar with it.

"Didn't you read the Report, Mr. Eisenberg?" she asked. She had meant the comment as a joke, but as she wrote in her notes, "There was a dead silence for 45 seconds (by the clock)." She assured Eisenberg she had just been kidding him, and Eisenberg resumed the conversation as if the remark had never been made. "He seemed to be somewhat offended by the (facetious) question."[41]

Sylvia mentioned the other letters she had written to former Commissioners and staff members, and how they had gone mostly unanswered. Eisenberg said that he had had inquiries from others about the Warren Report, but usually he didn't answer them; to do so, he said, would not be in good taste. He had replied to only one other inquiry. This was from a graduate student at Cornell University who was writing his political science thesis on the composition of the Commission.[42]

Their conversation went on until 11:15. The following day Sylvia dashed off a quick note thanking Eisenberg for taking the time to call her, and for his willingness to discuss the questions she had raised. She reiterated her promise to send him a copy of the Klein's advertisement, just as soon as she gained access to a photocopier. Eight days later she had it in the mail.[43]

On July 3, Sylvia composed another letter to Albert Jenner, asking again if he could clarify certain points of evidence. This time she suggested he telephone her at home, collect, and at his convenience. "I am anxious to have the requested clarification for purposes of a comparative study on which I am engaged."[44]

Barely one week later, she received a written reply. "Will wonders never cease?" she commented to Maggie Field. Yet Jenner's reply contained nothing of substance. He said her original letter reached him in the middle of a trial; now, he was about to leave town but promised to write her as soon as he returned.[45]

Sylvia replied to Jenner: "I shall look forward with much interest to your promised letter." But that letter never came. On August 20, she wrote again: "Forgive me if I say that I am surprised and concerned at the non-arrival of the letter you volunteered to write . . . I hope that I may still expect the promised reply?" This letter, too, went unanswered.[46]

On July 2, encouraged by her phone conversation with Melvin Eisenberg the night before, Sylvia had written to Alfred Goldberg, the Warren Commission historian who had prepared the "Speculations and Rumors" appendix to the Report. She invited him to write her or call her collect. She never received a reply.[47]

On August 1, Sylvia Meagher received a telephone call from Thomas Stamm, one of the men from the Warren Report class with whom she had kept in touch.

nm, who worked for the Ideal Toy Company in New York, said
ıst returned from Philadelphia the day before, where he had
th Vince Salandria. Stamm had read Salandria's "A Philadelphia
ʟawyer Analyzes the Shots, Trajectories, and Wounds" article in the
January *Liberation*, and a second article in the March *Liberation* called "A
Philadelphia Lawyer Analyzes the President's Neck and Back Wounds."
Impressed, Stamm wanted to meet the author and talk with him; he
found a man, he told Sylvia, who was completely committed to finding
the truth. Salandria's law practice had suffered from neglect due to his
assassination work. After his articles were published he was audited by the
Internal Revenue Service. Salandria, Stamm reported, thought this was
related to his articles.[48]

Stamm said Salandria was in touch with a young graduate student
at Cornell who was writing his Ph.D. thesis on the Warren Commission.
The student, whose name was Epstein, had interviewed a number of the
former Commission members and staff lawyers; Stamm said he was
writing a major attack on the Warren Report. "I believe Epstein must be
the young man mentioned to me by Eisenberg as the 'only other' person
to whom he had consented to talk," Meagher wrote in a memo of her
conversation with Stamm.[49]

Salandria had been very excited to hear that Sylvia had just visited
the National Archives to examine the Zapruder film color slides, and
asked for a copy of her notes. He was planning a visit there himself, and
hoped to have Stamm come with him. Salandria had been equally excited
to hear that Sylvia was preparing an index to the Warren Commission's
twenty-six volumes. This would be an invaluable research tool, he had
said, and he urged her, through Stamm, to keep at it and to publish it
when it was done.[50]

Stamm said that Salandria was about to go on vacation – not to
Washington and the Archives, but to Dallas for a second investigative
trip. As with his first Dallas trip, he planned to stop in Oklahoma to see
Shirley Martin and her family. Stamm added that perhaps the time was
right for all of them to get together in New York – Salandria, Meagher,
Lobenthal, and others from the New School class – for a meeting to
exchange ideas.[51]

After her conversation with Stamm, Sylvia decided it was time she
speak to Salandria personally, so she picked up the phone and gave him a
call. They talked about the National Archives and her notes, and the
subject index she was working on. "We also discussed a few other matters,
such as the need to avoid controversy and back-biting within the small

group that are working toward the same objectives, and the need to avoid proprietary attitudes about material turned up," Sylvia wrote in a memo. Salandria concluded by saying he might be in New York within the week. If he was able to, he would pay her a visit.[52]

In the March 1965 issue of *The Minority of One*, Harold Feldman published an article called "Fifty-one Witnesses: The Grassy Knoll." As with "Oswald and the FBI," the article was researched with Vince Salandria. Feldman dedicated it to Shirley Martin, "who was paid homage by the attorneys of the Warren Commission in being called in scorn, 'a self-appointed investigator.'" The piece surveyed 121 eyewitnesses in the vicinity of Dealey Plaza at the time of the assassination, whose statements were in the Hearings and Exhibits.[53]

By this time Shirley had been corresponding with Feldman and his brother-in-law for nearly a year. "Harold's article is pretty darn good, isn't it?" she wrote to Salandria after it appeared. If she had been flattered by the dedication she didn't admit it. "Why the ass had to put my name there I don't know. To make me feel cheap, I guess. I'll get hold of him some-day and pull his big nose for him."[54]

In evaluating the Commission's own Dealey Plaza evidence, Feldman demonstrated that the number of eyewitnesses – or ear witnesses, as he more properly called them – who heard shots from the grassy knoll area outnumbered those who heard shots from the so-called "sniper's nest."

> On the question of where the shots that killed the President came from, 38 could give no clear opinion and 32 thought they came from the Texas School Book Depository Building (TSBDB). Fifty-one held the shots sounded as if they came from west of the Depository, the area of the grassy knoll on Elm Street, the area directly on the right of the President's car when the bullets struck.[55]

Feldman wrote that Salandria's *Legal Intelligencer* article demonstrated that the ballistic and medical evidence pointed toward the grassy knoll as the probable source of the gunshots. "The chief weakness of the Warren Report was its absolute refusal to consider seriously any other source of shots besides the TSBDB, even though such a source is indicated by the largest number of direct witnesses."[56]

None of the Secret Service agents riding with the motorcade, Feldman wrote, voiced a suspicion that the shots had come from the Book Depository.

Some did say shots came from the "right rear," but none mentioned elevation. Some of the agents thought the noises they heard were police motorcycles backfiring, or firecrackers. Others had no opinion at all on the source of the shots.[57]

Presidential aide David Powers told the Commission that the shots came from "the right and overhead, but I had a fleeting impression that the noise appeared to come from the front in the area of the triple underpass." Kenneth O'Donnell, another aide, testified the shots came from the right rear. But years later he told Representative Thomas "Tip" O'Neill that in truth, the shots sounded to him as if they'd come from behind the fence on top of the grassy knoll.

"That's not what you told the Warren Commission," O'Neill said.

"You're right," O'Donnell replied. "I told the FBI what I had heard, but they said it couldn't have happened that way and that I must have been imagining things. So I testified the way they wanted me to."[58]

Feldman's article continued. None of the drivers or passengers of the first two cars in the motorcade – the lead car and the presidential limousine, in which Kennedy and Connally rode – indicated they thought shots came from the Depository. The reaction of numerous Dealey Plaza bystanders was to run in the general direction of the Triple Underpass, the grassy knoll, and the railroad yards behind it. The Warren Report conceded this fact, but presented it in terms that minimized its significance. A reading of the twenty-six volumes presented a different picture. "We would not learn from the Report itself, for example, that the 'many people' were in fact most people, the overwhelming majority," Feldman wrote. "We are drawn a picture of bystanders rushing westward of the TSBDB, 'some' to find the assassin, 'others' to escape him. But we are not told that practically none of the witnesses belonged to the second category, and that the 'some' who looked for the assassin in the vicinity of the grassy knoll included almost every deputy sheriff on duty in the area that day and most of the policemen."[59]

Feldman counted nineteen Depository employees whose observations were published by the Commission. Five of them had no opinion about where the shots came from. Six thought the shots had come from within the Book Depository, and eight thought they came from the grassy knoll area. Two of those who thought the shots came from within the building, along with a third employee, were on its fifth floor. Rather than running to the sixth floor they had looked out the west side of the fifth floor, toward the grassy knoll area. "Since everyone was running, you know, to the west side of the building, towards the railroad tracks, we assumed maybe somebody was down there," one of them said.[60]

The Warren Report stated: "No credible evidence suggests that the shots were fired from the railroad bridge over the Triple Underpass, the nearby railroad yards or any place other than the Texas School Book Depository." Harold Feldman found this appalling.

> No credible evidence! It is clear how the Commission reached this absurd conclusion. Once it was committed to the thesis that there could be only one assassin and no accomplices, it readily accepted the clues pointing to Lee Oswald in the TSBDB. Now that the assassin and his place were identified, it became "incredible" that any other assassin or any other source of shots could exist. Ergo, any evidence that there was another assassin and another shot source is not "credible."
>
> In what other murder case would the testimony of 51 sworn and many other unheard witnesses be dismissed so cavalierly as "no credible evidence"?
>
> We submit, on the contrary, that the earwitness evidence is quite credible. Taken together with the ballistic and medical evidence analyzed by Mr. Salandria, it is not only credible, it is convincing. There was at least one other assassin firing at President Kennedy from the vicinity of the grassy knoll.[61]

Feldman had developed other articles relating to the assassination. In the same month that "Fifty-one Witnesses: The Grassy Knoll" appeared, he published "The Kennedy Body Snatchers" in Paul Krassner's *The Realist*. This was the same periodical that had run Feldman's "The Unsinkable Marguerite Oswald" six months earlier. The new article recounted how the President's body was illegally taken from Parkland Memorial Hospital and flown to Andrews Air Force Base, after which it was routed to Bethesda Naval Hospital in Bethesda, Maryland, for autopsy. "The Bethesda autopsy was secret," Feldman wrote, "and no one, not even the doctors at Parkland Hospital in Dallas, could learn its findings. The public presentation of the autopsy report was made some 8 months later."[62]

An article called "Psychoanalysis and Lee Oswald" was never published. In it Feldman objected to Oswald's portrayal by the media, aided and abetted by mental health care professionals, as an unstable loner. This was the popular and prevailing view, but Feldman said it was without foundation.

> Oswald had just been arrested and Kennedy's body was hardly cold and still unburied when Dr. Silvano Arieti knew what it was all

about. "I am certain," he said about Lee Oswald whom he had never met, much less examined, "that he was fully conscious of what he was doing, and I believe he will be ruled legally sane." Dr. Arieti is a professor of clinical psychiatry and the author of *Interpretation of Schizophrenia*. Moving ahead unhampered by a concern for facts or that "benevolent skepticism" which Freud recommended to all analysts, he added, "The slayer is like Hitler in his extermination of the Jews—he felt he had to give meaning to his life."

O sapient doctor!

The midwinter 1963 meeting of the American Psychoanalytical Association buzzed with theories about Lee Oswald and the man who killed Oswald. Dr. Charles W. Socarides led the discussion. Kennedy's murderer may have had other ostensible grievances, political or personal, the good doctor admitted, but he knew the real reason for the Dallas pogrom. *The New York Times* (12/8/63) noted Dr. Socarides' opinion that Lee Oswald was a "classic example of the vengeful person." And having studied neither Jack Ruby nor Lee Oswald nor any firsthand material about the assassination, Dr. Socarides concluded that Kennedy, as president, was an authority figure made to order for Oswald's sharpshooting, and he noted, to show his fine penchant for detail, that "Jack Ruby does not emerge as clearly as Oswald does as a typical vengeful person, who is usually of a paranoid-schizophrenic type."

Please note that there is nothing here of that modest presumption that an accused man is innocent until he is proven guilty.[63]

In August of 1965 Harold Weisberg self-published a limited edition of his first book, *Whitewash*. This was a time of considerable frustration for Weisberg. For while he had written the book with a publisher's contract, and delivered it on time, the publisher had reneged on the deal. It was the first of a series of rejections that by his own count surpassed one hundred. In time, he would refer to *Whitewash* as "probably the world's most rejected book." None of the rejections, he always said, contained any adverse editorial comments.[64]

The publisher rejections were paralleled by disinterest on the part of would-be agents. "Seven literary agents, all interested in new clients, suddenly found themselves too busy to 'do justice to the book' once they learned its subject matter," Weisberg said. "One courageous agent alone read it, pronounced it 'a really excellent job,' but ultimately resigned with the explanation, 'No American publisher will now touch this subject.'"[65]

Particularly confounding, Weisberg recalled, was that most of the publishers who saw his manuscript were excited by it. "This is the most important thing I will do in my lifetime!" he quoted one of them. Another had declared it "extraordinarily important." Most, Weisberg said, told him it was well-written and well-presented, moderate, convincing – and marketable. Yet one after another, publishers declined to take on the book.[66]

Up to this point – the summer of 1965 – only a handful of books about the assassination had been published in the United States; no book-length analyses had appeared since publication of the Hearings and Exhibits in November 1964. Léo Sauvage had completed *L' Affaire Oswald,* but it had been published only in France. Sauvage had signed a contract with Random House for publication of his book in the United States. But like Weisberg's deal, Sauvage's contract had been broken.[67]

Sauvage had worked on the English-language edition of his book through the summer of 1964. At that time, of course, the Warren Commission's investigation was still underway, but Sauvage had his own research to draw upon, and would incorporate the official evidence when it became available. But after the Warren Report was published everything changed: "The enthusiasm of my New York publisher ebbed perceptibly."[68]

The Random House editor was a prominent figure in the publishing industry. In a letter dated November 4, 1964 – just over a month following the appearance of the Warren Report – he wrote in a letter to Sauvage:

> The problem is that the Warren Report has put the Oswald matter in a different light from what I had expected, and I'm now convinced that any book which attempts to question Oswald's guilt would be out of touch with reality and could not be taken seriously by responsible critics. This is by no means to say that the Warren Report is not without flaws – its treatment of the evidence, its indifference to many of the ambiguities which are evident in its pages, and its tendentiousness are clear. But for all this and for all the confusion earlier in Dallas, it is inconceivable that Oswald might yet be proven innocent. . . .[69]

Oswald, the editor conceded, was treated unfairly by the police and the media between the time of his arrest and the time of his murder. Had he lived, he might well have been acquitted on constitutional grounds. Now *that* would make an interesting book, the editor suggested, even with Oswald's guilt taken for granted. But Sauvage would have to revise his original concept, which he was unwilling to do. And with that the editor, at the direction of his superiors, "reluctantly" released Sauvage from the contract he had signed some eight months before.[70]

Weisberg and Sauvage were not the only critics to suffer broken contracts. Mark Lane was by this time working on a book and endured at least one cancelled contract; Maggie Field would suffer the same indignity. But Weisberg, Sauvage and Lane would in time find their way into print, and other books demonstrating the "omissions and distortions" of the Warren Commission were in development. The dam, before too much longer, would break.[71]

Chapter 18

Films and Photographs

In the seventh of his hypotheses on the Zapruder film, Ray Marcus had written:

> Hypothesis G: That head-shot at [Zapruder frame] 313 came from right front.
>
> 1. No doubt that 313 was a head shot.
>
>> a. cloud – presumably of blood and matter – at JFK's head.
>> b. marked change in head position from 312-314.
>> c. large, obviously bloody area visible on right side of head, color panel #6, LIFE, 10/2/64.
>
> 2. At instant of impact, JFK's head is facing somewhat leftward, and tilted sharply forward (see 312). From this position (which offered a broadside attitude to the grassy knoll), it moves sharply back and to the left; appearing to contact seat-back by 320, $2/5$ second later. The motion of his head in reaction to the head-shot is absolutely consistent with a bullet from the right front; and absolutely inconsistent with the bullet having come from the TSBD building.[1]

Most of the critics were certain that a shot had to have come from the grassy knoll, a tree-and-bush-lined hill above Elm Street to the immediate right front of the presidential limousine. The backward-to-the-left movement of Kennedy's head upon impact at Z-313 was, as Marcus said, absolutely consistent with someone's firing from there. What was lacking was hard evidence that a gunman or gunmen were in fact up on the knoll.

David Lifton believed he found proof. Lifton was the UCLA graduate student who late in 1965 confronted Allen Dulles with evidence that the Zapruder film did not support the theory that someone shot the president from behind. Early that same year he had contacted Ray Marcus after hearing that he had arranged some of Mark Lane's speaking engagements in and around Los Angeles. He also contacted Maggie Field and her friend Ronnie Solomon. All were wary of this unknown newcomer. Maggie said later that she considered Lifton bright but naïve, and that she was a little put off by his enthusiasm.[2]

Marcus, who had just completed his study of the Zapruder film, did meet with Lifton, and showed him how the President's head moved backward and to the left upon impact at Z-313. "I had been a physics major," Lifton later wrote. "I appreciated the inviolability of Newton's laws. What I was shown seemed no mere 'hypothesis,' but absolute proof that Kennedy had been shot from the front."[3]

Lifton was further impressed by Harold Feldman's "Fifty-One Witnesses: The Grassy Knoll," in the March 1965 issue of *The Minority of One*. This analysis of "ear witness" testimony amply demonstrated, Lifton believed, that a convincing number of Dealey Plaza witnesses heard gunshots coming from the grassy knoll area, proving at least one assassin had fired from there.[4]

Then, in May, Lifton made his important discovery. As he waited in line at a bookstore, he'd begun flipping through a commemorative magazine called *Four Dark Days in History*. The magazine contained a large reproduction of a Polaroid photograph of the assassination taken by Mary Moorman, a Dealey Plaza bystander. The photo, which had not been included in any of the Warren Commission's published evidence, corresponded to Z-313, the moment of impact, but showed the limousine from the opposite side of the street. One could plainly see the grassy knoll area in the picture's background. Standing there in the bookstore, Lifton was stunned to see, obscured in the shadows of the knoll, what he took to be a puff of smoke and the figure of a gunman in the act of shooting.[5]

Lifton bought the magazine. It marked the beginning of a period of intense research. "The Moorman photograph, and attempting to analyze it, and looking for images behind the wall, absolutely dominated my life in May and June of 1965," he remembered years later. Initially he simply examined the picture with a magnifying glass. But after noting the book had been published by a company not far from where he lived, he obtained from it a negative, then talked his way into a darkroom at a Hollywood photo lab. "That negative then produced even clearer images."[6]

Soon Lifton had more enlargements printed by a professional. The results solidified his view that he had stumbled upon a major and heretofore unknown piece of photographic evidence. As he examined the prints, he was surprised to find four more possible figures. Most of the five images were murky. "An act of photo interpretation was needed to 'see' my first discovery," he acknowledged. But the last one – the fifth that he had identified – was something else. "He was definitely there," Lifton later wrote, "visible from the waist up, and he was holding something in his hands in a horizontal position."[7]

Lifton finally convinced Ray Marcus to look at his work. Marcus was impressed. "We were both very excited about all of this," Lifton remembered. For reference purposes the two men numbered the images 1 through 5, left to right across the print. The image labelled #2 was the one Lifton had first seen while standing in line in the bookstore. Marcus considered it promising, but when it came to #5 – the one Lifton said "was definitely there" – he had no doubts. "After having enlargements made," Marcus later wrote, "we decided that since #2 (behind the 'puff of smoke') and #5 – and particularly the latter – were the clearest, we would concentrate our efforts on these two."[8]

Maggie Field was as impressed as Ray Marcus. "We had to admit that Dave had truly made a monumental discovery . . . if credit is finally to be due, it goes solely and entirely to Dave Lifton."[9]

Marcus remembered having seen Joseph Ball interviewed on Los Angeles television the previous February. Asked about the possibility of a grassy knoll gunman, Ball had replied, "There was a witness that was above that grassy knoll, in a tower, a railroad tower, who testified that in his opinion, the shots either came from the Texas School Book Depository or the overpass, and that no shots came from where his tower was located . . . there were no people there."[10]

The witness Ball referred to was Lee Bowers. Marcus took note that Ball misrepresented Bowers' testimony. Bowers had been stationed in a railroad tower behind the knoll area, and had in fact testified to seeing two men there behind the fence. He even described what they were wearing. But the important thing now was Ball's 1965 assertion that no one was in that area. Years later Marcus recalled: "I decided I wanted to get, if possible, a more explicit statement of Ball's denial. I did not want to leave open the possibility that, should #5 man be widely publicized, Ball (or others) could then say, yes, we knew about him – he was an innocent bystander – and we can produce him to corroborate that fact."[11]

So he wrote Ball a letter praising the Warren Commission's work. Just in case his own might be recognized as that of a Commission critic, he wrote under an assumed name. His letter included two specific questions: Had Ball heard of speculation that one or more men may have been behind a wall on the knoll? Was there any evidence to support this notion?[12]

Ball wrote back a week later. "I have heard of speculation that there were men secreted behind the wall on the grassy knoll just before the shooting of the President, but I have found no evidence to support such a claim."[13]

In the March 1965 issue of *The Minority of One* – the same issue featuring Harold Feldman's "Fifty-One Witnesses" article – there appeared, without editorial comment, a letter to the editor written by Lillian Castellano, one of the critics who had helped prepare Mark Lane for his Beverly Hills confrontation with Joseph Ball, A.L. Wirin, and Herman Selvin. Headed "Oswald Censored," Mrs. Castellano stated that she had seen a videotaped interview with Lee Oswald on a CBS program broadcast on September 27, 1964, when the Warren Report was first released. She remembered having seen the same interview – also on videotape – on the evening of November 22, 1963. She had paid particular attention to the 1964 replay, she wrote in *TMO*, because she remembered the interview as the only time Oswald appeared frightened. But the 1964 version was different. "The reporter told Oswald that he had been charged with killing the President; Oswald got the frightened look; and then – to my complete surprise – Oswald said, 'I'm a patsy!' That remark had not been in the videotape I heard at the time of the assassination; it evidently had been cut out."[14]

A few months later, on a program marking the first anniversary of the assassination, CBS broadcast another special which again featured numerous clips from the year before. "I set up my tape recorder," Castellano wrote in her letter. "CBS again reproduced the same video-taped interview with Oswald which I had heard twice before. This time, too, Oswald's remark, 'I'm a patsy!' was missing."[15]

The Warren Report conceded that Jack Ruby was among those in the crowded press room when Lee Oswald spoke briefly to the press. "Thus, after the assassination," Mrs. Castellano wrote, "the American public was not permitted by CBS to know that Oswald has said that he was a 'patsy.' But Jack Ruby was in the room when Oswald said it. The definition of a 'patsy' is someone who is being used by others to take the rap or the blame for something the others are guilty of. Jack Ruby certainly knew the meaning of the word."[16]

Mrs. Castellano had been interested in the assassination from the start. "My questioning began the moment I looked at the series of thirty-one small black and white pictures that appeared in the regular edition of *Life* magazine dated November 29, 1963," she said in 1965. Her involvement in Lane's debate with Joseph Ball and the others helped relieve her initial sense of isolation, but studying the case was still a lonely pursuit. "Nobody," she said, "pays any attention to my words concerning this evil set loose on the world by the assassination of our president."[17]

Before the Warren Commission published its report she compiled a long list of problems with the official story. Copies were sent to the Commission, to numerous media outlets, and to anyone else she could think of. "Not one answered me except Thomas Buchanan, the man who wrote *Who Killed Kennedy?*," she recalled. She could not understand the seeming lack of interest on the part of the media. "If it is for 'the good of the country' who is being protected?" she asked. "I do not wish to harm my country but why would it harm us to know the truth?"[18]

When Sylvia Meagher read Mrs. Castellano's letter to *The Minority of One* she wrote the magazine herself.

> Lillian Castellano is quite right in her recollection that Oswald told reporters that he was being framed. The handwritten notes of Seth Kantor, member of the White House Press Corps for Scripps-Howard Alliance, contains the following notation for Friday night:
>
> 7:55 "I'm just a patsy"
>
> Kantor's note is found in Volume XX of the Hearings, page 366, along with many other graphic and fascinating entries.[19]

M.S. Arnoni printed Meagher's letter in the May *TMO*. He sent a copy of the letter to Lillian Castellano before it appeared. Mrs. Castellano in turn wrote to Sylvia thanking her for her corroboration but adding a clarification. "The notation in Seth Kantor's notebook had reference to another time that Oswald referred to himself as a 'patsy.' NBC has the tape where he says 'I'm just a patsy' at 7:55 – CBS has the tape where he says 'I'm a patsy' at the Friday midnight press conference." It was, she felt, very significant – that Oswald had twice declared this to the press, and that on at least two occasions the declaration appeared to have been suppressed. She said she hoped to write Sylvia again in greater detail so that they might compare notes. "It makes me feel much better to know that there are many of us – all seeking the same thing – the truth."[20]

On Thursday, July 8, Sylvia Meagher received a package from Maggie Field. Enclosed were several photographs, and enlarged details of the photographs. In the jargon of that era's younger generation, the photographs blew her mind. "I am sitting here in a state of shock, even after the passage of twelve hours," she wrote to Maggie the next morning.[21]

The package was among that day's mail waiting for her when she arrived home from the World Health Organization. She opened it right away and saw some of the prints that David Lifton and Ray Marcus had been working on for the last few months. "I very nearly fainted," she wrote Maggie. "Not with surprise, for nothing could have surprised me less than the fact of those assassins hiding there on the grassy knoll behind the concrete – [but] with a sense of incredulity [that] here at last was physical evidence to confirm what one was convinced had really happened, and with a sense of rage and anguish for everything that has happened since that photograph was made."[22]

Immediately on that Thursday evening, she had called Joe Lobenthal, the Warren Report class instructor with whom she had remained in contact. "He dropped everything and came right over," Sylvia recalled. "He too saw the three men, as clearly as I did." But they had no time to talk much about what they were seeing and what it meant. Sylvia had to rush to the airport, where her niece was about to leave on a trip to Europe. Lobenthal offered to drive her there and she accepted the offer. She did not get back home for about three hours. Except for wishing her niece a safe flight, she thought of nothing but the photographs the entire time.[23]

When she got home it was nearly midnight, but she immediately telephoned Maggie in Los Angeles. There was no one there. "I shall try again tonight," she wrote the next morning, "but meanwhile, I just had to put this on paper, to try to tell you (and I really can't find words) how grateful I am that you sent me the photographs."[24]

When Sylvia called again, Mrs. Field was home. Maggie told her that the enlargements came from the Moorman photograph, which the Warren Commission had not published. Two men, whom she identified only as "a UCLA student" and "Ray," had done all the work on them. She urged Sylvia to use discretion in showing the photographs to others, and said if the authorities did not previously know about what the Moorman photograph revealed – that is, about the apparent figures in the shadows that emerged in enlargements – they almost certainly did now. That was because the UCLA student, who Maggie said was totally committed but impulsive, had already contacted several critics about the discovery.[25]

The two men were also working on pictures taken by assassination eyewitness Phil Willis, Maggie said. Willis had copyrighted his pictures, but they were asking for permission to use them. In notes on their conversation Sylvia recorded Maggie's reminder of "the danger of indiscreet disclosure, as well as personal danger, which she believes is real."[26]

A few days later Sylvia again showed the photographs to some people she trusted, inviting Bill Crehan, Thomas Stamm, Sylvia's friend Isabel Davis, and another friend named Norma Aitchison to her home. These four had been in Lobenthal's New School class. Also there that night was Curtis Crawford, a Unitarian minister and philosophy instructor at New York University whom Sylvia had come to know. Crawford had spoken on the radio just after the Warren Report was published in September 1964; he had criticized the Commission for what he considered a less than thorough job, but also said that Oswald was probably guilty. Sylvia enjoyed an uneasy relationship with Crawford. She felt he possessed the qualities needed for research and analysis, and indeed the two had briefly considered writing a book together on the case. Yet she could not understand how he could entertain doubts about and criticize the Commission's methods, and still support its conclusions. "I have never been able to grasp his rationale," Sylvia wrote to Maggie Field. "I was hopeful that if he saw the photographic evidence you sent me he might re-convert and apply himself again to the case."27

Everyone who looked at the pictures that evening saw the men in the shadows – everyone but Crawford. "If that was not enough, he was snide and unpleasant," Sylvia wrote, "and took his leave very abruptly and rudely. I think I will give him up as a hopeless case."28

When Maggie wrote Sylvia back a few days after getting her letter, she informed her new friend that their exchanges had given her spirits a much-needed boost. She had been feeling isolated because of her views. Her family and some of her friends, she said, were concerned about her obsession with the assassination. Other friends, she was certain, simply found the subject too painful to explore, and avoided her. They could not believe their government would offer a false document on some inconsequential matter, let alone on something like this. Still other friends, she suspected, simply did not care. Her feelings of isolation, of being so out of step, had led to serious self-doubt. "Despite what is revealed in the pictures," she told Sylvia, "I had reached a kind of impasse, prior to hearing from you, and felt utterly discouraged and spiritless."29

And yet, Maggie said, no matter how explosive and dramatic the implications of the pictures were, they did not represent, in and of themselves, absolute proof of an additional gunman or gunmen on the grassy knoll. "We have never deluded ourselves into thinking that they do or that they could materially alter the situation," Maggie said. The value of the photographs was in demonstrating to someone who had never read the testimony that there was good reason to believe shots were fired from somewhere other than the Book Depository. This was especially true when the photos were presented in combination with key testimony.[30]

Sylvia agreed. The figures the Moorman photograph appeared to reveal were not terribly clear, and while some saw them immediately – such as Lifton, who made out one of the figures even as he stood in line looking at the picture for the first time – others had to study them for a while. Maggie admitted that it had taken her twenty minutes to pinpoint them.[31]

Maggie loved everything her friend was doing. Sylvia's harassment campaign, she said, was inspired. She closed her letter with several questions. Had Sylvia shown the Moorman enlargements to Léo Sauvage? If so, had he seen anything? And second, had she shown anyone the panoply Maggie had sent to her? Was there any reaction to that?[32]

Another photograph arousing interest among the critics was made by a veteran Associated Press photographer named James Altgens. Altgens had taken a series of photographs as the motorcade passed through Dealey Plaza on November 22, including one from a vantage point on Elm Street just as the first shot was fired. "I made one picture at the time I heard a noise that sounded like a firecracker," he told the Warren Commission. "It was almost simultaneously with the shot."[33]

The Warren Commission published this photograph, Altgens' fifth, as Exhibit 203. But long before that, it had gained considerable notoriety. All of the attention was due not for its main subject – President Kennedy, who can be seen through the vehicle's windshield clutching his throat – but for a detail in its background. Standing among the spectators in the doorway of the Texas School Book Depository building was a man bearing an uncanny resemblance to Lee Harvey Oswald. The face seemed the same, and more telling, he seemed to be wearing the same open-necked, rough-textured shirt that Oswald wore when arrested a short time later. Harold Weisberg summed up the obvious: "Oswald could not have simultaneously been a sixth-floor assassin and a first-floor observer."[34]

The Associated Press had Altgens' picture on its wires within half an hour of the assassination. The resemblance between Oswald and the doorway man did not escape the FBI. As early as the evening of Saturday, November 23, agents from its Dallas office had identified and tracked down a Depository employee named Billy Nolan Lovelady. When they showed Lovelady the picture, he told them that the man in the doorway was none other than himself. "Right away I pointed to me and they seemed relieved," he told a reporter some months later. "They said they had a big discussion down at the FBI and one guy said it just had to be Oswald."[35]

In its Report, the Warren Commission stated unequivocally that the man in the doorway was Billy Lovelady, and indeed other Depository employees testified they were there with Lovelady as the President drove by. The Commission noted there was a "passing resemblance" between Lovelady and Oswald, but did not include any photographs to prove it, or do anything to demonstrate that the resemblance between Oswald and the man in the doorway was only a remarkable fluke. Thus most of the critics remained skeptical and were inclined to trust their own eyes. "The man in the doorway might be Oswald's identical twin," Sylvia Meagher observed. "Is the man nevertheless really Billy Lovelady?"[36]

Ray Marcus, already deeply immersed in the #5 man image and Zapruder film analysis, began studying the Altgens photo too. He had the man in the doorway's face greatly enlarged and began marking reference points on a clear sheet of plastic laid over it. The plastic sheet was in turn laid over enlargements of Oswald's face. "They seemed to roughly match," he recalled. "But then I heard the testimony. I said, well, my methods are too crude." Federal authorities undoubtedly had the skills and resources to settle the matter. But where were they? he asked himself. Where were these experts?[37]

Early in 1964 a well-connected New Yorker named Jones Harris was struck by the resemblance between Oswald and the man in the doorway. Harris obtained a print of the picture and arranged to have the man in the doorway detail professionally enlarged. The results served only to heighten his curiosity. Through his lawyer, he arranged a meeting with Warren Commission General Counsel J. Lee Rankin. Nothing was resolved: Harris was told that the Commission already knew about the man in the doorway and was "fascinated" by it. He was asked not to write the article he was then planning, but was not told the FBI had long since identified the man as Billy Lovelady.[38]

But a few weeks after his meeting with Rankin, Harris learned of the Lovelady identification. He was not convinced; he wanted absolute proof Lovelady resembled Oswald and thus might really be the man in the doorway. Things were complicated by the lack of a known photograph of Lovelady, so Harris hired a Fort Worth photographer to take Lovelady's picture surreptitiously. The man spent three fruitless weeks trying to get a snapshot. Ultimately Lovelady, who realized what was going on, confronted the man and called the police.[39]

Shirley Martin also wanted to see for herself what Lovelady looked like. She hired a private investigator to get a picture, but he too failed. Then she assigned the task to two of her children. "I remember walking around the Book Depository with my sister and a camera trying to get a picture of Billy Lovelady," Steve Martin recalled, "the assumption here being that no one would suspect two children." He and Teresa Martin hung around the loading dock watching employees come and go. "I remember they seemed to be mocking us," Teresa said. None of their pictures were useable.[40]

In the spring of 1964 Jones Harris flew to Dallas and managed to talk to Lovelady for about fifteen minutes. Lovelady told him that yes, it was he standing in the doorway in the Altgens photo. Harris conceded there was a resemblance between Lovelady and Lee Oswald. But Lovelady, according to Harris, added a confusing detail: on November 22 he was wearing a red-and-white striped sports shirt that was buttoned near the neck. "The figure in the picture does not appear to be wearing a striped shirt," Harris said.[41]

Eventually an FBI photograph of Billy Lovelady wearing the striped shirt surfaced, and Harold Weisberg published it in *Whitewash II* in 1966. He also found an FBI report stating Lovelady's striped shirt was the one he wore on November 22. And that, Weisberg was beginning to think, might be the ballgame right there. "The government presents no photographic evidence or any testimony or statements of any kind to support the belief that Lovelady is the man in question in the Altgens picture, although it is the crux of the entire case," he wrote, adding, "Any doubt that remains is doubt deliberately intruded by the government and can be interpreted by reasonable men only as proof that it was Oswald and not Lovelady in that doorway."[42]

In 1967 Weisberg received a phone call from a woman who said she was Lovelady's wife. "She insists it is 'my Billy' in the doorway," he reported, and "the FBI never asked [Lovelady] what shirt he had worn that day, and that he had worn a red-and-black check with a white fleck. The checks, she says, are about two inches." And while Lovelady reportedly told Jones Harris he was wearing a striped shirt, he later insisted he had said all along that he was wearing the checked shirt his wife described to Weisberg. Photographs taken the day of the assassination show Lovelady in police headquarters wearing the checked shirt.[43]

Although Harold Weisberg was unconvinced, in time Ray Marcus and others concluded that the man in the doorway really was Billy Lovelady, after all. And the checked shirt that Weisberg wrote about in

1967 may prove it. Fuzzy though they are, scrutiny of the "man in the doorway" enlargements reveal the shirt's apparently checked pattern.[44]

By the time her letter to the editor appeared in the March 1965 issue of *The Minority of One*, Lillian Castellano believed she had found further proof of a coverup in the assassination, "and an attempt to mislead the American public." This went beyond her suspicions engendered by Oswald's "I'm a patsy!" declaration.[45]

Mrs. Castellano had received her set of the twenty-six volumes in January of that year and began studying them closely. Her attention was quickly drawn to missing Z-frames 208 through 211, and the mutilated frame designated 212. "Frame 212 has obviously been torn in half," she said. "Look at the tree."[46]

She also began studying witness testimony, including that of FBI photo expert Lyndal Shaneyfelt, who had prepared the Zapruder film for the Warren Commission. Shaneyfelt had also prepared other photographic evidence, including photographs taken by a bystander named Phil Willis. Shaneyfelt testified that, based on his analysis of the Zapruder film and the fifth of Willis's pictures, the first shot to hit President Kennedy was fired "in the vicinity" of Z-210. He was not more precise than that.

Lillian thought it very strange that while Shaneyfelt believed the first shot came around Z-210, that very frame was among those missing from the film that Shaneyfelt himself had prepared as official evidence. She obtained a copy of a Dealey Plaza map from the surveyor who had made it for the Warren Commission. Using this she was able to establish that the photograph taken by bystander Willis lined up not with Z-210, as Shaneyfelt testified, but with Z-202. The time difference was only a fraction of a second, but was potentially signficant.[47]

Commission attorney Wesley Liebeler had asked Willis about the first shot. "You heard it just about the time you took the picture . . . ?"

"That's right," Willis replied.

"Prior to the time you took the picture . . . ?"

"Absolutely."[48]

Abraham Zapruder was visible in the background of the Willis picture, perfectly aligned with the left shoulder of Secret Service Agent Clint Hill, who was riding on the sideboard of the car just behind JFK's. Zapruder frame 202, meantime, was a reverse angle of the Willis photo; it too showed Hill's shoulder, but aligned with Willis. So the Willis photo, taken just as the first shot was fired, was at the same split second as Z-202. "Note well," Mrs. Castellano wrote, "that the occupants of the car were hidden from the sixth floor window by the foliage of the trees in Frame 202 and did not emerge to be viewed from that window until Frame 210." Which meant that the first shot could not have been fired from Lee Harvey Oswald's alleged sniper's nest.[49]

Sylvia Meagher believed Mrs. Castellano had found something very important. "You have done an excellent and very impressive job," she told her, "and I believe that you have been successful in demonstrating a crucial discrepancy between the 'evidence' and the thesis of the lone assassin." She urged Lillian to develop her findings into an article so that she might reach as wide an audience as possible.[50]

Ray Marcus was equally impressed. He got a copy of the surveyor's map from Mrs. Castellano and used it to make an ingenious chart that enabled him to re-create, for study purposes, Zapruder's camera angles and the movements of the limousine. Lillian's work on the timing of the first shot, he believed, was first rate. "She absolutely proved [the] idea that the first shot was someplace between 210 . . . and 225, was absolutely wrong, that it had been fired earlier."[51]

Over the summer of 1965, David Lifton and Ray Marcus worked steadily to create better and clearer enlargements from the Moorman photo. Lifton had obtained several prints and negatives of the picture from United Press International and the Associated Press. He concluded that the first negative he got – the one from *Four Dark Days in History* – produced the clearest images.[52]

As the summer progressed, Ray Marcus had many sets of enlargements produced. He assembled them into press kits that also included Zapruder film information he had developed, and his own written commentary. All of it, he was certain, pointed strongly to conspiracy.[53]

Marcus went about these tasks very methodically, and with short- and long-term objectives in mind. Only occasionally would the enormity of what he was engaged in be underscored. One such time occurred driving home alone from a photo lab after picking up some new enlargements of the #5 man image. The pictures were beside him on the front passenger seat. The car radio was on; a commentator mentioned a recent statement by Jack Ruby hinting at knowledge of a conspiracy in President Kennedy's assassination. Marcus glanced to his side and stared at the photograph of what almost certainly was a grassy knoll assassin.[54]

During this time Marcus continued his study of the Zapruder film frames; his exacting analysis made him intimately familiar with its most minute details. Before long he would amend his "Hypotheses" to include his belief that Kennedy was struck in the head not once, but twice: ". . . first from the rear, exiting [at the] right side; second, from the right front (probably exiting from the left or left-rear) which knocked him over." These nearly simultaneous shots, he believed, occurred at Z-312 and Z-314. The expert opinions he solicited on ballistics and the appearance of wounds bolstered this hypothesis.[55]

His ongoing study of the film frames led to a curious discovery: that Z-314 and Z-315, as published in the twenty-six volumes, were printed in reverse order. Marcus brought this to the attention of David Lifton and other critics, who agreed that the order of these two frames was incorrect. "In 313 the President's head explodes, visibly and unforgettably," Harold Weisberg said. "The reversal of the two immediately following frames has the effect of reversing the direction in which the President moved in response to the power of the bullet."[56]

In his Zapruder film photo panels, Marcus re-arranged the frames in their proper sequence. A few months later, David Lifton wrote the FBI to ask about the reversal; he received a reply from none other than J. Edgar Hoover. "You are correct in the observation that frames labeled 314 and 315 of Commission Exhibit 885 are transposed in Volume 18 as noted in your letter," Hoover wrote. "This is a printing error and does not exist in the actual Commission Exhibit."[57]

But to call it a mere printing error, Harold Weisberg declared, was indecent – even obscene. "And how many more unadmitted 'printing errors' do we have?"[58]

The press kits Marcus assembled that summer were mailed to about thirty journalists and other public figures. His objective was to influence someone with media access into publicizing the evidence showing the Warren Commission had, for whatever reason, produced an inaccurate Report. The response, he later wrote, was minimal. But there was one notable reply. On August 30 Ray sent one of the packages to Robert F. Kennedy, who had been Attorney General in his late brother's administration and was now a United States Senator from New York. "It is only after considerable hesitation that I send it to you," Marcus had written in a cover letter, "for I realize the personal anguish that the matter must cause you. However I feel an overriding obligation to bring the material to your attention."[59]

Two weeks later he received a brief reply from the Senator. The letter bore no typist's initials and Marcus assumed RFK had typed it himself.

> Dear Mr. Marcus,
>
> I have received your letter and the enclosed material. I just wanted you to know that your interest is appreciated.
>
> With best wishes,
>
> Sincerely,
>
> Robert F. Kennedy [60]

Marcus was very encouraged by this reply. "Although my course of action on the case would not have been affected had I not received a reply, or if it had been negative, his response in my opinion cannot be viewed as intending to discourage serious research."[61]

Writing to Maggie Field in mid-July, Sylvia Meagher said that Léo Sauvage had not been shown the Moorman photograph details that appeared to show gunmen on the grassy knoll. "Frankly, I am still very tempted to tell him about this development," Sylvia wrote, "but on the other hand, he is a working journalist and I am a little fearful." She did not elaborate, and her meaning is ambiguous. Did she fear that Sauvage, as a journalist, would consider the pictures a "scoop," and want to publicize them before any critics were ready? Or – perhaps most likely – did she think that he would be more skeptical than most?[62]

Sylvia said she had the impression that Sauvage's book, while it had yet to appear in English, might represent the end of his involvement in the case. Sauvage had told her that he was surprised she was still preoccupied with the assassination, although he did admit he was impressed that she had been in contact with Eisenberg. Sylvia was concerned about Sauvage's attitude toward Mark Lane, which was decidedly negative, and that he had engaged in a public back-and-forth with Thomas Buchanan in the "Letters" section of *The New Leader*, which had included what Sylvia considered some gratuitous insults. "So I continue to hesitate."[63]

Within a few weeks, however, Sauvage had seen the Moorman photographs. Ray Marcus sent him one of the press kits he had assembled. Sauvage called Meagher in late July on another matter, and then told her about the pictures. He had examined them closely, and with a magnifying glass, and while he thought there might indeed be one or more men in the shadows, he did not consider them particularly worthwhile as evidence. "He sees no weapon," Sylvia wrote in a memo, "and regards the claims about the photos as symptomatic of 'desperate and dishonest' people." The Warren Commission's own published evidence, Sauvage reminded her, was enough to disprove its conclusions.[64]

Sylvia told Maggie that personally, she remained interested in the photographs, although her initial excitement had subsided. "I no longer wake thinking about those murderers nor rush to the photo and the magnifying glass to be sure they are still there." She had shown the pictures to another friend from the New School to test her reaction. Sylvia did not tell her friend what she expected her to see. Rather she covered portions of the photograph and allowed her to inspect one section at a time. In several of the sections, the friend said she saw nothing. Good, Sylvia had told her; you weren't supposed to find anything there. "Then I uncovered the section where the assassins are seen. She did see the first man and the puff of smoke; the man in the hat, she was very uncertain about; the man at the end, she saw clearly."[65]

Sylvia didn't write Maggie anything about another question: Had she shown anyone the panoplies Maggie had sent?

"Panoplies" was the word Maggie Field was using for her adaptation and presentation of the official evidence as published by the Warren Commission in its Report and twenty-six volumes. "It is totally different from any of the other books that have been written on this case because it is not written in narrative," she said. She took the ten conclusions in the Warren Report and affixed each one to the top of a large poster board, one conclusion per board. "Then I've taken the actual testimony, the FBI reports, the Secret Service reports, the Commission exhibits, diagrams, and juxtaposed them against the stated conclusion to show that the evidence in no situation really supports the conclusion that they arrived at." Her objective was to demonstrate with great efficiency that the Commission's conclusions were false.[66]

The police reports and eyewitness testimony indicating shots fired from the grassy knoll area was compelling; when coupled with the photographic work of David Lifton and Ray Marcus they made a powerful case. "Someone who has never read the testimonies or the Report could recognize what we see in the photographs," Maggie said, "but would probably not be sufficiently sure of his ground to go any further than to agree that it is what it appears to be – but – for those of us who do know what the facts of the shots and wounds are, there can be a strong case made."[67]

The Warren Commission's first conclusion stated: "The shots which killed President Kennedy and wounded Governor Connally were fired from the sixth floor window at the southeast corner of the Texas School Book Depository." Maggie compiled a long list of witnesses whose official statements told a different story. These were assembled on a series of 3x5 cards and arranged on a large poster board as a single panoply:

Card 1.
Testimony of U.S. Secret Service Agent Paul Landis, who was riding in the follow-up car immediately behind the presidential car.
Vol. XVIII p. 755

". . . the shot came from somewhere towards the front, right-hand side of the road. . . ."

Card 2.
Testimony of Dep. Sheriff McCarley 11/22/63.
Vol. XIX p. 514

". . . I rushed towards the park & saw people running towards the RR yards . . . & I ran over & jumped a fence & a RR worker stated he believed the SMOKE from the bullets came from the vicinity of a stockade fence which surrounds the park area. . . ."

Card 3.
Testimony of Austin Miller, who was standing on the Triple Underpass bridge.
Vol. XXIV p. 217

". . . I saw something which I thought was SMOKE or steam coming from a group of trees north of Elm, off the RR tracks. . . . "

Card 4.
Testimony of Sam Holland.
Vol. XXIV p. 212

". . . I was standing on the top of the Triple Underpass . . . I heard what I thought for the moment was a fire-cracker . . . I looked over toward the ARCADE & TREES & saw a PUFF OF SMOKE come from the trees & I heard 3 more shots after the 1st shot . . . THE PUFF OF SMOKE definitely CAME FROM BEHIND THE ARCADE, THRU THE TREES."

Card 5.

Testimony of A. Zapruder (who took movies of assassination).

    Vol. VII p. 572

> Liebeler: "As you were standing on this abutment facing Elm St., you say police ran over behind the concrete structure behind you & down the RR tracks behind that, is that right?"
>
> Zapruder: "Yes – after the shots – some of them were motorcycle cops – I guess they left their motorcycles running – & they were running right behind me, of course, IN THE LINE OF THE SHOOTING. I guess they thought it came from right behind me."

Card 6.

Jack W. Faulkner – Nov. 22nd '63.

    Vol. XIX p. 511

> ". . . I asked a woman if they had hit the President & she told me that he was dead – that he had been shot through the head. I asked her where the shots came from & she POINTED TOWARD THE CONCRETE ARCADE ON THE EAST SIDE OF ELM ST. . . .
>
> There were many officers going toward the railroad yard & I joined them in the search for the assassin. . . .[68]

Maggie put in long days over many months in creating her first group of panoplies. "I've been working like a fiend – 8-12 hours per day (why I've not written) trying to get a new series of panoplies together and you know how compelling and absorbing it can be," she told Sylvia in August 1965. In spite of these long and absorbing days, she had started another project. Without being asked to and without seeking approval, she had obtained a copy of *L'Affaire Oswald* and begun translating it. "If you decide to call Sauvage again," she wrote Sylvia Meagher, "you might tell him that I have begun . . . and would be happy to continue and to send him the finished product if he is seeking an English translation." Given her interest in the assassination and all things French, the translation was probably a labor of love.[69]

Yet she was irritated with Sauvage over his attacks on Thomas Buchanan and Mark Lane. His differences with Buchanan, she felt, should have remained private; and to say that Lane had not made any real contributions to the case was unfair. Being human, Mark Lane of course had flaws. But "it was Lane who forced the Commission to face and to admit a number of very significant facets of the case which they would surely have either denied the existence of or omitted entirely . . . one must give him the very substantial amount of credit that is his due."[70]

Chapter 19

More Contacts

I n the early evening hours of August 4, 1965, the house phone in Sylvia Meagher's apartment rang, announcing a visitor at the building's main entrance. She answered the phone and heard a voice say: "This is Salandria."[1]

Although he was totally unexpected, Sylvia was delighted. "Come right up!" she said.[2]

So began the first in-person meeting between Meagher and Vince Salandria. They had a great deal to talk about. Once formalities were out of the way they got right to it. Salandria said he would be seeing the Zapruder film slides at the National Archives in less than one week. Zapruder's was easily the most important film of the assassination, but there were others, like those made by Orville Nix and Marie Muchmore. Salandria said he hoped to see these too, but Sylvia was doubtful. When she had been at the archives just a few weeks earlier, she'd been told there were no facilities for viewing motion pictures, and to the best of her knowledge no slides of these other films had been made.[3]

Salandria had brought something for Sylvia: a set of photographs, at least some of them similar to the Moorman photo enlargements Maggie Field had sent Sylvia nearly a month before. Like Maggie's, these copies had come from David Lifton, but Salandria saw a new detail: yet another man, whom Salandria believed was wearing headphones. He had first noticed this detail on page 19 of *Four Days*, UPI's minute-by-minute account of the assassination weekend. Salandria pinpointed the possible figure at "3 1/4 inches from the right of page 19 in the upper portion along the top of the wall." This image dovetailed with a theory of a radio-coordinated assassination developed by a man named Griscom Morgan of Yellow Springs, Ohio, a correspondent of Salandria's who had contacted him after reading his articles in *Liberation*.[4]

Morgan was so convinced that his theory represented important new evidence that he alerted both Earl Warren and Senator John Sherman Cooper. Warren didn't write him back, but Cooper, in what was plainly a formality, thanked Morgan for his interest. "As a member of the Commission, I can say we examined every aspect of the matter from many sources of testimony and evidence and it is my view that the conclusions of the Commission indicate as close as it is possible the events that occurred that tragic day."[5]

Salandria asked Sylvia about her subject index, which was nearing completion. In his opinion the Index would be very useful – not only an essential tool for anyone delving into the Hearings and Exhibits, but perhaps even lucrative to its author, since anyone with a set of volumes would need it. Sylvia was anxious to complete the index and get back to the case itself. She had never really stopped her research: at the time of Salandria's visit she was working on her comparative study of the Warren Report and the Hearings and Exhibits. The study would be published as *Accessories After the Fact* in 1967 and become a classic in the field, but in August 1965 it was still in development; almost no one had seen it. Sylvia had sent a few sections to Maggie Field in July, and Maggie had been the first to read them. Sylvia was deeply gratified by her favorable response.[6]

Salandria reacted with great enthusiasm when Sylvia showed him a manuscript section called "Where Did the Shots Come From?" It cited Harold Feldman's "Fifty-one Witnesses: The Grassy Knoll" to support the idea of shots coming from the right-front of the limousine. The Commission had conceded that none of the Secret Service agents assigned to the motorcade had stayed in Dealey Plaza after the assassination, instead accompanying the mortally wounded President to Parkland Hospital. Yet three Dallas officers – Seymour Weitzman, D.V. Harkness, and Officer Joe Marshall Smith – reported contacts, in the minutes after the assassination, with men identifying themselves as agents. Officer Smith told the Commission that he had searched the knoll area after an hysterical eyewitness directed him there. He encountered a man who immediately showed him Secret Service credentials.[7]

Sylvia was appalled that the Warren Commission had not followed up on what Officer Smith told them. If no Secret Service agents remained in Dealey Plaza, who could the man with the Secret Service identification have been? "I suggest that he was one of the assassins, armed with false credentials," Meagher wrote in her manuscript. "The men who identified themselves as Secret Service agents, to Harkness and to Smith, by the Commission's own account could not have been genuine agents . . . who, then, were the men who claimed to be but could not have been Secret Service agents? Was there any conceivable *innocent* reason for such impersonation?"[8]

Salandria had apparently not seen Officer Smith's testimony before, but he immediately grasped its importance. It represented a greater discovery, he said, than Sylvia realized. "This was a major find, in his view," she wrote in her notes, "because it furnished an essential link in his own theory by indicating a method by which the assassins could take over an area of the grassy knoll, with immunity from interference or suspicion, by posing as agents."[9]

Vince described to Sylvia the trip he had made to Dallas with Harold and Immie Feldman a year before. "Salandria has spent considerable time with Marguerite Oswald," Sylvia wrote in notes of the evening. "She is a very intelligent, shrewd but somewhat paranoic woman, with a strange regard and respect for the Government which Salandria feels corresponds with LHO's own seeming inconsistency – that of some genuine leftist convictions (which I personally regard as continuous and strongly motivating in his life) and his seeming role of undercover agent."[10]

Salandria told Sylvia a little about a man of whom he had grown very suspicious. "I am not too clear on this," she wrote in her notes, "but Salandria is on to a man named Boganov or something similar; he has obtained considerable information on Boganov through the mechanics of a credit rating check." Boganov was mentally unstable, a skilled rifleman, and was, Salandria believed, in Dallas at the time of the assassination. His investigation into this man was ongoing.[11]

The hour was growing late, but Salandria and Meagher remained deep in conversation. Vince said he could not understand why, right after Lee Oswald's arrest on November 22, the high echelons in Washington would have sent out word that there was no conspiracy in the assassination. There were no grounds for such a conclusion at that early time, and yet that message was sent to Air Force One and a Cabinet jet bound for Japan. Salandria also told Meagher about Shirley Martin, for whom he had a high regard. Vince would soon be visiting the Martin home in Oklahoma. From there, he and Shirley would travel to Dallas together.[12]

Salandria offered the opinion that Mark Lane was ill-mannered but had made some important contributions to the case, such as forcing the Warren Commission to confront some issues it would otherwise have ignored. A book by Lane, he said, could not fail to be interesting. George and Pat Nash had dropped out of the case – not only that, but were in support of the lone-assassin theory. Sylvia was astonished to hear that, but Salandria pointed out the Nashes were never really anti-Warren Report, as was plain from their article in *The New Leader*. He had not yet read Léo Sauvage's book, because he did not read French.[13]

Finally, Salandria stood to go. It was nearly midnight; they had talked for five hours.[14]

Five days later Salandria kept his appointment at the National Archives, arriving there early on the morning of August 9. In spite of Sylvia Meagher's prediction, he was ushered into a viewing room and shown, in motion, the home movies of the assassination taken by Orville Nix, Marie Muchmore, and Abraham Zapruder. To record his impressions he carried a small tape recorder.[15]

The viewing began just before 8 a.m. with the Nix film. This film was taken by air conditioning engineer Orville Nix, who had been positioned along Main Street just south of Houston. His view was opposite that of Abraham Zapruder. This reverse angle was about the same as Mary Moorman's Polaroid photograph, meaning the Nix film revealed the grassy knoll area. Salandria hoped it might reveal the man that David Lifton and Ray Marcus were talking about.[16]

Nix shot his home movie using indoor film and without a filter that would compensate for outdoor light, resulting in a graininess that Salandria noticed immediately. "The film is rather poor in quality and very blurred," he said into his microphone. He asked the projectionist to stop the film and repeat key sequences several times. "There is conceivably smoke on that concrete structure on the left hand side where Lifton thought it was. It looks like it could very well be." But he could not be sure.[17]

One of the most important features of the Nix film is that it plainly shows many of the witnesses in Dealey Plaza surging toward the grassy knoll area after the fusillade was over. Nix himself thought the shots came from behind the fence on top of the knoll's grassy slope.[18]

Following the assassination sequence, the film grew very dark. "Not too much value in the Nix film," Salandria concluded. It might yield more, he suggested, if slides were made from its frames. "Very poor quality film. Very poor."[19]

Next, the Muchmore film was threaded into a projector and shown. Marie Muchmore had also been opposite Zapruder, and her film is from an angle similar to Nix's. "I can say that on the area that Lifton said he saw smoke there conceivably is," Salandria said as the film played. He would not venture a more definitive statement. Salandria did not seem to have been too interested in this film; he had little else to say.[20]

The Zapruder film came next. "Here comes the car," Salandria said as it began. The presidential limousine is first seen having just turned onto Elm Street. It was escorted by several motorcycle policemen.

"Connally turns around, Kennedy reaches for his throat, and then 313 of course and Kennedy seems blown over to the left by the impact of the shot."[21]

After this Salandria was able to inspect all of the slides made from the Zapruder film. Generally his impressions were in line with those of Sylvia Meagher and Ray Marcus, but there was one important exception: determining at what point Governor Connally was hit. "My distinct impression is he was hit at 292, 293, 294, and he's falling back and reacting to the hit," Salandria said. "This I know is a minority view but I feel that this [is] when Governor Connally is hit."[22]

Salandria had spoken with Marion Johnson and, like Sylvia Meagher, asked him why frames 208 through 211 were missing. Although this question had recently come up, and remained an unresolved issue, Johnson said he thought the slides were easily at hand. "Oh, we have those frames," he told Vince. He went through his collection and, Salandria said later, seemed surprised that they were not there. "He assumed that the Archives had them. He was wrong and he learned then that he was wrong. I'm sure he was not pretending, he just did not know they were missing." Johnson did not have an adequate explanation, Salandria said, and Johnson seemed to realize his comments were totally inadequate.[23]

On September 2, Thomas Stamm visited the Archives for his own inspection of the available films. He spent a little over three hours there, and like Salandria saw the Nix and Muchmore films in addition to Zapruder's movie and slides. He was received and treated, he wrote in a nine-page report on his visit, very courteously.[24]

All three of the films, Stamm observed, were kept in ordinary commercial cardboard containers. Each bore a typewritten label identifying its contents a "Copy" film. But on each label the word "original" was handwritten in red crayon. Stamm thought that was to make the film title conform to the wording in the Hearing and Exhibits' Table of Contents.[25]

Stamm was in agreement with Salandria about the value of the first two films he was shown. "The Nix and Muchmore films are of poor photographic quality and have little, if any, evidentiary value," he wrote in his unpublished report. He had seen the #5 man enlargements from the Moorman photo the previous month in Sylvia Meagher's home, and like Salandria watched closely during the sequence when the grassy knoll area appeared. For Stamm, the film revealed nothing in this respect. "It was impossible to establish the presence of persons in front of or behind the pergolas." A little over one year later, an inspection of a single Nix frame would point to a different conclusion.[26]

Of the Zapruder film, Stamm wrote:

> As has been noted by other critics of the Warren Commission and its Report, frames #208-211 inclusive are missing, and frames #207 and #212 are spliced horizontally and crudely. No explanation for the omission is available at the National Archives. This omission may be characterized as an excision in view 1) of the splicing, and 2), as noted by others, the reproduction in black and white of frame #210 as Commission Exhibit 893 on page 89 of Volume XVIII of the Hearings. Whether these frames have any bearing on moot points cannot be determined in their absence . . . In the absence of these frames and of a definite and verifiable explanation for their omission, the motivation for their excision must remain a matter for speculation and of criticism of the Warren Commission for its mishandling of this important material.[27]

In motion, the Zapruder film took about half a minute to run, Stamm wrote. Since it afforded a continuous view of the occupants of the car, it was of decisive importance, establishing a context and frame of reference for the assassination. After his viewing of the film, Stamm concluded there was no longer any room for doubt about the question of conspiracy.

> Of greatest importance in the film is the sequence of the fatal shot and its aftermath. . . .
> The sudden explosive violence with which President Kennedy is slammed back against the rear seat is unmistakable. It is within the realm of speculative possibility that the violent backward thrust of the President was caused by the sudden acceleration of the limousine as Secret Service Agents Kellerman and Greer, in the front seats, made their effort to escape the murder site and obtain medical help at Parkland Hospital. Against that thesis is the fact that Mrs. Kennedy is obviously not thrust back but maintains her position while the President gyrates back, forward, and into her arms. Against that thesis, also, is the testimony of Governor and Mrs. Connally, as noted in the Report: "Mrs. Connally heard a second shot fired and pulled her husband down into her lap. . . . The Governor was lying with his head on his wife's lap when he heard a shot hit the President. At that point, both Governor and Mrs. Connally observed brain

tissue splattered over the interior of the car. According to Governor and Mrs. Connally, it was after this shot that Kellerman issued his emergency instructions and the car accelerated" (p. 50). No other testimony relating to this point is adduced in the Report and the Commission apparently accepted the testimony of the Governor and his wife as factual.

The violent backward thrust of President Kennedy occurs, to the eye, at the instant of impact of the fatal shot. The two events appear to be simultaneous and to have an obvious relationship of cause and effect. The service of truth requires no other explanation.

That President Kennedy could have been violently thrust back against the rear seat in consequence of a bullet fired from above and behind him, seems a manifest impossibility. This sequence in the Zapruder film, occupying a mere fraction of a second, invalidates the official autopsy finding and demolishes the Commission's thesis and findings of a lone gunman firing from the southeast corner, 6th-floor window of the TSBDB. It makes of the Report a monstrous fabrication erected to obscure the truth which must now be disinterred despite the official verdict.

Thomas Stamm
Sept. 8, 1965 [28]

By late summer 1965 Shirley Martin had been exchanging letters with Vince Salandria and Harold Feldman for over a year. Sometimes they sent audio tapes back and forth to speed up the process. Mostly their discussions centered on the assassination, but they occasionally drifted into personal areas. Vince began some letters "Dear Martin Family," and directed asides to specific family members. Shirley wrote warm letters to Vince's wife and young son. At Christmas in 1964, Mrs. Salandria had sent a fruitcake that was much appreciated. A few weeks later she commented to Shirley, "'Oswald' is the most spoken word in our house." [29]

But for the most part Salandria and Mrs. Martin stuck to the case, discussing certain points and sharing information. "I can't thank you enough for the article by Ruark," Shirley wrote. "We had missed this one completely and it has given us a shot in the arm second to none." This was an item by Robert C. Ruark, a newspaper columnist and amateur big-game hunter. Ruark related a conversation with his friend Walter Johnson, a professional hunter of many years' experience. "What Walter and I cannot understand, among other findings of the Warren Report, is how a bullet fired from behind could tear the back of President Kennedy's head off. I am speaking only as a semi-professional white hunter, but Walter is all pro, and he agrees with me . . . Walter Johnson and I have read the report scrupulously, several times, and the ballistic end of it makes no sense." Carl Marzani included the item in the *Critical Reactions to the Warren Report* anthology he published, and Mark Lane's CCI used it in one of its newsletters. "It is, of course, what all of us have been saying all along," Shirley wrote to Vince.[30]

Shirley occasionally chided Salandria about his dislike of JFK. "President Kennedy took the power he had so narrowly won and attempted to do with it what was possible. The impossibilities were not his cup of tea . . . he was never an Ivory Tower dreamer." A few days later Salandria wrote back: "In spite of myself I think that you are changing my view of JFK. I will confess that he was an enormously charming and courageous man. Now, there, beautiful Shirley, that must pass as a concession on my part."[31]

Shirley had become friendly with Marguerite Oswald to the point that she affectionately referred to her as "Mama O." She even invited her to visit the Martin home. Shirley was concerned for her welfare. "Mama O called this morning," she wrote Salandria. "She is still upset about the surveillance." Marguerite, a resident of Fort Worth, had been placed under police surveillance during a visit to Dallas by Vice President Hubert Humphrey. Fort Worth authorities confirmed the surveillance but declined to say who had requested it. It was maintained until after Humphrey left town. Marguerite said an officer had followed her car, and that it had been very obvious. "I thought the man was going to shoot me, or something else," she told *The Fort Worth Star Telegram*. "I'm a nervous wreck." The whole situation, she said, was asinine. Salandria was moved to write her. "Please allow me to feel ashamed for the police force of Fort Worth . . . this is a despicable business."[32]

By the spring of 1965 Salandria and the Martins were discussing the possibility of a joint trip to Dallas. Shirley had made multiple trips by this time but Salandria had been there just once. Travelling together seemed a logical step.

The families talked about it for several months. "The Dallas idea en masse sounds wonderful," Shirley wrote, "if we can go in separate cars. Vickie and I could go in one car and you people in another." They agreed that the Salandrias would drive to Hominy and, after a short stay, Vince would drive to Dallas with Mrs. Martin and Vickie. On May 13 Vickie wrote Salandria and teased, "Mother says to tell you she has a few repair jobs around the house and yard this summer, so bring your tools."[33]

The trip was planned as a one-day event. They wou'
through the night, talk to as many people as they cou'
back. As they left Hominy, local police pulled them o
an officer cautioned, "we see you are on your way on a ι.
With that they were allowed to continue. The drive atte.
uneventful and they reached Dallas shortly after dawn. They we..
straight to Dealey Plaza, arriving around 6:30 in the morning.[34]

They had not been there long when a man neither of them knew approached. He was a big man, wore sandals, and appeared to be in his mid-fifties. "How is Mark Lane?" the man said to Salandria.

Salandria stared back at him and, taken aback, said nothing.

"Do you know what this is?" the man asked, indicating the area around them.

"Dealey Plaza."

"No," the man said. "Do you know what it *is*?"

"I guess I don't."

"Well, this is a WPA project," the man replied. "A socialist project where a socialist president was killed. The next time you write an article, mention that."

Then, after telling Salandria that the Holocaust was an "historical accident," the man walked slowly away.[35]

Later they paid a visit to Helen Markham, the Dallas waitress who was the Warren Commission's star witness in the shooting of Officer Tippit. It was a wasted effort. As during the year before, Markham was reluctant to talk; again she said that she had to babysit her grandchildren. Salandria felt that what little she did say was evasive and self-contradictory.[36]

A stop by the home of Michael and Ruth Paine was a little more productive. It appears that the Paines were expecting Shirley Martin, but they didn't know Vince was coming. Yet Salandria recalled that Michael Paine immediately asked him, "Why are you working on the assassination? Why don't you stick to your work in civil liberties and civil rights?"[37]

A few weeks later Salandria described some of the conversation. "Michael Paine advised us under questioning of a cross-examination nature, that Oswald was serving as a spy in right wing organizations," he said. "I did not ask him, nor did he offer any explanation as to the reasons why and for whom Oswald was spying." Based on their discussions, he concluded that Michael Paine knew Oswald well – better than his Warren Commission testimony suggested.[38]

Their final stop that day was in Forth Worth, at the home of Marguerite Oswald. How long they stayed there and exactly what transpired are not known. But as he looked around the house it seemed to Salandria that Marguerite's financial situation had improved since his visit a year before. There was an uneasy period when Shirley and Marguerite talked privately as Salandria waited out of earshot. Salandria found this unusual.[39]

After they left, Salandria asked Shirley about Marguerite's improved finances. "Shirley told me that Marguerite had received money from good people who were interested in her welfare," he recalled. These people were not identified. Asked about this many years later, Shirley recalled the incident but did not give it any importance. Marguerite had always offered a spirited defense of her son. But had someone tried to buy her silence? "If Marguerite was bought off because she needed money," Shirley said, "she did it deliberately, and used the money, and didn't change her thinking one iota."[40]

Vince and Shirley began the long drive back to Hominy. Along the way, as Salandria recalled it, Shirley lost her temper for no apparent reason – the first time either had raised a voice toward the other. "She said that she would give up the work on the assassination, if she were provided with enough money so that she could raise horses." Long after the fact, Shirley was asked about this, too, but did not remember making that remark.[41]

Exhausted after a full day, and happy to get home, the travelers at last reached Hominy. Shirley was at the wheel and driving within the speed limit, but was pulled over and issued a speeding ticket.[42]

Many years later Salandria reviewed the circumstances of the Dallas trip. The most glaring fact, it seemed to him, was that he and Shirley were – or at least, he was – under surveillance, presumably by those connected in some way to the assassination plot. They had been pulled over by police as they left Hominy. Salandria had been approached in Dealey Plaza by a man who made it plain he knew who he was. Michael Paine also made it plain he knew who he was, and suggested Salandria stick to civil liberties work. Shirley Martin, perhaps under unknown pressures, had attacked him. They were pulled over a second time on their return.

"The only plausible explanation," Salandria concluded, "was that the killers were advertising to me that my efforts to maintain a low profile in the case were unsuccessful. They were also telling me that I could no longer trust my most loving friends. They were instructing me that I was being watched by the agents of the killers. They were advising me that I had a safe haven, if I gave up the assassination work and continued in my American Civil Liberties Union work . . . they were transparently advertising to me that they had great power, and that I had none."[43]

This surveillance, if it were really there, might have been extended to Shirley Martin as well. Federal authorities certainly knew of her activities. Ruth Paine had told two FBI agents about Shirley's visit to the Paine home in February 1964. And in the summer of 1964, during the same Dallas trip when she had interviewed Acquilla Clemons, Shirley had contacted eyewitness Lee Bowers. But Bowers told her he did not want to be interviewed, and had immediately notified the FBI that she had contacted him.[44]

Not long after he returned to Philadelphia, Salandria wrote to Sylvia Meagher and told her about the trip, and in a subsequent phone call told her even more. "He takes seriously Michael Paine's apparent allegation that Oswald was an infiltrator and/or spy in right-wing groups, and not necessarily for left-wing groups," Sylvia wrote in her notes. She thought that Salandria made a strong case for some sort of clandestine relationship between Oswald and a federal agency. But she tended to argue against it, she told a friend, on purely subjective grounds.[45]

Salandria talked at some length about a new article he was working on based on his viewing of the Zapruder film and slides at the National Archives. He was convinced, he told Meagher, that Governor Connally was hit at Z-292. He hoped to place the article in *Liberation*, but there was some kind of struggle going on within the magazine, with one faction opposed to any further articles on the assassination.[46]

At the beginning of August, Tom Stamm had suggested that the time had come for some of the critics to get together and exchange ideas. Sylvia agreed, and had begun to arrange such a meeting. The target date was sometime in early October, and it would be at Sylvia's apartment. Maggie Field would be passing through New York on her way to Paris, and she and Sylvia were already planning to meet at that time. If all went well, Mrs. Field would be able to attend. Sylvia asked Salandria if he would be interested in coming, and Vince said he would be delighted to. He would bring his wife along and plan to stay all day.[47]

There were ten names on Sylvia's original guest list, most of them people from the New School course. But Maggie Field was the one she was most looking forward to seeing. Yet she was apprehensive – concerned that work on her subject index had gone beyond mere compulsion and become something far more demanding. With her own energies similarly focused, Maggie might understand. "I should warn you that I am turning into some kind of monster – I find myself at times alien to myself, and understanding for the first time the kind of cold arrogant ruthlessness of men like Gauguin and others possessed by a force so compelling that they submitted willingly . . . I am confiding this against the impulse of self-protection, because I think that in your own way you are feeling similar stresses and strains, and above all a corrosive weariness and sometimes hopelessness that is black and evil. So please do be lenient with me, when we meet. . . ."[48]

The work the small band of critics was engaged in was important, Sylvia believed. Ultimately she hoped it would keep them united. "The few of us who are bound together by the WR must hold hands for comfort as we proceed deeper into the night of our discoveries."[49]

Chapter 20

The Meeting

As the summer of 1965 drew to a close Sylvia Meagher was working feverishly to complete her index to the Warren Commission's published material, sometimes going entire days without ever setting foot outside her apartment. "I did not even go out to the incinerator yesterday in my transport of indexing," she told Maggie Field. Reluctantly, in August, she took a few days off to fly to Miami to see her father. The trip meant more time away from the indexing that was consuming her, and was painful, she told Maggie, because it reminded her of the losses both she and her father had suffered, those that had left her feeling saturated with death. Equally painful was not having seen him in nearly a year.[1]

Adding to Sylvia's stress was concern over her other big project, the comparative study of the conclusions of the Warren Report and the evidence presented in the twenty-six volumes. "Will I ever find a publisher?" she asked Maggie in late July. "And if I do, am I prepared to sacrifice my job by publishing under my own name?" She would confront that if and when the time came. In the meantime her manuscript, by then 225 pages long and growing, would remain in development.[2]

Maggie Field was supportive: the index was important, she told Sylvia, because it filled a void. It would constitute a unique contribution that would be valuable to present researchers and those in the future. But in spite of this encouragement Sylvia was flagging. In late August she informed Maggie that work on the index was taking a severe toll on her health. "I am sitting here, nauseated and sick, fearful of a real collapse, because I have been grinding out the index so mercilessly." It was no joke, she said. She simultaneously held down her job at the World Health Organization, kept on track with the index and her comparative study, and looked after other assassination-related matters that, she said, seemed to crop up almost daily. At present Sylvia was rankled over an article in *Life* magazine about the alleged assassination rifle, which she had read with a mix of exasperation and rage. "This kind of development is one of the things that has made me, for the first time in memory, neglect my work at the office," she told Maggie. The article contained a number of contradictions and misrepresentations. For example, it quoted FBI firearms expert Robert Frazier's referring to the weapon as "a very strong, sturdy rifle." But it neglected another FBI expert, one in fingerprints, who told the Warren Commission it was "a cheap old weapon." Other testimony and documents in the Commission's twenty-six volumes spoke to its inferiority.[3]

Sylvia was so incensed that she called *Life* and got the article's author, Keith Wheeler, and outlined to him its deficiencies. "He was very interested," she reported to Maggie, "and I thought honest on the whole; his research in the Hearings and Exhibits was limited to consulting the sources indicated in the [Warren Report] footnotes – which of course is a trap and the very reason I am ruining my health and shortening my life by preparing the subject index."[4]

Wheeler had grown curious about how she was so knowledgeable, so she told him about the index she was preparing. "What a ghastly job!" he cried. But he was interested; he even recommended his literary agent after Meagher told him she was a novice writer. Perhaps in time, she told Maggie, she could develop this contact with Wheeler, and approach him about arranging to see the original Zapruder film, which *Life* then kept under lock and key.[5]

Once she was certain that Maggie would be passing through New York *en route* to Paris, and was interested in attending the critics' meeting, Sylvia grew excited. She warned her friend that she would be tempted to monopolize her time but promised to guard against that. She would invite as many critics and their associates to her home as possible, and make sure Maggie got to meet everyone.[6]

Sylvia had a word of caution, however. Some of the critics, like Tom Stamm, had suggested that they all organize their efforts in some way in order to work more efficiently. Sylvia believed that would be a serious mistake. "I think the degree of voluntary cooperation that we have now is heartwarming and good, and any attempt to formalize these relationships among individuals or small groups of collaborators would be disastrous." Better they all gather informally to exchange information and points of view, assess where they were and where they were headed.[7]

By early September the plans were firming up. Maggie would arrive in New York on October 2, a Saturday, and she and Sylvia would spend an evening getting better acquainted. The meeting would take place the next day. In addition to Maggie Field, Sylvia was expecting Vince Salandria and his wife, Joe Lobenthal, Léo Sauvage, Thomas Stamm, Bill

Crehan, and Sylvia's friends Norma Aitchison and Isabel Davis. Sylvia hoped that Fred Cook would also be in attendance, though she had not yet invited him.[8]

Meanwhile Maggie kept Sylvia apprised of developments as she heard them. Ray Marcus was "completely fed up" with David Lifton, at least in part because of Lifton's contacts with eyewitness Phil Willis, whom Marcus did not trust. Marcus had told Lifton not to call him any more. Mark Lane was in Europe finishing his book on the case, and hoped to have it published in England that fall. Ed Epstein, the Cornell student who had interviewed many Warren Commission members and staff for his doctoral thesis, would publish the thesis in book form early in 1966.[9]

As the day of the meeting drew closer, two more names were added to the list of attendees: Epstein and Jones Harris. Sylvia was a little irritated at how this had come about. She had called Harris, the man who had an early interest in the "man in the doorway" detail from the Altgens photograph, to invite him to the meeting. "To my surprise," Sylvia wrote to Maggie, "Harris had already been invited and was planning to come! It seems Salandria (without consulting or informing me) had invited Harris and that Ed Epstein, hearing that Harris was intending to be here, told Harris (but not me) that he would come in from Ithaca for the occasion and accompany Harris. I suspect you will join me in lifting at least one eyebrow at such dubious decorum – but in such a small coterie, I suppose we will have to take each other as we come." Sylvia had earlier called Epstein to invite him but he had declined. She was now expecting about a dozen people, "providing that Salandria is not planning to spring any more surprises, and I can just about manage enough chairs."[10]

Sylvia was not entirely happy that Jones Harris was coming. In telephone conversations he struck her as warm and outgoing, a man who was highly sophisticated, literate, and intelligent. But some of the things he said bothered her. During one conversation he slipped in "those vaguely patriotic and anti-Left remarks that put me off like nothing else." Harris was convinced that the Warren Commission would in time be discredited, she said, but gave no hint of anger or outrage over its Report. Where Sylvia was inclined to believe Oswald was innocent, Harris felt that he was definitely implicated in the assassination. He considered Oswald a man of no scruples who would engage in any antisocial or criminal act if there were a big payoff in store for him. Sylvia thought Harris was preoccupied with the fact that Bernard Weissman and Jack Ruby were Jewish, and was irritated when he asked Sylvia if she were, too. He assured her, in asking, that he was Jewish himself. "I pointed out that regardless of my origins or political sympathies," Sylvia said, "if I was personally satisfied that a Leftist, a Jew, or even Oswald was guilty, nothing on earth would persuade me to keep silent."[11]

When all was said and done, Sylvia wrote Maggie Field, it seemed to her that Harris's views on not only Oswald, but on the United States and politics in general, were in sharp contrast to her own and, she felt certain, to Maggie's – as well as Tom Stamm's, Isabel Davis's, and Salandria's. "This leads me to wonder how orderly and objective we can be when we are all together."[12]

On September 24 Sylvia called Fred Cook to invite him to the meeting. Cook was the journalist who, in the days after the assassination, had tried without success to convince *The Nation* editor Carey McWilliams that he was on to something important, after his preliminary investigations suggested the Mannlicher Carcano was an inferior weapon. McWilliams' lack of interest left Cook with no alternative but to return to the work he'd been developing before November 22. The overwhelming media approval of the Warren Report following its release nearly a year later deeply impressed him. He had not had the time to read it himself, but the endorsements of the major media – all three television networks, *The New York Times*, and the rest – convinced him that his initial skepticism had been unfounded.[13]

Then, alone one evening with nothing better to do, Cook began flipping through a paperback edition of the Report. In spite of his acceptance of the Commission's findings, two questions still nagged him: the identification of Oswald in a sixth floor window by Howard Brennan, seated along the motorcade route at ground level, and Governor Connally's certainty that he had been hit by a separate shot than the one which first struck President Kennedy.[14]

Just after the assassination, as he walked the streets of New York by himself, Cook had looked up at people in the fifth- and sixth-floor windows. "I found I couldn't tell how tall the men were or what they looked like," Cook said. "Yet the Commission had accepted Brennan's description, despite the physical difficulties involved."[15]

As for Connally, Fred Cook was impressed by the governor's account of the assassination and the fact that he had been around firearms for most of his life. That he was positive he had heard the first shot, and that a second shot had hit him, carried a great deal of weight. As Cook read through the Warren Report alone that night, he recalled long afterward, he found it "falling to pieces in my hands."[16]

And so he began outlining an article. As before he met with resistance: from his agent, from Carey McWilliams again, even from his wife. Finally, in the summer of 1965, he interested *Ramparts* magazine. With the assurance of a paycheck, Cook went ahead with the article.[17]

Cook limited himself to the assassination proper. He was convinced he was on very solid ground, and that he could demonstrate conclusively there was more than one assassin. The key, he believed, was the Zapruder film. As he wrestled with the meaning of all those black-and-white frames, he received some unexpected help.[18]

Ray Marcus was an admirer of Fred Cook and considered him a journalist of exceptional skills. He read his work in *The Nation*, and his books, like *The FBI Nobody Knows*, an exposé of the then-sacrosanct federal police agency. He had been expecting Cook to produce an article shredding the Warren Report and was surprised when none appeared. Undeterred by the experience with I.F. Stone, he wrote to Cook in the summer of 1965, and included one of the press kits with Moorman photo details, blowups from the Zapruder film, and commentary adapted from his Hypotheses.[19]

Cook wrote back excitedly. "Of all the fantastic coincidences!" he said. "You may not believe this, but it is true. Your package of material on the Kennedy assassination arrived here yesterday as I was sitting down to the typewriter, working on the first pages of a long article analyzing the Warren Report – and taking it pretty much apart. Some of the things you sent me helped a lot."[20]

Fred Cook described all of this to Sylvia Meagher on the telephone the night she called him. He simply could not understand the attitude of Carey McWilliams, he said; but the article was nevertheless done and *en route* to *Ramparts*. He said he wasn't sure he'd be able to attend the meeting, as he might be out of town. But if he were at all able, he'd be there.[21]

After she reached Paris, Maggie Field reflected on her brief stay in New York and on meeting Sylvia Meagher and so many other critics in person. The visit, she said, had been profoundly rewarding – for the colleagues she met, and in particular for getting closer to Sylvia, "a dedicated co-worker . . . but more importantly, a friend. I was truly touched by your hospitality, interest and attention in the midst of your staggeringly busy schedule."[22]

The meeting of what Sylvia was calling "Warrenologists" took place on Sunday, October 3, 1965. In addition to Sylvia and Maggie Field, those present included the Salandrias, Isabel Davis, Edward Jay Epstein, Joe Lobenthal, Tom Stamm, Bill Crehan, and Léo Sauvage. As it turned out, neither Fred Cook nor Jones Harris was able to attend, nor was Norma Aitchison.[23]

The idea for such a meeting was not entirely new. As early as July 1964, Vince Salandria had proposed such a gathering to Mark Lane. "He seemed to like it," Salandria told Shirley Martin at the time, "but he has made no follow-up." The plan seems to have gone no further.[24]

Most of those present had projects of one kind or another underway. Tom Stamm was circulating his paper, "On Viewing the Zapruder Film and Slides, and the Nix and Muchmore Films of the Assassination of President Kennedy," completed less than a month earlier; Sylvia ended up incorporating a portion of it in her comparative study. Joe Lobenthal was developing a play based entirely on Warren Commission testimony, and evidence found in Hearings and Exhibits.[25]

Léo Sauvage had just completed three articles that were about to be published in a national magazine. The first was due soon, in the November 22, 1965, issue of *The New Leader*. His book *The Oswald Affair* remained in limbo, but he was still looking for an American publisher.

Vince Salandria also had a new article, although it was still some months from publication. It was based in part on his recent trip to the National Archives, and he planned to read an excerpt at the meeting.

Finally things got underway. Maggie Field had brought with her a collection of photographs of Lee Oswald, and everyone looked them over, noting some of the anomalies she pointed out. In photographs taken only six months apart, Oswald in one had a full head of thick hair, and in another, thinning hair. And in Commission Exhibit 133-B, one of the notorious "backyard" photographs of Oswald armed with the Mannlicher-Carcano and a pistol, his left arm was positioned in a way Maggie thought was anatomically impossible. The group examined some of Maggie's panoplies, which she told them were designed to show a non-student of the case at a glance that the Warren Commission's assertions were fraudulent. These seem to have made an excellent impression; several of those present asked about buying copies.[26]

"Vince Salandria read a long portion of his first draft of an article on the Zapruder film and frames, in which he attempts to demonstrate that Gov. C was hit in frame 292, thus decisively demonstrating that there were at least two assassins," Sylvia wrote in her notes. "He feels certain that the Governor was shot from the TSBD but that the head shot in frame 313 had to come from grassy knoll." As Salandria had acknowledged, the Z-292 hit was a minority opinion among the critics. Ray Marcus had been surprised to hear about Salandria's opinion; he was certain Connally had been hit much sooner than at Z-292. He had seen a copy of Salandria's article a few weeks earlier, and told him: "I must frankly state my belief that the bulk of your article (the 292 theory) is as bad as your *Liberation* articles were good – and I thought the latter were very very good."[27]

Salandria cited his "four hour intensive analysis of the Zapruder films at the United States National Archives in Washington D.C. . . ." He described Zapruder frames 288 through 299, which represented about one-half of a second. At 292, where he argued Connally was hit, Salandria wrote: "His mouth is open. He seems to grimace in apparent pain. A hand seems to be thrown upward. He is still facing northeast." He was not presenting the 292 hypothesis as conclusive, he said; he urged that more work be done to determine exactly when the Governor was hit. But of one thing he had no doubt: the evidence against the single-bullet theory, "so crucial to the Warren Commission finding of a sole assassin," was overwhelmingly disproven by the Commission's own evidence.[28]

As it developed, the material presented that afternoon by Maggie Field, the reading by Salandria, the comments offered by other critics – all were merely a prelude to Edward Jay Epstein. Epstein was at this time an unknown commodity to most of those present, but he must have seemed like a godsend, because much of what he had to say confirmed what many of those present either suspected or had already concluded.

Epstein was the doctoral candidate from Cornell first mentioned to Sylvia Meagher the previous July by former Commission attorney Melvin Eisenberg. Somehow, Epstein had gained access not only to Eisenberg and the other Commission attorneys, but to all of the Warren Commission members except Senator Richard B. Russell and Warren himself. His remarks in Sylvia's apartment that afternoon, she said afterward, were utterly startling. "It is hard to believe or to understand why he was permitted to see so much – apparently he has strong backing from his University."[29]

Perhaps the most shocking of Epstein's revelations was described in Meagher's notes. "As late as September [1964], there was a series of panic memoranda from counsel, saying, alas, it's all over, there is really no evidence against Oswald, it's finished, the case has fallen apart. All these panic letters went to [assistant counsel Howard P.] Willens, who had the job of patching up the hole in the case, which each time he managed to do."30

Epstein made many other points, most of them equally startling. After each one, Sylvia asked him: "Do you intend to include that in your book?" He kept saying that he did.31

The Supreme Court justices, Epstein reported, were not happy with Earl Warren's decision to accept the chairmanship of the Commission. At least one had urged him to consider the implications. What if Jack Ruby's murder conviction came before the court? Warren would have to disqualify himself. What, then, if there were a 4-4 split among the remaining justices? That could cost Ruby his life. According to Epstein, Warren had listened, then replied, "None of your business."32

Commission members were furious with Gerald Ford because of his book *Portrait of the Assassin*. After the Commission had completed its work, Epstein said, its members met and came to a gentleman's agreement not to "break ranks" by discussing the case after the Report was published. Ford sat there and agreed to the arrangement, having already signed a contract to write his book.33

Joseph Ball and others who had examined Tippit eyewitness Helen Markham, Epstein told the critics that October afternoon, had concluded that she was a psychopathic liar. They urged that her testimony not be given much importance. Ball, of course, had more bluntly stated on a public platform that Markham was an "utter screwball." Members of the Commission nevertheless decided to use her and ordered that Joseph Ball's chapter four of the Report be rewritten.34

For at least a little while, the Warren Commission – or possibly the FBI or the CIA, Epstein was evidently not clear about this – had entertained a "Manchurian Candidate" theory – that is, that Oswald had been brainwashed in the Soviet Union via hypnosis and drugs. That might explain the hair loss noted in the photographs Maggie had brought. Echoing her sardonic remarks to WHO colleagues on the day JFK was slain, Sylvia wrote in her notes "that the Commission in contemplating the possibility of conspiracy limited the source and nature exclusively to a Communist plot." In any case, the theory was in the end discarded.35

The published testimonies in the Hearings and Exhibits were riddled with off-the-record discussions; this gave rise to speculation that important facts were being suppressed. Meagher had asked Epstein about that when she first telephoned him and thought he had indicated that some of these discussions might have been documented after all. But no, Epstein said that afternoon; based on his study, there were no transcripts of any of the off-the-record testimony.[36]

Virtually all of the work to produce the Warren Report, Epstein said, was done by its staff. The members of the Commission spent very little time on the investigation. When they were present, he said, it was mainly for background material and not the actual facts of the case. Some of the counsel even thought Earl Warren was rather stupid. Epstein himself had concluded that Warren was relatively well-informed and had made many important decisions.[37]

Epstein brought up the subject of Mark Lane. The FBI, he said, had so many tape recordings of his lectures on the assassination they would fill half of the room the critics then occupied. Sylvia noted that her living room was 21 by 14 feet. Epstein had seen the manuscript of Lane's book and considered it very poorly done – filled with inaccuracies, and including an irrelevant section about Jack Ruby's friendships with Dallas police officers, which was not in dispute.[38]

Lane, in his book, told the story of the supposed meeting between Officer J.D. Tippit, Ruby, and Bernard Weissman, the only signee of the notorious "Welcome, Mr. Kennedy, to Dallas" ad that had appeared the morning of the assassination. "All those present groaned," Sylvia wrote in her notes. A bad book by Mark Lane, they all felt, would be used to discredit all of them.[39]

Epstein was about finished when Léo Sauvage made a point that touched off a heated debate. He said that in its anxiety to refute Lane and Thomas Buchanan during the months before the Warren Report was published, the Commission succeeded only in making parts of its case more vulnerable. Sauvage cited as an example the Commission's efforts to prove that the police description of Oswald had "most probably" originated with Howard Brennan some fifteen minutes after the assassination. This, Sauvage said, raised a far more serious issue. If Brennan's eyewitness observation of a sniper in the sixth-floor window came at 12:45, as the Commission said, why didn't the police go straight to that window? Why was the sniper's nest not discovered for at least another fifteen minutes?[40]

"This discussion got us into a tremendous fracas," Sylvia wrote in her notes, "Sauvage and I versus Epstein and Stamm, the latter saying that it was perfectly understandable in the chaos and confusion that the police, even though having numerous reports that the shots came from that window, did not seal the building promptly nor go there immediately

– they 'waited for instructions,' etc. etc, the most appalling nonsense." Neither Meagher nor Sauvage would budge from their positions: the belated discovery of the sniper's nest, in spite of evidence that should have directed the police to it almost immediately, represented a serious, perhaps telling flaw in the Commission's version of events.[41]

As the intensity of this disagreement increased, Epstein stood and announced it was time for him to go. He had said earlier that he would be leaving soon, but Sylvia couldn't help wondering whether the argument had helped propel him toward the door.[42]

Precisely what was said during this "fracas" was not recorded, but Stamm clearly infuriated his hostess when he "reversed himself and reversed himself again, indulging in absurd arguments and making insulting statements to Sauvage and to me. Sauvage dealt with him politely but firmly, and devastated his whole position." As if that were not enough, Sylvia wrote,

> Stamm then got onto his eternal hobby horse – the political context of the assassination, deprecating our collective and individual preoccupation with the evidence (guns, bullets, all that nonsense) – what we needed . . . was economic study of the State of Texas!!!!!!!!
>
> I told Stamm he was crazy.
>
> I think he is, at times, and on this subject, just about paranoid.[43]

During the next month several letters were written that illuminate some of what must have been said during the fracas. On October 4 Sylvia wrote to Epstein: "Of course I am sorry that you had to leave before our rather heated discussion of the search of the TSBD was resolved, because I do believe and have always believed that this is a matter of cardinal importance." That being so, she spent the balance of her two-page letter reiterating why. At least four, and maybe five witnesses had reported seeing either a man or a rifle in a particular window. Why did the Dallas Police not send men to the sixth floor? "Personally I find it impossible to consider it inconsequential that neither the Warren Report nor any witness relates the search of the sixth floor southeast corner to the eyewitness reports of a man at a window in that location." After several more detailed paragraphs, Sylvia said "Enough of that . . . I hope we will stay in touch."[44]

Epstein wrote back with a polite request. Could Sylvia help in his effort to determine how many assassination witnesses reported hearing shots fired from somewhere other than the Book Depository, but were not called before the Warren Commission? Sylvia directed him to Feldman's "definitive article" from *The Minority of One*, "Fifty-one Witnesses: The Grassy Knoll." Epstein also asked for any insights she might have about the stretcher bullet – that is, CE 399, the so-called "pristine bullet" that the Commission said caused multiple wounds in Kennedy and Connally. This bullet had been found, in nearly perfect condition, on a stretcher at Parkland Hospital. Sylvia suggested Epstein contact Tom Stamm, who "did a much fuller treatment of the stretcher bullet in an unpublished article which he might be willing to send you."[45]

Epstein did contact Stamm, and Stamm did provide him with a copy of his unpublished article. "It is yours to do with as you see fit," Stamm wrote Epstein on November 3. Stamm used the opportunity to caution Epstein about "the lamentable fact that a number of those doing research on the Kennedy and Oswald assassinations and on the Warren Commission behave like dedicated zealots defending an esoteric truth against heretics. In reality, I suspect, they are engaged in an endless and, in the end, pointless hunt for error and discrepancy in the Report, which has become an end in itself. All errors have the same significance for them. Nothing is so unacceptable to them as definitive evidence of the Warren Commission's crime. They refuse point blank to draw conclusions from their findings. My statement, after you left, that the sum total of all the research done by all of us acting individually had demolished the Commission's case was rejected with emphasis. My suggestion that it was necessary to explore motive and the political genesis, context and aftermath of the assassination was regarded with scorn. The idea that political lessons must be drawn from these events was alien to them. I was even told that I was crazy."[46]

Like most of those at the meeting, Maggie Field had been favorably impressed with Edward Epstein. She found him intelligent and dispassionate, "and above all startlingly free with his information, which is vast and completely startling in nature." She, too, found it hard to believe Epstein had been granted such access to Commission members, attorneys, and their records. And yet she was encouraged. "He gave every evidence that he will condemn the Commission's work and its final outcome, that he regards the Report as spurious, that he believes there were a minimum of two assassins."[47]

When Sylvia Meagher first called Epstein to invite him to the meeting – before he in effect invited himself, through Jones Harris – she had asked him bluntly whether he believed Lee Harvey Oswald was guilty as charged. "He replied that it was not a question of who but of how many – that is, Oswald might or might not be implicated, there was not sufficient basis for a decisive judgment and there was no real evidence against him and no real eyewitness identification (he discounts the prints on cartons which Oswald normally handled anyway, discounts Brennan, etc.) – but he seems to feel that the assassination was carried out by a group of conspirators."[48]

She had also asked him whether his book would please the former Commissioners, and Epstein replied, "No." Nevertheless several guests at Sylvia's apartment a few weeks later found themselves wondering whether any of his sensational revelations about what went on behind the scenes with the Commission would actually find their way into print.[49]

About three weeks after the critics' meeting, Sylvia received several interesting telephone calls. The first came on October 26, and the caller was Melvin Eisenberg, the former Commission attorney with whom she had conversed the previous July. He called after Sylvia sent him copies of her unanswered letters to Albert Jenner, Wesley Liebeler, Alfred Goldberg, J. Lee Rankin, and Gerald Ford.[50]

"Mr. E commented that my unanswered letters, or some of them, revealed that I had drawn inferences and/or imputed personal motivation on the basis of errors that were perfectly understandable; that while my research was 'scholarly' my letters were subjective and unfair . . . he was sure that if he looked at my work he would find errors." Sylvia had agreed that he probably *would* find errors. But if there were a lot of them, and they all tended to support her arguments, she told Eisenberg he might well become suspicious.[51]

"In discussing my interpretation of the discrepancies between the Report and the H&E, Mr. E repeatedly said that I was 'intolerant,'" Sylvia wrote in her notes. "I emphasized that I was raising legitimate questions but not getting answers." She was sorry, she told him, that he found her attitude intolerant, but that she had not impugned his personal motives.[52]

Eisenberg expressed considerable interest in Sylvia's manuscript, as well as Epstein's. He was obviously very curious, especially about Epstein's work. Unknown until Eisenberg had mentioned him, Epstein and what he was about were by now very familiar to her, and she thought about telling Eisenberg that Epstein would find the Warren Report wanting. "But I ventured no diabolical hints about its probable verdict, much as I was tempted."[53]

As she had after Eisenberg called her in July, Sylvia made thorough notes about this conversation; she sent copies of each to Léo Sauvage. Two days later Sauvage telephoned to thank her for providing him the notes, which he called "extraordinary." He was envious, he said, that she had succeeded in getting Eisenberg to discuss the case with her.[54]

He wondered what Sylvia thought about Eisenberg. She replied that after her first conversation with him in July, she had thought he was fundamentally honest. But now she wasn't so sure. After their latest conversation, she said, she found it hard to reconcile his evasiveness about certain points of evidence with either honesty or integrity.[55]

Sauvage told her that he had recently encountered Dwight Macdonald at a luncheon, and had the impression that Macdonald had changed his mind about the Warren Report. Macdonald was the social critic and editor who had written a long critique of the Warren Report for *Esquire* magazine, which found the Commission's methods flawed but its lone-gunman conclusions correct. Like Sauvage, Macdonald had spoken at the New School's Warren Report class early in 1965. He had been very friendly at the luncheon. More than once he had said that someone should publish an English edition of Sauvage's book.[56]

Sauvage's instincts were on target: Macdonald had begun to doubt the Warren Report, and years later conceded that the work of some of the early critics led him "away from the solipsistic desert habitat of Lee and Jack into some more populous and fertile conspiratorial swamp." However, Macdonald never publicly expressed his doubts or recanted his *Esquire* critique.[57]

The same day that Sauvage had telephoned, Sylvia got a call from Jones Harris. He had been very disappointed at missing the critics meeting, but he had become seriously ill in Boston and had even undergone surgery. He was now back in New York and on the mend.[58]

Harris told her of a new book called *The Unanswered Questions About President Kennedy's Assassination*, written by a Pulitzer Prize-winning newspaperman named Sylvan Fox. Sauvage had mentioned the book too; both were impressed by it. Jones Harris had even called Fox to tell him how good it was. Sylvia not only knew about the book, she too had tried to contact its author, though he had not been home. By remarkable chance Fox lived just a block or so away.[59]

Sylvia had first heard about Fox's book from her friend Isabel Davis, who told her about it during a phone conversation. "I immediately rushed over to her place and appropriated the book," Sylvia later told Maggie Field, "rushed back home again, and sat down greedily with my prize. After reading 30 pages, I was so elated – needless to say, elated by the author's dissatisfaction with the Warren Report, the WC's conclusions, and the WC's composition, staff, methods, procedures, attitude, etc. – that I nearly called you in Paris." Meagher had suffered a bit of a letdown in the weeks following the critics' meeting. "This was just the shot in the arm I needed," she said, "and I felt exhilarated and recharged."[60]

The most interesting thing Harris had to say when he called, Sylvia thought, concerned some recent conversations he'd had with a man from Texas. This man was "the editor of a small newspaper or journal . . . who made it a point to look Harris up on a recent visit to New York," Sylvia wrote in her notes. "This editor has never lost interest in the case, and is especially interested in the 'peripheral crimes.' According to him, the Long Beach (California) newspaper man who was shot accidentally by a policeman in that city was among the reporters who entered Ruby's apartment on 11/24/63 and 'it is amazing how few of those men are still alive today.'" Sylvia was clearly intrigued by this Texas editor, whose name Harris did not reveal.[61]

Harris and Meagher spoke again the next day, and Harris told her a little about himself. He had done television work some years before, and some writing. But his true love was 16th century literature. In fact he was something of a conspiracy theorist in this area. "Take my word for it, Sylvia," he had said, "Shakespeare didn't write any of the plays or sonnets." The real author, he said, was someone who, for personal or political reasons, could not have it known that he was a literary man – perhaps Francis Bacon, or the Earl of Derby, or Edward de Vere, the Seventeenth Earl of Oxford.[62]

It was not the Bard of Avon, but the mystery writer Rex Stout, whom Sylvia soon found herself reading – and with great admiration. While Stout was a skilled writer, it was not his prose but his courage that most impressed her.

Isabel Davis had urged Sylvia to read Stout's new book, *The Doorbell Rang*. The novel was the latest in the author's Nero Wolfe saga. At first, the suggestion irritated Sylvia – "How often I use that word!" she said – because reading a popular mystery seemed a frivolous imposition on her busy schedule. "But how grateful I was that she had insisted!" she exclaimed later, when urging Maggie Field to read it, too.[63]

Nero Wolfe was the fictional detective who preferred orchids and *haute cuisine* to work, a cerebral sleuth who cracked most of his cases without ever leaving his New York brownstone. As Sylvia dug into the story, she could scarcely believe what she was reading. *The Doorbell Rang* centered on the FBI. Wolfe's entrée to the case was Fred Cook's *The FBI Nobody Knows,* copies of which Wolfe's wealthy, would-be client had sent to government officials, media bigwigs, bankers and publishers and corporate heads – as a public service, she said. Her contempt for the FBI thus known, she found herself under FBI surveillance, and turned to Wolfe for help.[64]

As it happened, Fred Cook had no idea that Stout had written a novel inspired by his exposé. The first he knew about it was the previous August, at the time he was beginning to work on his article for *Ramparts.* A copy of *The Doorbell Rang* arrived in the mail one day, inscribed to him by its author: "To Fred Cook, with admiration, esteem, and many thanks for priming my pump." Cook didn't quite understand what it was about and set the novel aside. But later that same day his daughter took a closer look and said, "Dad, did you notice what the little man on the cover is reading?" The little man was Nero Wolfe, and he was reading *The FBI Nobody Knows.* "Well, I'll be damned!" Cook said.[65]

"The whole book revolves about the FBI, which is the absolute bad-guy of the plot," Sylvia told Maggie Field. "That anyone should make so fearless an attack on the sacredest of cows *and* get published seemed incredible." Stout was a board member of the ACLU and during the 1950s had opposed McCarthyism. His one personal encounter with the FBI occurred when an agent questioned him about the reading habits of a friend. "I got so damned mad, I put him out," he recalled. Yet he told an interviewer he did not consider *The Doorbell Rang* an attack on the Bureau. J. Edgar Hoover probably did. Although officially Hoover's position was "No comment," a newspaper columnist wrote that the director had written him saying, among other things, "If a special agent ever conducted himself as depicted in Mr. Stout's book, he would be subject to immediate dismissal."[66]

Sylvia mentioned *The Doorbell Rang* to Léo Sauvage and urged him to read it. She was surprised to learn that Sauvage knew Stout and that both men were members of the Baker Street Irregulars, the society of Sherlock Holmes devotees. "I hinted that he should find out how Stout feels about the Warren Report," she said later, "and maybe enlist his razor brain and considerable prestige in our collective work."[67]

Chapter 21

No Exit

The "**Warren Commission's** Case Against Oswald," by Léo Sauvage, appeared in *The New Leader* on November 22, 1965, the second anniversary of President Kennedy's death. "And again this year, as last," Sauvage wrote, "it will be tacitly understood that there can be no casting of doubts on the official account of the President's assassination . . . Americans still do not seem capable of accepting the idea that one can criticize – and even reject – the Warren Report."[1]

The subject of conspiracy in the assassination of President Kennedy seemed taboo – so much so that the very periodical in which Sauvage's words appeared admitted that it printed them reluctantly: "We prefer not to be confronted once again by the ugly details of that day," *The New Leader* stated in an unsigned editorial. "We are content, in other words, as we stated in this space when the Warren Commission Report was issued, to accept its conclusions that Lee Harvey Oswald, acting alone, killed President Kennedy." Yet serious and responsible people such as Léo Sauvage disagreed, the magazine continued, and the dissent should be heard and commented on.[2]

The Warren Commission, Sauvage wrote, insisted it did not pass judgment on Lee Harvey Oswald – rather it "ascertained the facts surrounding the assassination" without reaching conclusions about Oswald's legal guilt. Yet the Commission had presented an eight-point summary which plainly labeled Oswald the assassin. These were at the end of the Warren Report's Chapter IV, appropriately titled, Sauvage said, "The Assassin." Here the Commission stated that 1) Oswald owned the assassination rifle, 2) he brought it to work on November 22, 3) he was present at the time of the assassination, 4) he killed Officer Tippit, 5) he resisted arrest, 6) he lied to police on key matters after his arrest, 7) he attempted to kill General Edwin Walker in April 1963, and 8) he possessed the necessary skills to commit the assassination.[3]

Sauvage wrote in his article that, unlike *The New Leader*, other publishers had not been as willing to present views opposed to their own. *L' Affair Oswald* had been published in Paris, but "The New York publisher broke the contract for the American version when he learned that I was not convinced by the Report and that I intended to say so."[4]

In Maryland, Harold Weisberg read Sauvage's article and the two that followed it, "Oswald's Case Against the Warren Commission" in the December 20 *New Leader*, and "The Case Against Mr. X," in its issue of January 3, 1966. He was impressed enough to write the magazine a letter that both praised Sauvage and promoted himself.

> May I express my appreciation for what today must be described as your courage in printing the three very worthwhile articles on the Warren Commission Report by Léo Sauvage.
>
> Almost unique among the limited writings about the Warren Commission, his pieces have been devoid of factual error, a failing that has characterized almost everything else I have seen. Like Sauvage, I have written a book on the Report. Like him, mine is also unpublished in the United States.[5]

Sylvia Meagher was also impressed with Sauvage's latest work, and wrote to congratulate the magazine for publishing the articles. Her letter appeared directly beneath Harold Weisberg's. The two did not then know each other, but Sylvia, intrigued by Weisberg's comments, wrote to him on January 31, 1966, in care of *The New Leader*. She said they were in close proximity – not only in the pages of the magazine, "but in degree of recoil from the Warren Report." She asked him about his book: his letter suggested it had been published abroad. She also told him about her comparative study, by then over 300 pages long, and her subject index, which had just been accepted for publication by Scarecrow Press and was due out that spring.[6]

"Gradually, this work has brought me into touch with more and more people, in various parts of the country," Sylvia told him. "Almost invariably, communication began with expressions of relief at a break in the isolation and the discouragement of seeming to be out of step with the rest of the world. Happily, there are quite a few heretics now, but not enough."[7]

Sylvia's letter worked its way through *The New Leader* and was duly forwarded to Weisberg, who replied on February 9. He was answering in haste, he said. Sylvia's letter was a welcome surprise. His own letter to *The New Leader* had not been meant for publication, although he did not object to it. He had enclosed a letter to Sauvage, as yet unanswered.[8]

"My book has not been published anywhere," Weisberg told her, "and the attitude of European publishers is a little less comprehensible than that of the Americans, who can at least tell themselves they might get hurt . . . if my experience means anything to you, unless you will labor for love, get an enforceable contract for your book before you go further." Some friends of his were exploring the possibility of a private printing. Weisberg did not mention the limited edition of *Whitewash* that had been published in August 1965. That early publication may have been for purposes of copyright registration.[9]

Weisberg expressed an interest in Sylvia's work, and hoped they would be able to talk before too much longer. He'd like a copy of the index – if it wasn't too expensive. He was now broke and in debt. "Meanwhile, do you know of any other such books floating around? By this I mean serious books, on the Commission, not such pot-boilers as *A Mother in History* and others like it, which, naturally, seem to find a ready market." He seemed to consider *Whitewash* definitive. What had been in Léo Sauvage's articles was "but a fragment of what I have mined" from the twenty-six volumes.[10]

On February 12 Weisberg wrote that he had arranged for a publisher then considering *Whitewash* to lend Sylvia the manuscript. On February 14 she picked it up in person, and spent the rest of that day and part of the night reading it start to finish. Her evaluation must have pleased him enormously. "I believe that you have written an outstanding and brilliant attack on the Warren Report, and I marvel that you completed the job as early as you did," Meagher told him. "The scholarship is extremely careful and in a number of instances you have seen much farther into the evidence than others – myself included – who have analyzed the same aspect of the case."[11]

Too, he must have been encouraged by her comments about the book's unpublished status. "It is appalling that your manuscript has been circulating for so long without the deserved results. Your book should have been published as a major and definitive work. To compare it with Sylvan Fox's book is almost indecent, and that had a remarkable commercial success."[12]

She included three pages of specific commentary on the manuscript, including what she termed some very minor errors. She enclosed copies of her unanswered letters to Warren Commission members and attorneys, and a chapter from her book entitled "The Proof of the Plot."[13]

A few days later Sylvia took Weisberg's manuscript back to the publisher, and told an editor there he should jump at the chance to publish it. He did not. "I've never been able to 'sell' on my own behalf," she reported back to Weisberg, "and I guess I don't do much better for third parties."[14]

On the day after Christmas 1965, Sylvia Meagher wrote a letter to Shirley Martin. She knew Shirley's name from its appearance in the Warren Commission volumes – she had indexed it – and because other critics, such as Harold Feldman in his article dedication, had mentioned it. But the two women did not yet know each other. "I have looked forward to being in touch with you ever since my first meeting with Vince Salandria last [summer], when he suggested that we should become acquainted for practical and moral support," she said. "Since you have incurred the displeasure of the Warren Commission, you are saddled with the admiration and perhaps effrontery of strangers like myself who are still going through the initiation rites."[15]

She was writing now, Sylvia said, to determine the source of an interview featured in an article by Dorothy Kilgallen in the September 25, 1964, issue of *The New York Journal-American*. The interview subject was not identified but seemed to be Acquilla Clemons. The article indicated the interview was from an official document, but this was nowhere to be found in the Warren Commission's published material. Sylvia had learned that Kilgallen may have obtained a transcript of an interview with Mrs. Clemons conducted by a non-official investigator, but she couldn't figure out who that might be. Jones Harris told her he hadn't talked to Mrs. Clemons, and it didn't appear as though "the Mark Lane people" had. George and Pat Nash had interviewed her but did not publish any quotations, and in any case Sylvia could not locate them. "Therefore, I would be most grateful if you could indicate whether you recorded an interview with Mrs. Clemons or whether you know of anyone else who did and who might have made the transcript available to Dorothy Kilgallen."[16]

Kilgallen's article raised serious questions about whether Oswald was the killer of Officer Tippit. The man her unnamed witness had seen was short and heavy – as Mrs. Clemons said, "kind of stocky-built. Stocky build. Whatever you call it." Ominously, Kilgallen reported, this unnamed witness had told her interviewer that a police officer had warned her to be careful, that she might get killed on the way to work.[17]

Shirley wrote back to Sylvia on December 28. She was pleased to hear from her; Salandria had mentioned her many times, always in favorable terms. "Yes, I interviewed Mrs. Clemons and I believe this interview was the basis for the Dorothy Kilgallen story. But how Miss Kilgallen got the story, I don't know. I was so sorry to hear of her death." Kilgallen had been found dead in her New York apartment less than two months before.[18]

In her reply Sylvia described her work on the case. Then she asked for additional information on Acquilla Clemons. Was their interview tape-recorded, or otherwise transcribed? If so, did Mrs. Martin have any idea who might have supplied a copy to Kilgallen? Shirley replied that she would have Vickie locate the Clemons tape, and send it along.[19]

Two weeks later Sylvia Meagher wrote to Martin with news of what she called "a *terrific* new development." She had just been contacted by an editor at *Ramparts* magazine. They had heard about her work on the Warren Report and wanted to see some of it; the magazine was about to open its pages to the work of the critics. "We plan to devote part of each issue to the subject," the magazine's news editor, David Welsh, had written her, "beginning with our April number – indefinitely, until the Warren Commission is reopened." In case she was not familiar with the magazine, he enclosed a copy of a recent issue.[20]

Sylvia was thrilled by *Ramparts'* interest. She was indeed familiar with the magazine, she wrote Welsh in reply. "In fact, I submitted material on the Warren Report in November 1964 and was disappointed at the lack of interest at that time." She described her comparative study and offered to make it available to *Ramparts*, in whole or in part. "If you feel that it is suitable I shall certainly be willing to consider making any necessary modifications in presentation for publication as an article or articles of individual chapters instead of the book which was the original scheme." Most of the chapters, she added, could stand alone as individual essays. Two days later, without waiting for a reply from Welsh, she sent the entire manuscript.[21]

In mid-February, after she had read *Whitewash*, Sylvia urged Harold Weisberg to contact *Ramparts* to see if it were interested in his work. Immediately he wrote a long letter to David Welsh. Weisberg described his book in great detail, including the publishing contract "which was broken by the excited and happy publisher, while raving about the advance-sale indications." More to the point, he said that "I believe I destroyed each and every one of the Commission's major conclusions and an awful lot more, all with its own evidence and nothing else." He ventured that Welsh might find it all quite exciting. At the same time, Weisberg said he was trying to interest another, unnamed magazine in either serialization or condensation of his book. But, he said, it might be unwise to think about magazine arrangements until the matter of book publication was resolved. "I'm really just thinking out loud with you."[22]

Some of the other critics had heard about the interest of *Ramparts* magazine, but were not as enthusiastic. "*Ramparts* has contacted us here, also," Ray Marcus told Vince Salandria in March. "They act like they really intend to start a campaign, but I'll believe it when I see it in print. I'm afraid this case has made me more cynical than I once was."[23]

The magazine had recruited Maggie Field and David Lifton to its "Kennedy Project," and Maggie was making a set of her panoplies available to them. Lifton submitted an article in the form of a dialogue between a critic and skeptical nonstudent of the case. But *Ramparts* already had at least one thing ready to go: Fred Cook's article, weighing in at 20,000 words, had been completed the previous September. It was to have appeared in its December 1965 issue, but for some reason the magazine had delayed publication. Neither did it appear in the January or February 1966 issues. In March Cook told Ray Marcus that his article was stuck in "a bottleneck at *Ramparts*. It was supposed to have been out before this. . . ."[24]

That same month *Ramparts* stunned Cook with what he remembered as "the worst double-cross I have ever had from a publisher." After Cook demanded to know what was holding up the article, *Ramparts* "made the incredible claim that it had never agreed to publish the article in the first place." In April Cook received a "token payment" of $500, along with his unpublished manuscript. He was frustrated and angry. It had been over a year since the night he had felt the Warren Report falling to pieces in his hands, and still he was unable to tell the story as he saw it.[25]

In time, Jones Harris stopped being cagey with Sylvia Meagher, and provided her with the name of the Texas editor he had mentioned to her in October 1965. It was Penn Jones, Jr. On November 21 Meagher wrote to Jones to introduce herself, subscribe to the *Midlothian Mirror*, and tell him about some of the work she had been doing.[26]

She also requested a copy of the *Mirror* from November 11, 1965. This issue contained "the story about Wanda Joyce Killam and John Carter, which I am very anxious to see."[27]

Jones wrote back promptly that he expected to be writing articles on the case "for about the next six weeks at least." He was probably underestimating this deliberately. Jones had begun his own investigation right after the assassination and, being so close to Dallas, had already spoken to a number of people connected to the case. Moreover he was advocating, in print, a re-opening of the Warren Commission probe.[28]

The article Sylvia was wondering about related to details of what Penn Jones considered one of the mysterious deaths associated with the assassination. It concerned "an unimportant person associated in a distant way to Ruby, and of that person's strange death far away from Dallas." The Warren Commission, Jones wrote, said that a possible connection between Jack Ruby and Lee Oswald was a man named John Carter, who lived in the same boarding house at 1026 North Beckley that Oswald lived in. Carter told the Warren Commission that he never heard of Ruby until Oswald was shot. Yet Carter was friendly with a woman named Wanda Joyce Killam, the Warren Report stated, who had known Ruby since the late 1940s, and worked for him at the Carousel Club from July 1963 until the assassination.[29]

Penn's interview with Wanda Joyce Killam revealed a different story. "Actually," Jones wrote, "she told me she had worked in Ruby's club for two years."[30]

John Carter was a house painter, as was Wanda Joyce's husband Hank Killam. The two were good friends, and worked some painting jobs together; Carter had been a guest in the Killam home. "How is it possible that he was such good friends with the Killams, whose wife worked for Ruby, and yet Carter never heard of Ruby?" Jones wrote.[31]

Wanda Joyce Killam told Penn Jones that after the assassination, her husband was constantly hounded by men she called "Federal Agents" whose constant contacts, she said, led to his losing a series of jobs. He finally left Dallas and eventually wound up in Pensacola, Florida, where he found work. He telephoned his wife to come join him there. But on the morning of March 17, 1964, he was found dead on a Pensacola street. His throat had been cut. It appeared he had gone through a plate glass window. But did he jump, or fall? Or was he pushed?[32]

As far as Penn could tell, things did not add up, and after learning of what happened to Hank Killam, the "unimportant person associated in a distant way to Ruby," he believed there were grounds for suspicion. "To this writer it seems more than passing strange that so little information is given on Carter by the FBI or the Commission . . . this writer has been unsuccessful in efforts to contact John Carter."[33]

That was the story, and Sylvia wanted to read it for herself. "Thanks for the subscription," Jones wrote her. He enclosed the article she had requested, along with two others. He flattered her by adding, "I want copies of all you publish – autographed." He was glad to know, he wrote in conclusion, "that more than two or three are interested in that great miscarriage of justice."[34]

Sylvia wrote back promptly. "I am *speechless* after reading your three articles on the Warren Report. I didn't think there was a newspaper in the country that still knew how to call a spade . . . I did not realize that you were taking such a determined and fearless editorial stand, and that delights me even more . . . incidentally, there are more than two or three who are interested, and interested full time, in the travesty of justice." She kept in touch with all of them, she said, as time permitted.[35]

She also told him that his work had given her spirits a lift. "Reading your editorials this evening gave me a moment of the kind of pride and optimism about the people of this country that I have not entertained for a hell of a long long time."[36]

Penn Jones, Sylvia soon learned, also considered the death of Dorothy Kilgallen suspicious. In spite of her public image as a gossip columnist and game show panelist, Kilgallen was a capable journalist. Before her September 1964 article quoting the unidentified Acquilla Clemons, she had been granted an exclusive interview with Jack Ruby. That was in March 1964 during a recess in Ruby's murder trial. That this meeting ever took place has been disputed by some, for the fact of the matter, according to Kilgallen's own biographer, is that she never published a word about it. But the biographer, Lee Israel, was certain that the meeting did in fact occur. She suggested several possible reasons for Kilgallen's withholding the story: that she was saving it for a chapter in a book she was writing called *Murder One;* that Ruby had given her a lead that she was still developing; that Ruby had extracted from her a promise of confidentiality; or that she had been acting as a courier. Whatever the reason, Kilgallen is said to have told a friend that she was about to leave for New Orleans and would soon be breaking the assassination case wide open. That was in late autumn 1965. On November 8 she was dead. While the cause of death was listed as a lethal combination of alcohol and barbituates – accidental or intentional was not established – Israel hinted that Kilgallen may have in fact been murdered. But there was nothing conclusive. What was certain, Israel wrote, was that nothing Kilgallen might have learned from her private meeting with Jack Ruby "has ever come to light."[37]

Penn Jones editorialized: "Is she another victim of possibly knowing the secret that still moves in the troubled mind of Jack Ruby?"[38]

Sylvia had sent Penn some excerpts from her compa‹
in manuscript form, and authorized him to photc
December 16, having done so, he returned them, reitera‹
autographed copies of whatever she published. If anything shu
ever rejected, he said, he'd be happy to publish it. He urged her to teh ‹
if she found any errors in his work.[39]

Jones mentioned having had a phone call from a Mr. Marcus in Los
Angeles the night before. "We need an organization of the true and
faithful," he observed. "Shirley Martin is a tireless worker in this field."
And he had a little news: he was planning to collect twelve of his assassination editorials from the *Mirror* into a book in order to raise some
research money. "It is very costly, but maybe the books would help a little."[40]

The article Vince Salandria had read in draft form at the critics'
meeting at Sylvia Meagher's home in October 1965 was finally published
over two issues of *The Minority of One*. The first part, erroneously credited
to "Victor" Salandria, appeared in the March 1966 issue as "The
Impossible Tasks of One Assassination Bullet." Part Two, "The Separate
Connally Shot," followed in April and contained explosive information
that Salandria did not have at the time of the critics' meeting.[41]

The Warren Commission's lone gunman conclusion was built on the
premise that a single bullet had passed through Kennedy and then
Connally. This bullet was officially designated Commission Exhibit 399.
From Salandria's first *Liberation* article in January 1965 to Ray Marcus's
"Hypotheses re: the Zapruder Film," the critics had demonstrated that
this single-bullet theory – sometimes referred to as a "weaving bullet"
theory or "double hit" theory – was simply not feasible. The doctors
attached to the government who supported the double-hit theory,
Salandria wrote in Part One, described the apparent trajectory of 399 in
vague and halting language that no critic of the Warren Report could
expect to get away with. "How could the Commission have fairly
concluded 'all the evidence' supported the idea that 399 had struck
Governor Connally and caused all his wounds?"[42]

Part Two of the *TMO* piece was meant "to establish finally and
objectively that Kennedy and Connally were wounded by separate
bullets." The evidence for this was inadvertently supplied by former
Commission attorney Arlen Specter.[43]

Salandria recalled Specter's appearance before the Philadelphia Bar
Association in October 1964, shortly after publication of the Warren

Report. It was this appearance that had sparked Salandria's *Legal Intelligencer* article. "Mr. Specter was asked during the questioning period whether the Commission had disagreed in any significant respect with the FBI report on the assassination. Mr. Specter replied that the FBI report concluded Governor Connally's hit was a separate one. Then he proceeded to take a large share of the credit for the double-hit theory. Since that time, I have endeavored to meet with Mr. Arlen Specter, now District Attorney of Philadelphia. I wished to assure myself that I heard correctly what he had said. He has chosen to ignore our requests to meet with him."[44]

Such a disagreement between the Commission and the FBI conclusions was no small matter. Could it be documented? Salandria applied to the National Archives and Records Service for permission to inspect the four-volume FBI Summary Report, which had not been made public. In due course he received that permission and on February 26, 1966, was able to visit the Archives and read the *Investigation of Assassination of President John F. Kennedy, November 22, 1963* – "which work bears the name of John Edgar Hoover, Director of the Federal Bureau of Investigation."[45]

On page 18 of the very first volume, Salandria reported in *TMO*, his search came to a successful conclusion. The FBI report stated:

> Immediately after President Kennedy and Governor Connally were admitted to Parkland Memorial Hospital, a bullet was found on one of the stretchers. Medical examination of the President's body revealed that one of the bullets had entered just below his shoulder to the right of the spinal column at an angle of 45 to 60 degrees downward, that there was no point of exit, and that the bullet was not in the body. An examination of this bullet by the FBI Laboratory determined that it had been fired from the rifle owned by Oswald. (Exhibit 23)

"Exhibit 23," Salandria wrote in *TMO*, "is labeled 'BULLET FROM STRETCHER,' and this bullet is none other than Commission Exhibit 399."[46]

That was it: CE 399 had *no point of exit.* If there was no point of exit, how could it have gone on to wound Governor Connally? Salandria had indeed heard correctly when Arlen Specter told the Philadelphia Bar Association that the FBI and the Warren Report were not in accord on a most fundamental point. Because of the timing proven in the Zapruder film, separate bullets meant separate gunmen – thus a conspiracy.

Finding official documentation in the FBI's report represented one of the most significant discoveries of the early critics, yet it was buried near the end of Salandria's article. Although Salandria had not examined it, the four-volume Summary Report was supplemented by a fifth volume dated January 13, 1964. It too supported a conclusion that the bullet that entered President Kennedy's back did not exit his body. This fact, completely undermining the Warren Commission's three-bullet thesis, was omitted from the Warren Report, which made but a sole, passing reference to the Summary Report in its Foreword.[47]

CE 399 was truly a remarkable missile. If the Commission's single-bullet theory of its trajectory was correct, it twisted and turned like a trapeze artist between the bodies of its two victims. And in spite of having passed through these two men, inflicting great damage that included smashed bones, the bullet was virtually undeformed. Its undeformed appearance was all the more striking when it was compared to a bullet test-fired by the FBI and entered into the record as CE 856. This bullet, the same type as 399, was fired only through the wrist of a human cadaver but was severely flattened at its front end. Equally striking about CE 399 was the absence of any blood or tissue on its surface. For all of these reasons some of the critics had come to refer to Commission Exhibit 399 as a "magic" or "pristine" bullet.[48]

Ray Marcus called it a bastard.

Marcus did not originally intend to write anything about CE 399. "I pushed Salandria to write it, and I pushed Lane to write it. You know, because they had mentioned the bullet," he recalled. "I said, 'Look. It's not enough to say that this bullet didn't do that. If it didn't do that, what is this bullet?' And they obviously were very, very busy with other things, and Lane said to me, 'Why don't you write it yourself?'"[49]

"It" was a detailed study of CE 399, which Marcus completed in mid-1966 and published as a 77-page monograph entitled *The Bastard Bullet: A Search for Legitimacy for Commission Exhibit 399*. Marcus was certain that CE 399 was not legitimate and that the single-bullet theory was invalid. But his approach gave the Warren Commission the benefit of the doubt. "If I was going to do an article at all on it, and do anything to contribute something that hadn't been touched on in that much detail, I felt I at least had to try, as objectively as I could, to examine any other hypothesis that could have legitimately explained that bullet."[50]

Once he'd finished it, Marcus offered *The Bastard Bullet* to a number of publishers including Dell and Pocket Books, but there were no takers. M.S. Arnoni offered to publish it in *TMO* if Marcus could cut it in half. But that couldn't be done, Marcus felt, without deleting elements too important to leave out. "So I was content to publish it myself."[51]

Marcus began by explaining, as he had in his unpublished "Hypotheses" a year earlier, how the Commission's lone-assassin position, coupled with the Zapruder film, imposed certain restrictions: the first shot in a lone-gunman scenario would have to have been fired at Z-frame 210, and the last shot fired at Z-313. Given the Zapruder film's 18 frames per second, the entire shooting sequence had to have occurred in slightly under six seconds. Given the time required to load another bullet into the Mannlicher Carcano's chamber, there had to have been at least 2.3 seconds between each shot. Therefore, "if any two hits are recorded by the Zapruder film in less than 2.3 seconds (forty-two frames) it would constitute *prima facie* evidence of a second assassin." And the Zapruder film recorded precisely that.[52]

But the central task of *The Bastard Bullet* was determining what role CE 399 played in the assassination. Could this nearly undamaged Commission exhibit really have passed through JFK, and then caused multiple wounds in John Connally? Marcus described how expert after expert told the Warren Commission that CE 399 could *not* have caused so many wounds in two men and remained virtually undamaged. Commission counsel Arlen Specter asked Commander James J. Humes, the Navy pathologist who led the autopsy team, whether CE 399 could have caused the wound in Connally's wrist. "I think that is most unlikely," Humes responded. X-rays taken in Dallas showed bullet fragments in Connally's wrist and thigh, while 399, Humes said, was basically intact. Colonel Pierre Finck, a certified forensic pathologist also present at JFK's autopsy, concurred. Other medical experts, as well as FBI firearms experts, testified to the bullet's near-perfect condition.[53]

Marcus also showed that tests performed to determine certain wound ballistics were inadequate in that they failed to properly re-create, insofar as it was possible, the conditions of the actual assassination. Test bullets were fired through gelatin blocks, goat and horse meat, and human cadavers, but these targets were never aligned so the bullets could penetrate all of them. "The tests as conducted are totally worthless as support for the Commission's theories," Marcus concluded. They did not account for the nearly-perfect condition of CE 399. Moreover a simple comparison between CE 399 and the badly deformed CE 856, which appeared side by side in *The Bastard Bullet*, demonstrated at a glance the improbability of 399 and the single-bullet theory.[54]

The weight of the evidence, Marcus wrote, tended to prove that CE 399 was not involved in wounding Governor Connally. Yet the bullet was discovered on the governor's stretcher at Parkland Hospital. How did it get there? The Commission said it worked its way out of Connally's thigh and fell onto the stretcher on which he was carried – first into a ground floor trauma room and then to the second floor operating room. Upstairs the governor had been moved from the stretcher to an operating table, and the stretcher was pushed into an elevator.[55]

That the bullet might even have fallen from Connally's thigh raised questions. Marcus consulted six experts who between them had examined some 15,000 bullet wounds. None had ever had a case of a bullet falling from a wound, or had ever heard of such a thing happening.[56]

Darrell Tomlinson, the hospital's senior engineer, was credited with finding the bullet. He testified that he had taken a stretcher off the elevator and placed it by another stretcher already in a corridor on the hospital's ground floor. The Warren Commission said it was on the stretcher Tomlinson took off the elevator that the bullet was found. But Marcus found the evidence inconclusive. Tomlinson's own testimony indicated the bullet was found on the stretcher already in the corridor.[57]

During the chaotic period when Kennedy and Connally were being treated, Tomlinson had acted temporarily as the elevator's operator. After removing the stretcher and placing it by the one in the corridor, he went back to the second floor. "I don't know anything about what could have happened to them in between the time I was gone, and I made several trips before I discovered the bullet on the end of it there."[58]

In his absence a doctor or intern had apparently moved one of the stretchers, which was blocking the door to the men's room. When he returned, Tomlinson pushed it back up against a wall, dislodging a bullet that rolled into view. "Tomlinson's implication that something 'could have happened' to the stretchers while he was gone, shortly before he discovered the bullet, suggests two possibilities," Marcus wrote.

> The first is innocent enough; that someone, on his way through the corridor or into the men's room, may have moved the stretchers around during Tomlinson's absence, thus confusing him as to whether the stretcher on which he 'found' the bullet was or was not the same one he discovered in the corridor. But the second possibility

is anything but innocent; that in his absence someone may have placed the bullet on the stretcher. Obviously, the second alternative immediately raises the dark cloud of conspiracy.[59]

Arlen Specter asked Tomlinson a series of questions that seemed designed to get him to say it was the elevator stretcher on which he found the bullet. To Marcus, it seemed that Specter was badgering the witness, but Tomlinson stuck to his guns: "I'm not going to tell you something I can't lay down and sleep at night with. . . ."[60]

In July 1966 Marcus interviewed Tomlinson by telephone. At that time Tomlinson stated unequivocally that the bullet had, in fact, come off the elevator stretcher. But he also told Marcus that the FBI telephoned him about one o'clock in the morning on November 23 and "told me to keep my mouth shut."

About the circumstances of his finding the bullet? Marcus asked.

"Just don't talk about it, period."[61]

Specter had not asked Tomlinson what he did with the bullet. The bullet, Tomlinson told Marcus, was "pretty clean" when he found it. He picked it up and put it in his pocket, and soon thereafter turned it over to O.P. Wright, Parkland's personnel officer. Marcus traced the chain of possession as Wright turned the bullet over to a Secret Service agent and it eventually reached an FBI special agent in Washington, D.C. But an FBI document in the twenty-six volumes showed inconsistencies with the possession. "Of the four individuals who supposedly handled [CE 399] from the time of its discovery by Tomlinson to its receipt by the FBI in Washington, none was able to identify it" in later questioning as the one they had possessed.[62]

The Warren Commission had failed to prove 399 inflicted all of the wounds it attributed to it, Marcus argued – "but also has done nothing whatever to investigate alternative possibilities as to its involvement. We shall have to do the Commission's work. . . ." He examined a series of possible explanations for how the bullet was involved in the assassination and how it could have wound up on a stretcher at Parkland Hospital. Perhaps it hit JFK in the back and worked its way onto his stretcher; or maybe it hadn't hit anyone but still, somehow, reached the stretcher where Tomlinson found it. In the end, Marcus found these possibilities unsupported by any evidence, and rejected them. Objective analysis of the known facts, he said, left no innocent explanation for the existence of Commission Exhibit 399.[63]

If its undistorted appearance, immaculate condition, suspicious discovery, and mysterious handling cannot be reasonably accounted for by any hypothesis implying legitimacy, the answer must lie elsewhere.

Indeed, it has been implicit at many junctures throughout our search; and it has now become as inescapable as it is ominous:

That bullet 399 is not a legitimate assassination bullet at all; that it was never fired at any human target; that instead, it was deliberately fired in such a manner as to prevent its mutilation; and then, with the intention of assuring its identification with the Mannlicher-Carcano rifle allegedly belonging to Lee Harvey Oswald, it was planted by person or persons unknown on the hospital stretcher where it was subsequently "found."[64]

In the aftermath of the assassination, newspapers continuously revised the nature of the President's wounds – where he was hit, and how many times. Was his throat wound one of entrance or exit? Was he hit in the back of the neck, or nearer the shoulder blades? What part of the skull was hit? The postmortem examination of Kennedy's body was of utmost importance in understanding what really happened. Yet the autopsy report offered few solid answers – a seemingly incomprehensible fact given the stature of the victim. Harold Weisberg said it was inexcusable that so many questions remained. "None should exist," he wrote. "This was not a Bowery bum; this was the President of the United States."[65]

The autopsy was performed at Bethesda Naval Hospital in Bethesda, Maryland, on the evening of November 22. Before it even began, Weisberg reported in *Whitewash*, the President's entire body was X-rayed and photographed. Additional X-rays and photographs were made during the course of the procedure. "With this elaborate photographic record," Weisberg asked, "why should there ever have been any question about the exact location of each wound?"[66]

The answer was that none of the photographs or X-rays were ever entered into the official record or viewed by members of the Warren Commission. Instead, the Commission relied on sketches made by a medical illustrator under the supervision of two of the autopsy doctors, Commanders James J. Humes and J. Thornton Boswell. "The doctors almost begged for the production of the photographs during their testimony, especially Dr. Humes," Weisberg said in 1966. "And finally, after this happened three or four times, the Commission asked, 'Well, would your testimony be any different, if you had the pictures here?' What was the poor doctor going to do – say he testified incompetently? or falsely? Obviously, he just said 'No. But – ' But he did put a 'but' in, and he insisted that the pictures would have been best. And he insisted that pictures and X-rays are basic and normal to an autopsy – apparently, everybody's autopsy but that of a President."[67]

Sylvia Meagher was also troubled by questions relating to the President's wounds and the autopsy. It wasn't only that descriptions of the wounds, as described in leaks to the press, kept changing. The autopsy report was not published until September 1964, and when it finally did appear was not dated. Commander Humes, the chief autopsy surgeon, acknowledged having burned his autopsy notes and even said he had been forbidden to talk.[68]

In view of this, Sylvia said, the autopsy report was highly suspicious. She would one day write: "Those who dismiss as preposterous, if not sacrilegious, the very notion that an autopsy report might be adjusted to serve police or political imperatives should consult David M. Spain's article 'Mississippi Autopsy' in *Ramparts*' special issue *Mississippi Eyewitness . . .* they will find incontrovertible proof of the falsification of autopsy findings in the case of James Chaney, who was murdered with Andrew Goodman and Michael Schwerner in the summer of 1964 in Philadelphia, Mississippi."[69]

In the spring of 1966, Sylvia was intrigued to learn that new doubts about the assassination were being expressed in the medical and legal communities. "Someone called my attention to a brief news item in the *NY Times* a few days ago," she told Ray Marcus, "reporting that at the annual meeting of the American Acadamey of Forensic Sciences there was some forthright criticism of the WR." Among those criticizing the Report, she went on, were a psychiatrist who was "appalled" at the conclusions the Warren Commission reached about Lee Harvey Oswald's personality and motives, and a lawyer who said the Report was based on evidence that would have been inadmissable in a court of law.[70]

At that meeting was a young doctor named Cyril H. Wecht, then the 34-year-old chief deputy coroner and chief forensic pathologist of Allegheny County in Pittsburgh, Pennsylvania. He was also the director of the Institute of Forensic Sciences at Duquesne University's School of Law. Dr. Wecht had been asked by the American Academy of Forensic Sciences to review the medical aspects of the Warren Report and deliver his findings at its annual meeting. Although he was not mentioned in the brief *Times* article Sylvia had seen, she and Dr. Wecht would soon be in contact.[71]

President Kennedy's autopsy, Dr. Wecht reported to his colleagues at the meeting, was a mess. "By standards found in most competent medical-legal investigative facilities, the autopsy report would not be deemed to be a complete one," he said. Two of the three doctors who performed the autopsy were not forensic pathologists – doctors trained in the specialized science of determing a cause of often violent death. This was a serious flaw in a case the magnitude of Kennedy's assassination; Wecht named five prominent forensic pathologists who could have reached the autopsy at the Bethesda Naval Hospital in an hour's flying time or less. Fortunately the third autopsy doctor, Colonel Pierre A. Finck, was a qualified forensic pathologist. "One can only conjecture how inadequate and incomplete the results of the autopsy findings would have been if Colonel Finck had not been present."[72]

Wecht said that all three autopsy doctors erred by failing to contact the emergency surgeons at Parkland Hospital in Dallas before starting the postmortem procedure. Had they done so, it might have eliminated subsequent confusion. Dr. Wecht had other criticisms, some of them minor – the Warren Report made no mention of Kennedy's adrenal glands – but perhaps the strongest was that the autopsy X-rays and photographs were not examined by the Commission. In spite of all this, Dr. Wecht said he agreed with the Commission's basic findings. There were only three shots fired, and they were all fired by Lee Harvey Oswald. The single-bullet theory was, in all likelihood, a valid one.[73]

Dr. Wecht's contacts with Sylvia Meagher and other critics would alter that point of view.

In March 1966 Meagher was able to tell friends that her index – formally titled *Subject Index to the Warren Report and Hearings & Exhibits* – was at long last finished and bound, and would be available no later than March 21. She had accepted an offer for publication the previous fall. And yet she had the feeling she was in a slump – in part, perhaps, from a sense of perfectionism. "I don't feel real elation about the index coming out . . . and I do feel some dismay at the thought of all the imperfections that I know about but others may never even discover."[74]

The *Subject Index* had a suggested retail price of four dollars. Scarecrow Press, its publisher, put out promotional material which said in part:

Researchers, scholars, professors, teachers, students, general readers . . . all now will be able to test the assertions and conclusions in the Warren Report against the facts contained in the huge, labyrinthine record of the investigation into the assassination of President John F. Kennedy. . . .[75]

Although his intentions were not stated, a message from J. Edgar Hoover to the head of the FBI's New York office suggests the government may have had a use for Sylvia Meagher's index, too. Hoover's message said in part: "The New York Division is instructed to purchase two copies of 'Subject Index to the Warren Report and Hearings and Exhibits' by Sylvia Meagher. One copy should be furnished to the Dallas Division and the other furnished to the Bureau."[76]

Another factor contributing to Sylvia's sense of malaise, probably more draining, was a secret she had sworn to keep. It had begun in late February when Sylvia was contacted by Edward Epstein, first by telephone and a few days later in person. Epstein had some big news: his book had been accepted by Viking Press, the very first publisher he had submitted it to. Viking was so enthusiastic that they offered him a big cash advance and, according to Sylvia, made the book a top priority in order to get it in bookstores as soon as possible. But it was all very hush-hush: Viking was concerned that if word got out there could be attempts to obstruct publication.[77]

The day after his visit, and at Epstein's request, Viking sent a copy of the manuscript by messenger to Sylvia's office at the World Health Organization. She took it home and read it over the next several nights, checking the accuracy of the text and its footnotes, and also making notes to herself about its content. "Ed has not only included all of the staggering items that he mentioned on that now-historical Sunday," she told Maggie Field, meaning the critics' meeting the previous fall, "but a great deal more that he had not mentioned that day." Much of the material that hadn't been mentioned – "at least not in my hearing," Sylvia said – was due in part to one of the Commission's own staff attorneys, Wesley J. Liebeler. "We must acknowledge that he not only attempted to do an honorable job during the investigation but fought a one-man battle to introduce some bit of objectivity into the WR, and then provided the ammunition which will be fatal to the WR and the WC – if there is any sanity left in America."[78]

Sylvia was to have the manuscript for four days only, but it stretched into a much longer period after she pointed out an obvious shortcoming: the book contained no index. The value of a thorough index was by this time a sensitive point for Sylvia, which is perhaps why she offered to prepare one for Epstein's book. Epstein thought it was a great idea, and Viking, too, was willing to turn the index over to her. And so she received the book's page proofs, its introduction, and its appendices. These appendices consisted of excerpts from the four-volume FBI Summary Report on the assassination, and its fifth volume, the Supplemental Report, which Epstein had obtained from Liebeler.[79]

Sylvia included all of this in a letter she wrote to Maggie Field on April 16, 1966. But due to its confidential character she did not mail the letter until June – a situation, she said, which distressed her greatly, "as I am not secretive by nature." She did not mention it, and perhaps it was not yet decided, but the name of Epstein's book was *Inquest*. The book, she was certain, would leave the Warren Commission in utter disgrace.[80]

By this time Sylvia's enthusiasm for the *Ramparts* project had cooled. In spite of its stated intention to devote regular space to the assassination starting in April, there had been delays. In view of Epstein's book, whatever *Ramparts* ultimately did now struck Sylvia as "anticlimactic and irrelevant." Furthermore she had been dismayed by what she regarded as a breach of trust. Somehow *Ramparts* had heard about Salandria's soon-to-be-published *TMO* article describing the FBI Summary Report and its description of CE 399 as having "no point of exit," invalidating the single-bullet theory. This was still confidential but *Ramparts* was eager to use it. On April 29 Sylvia sent David Welsh a telegram saying she was deeply shocked by this development, and was ending her relationship with *Ramparts*. She demanded they return her book manuscript.[81]

Inquest would enjoy intensive promotion and the endorsement of leading opinion-makers. There seemed to be a very real chance that the Warren Report would be discredited and discarded – but this would not be the end of the critics' struggle, only the beginning of a new phase. Sylvia told Maggie: "We must all do everything in our power to ensure that if a new investigation is undertaken, it must be in the framework of an adversary proceeding, if we are to have any hope of finding the truth."[82]

By the late spring and early summer of 1966 Harold Weisberg's book on the Warren Commission had been finished for over a year. Edward Jay Epstein's book had found a publisher. Mark Lane was known to be working on a book, and though Epstein said the manuscript was poor, rewrites were almost certainly underway. Sylvia Meagher's index was in print and her comparative study remained in development. Léo Sauvage had a published book on the case in France, and though frustrated in his efforts to publish it in the United States, he was not discouraged; he had a new contract with World Publishing and the book was due before the year was out. Penn Jones was readying an anthology of his editorials from the *Midlothian Mirror*.

A prolonged silence was about to be smashed, was about to undergo what Sylvia Meagher called "the dramatic transition from taboo to dialogue." It was a transition that she felt was long overdue – but was not especially easy for Harold Weisberg.[83]

"I think Weisberg panicked when he realized that Epstein, Lane, and Sauvage would have their books out by October," she told Maggie Field in May 1966. "He has very grandiose notions about his own book and wanted very much to be 'first.'" He was obsessed with his work, she said, but to his own detriment. Sylvia had just received a copy of a new private printing of *Whitewash*, which arrived by mail with no covering note, or any advance notice that he was planning to self-publish. In spite of her encouraging words to Weisberg some months before, she confided to Maggie now that she considered *Whitewash* "badly-written and very badly presented (tiny print, single space, minimal margins, no spacing between paragraphs, a real abuse of the eye.)"[84]

During the spring of 1966, Weisberg was concentrating on getting his book before the public. "I had to improvise," he once said, in recalling these efforts. He personally contacted eighteen bookstores, and a nineteenth placed a small unsolicited order. By late May he had placed 748 copies of *Whitewash* in these stores – a small number, really, but a number which, at that time, satisfied him. A distributor in Washington, D.C., also agreed to take some books. In June Weisberg attended a book-sellers convention to spread the word about *Whitewash*.[85]

In a four-page preface to his new privately printed *Whitewash*, written in April, Weisberg said the book was being published in "the least desirable of possible forms." The entire book consisted of typewritten pages that had been photographed, reduced, and bound. The preface recounted his unsuccessful struggle to find a commercial publisher and the decision to finally publish the book himself, originally in its limited edition in August of 1965. "With a few minor additions," he wrote, "this is that book – the book that could not be printed."[86]

The "minor additions" amounted to only seventeen pages, which Weisberg called a postscript. But what was in those pages was by no means minor. The principal topic was the FBI Summary Report of December 9, 1963 – what Salandria had written about in his *TMO* article, and what Epstein included in the appendices of his book. It appears that Harold Weisberg was completely unaware of the FBI report until its explosive contents were published in Salandria's April 1966 article, which Harold had first learned about, Sylvia said, from her. "True, Weisberg did go at once to the Archives and read the document for himself," she wrote to Maggie Field on May 18. "But his epilogue suggests that he found the document, without a word of acknowledgment of Salandria's earlier published work. And that seems to be outright dishonesty."[87]

Either Mark Lane or his publisher, it appears, also tried to take credit for finding this critical FBI report. In brochures promoting the upcoming publication of his book *Rush to Judgment*, the publisher, Holt Rinehart and Winston, stated that the FBI Summary Report would be evaluated in the book, and implied that Lane had discovered the document. For Sylvia, this was too much. "I love the way everyone is seizing credit for the FBI report actually found and published by Salandria!" she wrote to Maggie. "It is almost hilarious to see one pirate accusing the other, while the real 'finder' Vince, whose self-abnegation sometimes seems cloying, sturdily maintains an attitude of non-resentment and unconcern." She added that some of Salandria's friends "tease him with the appellation 'St. Vincent,' which I learned with amusement, and which he squirms to hear!"[88]

Salandria had known that Epstein would expose the Summary Report in his book; his first inclination, Sylvia reported, was not to write about it in his *TMO* article since it would be made public in due time. But *TMO* editor Arnoni disagreed, arguing that Salandria had a duty to inform the public; he insisted the report be included. "Ed feels that it was perfectly proper for Salandria to write the article," Sylvia told Maggie Field, "even though it reduced the shock value of his book and even though it had the unforeseen and unforeseeable effect of causing Weisberg and Lane to rush into print with claims of priority and credit which are wholly unwarranted and unprincipled."[89]

Chapter 22

Strange Authors

The distance from Memphis, Tennessee to Jackson, Mississippi is approximately 220 miles. Early in the summer of 1966 James Meredith proposed to walk this distance, saying it would be a personal test – not of his physical fitness, but of his courage. "Nothing can be more enslaving than fear," he said. His plan drew considerable media attention; some of the reporters dubbed it the "March Against Fear." Meredith said he hoped to inspire nearly half-a-million eligible black Mississippians to overcome their fear and register to vote.[1]

Meredith was a Mississippi native but lived with his wife and young son in New York, where he attended Columbia University law school. Except for a brief trip to Mississippi after his father died in 1965, he had not been there since graduating from the University of Mississippi in 1963. His admission to Ole Miss in 1962 had outraged white segregationists, whose rioting on the university's campus left two people dead and many more injured. Throughout his time there, Meredith was under the protection of U.S. marshals.

Meredith intended to make the walk to Jackson alone. "If anyone wants to go, it's his business," he said. "But I want to make it clear he's on his own." When he left for Jackson on June 5, Meredith said he expected it would take him about two weeks. He started at the Peabody Hotel, a Memphis landmark twelve miles north of the Mississippi state line. He wore a yellow pith helmet and a short-sleeved shirt in the 84-degree weather. For the first few miles he was accompanied by an entourage of well-wishers and reporters.[2]

While Meredith considered the journey a lone effort, some of those starting off with him that first day said they would accompany him, on and off, through the duration of the walk. In addition, the media photographed nearly every step. Their work recorded the white thugs who menaced him along the route: "Hurry up, nigger, you're gonna get killed in Mississippi!" On the morning of the second day, Meredith told reporters that "the tension is high. I can tell from the way the Negroes are acting along the way."[3]

Six men accompanied him as he headed out that second morning. As they walked Meredith told his press coordinator Sherwood Ross: "Nonviolence is not in the American tradition. The American tradition is to get out and work for what you want, to fight for what you want. I'm tired of all this begging and all this pleading. We've got to assert our rights."[4]

Shortly after four o'clock that afternoon, having walked some 28 miles of his proposed route, Meredith was shot in the back by a rifleman hidden in the brush alongside the highway.[5]

According to Sherwood Ross the sniper called out Meredith's name before opening fire. Ross shouted "James, he has a gun!" and the men scattered, throwing themselves onto the highway and scrambling for cover. Three shots were fired. Meredith was the only one hit; he pulled himself along the ground, crying out, "Oh, my God, oh, oh!"[6]

News bulletins flashed across the country that James Meredith had been killed. They were erroneous. At a hospital in Memphis, doctors removed between sixty and seventy shotgun pellets from his body, but the wounds were superficial and that same day he was listed in satisfactory condition. Clearly though, he was lucky to have escaped with his life. The night of the shooting Meredith, although sedated, called his wife and told her, "Except for being a little stiff, I feel as well as I ever did."[7]

At least one news photographer was present and took pictures of James Meredith as he lay bleeding along the roadside. These photographs were published in newspapers across the country the following day. Incredibly, one of them revealed the gunman, plainly visible as the wounded Meredith, sprawled on his hands and knees, looked back toward him. This photograph appeared in the *Los Angeles Times* on June 7. Ray Marcus saw it and was struck by the similarity between the man in the *Times* photo and the #5 man detail from the Moorman photograph. Not that he thought they were the same man: there was obviously no connection between the Meredith shooting and the Kennedy assassination. But there, in the *Times* photo, was a gunman largely obscured against a mottled background of leaves, light, and shadow. Yet his face and his rifle were conspicuous. Marcus decided it was worth keeping the photograph for purposes of demonstration and comparison.[8]

The man visible in the background of the photograph was arrested at the scene. He was identified as 40-year-old Aubrey James Norvel. Authorities said he was drunk when arrested. From his ranch in Texas, President Lyndon Johnson ordered a federal inquiry into the Meredith shooting.[9]

In its issue of June 13, 1966, more than a year and a half after he first proposed it, Fred J. Cook's article on the Kennedy assassination was finally published in *The Nation*. Editor Carey McWilliams had resisted Cook from the beginning, but had never seen the completed article. In desperation, Cook sent it to him after *Ramparts* rejected it. McWilliams was still reluctant, but Cook pointed out to him that Edward Epstein's *Inquest* was about to be published. Cook recalled telling McWilliams that "if he ever intended to do anything with my article, he had to get a move on. So finally he did."[10]

The article appeared in two installments, the June 13 and June 20 issues. Cook was bothered that both parts appeared with editorial disclaimers distancing the magazine from what it was publishing. This is what *The Nation* had done with Harold Feldman's "Oswald and the FBI" two-and-a-half years earlier.[11]

Part One was entitled "Some Unanswered Questions," and in it Cook restricted himself to the events of Dealey Plaza, discussing the Zapruder film and what it revealed, and the limitations it imposed on the Warren Commission's version of the shooting. Cook's arguments on the timing of the shots were in line with, and probably influenced by, the "Hypotheses re: the Zapruder Film," that Ray Marcus had sent him in the summer of 1965. "With this much established, the official description of one suspect, three shells, three shots begins to collide with fact," he wrote.[12]

One of Cook's most salient points was one that few, if any, other early critics had made: "*. . . not a single eyewitness* the commission heard," he wrote, "saw the action in the way that the commission decided it had happened. *All, without exception*, were convinced that the President and Governor Connally were felled by two separate, wounding shots."[13]

Yet his intention, Cook made clear, was not "to exculpate Lee Harvey Oswald . . . [he] was directly involved." He considered the evidence linking Oswald to the purchase of the weapon, to the same weapon discovered on the TSBD sixth floor, and the ballistics linking CE 399 to that weapon convincing. "To contend in the face of all this – and much more besides – that Oswald was innocent is to endorse absurdity." But, Cook added, it was virtually impossible for him to believe that Oswald acted alone.[14]

The second part of Cook's article was called "Testimony of the Eyewitnesses." He pointed out that in spite of the speed with which

Dallas authorities all but closed the case against Oswald, with a lone shooter, three-shots-fired theory, "a surprising number of spectators insisted with varying degrees of certainty that they had heard four, five or six shots." The location of the wounds on President Kennedy as described by documents and testimony in the Warren Commission also raised questions. FBI expert Robert Frazier had placed the back wound about 5 1/2 inches below the President's collar and an inch to the right of center of his jacket. As Harold Weisberg and others had already pointed out, the wounds were illustrated in the Commission volumes not with photographs, but schematic drawings prepared at the direction of Navy Commanders James J. Humes and J. Thornton Boswell. The first drawing, a side view of the President, showed the path of a bullet entering the base of his neck and exiting at his throat. "The second drawing," Cook wrote, "Exhibit 386, is a back view of the President's head and shoulders; it places the entry wound, not on a line with the tip of the shoulder, not almost in the middle of the back, but *well up above the shoulder level on the right side of the President's neck*. In other words, *the location of this wound has been changed!*" The discrepancy became more serious when the two drawings were compared to CE 397, which included the autopsy "face sheet" on which Kennedy's back wound was placed about where Humes described it in his testimony – that is, some five-and-a-half inches below the neckline and just to the left of the right shoulder blade.[15]

For some reason Cook failed to mention the certificate of Commander Humes that was also included in CE 397. This was Commander Humes' statement that he had "destroyed by burning certain preliminary draft notes" relating to Kennedy's autopsy.[16]

There was just too much that did not add up. The discrepancies – the omissions and distortions – suggested the possibility of a second gunman, Cook wrote, and "a Pandora's box of possibilities flies open. To admit so much is to admit that the man whose bullet actually killed President Kennedy may still be at large."[17]

Three issues later, *The Nation* ran an item entitled "The Vital Documents," written by a Yale history professor named Jacob Cohen. Cohen was said to be working on a defense of the Warren Commission, a book called *Honest Verdict.* The very first sentence of his *Nation* article set the tone for what was to come:

Several writers have recently suggested that Lee Harvey Oswald was not a lone assassin shooting at President Kennedy that black Friday in Dallas and publishers' fall lists promise several new books developing variations of the same theory.[18]

His first paragraph ended with the assertion that critics who rejected the lone-gunman theory would, by necessity, have to agree that "if there was more than one assassin, then the results of the autopsy which was performed on the President at Bethesda the night of the assassination must have been deliberately falsified. One can reach no other conclusion."[19]

The reason for this, Cohen said, was that the President's autopsy had been conducted by two experienced pathologists and a wound-ballistics expert, and their official report stated that two bullets had entered his body. Both were fired from above and behind him. One struck him in the base of the neck and exited from the lower third of the throat, and the other hit him in the back of the skull and exited through the right temple.[20]

The critics all disputed these official findings, Cohen wrote. Their articles suggested more than two bullets, argued that the shots came from different directions – most importantly, from the front – and placed the wounds in locations different from those reported by the official autopsy. If the critics were right, then the autopsy had to have been falsified.[21]

"Has it come to this, then?" Cohen asked – "the doctors' word against the word of Cook, Epstein, Salandria, et al?"

There should be an easy solution to the controversy: the photographs and X-rays of the President's body taken at the time of the autopsy. These would "either silence Cook and Epstein or win a Pulitzer Prize for one of them," Cohen said. But incredibly, those documents, "the only material evidence that could confirm or deny the observations of the autopsy doctors," were not included in the twenty-six volumes and were never examined by the Warren Commission and its staff. "Indeed," Cohen wrote, "after several months of part-time detective work, I cannot even be sure of the whereabouts of these documents."[22]

Cohen pointed out that FBI ballistics expert Robert Frazier had declined to say, during his May 1964 Warren Commission testimony, whether the bullet holes in the front and back of Kennedy's shirt were made by the same bullet. He wouldn't say because he had not seen the autopsy report. In June he had still not seen it, suggesting that the FBI did not have it, or X-rays or photos, when it prepared its Summary

Report in December 1963. "The point is crucial," Cohen said, "because, as Salandria and Epstein have stressed, the FBI report contradicts the autopsy in the Warren Report in several details. According to the FBI, Kennedy was hit in the back, not in the lower neck, and this bullet did not exit from his throat." Epstein had stated in *Inquest* that the FBI did have the autopsy report before submitting its Summary Report. But Cohen called that into question, saying that Epstein's only source for that claim was an interview with former Commission staffer Francis W. H. Adams. Cohen had interviewed Adams too; Adams said he did not remember ever talking to Epstein and did not have his name in his appointment calendar on the date Epstein said he had interviewed him. Simply put, Adams said he didn't know what Epstein was talking about.[23]

When Fred Cook saw Cohen's article, he was furious. Carey McWilliams had told him about the article before it appeared, but it was far different from what Cook had been led to expect. "The legitimate point of the article that Carey had mentioned to me was there, buried deep in the body of the piece. The whole approach, the whole tone, however, was slanted to ridicule critics of the Warren Report. The article was filled with snide references to me and to Vincent Salandria. . . ." Cook was so angry he wrote a letter to the editor and gave McWilliams an ultimatum: either run his reply without deleting a single word, or Cook would never write for *The Nation* again.[24]

The letter did appear, in *The Nation's* issue of August 22.

> Cohen leaps, by a process of logic that baffles me, to the conclusion that I hold the autopsy report in the Kennedy assassination to have been falsified. I have not said so nor am I convinced at this point that it was. There are certainly peculiar circumstances surrounding it. . . .
>
> Leaving all drawings and speculations about missing X-rays and photographs aside, Commander Humes's autopsy report specifically locates the wounds . . . these are fixed points . . . virtually a straight line through the body. . . .
>
> The schematic drawings by which the commission sought to reconcile the wounds with the projected downward trajectory were definitely falsified, either deliberately or possibly, though this seems difficult to believe, through asinine error.[25]

Edward Jay Epstein's book *Inquest* was published about a month before Cohen's article appeared in *The Nation*. It received a great deal of media attention and generally good reviews. An item in *The Atlantic* said the book showed some of the reasons why the Warren Commission failed to quiet doubts about the President's murder. The Commission's mistake "was to pretend that it could establish the whole truth, an effort doomed to failure from the start."[26]

Newsweek magazine gave *Inquest* a prominent position in its "National Affairs" section. In spite of the distinguished men of the Warren Commission, the magazine said, "the chorus of dissenters has never been stilled," although their continuing criticism represented "morbid curiosity." The judgments of critic newcomer Epstein were "harsh," but his book was serious and scholarly, declaring the Commission's work "extremely superficial," shaped by "an overriding desire to settle doubts rather than pursue the truth to its uncertain end." Epstein believed that the Commission's findings represented not absolute truth, but "political truth."[27]

In *The New Republic*, Epstein's book was reviewed along with Harold Weisberg's *Whitewash*. "Weisberg and Epstein have independently ransacked the twenty-six volumes of testimony and exhibits and the two FBI reports on which the Warren Report is based; additionally, Epstein interviewed members of the Commission and its staff, in pursuit of his master's thesis on government at Cornell University. He evoked some staggering admissions . . . the Warren Report may now have been shot to death and require a full autopsy."[28]

Léo Sauvage reviewed *Inquest* in *The New Leader* and called it "a fascinating book . . . the main preoccupation of the Commission was with 'national interest,' not with truth, and the real problem Epstein wound up studying concerned the place of what he calls 'political truth' . . . this is precisely what makes *Inquest* so fascinating."[29]

In *The Minority of One*, Sylvia Meagher wrote a positively glowing review. That she had prepared the book's index and was thanked by Epstein in its acknowledgments presented at least the appearance of a conflict of interest, but that seems not to have troubled M.S. Arnoni. She declared Epstein had "shot down the Warren Report for all time . . . the 'amateurs' and 'mischief-makers' who tried to warn a deaf and complacent public that Lee Harvey Oswald was not a 'lone assassin' and that the Warren Report was not an honest document have been vindicated."[30]

No book, of course, receives universal praise, and *Inquest* was no exception. The book was attacked in the pages of *Look* magazine in a long article by the novelist Fletcher Knebel, who declared that Epstein was guilty of presenting only that evidence which supported his thesis – the same thing, Knebel said, that Epstein accused the Warren Commission of doing. Knebel ended his article with a terse comment from former Commission member Allen Dulles: "If they've found another assassin, let them name names and produce their evidence."[31]

Inquest bothered Harold Weisberg, as well. "The more I think of the book and its line, the less I like both," he told Vince Salandria. He conceded that, if nothing else, it showed the willingness of a major publisher to print something critical of the Warren Commission. He also thought it was good that it documented that there were those who knew something wrong was being done, even as they were doing it. But overall Weisberg felt Epstein was not qualified to write on the subject, and it bothered him that some of the Commission critics, like Sylvia Meagher, thought so highly of him. "She speaks of a kind word from Epstein as though it were a divine dispensation."[32]

Salandria had written his own review of *Inquest* and sent it around to some of his fellow critics. It was never published in its original form and the earliest drafts no longer exist. But Salandria considered Epstein's book dishonest. "I wanted to excoriate him for writing that book!" he recalled many years later. "*Inquest*. I thought it was horrible."[33]

Before Salandria submitted his review – he hoped to publish it in *Liberation* – he was introduced to a young man named Ira Einhorn. Einhorn at this time was emerging as a leading figure in Philadelphia's flowering counterculture. He was also an iconoclast, a refugee from academia who nevertheless impressed virtually everyone he met with his lightening-fast mind and deep intellect.[34]

Einhorn read Salandria's review and thought it was too strident. He must have made some very good arguments, because Salandria allowed him to rewrite it; by the time he was finished, four people shared the byline credit. Einhorn's name came first, followed by Stephen Karpowitz, who had introduced Einhorn to Salandria; then Thomas Katen, a philosophy professor; and Salandria. "A Move Toward the Center" appeared in *Liberation's* August 1966 issue.[35]

The review said that reaction to the Warren Report had, since its appearance, been presented as falling into two broad categories: blind faith – belief in something for which there is no evidence, as Mark Lane was saying on public platforms – and demonology, which implicitly linked adherents to an evil spirit.

> By creating two diametrically opposed positions, the end points
> of battle are established with the further implication that the truth (in

the guise of Mr. Epstein's book) lies somewhere in the middle. This strategy which attempts to disqualify by categorizing the point of view from which the facts emerge rather than treating the facts has been all too prominent in the discussion so far . . . as soon as one impugns the honesty of the Commission or implies that Oswald did not kill Kennedy, one has left the carefully defined field of battle and is not allowed to play except under the rubric of "demonologist."[36]

This less-strident review touted Epstein's book as "brilliant and dispassionate in the best tradition of American academic scholarship" although its "carefully understated case leans much too far in the direction of excusing the Commission for a botched job. . . ." In the end, the reviewers found *Inquest* wanting.[37]

> The public cannot help but be disturbed by a situation in which the words "political truth" (Epstein) are used as a substitute for lies, and the phrase "morbid curiosity" (*Newsweek*, June 13, 1966) is applied to an attempt to honestly question the validity of a report whose veracity is being slowly dissolved with each passing day.
>
> The people will know. They must know, for the knowledge of this truth is vital to the continuance of our entire democratic system.[38]

Late in 1964, when Vince Salandria's first critique of the Warren Report appeared in *The Legal Intelligencer,* a young journalist named Gaeton Fonzi saw it and was intrigued. Fonzi, a senior editor for *Greater Philadelphia* magazine, thought the item could be developed for what was referred to as "the back of the book" – light and witty human interest stories to round out an issue. It might be an interesting character sketch, Fonzi thought – "a story about this crazy guy Salandria."[39]

He took it for granted that Salandria was crazy. "You have to remember," Fonzi said many years later, "what a discordant thing it was in 1964 to hear that an official government report might be wrong – especially a weighty one issued by a panel of men of public stature."[40]

But Gaeton Fonzi was in for a surprise. Salandria, it turned out, was a serious, very intense man who was deeply concerned about what had happened with the Warren Commission. "He didn't like the idea of the Commission holding secret hearings," Fonzi recalled. "He thought that was something basically contradictory to the process of government and that initially got him interested. Then, when he learned that they seemed to be leaning toward the conclusion that a lone assassin did it, someone who was totally unrelated to anybody else, he began getting suspicious. I remember he put it, 'If this had happened in Moscow or Minsk, no American would believe that a lone gunman could have killed the head of the government. But because it happened in Dallas, Americans are accepting it.'"41

Unexpectedly, Salandria had impressed Gaeton Fonzi; before long his arguments didn't sound so crazy. Yet Fonzi was not convinced. When the interview was over and Fonzi was about to leave, Salandria insisted that he take with him an extra set of the twenty-six volumes of Hearings and Exhibits to study the matter for himself. "And that's what I did, and that's what initially got me interested in the Kennedy assassination. But not only interested – it got me kind of angry about it."42

Fonzi began reading the Warren Commission material closely and comparing some of the Report's assertions against the raw material of the twenty-six volumes. Salandria had told him that if the assassination had occurred as the Commission said, the details would fit easily together. As Fonzi's study deepened he began to see that in fact, the details did not fit.43

When *Inquest* was published, Fonzi read the account in *Newsweek* that reported: "Epstein [says] the most crucial job – establishing all the basic facts of the assassination – fell impossibly heavily on one man, Arlen Specter, then a Philadelphia lawyer, now the city's new district attorney." This was a great local angle: the man responsible for establishing the basic facts of the assassination lived and worked in Fonzi's own back yard. Instead of a puff piece about a kook named Salandria, he would delve seriously into the case, with Specter as his point of departure. Fonzi called Specter's office to set up an interview. But before conducting it he talked to Salandria again, and together the two men prepared eleven pages of detailed questions to put before the former Commission assistant counsel.44

The first of what became two interviews was held on Tuesday, June 28. "As it turned out," Fonzi recalled, "I was the first one to ask Specter specific questions about the Report's inconsistencies. I couldn't believe the hemmings and hawings, the hesitations and evasions I got from the normally cool, collected and verbally masterful Specter. I had caught him off guard."45

Specter had been assigned to what the Warren Commission defined as Area I, the basic facts of the assassination. At age thirty-four, he was the junior counsel in this area; full responsibility fell to him after the senior counsel, Francis W. H. Adams, left the Commission. Adams was not asked to resign because General Counsel J. Lee Rankin was concerned it would give the impression of dissension within the ranks.[46]

Specter's most significant contribution to the Commission's case was probably his development of the single-bullet theory. This theory was the attempt to explain how one of the first two shots allegedly fired by Oswald wounded President Kennedy, then went on to inflict all of Governor Connally's wounds. That this bullet was also virtually unscathed was a related but separate issue.

This was one of the first things Fonzi asked Specter about. He answered at length, insisting that it was really an easy shot from the Book Depository's sixth floor to where the motorcade passed on Elm Street. "It was particularly a straight line shot which you can really only appreciate to the fullest when you're right there, look out of that window, and see it as we saw it on the reconstruction," he said. "At a hundred yards, less than a hundred yards, which was the range at all times – I forget the exact number of feet, but it ended up at about 275 feet I think that the head shot of the President, and less than 200 feet earlier, that is reasonably close with a four-power scope and it is not a very difficult shot for a guy with Oswald's background – so said the Marine experts who know this whole line."[47]

Specter offered to show Fonzi the Zapruder film. Each Commissioner and staff member had been given copies of this and other exhibits when the Commission's work was finished. Viewing the film, Specter said, might help Fonzi understand the difficulties in determining the shooting sequence. "You just can't tell when he was hit, uh . . . you can't tell on the films when he was hit."

"When Connally was hit?"

"When Connally was hit. You just can't tell. Connally, you see, says that he was hit by uh, by the second shot. Connally says that he heard the first shot, and then he was hit by the second shot. That's in Connally's testimony. Uh, but what you have on the Z-film is, naturally, just a two-dimensional film, and the governor is turning around and at some point he's hit, but I watched the governor watch those films – which, by the way, was fascinating to see – his response as he watched that film for the first time when he was at the Commission the day he testified – and even he can't tell exactly when he was hit, you know."

Fonzi asked Specter whether he agreed that if Kennedy and Connally were not hit by the same bullet, it meant there was more than one gunman. Specter did not agree.

"Why not?" Fonzi asked.

"Because I think it's entirely possible that Kennedy could have been hit before frame 207." Together Fonzi and Specter looked at the Warren Report, which contained a few of the Zapruder frames and FBI data relating to the shots. The FBI reenactments established that for a fleeting moment the presidential limousine was visible from the sniper's nest area through a gap in leaves and branches of the trees which otherwise obscured the vehicle entirely for several seconds. "There's a little opening in the tree here. He could have been hit at 186 – possible. Unlikely, I think. He could have been hit at 166, it's possible, unlikely. He went behind the tree, could have even been hit before he went behind the tree. Unlikely, but possible. You just, you just, you just really can't say with, with finality when the guy shot him, hit him."

Fonzi asked when Specter thought Connally was first hit; he replied that he couldn't tell for certain, but probably between Z-230 and Z-240.

What about Kennedy's back wound? The placement of this wound was a matter of controversy. The Warren Commission called it a neck wound and produced sketches as evidence. But some witnesses placed it on Kennedy's back, like Secret Service Agent Glen A. Bennett, who placed the wound about four inches down from the right shoulder, and Agent Clint Hill, who told the Commission it was about six inches below the neckline to the right of the spinal column. Commander Humes told the Commission this wound was about five-and-a-half inches below the collar, and just to the left of the right shoulder blade, and the autopsy face sheet placed it there, too. Photographs of the President's shirt and jacket showed bullet holes that supported all of these observations.

Throughout the interview with Specter, Fonzi was careful not to mention Vince Salandria's name; it might have upset him, Fonzi thought, since Salandria had questioned Specter on the pages of Philadelphia's law journal. For Salandria the holes shown in the President's shirt and jacket had a personal dimension. His father had been a tailor who was proud of his profession; Salandria couldn't accept the explanation that Kennedy's tailor would make a shirt and jacket so ill-fitting it would bunch up as he waved to the crowd. Yet this was the explanation Specter offered to Gaeton Fonzi. "Wave your arm a few times," Specter said. He got up from his desk and walked around to where Fonzi sat, as the obliging reporter lifted his arm. "Wave at the crowd." Specter jabbed one of his fingers into Fonzi's neck. "Well, see, if the bullet goes in here, the jacket gets hunched up. . . ."[48]

"Wasn't there only one single hole in the jacket? Wouldn't it have been doubled over?"

"No, not necessarily. It, it wouldn't be doubled over . . . when you sit in the car it could be doubled over at most any point, but the probabilities are that, uh, that it gets, that uh, this, this, this is about the way a jacket rides up. . . . " And the shirt? "Same thing."

Fonzi asked him about Zapruder frames 208 through 211, the ones missing from the Zapruder exhibit in the twenty-six volumes. "Missing frames on the Z film?" Specter replied with genuine surprise. "Which ones are missing?"

"There was a splicing and, a, missing, at any rate, from the National Archives. . . ."

"On the Z film?"

"Yeah."

"Well, I've got a copy of them frame-by-frame," Specter said, chuckling. He indicated his box of official evidence. "They're in the corner, and you're welcome to look at them."

Fonzi said the frames went missing just as Kennedy's head disappeared behind a street sign. "That's not so," Specter replied, "and I'll tell you now that I'll just reflect on it for a minute. Every frame in the Z-film is set forth in the exhibit and I've got the exhibit here. . . ."

The former Warren Commission staff counsel pulled it out. "See," Fonzi said, "it jumps from 207 to 212. And you can almost see the splice."

Specter must have been embarrassed. "Boy, you sure got me," he said. "207-212? Well, I've got the intervening frames. I don't think there's anything deliberate about that at all. I never knew that. I'm very much surprised. . . ."

"The point is," Fonzi said, "all this little stuff like this just seems to be adding fuel. A lot of these people who, as you say, are coming up with these conspiratorial theses, to me, seems to me that the Commission could clear up the whole matter."

"Well, Mr. Fonzi, you have the basic problem. The Commission is defunct. It's out of existence. People say to me, 'You ought to write a book, you ought to speak out. You ought to get permission from the Commission and really let loose.' Well, who's the Commission? The Commission doesn't exist any more. Earl Warren's just not available to talk about those things. There just isn't any Commission."

Fonzi was curious about why the Commission had accepted the sketches depicting President Kennedy's wounds. "Did you see the X-rays yourself?"

"No."

"You relied strictly on the testimonies of Finck and Humes?"

"Boswell and Humes."

"Did you ask to see the X-rays?"

"Did I ask to see the x-rays and photographs?" Specter repeated, chuckling. "Uhh, uhh, that question was considered by me and uh, the Commission decided not to press for the X-rays and photographs."

He paused. "Have I dodged your question? Yes, I've dodged your question." Specter stood and began pacing back and forth behind his desk. Finally he said quietly, "I don't want to dodge your questions."[49]

He continued: "As the assistant counsel in that area I was interested in seeing the photographs and X-rays. I was interested in every conceivable bit of evidence which would have any line on the issue of direction of the bullet. The Commission considered whether the X-rays and photographs should be put into the record and should be examined by the Commission's staff, and the Commission reached the conclusion that it was not necessary. And the reason for the Commission's decision was based, to the best of my understanding, on the considerations of taste, of taste and respect for the dead president. . . ."

Writing of this entire encounter many years later, Gaeton Fonzi recalled that when the interviews were finally over, he walked from Specter's office with a strange sense of uneasiness – what he called the numbness of disbelief. "I got the feeling he was still shaken by his inability to answer some of the questions," Fonzi said. Specter's evasiveness, his inability to explain the inconsistencies Fonzi had brought to his attention, were devastating. Fonzi's belief in the United States Government, he said, would never be the same.[50]

On the evening of June 30, two days after the first of the interviews between Gaeton Fonzi and Arlen Specter, Sylvia Meagher received a telephone call from Vince Salandria. He was "wildly excited," she wrote in her notes. The interview with Specter had yielded "unbelievable results – four hours of tape – invaluable material." Specter's answers to Fonzi's questions, Salandria felt, were further proof that the Commission's conclusions were an easily discernible fraud. He was not sure now, he told Sylvia, whether Arlen Specter was dishonest, or was just plain stupid.[51]

That same day Sylvia resumed her correspondence with Maggie Field. Maggie had written in May with the news that David Lifton had been hired as a consultant to *Ramparts*, in the magazine's stated commitment to publishing material critical of the Warren Commission. Meanwhile she was excited about the publication of *Inquest*. Just before it reached the stores a friend had told Maggie that booksellers were eager to get it, and confident it would "blow the lid off the Warren Commission."[52]

Sylvia replied that "I, too, am on needles of impatience, even though I have already read it." Her interest was so great that in May, she hired a press-clipping service to make sure she would miss none of the media commentary on the book. She told Maggie about a *New York Post* column by Maxwell Lerner in which Lerner admitted that *Inquest* had, for the first time, shaken his confidence in the Warren Report. "He was one of the die-hard 'liberals' who, like I.F. Stone, was ready to stake his life on the WR without even reading it. Well, better late than never . . . I suppose. . . ."[53]

Sylvia had recently given M.S. Arnoni three chapters of her comparative study and he had reacted very positively to them, which she found encouraging. Arnoni was giving signs he would like to publish something on the assassination in each issue of *TMO* for the foreseeable future. In fact the June issue carried an article by Sylvia: a review of *The Two Assassins*, a new book by Renatus Hartogs and Lucy Freeman. Hartogs was a psychiatrist who had examined the teenaged Lee Oswald when Oswald was confined, for about three weeks, to a youth home in New York. Later he testified before the Warren Commission. Coincidentally, Sylvia had known co-author Lucy Freeman slightly many years before.[54]

Privately Sylvia referred to *The Two Assassins* as a "contemptible piece of garbage" and "a dirty little book." Her published review was no kinder: "Hartogs might have been well advised to remain silent after his inglorious performance as a Warren Commission witness. Instead, he and his co-author, Lucy Freeman, have elected to give us a Freudian interpretation of the crime of the century which completely disregards the political setting in which the crime took place. . . ." Even the Warren Report acknowledged that Hartogs' May 1953 report did not indicate that Oswald, then a thirteen-year-old in trouble for truancy, was dangerous. Yet, as he had before the Warren Commission, Hartogs' book made that claim. He had also written that it was "interesting" that the letters making up "Alek J. Hidell," Oswald's pseudonym, could *almost* be re-arranged to form "Jekyll-Hyde." Meagher observed that "Renatus Hartogs" could be used to form at least two anagrams: "trash outrages" and "strange authors." She had come up with a third anagram but Arnoni deleted it: "Thor's great anus."[55]

One of the chapters Sylvia loaned to Arnoni was called "Oswald and the State Department." In researching this chapter, Sylvia told Maggie, "I began for the first time to suspect that there *was* a clandestine relationship" between Oswald and some government agency – "something which I had resisted all along." Nearly a year earlier she had argued against this possibility in a conversation with Salandria, although she admitted at the time that her objections were on "purely subjective grounds."[56]

On the surface, at least, Sylvia's relationship with Salandria remained very good. She had presented him with a copy of her *Subject Index*, which she inscribed: "To Vincent Salandria, whose encouragement helped me so much, in comradeship and warm affection." But she was dismayed by his negative reaction to *Inquest*. "With the help of three co-authors (!) he wrote a highly inflammatory 'review' of which he sent copies all around," she told Maggie Field. "Vince, in private conversation, goes so far as to suspect Ed of being an agent for the FBI or worse." But Maggie also had doubts about Epstein's book; she told Sylvia she was in agreement with Salandria's review. "A copy of it should accompany every copy of *Inquest!*"[57]

Sylvia was also angry with Salandria because he did not seem to be holding up his end of a bargain they'd made to share all documents each obtained from the National Archives. She had learned Salandria got copies of several important documents. But Salandria not only did not share them with her, he had given copies to Epstein. "Perhaps our conceptions of friendship, and of cooperation, are different," she said.[58]

Sylvia had heard that Penn Jones had ordered numerous copies of the *Subject Index,* which puzzled her. Why would he need more than one? Jones had purchased multiple sets of the Hearings and Exhibits, and sent them to libraries in Austin and New Orleans; he had even sent a set to France. He once told a journalist that he had purchased five copies of the *Subject Index* to go with his five remaining sets of the Hearings and Exhibits. "I have these other sets here to loan to anyone interested in studying them."[59]

The *Subject Index to the Warren Report* was drawing attention from unexpected places. In mid-July Sylvia received a letter from retired Major General Edwin Walker. Walker, who according to the Warren Report had been shot at by Lee Oswald in the spring of 1963, did not care for his index entry.

Official evidence. *The Warren Commission's Hearings Before the President's Commission on the Assassination of President Kennedy.* The twenty-six volumes were made public on November 23, 1964. (Photo by Beth Sanders.)

Above left: Mark Lane indicating the grassy knoll, October 4, 1964, at a press conference in Paris (AP/Wide World Photo). **Above right:** Philadelphia lawyer Vince Salandria with sketch demonstrating JFK head-snap, around 1966 (Courtesy Vince Salandria.).

Below left: Harold Feldman (left) with wife Immie (center), and Marguerite Oswald. Photo taken during the Feldmans' Dallas trip with Vince Salandria, summer 1964 (Photo courtesy Immie Feldman). **Below right:** This photograph of the Texas School Book Depository was taken by Vincent J. Salandria, summer 1964 (Photo courtesy Vincent J. Salandria).

Above left: Léo Sauvage, author of *The Oswald Affair* and numerous articles on the JFK assassination (AP/Wide World Photo). **Above right:** Sylvia Meagher, June 1977 (AP/Wide World Photo). **Below left:** Josiah "Tink" Thompson at the National Conference of COPA, the Coalition on Political Assassinations, Washington, D.C., October 1995 (Photograph © 1995 by John Kelin). **Below right:** Harold Weisberg, the author of *Whitewash*, framed by stacks of the 26 volumes (Photo courtesy of Hood College).

Above left: Penn Jones, Jr., edited and published *The Midlothian Mirror* from 1946 to 1974. This photograph was taken the morning after the *Mirror* was firebombed in 1962 (Photo by John Howard Griffin. Copyright © 2005 The Estate of John Howard Griffin). **Above right:** Raymond Marcus, June 1965, around the time #5 man was first identified (Courtesy Raymond Marcus). **Below left:** Maggie Field during the mid-1970s (Courtesy Gwen Field). **Below right:** Shirley Martin, who "started early and was interviewing witnesses before the Commission began taking testimony" (Courtesy Steven M. Martin).

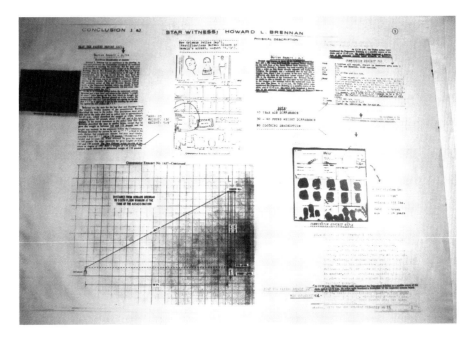

Above and below: The evidence. One of many "panoplies" produced by Maggie Field. No single panel, of course, can be representative of the entire work (Photo by author).

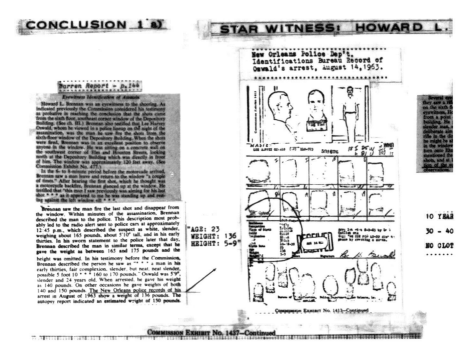

Gunman in the shadows? The #5 man image. This seldom-seen detail (circled above right, enlarged below) from a Polaroid picture by eyewitness Mary Moorman may reveal an armed man on the grassy knoll just as JFK was shot. Some scoff at its validity. But one analyst told Ray Marcus, "You don't need an expert to tell you what's there – it's a man" (AP/Wide World).

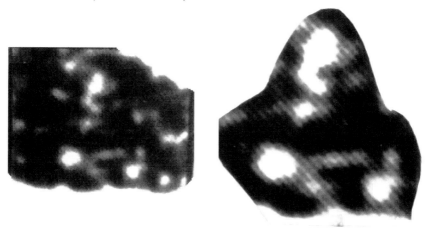

Above: James Meredith looks back at assailant (circled) just after being shot, June 1966 (AP/Wide World Photo). **Above, at left:** Meredith's assailant, enlarged. This image and the "#5 man" detail in the Moorman photograph were those confused by CBS executive Les Midgley. **Below:** Commission Exhibit 397. This certificate signed by JFK autopsy doctor James J. Humes, documenting that Humes "destroyed by burning" some of JFK's autopsy records, provided the early critics with powerful ammunition.

U. S. NAVAL MEDICAL SCHOOL
NATIONAL NAVAL MEDICAL CENTER
BETHESDA, MARYLAND 20014

24 November 1963

C-E-R-T-I-F-I-C-A-T-E

I, James J. Humes, certify that I have destroyed by burning certain preliminary draft notes relating to Naval Medical School Autopsy Report A63-272 and have officially transmitted all other papers related to this report to higher authority.

J. J. HUMES
CDR, MC, USN

Above: CE 399, at left, and CE 856. Many critics considered the juxtaposition of these images one of the most compelling proofs against the single-bullet theory. According to the Warren Commission, CE 399 first wounded President Kennedy, then went on to cause multiple wounds in Governor Connally. Yet CE 399 is virtually unscathed. In contrast, CE 856 (the same make and caliber as CE 399) was test-fired through the wrist of a human cadaver only.

Below: Zapruder frame 212, as printed in Volume 18. Harold Weisberg observed, "It has so amateurish a splice through it that a single tree in the upper section is a full quarter of the frame to the left in the lower section!" (Zapruder Film © 1967, renewed 1995, by The Sixth Floor Museum at Dealey Plaza. All Rights Reserved).

I note the indexing of 18 people, including Walker, E.A., as 'Right-Wingers and Neo-Nazi' (pp. 147-148).

Would you explain to me what you mean by neo-Nazi, how it is intended to apply to each of the 18, to me, and to the group as a whole?[60]

"He seems to take issue with my classifying him as a 'right-winger,'" Sylvia wrote to Lillian Castellano. "My publishers are shivering in their boots for fear that he will sue, which is silly, as he has no grounds whatsoever." Nevertheless she immediately drafted a reply in which she pointed out that Walker's name was mentioned a number of times in the Warren Report, in a sub-section called "Right-wing groups hostile to President Kennedy." The Report also stated that Oswald held an extreme dislike of the right wing, hence his alleged attempt on Walker's life. "Allow me to point out that, as stated in the preface to the *Subject Index*, the work is an attempt to classify the material in the Warren Report and the Hearings and Exhibits . . . and does not necessarily take a position with regard to the correctness or incorrectness of statements, exhibits, categorizations, or allegations in the Warren Report. . . ."[61]

General Walker had, according to at least one published report, once paid a visit to Byron de la Beckwith when Beckwith was incarcerated and awaiting trial for murdering Medgar Evers in June 1963. The retired general had shaken Beckwith's hand. The general was also prominent in the opposition to James Meredith's enrollment at Ole Miss in 1962. In urging civilians to defy the "anti-Christ" Supreme Court, Walker had declared himself "on the right side" of the issue.[62]

As James Meredith lay recuperating from his gunshot wounds in a Memphis hospital, leading civil rights activists came to see him. Visitors included Dr. Martin Luther King, Jr., of the Southern Christian Leadership Conference; newly elected SNCC chairman Stokely Carmichael; comedian Dick Gregory; and Charles Evers, Mississippi field secretary for the NAACP and brother of the late Medgar Evers. Reluctantly, Meredith endorsed their plans to continue the March Against Fear without him.[63]

The pilgrimage resumed the day after the shooting, at the very place where Meredith had been shot near the town of Hernando. It meandered through Mississippi toward Jackson along Highway 51. What started as the march of a single determined man was now growing steadily: each day it seemed there were more marchers than the day before. On June 8, the same day Meredith was discharged from the hospital and flew home to New York, there were about 150 marchers; the next day there were more than 200. They were escorted by state and federal authorities and as many as seventy-five journalists. King and Carmichael, representing sharply different points of view, were among the marchers. So were Floyd B. McKissick, the national director of CORE, and James Farmer, the former CORE director and a veteran of the Freedom Rides. Temperatures soared into the mid-90s and contributed to the fatal heart attack of a fifty-year-old marcher. Marchers were harassed intermittently along the way by whites, who shouted slurs and gave them the finger. Black volunteers organized to offer marchers food and shelter.[64]

On Tuesday, June 21, Dr. King and about twenty others left the main body of marchers and headed toward Philadelphia, Mississippi, to observe the second anniversary of the abduction and murder of Andrew Goodman, James Chaney, and Michael Schwerner. By this time Mt. Zion church, the burning of which Goodman, Chaney and Schwerner were investigating just before their disappearance, had been rebuilt. Inside was a plaque in memory of the three murdered men, "whose concern for others, and more particularly those of this community led to their early martyrdom."[65]

Once in Philadelphia, Dr. King and the others were joined by about 150 Neshoba County blacks. Together they marched to the Philadelphia courthouse square. As they approached, cars and trucks driven by white motorists came roaring toward them. The marchers did not disperse and most of the vehicles veered off, but one boy was hit by a truck and seriously injured. As they drew nearer the square, more and more angry whites were lining the streets, shaking fists and shouting. Police made no effort at crowd control.[66]

Before reaching the courthouse square, the marchers came to the jail where Goodman, Chaney, and Schwerner had been held in 1964. Here they prayed briefly before continuing. At the square Neshoba County Deputy Cecil Price personally blocked Dr. King's way onto the courthouse lawn, where King had intended to speak. "You're the one who had Schwerner and those fellows in jail?" Dr. King asked him.[67]

"Yes, sir," Price replied. Deputy Price was among eighteen men then facing federal charges of depriving Goodman, Chaney, and Schwerner of their constitutional rights. These charges were later dropped. But a year and a half later, in October 1967, Price and six others were convicted of violating the civil rights of the three murdered men. None would serve their full prison sentences; many more of the conspirators were acquitted.[68]

Blocked by Price, Dr. King addressed the marchers from the curb. "In this county Andrew Goodman, James Chaney, and Michael Schwerner were murdered. I believe in my heart that the murderers are somewhere around me at this moment. They ought to search their hearts. I want them to know that we are not afraid."[69]

During his brief speech Dr. King was heckled by whites who crowded the sidewalk across the street. When he had finished, the marchers led by King began to leave. They had not gone far when they were attacked by the surrounding crowd. Some of the black teenagers battled back. Finally the police jumped in and broke up the fighting, but a second attack followed. It too was quickly stopped. As they walked away Dr. King said, "This is a terrible town, the worst I've seen. There's a complete reign of terror here."[70]

That night, after King had left Neshoba County, white thugs unleashed scattered gunfire in the black section of town. The Philadelphia mayor blamed the trouble on "those rabble rousers, a bunch of foreigners that came in here."[71]

Dr. King later said that day in Philadelphia was one of the most frightening experiences of his life. Yet he returned a few days later vowing to use "all our nonviolent might" to influence the people of Philadelphia. This time leading citizens, including the mayor and the editor of the local paper, urged everyone to hold their tempers. The pleas were reinforced by a phalanx of highway patrolmen and auxiliary police officers who separated white onlookers from an estimated three-hundred marchers. Following the same route as a few days earlier, the marchers were this time allowed to rally on the courthouse square. In spite of the police presence, white onlookers hurled eggs, bottles, and other objects. Stokely Carmichael said, "The people gathered around us represent America in its truest form. They represent a sick and resisting society. . . ." Dr. King spoke next. Setting a conciliatory tone, he said, "We are going to build a society based on brotherhood and under-standing."[72]

A white man in the crowd shouted, "Go to hell!"

A white woman added: "Nigger – you're a nigger!"[73]

When it was over, the marchers returned to the black section of town. Along the way a car driven by whites sped into the line, scattering marchers and the reporters who accompanied them.[74]

A few days later, on June 26, the March Against Fear reached Jackson, Mississippi. A huge crowd estimated between 12,000 and 15,000 rallied at the State Capitol building. Many had joined the march that very day, coming from church in their Sunday best. James Meredith flew down from New York to be with the marchers on the last leg of the journey he had begun three weeks earlier. "From this day on," he told the rally, "our focus is going to be on the issue [of] freedom." Dr. King, having rejoined the March Against Fear, echoed his March on Washington speech of three years earlier in saying, "I have watched my dreams turn into a nightmare. I still have a dream . . . I still have a dream that one day right here in the state of Mississippi justice will become a reality for all of God's children." Stokely Carmichael, who during the course of the march had introduced the phrase "black power" to the American conscience, told the crowd that black Americans must "build a power base so strong in this country that we will bring [white people] to their knees every time they mess with us."[75]

About fifteen-hundred whites observed the rally from a distance. Some of them jeered and waved Confederate flags.[76]

Commentators would later refer to the March Against Fear as the last great march of the civil rights era. One of Meredith's stated objectives was to inspire eligible black citizens to register to vote. As many as four thousand people did precisely that. Among them was a man named El Fondren, a retired farmer who at the age of 106 was registered for the first time in his life. On June 11, 1966, El Fondren walked unsteadily into the registrar's office in Batesville, Mississippi. He leaned on a cane for support. After he was registered, several people lifted him onto their shoulders and carried him into a cheering crowd outside.[77]

PART THREE

It is not the light that we must fear; it is the darkness.

– Thomas G. Buchanan, *Who Killed Kennedy?*

Chapter 23

Developments Thick and Fast

Two books on the Kennedy assassination, long delayed, were at last due for publication in the late summer of 1966: *Rush to Judgment* by Mark Lane, and the English language edition of *The Oswald Affair* by Léo Sauvage.

For both men, publication must have been a satisfying vindication. Each had suffered broken contracts – Lane with Grove Press, and Sauvage with Random House. But both had at last placed their books with major firms. Holt, Rinehart and Winston was putting out *Rush to Judgment*, and *The Oswald Affair* was with World Publishing. Each received a good deal of media attention; Lane's book even topped best-seller lists.[1]

Mark Lane had written his book in London, where the Who Killed Kennedy? Committee maintained an apartment, and in Denmark, where he had married in late 1964. The first draft was completed by early February 1965, and that same month Lane returned to the United States. The sole copy of his manuscript was partly typed and partly handwritten. "I was possessed of neither the time nor the funds to have other copies made," he said. Shopping the book around to various publishers was thus a slow process. Recalling the broken contract and a series of rejections, Lane remembered this as a bitter and difficult period.[2]

Ray Marcus was still in regular contact with Lane's Citizens' Committee of Inquiry and was aware of Lane's progress on the book. He thought *Rush to Judgment* was a poor title choice. After discussing it with some friends, probably Maggie Field and Lillian Castellano, he told Deirdre Griswold that "the opinion was unanimously negative . . . all felt the failure to include in the title any mention of the assassination was a serious error." Marcus suggested modifying it to "The Assassination: Rush to Judgment." Griswold agreed, and hinted that Lane could be persuaded. But in the end, the book kept its original title.[3]

Early in 1966 Lane had returned to Dallas, this time with a film crew, and interviewed some key assassination witnesses. Portions of the interviews were incorporated into his book, but they also formed the basis for a documentary film on the assassination, also called *Rush to Judgment*.[4]

A year and a half had elapsed since *The Oswald Affair* first appeared in France and when it was finally published in the United States. It was the first book to critically evaluate the Warren Report and twenty-six volumes. In the end Maggie Field's translation was not used.

The book's content had not changed, although an eighteen page "American Postscript" had been added. In it Sauvage described his difficulty getting an English version of the book published, and the reaction to the Warren Commission by the American media and academia. "It is indeed a sad fact," he wrote, "that the Warren Report has been circulated among American readers mostly in the form of two paperbacks endowed with the Soviet-style prefatory brainwashing" of prominent opinion-makers.[5]

Sauvage also used the postscript to pay tribute to Sylvia Meagher, whose expertise with the Warren Commission material he had come to rely on. "I wish to express my gratitude to Mrs. Sylvia Meagher, author of an indispensable *Subject Index* and the only person in the world who really knows every item hidden in the twenty-six volumes of Hearings and Exhibits," he wrote. "With total unselfishness, Mrs. Meagher has always been available, to me as to others, for any needed information, verification, or reference."[6]

Just before leaving New York, Sauvage had sent Sylvia the galleys of his book. On reading it she concluded her French was not very good, since she got much more out of it than reading the original more than a year earlier. When she reached the end, with its effusive praise, she was flabbergasted. Her relationship with Sauvage, she told Maggie, had always been very businesslike. "After this whole year, we still address each other as 'Mr. Sauvage' and 'Mrs. Meagher' in the most formal manner, and exclude any personal conversation whatever. So his remarks come as a tremendous surprise, bringing me close to tears, whether of embarrassment or something else I am not sure."[7]

Other books were in the works that summer and fall. Harold Weisberg was writing a followup to his first book, which he was calling *Whitewash II*. Maggie Field was beginning to look at her panoplies as something publishable. And Ray Marcus was completing his examination of CE 399, *The Bastard Bullet*.

Sylvia Meagher's comparative study was nearing completion; an excerpt was published in the October issue of *The Minority of One*. This was the chapter she had loaned to Arnoni in June. Called "Oswald and the State Department," its research led Sylvia to suspect a clandestine relationship between Oswald and a government agency. Salandria was greatly impressed with Sylvia's work; he told her the article was "a five year thrust forward of the research."[8]

As more and more material about the murder of JFK was finally being published, the Central Intelligence Agency began keeping track of it, in time compiling a document called "Background Survey of Books Concerning the Assassination of President Kennedy." But this was not so much a survey of books as a catalog of the authors and their politics; it appears to have been an internal position paper for the spy agency. The anonymous author of this background survey took a dim view of the criticism of the Warren Commission, and argued that the critics either had put their egos at stake, had an axe to grind, or were out to make a quick buck.

> 1. Some of the authors of recent books on the assassination of President Kennedy (e.g., Joachim Joesten, *Oswald: Assassin or Fall Guy?*; Mark Lane, *Rush to Judgment*; Léo Sauvage, *The Oswald Affair: An Examination of the Contradictions and Omissions of the Warren Report*) had publicly asserted that a conspiracy existed before the Warren Commission finished its investigation. Not surprisingly, they immediately bestirred themselves to show that they were right and that the Commission was wrong. . . .

> 2. Some writers appear to have been predisposed to criticism by anti-American, far-left, or Communist sympathies. The British "Who Killed Kennedy Committee" includes some of the most persistent and vocal English critics of the United States, e.g. Michael Foot, Kingsley Martin, Kenneth Tynan, and Bertrand Russell. Joachim Joesten has been publicly revealed as a onetime member of the German Communist Party (KPD); a Gestapo document of 8 November 1937 among the German Foreign Ministry files microfilmed in England and now returned to West German custody shows that his party book was numbered 532315 and dated 12 May 1932 . . . Joesten's American publisher, Carl Marzani, was once sentenced to jail by a federal jury for concealing his Communist Party (CPUSA) membership in order to hold a government job. . . .

> 3. Another factor has been financial reward obtainable for sensational books. Mark Lane's *Rush to Judgment*, published on 13 August 1966, had sold 85,000 copies by early November. . . . The 1 January 1967 *New York Times Book Review* reported the book as at the top of the General category of the best seller list, having been in top position for seven weeks and on the list for 17 weeks. . . .[9]

The document said that some of the critics were publishing their versions of the assassination "simply because they were burning to give the world their theory." More were on the horizon: some favorable to the Commission, some not.

> 9.   Other books are yet to appear. William Manchester's not-yet-published *The Death of a President* is at this writing being purged of material personally objectionable to Mrs. Kennedy. There are hopeful signs: Jacob Cohen is writing a book which will appear in 1967 under the title *Honest Verdict,* defending the Commission report, and one of the Commission attorneys, Wesley J. Liebeler, is also reportedly writing a book, setting forth both sides. But further criticism will no doubt appear. . . .[10]

In August of 1966 an article by Gaeton Fonzi, first conceived as a minor feature about a nut named Salandria but now a serious examination of the Warren Commission, was published in *Greater Philadelphia* magazine. The article was long – the longest to have ever appeared in the magazine – and presented a detailed and damning account of the Warren Report's deficiencies. But Fonzi knew that his interview with Specter was a startling commodity, and it became the article's most striking element. He had written a powerful opening:

> It is difficult to believe the Warren Commission Report is the truth.
> Arlen Specter knows it.
> It is difficult to believe that "all the shots which caused the President's and Governor Connally's wounds were fired from the sixth floor window of the Texas School Book Depository."
> Arlen Specter knows it.
> It is difficult to believe that "the same bullet which pierced the President's throat also caused Governor Connally's wounds."
> Arlen Specter knows it.[11]

Fonzi recounted Specter's occasional evasiveness – "Have I dodged your question? Yes, I've dodged your question" – and his uneasiness, as when Fonzi asked him about the autopsy photographs and X-rays: ". . . he appeared visibly disturbed and made an apparent effort to retain his composure, uncharacteristic for a competent prosecutor who normally exudes self-confidence." Through no one's fault but his own, Specter looked bad – and by extension, so did the Warren Commission and its

Report. Yet Specter never attempted to answer the article – not with a press conference denouncing it, or an article of his own, or even a letter to the editor.[12]

Fonzi's article was greatly anticipated by those critics who knew about his interview with Specter, conducted barely a month before. In late July, after the magazine was on the newsstands, Sylvia Meagher sent Salandria a quick note with the letters "S.O.S." scrawled at the top: "Never did get the *Greater Philadelphia* with Fonzi's article, nor did Arnoni. Can you send me a copy, please?" Salandria, who called *Greater Philadelphia* "the most serious establishment organ which has taken a full plunge into the assassination work," promptly sent her one.[13]

Sylvia thought Fonzi's article was great. "I have just recaptured my breath after reading it with intense fascination and considerable admiration," she said. She wanted to contact Fonzi to compliment him, and also to point out a few small errors of fact, but did not have his address. And so she sent a letter to Salandria and asked him to forward it.[14]

She told Fonzi the article was "a masterful presentation of a highly complicated set of arguments." The letter was meant just for Fonzi, but to Sylvia's surprise it ended up as a letter to the editor, complete with corrections, in the September issue of *Greater Philadelphia*. She was pleased, she said, that the magazine's editors thought it was worth publishing.[15]

With little fanfare, Penn Jones published his collection of *Midlothian Mirror* editorials in May 1966, printing 7,500 copies of the book he called *Forgive My Grief* at his own expense. The small paperback appeared around the same time as *Inquest*, although at first it received almost no publicity outside of Texas – and not a whole lot there. The title was suggested by Penn's son Michael, who had studied Alfred Tennyson's long poem "In Memoriam A.H.H." in high school. He thought the sentiments it expressed – and one stanza in particular – best revealed his father's true feelings.

> Forgive my grief for one removed,
> Thy creature, whom I found so fair,
> I trust he lives in thee, and there
> I find him worthier to be loved.[16]

John Howard Griffin supplied a preface describing Jones as a man "moved by a profound sense of responsibility toward his country, toward truth and toward evidence. The truth risks being unspeakably ugly in this instance."[17]

Forgive My Grief was criticized by some who were otherwise inclined to support Penn Jones and his work. The book, they said, was in places poorly organized and overly speculative. This is a valid criticism, and particularly true of *Forgive My Grief's* later three volumes. But while Jones may at times have been unpolished as a journalist, a point he readily acknowledged, his work successfully connected facts demonstrating the gross weaknesses – the omissions and distortions – of the Warren Commission. And few doubted his sincerity or courage. Harold Weisberg once said, "I think Penn and his wife Louise are two of the bravest people I have ever met."[18]

Much of *Forgive My Grief* consisted of excerpts of witness testimony along with Penn's commentary. This selected testimony often suggested conspiracy but had been downplayed or ignored by the Warren Commission. One such instance was a sworn statement given to the Dallas Sheriff's Department by Julia Ann Mercer on the day of the assassination. Mercer, a Dallas resident, had driven through Dealey Plaza several hours before the assassination. A Ford pickup truck, apparently stalled on the side of Elm Street, compelled her to stop her car. As she waited for a chance to drive around the pickup, Mercer observed one man behind the steering wheel and another man at the back of the truck. This second man removed what Mercer took to be a rifle case from the truck and proceeded to carry it up the grassy knoll.[19]

"The deposition of Julia Ann Mercer was devastating," Jones wrote. "But she was not called as a witness . . . were her words so lethal to the Warren Commission's theory of no conspiracy?"[20]

Jones also described the testimony of Roger Craig, a Dallas deputy sheriff whose statements were among the strongest indicators of a Dealey Plaza conspiracy. According to the Warren Report, Lee Oswald fled the Texas School Book Depository on foot within minutes of the assassination. He caught a bus, but abandoned it in favor of a taxi, which he took to his rooming house in Oak Cliff. Yet in sworn statements given just after the assassination, and in testimony to the Warren Commission, Deputy Craig said he saw a man resembling Oswald flee the Book Depository some fifteen minutes after the fusillade. This man jumped into a waiting station wagon, possibly a Nash Rambler, driven by a second man who drove quickly away. Craig added that Ruth Paine, with whom Marina Oswald was then staying, owned a station wagon similar to the one he saw.[21]

Later in his testimony Craig related how he had come to the police station that same afternoon after hearing a suspect was in custody. Police Captain Will Fritz allowed him into the interrogation room and asked Craig if Oswald was the man he'd seen run from the TSBD and jump into a station wagon. Craig said yes. Captain Fritz, Craig testified, turned to Oswald and said, "What about this station wagon?"

"That station wagon belongs to Mrs. Paine," Oswald answered. "Don't try to tie her into this. She had nothing to do with it."

"All we're trying to do is find out what happened, and this man saw you leave from the scene," Fritz said.

"I told you people I did," Deputy Craig quoted Oswald. And he said Oswald added, "Everyone will know who I am now" – an enigmatic remark open to more than one interpretation.[22]

When Captain Fritz testified, Jones reported, he dismissed what Roger Craig had testified to under oath, telling the Commission, "One deputy sheriff . . . started to talk to me but he was telling me some things that I knew wouldn't help us and I didn't talk to him but someone else took an affidavit from him. His story that he was telling didn't fit with what we knew to be true."[23]

Penn Jones observed: "The next most obvious question for any lawyer would have been to determine how Fritz decided that Deputy Sheriff Roger D. Craig's testimony was untrue, other than it 'wouldn't help us.' But that question was never asked."[24]

Later Jones got to know Roger Craig, who became something of a *cause célèbre;* Jones was a staunch supporter and friend. He was convinced that Craig was absolutely truthful, even a genuine hero. Years later, long after Craig was dead, previously unknown evidence corroborating some of what he testified to seeing came to light.

Forgive My Grief also hammered on the "mysterious deaths" question, which remained one of the author's principal interests. He wrote about the meeting in Jack Ruby's apartment the evening after Ruby killed Oswald, and the deaths of three of those who attended: lawyer Tom Howard, and reporters Bill Hunter and Jim Koethe. He wrote about Earlene Roberts, who on November 22 witnessed a police car pull up in front of Oswald's rooming house and beep its horn while Oswald was in his room. "Now Mrs. Roberts has joined that long list of persons who had first hand information, but are now dead." He referred, albeit in passing, to the death of a stripper who worked for Jack Ruby and was said to be one of the last people to talk to Ruby before he shot Oswald, and to William Whaley, the cabbie who drove Oswald to his rooming house after the assassination. Whaley was killed in a two car crash in late 1965. Jones later said Whaley was the first on-duty cabbie killed in Dallas since the mid-1930s, but in his first book said "details on Whaley's accident are not available." Why would a cab driver pose a threat to conspirators? "Whaley had a chance to talk to Oswald alone after the assassination of President Kennedy." However, if Roger Craig's story were true, and Oswald left the TSBD fifteen minutes after the assassination and was driven from the scene by a presumed confederate, then Whaley's death might have been a simple, tragic accident.[25]

Dear Vince,

    I called you last night but I guess you didn't receive the message to call me. I just wanted to tell you the blood-chilling news I had received, that Lee Bowers Jr. had been killed in an auto accident on August 9th. First Whaley, now Bowers . . .

Hastily,
Sylvia[26]

It was another death of a key witness, and it got the attention of all the critics. The accident happened near Midlothian, Texas, and its proximity to him led Penn Jones to investigate. Bowers' car apparently crashed into a concrete bridge abutment after drifting off the road at a speed of about fifty miles an hour. Jones sought out the doctor who treated Bowers; according to Jones, the doctor said Bowers was in some sort of "strange shock" when he treated him in the emergency room. He did not appear to have suffered a heart attack. Jones felt the circumstances of this death were highly suspicious. He later reported that before the accident, Lee Bowers had been receiving death threats.[27]

It is difficult to understate the importance of Lee Bowers as an assassination witness. By nature a reticent man, he did not like discussing what he had seen on November 22. He once said that "the less others thought they knew the less problems they would have." On the day of the assassination Bowers was working in a railroad tower adjacent to Dealey Plaza. In the half hour or so preceding the ambush, he observed three cars drive through the parking lot near the fence; the driver of one of these cars appeared to be speaking into a microphone. This observation had helped fuel Griscom Morgan's theory of a radio-coordinated assassination. Moments before the shots were fired Bowers had witnessed several men behind the fence on top of the grassy knoll.[28]

On August 20, 1964, during the same Dallas trip in which she talked to Acquilla Clemons, Shirley Martin telephoned Bowers to ask for an interview. He had quit the railroad and was then working at the Green Clinic and Hospital in Dallas. Shirley identified herself as a private citizen conducting her own investigation into the assassination. Most of her questions, he recalled, had to do with what he had seen around the Triple Underpass area and the grassy knoll. But Bowers told Shirley he had no comment; he had reported what he knew to the Warren Commission.[29]

Their conversation lasted seven or eight minutes. As soon as it was over, Bowers called the FBI about it. The only reason he had even talked to her as long as he did, he said, was because he was curious about who she was and how much she knew about his previous interviews with law enforcement agencies. Some of her questions, Bowers said, indicated that she had full knowledge of his interviews with Dallas Police and the FBI.[30]

At the time of the first volume of *Forgive My Grief*, Jones calculated there had been thirteen suspicious deaths; he wrote that "more killings are going to be necessary in order to keep this crime quiet." The subject was given more attention in the second *Forgive My Grief*, published a year after the first. Merely glancing at that book's table of contents gives a numbing idea of what Jones believed was happening: Chapter 1. Deaths. Chapter 2. Deaths. Chapter 3. Deaths. Chapter 4. More Deaths. Chapter 5. And More Deaths. . . .[31]

The critics were, as a group, beginning to get publicity during this period, and while some of it was negative, this was not always so. In an editorial accompanying Sylvia Meagher's review of *Inquest*, M.S. Arnoni paid the critics this tribute:

> There are in our midst exceptional people whose minds can think and not merely calculate, and whose intellects maintain no neutrality as between truth and falsehood. From among these people come a few independent researchers, journalists and writers, amateur and professional, who have been making no less than heroic efforts to unravel the answers to how, why and what-for John F. Kennedy was felled. They do not know whether their investigations lead to 'good' or 'bad' results, yet they act out of that incorruptible human inquisitiveness that accounts for all progress. To them belongs the praise of future generations.[32]

Maggie Field was touched by this homage; she sat down and wrote her own tribute to *The Minority of One*.

> . . . thanks in large part to Lane, Epstein, Sauvage, Salandria, Feldman and a few others the unspeakable subject has become a matter for public discussion. To you goes one of the largest accolades, for you were able to assay the infamy correctly from the outset and you continued to pursue the question doggedly and enduringly when others had long since abandoned the campaign.
>
> Maggie Field
> (also for Ray Marcus and Lillian Castellano)[33]

Arnoni, Sylvia later told Maggie, said he was "moved to the very bones" by her letter, which he published in his September issue.[34]

But most of the notice the critics received was for the work that was finally beginning to appear. Much of the initial attention went to Edward Jay Epstein and *Inquest*, but certainly not all of it. On July 24, Harold Weisberg was interviewed by correspondent George Herman on *Mike Wallace At Large* on CBS radio. Introduced as a former investigator for a Senate civil liberties subcommittee, Weisberg declared: "The Commission set out to prove Oswald guilty, and it did just that. It did it by selecting what evidence it wanted to use, by ignoring the evidence it didn't want to use, by not looking for what it didn't want to find, and above all, as with any such inquiry, you have the built-in weakness of no representation of the other side. There was no cross-examination."[35]

Weisberg insisted that the Commission's own evidence demonstrated that Oswald had not shot anyone. "Are you maintaining," Herman asked, "that he did not carry a gun into the Book Depository, he did not go to the sixth floor . . . and he did not take a shot at the President?"

Weisberg said that the material in the twenty-six volumes showed that Oswald could not have carried the weapon into the building. "The only man who saw Oswald go into the building stoutly maintained that Oswald carried nothing."[36]

Herman ended the interview by asking, "Who killed President Kennedy?" Weisberg had to qualify his answer. *Whitewash* did not address that question because it was restricted to official evidence and did not speculate. But he was willing to offer an opinion. "I think you would have to have it in the plural. I think there was no one person. I doubt if, at this point, even if the people involved in the shooting were apprehended, we could determine which one fired which." President Kennedy, Weisberg told Herman, was shot by several people from several different directions. But that was just his personal opinion. "There is only one explicit conclusion in *Whitewash*. That is that the job hasn't been, and must be, done – and entirely in public."[37]

There is no record of how Harold Weisberg thought he fared in the George Herman interview. But he was aware of how powerful a good broadcast performance could be, and how much damage could come from a poor one. He was ridiculed by other guests during a radio appearance that summer, and Sylvia Meagher commended him for keeping his temper: "Congratulations on performing with dignity and forcefulness in discussing the evidence despite all the dirty pool by your opponents." Weisberg said that all of the critics should use similar care. "Everything any one of us says in public affects us all."[38]

With all the attention his book was getting, Edward Epstein was making broadcast appearances – he too had been on *Mike Wallace At Large*, a few weeks before Weisberg. But it seems that he made such appearances reluctantly. "He was pressured into accepting the *Today* show, next Friday, but is trying to disengage himself and cancel it," Sylvia Meagher told Weisberg around this time. Weisberg thought that was a good idea. He still believed that Epstein was simply not knowledgeable enough. "He'll get clobbered and hurt us all."[39]

Epstein did keep making appearances, and some of them were in fact disastrous, from the point of view of other critics. In August he debated former Commission counsel Wesley Liebeler in a program broadcast on public television in New York. "Horrible performance by Epstein," Sylvia wrote to Maggie Field. "Oily smooth well-acted Liebeler performance. Liebeler got the better of it, hands down."[40]

Epstein's poor showing had some of the critics buzzing. Arnoni called Sylvia the next morning and said the debate was "frightful." Her niece called shortly after that and said the same. Then Epstein himself phoned. Meagher minced no words: "I said that I thought his original decision – not to accept any radio/TV invitations – was correct and that he should not accept any more appearances, he was undercutting his own book, undercutting all of us, by giving ground constantly, speaking without conviction, failing to use devastating arguments which he had at his fingertips, and being an outright yellow-belly."[41]

In spite of these frustrations, Sylvia had reason to be optimistic that summer. Her comparative study, which seems to have been completed around this time, was on the verge of finding a publisher. On Friday, August 19, she received "out of the blue" a phone call from a senior editor at Random House who had somehow heard about her manuscript. He was very interested in reading it and offered to send a messenger by her apartment to pick up a copy. "I was blissful," she said.[42]

Then early on the following Tuesday – very early, at 3a.m., as she slept – Meagher had a telephone call from Jones Harris. "His record of effrontery is unmatched, but now he outdid himself," she later told Maggie Field. As Sylvia described it, Harris launched into a boastful tale about how he was luring Wesley Liebeler to what he called "our side." He told her that Liebeler wanted to write a book on his Warren Commission experience to make some money; Harris was personally taking Liebeler to a major publisher the next day. He declined to tell Sylvia who the publisher was, but she was certain it was Random House and that it was bad news for her own book. She asked him several times to tell her who the publisher was, but he refused. "Don't be offended," he said. "*Disgusted* is the word!" she shot back, before slamming down the phone. Harris immediately called back but she would not answer. She wound up tossing and turning for several hours before finally getting back to sleep.[43]

Meagher's reputation as a leading critic was growing. Even as her manuscript was at Random House – but before she learned about Liebeler's planned book – she was contacted by *Esquire* magazine, and agreed to be a consultant for an upcoming article on the Warren Report. She reviewed the article, written by Epstein, and found it to be full of errors, "most of which I hope I caught and removed." She also got a call from a small magazine called *Studies on the Left* and was asked to review four books on the Report: *Inquest*, *Rush to Judgment*, *Whitewash*, and *The Oswald Affair*. She agreed, although she had earlier rejected an offer from *Book Week* to review the Sauvage book, since his comments about her in his American Postscript might have affected her objectivity.[44]

Finally, CBS News asked her to provide background for a story they were preparing, and *The London Times* called with an urgent request for a copy of her *Subject Index* as they prepared their own examination of the Commission.[45]

Meagher was scheduled to have lunch with the Random House editor on Wednesday, August 24, so they might discuss her manuscript. But the day before, the editor called to ask if they could move it to Thursday so he could have enough time to finish reading it. She told him not to bother; she knew about Liebeler's conferences with them; he might as well reject her manuscript right then and there, over the phone. "He pleaded ignorance," she told Maggie. Later she learned that Liebeler's conference with Random House had not gone particularly well; in the end he never wrote his book. But neither did Random House accept Sylvia's comparative study.[46]

Rush to Judgment and *The Oswald Affair* were both published in August of 1966. They were written about jointly in *The New York Review of Books* in a curious analysis that went to great lengths to tell readers several things before discussing the books at hand. The first thing, reviewer Fred Graham wrote, was that eyewitness testimony is far less reliable than physical evidence. Next was that a "second round" of books on the assassination was being published "based upon more research and reflection" than earlier ones like *Who Killed Kennedy?* and *Oswald: Assassin or Fall Guy?*, which he claimed had been "largely discredited." Graham also pointed out that historian William Manchester had been commissioned by the Kennedy family to write a history of the assassination that might prove to be "the most interesting and definitive" study of the case when it was finally published.[47]

When he at last got to the point, Graham said that *Rush to Judgment* was "well-documented, persuasive, and restrained." But Sauvage, according to Graham, was so unsettled by what he observed in Dallas in the days immediately after the assassination "that he developed a deep suspicion of the authorities' version of the events, so that his book tends to waste its impact by being too quick to reject official explanations."[48]

On August 31, as Graham's review was on the newsstands, Sauvage was a guest on the Barry Farber radio show. The host asked him about the review. But first he read from it: "'. . . against the broad proof of Oswald's ownership of the rifle, his palmprint on the rifle, the three used shells from his rifle found near the window, the recovered slug traced ballistically to his rifle, his presence in the Depository building, his flight after the shooting, his murder of Officer J.D. Tippit, his resistance when finally caught, his personality, and the lack of evidence pointing to any other possible assassin, the Warren Commission had no choice but to smooth over the inconsistencies to the extent possible and brand Oswald the lone killer.'" Farber said that when he first read that, he found himself right back to where he was before reading *The Oswald Affair* – convinced that Oswald was guilty. "Maybe Europe demands a conspiracy, but I, for one, close the case."[49]

"Yes, well that's quite interesting," Sauvage replied. He was pleased that Farber had brought this up. There were ten points in the excerpt Farber had just read on the air. "I maintain . . . that all the ten points [Fred Graham] gives are either unsubstantiated, or have absolutely – are not relevant to the case." Each point was taken on the basis of faith. There was no real proof, for example, that Oswald killed Officer Tippit. "Spurious identifications, identifications made two months later on the basis of photos, and so on – there's nothing in it." Oswald's so-called flight after the assassination was a misrepresentation. If he had really wanted to flee, he wouldn't have gone home, gotten a jacket, and then gone to a movie theater. "Is that what anybody can call flight? Why didn't he go to Mexico?"

"Did he buy a ticket at that movie house?" Farber asked.

Sauvage conceded that according to the Commission, he did not. But theater employees gave conflicting statements, so it was hard to be certain of what really happened. "Mr. Graham has no right to give as one of his reasons of conviction his flight after the shooting."

Farber asked again about the Tippit murder, and admitted that this section of *The Oswald Affair* made him stop and think. Sauvage said that the description broadcast on police radio was so general it could have matched countless men in Dallas. But according to the Warren Report, it was from this broadcast description that Tippit recognized and stopped Oswald. "The description [had] nothing, for instance, like dress, or hair, or anything of the kind, which would attract attention. And this Tippit is supposed to have recognized Oswald on the street? I don't believe it."

In his review, Graham had written that it was "significant" that the critics – not just Lane and Sauvage, but Weisberg and Epstein and probably Buchanan and Joesten – "cannot get together on an alternative to the Warren Commission's conclusions." That same question came up on August 29, when Sauvage was a guest on *The Barry Gray Show*.[50]

"Mr. Sauvage," Gray said, "if Mr. Oswald did not commit – perform the assassination, or do the shooting, who did?"

"I don't know," Sauvage replied. "Do you?"

"No, I don't know . . . but everybody that's written a book like this says Oswald didn't do it, but then they say, 'I don't know who did.'"

"Listen. If I am accused – if some of *you* are accused – of killing your wife, all that your lawyer has to do is ask the prosecutor – the District Attorney – to furnish the proof. If the District Attorney cannot prove you did the murder, you are free. No one has ever asked a lawyer to find someone else."

By the fall of 1966 Penn Jones was working on the assassination full time, having entrusted weekly production of the *Midlothian Mirror* to three employees. Like many of the critics he was beginning to get a lot of publicity. In an interview broadcast on *The CBS Evening News,* Jones said, "I would rather be the sorriest bootlegger in Midlothian than to be in the shoes of Earl Warren in the eyes of history. If this is the democracy that we claim it is, then he flunked his final when his country needed him most."[51]

In late September Penn and L.A. flew to Los Angeles to meet with a book distributor and promote *Forgive My Grief.* He was interviewed by Pamela Mason, the ex-wife of actor James Mason, who hosted a radio program and lived near Maggie Field. "Pamela knows little about the case but is very interested in it, from our point of view," Maggie said later. Penn told Mason that there was definitely a conspiracy in the assassination, although he did not know who was behind it. "I think they got away with it, and I feel that they are continuing to kill to keep this thing hushed up." He now believed at least thirteen people with some kind of knowledge about the assassination had by then died under suspicious circumstances. "There are at least five others that I'm not yet ready to name, but I feel that they certainly were connected with the case."[52]

Afterward the Joneses headed for the studios of KTTV to videotape *The Lomax Show,* hosted by Louis Lomax. Lomax was not very well informed, but he was sympathetic to his guest and what he had to say. Jones described being at the Trade Mart in Dallas at the time JFK was shot, and his early investigative efforts. "I have talked to some witnesses, I have attempted to find others . . . I've knocked on many doors in Dallas, talking to, and attempting to talk to, people who were there." He did not think Lee Oswald was the lone gunman; in fact, in his judgment Oswald did not fire at all. "These were professional men, these were expert shots." Oswald was involved in some way, Jones continued – but at a low level of the conspiracy. He pointed out that Oswald himself had stoutly declared, "I'm just a patsy!"[53]

Maggie Field was in the audience watching the interview. She later assessed his performance: "Penn was on about twenty minutes or so, and while he's no dynamo, his complete sincerity and courage is effective . . . the fact that he's from Texas is not without dramatic impact. He isn't as forceful as I'd like to see him be, but I think he does implement the critics' cause."[54]

Inevitably, Lomax asked Jones who, if not Oswald, the real killers were? "What organization? What group? What people?"

"I think I'm being pretty brave to come out flatly and say that it was a conspiracy. I am not by any means ready to say who it was. I wish I knew. I wish I could tell you." But he was confidant, he said, that the case would be broken. "We have enough information."[55]

Another book published during this period was *The Second Oswald* by Richard Popkin. It was a short book, only 174 pages including nine appendices, and first appeared in condensed form in the July 28, 1966, issue of *The New York Review of Books*.

Most of the critics had never heard of the author. "Who is Popkin?" Harold Weisberg asked Sylvia Meagher in August. Popkin was then the chairman of the Department of Philosophy at the University of California in San Diego; he had previously published a book called *The History of Skepticism from Erasmus to Descartes*.[56]

Ostensibly, Popkin's article was a review of *Whitewash* and *Inquest*. Popkin acknowledged that the former was the first critical study of the Commission's case based on a close analysis of the twenty-six volumes, but said its power was diminished by its noisy and tendentious tone. *Inquest*, on the other hand, was "a remarkably effective book" that explained how the Warren Commission's main objective was presenting a politically acceptable account of the assassination.[57]

But the thrust of Popkin's article was a theory he felt explained the assassination based on the available evidence. The first-generation critics – and here Popkin meant not just Weisberg and Epstein, but Vince Salandria, Fred Cook, Sylvan Fox, and even Thomas Buchanan – did little more than raise questions that the Warren Commission had left unanswered. An alternative explanation was needed. As Allen Dulles had commented, if the critics had found another assassin, "let them name names and produce their evidence."[58]

The solution offered by Professor Popkin was what he called the "second Oswald" – a scenario derived from the official evidence suggesting that someone might have been impersonating Lee Harvey Oswald in the weeks and months before the assassination. The twenty-six volumes, Popkin wrote, contained numerous reliable reports placing Oswald in one location when equally reliable reports placed him elsewhere at the same time. Toward what end? "Critics have brought up the second Oswald as an insufficiently explored phenomenon that might throw light on the case."[59]

One of those critics was Harold Weisberg, who during the summer of 1966 was beginning to feel more optimistic about his work. *Whitewash* was about to be serialized in a Spanish newspaper and was selling well enough for him to have another five thousand copies printed. He also felt the attitude of the American press was beginning to change. He was being called more often to make speeches and to appear on radio and TV.[60]

When Weisberg read Popkin's article, he concluded Popkin had stolen his work. An entire chapter in *Whitewash* was devoted to what Weisberg called the "false Oswald," which he said proved there had been a conspiracy. Popkin's plagiarism was so obvious, Weisberg told Sylvia Meagher, that even her old associate Curtis Crawford had mentioned it to him.[61]

Meagher thought the allegation was absurd. "I am amazed at the suggestion that any plagiarism was involved," she told Harold. "What do you refer to? I am very careful always to take into consideration parallel discovery and reasoning, which is widespread among critics of the WR and almost inevitable."[62]

Weisberg declined to elaborate. But this was not the first time he had lashed out at other critics, and it was a cause of some concern for Sylvia; she was beginning to think Weisberg suffered from a persecution complex. The previous spring Weisberg had clashed with Vince Salandria after concluding Salandria could have placed a review of *Whitewash*, but did not, in *Liberation*. He had also been angry with M.S. Arnoni, who had dismissed *Whitewash* as having nothing new. "You are much too conceited about your book," Arnoni told him. Weisberg challenged this, but Arnoni would not be drawn into a debate.[63]

Vince Salandria had once warned his fellow critics to prepare for "a long, back-breaking excavation job, into the layers of waste material under which the answers in this case lie," and whatever the merits of Weisberg's opinion of Popkin, the story of the false or second Oswald was a case in point. There were many indications of a false or second Oswald. "Some are dubious, some possible," Popkin wrote. And while these indications came directly from the Warren Report, it was, as Weisberg put it, "unreflected in the table of contents, the headings, subheadings, or the index." The evidence, he said, was "hard and unrefuted proof that a group of men were deliberately fashioning a 'False Oswald.'" It was a trail that led to the shadowy world of anti-Castro Cuban politics in southern cities like Miami, New Orleans, and Dallas. In time, it would figure into a new investigation of the assassination, which in late 1966, unbeknownst to the critics, was getting underway in Louisiana.[64]

Early in his involvement, Ray Marcus knew that if there were going to be a grassroots movement opposing the official assassination story, he was going to be involved in it – but not as a leader. "I wasn't equipped to be, and I didn't *want* to be," he said. Apart from his specific areas of interest, Marcus saw his role as assisting those who were in the movement's vanguard. That was how, in December 1964, he had come to not only help prepare Mark Lane for his Beverly Hills confrontation with Joseph Ball, but had driven him to and from other engagements in the greater Los Angeles area, some of which he had also arranged.[65]

After the Warren Report was issued, Marcus noticed that some of the things that comedian Mort Sahl was saying suggested he did not believe the lone-gunman scenario to be true. At this time Sahl, known for his topical humor and political satire, hosted a popular television talk show in Los Angeles. None of his remarks were very specific, Marcus recalled, but they were enough to indicate his doubts. "I contacted his office, showed him the work I'd done on the Zapruder film, the Moorman photo; he got very interested in it." As time went on, Sahl began talking more and more, on the air, about the Kennedy assassination. He mentioned some of the recently published books on his program, and even showed *Rush to Judgment* and *Inquest* on camera. Sahl was thus a rarity: a public figure with access to the mass media who was not only sympathetic to the cause of the Warren Commission critics and unafraid to say so, but willing to get involved.[66]

In the fall of 1966 Mark Lane was busily promoting *Rush to Judgment* – both the book and the soon-to-be-released documentary film. The film version had great potential, as it featured on-camera interviews with witnesses like Lee Bowers and Acquilla Clemons. Sylvia Meagher attended a screening with M.S. Arnoni and wrote of her impressions to Ray Marcus – but cautiously, since she knew he thought so highly of Lane. While there were some good things in it, Sylvia thought that overall the movie was uneven and boring. Even worse, in some areas the film did not present all aspects of issues with which Lane had to be familiar. "I don't know beans about movie-making but it seems to me that they should have been able to make the whole thing more gripping with better use of camera and better editing."[67]

Marcus said she need not worry about offending him. While he admired Lane greatly, he was aware of his shortcomings. "I consider it an unfortunate fact that Lane – the leading critic in the public's eye – is an advocate, with all that implies by way of hyperbole and out-of-context case building." Regardless of how anyone felt, Marcus said, history would view Mark Lane in a positive light.[68]

Marcus made sure that Sahl and his producers were aware that Lane was coming to town. Lane appeared twice on *The Mort Sahl Show* that fall: first on September 4, and again on October 9. "What we're going to talk about tonight is the assassination," Sahl told his in-studio audience in remarks before the first of the programs began. "That's the whole show. Because I've been waiting to talk about it with somebody who knew . . . my own obsessive nature has brought it up, socially, enough since that date. But people normally say to me, 'I can't be as cynical as you – you're indicting our system, and our government,' and all that." The subject, he said, seemed to be taboo.[69]

As the broadcast began Lane reviewed the Warren Commission's version of the assassination, using a chart of Dealey Plaza to show how Kennedy's motorcade proceeded through the area: turning onto Houston Street from Main, and after one short block turning left onto Elm. Officially three shots were fired, all from the sixth floor of the Texas School Book Depository as the limousine drove west on Elm toward a railroad bridge. One shot hit Kennedy high on the back and exited through his throat before going on to wound Connally. Another shot hit him in the head and was the fatal wound. A third shot missed.

But there were reasons to doubt this scenario that were not adequately reflected in the Warren Report. Two-thirds of the Dealey Plaza witnesses, Lane said, reported hearing gunshots from the grassy knoll area, on top of which was a wooden fence. "There in fact were seven employees of the railroad company right up here on the top of this over-pass. All seven said independently – when the shots were fired he said he looked in this direction; each of the seven said he saw puffs of white smoke come from this area, right in front of the wooden fence." Lee Bowers had seen several men at the fence and noticed what he told the Warren Commission was a "commotion" and described to Lane as a "flash of light" as the shots were fired. Abraham Zapruder's home movie showed Kennedy's head driven back and to the left, as if reacting to a shot from the front.

Lane had with him some clips from his film that demonstrated his point. This was a very powerful moment: few if any assassination witnesses with testimony countering the official story had been heard by the general public. Lane had a portion of his interview with S.M. Holland, a railroad signalman and one of the seven men atop the railroad bridge.

"Did you look in any particular direction when you heard the shots?" Lane asked Holland in the film excerpt.

"Yes," Holland replied. "I looked over to where I thought the shots came from, and I saw a puff of smoke still lingering underneath the trees in front of the wooden fence. The report sounded like it came from behind the wooden fence." He described how two motorcycle cops left the motorcade and rushed up the grassy knoll slope, both with guns drawn. Holland ran toward where he'd seen the smoke, along with the other six railroad men. It took several minutes for them to reach the spot because of all the cars in the parking lot behind the fence. When the men got there they didn't see anyone, but did see muddy footprints.

"You were a witness who had as good a view of that scene as anyone in Dealey Plaza," Lane said as the excerpt neared its end. "Where do you think the shots came from?"

"Well, I *know* where that third shot came from."

"Where did that shot come from?"

"Behind the picket fence . . . there's no doubt whatsoever in my mind."

Holland's filmed statements to Mark Lane were especially potent because, while not taken under oath, they were identical to what he had sworn to in police statements given the day of the assassination, and later testified to before the Warren Commission. Lane played excerpts from interviews with several other railroad men whose observations were virtually the same as Holland's. These men had inexplicably not been called before the Warren Commission.

There were other excerpts from other witnesses, such as Charles Brehm, who was among those witnesses closest to the limousine when the shots were fired; he described seeing something, possibly a piece of Kennedy's skull, fly over the back of the limousine after the head shot.

"I know you don't like the burden of the truth," Mort Sahl told his audience as the show came to an end. "It isn't any fun to awaken America now. It's like walking into a party – everybody's been drunk for 175 years, and you're getting the tab for the liquor." The audience laughed as Sahl continued: "But we've gotta keep this thing going. As I always remind you . . . America is at stake."

With the spate of material published in summer 1966 – there were at least six books and many more articles, many critical of the Warren Commission – the critics were beginning to feel some momentum going their way. Public opinion polls from this time revealed that a majority of Americans did not accept the Warren Report, and there seemed to be a groundswell of support for re-opening the investigation into Kennedy's death. This reached a high point in late September when Theodore Kupferman, a Republican congressman from Manhattan, called for a new House-Senate Committee to review the findings of the Warren Commission. This committee, under Kupferman's proposal, would first determine whether there was even a need to go beyond the Commission's investigation.[70]

A public official's suggesting there might be a need to re-open the Kennedy investigation, and formally proposing a committee to begin the job – it seemed too good to be true. "About the Kupferman proposal," a skeptical Sylvia Meagher wrote to an equally skeptical Shirley Martin, "I don't know what is behind it and I agree that it seems to offer little if any chance of getting closer to the truth. Still, I am glad for the bare fact that 'respectable' figures go on record as believing that there is a need for some form of review."[71]

Around this time, Maggie Field wrote a series of letters to elected officials and media people, urging them to acquaint themselves with the Warren Commission's evidence. Her close study of the twenty-six volumes had convinced her, she said, that the conclusions published in the Warren Report did not reflect the truth. "The urgency of this request," she said in one letter, "is occasioned by the suspicion that our policies – both foreign and domestic – may well hang in the balance. . . . This is not a matter which can be set aside for future examination." A reply from Senator George Murphy of California acknowledged the proposal introduced by Theodore Kupferman, and that the 89th Congress had adjourned without taking action on it. "If a similar resolution is introduced in the 90th Congress, which convenes in January, I shall surely study it with your views in mind."[72]

In October, Wesley Liebeler announced that two teams from the UCLA law school, where he then taught, were reviewing the Warren Commission findings. These reviews were prompted by *Rush to Judgment* and *Inquest*. "What is needed at this point is one piece of work which sets forth both sides objectively," said Liebeler, who was overseeing both studies. "Lane doesn't. Epstein doesn't." Their two books would also be analyzed by Liebeler's students.[73]

Sylvia Meagher seems to have viewed this with a degree of amusement. Liebeler's true purpose, she felt, was to rehabilitate himself for his contributions to Epstein's book. That someone who worked for the Warren Commission was unable to defend its Report in its original published form, she said, "is in itself a total default to the opposition."[74]

That same month, the much-delayed assassination issue of *Ramparts* magazine was finally published. The issue bore little resemblance to what David Welsh had described early in the year. Sylvia Meagher had long since distanced herself from the project, but other critics had remained; *Ramparts* editor-in-chief Warren Hinckle had ultimately thrown out the lengthy article they produced. "It was a goddam legal brief," he said later. "I wanted something that would get people talking about the Warren Report with the cynicism they did about the weather report." Thus the magazine's assassination project became "In The Shadow of Dallas." Accompanying editorials called for a new official investigation and lamented the fact that it took private citizens to demonstrate the flaws in the Warren Report. But most of the coverage consisted of reprints from the *Midlothian Mirror*, and a profile of Penn Jones and his notion of mysterious deaths.[75]

Also in this *Ramparts* was a satire of the critics, in the form of a book review. The review was bogus from start to finish, in that the book in question did not really exist – although readers who didn't get the joke could not be blamed for taking the review seriously. Many, it seems, did. Hinckle later claimed that a single bookseller in Manhattan alone received over one hundred orders for *Time of Assassins* within twenty-four hours of the November issue's publication.[76]

Sylvia Meagher got the joke, but she was not amused. "Your editorial and cover story in the November issue are completely nullified by the cheap farce which appears in the book review section," she wrote in a letter to the editor. It was a cheap shot at the critics, and put *Ramparts* "in the same camp with the outright pornographers and other befouled merchants who are assassins of the human spirit." Ray Marcus called it "unfunny and totally stupid." For his part, Hinckle issued a tepid apology: "There is a best seller that isn't in print and that nobody can buy, and we suppose we are to blame . . . we thought the satire obvious, but we have been wrong before."[77]

Also appearing that November, but in a much more serious vein, was an item by Harrison Salisbury of *The New York Times*. In 1964 Salisbury had written that "the evidence of Oswald's single-handed guilt is overwhelming." Now he wrote that "enough questions have been raised, fairly and squarely, about the assassination, and about the Commission's findings, to warrant a reexamination." His opinion was given not in the *Times*, but in *The Progressive*, a small magazine in which Salisbury published a triple review of *Inquest, Rush to Judgment,* and *The Oswald Affair*.[78]

But the biggest surprise of all was probably the November issue of *Life* magazine. Its article, "A Matter of Reasonable Doubt," concluded that the Kennedy case should be reopened. "Now I *am* worried – *Life* magazine has joined our side," Sylvia joked to Maggie Field after seeing the article. "Actually, it is an index to the power of the attacks on the WR that even *Life*, committed as it has been to the WR, has had to reverse itself."[79]

In early November Sylvia told Maggie that her manuscript was at Bobbs-Merrill; an editor there had read excerpts in *The Minority of One* and requested to see the whole book. The book's working title, "Supreme Injustice," was discarded in favor of *Accessories After the Fact*. In spite of this editor's enthusiasm – he told her he considered it the best thing he had seen on the Warren Report – Sylvia thought the chances that Bobbs-Merrill would publish it were remote. The decision-makers there, she said, considered the market for assassination books glutted. Yet the editor promised her he would do everything in his power to persuade the firm to publish the book. Sylvia had taken a liking to this editor, whose name was Robert Ockene. "He is half-insane – as so many of us are – about the unspeakable atrocity of Vietnam," she told Maggie. "He obtains some relief by scrawling on subway walls, 'A. Hidell Lives!'" How, she asked, could one not like him for that?[80]

A lot was happening. The multibook review requested by *Studies on the Left* was about to be published, as was the December *Esquire*, which featured not only Epstein's article but one by Meagher called "Notes for a New Investigation." To Shirley Martin, Sylvia said there was "much excitement since *Life* came out. The developments are coming thick and fast."

But the fight, she knew, was far from over. The Warren Report still had its defenders, and the defenders still had easy access to the media. Among these many defenders were Professor Alexander M. Bickel of Yale; Arthur L. Goodhart, editor of *The Law Quarterly Review*; presidential aide John P. Roche; and John Sparrow, Warden of All Souls College, Oxford University. Probably just to relieve some pressure, Sylvia Meagher lampooned these men in verse.[81]

Defenders of the Gospel
According to Warren

Bickel, Sparrow, Goodhart, Roche –
No Clarence Darrow there, by gosh
To pit against Mark Lane,
Only a Sparrow-brain,
A scholar-in-residence,
An Ivy-legal-eagle, and
A White House Eminence,
To prop up Warren's bench.

Bickel, Goodhart, Roche and Sparrow –
Breathes there a don with mind more narrow,
to truth more fickle?
Professor Alex Bickel, to be sure,
Holds the key and has the cure:

> The illustrious Commission,
> Pure and good of heart,
> Remains above suspicion,
> While parties of the second part,
> The critics! are a mongrel pack,
> Nouveau-Roche and luster-lack –

> Place those villains on the rack!

Thus do the apologists
Dispose of "demonologists"
But bravely though they whistle
And bestow their benediction
The lone assassin and the single missile
Still take the prize for science fiction.[82]

– Sylvia Meagher

Chapter 24

An Ugly Question

Shirley Martin once wrote a letter to Vincent Salandria that among other things reminded him of a crush she'd had on Robert Vaughn, the handsome, dark-eyed actor who starred in the popular television series *The Man From U.N.C.L.E.* Now she informed Salandria that she also had a crush on an actor from another TV show, *Secret Agent*.

"Vickie and I find we like the English spy, Patrick McGoohan, who is blonde and blue-eyed, just as well. We figure this means we like spies. Vincent, I am joking. I am joking, Vincent. OK? You got that?"[1]

No doubt she was joking, but in truth this was no laughing matter. Salandria already felt the critical community was vulnerable to infiltration by intelligence assets who, acting on behalf of the true assassins, would try to confuse and misguide honest researchers, or failing that, attempt to discredit them. He would one day write: "Can we honestly expect that the powerful elements in our society who dispatched our President with that deadly Dealey Plaza fusillade and then sought to cover up the reasons why he was killed would leave to ordinary citizens to inform the public about the real meaning of the assassination of President Kennedy?"[2]

Salandria believed the critics were not merely vulnerable to infiltration; he was convinced it had already happened. But this was an area filled with pitfalls, for the one thing he could never expect to have was conclusive proof of another critic's true allegiances. Yet he was not hesitant to voice his suspicions, and some of his colleagues found this troubling. "So what else is new?" an exasperated Sylvia Meagher responded after Salandria told her that someone in their circle was probably an agent. "The list of persons similarly accused at one time or another is rather formidable."[3]

The list of persons similarly accused, or at least briefly guilty by association, included Sylvia herself. "How do I prove I'm *not* CIA-sponsored?" she had asked in early 1967. The cause of her concern was an article in *The Oakland Tribune* the previous February.[4]

> The Johnson Administration's own investigation of the Central Intelligence Agency's financial aid to private organizations is taking an intriguing turn.

Headed by Undersecretary Nicholas Katzenbach, the CIA study has been expanded to cover aid given Cuban refugee groups and several publication projects, including one dealing with the Warren Commission's inquiry into the assassination of President Kennedy.

The latter project, handled through a publishing firm, entailed the preparation of a comprehensive index by subject and name of the hundreds of persons involved in the commission's investigation . . . the index is the only accurate guide available, although those using it have no knowledge of the CIA's role in its preparation.[5]

The article had been sent to her by Harold Weisberg. "I am flabbergasted at the news of this 'CIA index' to the WR," she told him. "What are they talking about???? I hope no one forms the impression that my *Subject Index* is CIA-sponsored!" On April 5 she wrote to the *Tribune.* Her *Subject Index* was "a completely independent project . . . the CIA was in no way whatever involved. . . ."[6]

That may have ended this particular episode – but suspicions would in time touch many of the critics; no one was immune to the charge.

A panel discussion on the assassination was scheduled for Wednesday, November 30, 1966, at the Charles Street Meeting House in Boston. Billed as "Seven Judges, No Jury – A Second Look at the Murder of a President," the panel consisted of Penn Jones and Vince Salandria presenting the case against the Warren Report, with Jacob Cohen and four others, mostly academics, defending it. Edward Jay Epstein had been invited to participate but declined. Sylvia Meagher had also been invited, but had a scheduling conflict; she recommended Salandria to the organizers.[7]

Cohen was the Yale professor who had published "The Vital Documents" in *The Nation* the previous summer. He had written a second article, "The Warren Commission Report And Its Critics," which was in the then-current issue of *Frontier* magazine. He had also just appeared in a television discussion with Jones, Mark Lane, Léo Sauvage, and Harold Weisberg called "A Reexamination of the Warren Report." His book, *Honest Verdict,* had not yet been published but was still being mentioned as a work-in-progress. Cohen was emerging as one of the most prominent defenders of the Warren Commission.[8]

No complete record of the Boston discussion appears to exist. But Salandria was later quoted telling the audience, "Once the American

people are permitted to see what they have a right and duty
society which is still open, to wit: the Zapruder photographic
tation of the rude manner in which their President was disp
this world by a team of assassins, then the lone assassin theory of the
Warren Commission will be reduced to the proper place it deserves in
history as patent pap – improper sustenance for free minds."9

The evening contained a moment of theater – not high drama, but
a curious sort of burlesque. Cohen was doing his best to defend the
single-bullet theory when Salandria, the son of a skilled and proud tailor,
reached into his briefcase and withdrew a shirt and jacket with holes in
the same location as those in Kennedy's shirt and jacket. Moving toward
Cohen, he asked him to demonstrate how the President's finely-tailored
clothing could bunch up as the government claimed it did. Caught off
guard, Cohen refused to cooperate and threw the clothes back toward
Salandria.10

After the panel discussion, while Salandria was still on the stage, he
was surprised to see Edward Epstein and another young man approaching
him. Salandria had long since concluded that Epstein's book was dishonest. He further suspected, but could not prove, that Epstein had an
ulterior motive or unseen connection.11

Salandria recorded their exchange in notes later that evening.
"What are you doing in Boston?" Epstein asked, looking up at Salandria,
still at the podium.

"I'm telling the truth to the people."

Epstein extended his hand and the two men shook. "What are you
up to, Ed?" Salandria asked.

"I've changed, Vince."

Salandria looked at him evenly. "You mean that you made a deal.
That's OK, Ed. You made a deal and that's all right." His expression
hardened. "But if you get up before a television camera again and pretend
you're a critic I'll tell all about you, Ed Epstein."

Epstein smiled – "a sick smile," Salandria wrote in notes of the
encounter – and said, "You know what happened." Whereupon, he and
the other young man hurried away.12

Earlier that same day, when Salandria had checked into his hotel
room, he was surprised to learn a suite had been reserved for himself
and another panelist, who shall here be known as Robert Loeffler.
When he asked why, the hotel desk clerk didn't know; he could only tell

him it had been arranged by someone at Harvard University.[13]

Around 1 a.m., long after the forum had ended and Salandria was trying to sleep, there was a knock on his door.

It was Loeffler. "Vince, are you asleep?"

Salandria let Loeffler into the room. Loeffler, Salandria thought, appeared to be very agitated. "I feel horrible," Loeffler said. "I feel like a crumb."

"Why?"

"Debating the assassination is horrible," he replied.

"Well, you shouldn't feel like a crumb," Salandria said. "Your case is impossible to argue. No one can honestly defend the Warren Commission's work.

"But Bob," he continued, "you're brilliant. You know what happened in the assassination. Why do you do it? Why don't you just continue your academic career before you ruin it with this stupid case?"

"I'm not an academic anymore, Vince," Loeffler told him. "I can't stand professors. I like people too much." Before Salandria could comment, Loeffler continued: "Why is it that Sylvia Meagher can't stand me?"

Ignoring the direct question, Salandria replied, "Fred Cook, the reporter, thinks you may be a CIA agent. I don't believe that, myself." He watched closely for a reaction to this accusation, but saw none. He went on: "The case is nearly broken, Bob. It's all over in Europe, you know."

"Yes, I do know. I've heard about the European press."

"That's all I want: for this case to break. That's what we need – this society. We need to reexamine ourselves top to bottom, and benefit from this. Maybe the conservatives can do it. The liberal left and the Democrats are hopeless when it comes to the Kennedy assassination. Just hopeless."

"Yes," Loeffler agreed, "the conservatives may break it because they have the character. But the Birchers already know. And they're revolutionaries – they'll use it. They know this society can't digest a coup, and remain the same."

"Breaking the case could make us a better society," Salandria countered.

"We can't digest it."

"I think we can, Bob," Salandria said. "We need to become more American – we need to stop trying to act like a police state and go back to some of our original virtues, like skepticism of government and power. I can't live in a police state – not Russian, Cuban, or American."

"It's not a question of whether you want to live in a police state. You'll have to be killed."

This remark, Salandria thought, hadn't sounded all that speculative. "I agree," he replied. "And I'm prepared for that. You know I'm not afraid of that."

There was a long pause. Finally, Salandria continued. "You know, I'm not interested in having the conspirators punished. This society is already too violent. All I want is the truth, and the re-examination. But no punishment."

"That's impossible," Loeffler said quickly. "Our society isn't as compassionate as you. It will want – it will *demand* – retribution."

Salandria mentioned the President's autopsy photographs and X-rays, which had been the main topic of Jacob Cohen's article in *The Nation* the previous July. They were unavailable to non-government personnel, Salandria said. But Loeffler said no. "I have reason to think that we will see them." Salandria replied that they would almost certainly be forgeries.

Loeffler mentioned that Epstein had come to see him after the debate – just after he had seen Salandria, apparently. He was fawning like a little boy, Loeffler said contemptuously. "He was so eager to show me he was on my side. How weak he is!"

Loeffler reiterated that debating the assassination was horrible, and made him feel like a crumb. Salandria said he, too, was eager to be done with it and resume a normal life. Finally they said goodnight, and Loeffler left the room. "I detect he likes me," Salandria wrote in notes of the encounter. "I feel sorry for him and like him some."

Later that night – morning, really, for it had passed midnight – the telephone next to Fred Cook's bed began to ring. Startled from sleep, he answered groggily.

It was Salandria, who quickly described the panel discussion in Boston, and the subsequent encounter with Loeffler. "Fred, I told him that you had accused him of being a CIA front – and he did not deny it. He did not deny it!"

Salandria told Cook a little more about his conversation with Loeffler. "He's a very disturbed person, and I wound up feeling sorry for him. He has a lot of conflicts within himself, and he finally admitted that he knows we are right, but he said: 'The truth is too terrible. The American people would never be able to stand it.'"[14]

A few days later, Salandria began sending around to other critics copies of detailed notes he had made. The notes dealt mainly with his brief conversation with Epstein, and his longer conversation with Loeffler. The part that got the most attention was Loeffler's remark, "You'll have to be killed." Sylvia Meagher said she didn't quite know what to make of it. "Had Loeffler said, 'You would have to be...' instead of 'You will have to be,' I would be inclined to regard it as indicating merely that a rebel and critic in a police state would have to be liquidated if he would not or could not fall in line. The 'will' can of course have an ominous connotation."[15]

Meagher was flabbergasted by Salandria's remark that he felt sorry for Loeffler and liked him some. "Where I grew up, no one turned the other cheek – it was an eye (and an arm plus a leg) for an eye; and I have a keen and lively anticipation of the day of the WC's retribution – the WC and all its apologists and lackeys. If we don't have those little ceremonies the line of demarcation between good and evil is likely to get blurred."[16]

Early in 1967, a young journalist named Joe McGinniss attended a lecture by Salandria at a Philadelphia hotel and wrote about it a few days later in *The Philadelphia Inquirer.* "This was a political assassination and there was a lot of power behind it," Salandria had said. "A *lot* of power. If you want to find the men behind it you have to raise your sights. You have to screw your courage way up high. You have to look even higher than J. Edgar Hoover and the FBI."[17]

There were about fifty people in the audience, and McGinniss described their reaction. "It was Johnson," some whispered to others. "It sure makes sense." When the talk was over, many of them approached Salandria and told him how good it had been. "They said how terrible this conspiracy was," McGinniss reported, "and how important it was that they do something about it."[18]

This was a common response to Salandria's increasingly frequent public discussions, McGinniss wrote. "People know what happened," Salandria had told him. "They've always known. They just needed someone to bring it out into the open. That's what I'm trying to do. I'm trying to be a catalyst, to get other people to work."[19]

Later that evening McGinniss interviewed Salandria in his home in Philadelphia's Center City. He described a successful but rather ordinary man: a nice home, a pleasant wife, a son in second grade. There were a lot of things he could be doing, McGinniss observed, besides running around the country preaching conspiracy. Instead, he sat in his kitchen sipping lemonade and describing to McGinniss his ideas on the Kennedy assassination.[20]

There were so many ways, Salandria said, to demonstrate the Warren Report was false: the condition of CE 399, "the magic bullet." Or the Zapruder film showing the President being propelled back and to the left from a shot fired from the right front. "There was no single assassin. There were at least three and probably four and they were all in contact by radio. And Oswald was not one of them. He was standing on the front steps of the Depository when the shooting took place. The CIA had set him up as the perfect patsy."[21]

The CIA, McGinniss wrote, was very big in Salandria's theory. CIA and military leaders were afraid Kennedy would put an end to the Cold War and they would lose their power. But they could handle Lyndon Johnson, who would give them free reign in Asia. Johnson knew nothing of the plot against JFK until after the fact but agreed to go along with it. He assembled a commission of men who would also go along with it and forced Earl Warren to chair it. That, McGinniss wrote, was Salandria's theory, and it was crazy and horrible. Maybe, he suggested, Salandria had been working too hard.[22]

"The Kennedys know all about it," Salandria told McGinniss. "They were getting ready to expose the whole thing, then somebody made a deal. Somebody told them that Johnson would step down in '68 and Bobby could move right in. The Kennedys should never have done it. They should realize that these men won't give up their power. Sure, Johnson will step down and Bobby will move in, but how long will he stay? This was a bad deal. They'll get Bobby killed and they'll get us all killed . . . they'll turn this into a closed, totalitarian military society. The assassination was just the start."[23]

In 1964 another Philadelphia journalist, Gaeton Fonzi, had assumed Salandria was some kind of nut, but after interviewing him decided he wasn't so crazy after all. Joe McGinniss, however, was unconvinced. "No, I'm not a nut," he dutifully quoted Salandria. But his article concluded: "The sad part was that Vincent Salandria really believed in everything he said."[24]

Nearly a year before the McGinniss article appeared, a man named Josiah Thompson was one of several people arrested at an anti-Vietnam war demonstration in the Philadelphia area. Known as "Tink" to his friends, Thompson was then an assistant professor of philosophy at Haverford College. He was also a former Navy ensign who led an underwater demolition team when U.S. Marines landed in Beirut in the summer of 1958. His opposition to the war in Vietnam stemmed directly from his experiences in Lebanon. "The U.S. had invaded that country . . . on the basis of bad intelligence, [which] gave me a lot of sympathy for the guys that were actually in Vietnam. But absolutely no patience at all for the government that had sent them there."[25]

After his arrest Thompson and the others were taken to jail, where they were allowed to contact the American Civil Liberties Union. "We were brought out into the squad room," he remembered, "and an ACLU lawyer arrived. And his name was Vince Salandria. And he did one of the really classic jobs of bluffing the police that I've ever seen. Salandria's standing there talking to us in a loud voice so that all the gathered cops can hear him. And he says, 'Now, gentlemen, the ACLU has made contact with Attorney General Katzenbach, and when the FBI agents arrive – that should be in about fifteen or twenty minutes – I want you to tell them that not only have your civil rights been violated by these police officers here, but that you are suing for false arrest Captain so-and-so, Lieutenant so-and-so, Sergeant so-and-so, Patrolman blah blah blah,' went down the list. We were out of there in two-and-a-half minutes, if that. Released without any charges."[26]

Thompson had been mildly interested in the assassination when it happened. He traveled to Washington to walk through the Capitol Rotunda, where Kennedy's body lay in state, and even visited his local FBI office to tell them about contradictions in the official story he had noticed. But his chance meeting with Salandria proved to be a turning point. He had read and admired Salandria's *Liberation* articles; now he delved further into the case and gained considerable expertise in the evidence. By the summer of 1966 he and Salandria, with whom he had stayed in contact, were collaborating on what they conceived as a long magazine article.[27]

But before the summer was out the two had come to a sharp disagreement on the evidence, and Salandria dropped out of the project. "I immediately quit when Thompson tried to convince me that the Kennedy throat wound was a consequence of a bit of bone exiting from the throat which emanated from the head hit," Salandria once explained. This, he was certain, was not only incorrect, but would tend to exculpate the government. He told Thompson he would not be associated with it. Thompson viewed the impasse as a simple difference of opinion. "I was unwilling to say, unambiguously, that it was an entry hole," he recalled. "That sounds reasonable to me . . . In any case, I went on on my own." Before long Thompson's intended magazine article was expanded to a book called *Six Seconds in Dallas*, which was published by Bernard Geis Associates to great media attention in late 1967.[28]

The centerpiece of Thompson's book was to be an analysis of the Zapruder film. It was essential that Thompson see the best possible copy; he had heard that the *Life* magazine copy was far superior to any other. *Life* was then preparing a new article on the assassination. Thompson's Geis editor approached the magazine. *Life* was impressed with the young professor's work and asked him to serve as a consultant to their article, even as he continued working on his book. "The two projects," Thompson remembered, "fitted together beautifully."[29]

Ray Marcus heard about Tink Thompson in mid-1966 through his contacts with Salandria, Sylvia Meagher, and David Lifton. He was excited at the prospect of Thompson, with established academic credentials, writing a book based on a detailed study of the Zapruder film. He too was convinced that the film was the key to understanding the sequence of shots in Dealey Plaza but had no intention of writing such a book himself.[30]

Marcus was dismayed to learn that Thompson did not agree that JFK was first struck several seconds before the Warren Commission stated – just before Z-189, by his reckoning – and that Thompson in fact agreed with the Commission that JFK was first hit between Z-210 and Z-225. But he felt certain he could convince Thompson that this was incorrect. Marcus was planning a short business trip to Boston that October. He decided to extend it in order to go to the National Archives to meet in person some of the critics with whom he had been in touch for the past several years. Thompson was among those he wanted to meet. "I hoped I would have an opportunity to thrash this out with him in person."[31]

He also planned to visit Sylvia Meagher, Vince Salandria, and Harold Weisberg, each of whom he knew by letter and telephone but hadn't met in person. In addition he viewed the trip as a chance to tie up a few loose ends. Not long before leaving he telephoned I.F. Stone at his home in Washington, D.C. It had been two years since he had written his long letter to Stone questioning the venerable journalist's support of the Warren Commission findings – a letter that had gone unanswered. Now, on the phone, he asked Stone if the two of them could meet when Marcus reached Washington, so he could present some of the assassination evidence he had prepared.[32]

Stone's answer was immediate: *"I don't care about that asshole case!"* he shouted – and promptly hung up the phone. Marcus later remarked that had Stone made that comment in his *Weekly* of October 1964, instead of an ill-reasoned defense of the Warren Report, it would at least have had the virtue of being honest.[33]

In New York Marcus telephoned the offices of *Life* magazine. He had heard about *Life*'s new article and thought he could contribute something to it. He reached Ed Kern, one of the *Life* editors working on the article, which centered on Governor Connally; he told him he could show him where in the Z-film Connally had been struck, and that it was a separate hit. "If you can show us that," Kern replied, "you'll be showing us something we haven't been able to find in almost three years of looking at the film."[34]

Half an hour later Marcus was in *Life*'s offices and meeting with Kern and another editor, Loudon Wainwright. *Life* then owned all rights to the Zapruder film, and clear reproductions were not easily obtainable by private citizens. With Kern and Wainwright, Marcus was able to view, on a light table, a series of crystal-clear 4x5-inch slides prepared from the original film. Thirty-five years later he still recalled his astonishment at what he was shown. For several years he had been squinting at the reproductions published in Volume 18 of the Hearings and Exhibits. What the Commission published was low-resolution black-and-white, but *Life*'s slides were something else. "It was stunning to me," he said. "Here I was, working with these black and white fuzzies . . . what that did, it just – every hypothesis that I had come to in my own mind just was strengthened, greatly, by looking at those slides, where everything was so much clearer."[35]

Marcus showed the two *Life* editors the evidence he had documented in his "Hypotheses re: the Zapruder Film" a year and a half before, in particular the sharp drop of Connally's right shoulder between frames 237-238. Both men showed surprise and agreed that what Marcus was showing them was important evidence. They further agreed that Connally had indeed been hit by a separate bullet. This had been Connally's own conclusion. Connally too had been to the *Life* offices and had personally viewed the same slides.[36]

After they had spent some time examining the slides, Wainwright told Marcus that one of his colleagues was then in the *Life* offices. Marcus looked up and saw a man he did not recognize standing in the doorway to an adjoining room. He was pleased and surprised to be introduced to Josiah Thompson.[37]

By then Thompson was spending a great deal of time at *Life* . He was even able to arrange a screening of *Life*'s "camera original" Zapruder film that was attended by Sylvia Meagher, Republican Congressman Theodore Kupferman, and Dr. Cyril Wecht, the Pittsburgh-based forensic pathologist who had critiqued President Kennedy's autopsy. Just as Ray Marcus had been stunned by the clarity of *Life*'s Zapruder slides, the *Life* version of the film itself, Thompson still recalled years later, was "shockingly clear" – better, even, than the copy at the National Archives.[38]

Thompson's presence at the *Life* building on the day Marcus was there was a remarkable stroke of luck. Marcus had intended to contact Thompson so they could review the timing of the first Kennedy shot, which Marcus put at Z-189. Now Thompson was not only present, but so were two key journalists, and best of all, the crystal-clear Zapruder film slides that might enable them to reconcile their opposing views in a matter of minutes.[39]

Marcus was thus astonished when Thompson declined to look at the slides with him, saying vaguely that he did not have enough time. "For a moment, taken aback, I did not know how to respond to his refusal," Marcus remembered. "Here I was, having traveled cross-continent to visit and discuss matters with my fellow critics, including Thompson. He knew I was a serious researcher, having previously concurred with my conclusion of a frame 237-238 Connally hit, after earlier having believed he was hit much later; and also with my finding that JFK had been hit in the head twice between frames 313-315. Here we were in the same room with two *Life* editors preparing an important story based on the Z-film, and with their excellent slides on a light-table not more than ten feet from where he was standing, and he had just told me he didn't have time to look at the slides – an exercise that could not have required more than five minutes – to attempt to resolve our differing views on a vitally important question." Marcus could think of nothing better to say than to repeat his suggestion. Again Thompson declined. Marcus suggested they set up a meeting for another time but Thompson declined that, too. And with that, he left the room.[40]

Years later Thompson said that he had no recollection of this meeting, although he conceded that it probably happened. For his part, Marcus reflected: "I got the distinct impression that not only would he rather not meet with me again, but that he was less than delighted with our chance meeting."[41]

In January and February 1967 there were several incidents that put Sylvia Meagher and other critics on what might be termed "high alert." Sylvia had a couple of direct experiences with what she became convinced were well-thought-out strategies to discredit her and other critics. She became so concerned that she told Harold Weisberg: "I think that every one of us should view with extreme caution any allegations from strangers of 'breakthrough' information as I feel that part of the campaign will be the laying of some subtle traps."[42]

One such cause for concern involved a man known to the critics as Jules Striso, of Yonkers, New York. Striso was for a time in contact with Meagher, Shirley Martin, Harold Weisberg, and Vince Salandria. He hinted that he possessed important information. Presumably because of her proximity Striso telephoned Meagher on several occasions, asking to meet with her. After they agreed to an appointment for early February, however, Striso cancelled it.[43]

Striso had first contacted Shirley Martin in the fall of 1966. "I was leery of him from the start, as he harped so much on narcotics," she told Sylvia. He had told her, for example, that during a stay in China in 1950 he had witnessed several thousand tons of narcotics destined for the United States, adding that "we are a very sick nation and the illness like a cancer which courses through the body may already be incurable." More ominous were his warnings that some of the critics might be in personal danger.[44]

After cancelling his scheduled appointment with Sylvia, Striso unexpectedly reinstated it. He told her he might be in New York on February 6, a Monday, and if so, would call her. But instead of phoning, he showed up at Meagher's apartment around 9 pm. He was extremely drunk. Moreover he turned out to be a very large man, which coupled with his intoxication made Sylvia very uneasy. "He did not give any information except that he knew all the answers and that he was in touch with several Congressmen," a claim which Meagher later determined to be an exaggeration at best. "He also made dire warnings of what would happen to me if I accepted his information – all kinds of horrors and dangers, including acid in the face. That, I might say, is almost identical with another man who offered ultimate answers for $50,000, but whose real purpose seemed to be to throw us into terror."[45]

To Sylvia's relief, Striso did not stay long. He left of his own volition, saying that he did not wish to endanger her by telling her what he knew. She watched as he walked unsteadily toward the elevator and disappeared. Reflecting on his visit the next day, Sylvia began to wonder whether Striso had really been drunk or had put on a skillful performance. The entire episode left her anxious. "I want to urge you and Harold Weisberg," she told Shirley Martin, "to exercise great care if you continue to have any contacts with J.S. Something is very wrong here."[46]

The visit by Striso had come on the heels of a far more confusing event. On the last day of January 1967, Vince Salandria was contacted by a woman calling herself Rita Rollins, who said she had heard about Salandria and wanted to talk to him. She feared for her life, she said, and was desperate to talk to Salandria. Salandria was willing to have her come to his house, but Rollins insisted she would not do so unless she were picked up and driven there, a task which Salandria's wife agreed to perform.[47]

When she finally sat down with Salandria, Rollins had a fantastic story to tell. She was about fifty years old and was by training a nurse. She said that in 1963 she worked in a Dallas hospital and among her patients was a woman from a wealthy Texas family. Like Rollins herself, the patient was African-American. A member of the woman's family, Rollins had learned, was with the FBI and was formerly with the CIA. His name was Al, and Rollins believed he might have been involved in an assassination attempt in Africa. She had further learned that Al had taken target practice with five other men on the family's ranch around the time of the JFK assassination. She came to believe they had been part of an assassination team involved in the Dealey Plaza execution. The police detained Al after the assassination but let him go. Then, Rollins said, Al and another man went to a Dallas house to change clothes and dispose of their weapons. Others arrived in a Rambler station wagon. Later they were driven to the airport.[48]

Rollins was convinced that she knew too much, and that her life was in jeopardy. In December 1966 she was working at a hospital near Milwaukee, Wisconsin. She heard that unknown men had been asking questions about her: Did she talk a lot? Was she sociable? Around that same time, she told Salandria, her car was forced off the road by another car, in what she was certain had been an attempt on her life. She planned to leave the country within a week.[49]

The day after this meeting with Salandria, Sylvia Meagher received a phone call at her office in the United Nations building. It was M.S.

Arnoni. Salandria had just called him, he said, and wanted them both to come to Philadelphia immediately to meet Rita Rollins. After Arnoni outlined the Rollins story, Sylvia said, "I literally dropped what I was doing and left the office without a word of explanation, disappearing for the rest of the day. I took a train and was joined by Arnoni en route."[50]

On the way to Philadelphia, Sylvia told Arnoni she felt certain that Rollins was probably a fraud. But even if she were lying, her appearance might be significant. There was nothing random about it; if nothing else, she represented a well-thought-out operation.[51]

After Sylvia and Arnoni arrived in Philadelphia, they sat down with Rollins, Salandria, Salandria's wife, and Chris Kefalos, a former student of Salandria who had become a close family friend. "Despite my strong predisposition to regard Rollins as a fake, she very soon had me completely sold," Meagher reported to Maggie Field. "We listened for almost three hours." Rollins repeated the story she had told the night before and added more information. She had confided what she knew to her priest, who counseled that she must tell what she knew. One of the critics who had been getting so much publicity, he suggested, might have some ideas. Why did she choose Salandria? She had heard about the Joe McGinniss column, Rollins said, which said Salandria was working on a theory of government involvement.[52]

Did anyone involved in the assassination work in the Book Depository building? Sylvia asked. Rollins said she didn't know. Were there any Cuban exiles involved? No, but there was a Haitian.[53]

As the conversation progressed, Sylvia was increasingly certain that this was the real thing. It impressed her that Rollins was not a Caucasian. "How much more disarming her story, by that virtue," she told Maggie Field. "And she was fingering other non-whites, selling it as an integrated operation carried out by some of each hue."[54]

Arnoni, however, was increasingly skeptical. "Who knows of your coming to speak with Vince?" he asked.

"In Philadelphia, a Catholic Monsignor."

"Other than in the city?" Arnoni pressed.

"A reporter in Chicago and another ex-Secret Service agent . . . I came here because we heard about the McGinniss article."[55]

Arnoni's skepticism was plain to all. As they continued, Rollins began addressing herself more and more to Sylvia, who seemed to be a sympathetic listener, and was increasingly cold toward Arnoni. When they finally finished, Salandria drove Arnoni and Meagher to the railroad station while Rollins stayed behind. "We had a real hassle," Sylvia told

Maggie Field. "Vince remained certain that she was legitimate and had the ultimate answers; I was certain that either (a) she was legitimate, or (b) she nevertheless was a definite link to the ultimate answers for the simple reason that she was so skillful, the story so elaborate, the whole caper so professional, that it was a carefully prepared trap of some kind in which Rollins was fulfilling an assignment."[56]

But Arnoni was having none of it. Rollins, he was quite certain, was a lone nut with a lot of hearsay who had taken evidence already in the public record and embellished it. But why? Maybe, Arnoni suggested, to prod more of the critics into following the trail she felt needed to be followed.[57]

"I considered Arnoni's hypothesis absolutely idiotic," Sylvia said, "and we had a real good scrap. We missed the train." They drove back to Salandria's house to await the next train, due two hours later.[58]

They decided to put a few more questions to Rita Rollins. "Now this woman is *good*," Sylvia said, "not to say brilliant – but she did trip herself up on one point, in a way that resolved my indecision at once." The record is incomplete on this, but it appears Rollins may have faltered in answering questions about her purported profession, nursing. "I became certain again, as I had been almost sure before meeting her, that she was a fake who had been extremely well primed for the assignment and was doing a magnificent, an almost perfect performance."[59]

The meeting broke up in an air of uncertainty. When Salandria drove Sylvia and Arnoni back to the train station, Rollins went along, so they did not speak openly about what they thought. While Sylvia and Arnoni were both doubtful – Arnoni more so – Sylvia thought Salandria was inclined to believe Rollins. Long afterward Salandria said that was not so, that he was on to Rollins by this time as well. In any case Sylvia was trying to figure out just what was going on. "My bones and cells tell me that we are walking on a road that has been mined and that while Rollins' story is a clever fake, we are nevertheless making contact with those we are trying to find."[60]

On February 2, Salandria received a telephone call from Rollins. Still anxious, she told him that "they know full well what is going on. The government expects the Warren Report to be blown." She had spoken with a reporter from *The New York Times* and he was interested in her story; he wanted to talk to Salandria, too. Furthermore, she knew of persons in Toronto, whom she did not identify, who knew the secrets of Dallas but were not in a position to reveal what they knew. They wanted a prominent critic to act on their behalf. They would channel what they knew through him, although they expected he would do his own investigation to confirm the information. He could reveal the full story at a press conference. He would be well-paid for his services.[61]

Salandria asked how much money they were willing to pay; Rollins told him $12,000.[62]

Immediately after this conversation, Rollins telephoned Sylvia. When they had finished, Sylvia called Salandria. She reported that she had told Rollins that she was a very brilliant woman, but she had not fooled them – not Meagher, not Salandria, not Arnoni. She should go back to her employers, whoever they were, and so advise them.[63]

In August 1965, Salandria had told Sylvia Meagher about a man he was investigating whose name was "Boganov or something similar." In the year and a half since then, Salandria had learned more.

The man's first name was Igor, and the "something similar" was Vaganov. He was a 28-year-old Latvian émigré who had lived in the United States since he was nine years old. He was known to use the aliases John Nicholson, Kurt Kallaway, and Vince Carson. He was also known by the nickname "Turk." Tall and thin, a veteran of the United States Navy, Vaganov was believed to be a skilled rifleman with a sadistic streak: by one account he had a history of torturing animals for fun.[64]

In September 1963, Vaganov was employed as a credit manager at General Electric Credit Corporation just outside Philadelphia. Shortly after the White House announced President Kennedy's upcoming trip to Texas, Vaganov began requesting a transfer to the company's Dallas office. The request was made several times and each time was denied. In the first week of November he quit his job without giving notice, sold some of his belongings and packed up the rest, and left for Dallas, taking his girlfriend Anne with him. Along the way, they were married.[65]

Vaganov was driving a red Thunderbird convertible on which he still owed more than three thousand dollars. The vehicle was equipped with a two-way radio. Among Vaganov's luggage was a rifle and a .38 caliber pistol. He and Anne arrived in Dallas on November 10 or 11; on November 12 they moved into an apartment in Oak Cliff, the same part of town where Lee Oswald stayed in a rooming house.[66]

On the evening of November 21, Vaganov and his new wife argued, and a hysterical Anne called her sister in Conroe, Texas, crying that her husband was going to do "something horrible" the next day. On the morning of the 22nd Vaganov rose at noon, and according to his

landlord dressed in khaki pants and possibly a
12:45 p.m. his landlord told him about the Ke
watching a few minutes of television coverage
his red Thunderbird. Not long after this, I
Vaganov apartment, Dallas Police Officer J.I
with a .38 caliber pistol.[67]

A bit of serendipity had led Salandri
after the assassination a loan-officer friend noticed
report: a man named Vaganov had defaulted on his car loan. Attached
to the report was a note from Vaganov saying that he had abandoned
the car in a Dallas parking lot, where it could be recovered, and that he
could be reached via General Delivery in Mexico City. Noting that
some of the dates placed Vaganov in Dallas at the time of the assassination, and knowing of Salandria's interest, the loan officer passed along
a copy of the report.[68]

Some investigating established that Vaganov had been questioned
by the FBI after the assassination, after his wife's sister alerted them to
Anne's frantic phone call of November 21. But at this stage there was not
a whole lot more to go on; Salandria learned what he could about
Vaganov over the next few years. It was noted that he was an excellent
shot and had a .38 caliber pistol. The clothing he wore on November 22,
as well as his general build, matched the description of one of the two
men seen by Tippit witness Acquilla Clemons in the vicinity of the
Tippit shooting. And Tippit witness Domingo Benavides had reported
seeing a man in a red Ford.[69]

By 1966 both Josiah Thompson and Gaeton Fonzi were interested
in the Vaganov saga and helped out in the investigating. There was no
hard evidence tying Vaganov to either the Kennedy or Tippit killings,
just coinciding episodes and conjecture. Working independently,
Thompson and Fonzi attempted to find a link, focusing on a jacket found
near the Tippit murder site. The link was never established, but Fonzi
wrote another article for the *Greater Philadelphia* magazine that outlined
what was known about Vaganov, who was referred to as "Mr. Brown."[70]

By early 1967 Salandria had learned that Vaganov was back in
Philadelphia; he even found out where Vaganov was living. It was time to
talk to the man himself. Salandria and John Berendt, a writer developing
an article on Vaganov for *Esquire* magazine, went to his home and spoke
to him. Vaganov sat cross-legged on a couch and, puffing on a cigarette,
answered a series of questions. He was not inclined to cooperate for an
Esquire article, he told them, although he might. He had seen the *Greater*

a piece and was thinking about suing. He was aware that ~~h~~ad been checking up on him for the last couple of years. He ~~ne~~d to say where he was employed. At present he was not allowed to ~~lea~~ve the state of Pennsylvania without permission.[71]

That was about all Salandria and Berendt learned. Afterward, Salandria ruminated on the meeting. Vaganov, it seemed to him, had tried very hard to act nonchalantly. But Salandria thought he detected fear. "He's waiting for the answers, but right now he doesn't know what to say. I think he's in trouble."[72]

In Salandria's opinion, the assassination case was close to breaking. For him, the true nature of the case seemed clear enough: Kennedy had been killed for his efforts to end the Cold War. As he said at the lecture attended by Joe McGinnis, "You have to look even higher than J. Edgar Hoover and the FBI." The killing itself, he was certain, was carried out by the CIA. The true assassins were now attempting to throw the critics off their scent with a series of false leads. Vaganov might well have been such a false lead. As Sylvia had been doing, Salandria began warning his fellow critics to be on their guard. Most of them – Penn Jones, Ray Marcus, Harold Weisberg – said similar frauds had approached them, too.[73]

Perhaps coincidentally, the same night he returned home from the encounter with Igor "Turk" Vaganov, Salandria was first contacted by Rita Rollins.[74]

Around this time, there came the first hint of a major development in the city of New Orleans. In late January 1967, *New Orleans States-Item* columnist Jack Dempsey wrote obliquely:

> **DID YOU KNOW?** At least five persons have been questioned by the District Attorney's office in connection with another investigation into events linked to the Kennedy assassination.[74]

This was the extent of the first media reference to the investigation launched by District Attorney Jim Garrison several months earlier. Over the next few weeks, Dempsey gathered details on the probe with the help of several other *States-Item* reporters, and on Friday, February 17, the paper ran a front-page story on the Garrison investigation. By Sunday the investigation was front-page news in papers across the country. *The New York Times* had the story on Saturday, but relegated it to page 43. The brief item noted that an investigation was indeed underway but that

Garrison was calling it "routine." The focus appeared to be a New Orleans pilot named David Ferrie, whom Garrison had briefly detained and questioned in 1963, a few days after the assassination.[76]

Garrison would always maintain that he had meant to keep the investigation secret, but that the *States-Item* forced his hand. Left with no choice but to speak to the media, he cautiously told a press conference that the Warren Commission had consisted of honorable men whose investigation was nonetheless unsuccessful. "And that's where we came in. We have made progress. And there is no question in my mind but what there will be in time arrests of individuals following our investigation. And there is no question in my mind but what in time to come there will be charges, and there will be convictions based on the charges."[77]

The news was nothing short of electrifying. All of the critics' sacrifice and hard work over the preceding three years suddenly seemed on the verge of paying off. Asked about the Garrison probe, Mark Lane pledged to cooperate as much as possible. Sylvia Meagher was also ready to do what she could: a few days after the story broke, she sent Garrison a telegram.

> 2/22/67 3:30 pm
> District Attorney James Garrison
> New Orleans, LA
>
> Maggie Field of Beverly Hills, Calif. and I wish to offer you any possible assistance in your investigation of the assassination conspiracy stop If we can be of any service with our close knowledge of the Warren Report and Hearings and Exhibits or in any other way please contact us.[78]

Chapter 25

Counterattack

In the closing months of 1966 a reporter from the Italian magazine *Epoca* traveled around the United States interviewing many of the critics for an article planned to coincide with the third anniversary of the Kennedy assassination. Among those interviewed were Vince Salandria, Harold Feldman, Shirley Martin, Ray Marcus, Penn Jones, and Sylvia Meagher. "He even coaxed an old photograph out of me," Sylvia told Maggie Field. The reporter also talked to Theodore Kupferman, the Republican congressman who a few months earlier had proposed legislation to re-open the assassination investigation.[1]

The year had ended on a high note for Meagher: in spite of her uncertainty, Bobbs-Merrill accepted *Accessories After the Fact* for publication. In October Bob Ockene, the editor who had written "A. Hidell Lives!" on subway walls, enlisted Léo Sauvage to assess the book for Bobbs-Merrill – to give it, in effect, a peer review. As time went on but no verdict from Sauvage was forthcoming, Sylvia grew anxious. "I talked to our Eminent Reader on various matters but did not raise the subject of the manuscript," she told Ockene in late November. "Nor did he . . . if you are inclined to light a fire under the E.R., I promise not to holler for the Fire Department."[2]

Finally, on December 8, Ockene asked Sauvage if he had a rough idea when he would finish reading. Two days later he sent Ockene a two-page summary. In it he acknowledged his earlier praise for Sylvia Meagher in the "American Postscript" to *The Oswald Affair*. "After having unselfishly shared her information with most of the authors of recent books critical of the Warren Commission, most of whom neglected to acknowledge their debt, Sylvia Meagher has finally decided to publish a book of her own. It confirms not only her scientific mind and the exhaustive thoroughness of her research, but the penetrating insight she has brought to the study of the case." *Accessories After the Fact*, he told Bobbs-Merrill, would serve as a reference book on the case, and was an important contribution to the necessary re-examination of the Kennedy assassination.[3]

Sylvia was pleased, quite naturally, with Sauvage's assessment, although a bit chagrined that he had used the phrase "reference book" to describe it. But she knew that Ockene still had to sell it to his superiors. "If I were Bobbs, or even Merrill, I would not rush into this production," she quipped. In spite of her doubts, Ockene called her at work at four o'clock on Wednesday, December 28, with the best of all possible news: the manuscript had been accepted. She would receive a $1,500 advance with a 10% royalty on the first 7,500 copies sold, with a 15% royalty thereafter. Publication was expected in the fall of 1967. She was, she told friends, dazed and happy.[4]

During his first appearance on *The Mort Sahl Show*, in response to a question from a member of the audience, Mark Lane commented that America was entering the second phase of the aftermath of the Warren Report. The first phase, he said, was the critics' alerting the public that the Report was not merely a false document – it was, in fact, an obstacle to the truth. The second phase centered on the question: What can be done about it?[5]

One suggestion was the signing of petitions demanding that all of the evidence relating to the case be made public. The petitions could be delivered to the White House, Lane suggested, at a massive demonstration marking the third anniversary of the assassination, which was then just a few months away. He further said that it was crucial to support the bill to re-open the investigation introduced by Congressman Theodore Kupferman.[6]

There was no petition delivered to the White House, and no massive demonstration there, on November 22, 1966. But as it had been each year since the assassination, the date was marked in a variety of ways. In Dallas people gathered on the grassy knoll area, and Mayor Erik Jonsson dedicated a bronze historical marker nearby. Former JFK aide Arthur Schlesinger said public doubts about the Commission's findings warranted a new investigation. Senator Russell Long of Louisiana, whose father Huey Long had been assassinated in 1935, told reporters he believed there was more than one gunman involved in JFK's murder. But Oklahoma Representative Carl Albert said that the Commission had answered the basic questions, adding that "I never did get excited about minor inconsistencies such as an extra bullet."[7]

Speaking in Austin the following day, Governor John Connally said that in spite of a disagreement with the Warren Report on a single detail, he still supported its basic findings. His disagreement was then the topic of a cover story in the current issue of *Life* magazine: that he was not struck by the same bullet that hit President Kennedy – that, in short, he disagreed with the single-bullet theory. At the same time he dismissed the critics who argued that this disagreement was highly significant. Certain facts about the assassination, Connally said, would simply never be known. The Warren Commission had been composed of men of the highest integrity and unquestioned patriotism: he found it shocking that "journalistic scavengers such as Mark Lane, attempting to impugn the motives of these members individually, cast doubts upon the commission as a whole and question the credibility of the Government itself."[8]

Asked about the Texas Governor's remarks, Lane said they revealed "an abysmal ignorance of the implications of his own testimony. If the bullet that struck President Kennedy did not also strike the Governor, then there was no lone assassin." Connally's statements, Lane continued, questioned the loyalty and motivation of those who refused to accept a false governmental edict. It was the American people, after all, who had made *Rush to Judgment* a best seller.[9]

Much more bluntly, Penn Jones would say: "Connally has stated that he is satisfied with the conclusions of the Warren Commission. This is insanity. By persisting that he was hit by a separate shot, Connally destroys the Warren Report completely. How can he then state that he has no quarrel with the Commission's findings?"[10]

The article in *Epoca,* "La Verita e Vicina," appeared in its issue of November 27, 1966. The piece was generally favorable to the critics and their cause. But of course, it appeared only in Europe and only in Italian; it had no impact in the United States.[11]

Around the same time that the *Epoca* reporter was interviewing Warren Report critics, two other journalists, both Americans, were doing much the same thing. Lawrence Schiller and Richard Warren Lewis interviewed all of the first-generation critics, including Maggie Field, who had been overlooked by *Epoca,* and some of the second-generation critics like David Lifton. But unlike the man from *Epoca,* Schiller and Lewis did not lay all of their cards on the table. The end product of their labors was a widely publicized defense of the Warren Commission and its lone-assassin thesis, and an attack on the motives and personalities of the critics.

Schiller and Lewis made the most of their interviews, delivering them not only as a long-playing record album called *The Controversy,* but also as an article in *The World Journal Tribune* magazine *New York,* and later as a book. Both the magazine article and the book, written principally by Lewis, incorporated John Connally's "scavengers" epithet into their titles.

On November 23, 1966, the same day that Connally was disparaging "journalistic scavengers," Sylvia Meagher received a long-distance telephone call from Los Angeles. It was Lawrence Schiller, describing the proposed documentary record project. Meagher agreed to talk to him on the assumption she was merely sharing her expertise, and was interviewed in her home on Saturday, December 3, 1966. But as the lengthy interview progressed, Meagher began to feel very uneasy.[12]

"I couldn't even sleep last night for the feeling of taint and degradation that descended on me during the four-hour 'interview,'" she said the next day. When the interview was over, Schiller and Lewis left her with release forms, legal documents that, if she signed them, would allow the authors to use the tape-recorded interview on their record. Meagher read the forms carefully, did not like the terms, and decided not to sign.[13]

They telephoned her the next day to arrange a follow-up interview, but she declined to see them again. Meagher had by then written them a two-page letter describing her reasoning for not signing the release. She read it to them over the phone and then mailed it out. Her main reasons, she said, were that she didn't think it was possible to present the critics' case on a single album — on just one side of an album, in fact, according to what Schiller and Lewis had told her. She also couldn't agree to participate in a production over which she had no control on how her statements were used. In addition, between their initial contact and the interview there had been ever-greater expectations imposed on her. At bottom, she simply did not trust them. In time, she grew increasingly contemptuous of the duo and began referring to them as "Schlewis." But at this early juncture she told Maggie Field: "These scavengers are not worth the time it takes to tell them where to go; they don't give a good god-damn about this case, or they would have been in it from November 1963."[14]

Harold Weisberg agreed to the terms of the release, but came to regret it. "I am more and more impressed with the magnitude of my misjudgment of these wretched men," he commented not long after the record was out. Schiller and Lewis had told him, he recalled, that their purposes were scholarly. But, he wrote Schiller angrily, it was nothing of the sort: "What you did defames the gutter." Mark Lane said that they told him, on their initial contact, that they were producing an album that would be an objective examination of the Warren Report and its critics, with both sides adequately represented. But once they'd seen their work, all the critics felt they had been duped by a couple of con men, and were unfairly represented on the album, in the article, and in the book.[15]

As a group, the critics were characterized as "a keening pack of speculators" who had ransacked the official evidence in search of contradictions. They were also dealt with individually. Vince Salandria possessed a "strident nouvelle vague" voice; Shirley Martin was dismissed as an amateur detective with a passion for Agatha Christie mysteries. Ray Marcus was a "self-styled specialist" on CE 399 and a "distributor of signs reading 'For Sale' and 'Beware of Dog' and 'For Rent,'" while Maggie Field was little more than a housewife with too much time on her hands.[16]

Penn Jones, Jr., meanwhile, was "a drawling backwoods prophet." Schiller and Lewis recounted the story of the *Midlothian Mirror* fire-bombing, reporting that a troubled teenager had committed the crime – which neither Penn nor his wife ever believed. Penn's theory of mysterious deaths connected to the assassination was a "macabre doctrine" built on a foundation of error. Jones was further depicted as an alcoholic who carried a pint of bourbon in the hip pocket of his overalls. According to Penn, however, one of the interviewers had asked him for a drink. Not having any booze on hand, Jones said he "walked across town and borrowed a bottle *for him*."[17]

The most savage attacks were on Mark Lane, who was easily the critic with the highest public profile. "His wily showmanship helped sway millions of converts," narrator George Kennedy said on *The Controversy* record album. "But there were still millions more who realized that *Rush to Judgment* really belonged on top of the fiction best-seller lists." Nothing was offered to substantiate that claim.[18]

Lane was also denigrated for accumulating nineteen traffic tickets over a period of several years, for supporting, as a New York Assemblyman, a measure to abolish the House Un-American Activities Committee, and for his involvement in the civil rights movement in Mississippi in 1961. "He was arrested for breaching the peace in Jackson, Mississippi, where he and a Negro leader attempted to use segregated facilities at the municipal airport." Recalling that African-Americans of the civil rights era were merely asserting their constitutional rights, it is difficult to understand how supporters such as Lane – even those who may have viewed the issue with a cynical eye toward political advantage – could be faulted.[19]

Schiller and Lewis described the incident during Lane's 1961 New York State Assembly campaign when a thrown beer can opened a wound in his head. "It was never determined," they sneered, "whether its trajectory originated from the left front or the right rear." When Lane was in California, they reported, he often visited the home of Maggie Field, "where Lane likes to float around the swimming pool between engagements." The home, in posh Beverly Hills, was guarded by a vicious German shepard, the authors noted. Lane subsequently said that while he enjoyed visiting the Field home, he had never been in for a swim there. And the characterization of the dog as vicious was rather subjective. Brondo was a beloved family pet who apparently was not much of a watchdog. According to Maggie Field, he normally licked everyone's hand. But on the occasion of Larry Schiller's visit to interview Maggie, Brondo – to her horror – lunged at him and sank his teeth into his buttocks.[20]

Later there was some uncertainty whether it was Lewis or Schiller whom Brondo had bitten. Lane wrote that it was Lewis, but Ray Marcus and Maggie's daughter were certain that it was Larry Schiller. "Lawrence Schiller was the only person this dog ever bit," Gwen Field said. "He took an immediate dislike to him." In any case, once the true nature of Lewis and Schiller's work was known, the Brondo incident offered a measure of solace. Marcus recalled: "Memory of Brondo's attack, which had so mortified Maggie at the time, became for her – and for those of us she told about it – a source of satisfaction and justifiable retribution, exacted in this case in advance . . . good dog, Brondo."[21]

From Beverly Hills, Schiller and Lewis traveled to Oklahoma to interview Shirley Martin. Mrs. Martin generously offered to pick them up at the airport. "Schiller called himself 'James Bond,'" she reported to Sylvia Meagher. As they drove back to Hominy, they asked Mrs. Martin whether she had any dogs; pleased, she replied that she had twelve. "Lewis made me promise to lock up all my dogs before he would even get out of the car."[22]

In their magazine article and book, Schiller and Lewis made much of Shirley Martin's meeting with Father Oscar Huber in November of 1964. Father Huber had confirmed to Mrs. Martin that the newspaper article that said he had seen a "terrible wound" over the dead president's left eye was correct. But according to Schiller and Lewis, Father Huber denied that he had ever met Shirley Martin. His denial was not quoted directly; Lewis merely wrote that he denied it. But Huber was quoted as saying that President Kennedy's "face was covered with blood, but I saw no wounds . . . I did not know where he had been shot and I had no thought of looking for anything like that."[23]

"I was angry," Mrs. Martin recalled many years later. She could not understand why Father Huber would deny meeting with her. "If you can't trust a priest, who can you trust?"[24]

"He didn't know my sister had a tape recorder with the microphone wired through a purse handle," Teresa Martin added. "I suppose it's possible he forgot us or maybe just found it awkward later when confronted by it."[25]

Shirley later replied with "An Open Letter to Father Huber," which was published in the *Midlothian Mirror* and in *Latitudes*, a small arts magazine published in Houston. She said she regretted Father Huber did not remember her or her children, then recounted their meeting in great detail. "You told us the sight of the President's blood had not bothered you because as a young man you had participated in the slaughter of pigs and were accustomed to seeing blood 'all over the place.' You then described an accident you had once attended, concluding: 'No, no. The sight of blood never bothers me at all' . . . we are not accustomed to being called liars, either by a priest or a Hollywood 'journalist.'"

"The meeting definitely happened at his church," Teresa Martin remembered many years later. "I remember him touching his forehead in describing Kennedy's wound. He was an animated little guy."[26]

"We both agree," Shirley said of herself and Teresa, "that Huber was one of ten thousand priests – pathetic, shabby, pitiful."[27]

On January 3, 1967, Jack Ruby – sometimes referred to as the last living link to the Kennedy assassination – died in Dallas. He was fifty-five years old. The official cause of death was reported as a blood clot in the lungs, but Ruby had also been suffering from cancer. Curiously, Ruby died at Parkland Hospital, the same hospital where JFK and Lee Oswald also died.[28]

That same day, Sylvia Meagher was contacted by producers for the Barry Gray radio program, who wanted her as a guest that very evening. Gray had previously had other critics on his show, including Mark Lane and Léo Sauvage. Arrangements for Sylvia's appearance were hasty, and she assumed that the main subject would be Jack Ruby. Only after she arrived did she discover that the main topic of discussion would be *The Controversy*, the Schiller and Lewis record which had just been released, and that Lawrence Schiller himself was another of the program's guests. Also in the studio was attorney William Kunstler, who had served as moderator in the second Lane-Melvin Belli debate two years before and who had represented Ruby during his appeals process.[29]

The format of the program was to play *The Controversy*, with the panelists free to comment at any time. It was one of the first times the record was heard publicly. The first side of the record was an overview of the case – a general exposition of the known facts. The second side introduced critics and supporters of the Warren Report. "It became obvious and unmistakable that it was a piece of vicious ugly pro-WR propaganda, of the crudest and dirtiest kind," Sylvia Meagher later told Ray Marcus. "Both Kunstler and I protested." Its introduction of the critics, she said, was especially inflammatory, throwing doubt on the character of each before they were even heard. Although Meagher had not allowed her taped interviews to be used, the album contained a reference to her as "a researcher who closeted herself in her Greenwich Village apartment for nearly a year, and compiled her own polemic index to the twenty-six volumes" – the implication being, Meagher said, that she was some kind of nut.[30]

At one point Schiller jumped in to clarify something. "I have been involved in the case since three hours after President Kennedy was assassinated," he said. "I was there the four days of the assassination. I was there when Oswald was killed by Ruby and I have had subsequent dealings with members of the Ruby family in those three years that have followed." Those dealings included arrangements to tape record Jack Ruby as he lay on his deathbed and denied knowing Oswald or being involved in any conspiracy to kill JFK. The recordings of Ruby made up a central part of *The Controversy*.[31]

When the Barry Gray program was over, Meagher confronted Schiller: *The Controversy* was a dirty record, she told him, and he was a liar. He had lied with his promises of impartiality when first contacting her and other critics. "Not one of us would knowingly have touched so dirty a project had we known how it was motivated – that is certainly obvious."[32]

During the broadcast, each time one of Gray's guests had commented the record had been stopped. There had been so many comments that the record was not played all the way through, so a second program was scheduled for the following day. On that occasion Sylvia Meagher was accompanied to the studio by Bill Crehan and Dick Sprague, who were on the side of the critics and offered their moral support. Sylvia had not previously known Sprague, but he had a long-standing interest in the photographic evidence and had helped Sylvia document the photographic evidence that the Warren Commission ignored, assistance she later acknowledged in her book.[33]

Kunstler and Schiller both returned for the second night. Sylvia was outraged when Schiller attributed to her a statement she said she never made – that she was "drooling in anticipation of the money I would make from my book." Schiller replied that Richard Warren Lewis had tape-recorded the phone call he had placed to Sylvia a few nights before, when she allegedly made the comment. The program's host, Barry Gray, "immediately said that was actionable," Sylvia reported. "Schiller said it was taped with my knowledge. I said that was a lie. He then said there was a beep on the line that I must have heard. I said that there was no beep and it was a complete lie." According to Sylvia, Schiller "slandered every critic repeatedly, especially Mark Lane – and quoted Lane as saying that he had illegally taped telephone calls, and so had the other critics, all of them."[34]

The next morning Sylvia was thinking of suing. She wrote a letter to the U.S. attorney for the Southern District of New York, describing her appearance on Gray's show and Schiller's statements. Joe Lobenthal, who on occasion acted as Sylvia's attorney, reviewed the letter before she sent it. The U.S. Attorney's office in turn forwarded the letter to the New York County District Attorney's office, which informed Sylvia there had been no violation of any law.[35]

In time it became common knowledge among the critics that Schiller had acted as a business agent for Jack Ruby – which left his work on *The Controversy* on thin ethical ice. It appears that Maggie Field made the connection, but it was there for all to see, buried in the testimony of Jack Ruby's brother Earl, and his sister, Eva Grant. Just how Schiller got involved with Ruby is not clear, but in the aftermath of the Oswald murder Ruby needed to raise money for his defense. On Ruby's behalf, Schiller sold his story to the media. At the height of the publicity over *The Controversy*, Maggie photocopied a few pages of testimony from Volume 14 and mailed them to Sylvia Meagher:

> Mr. Hubert. How was it handled?
> Mrs. Grant. Earl.
> Mr. Hubert. Earl controlled the funds at that time?
> Mrs. Grant. At that time, yes. It came to the writer and the agent, Larry Schiller and Billy Woodfield. Larry sells the story, Billy wrote the story . . . I would say Larry Schiller and Billy Woodfield took 35 percent of the money. . . .[36]

"Under the circumstances," Mark Lane later observed, "one might have thought the word 'scavenger' might have been more sparingly employed by Schiller and Lewis."[37]

In February, Sylvia Meagher agreed to help Mark Lane when he asked her to come to a New York television studio where he was about to videotape a panel discussion. Lane was to appear with Albert Jenner and Alfredda Scobey, both former Warren Commission staff members, and Louis Nizer, a prominent attorney who had written an introduction to a mass market paperback edition of the Warren Report.[38]

Lane had by this time debated the Warren Report many times. He knew the case as well as any critic, and Sylvia felt he really didn't need her help. Nevertheless she conferred with him during breaks in the taping, supplying him with information and suggestions. Sylvia's niece had come to the studio with her, and they sat together as the taping progressed.[39]

The Commission supporters performed badly on the program, Sylvia thought, and Lane easily won the debate. But there was something else that night. In the past it had always seemed to her that Lane went out of his way not to acknowledge the other critics, but he surprised her by revealing a mellower attitude. "He in no way showed any feeling that he was in any special class, or 'the leader,' or the all-wise," she told Maggie Field. He defended the critics as a group after they were accused of besmirching the United States. "Lane responded that, leaving himself aside, the critics were courageous principled people to whom in due course the country would pay the homage they deserved – 'people like Sylvia Meagher, Penn Jones, Maggie Field, Ray Marcus, Léo Sauvage. . . .'"[40]

Albert Jenner was the most restrained of the Commission's supporters, Sylvia told Maggie. But, she added, he was not accurate or honest. He refused to comment when Lane quoted him as saying that the Commission's staff attorneys had all seen President Kennedy's autopsy photographs, even though the photographs had never been introduced as evidence. "Some members of the Commission saw both the film and the colored pictures, and the X-rays," Jenner had said. "We of the staff saw them ourselves."[41]

During the taping Sylvia and her niece had concluded, from observing her, that a young woman sitting directly in front of them was Albert Jenner's daughter. The young woman seemed surprisingly impartial, however, and Sylvia began to think maybe she wasn't Jenner's daughter after all. But when the taping was over her identity was apparently confirmed when Jenner walked into the audience and sat down next to her. "Now which is it," the young woman asked, "did you or didn't you see the autopsy photos?" To Sylvia's astonishment, Jenner shook his head no, he had not in fact seen them. "This – imagine it! – after he had sat before the cameras and denounced the critics for being 'irresponsible'!"[42]

In late January 1967, Ray Marcus attended a debate at UCLA between Mark Lane and former Commission attorney Wesley Liebeler. He was accompanied by his wife and by Maggie Field. The debate was highly anticipated on the UCLA campus, where Liebeler served as acting professor at its law school. In October, speaking on Mort Sahl's TV show, Lane had said he might sue Liebeler over statements he had made about *Rush to Judgment*. Liebeler had countered with published comments that *Rush to Judgment* and *Inquest* were not objective studies, and that he had yet to be served with any papers from Lane's lawsuit.[43]

Ray and Maggie, as well as the rest of the critics, were still stinging from the combined effect of *The Controversy* album and *The Scavengers* magazine article. So when Marcus overheard an audience member, during the course of the debate, say that Larry Schiller was in attendance that day, it got his attention. After the debate some of the audience members moved to an adjacent room to discuss the event. It was then that Marcus noticed a man moving freely about the room, making brief conversation with a number of those he passed. Marcus had never seen Larry Schiller before, but suddenly he was certain that this was he. "I watched him intently and with rapidly rising anger as he moved in our direction," Marcus recalled. The man got closer and closer to him, and finally, when he was just a few feet away, Marcus reached his boiling point. He abruptly stood and cocked his arm, fist doubled, prepared to deliver a shattering blow to Schiller's jaw.

Suddenly Maggie Field leaped to her feet and caught her friend's arm in both hands, crying out, *That's not him!*

In an instant, all movement in the room came to a halt, and heads turned to see what had happened. Fortunately, nothing much had. In years to come Marcus would marvel at how Maggie had divined what he was about to do – and be grateful for her intervention. "Besides the possible legal consequences for me, both civil and criminal, there was media present. I can imagine the news stories, had it not been for Maggie's presence of mind: 'Local JFK conspiracy-nut goes berserk – punches out innocent bystander. . . .'"[44]

Mark Lane once observed that, in the wake of the success of books critical of the Warren Commission, the publication of additional books defending it became a minor industry. The work of Lewis and Schiller was among these, although Lane dismissed it as the least important of the genre. Another such book was *The Truth About the Assassination*, by *Newsweek* correspondent Charles Roberts. Roberts had been in the motorcade when Kennedy was assassinated and was present on Air Force One when Lyndon Johnson took the oath of office. His 128-page book argued that the Commission's critics distorted and misinterpreted the evidence they used to damn the Warren Report.[45]

But the book that by far got the most attention was *The Death of a President*, by William Manchester. Manchester's book was an authorized account of the assassination. The author had been commissioned by the Kennedy family in early 1964 to write the story. The timing struck some of the critics as unusual, since the Warren Commission was then in session, and authorized by President Johnson to do precisely the same thing.[46]

Manchester's book had briefly been the center of a highly charged legal battle after he balked at changes in his manuscript requested by the Kennedy family. He had previously not objected to the Kennedy scrutiny imposed upon him by the terms of his contract. In the end, his book appeared only after numerous deletions – so many, some quipped, that the deletions had the makings of a best seller, in and of themselves.[47]

Whatever the merits of the claims against the book, *The Death of a President* received a great deal of publicity and was thus highly anticipated; it went on to become a best seller. When it finally appeared, Manchester was criticized for his writing style and his pro-Warren Report bias. In spite of this, reviews were generally favorable, but when M.S. Arnoni asked Sylvia Meagher to review it, her assessment was scorching.

> [Manchester] specifies the exact moment when Oswald felt desperate, when he felt rejected as a husband and a male, when he 'went mad,' when he fired a last shot—even that he slept soundly in his jail cell after the assassination. Here speaks a charlatan, not a historian. He exceeds even the Warren Commission in readiness to wrest incriminating 'fact' from inimical evidence, in doing violence to logic, in unconscionable and malicious departure from objectivity and simple fairness . . . when the real history of the assassination is written, it will perhaps become apparent even to Manchester that it was not a random lunatic individual act but a logical piece in a large

mosaic that is not yet complete. *The Death of a President* is not that history.[48]

In early February, Ray Marcus received a letter from Robert Richter of CBS News. The news organization was thinking of producing a new program on the Warren Report and was contacting some of its critics. One of them, Vincent Salandria, had given Richter a copy of *The Bastard Bullet* and described some of Marcus's other work. Perhaps Marcus would be willing to give CBS a hand.[49]

Marcus wrote back on February 14: "I shall be happy to assist as best I can." He described his Zapruder film analysis and his conclusions on the assassination shot sequence, and some of his photographic work, including the #5 man detail of the Moorman photograph. His opinion on whether the #5 figure was indeed a human had recently been strengthened by another discovery, which he described for Richter. It seemed to him that the figure he called #5 man should be visible in a frame from a film of the assassination taken by Dallas resident Orville Nix. *Esquire* had published the frame to accompany Edward Epstein's article the previous December. Marcus had not previously examined the frame, but he could see it would make sense that the figure might be there. Nix had stood on the south side of Main Street, farther from the motorcade than Mary Moorman but at a similar angle.[50]

Sure enough, Marcus found the figure. Unlike the Moorman #5 image, however, the figure in the Nix frame was scarcely distinguishable. He sent copies to other critics for comment; Sylvia Meagher said she thought she could see the figure, but wasn't sure. Marcus, though, considered it strong corroboration for the presence of the figure in the Moorman #5 detail. "The fact that on close inspection he was there," Marcus said, "is of more significance than the fact that the image in this reproduction is of very poor quality." But, recognizing his lack of expertise, Marcus approached a commercial photographer to evaluate both the Nix and Moorman images. Jacques de Langre's experience spanned over twenty years and included photography work for the War Crime Investigation Team for the United States Army following World War II. "I can state without question," de Langre told Marcus, "that the two angles of the subject are from the same person . . . [and] the subject is a man holding an elongated object."[51]

Marcus had agreed to help CBS any way he could, but a few months later nearly backed out. He was in Boston attending to some business interests when he happened to see an article in *The Boston Herald-Traveler* by the paper's television editor, Eleanor Roberts. The article's first sentence told most of the story. "A most unusual television experiment is taking place at CBS News – the preparation of a documentary on another look at the Warren Commission Report – which may never be telecast." Unless CBS could develop new information that weakened the arguments of the Commission's critics, Roberts wrote, the project might be shelved.[52]

Immediately, Marcus telephoned Roberts. She would not tell him the source of her story, but did say it was a CBS executive who had been a reliable contact in the past. A few weeks later Marcus heard again from Bob Richter. The CBS program was in development and he wanted to discuss Marcus's work with him. But Marcus said no, he had changed his mind; he had seen the Roberts article, and it was plain that CBS was not approaching the subject impartially.[53]

But Richter had a good comeback. "Some of us here are trying to do an honest job," he said, "and if those of you who have important information don't cooperate with us, you're just guaranteeing that the other side wins." Richter seemed sincere and his reasoning sound. Marcus agreed to meet with him.[54]

The two men met several times and Marcus outlined the work that he had done. Richter was impressed with the Moorman #5 man detail, which he agreed was almost certainly a man. He saw a series of ever-larger blow-ups of the picture, which Marcus had placed in a special portfolio. Richter arranged to have duplicates made of the entire set, and said he would show them to his superior at CBS, Leslie Midgley, the producer of the program.[55]

Midgley, it turned out, said he could not see anything resembling a man in any of the pictures when Richter showed them to him. But he agreed to meet with Marcus to go over the portfolio one more time. They met, along with Richter, in Midgley's office. Included in the portfolio was a detail from the photograph of James Meredith moments after he was shot – the photo that revealed his assailant in the shrubbery along the side of the road. Marcus had included an enlargement of the gunman for purposes of comparison to the #5 man detail, since the lighting and the figure obscured among leaves – this one known to be a man – were similar in appearance. Flipping through the series of #5 man enlargements, Midgley kept repeating that he couldn't see anything that looked human. Then he came to an especially clear photo, and he said, "Yes, that's the man who shot Meredith."[56]

Marcus and Richter immediately glanced at one another, in what Marcus took to be obvious and mutual understanding of what had just happened. Midgley was looking not at the photo of the Meredith gunman, but of the clearest enlargement of the Moorman #5 man detail, which he had previously looked at but dismissed.

Midgley understood what happened, too. He visibly reddened but did not acknowledge the error. Marcus must have felt completely vindicated, for this was an absolute, if tacit, admission: in order for Midgley to wrongly identify the #5 man detail as "the man who shot Meredith," he first had to be able to see #5 man in the picture.[57]

Marcus politely reminded Midgley he was looking at #5 man. The meeting ended shortly after this, without further discussion of what had just happened.[58]

Maggie Field traveled to New York in early March 1967 and had a relaxing visit with Sylvia Meagher. The two women grew closer during Maggie's brief stay; Sylvia said later that she gained new insight into her friend, which strengthened her conviction that Maggie was a remarkable woman with a range of excellent and beautiful qualities.[59]

But the main reason for Maggie's visit was not social. She carried with her to New York, in large leather portfolios, the panoplies she had assembled over the previous few years. She had developed them into a book she called *The Evidence,* and she was looking for a publisher. *The Evidence* was an utterly novel approach to the case, containing no narrative in the usual sense. Instead she took each of the Commission's ten main conclusions and, one by one, placed them at the beginning of a section of the book. "I've taken the actual testimony," she explained, "the FBI reports, the Secret Service reports, the Commission exhibits, diagrams, and juxtaposed them against the stated conclusion to show that the evidence in no situation really supports the conclusion that they arrived at."[60]

"She has had phenomenal success," Sylvia told Harold Weisberg. "Random House immediately accepted her work for publication, and the New American Library was equally eager. She accepted the Random House offer this morning." Meagher was thrilled at her friend's triumph; it was a just reward for someone who had worked as hard as she had. "The immediate enthusiasm and offer of publication by Random House is a tribute to the effectiveness of your work, a vindication of your unending labor . . . all of us are incredibly fortunate to have you in our midst."[61]

By the end of March, Maggie still had not received her contract from Random House but was not overly concerned. Before too much more time went by, the contract arrived and in due course she had signed it and received her first advance. Yet Random House had a poor record when it came to its dealings with the critics: it had previously broken its contract to publish Léo Sauvage's *The Oswald Affair*, and had contacted Sylvia Meagher with an interest in *Accessories After the Fact* only to turn it down. Mark Lane had submitted *Rush to Judgment* to that firm, only to have it rejected. This pattern would not change in the months ahead.[62]

Vince Salandria had not given up completely on Igor "Turk" Vaganov. Although Vaganov had said he didn't want to cooperate for the article John Berendt was developing for *Esquire*, Salandria and Berendt paid him another visit two weeks after they first spoke to him. Vaganov had opened his apartment door and beheld the two men. "I thought I'd be seeing you guys again."[63]

Vaganov's guests laid out a scenario: the assassination had been coordinated by radio – like the two-way radio in Vaganov's car. His role in the plot was to maintain radio contact with the other conspirators, follow Oswald, and perhaps identify him to the police. Vaganov was unable to account for his trip to Dallas or his whereabouts on the day of the assassination.[64]

Salandria said Vaganov's true role didn't matter all that much to him; he saw him merely as a cog in a machine. "It's the men who set it all up that we want to find. Tell us. You'll be forgiven; we'll help you get away."[65]

Vaganov was impassive; he would not say anything one way or the other. But the next day he reversed himself and agreed to cooperate with Berendt, provided he were paid the same fee *Esquire* paid its lead writers. Another interview was set up, this one at Salandria's house; Gaeton Fonzi and Tink Thompson were present. Now, though, Vaganov provided alibis for all of his movements. Months later Vaganov approached Salandria again, hinting he did indeed have something to tell, for a price. Salandria thought about paying him but concluded that Vaganov would, in all likelihood, provide false information. He was a red herring.[66]

Rita Rollins was another matter.

During the 1950s, the secretary of the Communist Party in Illinois was a man named Claude Lightfoot. On June 26, 1954, Lightfoot was arrested under the Smith Act, which made it a crime to advocate the violent overthrow of the United States government. He spent nearly four months in jail before supporters could raise the $30,000 bail. He was convicted the following January and sentenced to five years in prison and a $5,000 fine, a sentence later reversed by the Supreme Court.[67]

One of the witnesses to testify against Lightfoot was an FBI informant named Lola Belle Holmes. In later years she became an itinerant speaker for the John Birch Society, and in 1968 supported the presidential candidacy of George Wallace. One evening in mid-March 1967, shortly before 11 p.m., she knocked on Vince Salandria's door. While her visit was unannounced, it may not have been entirely unexpected, for she had recently had publicity in the Philadelphia area for her work in infiltrating the peace movement on behalf of the FBI. She and Salandria had met before, but she was calling herself "Rita Rollins."[68]

Holmes, making no pretense of being Rita Rollins, barged right into the house and told Salandria that he had most of the assassination story right. But he was wrong in assuming – as he had told Joe McGinniss – that the CIA was involved. As a matter of fact the CIA was presently helping Jim Garrison's investigation in New Orleans. The real plotters against Kennedy were Lyndon Johnson and J. Edgar Hoover.[69]

Salandria wasn't interested. He had no doubt that the CIA did it, he told her, and moreover had no doubt that she was in the CIA's employ. "I was looking closely for a reaction from her when I went on in this fashion," Salandria recalled, "and she merely shrugged her shoulders and did not agree or disagree." Before too much longer, she left.[70]

Chapter 26

Garrison

Early in 1967 there was a major development in the Kennedy case: the district attorney of Orleans Parish, Louisiana, had begun an independent investigation into the assassination. There was a conspiracy to kill JFK, Jim Garrison said, and part of it was hatched in New Orleans. Other people besides Lee Harvey Oswald were involved, the DA declared, and his investigators had learned the names of some of the conspirators. Arrests were on the horizon.[1]

By this time the handful of critical books on the Warren Report were being widely read and discussed; public confidence in the official version of the assassination was at its lowest ebb. According to a Gallup poll released in the second week of January 1967, 64 percent of Americans who were asked either believed more than one person was involved, or had uncertainty about the Warren Commission's conclusions. In spite of that, about the same number – 63 percent – said they were opposed to a new investigation.[2]

Jim Garrison's investigation appears to have been a not-too-closely guarded secret during its first few months. The DA and his staff worked quietly to avoid drawing attention to their activities, but at least half a dozen of the critics were made aware that something was going on. Then on Friday, February 17, 1967, *The New Orleans States-Item* broke the story in a copyrighted front-page article, and the investigation became public knowledge. This was not merely a public official suggesting that perhaps the case should be reexamined, as with the Kupferman proposal. This was an active investigation; it was professional law enforcement with subpoena power picking up where amateur critics left off. Garrison was not happy the investigation had been made public, and at first downplayed the *States-Item* article, insisting the probe was "routine." His investigators, Garrison said, had been making good progress until all the publicity, adding in his deep stentorian voice, "Let justice be done though the heavens fall!" Two days later Garrison said his office had been within a few weeks of making arrests, but with all the attention the case was getting, arrests were now months away.[3]

Garrison did not identify any of the witnesses or suspects targeted by his investigation. The life of one witness, he said, had already been jeopardized by the unwanted publicity. But the earliest press reports carried the name "David Ferry," and identified him as a former pilot who had been briefly detained by Garrison right after the assassination. One of Garrison's principal suspects at this time was indeed a man named David W. Ferrie, who may have known Lee Oswald in the mid-1950s when the teenaged Oswald was a member of the Civil Air Patrol in New Orleans, and Ferrie was the squadron leader. "Supposedly," Ferrie told *The New Orleans States-Item,* "I have been pegged as the getaway pilot in an elaborate plot to kill Kennedy." The Garrison investigation, he contended, was a big joke.[4]

But if David Ferrie possessed any knowledge that would help crack the assassination mystery, it died with him on February 22, 1967, just five days after the Garrison investigation was made public. On that day the 48-year-old Ferrie's body was found in his New Orleans apartment. Although two suicide notes were found, the Orleans Parish coroner did not immediately classify the death as a suicide, noting there were indications Ferrie may have suffered a brain hemorrhage. Garrison immediately announced that Ferrie had been a part of the Kennedy conspiracy. "The apparent suicide of David Ferrie ends the life of a man who in my judgment was one of history's most important individuals," he said. "Evidence developed by our office had long since confirmed that he was involved in events culminating in the assassination of President Kennedy . . . we have not mentioned his name publicly up to this point. The unique nature of this case now leaves me no other course of action." Just that morning, Garrison told reporters, a decision had been reached to arrest Ferrie within the week. "Apparently, we waited too long."[5]

At almost the same time, former Warren Commission staff attorney Wesley J. Liebeler told reporters that David Ferrie had already been investigated by the FBI back in 1963. "It was so clear that he was not involved that we didn't mention it in the report," said Liebeler, who had played a key role in the New Orleans phase of the Warren Commission inquiry. Garrison by this time no longer thought Ferrie had been a getaway pilot, but Liebeler said Garrison had failed to say what his role *had* been. "Garrison has a responsibility to indicate just why he thinks Ferrie might have been involved and so far as I can determine he has given no reason."[6]

Former Commission Chairman Earl Warren declined to comment on news of the Garrison investigation. Allen Dulles also said he had no comment. But former Commission member John J. McCloy, in what appears to have been the first public comment on the assassination by any former Commissioner, told the Associated Press that the Warren panel had always known that new evidence in the case might turn up. "We did not say that Oswald acted alone," McCloy explained. "We said we could find no credible evidence that he acted with anyone else."[7]

Lee Harvey Oswald spent the summer of 1963 in New Orleans. This simple fact was among the mass of data reported in the media the very day of the assassination. Jim Garrison said later it was the reason why, as the Orleans Parish District Attorney, he had been obligated in 1963 to learn what he could about Oswald's activities there. His investigators went out over the weekend of November 23 and 24 and, among other things, received a tip that Oswald had been seen that summer with David Ferrie. Moreover they learned that Ferrie had left New Orleans for Texas on the afternoon of November 22, accompanied by two young men. After Ferrie returned to New Orleans on Monday, November 25, he was brought in to Garrison's office for questioning.[8]

The interview did not go well for Ferrie. Garrison found him ill at ease; the story of his activities over the previous few days did not add up. When most Americans were watching the televised coverage of the assassination, Ferrie drove to Houston – reportedly through a severe thunderstorm – in order to go ice-skating. Although nothing linked Ferrie directly to the assassination, when the interview ended Garrison ordered him held for further questioning by the FBI. The FBI interrogation went much better for David Ferrie. He denied having known Oswald and was soon released. Garrison said later that as far as he was concerned, that was the end of it.[9]

By his own account, Garrison gave little serious thought to the assassination in the three years that followed. He heard about contradictions in the official story as reported in the press, but any anomalies, he was certain, had been thoroughly investigated and dispelled by the FBI and the Warren Commission. "The conclusion of these two weighty bodies that all the shooting had been done by one man aiming from behind the President satisfied me that the allegations about activity up front around the grassy knoll, and in the railroad yard behind it, were so much speculation," he recalled.[10]

That all changed after informal discussions Garrison had with Louisiana Congressman Hale Boggs, beginning in 1965. Boggs, a former member of the Warren Commission, told the district attorney about his misgivings over the lone-gunman scenario. Intrigued, and with the memory of Ferrie's arrest and release nagging at him, Garrison ordered the Warren Report and twenty-six volumes of Hearings and Exhibits and began studying them closely. As with his initial interest in David Ferrie in November 1963, Garrison said he was obliged to learn what he could because of Lee Oswald's summer in New Orleans.[11]

Jim Garrison started reading the critics' work soon after his encounter with Congressman Boggs, when he began searching out every book and magazine article questioning the official version of the assassination that he could find. "The works of the critics – particularly Edward Epstein, Harold Weisberg and Mark Lane – sparked my general doubts about the assassination," he told an interviewer. "But more importantly, they led me into specific areas of inquiry."[12]

By late 1966 Garrison's office had made contact with some of the critics. Most of these contacts appear to have been made on Garrison's behalf by a young man named Tom Bethell. Bethell was an Englishman, a graduate of Oxford University who had moved to the United States in the summer of 1962. He was interested in seeing America, but his true passion was jazz. "It was to me a mysterious and wonderful thing that a new musical form had arisen in the U.S. around 1900 – just at the time when it became undeniable that the European classical tradition was exhausted," he later said. Bethell found a teaching job at a prep school in Virginia. He had a vague but terribly erroneous idea that Virginia was somewhere near New Orleans. New Orleans was the cradle of jazz, and Bethell was very keen on going there to research the music's origins.[13]

By 1966 Bethell had rectified his geographical problem somewhat, after taking a teaching job at a secretarial school in Baton Rouge. He had also become interested in the assassination, and in a curious piece of serendipity met Jim Garrison and was hired as an investigator. On a weekend visit to New Orleans, a girlfriend there introduced him to an assistant DA she knew named John Volz. "Volz to my surprise took me immediately down a long corridor, to a comfortable panelled office in which the enormous figure of Jim Garrison (6' 8" I believe) was sprawled out on a sofa. I took to him immediately." Just how the topic of the Kennedy assassination came up is not clear, but according to Bethell, Garrison hired him "on the spot," without even asking any perfunctory background questions.[14]

Bethell's first assignment was to go to Dallas to learn what he could. He met Penn and Louise Jones around this time, and Mary Ferrell too, although Mrs. Ferrell recalled meeting Bethell before he was hired by Garrison. He had previously written to Vince Salandria at the suggestion of Matt Herron, the photographer. Later he visited Salandria on Garrison's behalf. Salandria recalled giving him "my usual spiel" that the true conspirators were CIA and military leaders who wanted to stop President Kennedy's effort to end the Cold War. Bethell made contact with Sylvia Meagher in late 1966 or early 1967, and may have alerted Harold Weisberg about the Garrison investigation in a letter written on New Year's Day, 1967. Bethell was also dispatched by Garrison to the National Archives.[15]

Most of these early contacts between the critics and Garrison were by necessity very discreet. But once the *States-Item* article was published, and the story was picked up by the national and international press, the critics began to give Jim Garrison serious attention. On February 23, the same day that David Ferrie's death was reported, Sylvia Meagher wrote to the DA: "It is difficult for me to tell you, without lapsing into extravagant prose, how deeply grateful my colleagues among the critics and I personally feel for your enormous courage and independence in this case." At Robert Ockene's urging she enclosed a copy of a chapter from *Accessories After the Fact* called "The Proof of the Plot," which Ockene thought might be particularly useful to the Garrison investigation. Then, quoting Garrison's own public pronouncements, she concluded: "Let justice be done, though the heavens fall."[16]

That same day, Shirley Martin wrote to Sylvia; she too was thrilled with the developments in New Orleans. "I sent a wire to Marguerite; I was so elated I couldn't help it." Two days later Shirley wrote again, in much the same vein, adding that perhaps the Garrison investigation was "the light at the end of the tunnel."[17]

Sylvia was particularly encouraged after hearing from Philippe Labro, a French journalist of her acquaintance, who during this early phase of Garrison's investigation had already been to New Orleans and spent some time with the DA. Labro was the reporter who had interviewed John Howard Griffin in 1963, about a month after the assassination. Penn Jones had been on hand for that interview and had gotten to know Labro; he subsequently put him in touch with Sylvia Meagher. Garrison, Labro assured Meagher, was no Southern politician out to get publicity – although he was, of course, politically ambitious. In Labro's opinion Jim Garrison was an honest man, serious and cultured.

He possessed an excellent knowledge of the case, knew of Sylvia's work, and considered it important. Garrison's case was not well-defined at this stage, but, Sylvia wrote in her notes, "Labro believes he will come up with something." Labro also predicted, however, that there would be an effort to destroy him.[18]

Soon after news of the Garrison case was reported in the press, Vince Salandria wrote a short note to Sylvia. He had just heard that arrests in Garrison's case, once thought to be imminent, were now months away. "That has to mean never," he wrote gloomily. "Back to the drawing board."[19]

But Salandria was wrong. On the first day of March, exactly one week after David Ferrie's death, Jim Garrison announced the arrest of a man named Clay Shaw. Shaw was 54 years old and a retired businessman, the former director of the International Trade Mart in New Orleans. Like Ferrie, he had already been targeted by Garrison's investigation and had been interviewed by an assistant DA in December 1966. At the time of his arrest, a Garrison investigator named William Gurvich said Shaw would be charged with having taken part in a conspiracy to assassinate Kennedy. Bond was set at $10,000. It was quickly posted and Shaw was released.[20]

In spite of the arrest, linking Shaw to a conspiracy to assassinate JFK would be a contentious matter. Almost immediately, United States Attorney General-designate Ramsey Clark told reporters that Clay Shaw "was involved in an FBI investigation in the New Orleans area in November and December, 1963 . . . there was no connection found" between him and the assassination.[21]

The difficulty facing Garrison would be connecting Clay Shaw to Lee Harvey Oswald, and demonstrating that Shaw was the true identity of a mystery man known as "Clay Bertrand." On the day after the assassination, a man using that name telephoned a small-time New Orleans lawyer named Dean Andrews, and asked him to come to Dallas to defend Oswald. Bertrand was not unknown to Dean Andrews; he had telephoned him in the past asking him to represent homosexuals who had been picked up by New Orleans police.[22]

Andrews also knew Oswald, who had come into his New Orleans office several times during the summer of 1963, looking for help in upgrading his Marine discharge and seeking advice about his Russian wife's citizenship status. On his first visit, Oswald had been accompanied by several Mexican "gay kids." Furthermore, Andrews told the Warren Commission he had seen Oswald in front of the Maison Blanche Building, where Andrews kept his law office, handing out pro-Castro leaflets.[23]

Andrews, who was known for his colorful speech, had been hospitalized with pneumonia at the time Clay Bertrand called him. After Oswald was killed, he notified the Secret Service about the phone call and Oswald's visits to his office. There were repeated interviews with FBI agents, or "Feebees" as Dean Andrews called them, and it appears that he was pressured into stating that, while under sedation, he had imagined the phone call from Bertrand.[24]

Commission counsel Wesley Liebeler asked him, "You finally came to the conclusion that Clay Bertrand was a figment of your imagination?"[25]

"That's what the Feebees put on," Andrews replied. "I told them, 'Write what you want, that I am nuts. I don't care.' They were running on the time factor, and the hills were shook up plenty to get it, get it, get it. I couldn't give it to them. I have been playing cops and robbers with them. You can tell when the steam is on. They are on you like the plague. They never leave. They are like cancer. Eternal."

When Sylvia Meagher wrote to Jim Garrison on February 23, she told him that Bob Richter of CBS had asked for a copy of her *Subject Index,* which he intended to send to Garrison. CBS had spoken with Sylvia and several other critics for the program they were producing. It was scheduled to be broadcast over four consecutive nights beginning June 25; as the air date drew near the network began promoting it as an unprecedented re-examination of the Warren Report and its findings. An advertisement informed the public the documentary "could very well be the most valuable four hours you ever spent with television."[26]

Ray Marcus, who had seen the item in *The Boston Herald-Traveler* suggesting the program might not be objective, was concerned. After the incident in Les Midgley's office, during which Midgley wrongly identified a Moorman photo enlargement as "the man who shot Meredith," Marcus had met again with Richter and stayed in touch with him by telephone. On June 19, the broadcast date drawing near, Marcus wrote an eleven-page letter to Midgley describing the incident in great detail, and calling the mis-identification "a very understandable error. But one which would have been impossible for you to make had you not promptly recognized the #5 image as a human figure, despite your earlier denials that you saw anything in the pictures that looked like a man." With its vast resources, both technical and financial, CBS was obviously capable of presenting the #5 man image during its documentary clearly and objectively. "Need it be stated," Marcus told Midgley, "that if CBS fails to do so – *especially considering your positive reaction to #5 man* – that fact in and of itself will constitute powerful evidence that the entire CBS effort was designed to be what I fear it to be: a high-level whitewash of the Warren Commission findings?"[27]

The next morning Marcus mailed the letter to Midgley and enclosed additional copies of #2 and #5 man and other photographs. That same day he telephoned Bob Richter in New York. He wanted Richter to confirm, in writing, the mis-identification of the #5 image that had taken place in Midgley's office, which Richter agreed to do. Then Richter, while cautioning that Marcus would probably be unhappy with the overall content of the four programs, added that some of the Moorman details might make it into the final edit of the show. Richter described one of them, but Marcus said it was not the best one to use. Which one was? Richter asked. The most advantageous one to show, Marcus replied, would be the clearest one of the bunch – the one Richter's boss, Les Midgley, had mistaken for the man who shot Meredith.[28]

Fidel Castro came to power on New Year's Day 1959, after right-wing military dictator Fulgencia Batista fled the country just hours ahead of Castro's rebel forces. Within a few months Castro's communist allegiance was known. This was the realization of one of Washington's deepest fears: a communist government just ninety miles from American shores. Accordingly, the government took steps, covertly, to eliminate Fidel Castro. In March 1960 President Dwight Eisenhower authorized the CIA to organize Cuban refugees into a guerilla army to overthrow Castro. At the same time the CIA began recruiting organized crime figures to assassinate him.[29]

More than 100,000 Batistiano exiles were dispersed across the southern United States by early 1961. Most were in Miami, but many were in cities like New Orleans and Dallas. Before too long, it was well known within Cuba that a political structure dedicated to overthrowing Castro was in the United States, and that a well-financed liberation army was in place. At first, the Cuban exiles viewed their American benefactors with absolute trust. That changed dramatically after the April 1961 Bay of Pigs disaster when, at the direction of the CIA, the exile army launched an invasion of Cuba. It failed badly: Castro's forces crushed the invasion and captured most of the exiles. Exile leaders were convinced the invasion failed because promised air support never materialized. When President Kennedy publicly accepted full responsibility for what happened, the exiles' attitude toward the United States transformed into bitter hatred.[30]

It is in the context of the CIA's secret war against Castro that Jim Garrison's investigation took place. During the early 1960s, New Orleans was second only to Miami in its importance to anti-Castro activity. A central locale for anti-Castro operations there was a three-story granite structure known as the Newman Building, which occupied a corner lot at Lafayette and Camp streets. The anti-Castro Cuban Revolutionary Council maintained an office in this building from October 1961 to February 1962.[31]

Due to its corner location the building had two entrances, one from each street. Using the address 531 Lafayette, the building also housed the office of Guy Banister Associates. Ostensibly a private detective agency headed by former FBI agent Guy Banister, the office was also the hub of CIA-backed anti-Castro operations in New Orleans. The other entrance, with a 544 Camp Street address, was used by two labor unions. Aside from a small coffee shop on the building's street level, these were the only three occupants in the building during the summer of 1963.[32]

Oswald has been indisputably linked to the Newman Building. On August 9, 1963, he was distributing pro-Castro literature on Canal Street in New Orleans, when he was confronted by three anti-Castro exiles, one of whom had met Oswald a few days before and thought he too was against Castro. A fight broke out and all four men were arrested. Oswald's literature was confiscated by the police, and after the assassination was turned over to the Secret Service. On the inside cover of one pamphlet investigators found a hand-stamped address:

FPCC
544 Camp Street
New Orleans, LA[33]

This was a curious anomaly: why was Oswald, a presumed supporter of Castro, handing out literature stamped with the former address of an anti-Castro group? "FPCC" was the pro-Castro Fair Play for Cuba Committee. Oswald was the president and sole member of its New

Orleans chapter, which was not recognized by the FPCC's national office.[34]

Eight days before his arrest for the street fight, Oswald had written the FPCC's national president. Among other things he said he had rented an office for the FPCC New Orleans chapter, but had to move after just three days. He did not disclose its location, but after the assassination, the 544 Camp Street address having come to their attention, the FBI contacted the Newman Building's owner. Sam Newman told them that Oswald had not rented space in his building. Likewise none of the building's other tenants could recall him. Guy Banister was interviewed by telephone on November 25, 1963, but was not asked about Lee Oswald. The Warren Commission acknowledged that "544 Camp Street" was stamped on some of Oswald's literature, but said in its Report that extensive investigation had not linked him to the Camp Street address.[35]

After Jim Garrison began re-investigating the JFK assassination, one of his first acts was to find the source of the tip that first led his investigators to David Ferrie. It turned out to be a man named Jack Martin, a part-time private eye and writer who had worked for Guy Banister and had known Ferrie for several years. He tipped the DA's office to his suspicions about Ferrie after Banister had assaulted him on the evening of November 22, 1963, when, during an alcohol-fueled argument, Martin angrily challenged, "What are you going to do – kill me like you all did Kennedy?" Banister responded with a savage pistol-whipping. Martin later contended that if Banister's secretary had not intervened, Banister would have killed him.[36]

In some respects Jack Martin was a stereotypical gumshoe – chain smoking, black coffee, porkpie hat, seedy office. But as Jim Garrison would later recall, Martin was also an innocent bystander to significant episodes, an unnoticed fly on the wall who provided otherwise missing links between suspected people, places, and events. As Garrison's investigation started up again, Martin was interviewed several times over several weeks. He described the Guy Banister Associates office in the Newman Building as a nerve center for the activities of anti-Castro Cuban exiles and soldiers-of-fortune – people like David Ferrie and Lee Harvey Oswald. According to Martin, Banister's office was part of a network providing war matériel to the CIA-backed guerilla army seeking to depose Fidel Castro.[37]

Early in the investigation the DA's office interviewed Guy Banister's widow. She did not provide much information but did recall finding, among her late husband's effects, stacks of leaflets like the ones Lee Oswald was handing out when he was arrested in August 1963. Mrs. Banister also recalled that federal agents had removed locked file cabinets from Banister's office within a few hours of his death. The index cards to those files had somehow ended up in the hands of the Louisiana State Police, some of which Garrison was able to recover.[38]

"From this index list," Garrison recalled, "we were able to determine the general nature of the Banister files seized by the federal government." None of the cards the DA's office retrieved referred to local or private matters. Subject headings included the CIA, Ammunitions and Arms, the Civil Rights program of JFK, the International Trade Mart, the General Assembly of the United Nations, and the Fair Play for Cuba Committee. This last file contained data on Lee Harvey Oswald.[39]

It was, Garrison observed, a most unusual set of files for a private investigator.[40]

In February 1967, Philippe Labro told Sylvia Meagher there was a lack of definition in Jim Garrison's case. But by March, its focus seems to have sharpened.

Chapter 27

The Proof of a Plot

Two weeks after Clay Shaw's arrest, his preliminary hearing began before a three-judge panel. The hearing was considered a safeguard for the defendant, in that it would determine whether there were sufficient grounds for bringing the case to trial. It was an unusual move, almost unheard of, in that it was sought not by the defense, but by Garrison, who said he requested it due to the gravity of the charges.[1]

Among the witnesses who testified were two who would become controversial figures in the prosecution's case. One was an insurance salesman from Baton Rouge named Perry Raymond Russo, who testified he had seen Clay Shaw and Lee Oswald together at David Ferrie's apartment in September 1963. They were introduced to him as Clay Bertrand and Leon Oswald. Along with several anti-Castro Cubans who were also present, Russo said, they had discussed a plan to assassinate JFK.[2]

The second witness was Vernon Bundy, a heroin addict who said he had seen Shaw and Oswald rendezvous along the Lake Pontchartrain seawall in June or July 1963. Shaw and Oswald, Bundy testified, talked for fifteen or twenty minutes, during which Shaw gave Oswald some money. As Oswald tucked the money into his back pocket, some papers fell unnoticed to the ground. After the two men left Bundy retrieved one; he recalled that it was a leaflet that said something about Cuba.[3]

After four days, the three judges ruled that there was sufficient evidence against Shaw and ordered him to stand trial. As an additional precaution Garrison next presented his case to a grand jury. At the request of the DA's office, several of the Warren Commission critics agreed to testify, offering their expertise in the subtleties of the Commission's evidence.[4]

Some of them had already begun gravitating toward New Orleans. Sylvia Meagher was tempted but remained in New York. She had to resist the impulse, she said, to take the nearest plane to the Crescent City. She reiterated her offer to assist Garrison in any way possible, and by early March had compiled and sent to him a list of Commission exhibits that related to New Orleans. Garrison replied with a letter of thanks, adding that her *Subject Index* had been very useful to his staff. Sylvia cautioned him about the CIA-sponsored index to the Warren Commission material that had been written about in *The Oakland Tribune.* She assured him that her index was an independent effort.[5]

Among those who did go to New Orleans was Mort Sahl, whose interest in the case remained high. Since first having Mark Lane on his program in September 1966, he had interviewed Penn Jones and Ray Marcus, and had Lane back. Soon after hearing about the Garrison probe, Sahl flew to New Orleans and went straight to Garrison's house. The DA answered the door wearing a bathrobe. "I'm Mort Sahl," Sahl said, "and I want to shake your hand." Grasping the extended hand, Garrison replied, "I hope you're available to do a lot more than that." This marked the beginning of Sahl's involvement in the Garrison case, which extended over the next several years.[6]

One of the first to appear on Sahl's radio show after the Garrison case broke was Mark Lane. Lane was one of those critics whose work Garrison cited as influencing his thinking about the case; he was also one of the first to get involved in Garrison's investigation. On March 29, not long after Clay Shaw was ordered to stand trial, Lane did a telephone interview with Sahl from New Orleans and described his initial conversations with Garrison and his staff. "We haven't gossiped idly, we've exchanged information," he said. Garrison's approach to the case, Lane said, was different from his own. Lane had examined the empirical evidence of the assassination, such as ballistics and eyewitness testimony, while Garrison studied his suspects. "He presents [his case] with great detail," Lane told Sahl, "and he presents it with such detail that it is impossible not to accept it." Lane could not comment further on the evidence without jeopardizing Garrison's case, he said. "But the evidence that he has is massively detailed and shows that very powerful forces, I think I can say this, that the evidence is conclusive that no foreign power was involved, none at all, but a very powerful domestic force was involved in planning the events which culminated in the death of President Kennedy and that the persons that actually participated in the conspiracy and in the assassination are known to Mr. Garrison, to his staff, and now to me." When the details of Garrison's case were known, Lane said, the American public would be stunned and outraged.[7]

A few days later Garrison himself was on Sahl's show, along with Lane. He told Sahl that one of the biggest problems his investigators had faced up to that point was a lack of interest by those with important information. "We're encountering indifference every day from witnesses who don't want to be involved, who know who Oswald associated with here, who know the special mission that Oswald was a part of here, who know what Oswald was doing here and the people associated with him, and who know who employed Oswald. But they say nothing about it, because they don't want to be involved. And many of them are honorable men. Of course, these are the kind of men who killed Caesar. But we have in New Orleans, too, honorable men who don't want to be involved because they're indifferent."8

This appearance with a sympathetic interviewer was not the only positive publicity for Jim Garrison during this period, but the positive was far outweighed by the negative. From the moment Garrison's case broke, the media in general presented it with more than the healthy skepticism one would expect from an impartial press. In May there were several outright attacks: first in *The Saturday Evening Post*, then in *Newsweek*. The latter was an article written by Hugh Aynesworth, the same reporter who had harshly reviewed Joachim Joesten's *Oswald: Assassin or Fall Guy?* in 1964. Aynesworth declared that Garrison's investigation was "a scheme to concoct a fantastic 'solution' to the death of John F. Kennedy," and that his investigators had attempted to bribe at least one witness.9

In June came the most damaging of all, an hour-long documentary on the NBC television network called "The JFK Conspiracy: The Case of Jim Garrison." As with *The Saturday Evening Post* and *Newsweek*, the credibility of Garrison's methods and witnesses was called into doubt. The common theme was that Clay Shaw had been falsely accused by a prosecutor who was using him to further his political ambitions, or was drunk with power – or was simply mad. "I only wish the press would allow our case to stand or fall on its merits in court," Garrison lamented. "It appears that certain elements of the mass media have an active interest in preventing this case from ever coming to trial at all." 10

Sylvia Meagher had successfully resisted her impulse to fly to New Orleans, yet she was still able to give the DA some long-distance help. The chapter she sent to him, "The Proof of the Plot," dovetailed perfectly with the Garrison probe, drawing on some of the same strands that the DA was working with.

The chapter described an episode in the Warren Commission's own evidence that, perhaps more than any other, demonstrated a conspiracy. According to the Commission, Lee Harvey Oswald left New Orleans on September 25, 1963, bound for Mexico City, with the intention of obtaining a visa for travel to Cuba. He arrived in Mexico City on the 27th. But the experience of Mrs. Silvia Odio, published in the Commission's evidence only to be refuted, belied the official account.[11]

In the fall of 1963 Mrs. Odio, a divorced, twenty-six-year-old Cuban émigrée, was living with her four children in Dallas. Mrs. Odio was active in anti-Castro politics as a member of the Cuban Revolutionary Junta, or JURE. Her father and mother were political prisoners in Cuba. One evening late in September, probably the 26th or the 27th, she was visited at her home by three men she did not know who said they too were members of JURE and wanted her help in JURE fundraising. At first, the men stayed on the porch while a cautious Mrs. Odio remained inside, the door's security chain still in place. After they exhibited personal familiarity with her father she relaxed a little and unhooked the chain. Two of them appeared to be Cuban or Mexican; they gave her their fictitious "war names," one of which was Leopoldo, while the other was "something like Angelo." The third man was an American, and Mrs. Odio told the Warren Commission that Leopoldo, who did most of the talking, introduced him as "Leon Oswald."[12]

Before long Silvia Odio's sister Annie came to the door to see what was going on; she too got a good look at the three visitors. The three had just come from New Orleans, Leopoldo told Silvia, and indeed they appeared tired and unkempt. They were about to leave on a trip, although Leopoldo did not name their destination.[13]

Although the men seemed to know Mrs. Odio's father, something about them made her uneasy. Batistiano exile politics was rife with intrigue, and her father had warned her about the risks of trusting strangers, regardless of the circumstances. The conversation did not last long before the men departed, having gained nothing from their effort.[14]

But the next day Leopoldo unexpectedly telephoned Silvia Odio. "At first, I thought he was just trying to get fresh with me," Mrs. Odio recalled. But no: Leopoldo talked a lot about his American companion, Leon Oswald. He was an ex-Marine and an excellent marksman. Leopoldo said he was thinking about introducing Oswald into the anti-Castro underground "because he is great, he is kind of nuts." Furthermore, Leopoldo continued, Leon Oswald had said that the Cubans "don't have any guts . . . because President Kennedy should have been assassinated after the Bay of Pigs, and some Cubans should have done that," because Kennedy was the one holding the freedom of Cuba.[15]

Two months later, upon hearing of President Kennedy's assassination, Silvia Odio fainted dead away, and had to be hospitalized. Her immediate thought, before she ever saw any pictures of the alleged assassin, was that the three men who came to her home in September had something to do with it. And once she saw his photograph, she had no doubt that "Leon Oswald" was actually Lee Harvey Oswald.[16]

The testimony of Silvia Odio and the corroborating recollections of her sister Annie were an enormous problem for the Warren Commission. If nothing else, the Commission stated it meant that "Oswald may have had companions on his trip to Mexico." But the linking of Oswald to an assassination plot two months before it actually happened had far more sinister implications.[17]

The Warren Commission allowed the Odio matter to stagnate until July 1964, as it neared the end of its work. Staff attorney W. David Slawson prepared a report that tried to demonstrate that Oswald could not have been in Dallas at the time in question. According to Slawson, Oswald was in New Orleans on September 25, and by the 26th had traveled to Houston, where he boarded a bus bound for Mexico City. There were only a few hours unaccounted for in this analysis. But after reading it, Wesley Liebeler submitted his own memo demonstrating that Oswald could have been in Dallas on the 26th and still made his bus for Mexico City. When General Counsel J. Lee Rankin saw Liebeler's memo, he commented, "At this stage, we are supposed to be closing doors, not opening them."[18]

The Commission, in its report, said the FBI had located a man named Loran Hall who said he was active in anti-Castro activities and had visited Silvia Odio in Dallas accompanied by two men, whom he identified as Lawrence Howard and William Seymour. Hall said further that Seymour resembled Lee Oswald. That was enough for the Commission: the door was slammed shut. "The Commission has concluded that Lee Harvey Oswald was not at Mrs. Odio's apartment in September of 1963."[19]

Yet the Commission, Meagher wrote in "The Proof of the Plot," sent its Report to press *before* the FBI's Odio investigation was even completed. This was an "unbelievable denouement." Even if it had been a thorough investigation, even if it really was Hall, Howard and Seymour who visited Silvia Odio, and even if the Odio sisters really had mistaken Seymour for Oswald, the incident was nothing less than proof of a plot.

> Is there any other way to explain Seymour's introduction as "Leon Oswald" or the telephone call that Mrs. Odio received from "Leopoldo" the next day when he carefully told her (1) that "Leon Oswald" was a former Marine; (2) that "Oswald" was a crack

marksman; (3) that "Oswald" felt that President Kennedy should have been assassinated after the Bay of Pigs, and (4) that "Oswald" was "loco" and the kind of man who could do anything, like "getting" the Cuban underground or killing Castro?

Whether the visitor was Oswald himself, or Seymour impersonating Oswald, "Leopoldo" took pains to plant seeds which inevitably would incriminate Oswald in the assassination carried out on November 22. . . .[20]

Harold Weisberg had also studied the Cuban exile milieu closely, including the Odio matter. This incident, he wrote in *Whitewash*, fit the pattern of what he called "the false Oswald" – recurring and reliable reports placing Lee Oswald in one location when he was known to be elsewhere, far away. This was precisely what the Commission had been faced with in the Odio incident. "How could it ignore the existence of a 'False Oswald' until the bitter end?" Weisberg wrote. "How could it close up shop, with its files interred for 75 years, knowing a 'False Oswald' existed?"[21]

Silvia Odio was unquestionably an important witness. Everything she told the authorities about the visit to her home in September 1963 checked out. But her story seriously undermined the lone-gunman scenario; consequently, Weisberg wrote, "we find aspersions about her sanity." While Silvia Odio had had a privileged upbringing in Cuba prior to the Castro revolution, the years immediately afterward were difficult – a life in exile highlighted by the breakup of her marriage. The emotional strains were such that she sought the help of mental health professionals. This was played up in FBI background reports to imply that she suffered serious emotional problems.[22]

On April 28, 1967, Weisberg appeared before the Orleans Parish Grand Jury. Before he got to the specifics of Clay Shaw's alleged role, Jim Garrison needed to demonstrate that there had been a conspiracy to kill JFK. He needed experts who could speak with authority on the deficiencies of the Warren Commission's published work, so Weisberg had agreed to testify. Mark Lane and Ray Marcus would follow him over the next two weeks.

Weisberg had just completed a book called *Oswald in New Orleans: Case for Conspiracy with the CIA*, which was not yet published. It was his third completed book relating to the assassination. As its title suggested, it delved into the very aspects of the case that the Garrison probe went into. But, Weisberg said, "I am happy to abandon this facet to the New Orleans District Attorney with the sincere hope he develops a case he can take to court." The Kennedy assassination, he said, desperately needed to be tested in an adversarial proceeding.[23]

Weisberg was convinced that it was not the real Lee Oswald who visited Silvia Odio's apartment with Leopoldo and Angelo. Based on documents he had found in the National Archives, Weisberg thought it more likely that it was indeed Loran Hall and Lawrence Howard who visited Odio's apartment in September 1963. The third man may have been William Seymour, but may also have been a Cuban named Celio Alba. They were all based in Florida and involved in CIA-backed training of Cuban exiles for an invasion of Cuba. They were also involved in running guns and drugs across the southern United States; Hall and Seymour had been arrested in Dallas in October 1963 on a drug charge. Hall and Howard appeared, as Odio had described her visitors, to be Cuban or Mexican.[24]

In his grand jury testimony, as in his published writings, Weisberg was very critical of the authorities who had investigated the Odio affair. Deliberately or not, they had failed to ask the right questions of many of those they had interviewed. "Unlike Mr. Garrison," he told the jurors, "who reminds me of things that I should tell you, nobody ever thought to try and refresh Mrs. Odio's recollection or suggest 'could it have been this, or this?'" A relevant example was the war names used by the men who had visited Mrs. Odio. She recalled them as "Leopoldo" and possibly "Angelo." Weisberg had learned that Loran Hall's war name was "Lorenzo," and Lawrence Howard's was "Alonzo." If this were correct, he said, then perhaps Mrs. Odio recalled both war names by the right first initial and names that sounded like the actual war names of Hall and Howard. "I think if she were asked were it not 'Angelo' but was it 'Alonzo,' I think her face would light up again."[25]

"We can't talk to Silvia Odio, incidentally," Garrison pointed out, "and [she] is probably the most important witness in the entire twenty-six volumes, probably. We went to Puerto Rico and she is so scared, scared to death, and she won't talk to anybody."

"I don't blame her," Weisberg replied. "She tried in every way she could and what they did to this woman is a disgrace. These FBI reports are dedicated to the destruction of her character, to undermine her credibility, and I am telling you that everything she says backs up. They couldn't break down anything she says."[26]

But the important point remained what Sylvia Meagher said was the proof of the plot. Regardless of who the visitors really were, Lee or Leon Oswald's name was linked to assassinating President Kennedy two months before it happened. "That leaves two possibilities," Sylvia had written in the chapter she sent to Garrison. "That the real Oswald visited Mrs. Odio with two companions, one of whom deliberately planted highly incriminating information about him without his knowledge; or that a mock-Oswald visited her, to accomplish the same purpose."[27]

Harold Weisberg addressed much more than the Odio incident during his testimony before the Orleans Parish Grand Jury. He told them about the first FBI Summary Report of December 9, 1963 – the report that Weisberg had hastily added as a "postscript" to the first *Whitewash*, which stated plainly that the bullet that hit Kennedy in the back had "no point of exit." Moreover, Weisberg told the jurors, "the FBI didn't mention the wound in front of the President's neck and didn't mention the missed shot."[28]

He told them how one of the president's three autopsy surgeons, Dr. James J. Humes, had been ordered not to talk about the autopsy, and how Humes personally burned the original draft of his autopsy report in the fireplace of his home's rec room. "And what a ghoulish thing to do in a recreation room . . . this was an historical document. This was an important paper. Nobody ever asked him why he burned it."[29]

Weisberg discussed some of the photographic evidence, including the Zapruder film, which he said showed conclusively that the president's fatal head shot came from the front. He also described the photograph taken by Associated Press photographer James Altgens, which he said corresponded with Zapruder frame 255. This was the picture showing JFK grasping his throat in reaction to the first shot, and, in the background, a man in the Book Depository doorway who appeared to be Lee Oswald. Weisberg was convinced this man *was* Lee Oswald. To the grand jury, he stated the obvious: "How could Oswald be on the first floor of the Texas School Book Depository Building observing the assassination that he was committing on the sixth floor at the same time?"[30]

There was an unseen connection between Lee Oswald and the Central Intelligence Agency, Weisberg told the grand jury. One indicator of that, he said, was the fact that a member of the Russian community in Dallas had once phoned the FBI after noticing communist literature in Oswald's home, and was told that Oswald was "all right." Another was the fact that while in the Marines Oswald was stationed at a top-secret Air Force Base in Japan. Weisberg had interviewed a man who claimed to have been stationed with Oswald there. This man told Weisberg that "Oswald was one of five men who had a security clearance that I have never even heard of, higher than top secret." He did not tell the jurors, but in *Oswald in New Orleans* Weisberg wrote that Oswald's security level was that of "crypto clearance." It all reminded Weisberg of the testimony of Nelson Delgado, a Marine buddy of Oswald, who was stationed with him at a Marine base in Santa Ana, California. Both men worked in a radar control room and had access to classified information – "not exactly where one expects the Marine Corps to assign 'Communists.'"[31]

In response to a juror's question, Weisberg described how, following his arrest in Dallas, Lee Oswald was denied every one of his legal rights.

"Isn't there a transcript from the more than twelve hours of questioning?" Garrison asked.

"No tape recording."

"They said," Garrison continued, "the room was too small to get a stenographer in."

"By the way, I went into all of that," Weisberg replied. "I went into all the empty rooms they had available including the jail in which Oswald was, and all the people who were there serving no purpose who could have been replaced by a police stenographer, and Chief Curry said he had put in his budget a request for a tape recorder and didn't have any. Poor Chief Curry; he couldn't go out and spend $50.00 of his own money, he couldn't ask the FBI to lend him theirs or the Secret Service to lend him theirs. Or the credit of Dallas was no good and he couldn't rent one. Or there was no public spirited citizen to come forward with one. They had five detectives and they were guarding Oswald with hands handcuffed behind his back. For what purpose?"[32]

After he got back home from New Orleans, Weisberg wrote Sylvia Meagher and described some of his experiences. He had spent a great deal of time with Garrison and his staff, sometimes working into the wee hours of the morning. The DA had some very exciting information and Weisberg was very impressed by him. "I have no doubt about the sincerity or integrity of Garrison or any of his staff," he said. "They are convinced of Cuban-FBI-CIA involvement, as my own work proves." Weisberg and Garrison's staff disagreed on at least one point: that it was the real Oswald who made such an impression in New Orleans over the summer of 1963. Weisberg was certain most or all of these were the "false Oswald."

Nevertheless, Garrison had assembled a dedicated and hard-working team. Garrison, it seemed to Weisberg, kept himself going at the office by a steady consumption of Metrocal.[33]

Garrison faced great opposition, Weisberg told Meagher. Some of his witnesses had been intimidated. But his biggest concern was that Garrison was too trusting. Many of the people he was dealing with were of unknown character, but he seemed to take most of them at face value; he was bound to be hurt by this. But Weisberg's grand jury testimony had gone very well. "I was before the grand jury for three hours. It is one of the remarkable wonderful accidents in our history, it is that good a grand jury."[34]

Mark Lane testified to this grand jury on May 10. His initial remarks resembled the countless speeches he had delivered over the preceding three years, outlining the basic reasons for doubting the official version of the assassination.

But before long Lane got to some material that bore more directly on Jim Garrison's investigation. "I read the testimony of Dean Andrews, who mentioned Clay Bertrand, and it appeared to me that he might have been an important person in the entire episode." Accordingly Lane arranged an interview with Andrews when he was documenting witness statements for the film version of *Rush to Judgment*. He drove to New Orleans with a film crew and went to Andrews' office in the Maison Blanche Building. When they got there, Andrews said that there had been a mistake. He would not grant an interview. "'Washington, D.C. has told me that I cannot talk with you about this,'" Lane quoted Andrews. "'I have been threatened,' he said, 'and I have been told that a hole will be put in my head if I give you a filmed interview about Bertrand or any other of my testimony.'" Lane assured Andrews he was not an official investigator; he was just trying to make a documentary film. "He said, 'I repeat, I cannot tell you, I am threatened,' and then he repeated the thing about the hole in his head, and he said 'if there is a hole in my head blood will run out and I don't have too much blood to start out with.'" Lane tried to convince Andrews to change his mind, but Andrews wouldn't budge.[35]

Some witnesses with relevant information were never called to testify to the Warren Commission, Lane told the grand jury, and attempts had been made to get other witnesses to change their stories. Dean Andrews was a perfect example. "The FBI sought to convince him that there was no such person as Bertrand, that in fact he never received a phone call on November 23," Lane said. In the end Andrews had told the

FBI to "write what you want, that I am nuts. I don't care." The Warren Report stated that Andrews believed he had been contacted by phone on November 23 and asked to represent Oswald, but that he had been under heavy sedation at the time of the call.[36]

Lane said that over the preceding three years he had spoken to audiences at one hundred an fifty universities, and had made countless radio and television appearances. Consequently he had a feel for how the nation viewed the Warren Report: almost no one believed it any more. "That there is a false Report has raised more speculation and conjecture than the result of a truthful report telling whatever the facts are. Truth would have satisfied the American people. They don't have it there, and they are looking for truth. They would like to know who killed their President, but there is nobody to tell them but Mr. Garrison, and his staff."[37]

There were many more witnesses still to come before the Orleans Parish Grand Jury, but the last of the critics to offer his expertise was Ray Marcus, who testified the day after Mark Lane. Perhaps sensing a curiosity from some of the jurors, Marcus began by talking about his involvement in the case. "I have asked myself many times in the last three and a half years, what am I doing? Why? And what are my qualifications? And they are legitimate questions." Though a layman, he had done extensive work in photo analysis and ballistics because those experts who were most qualified to do the work had not done it. "Mr. Lane was here yesterday, and of course he is a lawyer so he has qualifications in this area, criminal area. But I am not, but I guess the only qualifications that matter are a sincere desire to find out who killed President Kennedy."[38]

On November 22, 1963, with the world reeling from news of the President's violent death, Lee Harvey Oswald had been presented as the sole assassin. "Now it was obvious to anybody who had recovered sufficiently from the shock that the Federal Government was making a statement which they could not know to be true. At that time it might have eventually worked out to be true, but they certainly could not know at the time they made the statement." That had raised his initial suspicions, Marcus said. Once the Warren Report was published, it didn't take a long, painstaking analysis to see that it was a false document. He told jurors that anyone who wanted to keep believing the Warren Report shouldn't read it. "But I think history obliges some of us to take a different view."[39]

He described studying the Zapruder film frames published in the November 29, 1963 issue of *Life* and noticing a detail in one frame suggesting that Governor John Connally could not have been shot from the direction of the Texas School Book Depository. From that simple but key observation came his intensive analysis of the Zapruder film. Marcus had amended his views since completing his "Hypotheses re: the Zapruder Film" two years earlier. "I want to mention that I believe, and there is one of the other critics that independently came to [this conclusion], Professor Thompson, that President Kennedy was struck in the head by two bullets, approximately frame 312 and 313" – in other words, almost simultaneously. This opinion was based on further analysis of the Zapruder film; two head shots were in addition to a throat wound and a back wound. Marcus explained how he used the curb on Elm Street as a fixed reference point and measured the movement of the President's head. "The first shot I infer came from the left rear which moved his head forward, down and somewhat to the right, more toward the center of an upright position." It did not come from the Book Depository. The second, almost simultaneous head shot came from the right front and slammed Kennedy's head back against the car seat. All told, Marcus told the grand jury he believed the President was hit four times, while Governor Connally's multiple wounds were probably caused by just one bullet.[40]

Marcus told the jurors he wanted to discuss the single-bullet theory, "which probably bores you at this point. But we have heard so much about it. I think you are all aware by now that the Commission's entire case depends on a single-bullet hypothesis." The single-bullet theory stated that the first shot in the entire assassination sequence hit the president in the back of the neck, exited his throat, and went on to cause all of Governor Connally's wounds. The single-bullet theory was crucial to Warren Commission, Marcus said. "Without it they have no case."[41]

Marcus showed the grand jury a copy of an enlarged Z-232, "which proves that Connally was not hit by the first bullet that hit Kennedy." In this frame, the president is plainly reacting to a wound – which according to the single-bullet theory was the first he received. But Connally, who according to the Warren Commission was also hit by this bullet, is not reacting at all. Moreover his right hand is visible. "Kennedy has already been hit and the Commission's version says Connally has been hit by this time too, but Connally's wrist is totally out of position to take a bullet" in the way the Warren Report described. It wasn't a matter of the Governor's raising a wounded arm. Marcus had sought the opinion of an orthopedic surgeon. "He gave me his opinion willingly but would not let me use his name. He said it was a physical impossibility to hold a wrist and hand in that position after the wrist had been shattered in seven pieces, the tendons were torn; he said it was a physical impossibility to do that."[42]

After demonstrating to the grand jury that the assassination could not have happened the way the government said it did, Marcus turned to the evidence he had developed placing gunmen on the grassy knoll. The jurors had already heard considerable evidence of this. Marcus had just shown them the back-and-to-the-left motion of the President's body after the head shot in the Zapruder film; Harold Weisberg and Mark Lane had already introduced much. The gunsmoke seen by S.M. Holland hanging among the trees along the knoll, and the "commotion" and "flash of light" described by Lee Bowers in that same area, all indicated shots from the right front. Bowers had also seen, Marcus said, three cars cruise through the parking lot behind the knoll just before the assassination, and observed that the driver of one appeared to be speaking into a microphone.[43]

Marcus showed the grand jury his enlargements from the Mary Moorman photograph – blow-ups that made grassy knoll gunmen very real, very lethal entities. First he brought out the full photograph, which coincided with Zapruder frames 312-313, the moment of the head shot. This photograph, he told them, had been widely published – among other places, in a magazine called *Four Dark Days in History*. "David Lifton sees this photograph in there and he begins to study," Marcus said. "He was convinced by now that some shots had to come from behind that knoll, and just maybe we can see something, or somebody, and he studied very, very carefully. And he called up in a high state of excitement one day, and said 'I think I found something.' He came over to the house and he pointed out some images that he thought he saw there, and I didn't see them at first. They are very, very tiny. Then we had blowups made of the images, and I want to show you what emerged."[44]

Lifton had identified five possible figures in the picture's shadows, Marcus explained. First, he passed around an enlargement of the area where the five possible figures appeared. "I am not asking you to draw a conclusion that these are men. I am only saying, do you see images?"[45]

The jurors got a good look. "I see one man's face," one of them said. "Clearly."[46]

"I will tell you now what I see," Marcus said. Separate enlargements of #2 man and #5 man were passed around. Marcus spoke first of #5 man, which he was convinced was indeed a human figure. "Here is his face in full view, you can see slight ear bulges, eye holes, one very dark point which is a blemish on the film, very dark. I can see the right point of his collar. Anybody see that? Right collar point. I can see what I believe to be his left hand and his right hand and a straight object, an elongated object held between his hands. I am not saying the elongated object is a rifle – I cannot say that. But I can see an elongated object, straight appearing object in his hands." Whether it was a rifle or not, the figure did not appear to be in a firing position.[47]

The other image, #2 man, was another matter. "This man," Marcus said, "if it's a man, is in a firing position." The figure appeared to be aiming at a downward angle, but Marcus stopped short of saying the figure held a weapon. "All I will say about that object sticking down is if someone were pointing at you with a rifle or a broom handle, or anything from that angle, that is about what you would see in the photograph."[48]

Marcus concluded his photographic presentation by showing the jury the wire-service picture of the man who shot James Meredith. Like the Moorman blow-ups, the Meredith photograph had a heavily foliated background. "This is the standard because we know this is a face," Marcus said of Meredith's assailant. He indicated the #5 man blow-up. "See how strikingly similar it is?" What did the two Moorman enlargements reveal? "Giving it a conservative interpretation, we are looking at unknown, unauthorized individuals behind a fence. In giving it a less conservative but probably true interpretation, we are looking at some of the assassins."[49]

Vince Salandria did not travel to New Orleans during this phase of the Garrison investigation; he would not personally meet with the district attorney until August. But he was pursuing several other areas that interested him greatly, one of which he believed, as much as the Silvia Odio incident, demonstrated proof of a plot.

By November 1964 Salandria had discovered that there were two conflicting versions of the October 2, 1964, issue of *Life*. The issue marked the publication of the Warren Report in an article by former Commission member Gerald Ford. Before long Salandria found a third version of that same issue. The differences between them were slight but critical, since they went to the question of what direction the rifle fire came from in Dealey Plaza.[50]

Eight frames from the Zapruder film had accompanied Ford's article; all but the first illustrated a key sequence in the assassination. The sixth of these was Z-313, a horrific image showing Kennedy's head at the

moment it was blown apart. The caption stated that
struck the right rear portion of the President's sku
wound and snapping his head to one side." This
reasoning to Salandria. A head struck from the rea
side ran counter to a Newtonian law of motion;
snapped forward and downward.[51]

In the second version of the magazine, the caption was changed to
read, "The direction from which shots came was established by this
picture taken at instant bullet struck the rear of the President's head and,
passing through, caused the front part of his skull to explode forward."
The picture was different, too: Z-324, barely half a second after Z-313,
showed Kennedy's head and shoulders slammed back and to the left into
the car seat – powerful evidence that the shots came not from the rear,
but from the grassy knoll area to the President's the right front.[52]

Like the first version, the third version of *Life*'s October 2 issue used
Z-313 for its sixth picture. The caption, however, was the same exploding-
forward caption from the second version of *Life*. Salandria wrote about the
three versions of *Life* in an article published in the January 1965 issue of
Liberation.

Two years passed before Salandria asked anyone at *Life* about the
three versions. "I knew whose side they were on," he said. The magazine
had already published some questionable material on the assassination,
perhaps most significantly the item in its December 6, 1963, issue stating
that Kennedy had turned around in his seat, thereby explaining how he
was wounded in the throat by a gunman firing from behind him. Mark
Lane had pointed this out to the Commission during his testimony in
March 1964 – and that *Life* had already published Zapruder frames
showing unequivocally that he had *not* turned in his seat.[53]

In its issue of November 25, 1966, *Life* published its article "A
Matter of Reasonable Doubt," which editorialized that the assassination
investigation should be re-opened. Salandria used this as an opportunity
to write to Ed Kern, a *Life* editor who had worked on the article. "Can you
cast any light on why *Life* saw fit to have three versions on the same press
run?" Salandria asked him. He enclosed a copy of his *Liberation* article that
outlined the problem.[54]

Kern wrote him back at once. "I am at a loss to explain the discrepancies between the three versions of *Life* which you cite," he said. "I've
heard of breaking a plate to correct an error. I've never heard of doing it
twice for a single issue, much less a single story." No one in the office, he
explained, seemed to remember who worked on that article.[55]

But for Salandria there was no real mystery about it. Reflecting on many years later, he said that *Life* both censored the Zapruder film and lied about its contents. "To me the three versions of *Life* and *Life*'s lies about what the Zapruder film revealed show in microcosm an elegant example of how the U.S. media criminally joined with U.S. governmental civilian personages, and with the national security state apparatus to employ deceit in seeking to prop up the Warren Report."[56]

As much as the three versions of *Life* seemed to reveal, there was something that Salandria thought revealed even more – in essence, proof of a plot formulated at the highest levels of the United States government. He had mentioned it to Sylvia Meagher on the occasion of their first meeting in August 1965, when he said he could not understand why, on November 22, 1963, high government officials in Washington had sent out word that there was no conspiracy in the assassination. He had learned of this in a book entitled *The Making of the President – 1964*, by the Pulitzer Prize winning journalist Theodore H. White. White had recounted the tumultuous day when the assassination elevated Lyndon Johnson to the presidency; he described the flight of the presidential party from Dallas back to Washington on board Air Force One:

> On the flight the party learned that there was no conspiracy; learned of the identity of Oswald and his arrest; and the President's mind turned to the duties of consoling the stricken and guiding the quick.[57]

If this was correct, Salandria believed it to be a telling anecdote. Air Force One had arrived at Andrews Air Force Base at 5:59 pm Eastern Standard Time. Back in Dallas it was 4:59. Lee Harvey Oswald was by then under arrest, but he had not been formally charged with the murders of either the President or J.D. Tippit. How could the presidential party be informed at this early time that there was no conspiracy in President Kennedy's assassination?

On November 11, 1966, Salandria wrote to Theodore White asking him where he heard about this: "I would much appreciate your providing the source of this information and a designation of the nature of the communication to Air Force One, i.e. whether it was commercial TV, government radio, or whatever." White replied in an undated note he scrawled at the bottom of Salandria's original letter: "By government radio – all relays go through a big Signal Corps center in the Midwest – and the White House was in constant communication with the plane."[58]

White's book had also stated there was a tape recording of all conversations between Air Force One, the Joint Chiefs communication center, and the White House communications center in Washington. The Cabinet plane, over the Pacific Ocean bound for Japan, was also part of the conversation. The tape recording, White wrote, ended up "in the archives of the government." Exactly one year after he had written to White, Salandria addressed a letter to Dr. Robert H. Bahmer of the National Archives: "Will you kindly arrange to have a copy of the said tape sent to me, or in lieu thereof, a transcript, or in lieu thereof, provide me with an opportunity to listen to the same at the Archives?"[59]

But when Dr. Bahmer replied, he said the National Archives did not have the recordings in question. "Apparently Mr. White is here using the word 'archives' in its generic sense . . . we have no knowledge of the existence or location of the tape recording mentioned by Mr. White." He suggested that Salandria ask White for more information, but White never supplied any.[60]

Salandria turned next to Pierre Salinger, President Kennedy's former press secretary, who had just published *With Kennedy*. At the time of the assassination Salinger had been aboard the Cabinet plane flying to Japan for an economic conference. He wrote of hearing the stunning news of the assassination, the subsequent communications between the Cabinet Plane and the White House, and while still on the plane, about Lee Harvey Oswald.[61]

"What I am about," Salandria told Salinger, "is the verification of what Mr. White stated was on the tape, to wit: 'On the flight the party learned that there was no conspiracy; learned of the identity of Oswald and his arrest; and the President's mind turned to the duties of consoling the stricken and guiding the quick.' If such was said, before there was any evidence against Oswald as the assassin, and while there was overwhelming evidence of a conspiracy, then the White House is in the interesting position of being the first to designate Oswald as the assassin and the first to have ruled out in the face of impressive evidence to the contrary, that there could have been a conspiracy." Could Salinger provide him with a copy of the tape?[62]

Salinger's reply came three weeks later. The section of his book describing the conversations between the White House and the Cabinet plane, he said, was taken from a transcript of the tape made by the White House Communications Agency. He hadn't seen a similar transcript for the White House-Air Force One tapes, nor had he heard those tapes themselves. But the Cabinet plane transcript was in his personal files, which had been turned over to the National Archives for placement in the Kennedy Library. He had no objection to Salandria's seeing it.[63]

But this search, too, would end in frustration. After letters to the National Archives and to the Kennedy Library, Salandria was informed by Dr. Bahmer that "a careful examination" of Salinger's papers did not yield the transcript in question. And Air Force Colonel James U. Cross wrote to Salandria that tapes and transcripts of military aircraft, which included Air Force One, were kept for official use only; they were not releasable, nor were they obtainable commercially.[64]

And yet, Salandria said, they were obtainable: Theodore White and Pierre Salinger both got them, and for unofficial use. But the important point was what the tapes, as described by White, revealed. The first announcement of Oswald as the lone assassin came from the White House Situation Room, no more than four and a half hours after the Dealey Plaza ambush. No one, Salandria reasoned, could have known so early that Oswald was the killer and there was no conspiracy. Only the true assassins could have made such an announcement. "Can there be any doubt that for any innocent government, taken by surprise by the assassination – and legitimately seeking the truth concerning it – the White House Situation Room message was sent too soon?" This, Salandria said, was the proof of the plot – conclusive evidence of high-level U.S. governmental guilt.[65]

The investigation and eventual prosecution of Clay Shaw involved many elements, but one that would prove to be divisive was an entry in Clay Shaw's address book, seized during a search of his home in New Orleans' French Quarter soon after his arrest. The entry in Shaw's address book, made public in May of 1967, was as follows:

Lee Odom
P.O. Box 19106
Dallas, Tex[66]

Shaw's "19106" was matched to the same number in Lee Harvey Oswald's notebook, published in the Warren Commission's twenty-six volumes. But Oswald's "19106" appeared to be preceded by two Cyrillic letters, which did not necessarily correspond to the letters "P.O." Was it still a match? And if so, what did it mean?[67]

Clay Shaw's attorneys said the notation in Shaw's address book was written in 1966, by which time Lee Oswald was long dead. It was an address, they said, for a Dallas businessman and promoter named Lee Odom, with whom Shaw had discussed the possibility of staging a bullfight in New Orleans.[68]

But Garrison said that Shaw's and Oswald's both having, by sheer coincidence, "19106" written in their personal papers stretched the limits of believability. "19106," he argued, was really a coded version of Jack Ruby's 1963 telephone number, WHitehall 1-5601, and it established a link among Ruby, Lee Oswald, and Clay Shaw.[69]

Sylvia Meagher was concerned with this development. In mid-May she wrote to Garrison:

> Two problems arise with respect to the notation "19106" in Oswald's address book which raise a question about its correspondence, when decoded, with the unpublished number WHitehall 1-5601. The symbols which precede the digits "19106" in the notebook (XVI page 58) seem to me to represent the Cyrillic letters "DD" rather than the English letters "PO" . . . if the correct reading is "DD 19106" decoding would not produce the WHitehall exchange.
>
> The second problem is that this notation, which I read as "DD 19106," appears on a page of the address book which seems to have been written during Oswald's stay in the Soviet Union. This is the inference I draw from the contents, the script, and the consistency of the ink, which is all distinguished from the facing page of the address book which appears to been written after Oswald's return to the U.S. While it is plausible that Oswald would have recorded a cryptogram of Ruby's telephone number sometime in 1963, it is hard to believe that Oswald would have done so during his time in the Soviet Union.[70]

These points, Sylvia concluded, may already have occurred to Garrison and been dealt with. She took it for granted, however, that Garrison would want the problem brought to his attention.[71]

On Tuesday, May 16, Sylvia sent the letter to Garrison by registered airmail, special delivery, ensuring he would get it by the next day. On Wednesday she got a phone call from Garrison at work. The call was placed by Garrison's secretary, who asked her to hold. "As I waited two or three minutes for Garrison to come on the line, I tried to steel myself for a possibly angry, hostile, or irritated reaction to my letter," she said.[72]

But when Garrison at last came on the line, he began talking about an alleged CIA photograph showing Lee Oswald with a known CIA operative in Mexico City. As he talked, Meagher began to think that her letter must not have arrived yet. Finally, she asked him. "He said, oh, yes, he had it, and that my points were well-taken; but that he had also decoded from other notations in the same LHO notebook (CE 18) the phone numbers for (1) Clay Shaw (2) the local FBI office (3) the local CIA office. The press had blacked this out, in Garrison's opinion because the CIA had put the pressure on." Perhaps, the DA suggested, Sylvia could interest someone in the New York press, specifically Sylvan Fox, author of *Unanswered Questions About President Kennedy's Assassination*, who was by then at *The New York Times*. Garrison then gave her a detailed description of the entries and the method of decoding.[73]

Sylvia Meagher did reach Sylvan Fox by phone that day. He took Garrison's phone number and said the *Times* had a reporter in New Orleans on the whole Garrison story, but was non-committal. Sylvia, meantime, was disappointed that Garrison had not even dealt with her questions about "DD 19106" beyond saying they were well-taken. "I feel uneasy because Garrison said several times while he was giving me the data that there was an element of subjectivity. I think he meant on LHO's part; but perhaps there is some subjectivity on his own part, too."[74]

Chapter 28

Fatal Ruptures

In its **June 10, 1967,** issue, *The New Yorker* magazine published an article about the Warren Commission critics by Calvin Trillin called "The Buffs." By documenting the phenomenon of a spontaneous, mostly grass-roots response to an unacceptable Warren Report, the urbane magazine became one of the first mainstream publications to identify most of the critics as a group, and discuss, even-handedly, their work in detail. The piece consisted of a series of critic profiles and in general was quite friendly, although Sylvia Meagher said she wondered why anyone would care about the personalities of the critics. "There are certainly regrettable omissions – mainly on evidentiary questions," she said. "But at least it is no Schlewis-type exercise in slander which, given the greater sophistication of *New Yorker* writing, could have been brutal."[1]

Some found the article's title irritating, since the term "buff" implied a casual or frivolous pursuit. The phrase was repeated throughout the piece. Trillin himself noted that the preferred terms were "'investigators' or 'researchers,' or most often, 'critics.'" He distinguished between the "first-generation critics," who began tracking developments on November 22, 1963, and those who came later, like David Lifton and Tink Thompson. "The discovery that they were not alone struck most of the buffs as monumental," Trillin wrote. "They finally had somebody to *talk* to."[2]

"The Buffs" sketched most of the critics: Meagher, Field, Salandria, Ray Marcus, and Lillian Castellano. There was no mention of Penn Jones, Jr., or Mary Ferrell, and only passing references to Mark Lane and Harold Weisberg. There was a brief reference to "James" Garrison, who had "launched an investigation of his own as district attorney of New Orleans." Trillin could not have known it, but by the time his article appeared, Jim Garrison's investigation was causing a serious rift among the people he had written about.[3]

As early as March 1967, Sylvia Meagher had noticed among the critics a wide range of reaction to Jim Garrison. "It is interesting to see how many differing interpretations three or four of us, otherwise so united in thought and analysis, placed upon the same set of events," she said.

"We all agree that Garrison is with us, in every sense of the word, and that he is working on the hypothesis of a Batistiano exile/CIA conspiracy." But she was concerned that Garrison was relying too heavily on insufficient evidence. Maggie Field and Ray Marcus were certain that he had all the evidence he needed, but was vulnerable to character assassination in the mass media, which seemed determined to discredit him. Meanwhile Salandria, Sylvia wrote, was predicting that in the end, the official story would be amended to state that a CIA-sponsored plot against Fidel Castro, to be carried out by Cuban refugees, was re-directed toward JFK. "It will be interesting, three or six months from now, to see who was closest to the mark."[4]

But by late May, Sylvia Meagher had lost all confidence in Jim Garrison. The theory of the postal code was completely wrong, she determined; what's more, she believed Garrison knew it was wrong, but would not publicly say so. "The so-called decoding of identical notations ('PO 19106') in both Shaw's and Oswald's address books is not valid," she wrote to Vince Salandria in a terse note dated May 30. "Garrison has acknowledged that the 'PO' in Oswald's book is in fact the Cyrillic 'DD.' Therefore, the notation in his book cannot be a cryptogram for Ruby's unpublished telephone number in Dallas in 1963." Moreover there really was a Lee Odom who used that post office box number and who knew Shaw slightly.[5]

Two days later, Sylvia told Harold Weisberg: "My position with respect to Jim Garrison is very simple – it is also final and not negotiable. He has 'decoded' the notations 'PO 19106' into Ruby's unlisted 1963 phone number in Dallas. I am ready to grant that his 'decoding' was done in good faith (if without sufficient care and objectivity). But it is in error, for what he read as 'PO 19106' in Oswald's book is in fact 'DD 19106.' The entire decoding is therefore invalidated." Garrison had conceded that the "PO" was in fact "DD," but did not intend to retract his public statements about the alleged cryptographic evidence establishing a link between Lee Oswald, Clay Shaw, and Jack Ruby. "In other words," Sylvia continued, "he is allowing a lie to stand on the record."[6]

On Sunday, June 25, 1967, *The New York Times* carried a front page story headlined "Meredith Marching in Mississippi Again." A year after gunfire had ended his first attempt to walk from Memphis, Tennessee, to the state capitol in Jackson, Meredith was resuming his March Against Fear at the very location he had been shot. He arrived at the spot along

Highway 51, near Hernando, Mississippi, on June 24 around 10 a.m.. Emerging from a blue Thunderbird, he handed out leaflets to the reporters there to see him off. The leaflets declared that three things were necessary for Black Americans to overcome racism in the United States: the elimination of fear, unconditional participation in the political process for all citizens, and the complete enjoyment of the fruits of the country's economic system. "I think," Meredith told reporters, "we will find total freedom here." He walked seventeen miles that day. The column of marchers grew to nineteen before that day was out; they were accompanied by as many as fifty newspaper and TV people.[7]

That same evening, CBS television broadcast the first of its four-part *CBS News Inquiry: The Warren Report*. This was the documentary that CBS was touting as "the most valuable four hours" its viewers might ever spend in front of their TV sets. It was anchored by Walter Cronkite, a broadcasting legend already considered the dean of American television newsmen. Cronkite said later it would have been "the crowning moment of an entire career – of an entire lifetime – to find that Oswald had not acted alone, to uncover a conspiracy that took the life of John F. Kennedy." But, he continued, "We could not."[8]

Each segment of the *CBS News Inquiry* posed a series of questions and answered them with an unbiased evaluation of the evidence. That, at any rate, was the stated intent. The actual content of the four programs left many wondering whether CBS had really taken a disinterested approach to the subject. *The Boston Herald Traveler* article Ray Marcus had seen, stating that the CBS documentary might really be aimed at "weakening the arguments of those who criticize" the Warren Report, may have been accurate, after all.

"I decided to watch the CBS effort very closely," Mark Lane said later. Like Ray Marcus, Lane had met with Bob Richter in the months preceding the broadcast, and had also been interviewed for the documentary. After watching the series he concluded that the programs were highly deceptive. "What had evidently been the original approach – to present the evidence and permit the viewer to draw his own conclusions – bore no resemblance to the final concept."[9]

In his 1964 book *Who Killed Kennedy?*, Thomas G. Buchanan observed that the facts of the assassination as they were initially reported in the media changed several times, but the conclusion of Oswald's lone guilt never changed. "If, as a statistician, I were solving problems with the aid of a machine and I discovered that, however the components of my problem were altered, the machine would always give me the same answer, I should be inclined to think that the machine was broken."[10]

CBS was such a machine. It altered its components with firearms and ballistics tests that improved on the original FBI tests; with new analyses of the Zapruder film; and with new interviews with witnesses to the events of November 1963. But its answer was the same one it had always reported, the same one delivered by the Warren Commission: Lee Oswald, for reasons not entirely fathomable, had murdered President Kennedy without direction or help from anyone.[11]

To answer the questions it posed, CBS used a number of experts. One of them was Lawrence Schiller, the photographer and journalist who had once acted as Jack Ruby's business agent and had played a role in developing what became *The Controversy* record album, and *The Scavengers and Critics of the Warren Report.* Schiller was brought in to refute the allegations first made by Mark Lane before the Warren Commission that a photograph of Oswald brandishing the alleged assassination rifle was a forgery.[12]

Schiller, Walter Cronkite said, had studied both the original photograph and its negative. Appearing on-camera, Schiller said that the critics "say that the disparity of shadows, a straight nose shadow from the nose, and an angle body shadow proves without a doubt that [Oswald's] head was superimposed on this body." He had gone to the precise location in Dallas where the original was taken, and on the same date, at the same hour, had taken a photograph of his own. This picture, Schiller said, perfectly reproduced the controversial shadows, indicating the Oswald picture was genuine.[13]

Mark Lane was not able to respond to Schiller on the CBS program. But he later said that the negative for the photograph was never recovered by the authorities, suggesting the photograph was not genuine. "It is interesting to fathom the CBS concept of the life of the average American if it imagined that watching Jack Ruby's business agent after he studied a nonexistent negative might constitute 'the most valuable' time spent watching television."[14]

On the second installment Dr. James J. Humes, the Navy doctor who had been in charge of the president's autopsy and had burned his autopsy notes, was interviewed. Asked about the discrepancy between the schematic drawings that placed an entry wound at the base of the neck, and the autopsy "face sheet" that indicated this wound was really lower down on the back, Humes said that the face sheet was "never meant to be accurate or precisely to scale." The exact measurements were in fact written in the face sheet margins, and conformed to the schematic drawings.[15]

Sylvia Meagher was so incensed that she wrote to CBS News President Richard Salant. The CBS documentary was "marred by serious error and fallacious reasoning which inevitably will have mis-led and confused a general audience." In the case of Dr. Humes, while he insisted the measurements written in the face sheet margin were correct, "CBS failed to pursue or challenge this explanation, as in conscience it should have done, by pointing out no marginal notations giving precise measurements for any other wound, cut-down, or physical characteristic appear on the diagram; that every other entry in the diagram appears to be accurate, as opposed to the crucial bullet wound in the back; that the clothing bullet holes match the diagram, not the schematic drawings; that a Secret Service agent saw a bullet hit the President four inches below the neck; and that another Secret Service agent, summoned to the autopsy chamber expressly to witness the wound, testified that this wound was six inches below the neck."[16]

The third part of the CBS special proved to be especially newsworthy. A portion of this segment was devoted to the Garrison investigation, although for much of it Garrison was put on the defensive. CBS included a sound bite with Clay Shaw, who said: "I am completely innocent . . . I have not conspired with anyone, at any time, or any place, to murder our late and esteemed President John F. Kennedy, or any other individual . . . the charges filed against me have no foundation in fact or in law."[17]

Most damaging to Garrison was the appearance of William Gurvich, a former Garrison investigator introduced as his "chief aide" who, Cronkite told his viewers, had just resigned from the DA's staff. Asked why he quit, Gurvich said that he was dissatisfied with the way the investigation was being conducted. "The truth, as I see it, is that Mr. Shaw should never have been arrested." Gurvich said he had met with Senator Robert F. Kennedy "to tell him we could shed no light on the death of his brother, and not to be hoping for such. After I told him that, he appeared to be rather disgusted to think that someone was exploiting his brother's death." The allegations of bribery by Garrison investigators, Gurvich said, were true. Asked whether Garrison had knowledge of it, Gurvich answered: "Of course he did. He ordered it."[18]

Garrison himself was interviewed by Mike Wallace. Reflecting on all the bad publicity he was getting, which included allegations of witness intimidation and bribery, the DA said, "This attitude of skepticism on the part of the press is an astonishing thing to me, and a new thing to me. They have a problem with my office. And one of the problems is that we have no political appointments. Most of our men are selected by recommendations of deans of law schools. They work nine to five, and we have a highly professional office – I think one of the best in the country. So they're reduced to making up these fictions. We have not intimidated a witness since the day I came in office."[19]

Not missing a beat, Wallace pressed on: "One question is asked again and again. Why doesn't Jim Garrison give his information, if it is valid information, why doesn't he give it to the federal government? Now that everything is out in the open, the CIA could hardly stand in your way again, could they? Why don't you take this information that you have and cooperate with the federal government?"

"Well, that would be one approach, Mike," Garrison countered. "Or I could take my files and take them up on the Mississippi River Bridge and throw them in the river. It'd be about the same result."

"You mean, they just don't want any other solution from that in the Warren Report?"

"Well," the DA replied, "isn't that kind of obvious?"

Garrison had told Wallace there was a photograph in which assassins on the grassy knoll were visible. He referred, of course, to the Moorman photograph. As he had CBS, Ray Marcus had supplied Garrison with a portfolio of images from the picture, including the clearest copies of the #5 man enlargement.

"This is one of the photographs Garrison is talking about," Wallace told his viewers, holding up one of the Moorman pictures Marcus had given to Bob Richter. It was not the one that Marcus had recommended to Richter. Instead Wallace held up a smaller version – the smallest one, Marcus recalled, that he had given CBS. "If there are men up there behind the wall," Wallace said, "they definitely cannot be seen with the naked eye."[20]

Marcus had urged Bob Richter to use the enlargement that the producer of the *CBS New Inquiry,* Les Midgley, had mis-identified as "the man who shot Meredith." Some months after the airing of the CBS documentary, Midgley was asked to reflect on the broadcasts. Echoing Walter Cronkite, Midgley said, "Nothing would have pleased me more than to have found a second assassin. We looked for one and it isn't our fault that we didn't find one. But the evidence just isn't there."[21]

Before the last of the CBS segments even aired, Ray Marcus telephoned Bob Richter again. He trusted Richter, at least up to a point; Richter had, after all, assured him that some of those at CBS were trying to do an honest job. Marcus sent Richter a copy of his eleven-page letter to Les Midgley and hoped now to elicit from him a corroborating opinion that Midgley had, in fact, looked at the clear #5 man blow-up and, though he had previously said he couldn't see a man there, identified it as "the man who shot Meredith."

Richter agreed to that basic truth, and even put it in writing in a note to Marcus written that same day. But as they talked on the phone Richter attempted to take the blame for his boss, saying he had made the same mistake himself; he implied that his own power of suggestion may have led Midgley to misidentify the photograph. But Marcus said that was beside the point: Midgley couldn't have mis-identified the #5 man detail as "the man who shot Meredith" if he hadn't seen a human form there to begin with. "'With the naked eye, you can't see anything,'" Marcus said, paraphrasing Mike Wallace. "Well, that wasn't what Midgley said, of course."[22]

They discussed the appearance of William Gurvich on the CBS special. Regardless of whether there was any truth to what he said, Marcus said that as propaganda it was a powerful blow against Jim Garrison.

"You met him, didn't you?" Richter asked, meaning Gurvich.

"Yes; I spoke to him, oh, for a couple of hours, I'd say, on and off."

"He seemed like a fairly honest person."

"Well, *seemed* like an honest person, yes – I don't know what that means. 'He seemed like an honest person.' He's now said some things on national television which were grossly *dis*honest."

Gurvich was not finished. On June 28 he appeared before the Orleans Parish Grand Jury and repeated his allegations of "misconduct and malfeasance" on the part of Garrison's office in its effort to build a case against Clay Shaw. Stopped by reporters as he entered the grand jury room, Gurvich said that for several months Garrison had information that Clay Shaw was not, in fact, Clay Bertrand, but was still going ahead with his case. The source of that information, he said, was Dean Andrews, the lawyer who had first brought up the name "Clay Bertrand" during interviews with the FBI. Gurvich was asked why Garrison had ignored Andrews' latest assertion.[23]

"Because," Gurvich answered them, "he is an unmitigated liar and a psychopathic paranoid. He is nuts."[24]

Garrison later said that he should have been more cautious about hiring William Gurvich. According to the DA, Gurvich had appeared at the district attorney's office one day before the case was made public, offering his services as a private detective. Garrison was then desperately understaffed and agreed to take Gurvich on, and for a few months – working without pay – he did an adequate job. In time, although he had no proof of improper behavior, Garrison began to suspect William Gurvich, and removed him from the more sensitive areas of the investigation. Eventually Gurvich stopped showing up, and Garrison was certain he made off with a copy of Garrison's master file.[25]

The DA came to believe Gurvich had been in his office in a double-agent capacity. "Let me stress that I have no secret documents or monitored telephone calls to support this hypothesis," he said. "It just seems to me the most logical explanation for Bill's behavior."[26]

The final segment of the *CBS News Inquiry* on the Warren Report was broadcast on the evening of June 28. It posed viewers with the question, Why doesn't America believe the Warren Report?[27]

"As we take up whether or not America should believe the Warren Report," said correspondent Dan Rather, "we'll hear first from the man who perhaps more than any other is responsible for the question being asked." That man was Mark Lane.

Lane said that the only Warren Commission conclusion that was beyond dispute was that Jack Ruby had killed Lee Harvey Oswald. "But, of course, that took place on television," Lane said. "It would have been very difficult to deny that." Beyond that, Lane continued, there was not a single important conclusion that was supported by the facts. The problem was compounded by so much of the Commission's evidence being locked up in the National Archives where no one was allowed to see it.

The photographs and X-rays of the President's body, which represented some of the most important evidence in the entire case, were not seen by any of the Commission members, Lane said. This was a very serious shortcoming, since these films could show decisively how many wounds the President had suffered and precisely where they were located.

Rather than immediately address this, however, CBS chose to question Lane's credibility, presenting a Dealey Plaza eyewitness named Charles Brehm, who accused Lane of misrepresenting his statements in *Rush to Judgment*.

But the most notable feature in the final installment of the CBS documentary was the appearance of former Warren Commission member John McCloy. Aside from his comments to the Associated Press the previous February when the Garrison case first broke, these were his first public statements about the Warren Commission investigation. "I had some question as to the propriety of my appearing here as a former member of the Commission, to comment on the evidence of the Commission," McCloy told Walter Cronkite as their in-studio interview began. "I think there is some question about the advisability of doing that. But I'm quite prepared to talk about the procedures and the attitudes of the Commission."

The Warren Commission, McCloy said, was not beholden to any administration. And each Commission member had his integrity on the line. "And you know that seven men aren't going to get together, of that character, and concoct a conspiracy, with all of the members of the staff we had, with all of the investigation agencies. It would have been a conspiracy of a character so mammoth and so vast that it transcends any – even some of the distorted charges of conspiracy on the part of Oswald."

McCloy insisted that the Warren Commission had done an honest job. Its Report may have been rushed into print a little too soon, he said, but the conclusions in it were not rushed. McCloy did, however, indulge in a little second-guessing. "I think that if there's one thing I would do over again, I would insist on those photographs and the X-rays having been produced before us. In the one respect, and only one respect there, I think we were perhaps a little oversensitive to what we understood was the sensitivities of the Kennedy family against the production of colored photographs of the body, and so forth. But . . . we had the best evidence in regard to that – the pathology in respect to the President's wounds."[28]

At the outset of this last installment of the *CBS News Inquiry*, Walter Cronkite had informed his audience: "The questions we will ask tonight we can only ask. Tonight's answers will be not ours, but yours." In wondering why America didn't believe the Warren Report, CBS asked two underlying questions: *Could* and *should* America believe the Warren Report? "We have found," Cronkite said at the program's conclusion, "that wherever you look at the Report closely and without preconceptions, you come away convinced that the story it tells is the best account we are ever likely to have of what happened that day in Dallas." He criticized the Commission for accepting, without scrutiny, the FBI and CIA denials that there was any link between Lee Oswald and their respective agencies. And he criticized *Life* magazine for its suppression of the Zapruder film, and called on Time-Life to make the film public. Nevertheless, Cronkite said that most objections to the Warren Report vanished when exposed to the light of honest inquiry. Compared to the alternatives, the Warren Report was the easiest explanation to believe.

"The damage that Lee Harvey Oswald did the United States of America, the country he first denounced and then appeared to reembrace, did not end when the shots were fired from the Texas School Book Depository. The most grevious wounds persist, and there is little reason to believe that they will soon be healed."

A week after this broadcast, on July 4, James Meredith walked into the nearly deserted courthouse square in Canton, Mississippi, about twenty-five miles north of Jackson. He sat down on the courthouse steps and remarked casually, "We made it." Eleven days and 162 miles after resuming his "March Against Fear," he had completed his journey. While the original destination was Jackson, he had said along the way that he might stop after Canton, where a year before a crowd of several hundred of his supporters, carrying on the march after Meredith was shot, were tear-gassed by Mississippi authorities.[29]

In the year between the shooting and the resumed march Meredith's assailant, Aubrey James Norvel, had come before the De Soto County Circuit Court. He was charged with assault with intent to kill. After Judge Curtis Swango denied defense motions to dismiss the charges, Norvell entered a surprise plea of guilty. Norvell, a former Memphis hardware salesman, was sentenced to five years in prison, with three years suspended.[30]

CBS News Inquiry: The Warren Report had the unexpected effect of improving the relationship between Maggie Field and her husband. While never discouraging his wife's work on the assassination, Joe Field never shared it, either. Most of those in their social circle came to view Maggie as obsessive on the subject of Kennedy; Joe, an outgoing man who loved being with people, began attending social functions by himself. "Maggie told us her heavy involvement in the case was the cause of the only extended period of tension in their marriage," Ray Marcus recalled. "But watching CBS's spurious documentary convinced Joe that Maggie had been right all along, and greatly eased the strain."[31]

While this was a welcome development, Maggie was at this time enduring a major setback with her book, *The Evidence*. It had been accepted for publication by Random House earlier that year and she had traveled to New York to sign a contract. By June she had received her first advance. Then, quite unexpectedly, Random House cancelled the contract. "The reason I was given was that the production costs were too great," Maggie said not long afterward. She conceded that the unconventional format of the book, with its lack of narrative and emphasis on facsimile documents, photographs, and other graphics, did pose certain production difficulties. Yet she did not think that was the real reason that Random House cancelled the contract. "They were in consultation with a production man in New York, and he was so excited about the book that he said, 'I will waive my fee, and take it in royalties, because I believe it is an important book. . . .' Then they still told me that there was a production problem. At that point I felt that I really couldn't accept that as a valid excuse."[32]

Léo Sauvage, whose Random House contract on *The Oswald Affair* had been broken two-and-a-half years before, was surprised to hear that Random House had broken another contract for a book on the same subject. Sylvia Meagher discussed it with him and reported back to Maggie. "He thought that as mere businessmen, they would be more prudent," she said. "He thinks there is less excuse for Random House in your case than in his, as his contract was signed before the Warren Report was published and before the issues were clearly arrayed." Sauvage believed Maggie might have enough leverage to force Random House to pay the balance of the advance stipulated in her contract, since she had fulfilled her obligations. It might even be possible through legal action, he thought, to force Random House to publish the book. "But he advises against it because it will cost a fortune in legal fees and because even if you succeeded, they would publish 'pro forma' and not promote or otherwise help the book."[33]

Sylvia urged Maggie not to give up. "No one could have deserved less the foul blow you have suffered at the hands of those rotten Random House people," she told her. "They are yellow-belly sycophants, handmaidens to LBJ, and they don't deserve the honor of publishing your work." Another firm would accept it, Sylvia assured her, and it would make an impact.[34]

As the summer wore on, the split among the critics over the Garrison investigation widened into a chasm. In July Ray Marcus sent to Sylvia Meagher a copy of his letters to Les Midgley of CBS and invited her to visit him in Boston, where he was living temporarily. She wrote back at length describing her workload, which between her professional responsibilities and preparing *Accessories After the Fact* for publication was very heavy. "I have explained this all in detail, lest you think that I am reluctant to accept your invitation because of our differences about Garrison. I remain hopeful that these differences will be very short-lived (whether I come to change my views, which I only wish I could, or whether you and the others change). And I would like in every way to protect my long and greatly valued and genuinely warm relationship with you, Vince and others, from being affected by differences on Garrison. Perhaps this is not realistic."[35]

Sylvia continued to go back and forth with Salandria over the question of Jim Garrison's credibility. "Let me try once again to explain my views on Garrison," she wrote to him. "I am willing to commit myself in writing, against the future risk of being proven wrong." She reiterated her position on the postal code – it was in error, but it was compounded by Garrison not admitting he was wrong. She was also unable to accept two key witnesses, Perry Russo and Vernon Bundy. Russo was the Baton Rouge insurance salesman who claimed he saw Oswald and Shaw at a party at David Ferrie's apartment in September 1963, while Bundy was the junkie who said he saw Oswald and Shaw together at the Lake Pontchartrain seawall several months before that. Sylvia was convinced they could not and should not be believed. Russo's story linking Clay Shaw to David Ferrie, Lee Oswald and an assassination plot was enhanced at Garrison's suggestion by the use of sodium pentathol, a "truth serum," and also by hypnosis. Bundy's story of witnessing a meeting he should have no reason to recall, told several years after the fact, was extremely dubious. "Their credibility was no greater than that of Markham, Brennan, and other WC witnesses whom all the critics rejected and denounced." Later she added that she was bitterly unhappy about the conflict between them, but that she could not and would not yield on what to her was a matter of principle. "On the day that I accept Russo and Bundy, I will also accept Markham and Brennan – and you may be sure that that will never come to pass."[36]

Salandria rejected outright the comparison between Russo and Bundy and Markham and Brennan. This was based in part on his personal experience. "Markham lied to me in the summers of 1964 and 1965 out of plain terror," he told Sylvia. "This terror she felt while she was doing business with the FBI, Secret Service and Dallas Police . . . Russo and Bundy have no such powerful protectors . . . Markham and Brennan provide lies which support a myth we know to be wrong. Russo's and Bundy's assertions support what we have to know is close to the truth." Salandria conceded that Russo and Bundy might be liars. "But they have not been proven to be so."[37]

In late July Penn Jones telephoned Sylvia to correct an error. He had recently informed her about the death of another assassination witness;

now he told her the witness was still alive. Then the subject of the Garrison investigation came up, and Sylvia expressed her contempt over the erroneous postal code. Chuckling, Penn said, "Do you expect Garrison to retract the cryptography publicly, just to satisfy *you*?"[38]

"No," Sylvia replied. "Just to satisfy the requirements of honesty and integrity."

"How can you criticize Jim Garrison? What do *you* know? You've never held public office."

"You've never asked what credentials I had for attacking the Warren Report. Those same credentials qualify me to dismiss Garrison as a fraud and a charlatan, and as a menace to honest criticism."

"You don't know what evidence he has," Penn replied, "and you don't even know any of his investigators."

"I know Tom Bethell – "

"Bethell is not one of the important ones – "

" – and when Garrison personally told me about some of his evidence, I had wondered if he was even rational."

They argued about Bill Gurvich, whose denunciations of Garrison in the media were so devastating. Penn insisted he was never a key figure in the DA's office, while Meagher countered that prior to his defection he was described by several critics who had been to New Orleans as Garrison's chief investigator.

Penn said she was running the risk of becoming completely isolated from the rest of the critics. "We must be working toward different objectives," he said. "I'm trying to save the country."

"I'm not working just to put a new set of liars into power. Garrison is a menace to the integrity and credibility of all of the critics."

"Well," Penn said at last, "good luck to you."

"And to you."

They both hung up.

Troubled by their conversation, Sylvia wrote to Penn Jones the very next day, apologizing for getting into the argument. "Our disagreement was not the first I have had on this subject – in fact, it was one of the mildest. You should have heard Ray and me, or Vince and me! Never mind, I am still friends with them, and with you, no matter how apart our feelings on Garrison. The prospect of 'being alone' does not worry me in the least." Many people still believed in the Warren Report because of their faith in Earl Warren. "The critics have spent four years trying to reach those people and tell them the facts. Are we now to subordinate facts and truth to faith in Mr. Garrison?"[39]

That summer Ray Marcus saw a movie called *Blow-up*, the first English-language film by the Italian director Michaelangelo Antonioni. The film was considered groundbreaking on several levels, including its depictions of nudity and recreational drug use. *Blow-up* is the story of a man named Thomas, a jaded photographer living in swinging London. One day he wanders through a park and sees a man and a woman secluded among some trees. He does not know them but assumes they are lovers; he takes a series of candid photographs. Back home in his darkroom, Thomas begins printing the pictures and becomes intrigued by a small detail in one of them. He prints a series of ever-larger blow-ups of the detail, which reveal a shadowy figure holding a pistol, hiding by a fence among the leaves near the two lovers. Further inspection reveals a body lying on the ground, and when Thomas returns to the park that night, he discovers the corpse.

The parallels between *Blow-up* and the #5 man detail were too close to have been a coincidence. "You had a grassy knoll. You had a picket fence," Marcus recalled years later. "And he blows it up, and there's the image." When Antonioni was in Los Angeles promoting the film, Marcus was able to meet with him; the director acknowledged having seen some of the Moorman details that appeared in several European magazines a year or so earlier. The articles had been written by Thomas G. Buchanan, one of the recipients of the Moorman press kits Marcus and David Lifton had sent out during the summer of 1965.[40]

Marcus had never stopped developing what information he could about the #5 man detail. The previous spring he had been surprised when the Massachusetts-based Itek Corporation, a leading photographic laboratory, announced that it had completed an analysis of the Nix film that proved there was no grassy knoll gunman. The image had first been publicized in the December 1966 issue of *Esquire* magazine, but was not the same Nix detail Marcus had found, which he felt corroborated #5 man. The Nix detail that Itek analyzed, Marcus believed, was extremely unconvincing. No recognized Warren Commission critic had ever promoted it; it was first identified by Jones Harris. Marcus was immediately suspicious. By this time the #2 and #5 man image details had been circulating for nearly two years. If the Itek study had been serious, it would have considered them, too. Itek, Marcus said, got at least sixty percent of its business from the federal government, and he wondered whether their analysis was done on its behalf. Perhaps the question had been raised so that it could be publicly discredited, thereby casting doubt on any similar story.[41]

In October 1967 Marcus published an article about the #5 man image in an alternative weekly called the *Los Angeles Free Press.* Antonioni had borrowed the notion of enlarged photographic details revealing stunning secrets, so Marcus borrowed the title "Blow-up" for his article. He told how David Lifton first noticed the five possible figures in the spring of 1965, and how the two of them had decided that the #2 and #5 man images were the most viable. He described sending copies to Robert F. Kennedy and RFK's seemingly favorable reply. He wrote about the Itek study and his suspicions about it, and described Robert Richter of CBS agreeing that #5 in particular was indeed a man hidden on the grassy knoll – and Richter's boss Les Midgley's inadvertently admitting he too saw the figure by calling it "the man who shot Meredith."[42]

But the opinions of a dozen photographic experts, whose judgments Marcus had solicited, were the article's most compelling feature. None of the experts, whose credentials included the Massachusetts Institute of Technology, UCLA, and the Jet Propulsion Laboratory, had been told that they were viewing an assassination photograph until after they had rendered an opinion, and none had been told what the other experts had concluded. Although only four of the twelve were willing to sign statements, Marcus reported,

> a total of ten said they believed that No. 5 was a man, their opinions ranging from "probable' to "positive." The remaining two said they could detect no discernible shape.
>
> Among those who were "positive" of the validity of No. 5, but who refused to sign a statement, was a photo analyst employed by a leading government-affiliated aerospace organization. He viewed the enlargements briefly and said, "You don't need an expert to tell you what's there – it's a man."[43]

After the article was published Joseph Ball, the Warren Commission attorney in charge of investigating what, if anything, happened behind the grassy knoll, was contacted by a Los Angeles radio newsman and asked to comment. Ball had not seen the *Free Press* article but remembered the photos. "Somebody sent me a picture two years ago so dark that I was unable to decipher anything out of it, and there's obviously no man in the picture."

"Well," the newsman replied, "the copies I saw of the picture were pretty darn convincing."

"Oh, Christ," Ball said, scornfully. "You can imagine anything. Did you ever take the Rorschach Test? You can see all kinds of things in shadows. Get a good picture of it, and examine it . . . there's no man there – that's a lot of damned nonsense."

Asked for a more thoughtful response for the record, Ball said, "I say it's nonsense, and there's no more [man] in there than anything else, and anybody can see one has got a terrific imagination. They ought to go to a psychiatrist. That's my reaction to it."[44]

The Garrison investigation produced no apparent strain between Maggie Field and Sylvia Meagher during the summer months of 1967, although Maggie supported the DA's work while Sylvia had stated her position was not negotiable. Some of Sylvia's statements on Garrison, so uncompromising to other critics, were softened in her letters to Maggie Field. "I am sorry that Garrison has decided to speak in the capacity of a WR critic full-fledged," she wrote on July 17. "I don't think his knowledge of the twenty-six volumes is complete or secure." In August she told Maggie she had heard that Salandria had been to New Orleans, had reviewed Garrison's evidence against Clay Shaw, and concluded that Garrison did not have much of a case. A few weeks later she told Maggie that insofar as Garrison was concerned, her overriding interest was that criticism of the Warren Report should continue if Garrison's case did not succeed.[45]

While Maggie Field remained a strong supporter of Garrison – she held a fundraiser on his behalf at her Beverly Hills home, and had agreed to travel to New Orleans as a representative of KPFK when the Shaw trial finally began – she did have some doubts, although whether they were ever expressed to Sylvia Meagher is not known. "I have feelings of uneasiness in a few areas," she confided to Vince Salandria. "I don't feel assured of the solid nature of his findings in spots – but I do feel that his intentions are right and that he does, indeed, have very significant evidence along certain lines." While Salandria conceded he had indeed said that Garrison had no case, he maintained he was speaking in a legal sense – that Garrison, on whom fell the burden of proof, would be unable to convince twelve jurors beyond a reasonable doubt of the charges against Clay Shaw.[46]

In the aftermath of its rejection by Random House, Maggie had begun revising *The Evidence* – a "complete and total revamping of each page," she said. The result, she was confident, was a much stronger and better book. She was working with a layout man to prepare new sections for a meeting she had scheduled with another publisher. She remained optimistic about her chances of getting it into print.[47]

Maggie had seen copies of the correspondence between Sylvia and Salandria in which the pair's opposing positions were clearly spelled out. "I was saddened by your letter to Vince," she wrote Sylvia. "I understand your feeling the need to send it. I just regret that circumstances necessitated your doing so." She expressed her hope that their differences were not irreconcilable.[48]

Yet the Garrison investigation was an unavoidable issue among the critics that summer, and by September Sylvia and Maggie were forced to confront it. "He has made some errors, but he is not a knave or a fool," Maggie wrote in early September. "This has been my position from the beginning and it is my position now. I think he has a case and I am willing to give him a chance to prove it." Sylvia wrote back a few days later and said she was happy that Maggie would be going to New Orleans for the trial; KPFK would be represented by one of the few people in the world who had complete mastery of the case. "If I can write you or call you at the time of the trial in order to say that your confidence was warranted, it will give me a satisfaction that I think will outweigh any distaste at having to admit that my estimate of the man and of his case were wrong." However far apart they might be over Garrison, Sylvia added, "we certainly have no differences in our desire for the truth about Dallas."[49]

It would be another year and a half before Clay Shaw would come to trial, but the relationship between Maggie Field and Sylvia Meagher, which began with a letter of inquiry to The New School but blossomed quickly to a warm and loving friendship, was nearing an irrevocable end. In mid-September Maggie and her husband traveled to New York for a meeting with a publisher. At the end of a long day Maggie telephoned Sylvia for what, it developed, was the final time.

"How was your day?" Sylvia asked.

"Well, there was a lot of running around, but nothing much to report," Maggie replied. "It looks as if I'll have to stay on after Joe leaves. I hate that; I'm such a coward about being alone in a New York hotel."

"This time I won't be able to be of much comfort to you, because this Garrison thing has created such an unbridgeable gulf between us."

"Yes," Maggie conceded. "It has."

"I beg you, Maggie, please consider how much you're compromising three years of work by your position on Garrison."

"What do you mean?"

"You're attacking, in your book, the lies of the Specters and Liebelers. But you're condoning the lies of Garrison."

"What lies? He's told no lies."

"Hasn't he?" Sylvia countered. "What about that foul fabrication of the telephone number code?"

"That was a mistake."

"What's the difference between the mistakes of the Specters and Garrisons?"

"They made so many . . . but I don't want to talk about it."

"If we can't talk about that, we have nothing to talk about at all."

"No."

"So be it. Goodbye."

"Goodbye."[50]

As she had after her argument with Penn Jones in July, Sylvia wrote Maggie a letter the very next day. But now her words were utterly uncompromising. "Our conversation last night merely formalized a de facto rift which neither of us was hitherto willing to verbalize. The worst of the rift is that it has been produced by differences so fundamental as to nullify our relationship in the past as well as in the present and the future. The intimacy and the loyalty between us were based on false assumptions each of us made about the other. I will not be a party to incriminating Oswald in the assassination on the lies and fabrications of the Warren Commission, or on the lies and fabrications of Garrison, and I intend to speak out against both of them and against their supporters and collaborators."[51]

A few days later Sylvia discussed this development with Harold Weisberg. "There has been a fatal rupture the other day on the issue of Garrison," she said. She described her last conversation with Maggie. "We had brief but bitter words." Weisberg said it wasn't right to call Maggie Field unprincipled. "What is between you and her and you and others is really your attitude toward Garrison. As I tried to tell you, I believe you should let history, not passion, write the answer. None of us knows what he really has or doesn't have."[52]

"I am afraid that, for the moment at least, nothing is to be done," Sylvia replied. "I did not call Maggie 'unprincipled' although you may consider that implicit in the remarks I did make. I would like to make it clear now that I do not believe for a moment that she ever does anything which she consciously knows to be unprincipled." But Maggie was using a double standard where Garrison was concerned. The postal code may have been an honest mistake, but he never retracted it and even repeated it after he knew it was wrong. "Is that an honest man? That code is no less dishonest and contrived than the single-missile hypothesis to which Specter gave birth . . . since Maggie was not willing even to discuss this with me, I could not see, as I said to her, that we could discuss anything." Much the same was true of Salandria, she said, although they had not had an explicit break. Her relationship with Ray Marcus was healthier, she said. "He at least acknowledges readily that he believes the ends justify the means."[53]

Sylvia continued to denounce Garrison to her fellow critics, most of whom were staunch supporters of the New Orleans investigation. She became estranged from all but a few of them. "It seems I have become the villainess of the piece," she told Marcus.[54]

Then, in the midst of this divisive controversy came a horrific intrusion. In early October Sylvia had written to Shirley Martin. "It seems a long time since I heard from you," she said. She had some news: *Accessories After the Fact* would be officially published on November 30, although she expected to have some advance copies before that date. She had split completely from Maggie Field and several others over Garrison. Garrison had accused an ever-wider range of people with involvement in the assassination; "he is bound to hit on someone who was really involved, if he names enough groups." The October issue of *The Minority of One* contained an unsigned anti-Garrison editorial which some thought Sylvia had written – although she had not.[55]

A few days later, Sylvia got a brief reply. "Sylvia, Sylvia," Shirley wrote. "I haven't forgotten you. I love you more than ever. Vickie is dead, killed in a terrible automobile accident. I think I am dead, too. Pray for us. Love, S."[56]

Vickie Martin, the beloved daughter who in 1964 had traveled to Dallas with her mother to interview assassination witnesses, who had secreted a microphone in her purse to tape record Acquilla Clemons and Father Oscar Huber, and who had later transcribed some of the recordings, died on September 12, 1967. She had been a passenger in a Volkswagen Beetle that was sideswiped by another car. The accident occurred as Vickie and a colleague named Candy were driving on their lunch hour. Vickie sustained twenty-four broken bones in the crash. The two young women were rushed to separate hospitals; Candy died the next day. Vickie lingered for four days before she too finally died. She was twenty-two years old.[57]

Sylvia called Shirley immediately to offer her condolences and support, then wrote to several other critics to tell them the news. "This is the greatest tragedy that Shirley could have suffered, and she needs her friends very much . . . I would give anything not to be giving you such horrible news."[58]

Shirley Martin was instrumental in Mark Lane's early work; it was she who initially put Lane in touch with Marguerite Oswald. Without her he might never have become as involved in the case as he did. During the early years of the case he had come to know the entire Martin family. In the fall of 1967 Lane was completing his second book on the Kennedy assassination, detailing his experiences as a Warren Commission critic. He called it *A Citizen's Dissent*, and he dedicated it to Vickie Martin.

Chapter 29

Single-Spaced Letters

In the fall of 1966, Mark Lane had identified the first phase of the assassination case as critics alerting the public to an erroneous Warren Report. The second phase, he went on, was doing something about it. Now, in October 1967, Ray Marcus said that like it or not, they were clearly in the Garrison phase; it remained the dominant issue among the critics throughout that fall. He told Sylvia Meagher he deeply regretted her severed relations with Maggie Field and hoped it was only temporary. But it was apparent now, he said, that the subject of Jim Garrison could not be ignored in conversations among critics.[1]

The publication date for *Accessories After the Fact* was getting close. Sylvia admitted to some anxiety as the book's appearance drew near. "I would be less apprehensive, I guess, if I still felt part of the 'group' which turns out to have been illusory," she confided to Shirley Martin. "Most of our colleagues are devotees of Garrison, which to me is practically the same as being apologists for the WR." Months earlier Sylvia had revised the ending of the book to reflect her views on the Garrison case. As originally drafted, the book included two appendices. One of them had been deleted. It was called "The Mystery of the Unanswered Letters," and documented her attempts in the summer of 1965 to get various Warren Commission personnel to comment in writing on questions she raised about the Report. The sole reference to these letters in the published book was in a footnote in its Foreword.[2]

The second appendix called for a new investigation into the assassination. Such a probe should begin with a complete re-evaluation of the evidence against Lee Harvey Oswald as presented in the Warren Commission's published record. "The new body must also be given access to the secret and suppressed documents of the Warren Commission. The 75-year time vault must be opened and its contents must be put before the new body – and, at the appropriate moment, before the public, within our lifetime." The investigation she proposed would, almost inevitably, point to the true assassins.

The American people have a debt to the memory of the slain President, and that debt has not been paid. If we do not rectify and rewrite this sordid page of our history, those who come after us will do it. We will have earned contempt and disgrace if we leave them a heritage so great in dishonor.[3]

This paragraph was cut from the published text and replaced with three paragraphs completed in June 1967. "In advocating a new investigation," she wrote, "I do not have in mind the inquiry in progress in New Orleans – even though it will not have escaped notice that District Attorney Jim Garrison of the Parish of New Orleans, in accusing anti-Castro Cuban exiles and CIA agents of complicity in the assassination, has postulated a theory which has much in common with the hypothetical construct" she had suggested earlier in the book – the "Batistiano exile/CIA conspiracy" she had described in March. Such a conspiracy, she had speculated, may have had the dual function of avenging the Bay of Pigs, blamed on Kennedy, and avenging a suspected double-agent, Oswald, who had tried to infiltrate the anti-Castro movement.

> But as the Garrison investigation continued to unfold, it gave cause for increasingly serious misgivings about the validity of his evidence, the credibility of his witnesses, and the scrupulousness of his methods. The fact that many critics of the Warren Report have remained passionate advocates of the Garrison investigation, even condoning tactics which they might not condone on the part of others, is a matter for regret and disappointment. Nothing less than strict factual accuracy and absolute moral integrity must be deemed permissible, if justice is, indeed, to be served.[4]

As fall deepened, Sylvia's relationship with Harold Weisberg, always rather uneasy, was becoming strained over Garrison. "I am weary beyond words of explaining why I regard this man as a menace to legitimate criticism," she wrote him at the end of September. Weisberg had told her that Garrison did not believe Oswald was part of the conspiracy to kill JFK. "Harold," she replied, "how else can one interpret the Garrison allegations about 'P.O. 19106' with which he links Oswald personally (not a mock-Oswald) to Shaw, whom he has accused?"[5]

Around that time, Weisberg's book *Oswald in New Orleans* was finally published. Its contents paralleled the Garrison investigation and contained a foreword written by the district attorney, which, although waiting for it delayed the book's appearance, Weisberg considered an excellent piece of writing. Curiously this foreword made no mention of either *Oswald in New Orleans* or its author.[6]

In Weisberg's chapter examining the testimony of Dean Andrews, Sylvia was surprised to come across several sentences she said were grossly unfair and highly prejudicial. "During the course of our widening disagreement on Garrison," she wrote Weisberg on November 1, ". . . you have often argued that I should suspend judgment until he has his day in court, until the judicial process has had the opportunity to function and the charges have been tested by cross-examination and fair trial . . . that being so, I was astonished to find in your book, *Oswald in New Orleans*, on page 107, the following paragraph:

> [Clay Shaw] attracted the greatest attention to the Trade Mart when he was arrested on March 1, 1967, charged with conspiracy to commit murder in the assassination. He was first publicized in connection with the assassination in *Whitewash*, where I brought him to light under the alias by which he was known to Dean Adams Andrews.

Meagher continued: "It is clear that in spite of your stated position on the need to await trial, and in spite of the entitlement of any accused person to the presumption of his innocence, you have already found Clay Shaw guilty of having used the alias Clay Bertrand (or Clem Bertrand) and, implicitly, of participation in the conspiratorial meeting with Ferrie and Oswald to which Perry Russo testified at the preliminary hearing. Your assertion has no foundation in fact or in law."[7]

When he read this, Weisberg was livid. "I would like to prevent your making enemies of all the friends you have, as you seem intent upon doing," he replied. He acknowledged the section of his book linking Shaw and Bertrand. But what Sylvia failed to point out, he said, was that starting on page 212 of *Oswald in New Orleans* Weisberg recounted Attorney General-designate Ramsey Clark's tacit admission, as reported in an Associated Press dispatch published in *The Washington Star,* that Shaw was Bertrand. George Lardner of *The Washington Post* acknowledged this and quoted an unnamed Justice Department source saying, of Shaw and Bertrand, "It's the same guy."

The Shaw case, Weisberg told Sylvia, belonged in court. "How dare you say, 'Your assertion has no foundation in fact or law' when the Attorney General made the statement and the Department of Justice reaffirmed it to two major newspapers, separately?"

At this juncture, Weisberg and Sylvia broke off communications.[8]

Like Sylvia Meagher, M.S. Arnoni had initially supported Jim Garrison's investigation but soon concluded that the DA in fact had nothing. But it was not until the October issue of *The Minority of One* that he editorialized against him. "The District Attorney's 'scientific' methods, such as administration of sodium pentothal, use of hypnosis and lie detectors on witnesses, hardly bespoke a man aware of the differences between scientifically determined evidence and black magic." He continued:

> At the same time, Mr. Garrison was ever more heavily relying on independent, private researchers of the published evidence. These people fall basically into two categories: students of the released Hearings and Exhibits of the Warren Commission and other related evidence, and political hypothesizers. Garrison wanted them all in his corner and carefully cultivated their friendship and support. He has been doing this with such determined solicitude as to suggest dependence on their work.[9]

Some of these critics, Arnoni wrote, did not demand from Jim Garrison the same objectivity they had criticized the Warren Commission for not having. Moreover the erroneous postal code deciphering and the defection of William Gurvich were disasters to Garrison's case. Although he did not mention her by name, Arnoni allowed that it was conceivable Garrison had been duped by a Lula Belle Holmes-style trap. If so he could, by virtue of his high public profile, do much damage to the critics' work. "Indeed, such precisely may have been the intent of whomever got Garrison into these deep waters in the first place." And yet, Arnoni reminded his readers, however counter productive Garrison might prove to be, the Warren Report was still discredited.[10]

Garrison himself replied to Arnoni's criticisms in a letter to the editor published in *TMO*'s November issue. "I really do not care greatly whether anybody thinks I am wrong or right about the assassination. Since I happen to be right, the problem is theirs and not mine." To this he appended a postscript that was twice the length of his letter. In it, he declared the postal code was still valid. Even had it not been, he was justified in pursuing it because it allowed his office to retain Clay Shaw's address book for its potential evidentiary value. As for Gurvich, "it is simply not true that he was my Chief Investigator and there really is no conflict about that point at all." Gurvich had volunteered his services and was never a paid member of the staff.[11]

Garrison concluded his lengthy postscript with the observation that he was the only public official to date to take a stand against the Warren Commission. "The point is that we are fighting and we are not going to quit and that we have found out what happened. This is all that is important."[12]

The December issue of *TMO* featured still more letters in response to Arnoni's October editorial. "If Garrison's case deserves any skepticism, it must be a benevolent skepticism," wrote Harold Feldman. "You cited the fake 'leads,' which were being foisted on the critics a few months ago with the probable intention of misleading and discrediting them. One obvious difference between such leads and Garrison's work is that he has, undoubtedly, and unerringly, located the plot to kill Kennedy in its actual locales and its evident milieus. Another difference is that Garrison has bet his life on the outcome."

Maggie Field also wrote of her dismay over the editorial. She conceded, as she had privately to Salandria, that there were troublesome aspects to Garrison's case. But she challenged Arnoni's assertion that "Garrison wanted [all of the critics] in his corner and carefully cultivated their friendship and support." This, Maggie said, was a total misrepresentation, "at least so far as I am concerned." Clay Shaw had been bound over for trial after a preliminary hearing and grand jury hearings, so Garrison should be allowed to proceed with his case "and to stand or fall on the evidence presented in a courtroom."

Léo Sauvage called the editorial "a refreshing and heartening reaction to the headlong plunge most of the ex-critics of the Warren Report have taken into District Attorney Jim Garrison's arms. I say ex-critics because the critics of the Warren Report have any valid existence as such only if their ethical, logical and factual standards are better than those of the Commission they criticize, or, for that matter, of the Dallas authorities."

But Penn Jones accused Arnoni of following "the pack of the hundreds of American editors screaming for Jim Garrison's scalp. For the first time John Kennedy's assassination is being investigated inside and under the rules of the American judicial system. This is the difference between Garrison and Earl Warren. If Garrison makes no case, I had rather hoped you would join me in a dark corner for a heartbreaking cry."[13]

This same issue of *TMO* also contained a review of *Accessories After the Fact* written by Conor Cruise O'Brien, an author, former Irish diplomat, and professor in the humanities at New York University. O'Brien had been asked to read *Accessories* as early as June 1967, originally so that he could provide a dust jacket quote. In September he told Sylvia Meagher he had not read the book as carefully as he would have liked but was impressed with what he had read. But his review, rather than reflecting a partial reading, was a careful analysis; O'Brien gave the book an enthusiastic endorsement. "*Accessories After the Fact* is not a case against the Report but a methodical and exhaustive critique of it . . . Mrs. Meagher does not conceal her feelings about these proceedings, but she keeps them well under control . . . her writing is lucid and crisp, touched at times by a dry wit, which one feels she would have liked to resist but which is almost imposed on her by the character, at once sly and ludicrous, of the Report itself. . . ."14

Accessories After the Fact: The Warren Commission, the Authorities and the Report was published at the end of 1967. The author dedicated the work to "the innocent victims of a society which often inflicts indignity, imprisonment, and even death on the obscure and helpless." Deleted from the published version were these lines:

> It is dedicated in particular to Lee Harvey Oswald, whom I believe to be innocent of the murders and crimes of which he has been accused by the Warren Commission.15

In spite of the differences over Garrison which led her to sever all ties with many critics who had been close to her, Meagher left untouched the book's acknowledgments which included expressions of gratitude to some of those with whom she was now at odds, including Vincent J. Salandria, Harold Weisberg, and Maggie Field. She also acknowledged Léo Sauvage, who provided the book's Introduction. Here Sauvage made much of the attacks directed at those critics who, especially in the earliest days, declared the Warren Report to be seriously flawed or worse. Commercial works touting the official lone-nut story, such as the mass market paperbacks of the Warren Report and William Manchester's *Death of a President*, typically made vastly greater profits while failing to provoke any debate on the merits of the Commission's case. Sylvia Meagher's work was another matter. "Of all the books written on the Kennedy assassination, including the Warren Report,

Accessories After the Fact comes closest to being *the* reference book on the subject."[16]

Sylvia had received one advance copy of the book on October 17. That was a Tuesday. By the end of the week she had received forty-one additional copies, which almost immediately she began distributing to friends and colleagues. "I have just finished your book, which arrived yesterday, and for which I thank you most sincerely," Ray Marcus wrote her on November 3. "It is, quite simply, a tremendous achievement. The fact that I profoundly disagree with the thrust of the final paragraph re: Garrison should not and does not alter my view that *Accessories* is clearly – and by a considerable margin – the finest book yet produced."[17]

"Your book is a milestone in the literature," Vince Salandria told her. "It is far and away the best done." L.A. Jones wrote to Sylvia on November 22. "What a damn day to write a letter," she said. Penn was at that moment off to Dealey Plaza to lead a moment of silence for President Kennedy, as he had for the previous few years, but L.A. had been unable to go with him. And so she used the time to write to Meagher. "Kid, I am an author's dream: I look up words in the dictionary; if momentarily I am distracted and lose the author's thought I go back several paragraphs and pick up the thread; and if I honestly genuinely like the book I will read it three, four, even five times. So your book is going to get pretty dog-eared." Similar praise came from Harold Feldman, Ed Epstein, Gaeton Fonzi, Joe Lobenthal, Philippe Labro, Thomas Stamm, Rep. Theodore Kupferman, and even United Nations Secretary-General U Thant.[18]

Maggie Field wrote in early November. It had been a month and a half since their harsh words over Garrison. Reading between the lines, Maggie's letter appears to be a more considered farewell to a once-cherished friend. She was thrilled, she said, to finally see the book in print. "I told you a long time ago that I felt it would be the definitive book on the subject. Although I have not read more than about one-third of it to date, I have no reason to qualify my original conviction. . . . You know that I wish you the fullest measure of success for your truly outstanding contribution to the cause in which we have both been engaged and to which we have both been committed for so long."[19]

Accessories After the Fact was critiqued in a double book review in *The New York Times Book Review* by Fred Graham, the same lawyer-journalist who had jointly reviewed *The Oswald Affair* and *Rush to Judgment* in

1966. The new review was called "Studies in Disbelief," and Graham
began with an argument the critics had been parrying since the beginning.
"[D]espite the fact that embarrassing gaffes by the Commission and
inconsistencies in the evidence have been pointed out, none of the critics
have been able to suggest any other explanation that fits the known facts
better than the Warren Commission's." Léo Sauvage had spoken to this
question in a 1966 radio interview when he said that in a trial, the prosecution bears the burden of proof; the defense is not obliged to provide
another suspect if the DA can't prove his case. Penn Jones had referred to
it in a 1966 interview with Louis Lomax. Sylvia addressed it in her
book's foreword: it was, she wrote, a "characteristic non sequitur" of
Warren Commission defenders.[20]

Graham acknowledged the widespread public doubts about the
Warren Report as if it were an American virtue and nothing more:
"Disbelief is a precedented form of political dissent in this country – the
old guard could never believe that FDR didn't know about Pearl Harbor
in advance." Warren Commission criticism was in this tradition. Sylvia
Meagher, he reported, had previously compiled a subject index to the
Commission's published data. "Unfortunately, her meticulous skills as an
indexer carried over to produce a book that is a bore . . . there is little
organization and no change of pace."[21]

The second book in this double review was Josiah Thompson's *Six
Seconds in Dallas*. This was the book on which Vince Salandria had
briefly collaborated before dropping out due to sharp disagreement
with Thompson over the nature of the President's throat wound. "Mr.
Thompson's method is to magnify, measure and analyze every available
shred of physical evidence of the fatal six seconds," which Graham
considered a novel approach. Thompson relied heavily on assassination
photographs, in particular on the Zapruder film, which Thompson called
the single most important piece of evidence in the case; he concluded that
at least three snipers fired at least four bullets at the presidential limousine. But Graham said it was a flawed technique: "By ignoring the larger
logic of the Warren Report, Mr. Thompson's analysis ultimately makes
little sense."[22]

Accessories After the Fact and *Six Seconds in Dallas*, Graham wrote,
might represent a "sweet climax" to the flow of anti-Warren Report
books. "Neither adds any important disclosures, and unless someone can
come up with a new slant, as Mr. Thompson did, further books would be
hard to justify." The release of X-rays and autopsy photographs of
President Kennedy, then expected in 1971, should confirm the Warren

Commission conclusion that only one bullet struck the President's head, and might even confirm the single-bullet theory. That would resolve the most controversial issues. "Time or politics must eventually take care of the rest."[23]

Just before Josiah Thompson's book was published, it was condensed in *The Saturday Evening Post*, which made it the cover story to its December 2, 1967, issue. The magazine's editor, William Emerson, commented that it was painful to relive the events of November 22, 1963, but necessary: "I think we remain dishonored until we solve the murder of our President." He was convinced the official solution was not correct, and that Thompson's work "demolishes the Warren Report."[24]

In the *Post* condensation, Thompson declared there was "much evidence that has either been overlooked or improperly interpreted." He described witnesses whose statements were problematic to the lone-gunman scenario, and asserted that at least three gunmen were involved; he offered a likely shot sequence based on the Zapruder film; he discussed Kennedy's wounds as described in the official autopsy. Kennedy's throat wound, he hypothesized, was caused not by a gunshot, but by "a bullet fragment, or more likely a bone fragment" from a wound to the head. There was great emphasis on how precarious it all made the Warren Commission's version of events, but Thompson stopped short of saying outright that there had been a conspiracy.[25]

> What does this collection of new evidence prove? It does not *prove* that the assassination was a conspiracy, and that two men were together on the sixth floor of the depository at the time the shots were fired. Nor does it *prove* Oswald's innocence. What it does suggest is that there are threads in this case that should have been unraveled long ago instead of being swept under the Archives' rug. It also shows that the question of Oswald's guilt must remain – four years after the event – still unanswered.[26]

During this period Ray Marcus and Vince Salandria began discussing Thompson's work and motivations. Marcus had been uneasy with Thompson since their chance meeting at *Life* headquarters in October 1966, when Thompson declined to look at *Life*'s high-quality Zapruder film slides. Marcus had hoped to convince him that President Kennedy was first struck at Zapruder frame 189, rather than between Z-210 and Z-225.[27]

But after Marcus saw the *Post* article he was outraged. It seemed to him that Thompson had used elements of his early work in several instances but not credited him. In particular, Marcus said Thompson used his discovery of Governor Connally's shoulder dip, visible in Z-238, which Marcus had written about in his "Hypotheses re: the Zapruder Film" completed in March 1965. He immediately wrote Thompson and accused him of plagiarism. "If you have any integrity at all, you will immediately exert your influence to see that the *Post* sets the record straight."[28]

A flurry of letters followed. Some were quite long and detailed. One by Ray Marcus, presenting his case in exacting detail, ran 23 single-spaced, typewritten pages. Lest his fellow critics think he was being petty and territorial, he pointed out that without his discovery of Connally's shoulder-dip, "there would be no conclusive proof indicating the frame at which Connally was hit, making it difficult if not impossible to disprove the Commission's essential single-bullet theory."[29]

Copies of these letters were sent to Salandria, M.S. Arnoni, Sylvia Meagher, and a few others. Meagher read them and replied, but her involvement was reluctant: her combined workload with the World Health Organization and promoting *Accessories After the Fact* was enormous, and made far more stressful by her elderly father's illness. She had just been with him in Miami and was prepared to return at a moment's notice should his condition deteriorate. Yet she told Thompson, "It verges on surrealistic comedy, or nightmare, that so many of us are writing so many long single-space pages, in order to pick so many nits . . . the temptation to say a plague on both your houses is not inconsiderable." She urged everyone concerned "to cool it, so that we can all go back to the real work that remains for all of us to do."[30]

Copies of Meagher's letter went out to Ray Marcus, Arnoni, and others. To Marcus, Sylvia added that "both Epstein and Thompson have made a solid, significant, and probably historic impact against the fraudulent Warren Report." Their overall contributions outweighed any shortcomings, she believed, "yet both have been the subject of bitter, dogmatic, and even vicious attack by other critics."[31]

By mid-December Marcus was beginning to think that there was more going on that just plagiarism. Perhaps Thompson was a covert federal agent. The more he thought about it, the more sense it seemed to make. Thompson, Marcus believed, consistently avoided obvious conclusions, such as his failure to state that three assassins, which Thompson postulated, meant there had to have been a conspiracy. His argument that a bone fragment caused JFK's throat wound went against evidence of a grassy knoll rifleman. And he seemed to enjoy easy access to major media outlets. Marcus shared this view with Vince Salandria, who said he was inclined to agree with him.[32]

Marcus was also suspicious about a meeting between Thompson and Sylvia Meagher in February 1967, which had taken place in Salandria's home. Maggie Field was present, but Thompson and Sylvia left her waiting in another room as they met behind closed doors for over two hours. Sylvia said there was nothing wrong with it. "What he did," she said, "was to offer me every single one of his findings – documents from the Archives and accounts of his interviews with Dallas witnesses." She could use any or all of it in *Accessories After the Fact*. Sylvia found that extraordinarily generous; surely Thompson was motivated by a desire to put all the facts before the public. By now openly skeptical, Marcus said Thompson was really trying to flatter Sylvia with special attention, and thereby win an important ally.[33]

When M.S. Arnoni heard the case against Thompson, he said it was nonsense. "In my considered judgment, the whole structure of the 'evidence' involved is classically psychological, bespeaking Thompson's pursuits in no way whatsoever, but rather reflecting the frame of mind of whomever begot the suspicion and proceeded to add 'convincing' details and deductions."[34]

Meanwhile Thompson's *Saturday Evening Post* article was well-received; many readers found it a revelation. "Thanks to Thompson and the *Post* for presenting meticulous medical data and eyewitness reports that clearly validate the re-opening of the case," wrote a Detroit reader. Another wrote, "Hopefully the members of the Commission were as deeply disturbed by Josiah Thompson's analysis as I was." Yet another wrote: "Though Mr. Thompson's article is not the answer, it does shed light on facts that should not be ignored." One letter was from Thompson himself. "It was not I, but Raymond Marcus of Los Angeles, who first noticed the buckle of the Governor's shoulder at Zapruder frame 238," he said.[35]

Ray Marcus and Sylvia Meagher kept going back and forth about Thompson. "I cannot take seriously the suggestion that Tink is a CIA plant," Sylvia wrote on January 11. "Nor can I in honesty agree that he has committed deliberate or inadvertent plagiarism." Increasingly upset, Marcus wrote another long, single-spaced letter on January 18; his comments were very direct and very harsh. When it came to Josiah Thompson, he said, Sylvia had relinquished any objectivity she may have had in the matter. But he was not disappointed because he had seen it coming. Thompson, he charged, had completed his objective of intellectual seduction. "You have been had, Sylvia – most outrageously and ingloriously had. In the midst of this historic struggle, in which you have made a magnificent contribution, you have chosen to turn your back on trusted and proven comrades." This was the most painful letter he'd ever had to write, he said, and he urged her to re-evaluate the entire matter.[36]

After mailing this letter, Marcus learned that Sylvia's father had just died. Horrified by the timing, he immediately sent off a telegram expressing his condolences. "I mailed you yesterday a brutally frank letter which I felt obliged to write. Although it was not written dispassionately I don't believe the contents were distorted by emotion, but I certainly would not have sent it now had I known of your father's death. In retrospect, even my knowledge that he was seriously ill should have dictated my delay. I sincerely apologize for the ill-considered timing."[37]

It was early 1968. Marcus and Sylvia would not be in contact again for more than five years.

After its *Saturday Evening Post* condensation, *Six Seconds in Dallas* was finally published. "I went on the usual book tour," Thompson recalled years later, "and in one major city, started being attacked as a CIA agent. And it became clear, within a day or so, that that charge was coming from Ray Marcus and Vince Salandria. Vince Salandria was the guy who started me in all this!"[38]

In March 1968, Salandria had written him a short letter. "I feel that you should know that I consider the data on whether you are a United States government agent or not incomplete, but that I entertain a suspicion at this time that you are," he told him. "It will be a pleasure to admit to you later, should you do work to rectify the damage which you have done by failing to confront the truth in the assassination, that I have been egregiously wrong about you."[39]

Thompson wrote back an even shorter reply: he told Salandria he was out of his goddam mind. But that was all right, he said; at times he wondered about his own sanity. "But a government agent? Jesus!"[40]

Chapter 30

The Trial

Nineteen sixty-eight was a tumultuous year in the United States, with the assassinations of Dr. Martin Luther King Jr. and Robert F. Kennedy and rioting at the Democratic National Convention in Chicago. But as far as the Shaw case went, it was a period of waiting.

Clay Shaw and Jim Garrison continued to generate much public interest, and the DA continued to be criticized in the media. In July *The New Yorker* published an article by Edward J. Epstein entitled simply "Garrison," a lengthy attack on the district attorney that portrayed him as a wild opportunist, and included unflattering references to Mark Lane, Harold Weisberg, Ray Marcus, and several other critics.[1]

Soon after the article was published, Penn Jones wrote in the *Midlothian Mirror* that "Epstein, author of *Inquest* . . . took one look inside Pandora's box, wrote a good book, and has been running scared from his book ever since its publication." Garrison, Jones said, was a brilliant attorney whose case was good enough to obtain grand jury indictments against Clay Shaw. He had also won a conviction against Dean Andrews for lying to the grand jury when he testified that Shaw was not the Clay Bertrand who had called him after the assassination to ask him to represent Oswald. "There are some people in this nation who feel that honesty and truth are the best protection for a democracy," Jones wrote. Epstein, he concluded, did not appear to be one of them.[2]

Epstein's article had stated that Ray Marcus influenced Garrison for the worse when he "came along with a blow-up of some trees and shadows on the grassy knoll, claiming that this revealed four gunmen in cowboy hats, and Garrison added four more assassins" to an ever-growing, increasingly absurd assassination scenario. Immediately, Marcus wrote to the magazine demanding a retraction: "The statement is false. I have never held the view Epstein attributes to me, nor have I made such a statement, verbal or written." Marcus's views on #5 man, he continued, had been published in *The Harvard Crimson* and the *Los Angeles Free Press,* and the image's validity had been confirmed by photo experts at MIT and UCLA. An academic of Epstein's stature, Marcus said, should have known that.[3]

Milton Greenstein, a *New Yorker* vice-president, wrote back promptly. "We see no warrant for printing any correction in connection with the statement quoted in your letter," he said.[4]

Earlier that year, Jim Garrison had been a guest on NBC's *The Tonight Show*. NBC was the network that had portrayed him so unfairly in 1967; it was required to grant him equal time to respond to its *White Paper* program. Garrison's appearance on *The Tonight Show* was arranged after Mort Sahl told host Johnny Carson, during an appearance of his own, that he was working as an investigator for Garrison, and that Garrison would make an interesting guest. He was the most important man in the country, Sahl said. One week later the DA was at the NBC studios in New York.[5]

While Johnny Carson's best years as host of *The Tonight Show* were still before him, both he and the program were already enormously popular. Thus Garrison's appearance was considered very important. Both Sahl and Mark Lane, each of them a seasoned media veteran, rehearsed him, asking some tough questions they thought could rattle him. The DA withstood the grilling, and Lane said later that he considered Garrison's performance on the program nearly flawless. "Jim got tremendous applause from the audience . . . it was the first time the American people had heard that kind of allegation on network television."[6]

As the show began, Carson said, "I felt, personally, as an individual, that enough theorists, including Mark Lane, Buchanan, and many many others – Weisberg – had proposed enough theories, and the American public was confused enough. And then about a year ago, the District Attorney of New Orleans, Mr. Jim Garrison, came up with something that kind of astounded the world, when he announced that he had solved the Kennedy assassination." Garrison was a different class of Warren Commission critic, Carson said, and so he invited him onto the show.[7]

Garrison was the sole guest that evening. Carson said he hoped they could have an informal discussion that would help illuminate what the New Orleans investigation was all about. Garrison said that was fine with him; Carson could ask anything he wanted, except for questions about Clay Shaw.

Throughout the program Carson played devil's advocate, defending the Warren Commission and its conclusions as Garrison tried to make his case. He read what he said was a chronology of events from the Garrison investigation that seemed to be at odds with one another: statements by the DA about different numbers of assassins shooting from different locations in Dealey Plaza, sponsored by different groups – Texas oil men, neo-Nazis, anti-Castro Cubans, the CIA. "Isn't that terribly confusing?" Carson asked. "And don't you seem to be riding off in all directions?"

"It seems like it, doesn't it?" Garrison replied.

"Yes, it certainly does."

"Right. Let me ask you first," Garrison continued, "how many hours do I have to answer this list you just went over?"

"Well, I don't – we have the rest of the program this evening – I understand that we can't sit here and completely re-create, or theorize on what happened. . . ."

Replying at length, Garrison said that his statements were really consistent, but they had not been presented consistently in the media. "In other words, there hasn't been a great deal of change in the matter as we see it in the last nine or ten months. Certainly, there have been refinements. My God; an investigation is a developmental thing. If we didn't know more about it now than we knew thirty days ago, then we wouldn't be doing much."

The real function of the Warren Commission, Garrison said, was to convince the American people that the assassination of Kennedy had been looked into and that the case was closed. He was no longer impressed by men with distinguished credentials and reputations. "The fact that [a man is] important in Washington doesn't mean a thing to me, because I've seen what the members of the Warren Commission did."

Although Carson repeatedly interrupted his guest, the DA was still able to make a number of important points. The Commission had failed to call many eyewitnesses whose statements to police indicated shots came from in front of the President. Certain witnesses said their sworn statements had been altered. The Zapruder film was being suppressed. And neither the Warren Commission members nor any of its staff had ever looked at any of the President's X-rays or autopsy photographs; moreover Commander James J. Humes, who led the autopsy, had burned his autopsy notes.

This seemed to catch Carson off guard. "Is that a fact?" he asked.

"Of course it is," Garrison shot back.

More than once, Carson demanded to know whether what Garrison was saying was a fact. Garrison said he wanted to show one of the methods the Commission used to conceal evidence. "Now again," Carson cut in, "when you say 'let me show you methods' – I hate to interrupt . . . but when you say, 'let me show you methods the Federal government used to distort,' that is not a *fact*, is it? Isn't it what your opinion is? Or just the way you think it happened?"

"Now, you understand that I'm a human being," Garrison replied. "And it's very difficult for any human being, including a scientist, to speak with total objectivity. So when I say, 'let me show you some examples of how distortion was accomplished,' obviously, these are examples of how I *think* it was accomplished."

"All right."

"You may or may not agree."

"All right. That's what I wanted to make clear."

As the program drew to a close, Garrison told Carson, "I am trying to tell you that there is no question, as a result of our investigation, that an element of the Central Intelligence Agency of our country killed John Kennedy, and the present administration is concealing the fact. There's no question about it at all."

"That is your opinion."

"No, it is not; I *know* it, and if you will just wait, you will see that history will support this as fact."

When Carson said that Garrison's evidence still had him confused, the DA spoke more bluntly than he had before. "I'm trying to tell the people of America that the honor of this country is at stake. And if we don't do something about this fraud, we will not survive, and there is no way to survive if we do not bring out the truth about how our President was killed four years ago. And the investigation by the Warren Commission wasn't even close."

On the first day of June 1968, Sylvia Meagher wrote a letter to Clay Shaw. Shaw was probably already aware, she told him, that she considered Jim Garrison a dangerous charlatan and an unscrupulous demagogue; she was convinced that Shaw was completely innocent of all charges against him and that he was being unjustly victimized. Yet she was disturbed to hear that Shaw's attorneys were petitioning the Federal District Court in New Orleans to rule that the Warren Report was a valid, accurate, and binding document. Should the petition with respect to the Report's status be seriously considered by the District Court, she said, "I would consider it my urgent and foremost duty to seek to testify, as a friend of the Court, as to the fraudulent character of the Report, and to urge my fellow-critics to do the same." She urged Shaw to have his attorneys discard that strategy.[8]

Shaw replied a month later. "As for the Warren Report," he said, "I see no reason why I should not introduce it as evidence, since it contradicts in important particulars, the theories and fantasies which Garrison will undoubtedly produce in court. It is, after all, an official government document. . . ." He complimented her on *Accessories After the Fact*, but added she had become "bogged down in minutiae."9

In between the writing of these letters, Robert F. Kennedy was shot at near point-blank range after delivering a victory speech in the California presidential primary election. He died early the next morning. As with JFK's murder, this assassination was blamed on a lone nut.

A few days after Robert Kennedy was shot, Vince Salandria spoke at a rally in New York's Central Park, held in memory of RFK, his brother JFK, Dr. Martin Luther King, Jr., and Malcolm X. Salandria sensed a relationship among these murders. "People, how can it be that diverse madmen, such as the candidates we are asked to accept as the murderers of the four martyrs whom we honor today, are so focused in their madness that they shoot only those great men who are joined with one common thread – dedication to sparing mankind from the oppression and violence visited upon it by our warlords?"10

President Kennedy's assassination, he said, was a foreign policy killing done at the behest of the U.S. military, and carried out by operatives of the Central Intelligence Agency. After the assassination Kennedy's announced intention of withdrawing American troops from Vietnam was reversed. "I submit that the military fired John F. Kennedy," Salandria said. Kennedy himself said it could happen. Salandria read a portion of a book called *The Pleasure of His Company* by Paul Fay, the former Undersecretary of the Navy and JFK's longtime friend. "It's possible," Fay had quoted Kennedy. "It could happen in this country, but the conditions would have to be just right. If, for example, the country had a young President, and he had a Bay of Pigs . . . then if there were another Bay of Pigs, the reaction of the country would be, 'Is he too young and inexperienced?' The military would almost feel that it was their patriotic obligation to stand ready to preserve the integrity of the nation. . . . Then, if there were a third Bay of Pigs, it could happen. But it won't happen on my watch." There was a Bay of Pigs in which the CIA betrayed President Kennedy, Salandria said. There was a detente with Russia, followed by a test ban treaty which encountered heavy military resistance. And when Kennedy sought to change United States policy in Vietnam, he was himself fired by the military – killed on his watch. "Upon his death, the military became the dominant force in our government."11

The CIA, Salandria warned, was promoting disorder and chaos in the United States – was, in short, using a divide-and-conquer strategy as a means of keeping American citizens confused and unorganized. He called on everyone to continue the unifying work of the Kennedys, King, and Malcolm X. "If we do not quickly join together, brothers, the guns will pick us off one by one, and join us together – in death. This is the lesson to be learned from the killing of President Kennedy, Malcolm X, Martin Luther King and Senator Kennedy."[12]

Salandria was in intermittent contact with Sylvia Meagher through 1968. Their differences over Garrison by now well established, these contacts were brief and often icy, as when Salandria telephoned her on the evening of March 9, a period when the Orleans Parish grand jury was still in session. "Have you heard the news?" he asked.

"No."

"A judge has ordered Allen Dulles to testify, and I'm calling to ask if you would be willing to cooperate and help prepare his examination."

"No," Sylvia answered, "I would not."

There was a long silence. Finally Salandria continued, "Uh . . . well, how are you?"

"I am very well, thank you."

Another silence followed.

"Well," Salandria said at last, "good-bye."

"Good-bye."[13]

Dulles never did testify.[14]

Later in the year Salandria wrote Sylvia a short note. "I get the urge to try to get in the last words in an argument with a woman," he said. "Our differences over Garrison notwithstanding, you, Sylvia Meagher, are eloquent, brilliant, consistent, honest, brave, stubborn, selfless, tough, and I love you."[15]

This note went unanswered, but Salandria soon followed it up. "May I have a final, final word?" he wrote. A man that both he and Sylvia had been in contact with nearly two years before had, in fact, been a government agent, he informed her. "This species apparently abounded in our work. If we ever talk again, and let me make it clear that I am always willing to talk to you, I will tell you what I learned and show you some supporting documents on this ugly subject."[16]

This time Sylvia responded, and within just a few days. Salandria's declaration about a presumed agent among them was not surprising, she said. Salandria had accused so many: "Epstein, Thompson, Jacob Cohen, William Gurvich . . . not unnaturally, then, the cry wolf may not raise any hackles even if a real one is finally in the chicken coop."

She had not answered his previous letter, she said, in order to grant him his apparent desire to have the last word with her. "But perhaps I should make it clear that no question of unwillingness to talk is involved on my part – it is just that I do not know what we can talk *about.* 'Our differences on Garrison' cannot be, so far as I am concerned, 'notwith-standing.'"

She concluded her reply with what she called melancholy news. M.S. Arnoni had been forced to suspend publication of *The Minority of One* due to financial difficulties. He and his family had, in fact, left the United States and relocated to Israel.[17]

Shortly before the Clay Shaw trial was scheduled to begin, apparently eager to re-establish their relationship with Meagher, Salandria wrote again. "Think over this proposition," he said. "After the Jim Garrison matter is over, win or lose, let's make up."[18]

This short note irritated Sylvia Meagher considerably. "You misunderstand me so persistently that I can only think that you don't wish to understand me," she replied a few days later. "I don't look on the 'Jim Garrison matter' as a game, a gamble, a sporting event, or as enter-tainment. After it is 'over,' as you put it, the 'code' will still be a clumsy and unconscionable fabrication. . . . I will still find it dismaying and frightening as well as incomprehensible that anyone who claims to be striving for truth and justice in the assassination could aid and abet a hysterical, unscrupulous half-wit like Garrison." Should Garrison win the case, she continued, it would mean another innocent man sacrificed by the State for its own purpose.

"The relationship I had with you and one or two others was built on comradeship, unselfishness, trust, and love rarely experienced in life. If you miss our friendship, how much more do I miss it, having lost the other friendships as well? But I must live with myself, even if I live apart from everyone who has ever been dear to me. This is no capricious personal tiff, to be erased by agreeing to kiss and make up . . . please try to understand me this time, Vince. I am in dead earnest."[19]

At this time the Shaw trial was at long last getting underway. After some 1,400 prospective jurors had been screened, an all-male jury was seated by February 5, 1969.[20]

After they were sworn in, Criminal District Judge Edward A. Haggerty accompanied the twelve jurors and two alternates to a nearby motel, where they were photographed by the media. Haggerty offered racetrack passes to some of the reporters before retiring to the motel bar for a drink. As he sipped a scotch, the jurist told reporters that although Clay Shaw was charged only with conspiracy, he would allow the prosecution to present evidence relating directly to the Kennedy assassination. "If [the prosecution] wants to overprove its case, that's its business."[21]

Even as Clay Shaw's criminal trial was beginning in New Orleans, a related legal battle was playing out in Washington, D.C.: the concluding episodes of Jim Garrison's attempts to secure the still-secret JFK autopsy photographs and X-rays. They had been given to the National Archives by the Kennedy family in October 1966 with the stipulation that until 1971 they could be seen only by government investigators and experts approved by the Kennedys. After that they could be seen by recognized experts in pathology or related fields.[22]

These terms had stymied Theodore Kupferman, the Republican congressman who had introduced a resolution calling for an official review of the Warren Commission's findings. In late 1966 Kupferman petitioned the Archives for a review of the X-rays and autopsy photographs by himself and three others: Sylvia Meagher; Dr. Cyril Wecht, the Pittsburgh forensic pathologist who had studied the autopsy findings for the American Academy of Forensic Sciences; and Dr. Milton Helpern, medical examiner of New York City. Kupferman's petitions were denied.[23]

It was critical, Jim Garrison believed, to get access to the autopsy photographs and X-rays and introduce them as evidence in Shaw's trial. Legally, these materials were in the custody of Dr. James B. Rhoads of the National Archives. The DA obtained a court order for them in May of 1968, but authorities in Washington, D.C., declined to serve Dr. Rhoads with a subpoena. The legal skirmish that ensued dragged on for many months. In early January 1969 federal judge Charles Halleck ordered Dr. Rhoads to appear before him to explain why he should not have to provide Garrison with the autopsy materials. But on the eve of Dr. Rhoads' scheduled court appearance the government announced that a panel of medical experts, secretly appointed by Attorney General Ramsey Clark a year earlier, had reviewed the autopsy photographs and X-rays and said they confirmed the conclusions of the Warren Commission.[24]

Harold Weisberg was due to testify as an expert witness on the same day Rhoads was to appear before Judge Halleck. But after getting news of the Clark Panel announcement, his strategy was revised. Weisberg stayed up until 3 a.m. reviewing the Clark Panel material with attorney Bud

Fensterwald, who was handling the Washington case for Garrison, and Garrison assistant Numa Bertel. Weisberg concluded that the new Clark material proved nothing. The new strategy, he recalled, was to put him on the stand and have a scripted exchange with Bertel, who would ask: "Have you studied the autopsy report?" Weisberg would reply, "Which one? The one the doctor burned, the one he turned in, or the one the government turned out, none of which agrees with the others?" That, Weisberg believed, was sure to get Judge Halleck's interest.[25]

But at the last minute Garrison's chief assistant DA telephoned Bertel and ordered him not to put any witnesses on the stand. To do so would amount to arguing a Louisiana case in a Washington court. "It was so frustrating!" Weisberg recalled. He could hardly believe it. He considered Judge Halleck honest. He was about to take the stand and had the pertinent documents with him. The keeper of the autopsy photos and X-rays, Dr. Rhoads, was in court. Weisberg was sure they would destroy the Warren Report, or at least the autopsy report, but were thwarted by those who needed the very pictures and X-rays they sought.[26]

Weisberg came to believe that Vince Salandria, then in New Orleans and available to Jim Garrison and his staff, had influenced the decision. "For the first time, in a court of law – and in Washington! – we had a chance of doing what had never been done and what had never before been possible, and you prevented it!" he angrily rebuked. "You saved the government and its henchmen."[27]

Salandria denied having counseled Garrison. In any case, Garrison still had another move to make.[28]

In New Orleans, Garrison's opening statement in the Shaw trial was delivered on February 6. "The defendant is charged in a bill of indictment with having willfully and unlawfully conspired with David W. Ferrie, Lee Harvey Oswald, and others, to murder John F. Kennedy," he told the jury. The murder had been planned during the summer and fall of 1963 at two parties held in New Orleans.[29]

Garrison said the prosecution would disprove the Warren Report's lone-assassin thesis. Defense lawyer Irvin Dymond objected: "The Court has repeatedly ruled that the actual assassination in Dallas has no place in this case." Judge Haggerty overruled the objection, reiterating that if the prosecution wanted to overprove its case, it was free to do so.[30]

In his own opening remarks, Dymond said that he would not be defending the conclusions of the Warren Report. "That is not this case at all, and should not and is not to be confused with the issues in this case." Rather, he would "strike at the very core of the State's case – that is, the alleged conspiratorial meeting between David Ferrie, Lee Harvey Oswald, and Mr. Clay Shaw." The meeting, Dymond said, never took place, and the man who said it did, prosecution witness Perry Raymond Russo, was a liar.[31]

In addition to Russo and Vernon Bundy, the witnesses Garrison intended to put on the stand included residents and elected officials from the small town of Clinton, Louisiana. They would testify to seeing Shaw, Ferrie and Oswald together in Clinton during the summer of 1963 at a CORE-sponsored voter registration drive.[32]

Another possible witness was a man Garrison had interviewed before the start of the trial. Richard Case Nagell claimed he was a federal intelligence agent for a super-secret spy agency he would not identify. He had learned of a plot against the life of President Kennedy in the summer of 1963, Nagell said. Among those he had been in contact with that summer was Lee Harvey Oswald. After his warnings to the FBI were inexplicably ignored, Nagell began to fear he was being drawn too deeply into the plot, so he fired his pistol inside a federal bank in El Paso, Texas. This, he hoped, would earn him a short stretch in jail – just long enough to provide an airtight alibi when the assassination occurred. Instead he spent nearly five years behind bars.[33]

Nagell had been out of prison for only a few weeks when he met with Garrison in May 1968. Garrison flew to New York to meet with him in person. Although the DA was impressed with Nagell's account, and he went to New Orleans prepared to testify, in the end Garrison elected not to call him as a witness. Nagell remained adamant about not identifying the agency he had worked for, and Garrison concluded that the defense would destroy him on cross-examination. "One such incident, one such discrediting, is all it takes to undo an entire case," Garrison said.[34]

And yet the case was largely undone by one such witness. "The bomb that shattered our case exploded quickly enough," Garrison recalled long afterward. "His name was Charles Spiesel." Spiesel, an accountant from New York, was a surprise witness when he took the stand on February 7. His testimony was much like Perry Russo's: He too had been at a party in the New Orleans French Quarter, he said, and heard Clay Shaw and David Ferrie casually discussing a plan to assassinate JFK. That was in June 1963. But on cross-examination, Spiesel said he was sometimes hypnotized and tortured until he revealed unspecified confidential information. He did not always know who was doing the hypnotizing.

Furthermore he sometimes fingerprinted his daughter before she went off for school so that, he said, he would know that when she returned she was not an imposter.[35]

The following day Spiesel led the fourteen jurors, Judge Haggerty, lawyers for the prosecution and defense, and even Clay Shaw through the French Quarter in a search for the apartment where the alleged party took place. Spiesel led them all to an apartment at 906 Esplanade, where the scene escalated into near-chaos. Photographers and curiosity seekers converged outside the building and a traffic jam grew to monumental proportions. Spiesel said the apartment was probably the one at which he attended the party.[36]

It appears not to have come out at the trial, but it was later reported that the building Spiesel led the jurors to was once owned by Clay Shaw. At the time of the party Shaw also owned an adjoining property at 908 Esplanade, and both of these properties neighbored Shaw's own residence at 1313 Dauphine Street.[37]

Perry Russo, who had testified to the grand jury in 1967 that he heard Shaw, David Ferrie, and Lee Harvey Oswald at a party discussing a plot to assassinate Kennedy, testified at the trial on February 10 and 11. He told essentially the same story, but as it was reported in the press, Russo seemed to have some doubt about whether he did, in fact, hear a conspiracy under discussion. Under cross-examination Russo said that he had come under enormous pressure after coming forward as a witness, and all the pressure had led to some self-doubt. "I said all these people are pressing me and saying I am wrong and inaccurate and other things, that it was hard to tell whether he was there or not."[38]

Garrison's case against Shaw was seriously damaged, but powerful moments remained. On February 13, for the first time ever, the Zapruder film was given a public showing. Garrison had had to subpoena *Life* to obtain it. The film was screened at least five times, drawing loud gasps from the crowded courtroom as President Kennedy's head was shown being blown to bits. *New York Times* reporter Martin Waldron wrote that "the President appeared to be knocked backward against the rear seat" when he was hit in the head, and that Garrison was arguing that this proved Kennedy was shot from the front.[39]

Penn Jones said there was no other way to interpret the film. He had seen it first during the trial, and wrote in the *Midlothian Mirror*: "No sane person can see that film and still protest that Kennedy was shot only from the back . . . it is the most important little piece of film ever exposed on this planet."[40]

Garrison was ordered by *Life* magazine not to copy the film. But when asked years later whether he had, he replied, "Hell yes, I did!" In fact, Garrison, Mark Lane, and Penn Jones all arranged for bootleg copies of the Zapruder film. Jones even sold inexpensive copies, and included order forms in subsequent editions of *Forgive My Grief*.[41]

By the time of the Shaw trial the question of missing Z-frames 208-211 had been resolved, if not satisfactorily. Early in 1967 *Life* announced it would release the missing frames, and late that year they appeared in Josiah Thompson's *Six Seconds in Dallas*. Ironically, *Life* had denied Thompson permission to use the remaining Zapruder frames in the book, and on advice of counsel he used sketches instead. Nevertheless *Life* sued, claiming copyright infringement, but lost its case.[42]

Roger Craig, the Dallas Deputy Sheriff on duty in Dealey Plaza at the time of the assassination, testified at the Shaw trial. He told the jury he saw Lee Oswald flee the murder scene by car some fifteen minutes after the shooting. He later saw Oswald in custody at police headquarters and identified him as the man he had seen escape the building. "He said that the station wagon belonged to Mrs. Paine," Craig testified, meaning Ruth Paine. But Oswald had added, "Don't try to drag her in this." Shortly after this, Craig said Oswald had leaned back in his chair and said dejectedly, "Everybody will know who I am now."[43]

In Washington, D.C., the matter of the autopsy photographs and X-rays was nearly settled. These materials, Garrison contended, would prove that JFK had been struck from at least two directions and thereby prove there had been a conspiracy in his assassination. Garrison had sought the opinions of several expert witnesses, including Dr. Cyril Wecht. After Garrison obtained an additional court order for archivist Rhoads to appear before Judge Halleck, Wecht took the stand on Friday, February 14 and testified to the relevance of such autopsy records to any homicide investigation. That same day Halleck ruled that Wecht must be allowed to inspect the autopsy photos and X-rays, and gave the government until the following Monday at 4 p.m. to allow him to examine them.[44]

On Monday government lawyers informed Judge Halleck that Dr. Wecht could not see the photos and X-rays. The judge, in turn, signed a court order directing Dr. Rhoads to produce the materials at Shaw's trial in New Orleans within 48 hours. The government appealed. But before the matter could fully play out in court, the prosecution rested its case against Clay Shaw. Garrison informed the Justice Department that the materials were no longer needed by the State of Louisiana.[45]

It would take another three years, but Dr. Wecht would eventually see the JFK autopsy materials. He was the first Commission critic allowed to see them, but when he did, he would report that the late President's brain, along with microscopic slides of tissues taken from his wounds, were not among the materials in the National Archives. No one seemed to know why.[46]

A key prosecution witness was Aloysius J. Habighorst, the New Orleans police officer who booked Clay Shaw after his arrest on March 1, 1967. Officer Habighorst testified that during this procedure, he asked a series of routine questions, such as name and date of birth, and any other names the arrested man was known by. Habighorst said that Shaw had told him "Clay Bertrand." That name did in fact appear on Shaw's fingerprint card, which Shaw had signed. But Shaw, who took the stand shortly after Habighorst, insisted that the fingerprint card he signed had been blank, implying that the information on it – including the damning "Clay Bertrand" alias – was filled out afterward. Habighorst, Shaw said, had asked him no questions. Shaw's attorneys argued that in any case, if Habighorst had asked the routine questions and filled out the card, he had done so when Shaw's attorneys were not present, which was a violation of Clay Shaw's rights; they asked the judge not to allow Habighorst's testimony.[47]

Judge Haggerty ordered the jury to leave the room when he announced his decision on this matter. "He did not forewarn Mr. Shaw of his right to remain silent on an inculpatory statement such as 'do you have an alias?' So even if Officer Habighorst is telling the truth about what he did testify to – and I doubt it very seriously from all the circumstances – "

Assistant DA James Alcock was shocked. "Your Honor!" he protested.

"Wait a minute. Let me finish my reasons for ruling."

"Are you passing on the credibility of the State's witnesses in front of the press and the world?"

"The jury is not hearing it, that is the main thing; the whole world can hear it. I do not believe Officer Habighorst, I do not believe him – "

"If Your Honor please – " Alcock pleaded.

"Let me finish my reasons for ruling."

"I move for a mistrial."

"Mistrial is denied."[48]

But it was already too late for the prosecution. On March 1, two years to the day since his arrest, the jury acquitted Shaw after deliberating for less than one hour.

Not long after the verdict was reached, one of Shaw's defense lawyers said that if the defense team had not succeeded in getting information about Charles Spiesel's background, Clay Shaw might well have been convicted. Garrison agreed that the testimony of Charles Spiesel had been particularly devastating but felt his case was sabotaged by a "clandestine operation" of the opposition – presumably the CIA. "Destroying an old-fashioned state jury trial," he ruminated, "was very much like shooting a fish in a barrel with a shotgun." Even Judge Haggerty had his doubts; long afterward, he said he believed Clay Shaw had lied under oath and "pulled a con job on the jury."[49]

Nevertheless Clay Shaw, who all along had denied the charges against him, was a free man. And rightly or wrongly, the verdict was perceived by many as a complete vindication of the Warren Commission's lone-assassin conclusion.[50]

Watching from a distance, Sylvia Meagher took no pleasure from the verdict, in spite of her complete agreement with it. A week after it ended she completed a blistering critique of the trial, an article she called "Not with a Roar but a Whimper: The Shaw Trial, the Garrison Wreck." The prosecution's case, she said, had been humiliatingly rejected.

> A "surprise witness," Charles Spiesel, a New York City account-ant, probably surprised the prosecution more than anyone else . . . as rich as this testimony was in comic pathos, it was no help to Garrison that he placed so ridiculous a witness on the stand – with, or with-out, prior knowledge of his case history.
>
> Finally, Perry Russo himself, the indispensable witness but for whom there could be no "case" against Clay Shaw, delivered the coup de grace to Garrison by recanting those parts of his earlier testimony which were crucial for the incrimination of Shaw as a conspirator. . . .
>
> But it was not Shaw alone who was on trial at New Orleans. All parties agree on this one thing at least – that Garrison used the trial to place the Warren Report (WR) in the dock. Indeed, there are some among his adherents who always believed that his charges against Shaw were nothing but a device by which the WR evidence could be tested for the first time in a court of law (and they condoned this means – the pillorying of an innocent man – to that necessary and desirable end).

The prosecution did succeed – "almost in spite of itself," Meagher said – in casting serious doubt on the Warren Commission's case. It made good use of the Zapruder film; even the press acknowledged that JFK was thrust backward by a shot that supposedly originated from behind. And assassination eyewitnesses gave testimony that had an impact on the jury, such as William and Frances Newman, who had not been called to testify before the Warren Commission. They both described gunfire they believed came from behind them on the grassy knoll, causing them to throw themselves to the ground and shield their young children with their bodies. The testimony most damaging to the Warren Report, Sylvia said, was in the cross-examination of defense witness Pierre Finck, one of the three autopsy surgeons at Bethesda. Dr. Finck said that top military brass were present at the autopsy, and that one of them had declared himself to be in charge of the proceedings. A Navy admiral told the surgeons not to dissect the neck wound to determine the path of the bullet that made it. And though Dr. Finck said he was positive one of the President's wounds was one of entry, an admiral told the doctors to describe it as "presumably of entry."[51]

The problem was linking Clay Shaw to all of this – something Garrison utterly failed to do.

> The repugnant spectacle of Garrison's trial of Clay Shaw, and the opportunism or defection of critics and pseudo-critics of the WR, confirms me in the conviction I first expressed in September 1967 in a letter to *The New York Review of Books:* that one is not obliged to take sides in gang warfare in which both factions – the Warren Commission, and the New Orleans District Attorney – have nothing but contempt for truth.[52]

In the opinion of Penn Jones, "Jim Garrison carried the ball as far as he could." Jones had been critical of certain aspects of Garrison's handling of the case, but remained a supporter even after the case came to its controversial end. He was troubled by a theme that emerged afterward:[53]

> "Yes, Garrison has proved a conspiracy, but Clay Shaw was not involved." How can one who cares for his country make such a statement in casual conversation? It could just as properly be restated: 'Yes, Earl Warren, Chief Justice of the United States, and his six associates on the Warren Commission lied and perjured themselves, but Clay Shaw was not involved." When a democracy has died, tears should be shed.[54]

Jones was in sharp disagreement with Garrison over the matter of Bill Boxley, a former CIA agent who was hired as a Garrison investigator in April 1967. His real name was William Wood, and he said he had not worked for the CIA since 1953, when he had been fired for alcoholism. In the years since, he had dried out and become a journalist. At the time he approached Garrison Wood was working for a newspaper in Austin, Texas. Garrison thought he would be a useful addition to his staff and hired him, but had him use the name Boxley after deciding it was best to keep it quiet that there was a former CIA man on his staff.[55]

In late 1968 Garrison fired Bill Boxley on the grounds that he not only still worked for the CIA, but had been planted in Garrison's office with the goal of discrediting its investigation. Boxley had apparently pushed for the arrest of a man named Robert Perrin, a gun-runner who reportedly committed suicide in 1962. Boxley said Perrin was in fact still alive. According to Jones, Harold Weisberg and Vincent Salandria both became suspicious of Boxley over his investigation of Perrin and urged Garrison to fire him. Jones, however, said he was certain that Boxley's investigation was legitimate. Years later Weisberg told an interviewer that Boxley was, in fact, loyal to Garrison. Garrison himself remained convinced that Boxley had infiltrated his office to destroy his case; he credited Salandria with seeing through Boxley's facade.[56]

Garrison's case suffered another setback when Tom Bethell, the Englishman he hired who had made early contacts with many of the critics, gave the prosecution's list of witnesses to the defense, which under Louisiana law Garrison was not obligated to do. Confronted with his treachery six months later, Bethell made a weeping confession to other Garrison staffers. But when he recalled it in 1975, Bethell was almost boastful: "After a while it became clearer and clearer that [Garrison] had no case at all...and I ended up betraying Garrison to Shaw's attorneys."[57]

In the years ahead Vince Salandria remained a Garrison supporter, but maintained the case against Clay Shaw was and always had been unwinnable. "The power behind the assassination would never have permitted Shaw to be prosecuted successfully. I knew the case could not be won by the prosecution. I strongly suspected that Garrison also knew. Given the rules of evidence, given the limitations of funds, given the infiltration of the staff, given the ability of the government to bribe, threaten, cajole or to kill potential witnesses, jurors, staff members, the judge, what had to have been done would have been done to defeat Garrison. I think Jim knew that. Jim fatalistically went in and took his beating.

"I was with him after we received the verdict," Salandria continued. "He said simply, 'Now, everyone will know who I am.' He consciously or unconsciously identified with Lee Harvey Oswald. Jim was a patsy who took the government's punishment for me, and for all of us."[58]

On the same day the verdict was announced, Ray Marcus wrote the DA a letter. "I did not expect it would be possible for you to convict Shaw," he said. "It has been my feeling that the forces in and/or connected with the federal government that were powerful enough to suppress the facts of the assassination (not to speak of the probable involvement before the fact of some of these forces) were certainly powerful enough, at least for the present, to prevent their exposure in a court of law."[59]

By this time Marcus was giving serious attention to an obscure article written by former President Harry S. Truman, and published in *The Washington Post* on December 22, 1963. He had heard of it only recently, in Roger Hilsman's book *To Move a Nation*, but in the years ahead would come to regard it as an important public policy statement. As far as he could tell, it appeared in only one edition of the *Post*; it was omitted from later editions of that same day's paper. Neither did it appear to have been picked up by any other newspapers or discussed by any columnist or broadcast commentator. "I'm amazed it has received so little notice," Marcus told Vince Salandria. "Or perhaps not so amazed."[60]

Truman's article was called "U.S. Should Hold CIA to Intelligence Role," and was no less than a call by Truman, under whom the Central Intelligence Agency had been established, to rein in an agency that had gained too much power. The CIA had become diverted from its original assignment. "It has become an operational and at times a policy-making arm of the Government," Truman wrote. "This has led to trouble and may have compounded our difficulties in several explosive areas. I never had any thought that when I set up the CIA that it would be injected into peacetime cloak and dagger operations . . . there is something about the way the CIA has been functioning that is casting a shadow over our historic position and I feel that we need to correct it."[61]

What was most striking to Marcus was the timing of this article, which was published one month after President Kennedy's assassination. "I can't read it any other way but [as] a warning by him that the CIA was involved in the assassination," Marcus told Salandria. "If that wasn't what he meant then I can't imagine he would have written and/or released it then for fear of having it read that way." When the article appeared, Marcus reasoned, the nation was still reeling from the assassination. There were all sorts of rumors about possible conspiracies, even as the government insisted otherwise. It would have been irresponsible, Marcus speculated, for Truman to publish such an article so soon after Kennedy's assassination unless he were trying to alert the nation to the possibility of CIA culpability. Such a warning, he felt, may have been as overt as Truman dared make under the circumstances.[62]

By the time the trial of Clay Shaw came to an end, Marcus was withdrawing from active involvement in the Kennedy case. He had worked steadily on it since the day of the assassination, but by 1969 concluded he simply had nothing more to contribute. "That this occurred at the time the Shaw trial was coming to an end was coincidental – but there's no doubt Garrison's failure to convict Shaw was a psychological setback for the critics."[63]

All along Marcus had been contacting influential public figures and trying to interest them in the Kennedy case. In late May 1967, nearly two years after first writing Robert F. Kennedy, he tried contacting him again to urge him to contact Jim Garrison and see for himself whether the district attorney was on to something important.[64]

He succeeded in reaching RFK's press secretary, Frank Mankiewicz, who remembered the packet of material Marcus had earlier sent. "Our minds are open on the case," Mankiewicz told him, and invited Marcus to meet with him in Senator Kennedy's Washington office. The senator would not be there himself, but Mankiewicz assured Marcus he would bring his views, and his appraisal of those views, to RFK's attention.[65]

The meeting lasted about two hours. Among other things, Marcus had with him some additional prints of the #5 man image, which were clearer than the images he had sent to Robert Kennedy in 1965. When the meeting ended, Mankiewicz invited Marcus to come to his home to show his material to another Kennedy aide, Adam Walinsky. They saw both the #5 and #2 man images, and both indicated they considered the images to be men. Afterward Mankiewicz and Walinsky drove Marcus to National Airport. Along the way, Marcus observed that if Senator Kennedy entertained any doubts about the Warren Report, it was important that he go public with them. Walinsky replied, "What good will it do the country for Robert Kennedy to stand up and say, 'I don't believe the Warren Report'?"[66]

Just over a year later Marcus was watching televised coverage of RFK's victory in the California presidential primary when Senator Kennedy was assassinated. "Walinsky's words flashed through my mind," Marcus recalled, "followed immediately by the thought that he might not have been shot."[67]

Marcus also tried to convince Wesley Liebeler to publicly call for a new investigation into President Kennedy's death. In the fall of 1967 he called the former Warren Commission attorney at the UCLA law school to set up a meeting. His plan was to show Liebeler his portfolio of assassination photos, including the #5 man enlargement. Marcus didn't know it, but David Lifton had shown Liebeler the #5 man images a few years before, and Liebeler had tacitly conceded their validity.[68]

Marcus showed Liebeler his photographs, including a much clearer version of #5 man. Jim Garrison's investigation was then commanding headlines; it was only a matter of time, Marcus insisted, before the official story fell apart. "I urged him to consider his responsibility as a citizen, and said that he would not dishonor himself – quite the contrary – if he was to be the first Warren Commission attorney to call a press conference and say something like, 'We did the best we could under the circumstances, but there is now sufficient evidence to warrant a reopening of the case.'"[69]

When Marcus had finished, Liebeler didn't say anything right away. Instead he looked at him for about half a minute. Finally, he spoke. "Mr. Marcus, sometimes we get caught up in things that are bigger than we are."[70]

Epilogue

In 1967 **Penn Jones** was profiled in a small magazine called *The Texas Observer*. He emphasized that as far as he was concerned, the Warren Commission had been thoroughly discredited many times over. "Just how many times must we prove conspiracy?" he asked. "The combined work of Lane, Meagher, Salandria, Shirley Martin, Ray Marcus, Weisberg, and myself should be enough to warrant a new investigation. But I doubt that it will come before ten years."[1]

Nine years later the case was in fact reopened by the House Select Committee on Assassinations, which concluded, albeit tepidly, there had been a conspiracy in President Kennedy's assassination.

> The committee believes, on the basis of the evidence available to it, that President John F. Kennedy was probably assassinated as a result of a conspiracy. The committee is unable to identify the other gunman or the extent of the conspiracy.[2]

Gaeton Fonzi, the former *Greater Philadelphia* magazine senior editor, was a staff investigator for the HSCA. He had come to the HSCA by way of the Church Committee, to which he had been recruited by an associate from his magazine days in Philadelphia. Fonzi made several important contributions to the work of the HSCA; by the time it was over he was convinced he had identified a man – a former high-ranking CIA official – who had played a key role in the conspiracy to assassinate President Kennedy.[3]

Before beginning his work with the Church Committee in 1975, Fonzi visited with Vince Salandria, whom he had not seen in a number of years. Salandria, he discovered, had largely repudiated his earliest work on the assassination, which he had labeled the "microanalysis" of the events in Dealey Plaza. Not that he had any doubts about his early evaluations: but to be pursuing them so many years later, Salandria now believed, was a waste of time. "We spent too much time and effort microanalyzing the details of the assassination when all the time it was obvious, it was blatantly obvious that it was a conspiracy," he told Fonzi. But the powerful forces that conspired to kill President Kennedy, which Salandria referred to as the National Security State, were unconcerned with those still microanalyzing the assassination's details. "That's exactly what they want us to do. They have kept us busy for so long. And I will bet, buddy, that is what will happen to you. They'll keep you very, very busy and, eventually, they'll wear you down."[4]

Fonzi was indeed kept very busy over the next three years, and he pursued several avenues he came to believe were false leads made enticing by unseen forces. But there were important avenues as well. He interviewed Silvia Odio and her sister Annie, the Cuban émigrés visited in Dallas by three men, one of whom may have been Lee Harvey Oswald, several months before the assassination. Fonzi considered Silvia Odio one of the most important Warren Commission witnesses, since she linked Oswald's name to the assassination long before it happened. Now, more than a decade later, her statements, coupled with Annie's, were just as significant. "Their story held up through my subsequent heavy checking and I was absolutely convinced they were telling the truth." In fact, Fonzi later wrote, he was confidant the JFK assassination was a conspiracy based solely on Odio's story.[5]

Even more important were Fonzi's contacts with another Cuban émigrée, a man named Antonio Veciana. Veciana had been an accountant in Havana before the Castro revolution. When Fonzi met him, he was living quietly in Miami's Little Havana. He had just completed a prison sentence following his conviction on what he insisted was a false drug conspiracy charge. But in the early 1960s Veciana had founded the anti-Castro organization Alpha 66, probably the most militant of the anti-Castro groups then active. Alpha 66 was directed by the Central Intelligence Agency; Veciana's CIA contact was a man he knew as Maurice Bishop. According to Veciana, Alpha 66 was Bishop's brainchild. All of the group's activities, including at least two assassination attempts on Fidel Castro, were at his instigation. "Bishop's main thesis was that Cuba had to be liberated by Cubans," Veciana said. As Fonzi interviewed Veciana and began probing his background, he was stunned to hear him casually mention having once seen Lee Oswald – in Dallas, in the presence of Maurice Bishop.[6]

This had occurred, Veciana explained, in early September 1963. Bishop had contacted him and asked to meet him in Dallas. They rendezvoused in the lobby of a downtown office building. When Veciana arrived, Bishop was already there, talking to a young man Veciana did not recognize. As Bishop concluded this conversation, the three men walked outside together, where the young man, whom Bishop did not introduce or identify, walked away. Bishop and Veciana walked to a nearby coffee shop and discussed Alpha 66 business.[7]

After the assassination, when Oswald's face saturated the media, Veciana immediately recognized him as the young man he had seen with Bishop several months earlier. But the clandestine world, Veciana knew, operated on a need-to-know basis, and he knew better than to ask Bishop about Oswald. He was uneasy to be in possession of knowledge he did not want.[8]

It was taken for granted that "Maurice Bishop" was a pseudonym. Fonzi was determined to learn his true identity. To help this effort a composite sketch was drawn by a police artist under Veciana's direction. It was this sketch that made the difference: Senator Richard Schweiker saw it and was reminded of David Atlee Phillips, the former chief of the CIA's Western Hemisphere Division, who had come before Schweiker and the Church Committee on several occasions. Shown a series of photographs of Phillips, Veciana said he was not Bishop, then added, "But I would like to talk with him . . . he is CIA and maybe he could help."[9]

At the time of the Kennedy assassination David Phillips was the CIA's Chief of Cuban Operations in Mexico City. Although Veciana had failed to identify photographs of Phillips as Bishop, Senator Schweiker arranged to bring Veciana and Phillips face-to-face at a luncheon of Phillips' newly-formed Retired Intelligence Officers Association. Of course, Phillips knew nothing of it: he was essentially ambushed by the presence of Antonio Veciana. The two men spoke in Spanish; Phillips confirmed to Veciana he had been in Havana during the relevant periods and that they knew some of the same people. Phillips, Fonzi recalled, appeared shaken by the confrontation; his hands had trembled. Afterward, though, Veciana said, "No, he's not him." There was a long silence before he added, "But he knows."[10]

"What do you mean, he knows?" Fonzi demanded.

"He knows," Veciana repeated without elaboration.

Fonzi was skeptical about Veciana's denial of this most critical point. Veciana had a renewed interest in anti-Castro activities and had even expressed a desire to re-connect with Bishop for that purpose. After additional investigating into Phillips' background, Fonzi was more convinced than ever that Maurice Bishop and David Atlee Phillips were one and the same. In 1978 Phillips gave sworn testimony to the HSCA that he had never used the "Maurice Bishop" alias and had never known Veciana. Fonzi was certain Phillips had perjured himself and that the Committee could have easily proven it and convicted him. But Chief Counsel G. Robert Blakey declined to bring perjury charges against Phillips and, officially, the matter went unresolved.[11]

Several years later, after the HSCA had concluded its work and issued its report, Fonzi confronted Veciana again. He believed everything Veciana had told him, he said – except when he said that Phillips was not Maurice Bishop. He also said he understood that to Veciana, the liberation of Cuba from Fidel Castro was far more important than the Kennedy assassination; moreover he appreciated that the CIA and Bishop, or Phillips, had aided that objective in the past and might again in the future. Having laid that out, Fonzi said: "I would like you to tell me this one time very truthfully: Would you have told me if I had found Maurice Bishop?"

Veciana, Fonzi was certain, was grateful that the question was phrased so carefully. Veciana smiled as he phrased his reply: "Well, you know . . . I would like to talk to him first."

After a moment, Fonzi began to laugh. Veciana laughed with him.[12]

Sylvia Meagher and Maggie Field never did re-establish their relationship. About a year and a half after their last phone conversation, Sylvia heard that Maggie was in New York for a short visit. "I must admit that I have been answering phone calls all day with a certain degree of trepidation," she told a friend. But the call from Maggie never came.[13]

Around the time of the Shaw trial, Sylvia resumed her correspondence with Harold Weisberg and they continued to discuss the assassination by mail. But she never mended fences with Vince Salandria or Penn Jones. Indeed, she seemed to have particular disdain for Salandria in the years following the Garrison investigation.

In late 1971 Salandria delivered a speech he called "A Model of Explanation" in Cambridge, Massachusetts, to the Women's International League for Peace and Freedom. In it he attempted to put the Kennedy assassination into a political context. Salandria outlined his repudiation of microanalysis, calling himself one of the earliest and guiltiest of the first-generation critics to undertake a protracted analysis of how the assassination took place. This had concerned him as early as 1964, when he told Deirdre Griswold that the twenty-six volumes made such easy pickings, he thought perhaps the critics were meant to dine on them. "There has been almost no systematic thinking on *why* President Kennedy was killed," Salandria said. "We have neglected this essential work of constructing a model of explanation which fits the data of the assassination and explains the why of it."[14]

Consistent and credible evidence of a conspiracy was always there, Salandria contended, thanks in large part to the Warren Commission's

Report and twenty-six volumes. Yet the government "from the very first and continuously to date has publicly refused to act on that evidence . . . the unvarying governmental pattern of consistently and publicly supporting the lone-assassin myth, and equally uniformly rejecting the irrefutable conspiracy evidence, was too studied to be the function of mere bureaucratic stupidity or accident. I propose the thesis that this uniform governmental pattern did not speak to official innocence or ignorance but rather to the guilt of the government at the very highest echelons."[15]

Thomas Stamm read the speech but didn't think Salandria made his case; he wrote an analysis and sent it to him. Sylvia Meagher thought Stamm's review devastated Salandria's position. "Your letter makes Salandria appear not only sophomoric – as I had thought when I read his long boring speech hastily and superficially – but decidedly ignorant, devoid of any semblance of interior logic, and almost imbecilic," she told Stamm, adding icily, "I hope he feels every thrust, parry, cut and slash."[16]

A few years later, Meagher commented on the speech again, this time with less rancor. "There is much merit to seeking a political framework and motivation for Dallas," she told Ray Marcus, "but it can be perilous . . . and in any event, it is simply impossible to disregard the forensic evidence." Explanations on the why of Dallas, she said, which were numerous, contained many pitfalls. "How does one choose between them, when all such hypotheses are compelling to a degree? After all these years, I still do not know if it was the CIA, the military, LBJ, the Cubans, or the Mafia, or any combination of them. But I always knew, know, and will always know for a certainty that CE 399 is a fake, that the autopsy is a fraud, that much of the other hard evidence is suspect or tainted, and that the Warren Report is false and deliberately false."[17]

By this time Marcus and Meagher had renewed their friendship. Neither had changed views on Garrison; they simply agreed to disagree. "We could mention his name in a brief reference to each other without arguing," Marcus recalled. "We really didn't have conversations about him." They remained in intermittent contact into the 1980s and visited on several occasions.[18]

When the HSCA began its work, all of the critics were, of course, interested to some degree; at last, it appeared that a genuine investigation of the Kennedy assassination might take place. In 1977 Marcus supplied the Committee, at its request, with copies of his work, including *The Bastard Bullet*, Zapruder film analyses, and reproductions of #5 man.[19]

Like Salandria, Sylvia Meagher was skeptical that anything of substance would come from the new investigation, which was reopening not only the JFK assassination but the killing of Dr. Martin Luther King, Jr., as well. The new investigation, she predicted, would be abortive or a failure, and likely set the case back. But she added, "I hope I am wrong."[20]

In September 1977 the Committee learned of a tape recording of radio transmissions between Dallas police dispatchers and a motorcycle cop riding with the presidential motorcade at the time of the assassination. Acoustical analysis showed that the tape had recorded the sounds of shots fired from the front of the President – from the direction of the grassy knoll. Even the HSCA's Chief Counsel G. Robert Blakey embraced this as evidence of a conspiracy. "It is ironic," Meagher observed, "that all the evidence of shots from the grassy knoll cited by the critics – the earwitnesses, the photographs, the puff of smoke, the fake Secret Service agents – have suddenly been given legitimacy by Blakey. That evidence was no less strong before the acoustical findings but was ignored by the HSCA as by the Warren Commission before it."[21]

The HSCA, it developed, was a highly politicized body that in its own way was as determined as the Warren Commission had been to conduct a less than full and honest investigation of President Kennedy's assassination. It did not make use of the #5 man images Ray Marcus sent, instead restricting itself to the original Moorman Polaroid, which had greatly deteriorated in the years since it was taken. The Committee declared that its analysis of the picture, performed in part by the Rochester Institute of Technology, yielded no new data.[22]

Marcus had sent his most up-to-date #5 man images to Sylvia Meagher. She had, of course, seen these and related images in the summer of 1965; at the time she said they had left her in a state of shock. The images Marcus developed later were far superior to the initial efforts. "I am very, very impressed by the No. 5 man," she told him. "How could the HSCA have disregarded or 'disproved' it? It seems impossible that the figure can be only an illusion, a trick of the eye. It seems to be an indisputable human male figure, with a very large forehead and pinched facial features."[23]

Like the Warren Commission, the House Select Committee on Assassinations published a single-volume Report appended by a multiple-volume set of supporting evidence. By the time it was published, Sylvia Meagher had retired from the World Health Organization. Whether that factored into her decision to index this material is not known, but as she had done more than twelve years before with the Warren Commission, she produced an index for the entire HSCA body of published evidence

– an achievement as remarkable as the original. It was published in 1980 by Scarecrow Press, the same publisher that had first published her *Subject Index to the Warren Report.* The new book was called *Master Index to the JFK Assassination Investigations,* and included a slightly revised version of Sylvia's original Warren Commission index.

In the earliest days of their friendship, Shirley Martin was impressed by something Vince Salandria had told her about the work they were engaged in: "No matter what comes of all this, we have involved ourselves in the worthiest cause of our lives." Her hopes for a definitive solution to the assassination were raised by Jim Garrison, but in the end she concluded Garrison's was not a legitimate investigation.[24]

She periodically grew disillusioned, and thought about dropping out of the case altogether. "Sometimes she 'quits' but then resumes her detective work," Sylvia Meagher noted early on. But following the death of her daughter Vickie in September 1967 Shirley began to withdraw in earnest. "I really dropped out of almost everything," she recalled many years later. "I really kind of lost heart."[25]

There was a long period of no contact between Shirley and Vince Salandria, who had been a favorite in her circle of critic-friends. Salandria attributed this in part to their trip to Dallas together in the summer of 1965, when, as he recalled it, Shirley had inexplicably lost her temper and said she would rather raise horses than keep investigating the assassination. Sylvia once confided to a friend her opinion that Salandria also felt guilty, especially after Vickie's death, for not living up to a pact he and Shirley had made to share with one another every scrap of information they turned up.

They corresponded briefly in the summer of 1969. By this time Salandria had begun working in labor relations with the Philadelphia public schools: "It appears that I am not without some talent in serving as a mediating force in impasse, crisis situations," he told Shirley. He gave her an insider's perspective on the Garrison case. The DA was "no ordinary man . . . his strengths make him, taken all in all, about the best person I know. The Shaw trial work product, given the obstacles which were thrown in his way, is not a bad accomplishment . . . the complete record will demonstrate to history that the case was not without substance."[26]

In the years after it ended, Jim Garrison's failed prosecution of Clay Shaw remained controversial. Even by the turn of the new millennium, the complete record had not yet emerged. Much of it, however, had, and the case against Shaw appeared to have much more substance than it did at the time of the trial. A 1967 memo from CIA headquarters to its New Orleans office, written after the Garrison investigation had become public knowledge, urged the use of local contacts to gather information on the probe. "We have means of getting this information on to [Shaw defense attorney] Dymond for use in preparing Shaw case. . . ." In other words, the CIA was covertly assisting in Shaw's defense. And in a 1975 interview, a former high-ranking CIA staff officer named Victor Marchetti said, "During the Clay Shaw trial I remember the Director [Richard Helms] on several occasions asking questions like, you know, 'Are we giving them all the help they need?' I didn't know who *they* or *them* were. I knew they didn't like Garrison because there were a lot of snotty remarks passed about him."[27]

Moreover it appears that in the assassination's aftermath, Clay Shaw did receive more official interest than has ever been acknowledged. Attorney General-designate Ramsey Clark said as much after Shaw's arrest, although a Justice Department statement released several months later stated that Clark had been in error. But FBI assistant director Cartha DeLoach wrote in a March 1967 memo that "Shaw's name had come up in our investigation in December 1963 as a result of several parties furnishing information concerning Shaw." There were more indications that Shaw did in fact use the "Clay Bertrand" alias, as Dean Andrews had originally stated. One such indication came from Lawrence Schiller. On March 22, 1967, he told the FBI that while he remained an advocate of the Warren Commission's conclusions, he "volunteered that he recently had been interviewing homosexual sources available to him, and in the course of these interviews three homosexual sources in New Orleans and two homosexual sources in San Francisco have indicated that Clay L. Shaw was known by other names including the name of Clay Bertrand." Three months later Schiller clouded the issue, telling the FBI that "Clay Bertrand" was, in fact, a code name used by homosexuals "to signify that they or fellow homosexuals are in serious trouble and that assistance is required."[28]

Finally, on September 1, 1977, HSCA staff counsel Jonathan Blackmer wrote a fifteen-page memo to Chief Counsel Blakey and other staff members that concluded: "We have reason to believe Shaw was heavily involved in the anti-Castro efforts in New Orleans in the 1960s and possibly one of the high level planners or 'cut out' to the planners of the assassination."[29]

In 1969 Vince Salandria ended his brief exchanges with Shirley Martin by observing, "Shirley, the assassination work is over. Wasn't it long ago? How much all of us learned from it! . . . I am only sorry that our little critical community could not have been somewhat less critical of one another and more supportive of each other. I found much to get from each of them, and feel indebted for the exposure to their fine minds and courageous character structures."[30]

Of course, the assassination work was not over. Even Salandria had more to contribute, as in his "Model of Explanation" speech in 1971, later published in a small technical magazine called *Computers and Automation*, whose editor had an interest in the Kennedy case.

Nor was the assassination work over for Maggie Field, and after the murder of Robert F. Kennedy in June 1968 – in her hometown, no less – she began working on that assassination conspiracy, too. But as in her youth, Maggie remained prone to illness, and her years of relentless probing exacted a physical and emotional toll. Late in 1967 she and her husband traveled to France, which she found revitalizing. Paris, she said, had never been more beautiful. "I walked and walked for blocks regaling in all the sights, sounds, smells and colors of every possible quarter I could cover on foot – each one with its own character and particular beauty or ugliness. When I became tired I'd stop in a café and have a strong hot cup of coffee and a piece of incomparable French bread – or I'd stop and eat 4 or 6 freshly chucked oysters, which come for about 50¢, with a slice of brown bread and a glass of chilled white wine . . . how fortunate we are to be able to make this kind of journey and I'm making the most of it."[31]

During this same trip she received a letter from Joachim Joesten, who told her he could arrange to have *The Evidence* published by his British publisher. Joesten was apparently not familiar with the book's unconventional form; he asked that she send him a copy of the manuscript. "Are you ready for *that?!!!*" she exclaimed. Whatever the exact circumstances of Joesten's offer, in the end he was unable to help get the book into print.[32]

In 1970, their children grown, Maggie and Joe Field moved from Los Angeles to Paris. The move came after a series of illnesses for Maggie, illnesses so serious that for a time Joe Field thought she might die. But once again Paris restored her health, and in 1971, though it was to have been only temporary, the Fields decided to make the move permanent. That same year they invested in Chateau Bouscaut, a vineyard in Bordeaux, which Maggie hoped would increase her thoroughly American husband's interest in France. They remained there for nearly a decade, returning to the United States in 1981 when Joe's own health began to fail. After battling cancer for more than a year, he died in Los Angeles early in 1982.[33]

Maggie survived her husband by another fourteen years. Not long after his death she returned to France, where she spent most of the rest of her life. She would come back to the United States periodically, often during the holidays. In the late 1980s, after recuperating from a broken hip, she traveled to Rio de Janiero with several friends and took part in Carnaval celebrations.[34]

She returned to the United States for good in early 1996. In 1997 a lifetime of poor health caught up to her; she became seriously ill early that year. "She felt that the quality of her life had been compromised enough by her health issues, and asked the doctor what would happen if she refused any treatment," her daughter Gwen recalled. "She had a blood disease. And the doctor said, 'Well, you'll die in eight weeks.' And she said, 'Okay.'" Maggie refused further treatment, opting instead to depart on her own terms, giving her a chance to say goodbye to her loved ones. On July 31, 1997, she died quietly in her daughter's home.[35]

The original poster boards comprising Maggie's unpublished book remained in the oversized artist portfolios she first stored them in. For a number of years they were kept among her daughter's possessions in a storage facility. There are least fifty of these poster boards. When they were inspected by a curious journalist in December 2001 they had long since begun to deteriorate. The boards represented years of diligent work that due to circumstances beyond Maggie Field's control never came to fruition. "I know she was frustrated and disappointed about this, although she rarely said so – it would be super human for her not to be," Ray Marcus once said. He remained convinced that had it been published, *The Evidence* would have been one of the most important books on the case.[36]

In 1967 Maggie was interviewed by a reporter for the *Los Angeles Free Press,* an alternative newspaper which had taken an interest in the assassination. "Until we can get to the bottom of the Kennedy assassination, this country is going to remain a sick country," she said. "No matter what we do. Because we cannot live with that crime. We just can't. The threat is too great. There are forces in this country who have gotten away with this thing, and will strike again. And not any one of us is safe."[37]

Harold Feldman died unexpectedly in the summer of 1986. By the time of his death he had withdrawn from active involvement in the JFK case and kept busy writing and teaching. In August of 1986 he began feeling poorly. At first this was thought to be a stomach inflammation brought on by medications he was on. When he did not improve he was hospitalized, and a few days later was diagnosed with liver cancer. "And the doctor told me that he probably had six months to live," Immie Feldman recalled. Two days later, Harold Feldman died at the age of 67.[38]

Among Feldman's important contributions to assassination criticism was his analysis of Dealey Plaza witnesses, "Fifty-one Witnesses: The Grassy Knoll," which demonstrated that most of those nearest to the assassination thought that at least some of the shots had originated from the grassy knoll area in front of JFK. But in eulogizing him, Vince Salandria said that even more important was Feldman's view of the big picture. "Harold was crucial in helping me think about the assassination of President Kennedy and to use this understanding as a prism through which I would better examine and gain insights into the nature of the society," he said. "Harold was a brilliant thinker and a revolutionary one. He was willing to oppose power and to [seek] justice for the powerless."[39]

In 1965, during his correspondence with Shirley Martin, Feldman once turned from the subject of the Kennedy assassination to muse about life. "The sun has been shining fresh and dry for days now and my favorite neighbor kids play up and down our alley for hours and I have to stay indoors and chew this legal lumber until it tastes like cotton, when I want to go out and toss them around and have them beg for stories – not to mention the Elke Sommer who lives two doors down. The world is a carnival while it lasts but we're taught from birth that it is at best a church picnic."[40]

In 1975, Léo Sauvage resigned from *Le Figaro*, for which he had written for 25 years, after the paper was sold to a man Sauvage believed was a former Nazi collaborator.[41]

Sauvage remained in New York, which he had grown to love, and continued to write. He had been a contributor to *The New Leader* for many years, and joined its staff as a theatre critic. But again, his writing sometimes went beyond its prescribed boundaries, as in a 1978 article on the American Nazi Party and its efforts to march in Skokie, Illinois. "America's Nazis and their Defenders" described the party's defense by the ACLU, on the grounds that it had a constitutional right to exist and demonstrate wherever it wanted to. Sauvage suggested it was a strange state of affairs when the Constitution protected the rights of Nazis marching in uniform, but not the rights of a citizen who wanted to march naked down Fifth Avenue. Wasn't that, Sauvage asked an ACLU attorney, in conflict with the First Amendment?

"Well . . . I suppose," the attorney replied. "The ACLU has always had difficulties with any kind of regulation." On the other hand, the attorney observed, marching naked was probably not a question of free speech.

"You would not defend the nudist?" Sauvage asked.

"I'm not saying I would not defend them," the attorney replied. "I'm just saying I would predict they would lose."

"Would you defend them with the same energy and conviction you brought to the defense of the Nazis?"

"I can't tell you what the position of the ACLU would be in that particular case."[42]

Sauvage wrote several more books in the 1980s, including *Les Americains,* which became a bestseller in France, and *The Lumière Affair: From Myth to History,* about the development of motion pictures. He died in Manhattan on October 30, 1988, at the age of 75.[43]

After the publication of her *Master Index to the JFK Assassination Investigations* in 1980, Sylvia Meagher seems to have largely retired from the case. She had become interested in baseball a number of years earlier, after the "Miracle Mets" upset the Baltimore Orioles to win the 1969 World Series. The interest stayed with her for the rest of her life. "Baseball opens," she wrote in her appointment book on April 7, 1987, at the start of a new season. She would track the team's progress in the book as the season progressed. Her April 7 notation continued: "Mets 3-2. DS HR." The Mets defeated the Pittsburgh Pirates that day and their star slugger Darryl Strawberry belted a three run home run.[44]

She also used the appointment book to remember, amid notations about birthdays, dentist appointments, and the poker games she had begun to enjoy, the friends and loved ones who had died. "Father RIP 1968," she noted on January 15. On June 20: "Isabel Davis RIP 1984." On October 3: "Tom Stamm RIP 1980." And on November 22: "JFK RIP 1963."[45]

On April 10, 1987, she recorded in this calendar: "Rec'd Marrs MS 6 pm." This is a reference to a manuscript by Texas journalist Jim Marrs.

The book, a survey of the JFK case, was being considered for publication by Simon and Schuster, and Meagher had been asked to review it. "The accuracy of the manuscript in dealing with a vast body of complex evidence is nearly impeccable," she concluded. "There are only a few factual errors of a marginal nature . . . there are in the manuscript numerous new allegations, but they are subject to tests of credibility which they may not pass . . . the manuscript is, in my opinion, a fine and admirable work." Simon and Schuster nevertheless decided against publishing the book, although it was later published as *Crossfire* by Carroll and Graf. It became one of two books drawn upon for the screenplay to Oliver Stone's controversial 1991 film *JFK*.[46]

The other book was *On the Trail of the Assassins*, Jim Garrison's account of his investigation and eventual prosecution of Clay Shaw. Ironically Meagher had reviewed that book in manuscript form as well. One wonders whether the Prentice Hall editor who sought Sylvia's opinion was aware of her strong anti-Garrison stance. Regardless, the request was made in late 1986, and any personal distaste she may have had seems not to have figured into her initial evaluation. "The manuscript on the assassination of President John F. Kennedy which you have asked me to vet is publishable," she wrote. She was especially pleased to see that Garrison now stated that Lee Oswald had nothing to do with killing either JFK or Officer Tippit.[47]

Prentice Hall was particularly interested in Garrison's chapter outlining his thesis that the CIA planned and carried out the JFK assassination. Sylvia wrote:

> The general argument for that conclusion appears in Chapter 13, "The Secret Sponsors." This is a superlative chapter, which provides a historical account of and a convincing perspective on the CIA's resort to assassination plots. This chapter is superb writing, well-documented, and very persuasive indeed. It passes the test of credibility with flying colors.
>
> It is clear that prodigious study and effort went into this work. . . .[48]

Nine days later, however, Meagher's assessment was sharply revised, although not because of the chapter on CIA culpability. She had a nagging feeling that something wasn't right about Garrison's description of the motorcade route through Dallas – that unlike what Garrison had written, the route traveled on November 22 was the route intended all along. Finally she double-checked his citation to the Warren Commission testimony of Secret Service agent Forrest Sorrels. "I was appalled to find that in taking a short excerpt and quoting it out of context, Garrison had completely distorted and misrepresented the real meaning of Sorrels' testimony," she wrote. The route had not been changed to force the motorcade to slow down as it turned sharply from Houston Street onto Elm, thus making Kennedy an easier target. "I am afraid that this removes any vestige of validity from Garrison's arguments about the motorcade route and will require a complete revision of the relevant parts of the manuscript." That seems to have been the deciding factor for Prentice Hall editor-in-chief Philip Pochoda, who decided against publication.[49]

About a year and a half later, in the fall of 1988, Jim Garrison telephoned Sylvia in New York. *On the Trail of the Assassins* was published that year by Sheridan Square Press, with the motorcade route thesis intact – but it does not appear Garrison called to gloat. "She described him to me as being very gracious and conciliatory," a friend recalled. "She indicated that she had stood her ground on her disagreements with his case against Shaw, but she was nevertheless impressed by Garrison's gesture in calling." They even made vague plans to meet during Garrison's next trip to New York, although this meeting never came to pass.[50]

The assessments of *On the Trail of the Assassins* and *Crossfire* were among the last things Sylvia Meagher did relating to the Kennedy assassination. By 1988 she was in declining health, suffering from diabetes and emphysema. She died on January 14, 1989, at St. Vincent's Hospital in New York at the age of 67.[51]

Sylvia Meagher's *Subject Index to the Warren Report and Hearings & Exhibits*, it is generally agreed, remains an indispensable tool for anyone researching the JFK assassination, and *Accessories After the Fact* is probably the best analysis of the Warren Commission's case produced by the first-generation critics. Long after her death a friend observed, "Her work on the case was the most important thing in her life. It was her identity, and it was the only legacy that she cared about leaving behind."[52]

Jim Garrison once was asked whether, if he had it to do over again, he would pursue his investigation of the Kennedy assassination and the prosecution of Clay Shaw. "I wish I could say, in heroic words, that 'Yes, I would do it again,'" he replied. "But actually what the investigation cost me – a magnificent office which took years to build up – and a tremendous amount of emotional involvement, not unrelated to my personal concerns about what happened to John Kennedy, and what was obviously happening to America – I'd say that, I don't know if I would do it again, because of the emotional price I paid." He still believed in the case he brought to trial, although he acknowledged he never had a real chance to win it, as illustrated by the witness Charles Spiesel. "He simply helps illuminate what we were up against, how naïve we were in the over-all strategic game we were caught up in and – in the final analysis – how very naïve we probably were to enter the game in the first place."[53]

In 1991 Garrison re-emerged on the national scene with the release of *JFK*, Oliver Stone's telling of the Kennedy assassination and Garrison's investigation. The film was curiously devoid of references to any of the early critics. Garrison was played by Kevin Costner, at the time one of the top box-office draws in the movie industry. The real-life DA himself had a small role in the film. In what must have seemed to director Stone like a delightful casting irony, Garrison played Earl Warren and appeared in several scenes.

Most of the first-generation critics could not help but be interested in Hollywood's take on the Kennedy assassination; several were in due course asked their opinion of the movie by one media outlet or another. "The greatest contribution to a discussion in America about the subject since the [assassination] is being made by Oliver Stone," Mark Lane told *Life* magazine. "He's placed it on the agenda, and I salute him."[54]

Vince Salandria was asked about the film by *The Legal-Intelligencer,* the same newspaper that had published his analysis of the Warren Report in 1964. "The movie *JFK* has come under fire for pandering to the paranoid fantasies of a young audience, whose nerve endings were feared to have been dulled by years of MTV," he said. "It really makes no difference whether or not Oliver Stone and Jim Garrison were looking for their long-lost fathers in President Kennedy, or if the movie idealizes Garrison, or even if Kevin Costner can act." What mattered, Salandria told the paper, was that the movie was a truer account of the assassination than was the Warren Report.[55]

But in the same article Arlen Specter said Stone's film might have the opposite effect than that intended. "In a curious way, this absurd movie, which no one is taking seriously once acquainted with the facts, may lead people to read and accept the extensive factual analysis and sound conclusions of the Warren Commission's Report."[56]

According to her daughter Gwen, Maggie Field thought the movie represented the truth. "When Oliver Stone's movie *JFK* came out, she was very excited about it, because she really did feel that he nailed it." But the subject of Jim Garrison remained divisive among the early critics.

Had she still been alive, a friend was certain, Sylvia Meagher would have distanced herself from the movie. And Harold Weisberg acknowledged playing a role in getting an early, pre-production draft of the screenplay into the hands of an unfriendly journalist who, six months before it was released, attacked the film in the pages of *The Washington Post*. "My only opposition to what Oliver Stone did," Weisberg said later, "was to lie to the people in telling them that his work would be of nonfiction, when it was clearly a work of fiction. Other than that he's got a right to say anything he wants to say."[57]

While the film was still in production, Ray Marcus had tried without success to interest Stone in the #5 man image. Later, while it was in the theaters, he wrote Jim Garrison a letter. "I have just seen the film *JFK* for the second time in a week," he said. "As before, the audience sat transfixed for the entire three hours." There were a few moments of stunned silence at the film's conclusion before the audience burst into applause. "The accessories-after-the-fact in government and media who labored so hard and long to promote the official lie, and to destroy the work and reputation of the only public official who attempted to expose the conspiracy in a court of law, now see their victory being undone by a motion picture inspired by that same individual." It was, Marcus said, a wonderful example of poetic justice.[58]

Most of the critics who supported Garrison through the Shaw trial remained supportive in the years that followed. "He's the only public official in twenty-eight years to give a damn about who killed the President of the United States," Mark Lane said in 1991, "and to risk everything in an effort to find out who did it and to tell the truth to the American people."[59]

Jim Garrison died at the age of 70, on October 21, 1992, after years of poor health.[60]

Harold Weisberg had turned on Jim Garrison years before Oliver Stone's movie, although precisely what led to his change of heart is unclear; he was still writing him friendly letters a year and a half after the Shaw trial ended. Weisberg told several interviewers late in his life that he had concluded that Garrison never really had a case. Why then, he was asked, did Garrison proceed? Was it simply a matter of arrogance – a man who couldn't admit he was wrong?

"No," Weisberg answered without hesitation. "I think we never had a chance to know what he was really driving at. And I think most of us began by assuming what the hell, if the District Attorney of a big city is going to take a case to trial, he's gotta have something. Nobody, none of us ever dreamed, to begin with, that his case was so barren. But then it became pretty obvious that it wasn't possible."[61]

How then could all of the critics who were in contact with Garrison – all of them honest people in search of the truth – come to have such uncompromising opinions on the DA? Why did the case prove to be so divisive? "That's a legitimate question," Weisberg conceded. "And I'm ashamed of myself for not coming to it earlier. I've thought about it often. I think a lot of it was wishful thinking – that we wanted it to be true, even though we had doubts. In my case, after I had doubts, I wanted the Shaw case to go to trial.

"Garrison was pretty glib. And he conned most of us. I'm sure I'm not the only one who expressed doubts. I'm sure he gave others explanations that they believed. He was just that slick." In the end, Weisberg said, Garrison had no one to blame but himself for the failure of his investigation. Stories that Garrison's office was infiltrated and his case sabotaged were nonsense. Even though Weisberg had, as a young man in Kentucky, experienced first-hand how a power structure could manipulate the outcome of a trial, he didn't believe it was a factor in the Garrison probe.[62]

Weisberg once estimated that he had written fifty books, most of them on the JFK assassination, although he also became involved in the Martin Luther King, Jr. case. He saw all of his books as connected: "What I am writing is one big book. This is one of its parts," he wrote in the introduction to 1967's *Photographic Whitewash*. Most of the books remained unpublished, and Weisberg often said they were intended as a record for history.[63]

Throughout his written work, Weisberg insisted on absolute fidelity to the written record. If he was unable to substantiate something, he did not publish it – and reserved great scorn for writers who resorted to speculation. Beginning in 1966, he was using the Freedom of Information Act to get at assassination records the government had locked away. These efforts continued over many years and involved more than a dozen lawsuits. By the 1990s he had amassed a vast collection of documents, housed in dozens of metal filing cabinets in the basement of his Maryland home. These records were used in his own work, but also were made available to the growing body of independent, private researchers who came after the first-generation critics.[64]

"The thrust of all of my work that most people don't perceive, but many do," Weisberg once said, "is that in that time of great crisis, and ever since then, all the institutions of our society had failed. And that represents a great danger to our society, and the form of our society.

"I'm a firm believer in the democratic system and representative society. In spite of all of its many failings I think it is still the best system of freedom through self-government that man has yet devised. And I think that the greatest political thinkers of all time were those we know as our Founding Fathers. And it is in this sense that I have done this work."[65]

Weisberg was in increasingly poor health over the last decade of his life, suffering from a heart condition, diabetes, and a host of infirmities brought on by advancing age. He was 88 years old when he finally died on February 21, 2002. About six months earlier, he had commented: "I think very often of Frost's words, 'Promises to keep. And miles to go' before we sleep. And right now my regret is that I can't look forward to as many miles as I need to finish what I'm doing."[66]

Marguerite Oswald, who had vowed to fight to her last breath to clear her son's name and never did give up, died of cancer in Fort Worth, Texas, in January 1981. She was 73 years old. Shirley Martin had befriended Marguerite during the 1960s, but by the time of Mrs. Oswald's death had lost contact with her. "When she died, and I read that she died alone, I felt terrible," Shirley said. She fondly recalled a visit with Marguerite during which Shirley enumerated the reasons why she felt Lee Oswald was not as the media portrayed him. Rather, he was industrious, he had learned the difficult Russian language, he had earned his high school equivalency diploma while in the Marines. To all this, Marguerite asked Shirley, "Who's the mother here?"[67]

Though Shirley had withdrawn from active involvement in the case she remained interested in it, and kept up with most of the literature as it appeared. She also kept up with the basic evidence. Although the blue bindings were becoming tattered and worn, and on some volumes were beginning to fall off, she was still reading testimony from Warren Commission data as late as 2004. While she felt that the truth about the Kennedy assassination would probably never be known, she was also convinced that if a researcher – someone younger and more energetic than herself – could, from the available record, piece together the movements of everyone who was in the Texas School Book Depository building on the day of the assassination, a clearer picture of what happened on November 22, 1963, would emerge.[68]

"I still feel that Lee was innocent," she said not long after the fortieth anniversary of the assassination. "And there's something about that that just haunts me. I think to myself, imagine being shot down, and murdered, because of something you didn't do. And it makes me so angry."[69]

Almost without exception, members of the Warren Commission and their staff attorneys have never wavered from public support of the original Commission finding published in 1964. Thus history is left with two official and opposing versions of the crime: the Commission's lone-assassin version, and the House Select Committee's 1978 conclusion that there was a conspiracy. In 1991 Gerald Ford insisted that the Warren Commission had been right all along. "I resent and reject all these speculative stories," he said. "There has been no new credible evidence." Ford and staff attorneys David Belin, Arlen Specter, and W. David Slawson all published work in defense of the Commission. HSCA Chief Counsel G. Robert Blakey also wrote a book on the case, laying blame for the assassination on organized crime.[70]

David Belin published not one, but two books in defense of the Commission: *November 22, 1963: You Are the Jury* was published in 1973, while *Final Disclosure* was published in 1988. He also wrote several articles for such diverse publications as *The New York Times* and *The Texas Observer*. "In my work with the Warren Commission," he wrote in the *Times* in 1971, "I served as an independent lawyer from Des Moines, beholden to no one. There is not a person in the world who could have made me write any portion of any report if I disagreed with its ultimate conclusion. I know that truth was my only goal. . . ."[71]

Arlen Specter, who in 1966 was nervously dodging questions put to him by Gaeton Fonzi, became a polished defender of the Commission. The first-generation critics, in particular the "Hypotheses" of Ray Marcus, had long since invalidated the single-bullet theory. But in a memoir published in the year 2000, Specter declared: "I now call it the Single Bullet Conclusion. It began as a theory, but when a theory is established by the facts, it deserves to be called a conclusion." He stated further that one of the biggest problems in the United States is distrust of government. "Many Americans believe that their elected representatives are for sale and that their government lies to them. When momentous historical events occur, such as the assassination of President Kennedy, the popular reaction is that the government deceives and covers up through an explanation like the Single Bullet Theory." One of his book's objectives, he said, was to combat that distrust; he urged all Americans to participate in the democratic process.[72]

Edward Epstein had told the "Warrenologists" who met in Sylvia Meagher's apartment in October 1965 that the Warren Commission members had reached a gentlemen's agreement not to "break ranks" and discuss the Commission's findings publicly. And while Senator Richard Russell adhered to that pact, it appears that he was, in fact, in disagreement with the Commission's findings.

"He was satisfied there had been a conspiracy, that no one man could have done the known shooting, and that 'we have not been told the truth about Oswald,'" Harold Weisberg wrote in the early 1970s. He had come to know the senator in the years after the Commission completed its work. Weisberg claimed that Senator Russell had agreed to sign the Warren Report only after forcing a secret Commission session at which he laid out his disagreement. He would sign the report, but there would at least be a record of his dissent. But, Weisberg said, unbeknownst to the senator, that record was destroyed on orders from General Counsel J. Lee Rankin, probably with Earl Warren's approval.[73]

Moreover Commission members John Sherman Cooper, and to a lesser extent Hale Boggs, were also in disagreement with the Commission's most basic finding, although they signed the Report anyway. "This means," Weisberg wrote, "that there was not what the official record says, unanimous Commission agreement that Lee Harvey Oswald was the lone assassin."[74]

In 1973, on the occasion of the tenth anniversary of President Kennedy's assassination, Penn Jones wrote: "We know we will never see that crime brought to justice. A small band of us have been laboring to point out some of the monumental lies – to bring to the attention of the people the deliberate distortions of the Warren Commission. All of us know there is no hope.

"At times we quote: 'Ten thousand years from now, when a man picks us up as a hunk of clay to chink a crack against the wind, he may pause and say, 'Damn, that's good clay.'

"With that thought, and this work, we can sleep at night."[75]

Jones sold the *Midlothian Mirror* in 1974. Within a year he began publishing a newsletter specializing in the assassination called *The Continuing Inquiry*. By this time he was convinced that the assassination was the work of the United States military, although he also felt that Lyndon Johnson was somehow involved.[76]

"I met both John and Robert Kennedy," Jones wrote late in his life, "and they were two of the finest, bravest and most honest men ever to serve in politics. They gave their all for this country and took nothing in return. We will never see the likes of them again. Men of their type don't turn up more than every few generations. The best of all is gone and we are left with the dregs. . . .

"We lost our democracy on November 22nd and we have never regained it yet. I won't live long enough to see it return, but I hope you do."[77]

A few months earlier he had been an invited guest at a remembrance ceremony for JFK held in Dealey Plaza on the thirtieth anniversary of the assassination. The once-feisty country editor, then 79 years old, appeared frail as he spoke.

"I'm an old man now," he began, "but years ago I wrote four books on the assassination of John Kennedy. I think there were nine guns firing right in this area – two of them from the top of the jail. And it was well-arranged and well-organized, so that there was no chance for the president to escape. I hope someday we'll overcome this, but it will be a long time before we will overcome it."[78]

Penn Jones, Jr., lived for another four years, but during that time battled the debilitating effects of Alzheimer's disease. He died in a nursing home in Alvarado, Texas, on January 25, 1998.[79]

By the 1990s, Ray Marcus had retired but still lived in Los Angeles, where he had lived most of his life. Oliver Stone's *JFK* helped to rekindle his interest in the JFK case: he wrote and self-published several monographs during the 1990s, including *#5 Man, November 22, 1963*, a brief history of his involvement with the #5 man detail of the Moorman photograph. He produced new copies of *The Bastard Bullet*, its first re-printing since the original in 1966. And he joined an informal circle of mail correspondents, the principal subjects of which were the Kennedy assassination and the state of the world. The group was formed by Vince Salandria, and included Gaeton Fonzi, several university professors, and other like-minded individuals.

Marcus was as convinced as ever that there had been a conspiracy in the assassination of President Kennedy. "Every once in a while I'd think through some of the evidence I had worked with, and I said, 'Could I be wrong in total?' Not just this detail or that – in other words, is there an innocent explanation for this and that? And I would think it through, and I would always come up negative. No, it couldn't be."[80]

In the spring of 2001 Marcus was encouraged by a new scientific study confirming the HSCA's acoustical analysis of police radio transmissions, which supported shots fired from the grassy knoll. That HSCA conclusion had been thrown into doubt by an analysis of the same radio transmissions by the National Academy of Sciences in the early 1980s. But the peer-reviewed 2001 study said that the NAS finding was in error, and that at least one shot had indeed come from the grassy knoll. That in turn bolstered the validity of the #5 man image, on which Marcus had worked so long.[81]

By this time a debate had been raging for several years, centering on the validity of the Zapruder film. Many had come to believe it had been tampered with from the very beginning and cited different aspects of the film and its early handling in support of this contention. Marcus considered the issue deliberately misleading – perhaps the work of agents whose strategy was the promotion of confusion and mystery. "They've tried to take evidence that's both clear and convincing that you get over to a lay public – that's the crucial thing, they don't care about a few people – that a lay public can understand," he said, "and to render them seriously arguable."[82]

But chances of solving the assassination, in the usual sense of the term, seemed remote at best, Marcus felt. "What remains now is historical truth. That brings up the question as to whom is the truth important? Well, it's *not* important to a lot of people. But I think historical truth is important to the nation . . . I do feel this is the greatest country on Earth, the greatest country in the history of the world. If my own parents had not decided to leave eastern Europe, they probably would have died in the Holocaust. I probably would never have been born . . . so, for personal reasons, and reasons stepping out of it objectively, I just think this is a great country, a tremendous country. And those few of us who feel that the historic truth of a country is important to its people, important to its future – then that's the spur to do this."[83]

In the aftermath of the movie *JFK*, Congress passed Public Law 102-526, The President John F. Kennedy Assassination Records Collection Act, signed into law by President George H. W. Bush. Under the law, all records relating to Kennedy's assassination "should carry a presumption of immediate disclosure." To implement the Act, President Bill Clinton appointed a five-member panel called the Assassination Records Review Board (ARRB), described as "an independent federal agency created to oversee the identification and release of records related to the assassination." Board members, following Senate confirmation, were sworn in on April 11, 1994. Under terms of the Act, the Board had until October 1, 1996, to fulfill its mandate, with an extra year available if it deemed it necessary. It would actively seek previously unknown records from private collections, and from federal agencies that had resisted making them available in the past. The ARRB did not have any investigative authority.[84]

"Thirty years of government secrecy relating to the assassination of President John F. Kennedy led the American public to believe that the government had something to hide," the Board said in its final report. It stressed the need for more government accountability in the future. In establishing the JFK Act, Congress stated that records relating to the assassination would "carry a presumption of immediate disclosure."[85]

The Board released thousands of previously unseen documents that by one estimate totaled about a million pages. "Who in the world is going to be able to buy, store, and read one million pages?" Harold Weisberg wondered. A new generation of critics tried. None truly expected to find a smoking gun in the case, and none did, but important material was uncovered. A November 23, 1963, FBI report located in the National Archives in 1997, for example, offered strong corroboration for Roger Craig's story of seeing a man resembling Lee Oswald exit the TSBD about fifteen minutes after the assassination, get into a waiting Nash Rambler driven by another man, and drive off. This and a similar report that surfaced in the 1970s came too late to vindicate Craig, who by 1967 had fallen into disfavor with the Dallas sheriff and was forced out of his job. Penn Jones tried to help Craig rebuild his life, but it wasn't enough. Roger Craig committed suicide in 1975.[86]

Oliver Stone's movie also touched off a groundswell of renewed public interest in the assassination. Several non-profit organizations were formed to facilitate new research, including the Dallas-based JFK Lancer, with which Mary Ferrell was closely associated, and the Washington-based Coalition on Political Assassinations, or COPA. COPA's stated purpose was to "secure full disclosure of U.S. and international government records" relating to the JFK, Robert Kennedy and Martin Luther King, Jr., murders, by working closely with the ARRB. The group would also serve as a watchdog on Congress and the media, and to seek the historical truth about the major political assassinations of the 1960s.[87]

Toward that end, COPA held regional and national conferences each year beginning in 1994. In 1998, Mark Lane and Vincent Salandria were among those invited to COPA's national conference, held that year in Dallas. It was Salandria's first time there since his visit with Shirley Martin in 1965.

Salandria had once told Gaeton Fonzi that a conspiracy in the assassination was "obvious," and while his was the perspective of one intimately familiar with the evidence, it appears that most Americans were and are in accord with this view. Public opinion polls from as early as December 1963 showed that most of those who were asked rejected the lone-gunman scenario. "A majority of the American public [hold] the view that some group or element – or other individual – was also involved in the assassination," wrote George Gallup, director of the American Institute of Public Opinion, within two weeks of the assassination. This general belief remained consistent in the decades that followed. From the very start, then, it seems the critics were telling Americans what, in their bones, many of them already knew.[88]

On the first night of COPA's 1998 conference Salandria delivered a speech summarizing his work on the assassination from the day it happened through the early 1970s. He described his initial work with Harold Feldman and their suspicion, later a certainty, that Oswald had intelligence connections; his early articles in *Liberation* and *TMO*; and his pursuit of the Air Force One tape recordings, when the plane's occupants were told that the assassination was the work of one man and there had been no conspiracy. Later an ARRB staff member named Doug Horne said the Board's failure to locate those original Air Force One tapes was one of his greatest disappointments while serving on that panel.[89]

"I have asked, and ask again," Salandria said in Dallas that night, "can there be any doubt that for any innocent government, taken by surprise by the assassination – and legitimately seeking the truth concerning it – the White House Situation Room message was sent too soon? The government could not have *known* at that time that Oswald was the killer and that there was no conspiracy!"[90]

The motive for the assassination, Salandria had long since concluded, was President Kennedy's transition from Cold Warrior to peacemaker. Kennedy had articulated his vision in a speech at American University five months before his death: ". . . is not peace, in the last analysis, basically a matter of human rights – the right to live out our lives without fear of devastation – the right to breathe air as nature provided it – the right of future generations to a healthy existence? While we proceed to safeguard our national interests, let us also safeguard human interests."[91]

This, Salandria said, was the crux of the matter. "President Kennedy was killed for seeking to reduce the planet-threatening tensions of the Cold War. He was killed for accomplishing the test-ban treaty . . . [he] was killed because he had refused to bomb and to invade Cuba at the Bay of Pigs, although the Joint Chiefs and the CIA were much for this course of action. Later he had refused, when opposed by the Joint Chiefs and the CIA, to consent to invading Cuba during the missile crisis."[92]

It was easy, Salandria said, to lull oneself into thinking the assassination was a mystery that could never be solved – but this was a form of denial. "Because of his quest for world peace and his struggle to preserve the human race from a devastating thermonuclear war, President John F. Kennedy was killed by the highest levels of our national security state . . . by understanding the nature of this monumental crime, we will become equipped to organize the struggle through which we can make this country a civilian republic in more than name only."[93]

The day after Salandria's speech was November 22, 1998 – the thirty-fifth anniversary of the assassination. COPA held a brief remembrance ceremony on the grassy knoll, at which a series of speakers addressed several hundred people.

Among the speakers was Mark Lane. The years since his involvement with the Garrison investigation had not been without controversy. In 1970 he published *Conversations with Americans*, a collection of interviews with American soldiers who described atrocities they committed in Vietnam. A decade later he published *The Strongest Poison*, an account of the People's Temple tragedy in Guyana. Lane had been hired by the Reverend Jim Jones in 1977 to assist in the legal defense of Jonestown, and was in Guyana when a series of events, beginning with the murder of California Representative Leo Ryan, led to a mass suicide in which at least 900 people died. Between these two books, Lane co-authored a novel on the JFK assassination called *Executive Action* with Donald Freed in 1973, and a book on the Martin Luther King, Jr., assassination called *Code Name: Zorro* with Dick Gregory. In 1991 he published *Plausible Denial*, which placed responsibility for the Kennedy assassination directly on the CIA.

When Lane spoke that day on the grassy knoll, it was sunny and warm – an early afternoon much like the day Kennedy was assassinated. He began by remembering some of the eyewitnesses whose statements helped bring out the truth: "There were a number of brave, courageous residents in this city, longtime residents of Texas, who had the courage to speak truth to power – in the face of threats and intimidation." These were people like Jean Hill, Lee Bowers, and railroad man S.M. Holland – all of them deserving remembrance for courageous, unsung roles in American history.

Lane's comments met with enthusiastic applause. As his listeners clapped, Lane paused, gazed at some papers in his hand, then looked out over a crowded Dealey Plaza. "This is the place where our leader was murdered," he said as the applause subsided. "This is hallowed ground – and the people of this country know it. This is supposed to be the largest tourist attraction in Dallas. . . . I was here yesterday and this morning, and people were all over the grassy knoll, looking at the area. . . . I didn't see them all looking up at the sixth floor of the Book Depository Building, because the people of America know the truth, even though the government is unwilling to share the information with us."

Lane, who was then 71 years old, had begun slowly, but as he warmed to the subject his voice swelled to the *fortissimo* first described by *The New York Times* some thirty-six years earlier. "That day in Dallas – this city, at this location – when the government of the United States executed its own President – when that happened, we as a nation lost our code of honor – lost our sense of honor – that can only be restored when the government of the United States – and it will not do it without us insisting, and marching, and fighting, and voting, and putting this matter on the agenda – but when the day comes, that the government of the United States tells us the truth, and all the factual details about the assassination, including *their role* in the murder – when that day comes, for the first moment, honor will be restored to this nation."[94]

Appendix A

New Developments

On February 19, 2007 – Presidents' Day in the United States – the Kennedy assassination made news again, with the startling disclosure of a heretofore-unknown film shot by a spectator along the motorcade route on November 22, 1963. The film is in the possession of The Sixth Floor Museum at Dealey Plaza, and as of March 2007 is posted on its web site.[1]

The film was taken by a man named George Jefferies, who worked at a Dallas insurance firm. Like the more famous Zapruder film, it is a silent eight-millimeter color home movie. Unlike the Zapruder film, it does not show President Kennedy's final moments; the President and First Lady Jacqueline Kennedy are seen only briefly.

Although George Jefferies was still alive, it was his son-in-law Wayne Graham who contacted museum curator Gary Mack in late 2005 and asked if the film, which Mr. Jefferies apparently believed had no historical value, was of any interest. Mack assured him that it was. Graham agreed to donate the film to the museum, and after arrangements for transfer of ownership were made, the film was restored by eight-millimeter film specialists in Massachusetts. "The Jefferies reel, which was comprised of several 50-foot rolls of film, was inspected, cleaned, splices were repaired or redone, and the film was evaluated for transfer to video," Mack said.[2]

Jefferies shot his film about four blocks from the scene of the assassination. By Mack's calculations it was about ninety seconds before the shooting took place. Jefferies had planned to walk all the way to Dealey Plaza, but was accompanied by a co-worker who suffered from emphysema and literally ran out of breath. So they stopped at Main and Lamar.[3]

Predictably, the new film generated a great deal of interest, although Mack said he did not anticipate the level of response it got. "We were very surprised, albeit quite pleased, to have such a huge, worldwide reaction," he said. Press reports emphasized Mack's observation that the Jefferies film was "the clearest, best film of Jackie in the motorcade." But much was also made of the fact that, although President Kennedy is seen only briefly, there appears to be a slight bunching up of his jacket in the area between his shoulders.[4]

Among those weighing in on the film was author Ron Rosenbaum, who according to Slate.com has "written extensively about JFK conspiracy theories." Rosenbaum says the Jefferies film is not very important. "Its significance is almost its lack of significance," he told Slate.com's Andy Bowers. "The real mystery is why the person who took this film waited forty-five years, almost, to show us something that doesn't really show us anything."[5]

Bowers asked about the bunching of the jacket. "The question is the trajectory of the bullet that hit JFK," Rosenbaum said. "There's been a lot of controversy because the hole in the back of JFK's jacket and the hole in his body seemed to be at different points. But the fact that the jacket could have been bunched up might resolve this discrepancy."

"So this might debunk part of the conspiracy theory?" Bowers asked.

"I think the real mystery," Rosenbaum replied, "is not whether Oswald acted alone. I believe he acted alone. He was the only one firing the gun. The real mystery is what is going on inside Oswald's head: what prompted him, what his motive was, what his allegiances were. Those are still unresolved questions."

Rosenbaum was perhaps a bit cavalier in describing the back wound/jacket hole discrepancy. The early critics, and Vince Salandria in particular, argued that this discrepancy overturns the Warren Commission's entire case. The Commission's Report puts a bullet wound high on Kennedy's back. But photos of JFK's shirt and jacket show holes further down, about five inches below the collar line. This may seem like arcane quibbling, but a higher wound would make the single bullet theory more plausible. According to that theory, the bullet that caused the high back wound exited from Kennedy's throat and went on to cause multiple wounds in Governor Connally.

Two very reliable witnesses, both Secret Service agents, placed JFK's back wound in line with the clothing holes. As Salandria noted in an article written in 1964, Glen Bennett was positioned behind JFK in the motorcade, and put the back wound about four inches down from the right shoulder. Agent Clint Hill was present at the autopsy and said this wound was about six inches below the neckline to the right of the spinal column.[6]

Forty years before Ron Rosenbaum, Arlen Specter cited a bunched-up jacket to try explaining the discrepancy between the holes in Kennedy's clothing and the (presumed) holes in his body. (This is described in detail in Chapter 22, "Strange Authors.") It happened as Specter was interviewed by Gaeton Fonzi. Using Fonzi as a stand-in for JFK, Specter asked him to wave as the President had done. "Well, see, if the bullet goes in here," Specter said, jabbing at Fonzi's neck, "the jacket gets bunched up. . . ."

"Wasn't there only one single hole in the jacket?" Fonzi asked. "Wouldn't it have been doubled over?"

"No, not necessarily. It, it wouldn't be doubled over . . . when you sit in the car it could be doubled over at most any point, but the probabilities are that, uh, that it gets, that uh, this, this, this is about the way a jacket rides up. . . ."[7]

Vince Salandria remains certain that the holes in the back of Kennedy's custom-made jacket and custom-made shirt *do* line up precisely with the wound in Kennedy's back, and that the placement of the wound high on the back is fraudulent. "Specter made a fool of himself with Fonzi in trying to defend the single bullet theory," he recalled in 2007, in discussing the Jefferies film. "If he could not defend the single-bullet concept, then it is not defensible."[8]

How extensively the Jefferies film will be used to further the cause of those promoting the theory of jacket bunching to explain the clothing/body discrepancy remains to be seen. And while the Jefferies film and others like it are fascinating, the best visual record of the assassination is still the Zapruder film. "It's so obvious that the big head hit came from the front," Salandria said in 1967, two years after he first saw the film in motion at the National Archives.

"No sane person can see that film and still protest that Kennedy was shot only from the back," Penn Jones said in 1969.

"The Zapruder film," Thomas Stamm concluded in 1965, "invalidates the official autopsy finding and demolishes the Commission's thesis and findings of a lone gunman firing from the southeast corner, sixth-floor window of the Texas School Book Depository building."[9]

But the vast majority of Americans did not see the Zapruder film during the 1960s. It was, however, described on national television immediately after the assassination by CBS correspondent Dan Rather. There is some dispute about just when this occurred. Rather recalled that it was Saturday, November 23, the day after JFK was killed, but other accounts indicate it took place as late as Monday, November 25.

Whenever it was, the film was screened for Dan Rather and several others in the office of Abraham Zapruder's lawyer. Each was expected to see the film and make a bid on it; as it developed, *Life* magazine bought all rights. Rather said he briefly entertained a notion that could have significantly changed the course of events. "For a moment," he recalled, "I thought, if I have to, I'll just knock him down and grab the film, run back to the station, show it one time and then let him sue us." If only he had. Instead, he viewed the Zapruder film once and "fled back to the station" without even making a bid.[10]

In his autobiography *The Camera Never Blinks*, Rather says that he was on the air within seconds of his return. Despite having seen the film only once and despite not having been allowed to take notes, he provided a remarkably detailed description that included the correct placement of each occupant in the limousine, the observation that JFK had put his hand up to his right eye moments before the shots were fired, and that Jackie Kennedy was not looking at her husband.[11]

Yet for all of that detail, Dan Rather incorrectly described the single most important and obvious point. The impact from the fatal head shot, Rather told a national TV audience, drove JFK's head "forward with considerable violence."

Of course, the Zapruder film shows the exact opposite – vividly and unforgettably. "The President," wrote a *New York Times* reporter who saw it in 1969, "appeared to be knocked backward against the rear seat."[12]

Penn Jones suspected Dan Rather's description was no accident. He was so disturbed by it that he said Rather should not be allowed to continue working as a journalist. "Newsmen were granted freedom of the press under the First Amendment in an effort to be assured of an informed citizenry," he said in the early 1970s. "Rather has knowingly violated this duty, and his credentials should be lifted."[13]

Dan Rather later called his errant description "an honest error," and indignantly defended himself. "I challenge anyone to watch for the first time a twenty-two second film of devastating impact . . . then describe what they had seen in its entirety, without notes."[14]

By the cyber age, an audio clip of Rather's description was circulating on the Internet. In the early 1970s the clip was hard to come by, but "with the help of some young men in California, Rather's words have been synchronized with the action of this [Zapruder] film," Jones wrote. The effect was very powerful: as Rather says JFK's "head went forward with considerable violence," the president's head and upper body are seen being slammed back and to the left.

"The impression was given," Rather protested in *The Camera Never Blinks*, "that Dan Rather was part of the conspiracy. Either that or he was a Communist dupe, or something, how else could he have seen the film, etc., etc."[15]

"No one that I know ever thought Rather was a Communist dupe," Penn Jones countered. "All I wanted Rather to do was admit his error to the television audience he had misinformed. Grudgingly, he admits the error in his book, but that is not the same as saying so on CBS Evening News."[16]

Of course, "new" film relating to the JFK assassination is not unprecedented. When the Assassination Records Review Board was in existence during the mid-1990s it actively sought previously unknown records, including still and motion pictures, for inclusion in the JFK Collection of the National Archives.

Among the ARRB's finds was forty-five minutes of news footage shot by KTVT cameraman Roy Cooper. For reasons unknown, the silent, black-and-white film was not broadcast by KTVT in 1963, and Cooper literally salvaged it from an editing room wastebasket. According to CBS News, which in 1996 broadcast portions of the Cooper film after the ARRB made it public, Cooper tried unsuccessfully to sell the film, then stored it in his home for many years.

The unedited film documents the President's Texas trip from Fort Worth on the evening of November 21 through its tragic end the next day. There are no shots of the motorcade under fire, but police and witnesses are seen running toward a rail yard adjacent to the grassy knoll area immediately afterward. Later, new president Lyndon Johnson is briefly seen leaving Parkland Hospital, and Lee Oswald appears in several sequences at the Dallas police station after his arrest.[17]

Other previously unknown film has turned up periodically over the years, such as that shot by Jackie Tindel showing the motorcade several minutes before the assassination. Like the film of George Jefferies, the Tindel film was acquired by the Sixth Floor museum and made public in 2002. Some have wondered if more images might one day be discovered, and Gary Mack is confident that some will. "I know there are pictures out here that have not surfaced," he said at the time the Jefferies film was announced. "The museum is always on the lookout for pictures."[18]

Mack will probably be rewarded with more discoveries. The value of any such film, of course, cannot be known until it is discovered. But an estimated 150,000 people lined the motorcade route between Love Field and Dealey Plaza, and many of them took pictures and home movies. Federal investigators were not interested in most of it.[19]

Not long after the assassination, a Dallas woman who was among those along the route started collecting film clips because her own camera had malfunctioned on November 22, and she wanted a record of the historic event. She made contact with a number of amateurs who had shot film, and soon her collecting expanded into a commercial project. Dallas Cinema Associates, as the amateur filmmakers were incorporated, released a short eight-millimeter film in 1964 called "DCA Presents/President John F. Kennedy's Final Hour/Dallas, Texas, Nov. 22, 1963." Rights were eventually sold to Wolper Productions, a subsidiary of Metromedia, which produced a sixteen-millimeter version of the film.[20]

This appendix has been written to provide some information about, and context to, the George Jefferies film. But I would like to use this opportunity to note the passing of Shirley Martin, who died in Oklahoma on September 30, 2006. I had developed a particular fondness for Mrs. Martin during the course of many interviews and was saddened to hear of her death. [21]

It is a truism that anyone undertaking a project such as the one that led to this book must be prepared to ask what are sometimes difficult questions. But it was only after a great deal of soul-searching that I was able to steel myself to ask Mrs. Martin about the death of her first child, Victoria, who played a small but significant role in the events described. I need not have worried. The matter arose spontaneously as we discussed Shirley's trip to Dallas in 1965 with Vince Salandria. Mrs. Martin was very open about the entire matter and told me everything I needed to know – more detail, in fact, than I would dared have asked.

Her daughter's death marked the beginning of the end of Shirley's involvement as a Warren Report critic. "I gradually withdrew from the case after that," she told me. "That was 1967, when Vickie died. I was out of it by '68."[22]

As we finished our conversation that day I apologized for making her re-live such a terrible episode, but she told me not to worry about it. "I can always retreat into Mahatma Gandhi when I get depressed."[23]

NOTES

Chapter One – Air Force One

1. Air Force One: *The Making of the President, 1964,* by Theodore H. White, p. 33. AF1 arrived at Andrews AFB at 5:58 p.m. EST, November 22, 1963: *Report of the President's Commission on the Assassination of President John F. Kennedy* (The Warren Report), p. 59. Hereafter cited as The Warren Report. Oswald charged in Kennedy's death: approximately 1:30a.m. CST, Saturday, November 23, 1963: Warren Report, p. 16.

2. Cabinet plane: see *With Kennedy,* by Pierre Salinger, p. 10, and *Let Us Begin Anew,* by Gerald S. and Deborah H. Strober, p. 451. Situation Room: *The Day Kennedy was Shot,* by Jim Bishop, p. 273.

3. Speech to Coalition on Political Assassinations, November 21, 1998. See also *False Mystery: An Anthology of Essays on the Assassination of President Kennedy,* by Vincent J. Salandria, p. 119, privately published, 1999.

4. Estimate of "First Generation" critics: *Addendum B: Addendum to the HSCA, The Zapruder Film, and the Single Bullet Theory,* by Raymond Marcus, p. 20, and Ray Marcus interview, July 12, 2000.

5. *Addendum B,* p. 20.

6. Ten blocks from Dealey Plaza: Mary Ferrell, speech to JFK-Lancer November in Dallas conference, November 22, 1997; "The Dallas police were not gifted with ESP..." Mary Ferrell interview, November 18, 2000.

7. Harold Weisberg interview, November 30, 2000.

8. *Hearings Before the President's Commission on the Assassination of President Kennedy,* Volume VII, p. 535, testimony of Dallas Police Officer Joe Marshall Smith. Hearings cited hereafter as "WC Vol." with appropriate volume and page numbers, e.g. WC Vol. VII, p. 535.

9. Vincent J. Salandria to David Starks, videotaped interview, 1993.

10. The Warren Report, Appendix II, p. 472.

11. *The Dallas Morning News,* December 9, 1963. Reprinted in *The Assassination Story: Newspaper Clippings from the two Dallas Dailies,* privately published.

12. Senate Committee investigation: *The New York Times,* November 27, 1963. Quote: *The New York Times,* November 30, 1963, p. 12.

13. The Warren Report, Appendix II, pp. 475-6.

14. *Inquest,* by Edward J. Epstein, p. 36. "Of the 489 witnesses..." *Accessories After the Fact* by Sylvia Meagher, p. xxx.

15. Details on mass publication of the Warren Report: *Publisher's Weekly,* October 5, 1964, and *Saturday Review,* November 7, 1964. *The New York Times* version: September 28, 1964.

16. Commission's twelve conclusions: The Warren Report, pp. 18-25.

17. Raymond Marcus interview, July 12, 2000, and *Addendum B,* p. 20.

18. Forbidden to talk: "Kennedy Slaying is Reconstructed," *The New York Times,* December 6, 1963, p. 23. Quote: *Journal of the American Medical Association,* February 15, 1965, "Letters."

19. "...one of the few certainties in Dallas..." "Oswald in Dallas: A Few Loose Ends," by Léo Sauvage, *The Reporter,* January 2, 1964, p. 24.

20. Distinction between secret and private hearings: *New York University Law Review,* May 1965, p. 405, footnote #3. "I became disturbed..." Vincent J. Salandria to Phoebe Leider, WPEN Radio, June 12, 1968. "With the Commission working in secret..." *Whitewash II: The FBI-Secret Service Coverup,* by Harold Weisberg, p. 5. "I have always felt..." Harold Weisberg to David Starks, videotaped interview, May 1997.

21. FBI supplied bulk of investigatory data: The Warren Report, "Foreword," pp. xi-xiii. "In 1965 one critic told his colleagues..." Edward J. Epstein to Sylvia Meagher, "Notes on Meeting of Warrenologists, Sunday 3 October 1965," by Sylvia Meagher, p. 7. Sylvia Meagher Collection, Special Collections and Archives of the Beneficial-Hodson Library, Hood College, Frederick, Maryland. CIA memorandum: CIA Dispatch Document No. 1035-960, Countering Criticism of the Warren Report, reproduced in facsimile form in *Addendum B*, by Raymond Marcus, pp. 22a-22b.

22. "...another bitter attack..." FBI memorandum, January 25, 1964, regarding "Oswald and the FBI" by Harold Feldman, *The Nation*, Volume 158, No. 5.

23. "I did the research" and statement regarding insurance: Vincent J. Salandria interview, Spring 2000. "Mysterious deaths": Penn Jones, *Forgive My Grief*, Vol. I, pp. 1-6; and *Forgive My Grief*, Vol. II, pp. 1-37 (Chapters 1-5).

24. Harold Weisberg to David Starks, videotaped interview, May 1997.

25. Quote: Ray Marcus interview, September 20, 2000.

26. "It would later emerge..." See "The Media and the Murder of JFK," by Jerry Policoff, *New Times* magazine, August 8, 1975; "JFK: How the Media Assassinated the Real Story," by Robert Hennelly and Jerry Policoff, *The Village Voice*, March 31, 1992, reprinted in *JFK: The Documented Screenplay*, by Oliver Stone and Zachary Sklar, et al; "The CIA and the Media," by Carl Bernstein, *Rolling Stone*, October 20, 1977. "Covert assets..." Propaganda Notes, September 22, 1964, "Warren Commission Report," ARRB Number 180-10094-10117.

27. "My sense of the critical community..." Vincent J. Salandria, cover letter to correspondence group, October 5, 1993.

28. Ray Marcus interview, September 20, 2000.

29. "A public official armed..." *Accessories After the Fact*, by Sylvia Meagher, p. 457.

30. Mary Ferrell, October 1992, quoted in *The Last Investigation*, by Gaeton Fonzi, p. xiv. Probable conspiracy: Report of the Select Committee on Assassinations, U.S. House of Representatives, 95th Congress, 2nd Session, p. 1.

31. Harold Weisberg to David Starks, videotaped interview, 1993.

Chapter Two – The Beplumed Knight

1. Mark Lane to Earl Warren, December 17, 1963: WC, Vol. XXIV, p. 444, Commission Exhibit 2033. See also, *A Citizen's Dissent* by Mark Lane, p. 255. Rankin's reply: WC Vol. XXIV, p. 445.

2. Raymond Marcus interview, July 12, 2000.

3. "The most important person to read the brief..." *A Citizen's Dissent*, by Mark Lane, p. 8. One of the journalists inspired by Lane's brief was Joachim Joesten, who acknowledged Lane and the brief in the dedication to his own book, *Oswald: Assassin or Fall Guy?* See Chapter 15.

4. Wade press conference: transcript published in *The New York Times*, November 26, 1963. "Perused lightly..." – "Defense Brief for Oswald," by Mark Lane, December 1963, reprinted in *Plausible Denial*, by Mark Lane, 1991.

5. "Defense Brief for Oswald," by Mark Lane, December 1963, reprinted in *Plausible Denial*, by Mark Lane, 1991.

6. "Defense Brief for Oswald," by Mark Lane, December 1963, reprinted in *Plausible Denial*, by Mark Lane, 1991, p. 339. Witness quotation appears in *Newsweek* magazine, Dec. 9, 1963, p. 41.

7. "Defense Brief for Oswald," by Mark Lane, December 1963, reprinted in *Plausible*

Denial, by Mark Lane, 1991.

8. *Ibid.*

9. *Ibid.*

10. *Ibid.*

11. Shirley Martin sees *Times* article, "something fishy in Dallas..." Shirley Martin interview, 2000.

12. *New York Times* article, "Lawyer Urges Defense for Oswald at Inquiry," December 19, 1963. Shirley Martin clips article: Shirley Martin interview, spring 2000.

13. Shirley Martin interview, June 1, 2000.

14. *A Citizen's Dissent,* by Mark Lane, p. 9. Shirley Martin-Marguerite Oswald-Mark Lane connection also recounted in Mark Lane interview, February 10, 2004.

15. ... "not offering" to defend...*The New York Times*, December 19, 1963. "He's being tried..." *A Citizen's Dissent,* by Mark Lane, p. 9.

16. *Document Addendum to the Warren Report,* David Lifton, (ed)., Sightext Publications, 1968, p. 184.

17. *The New York Times*, December 30, 1963.

18. *The New York Times*, January 25, 1964.

19. Lane background: Mark Lane interview, February 10, 2004; *The New York Times*, "Campaigning Legislator," December 22, 1961; "Background Information on Mark Lane," from National Archives, Assassination Records Review Board Record Number 179-10001-10010. "My clients were..." *Plausible Denial*, by Mark Lane, p. 12; pretrial publicity: *Plausible Denial*, p. 12; *A Citizen's Dissent,* by Mark Lane, p. 3.

20. *The New York Times*, December 22, 1961.

21. Lane and Santangelo: *The New York Times*, December 22, 1961. Lane and New York Committee for Democratic Voters: *Plausible Denial*, by Mark Lane, Chapter 1; *The New York Times*, December 30, 1959; *The Making of the President, 1960*, by Theodore H. White, p. 140.

22. *Plausible Denial*, by Mark Lane, pp. 9-10; *A Citizen's Dissent,* by Mark Lane, p. 3; *The New York Times*, December 30, 1959.

23. *Plausible Denial*, by Mark Lane, p. 10.

24. Threats: *The New York Times*, June 7, 1960; Lane struck on head: *The New York Times*, August 30, 1961, and *Plausible Denial*, by Mark Lane, p. 11.

25. *Plausible Denial*, by Mark Lane, pp. 11-12; "Of the slightly more than..." *The New York Times*, November 10, 1960.

26. *Plausible Denial*, by Mark Lane, p. 10.

27. Dim sum and chrysanthemum tea: *Plausible Denial*, by Mark Lane, p. 13; "The scene was immediately..." *A Citizen's Dissent,* by Mark Lane, p. 4.

28. *Plausible Denial*, by Mark Lane, p. 13; *A Citizen's Dissent,* by Mark Lane, p. 4.

29. *Plausible Denial*, by Mark Lane, p. 14.

30. *Plausible Denial*, by Mark Lane, p. 14; *A Citizen's Dissent,* by Mark Lane, p. 4.

31. The exchange between Lane and the judge is related in *Plausible Denial*, by Mark Lane, p. 14, and *A Citizen's Dissent,* by Mark Lane, p. 4.

32. *A Citizen's Dissent,* by Mark Lane, p. 4.

33. *The New York Times*, January 15, 1964.

34. *A Citizen's Dissent,* by Mark Lane, pp. 9-10.

35. Shirley Martin helpful: *A Citizen's Dissent,* by Mark Lane, p. 11. Lane's speaking schedule tracked through documents obtained from the National Archives.

36. Buffalo speech demonstrators: FBI report, March 6, 1964, ARRB record number 179-10002-10091.

37. FBI report, March 2, 1964, on Lane in Detroit – ARRB record number 124-10193-10019; FBI report, March 6, 1964, Lane in Buffalo – ARRB record number 179-10002-10091.

38. Office of Naval Intelligence document, obtained from National Archives, ARRB record number 173-10011-10052, dated April 1, 1964. Marguerite Oswald before Warren Commission, represented by Doyle: WC Vol. I, p. 127.

39. Office of Naval Intelligence document, obtained from National Archives, ARRB record number 173-10011-10052, dated April 1, 1964. Disgrace to free speech: *The New York Times*, February 19, 1964, p. 30.

40. Office of Naval Intelligence document, obtained from National Archives, ARRB record number 173-10011-10052, dated April 1, 1964; "An Interview with Mrs. Oswald," *The Ladies Home Companion*, undated issue obtained from the Dallas Public Library historical collection. See also *The New York Times*, February 19, 1964, p. 30.

41. Office of Naval Intelligence document, obtained from National Archives, ARRB record number 173-10011-10052, dated April 1, 1964. Marguerite Oswald quote: "An Interview with Mrs. Oswald," *The Ladies Home Companion*, undated issue obtained from the Dallas Public Library historical collection.

42. Office of Naval Intelligence document, obtained from National Archives, ARRB record number 173-10011-10052, dated April 1, 1964.

43. *The New York Times*, March 5, 1964.

44. *Ibid.*

45. *A Citizen's Dissent,* by Mark Lane, p. 19.

46. WC Vol. I, p. 187.

47. Lane's testimony: WC Vol. II, p. 32. Walter Craig's appointment: Warren Report, pp. xiv-xv; *The New York Times*, February 26, 1964. Comments on Craig and his representatives: *Accessories After the Fact*, by Sylvia Meagher, p. xxix.

48. WC Vol. II, pp. 32-3.

49. WC Vol. II, p. 33.

50. Warren quotes: WC Vol. II, p. 34; first public hearing: *The New York Times*, March 5, 1964. Only public hearing: *Inquest*, by Edward J. Epstein, p. 107.

51. WC Vol. II, p. 34.

52. Warren Report, pp. 608-9.

53. WC Vol. II, p. 35.

54. WC Vol. II, pp. 35-6.

55. Lane-Warren exchange: WC Vol. II, p. 37.

56. WC Vol. II, p. 40. *Life* article: "End to Nagging Rumors: The Six Critical Seconds," by Paul Mandel, December 6, 1963, issue, p. 52F.

57. Dialogue from WC Vol. II, p. 40.

58. WC Vol. II, pp. 42-46. Weitzman credited with finding rifle: WC Vol. XXIV, pp. 228, 297. Boone and Fritz: WC Vol. III, p. 295, and Vol. XIX, pp. 508-509.

59. WC Vol. II, p. 46.

60. WC Vol. II, p. 58.

61. Dialog from WC Vol. II, p. 60.

62. WC Vol. II, p. 60.

63. *Rush to Judgment*, by Mark Lane, p. 249

64. *The New York Times*, March 5, 1964.

65. *Ibid.*

66. WC Vol. V, pp. 503-505.

67. Commission Exhibit 1031, Warren Report, p. 294.

68. *Ibid.*

69. WC Vol. 5, p. 505.

70. *The Day Kennedy was Shot*, by Jim Bishop, p. 20.

71. Weissman leaves Dallas: *The New York Times*, December 4, 1963.

72. Dialog from WC Vol. 25, pp. 664-67, CE 2475-C, "Excerpt from the two reels of tape covering the 'Contact' program of February 18, 1964, over radio station WINS, New York, New York, being the contents of the telephone conversation between Murray Burnett, Mark Lane, and Bernard Weissman."

73. *Ibid.*

74. Lane no longer representing Marguerite Oswald: *The New York Times*, April 2, 1964. CCI press release: "Independent Citizen's Committee Formed for Assassination Inquiry," April 1, 1964.

75. Shirley Martin to Mark Lane, 1964 letter, exact date unknown.

76. CCI press release: "Independent Citizen's Committee Formed for Assassination Inquiry," April 1, 1964. Author's collection.

77. Vincent J. Salandria to Mark Lane, March 18, 1964

78. Vincent J. Salandria to Mark Lane, April 2, 1964.

79. "The Unsinkable Marguerite Oswald," by Harold Feldman, *The Realist,* September 1964.

Chapter Three – Oswald and the FBI

1. Speech to Coalition on Political Assassinations, by Vincent J. Salandria, Nov. 20, 1998.

2. *Infamy: Pearl Harbor and its Aftermath,* by John Toland. "The whole truth concerning..." ibid, p. 29.

3. See *Infamy: Pearl Harbor and its Aftermath,* by John Toland; *Pearl Harbor: Final Judgement,* by Henry C. Clausen and Bruce Lee; *Pearl Harbor: The Verdict of History,* by Gordon W. Prange, with Donald M. Goldstein and Katherine V. Dillon; and *Day of Deceit,* by Robert Stinnett.

4. Vincent J. Salandria interview, April 24, 2000.

5. "I'm particularly sensitive..." "The Warren Commission, The Truth, and Arlen Specter," by Gaeton Fonzi, *Greater Philadelphia* magazine, August 1966.

6. Vincent J. Salandria interview, April 24, 2000.

7. Vincent J. Salandria to Shirley Martin, October 12, 1964.

8. Speech to Coalition on Political Assassinations, by Vincent J. Salandria, November 20, 1998.

9. Tells students the CIA may have killed Kennedy: Vincent J. Salandria interview, April 24, 2000. Helps students obtain WR copies, some write term papers: Vincent J. Salandria to Shirley Martin, October 12, 1964.

10. Vincent J. Salandria interview, April 24, 2000.

11. *Ibid.*

12. "Italian ghetto": Vincent J. Salandria interview, September 18, 2000. Salandria family background: Vincent J. Salandria interview, May 31, 2001. "When we were kids..." Vince Salandria to Steve Martin, May 3, 1965.

13. "Since I cannot deal with blood..." Salandria to correspondence group, June 13, 1994.

14. Roberts as dean of Penn Law: Speech to Coalition on Political Assassinations, by Vincent J. Salandria, November 20, 1998. "I did not want to harm..." Vincent J. Salandria interview, September 18, 2000.

15. Speech before the Coalition on Political Assassinations, by Vincent J. Salandria, November 20, 1998.

16. Vincent J. Salandria interview, April 24, 2000.

17. Recollections of Fred Feldman, February 19 and May 6, 2001.

18. Harold Feldman background: Irma Feldman interview, December 10, 2000. Psychology of assassins article: "The Hero As Assassin," by Harold Feldman, *Psychoanalysis*, Vol. 3 No. 1, Fall 1954. Quote: *The Scavengers and Critics of the Warren Report*, p. 142. Note: I would like to comment here on my use of *The Scavengers* as a source. Since I view it as a dishonest book, which I think is amply demonstrated in Chapter 25, it was with extreme reluctance that I even considered using it. It appears that generally, the quotations are accurate, but that Schiller and Lewis gave them a negative spin. Since the book has comments that were otherwise unobtainable, I decided to use some of them. Ray Marcus told me on July 25, 2001, "I think a lot of the quotes, to my experience, in *The Scavengers*, at least the ones with Maggie [Field] and with me, that I knew about, were accurate. The quotes were accurate...the title is the spin."

19. Harold Feldman to Shirley Martin, February 2, 1965.

20. Vincent J. Salandria interview, April 24, 2000.

21. "If Oswald is killed this weekend..." Vincent J. Salandria interview, November 7, 2000. Feldman's intuititve "they'll get a Jew": Fred Feldman to author, May 22 and 23, 2003. "A Jewish killer would frighten the Left..." Salandria, cover letter to correspondence group, December 14, 1994. "The investigation of it would have to be undertaken by private individuals..." Salandria to David Starks, videotaped interview, 1993.

22. Vincent J. Salandria interview, April 24, 2000; Salandria, cover letter to correspondence group, December 14, 1994; Salandria, Harold Feldman eulogy, undated, circa 1986.

23. *The Nation*, Volume 158, No. 5.

24. "Oswald and the FBI," *The Nation*, January 27, 1964, p. 86.

25. "Three weeks before the Warren Commission..." – *Portrait of the Assassin*, Gerald R. Ford and John Stiles, Chapter 1. "Fantastic rumor" – "Oswald Rumored as Informant for U.S.," *Houston Post*, January 1, 1964. "The Federal Bureau of Investigation tried to recruit..." *Philadelphia Inquirer*, December 8, 1964.

26. Gerald R. Ford and John R. Stiles, *Portrait of the Assassin*, Ballantine paperback edition, 1966, p. 17.

27. Executive Session, January 27, 1964, transcript published in facsimile form in *Whitewash IV: JFK Assassination Transcript*, by Harold Weisberg, pp. 39-41. Jaworski interviews Hudkins: *Inquest*, by Edward Epstein, p. 52. Hudkins naming Sweatt: Secret Service interview of Hudkins, report number 767, published in facsimile form in *Whitewash IV: JFK Assassination Transcript*, by Harold Weisberg, p. 141.

28. Executive Session, January 27, 1964, transcript published in facsimile form in *Whitewash IV: JFK Assassination Transcript*, by Harold Weisberg, p. 48.

29. Warren Report, pp. 659-60.

30. *Portrait of the Assassin*, Gerald R. Ford and John R. Stiles, Ballantine paperback edition, 1966, p. 17.

31. "You know that we made one mistake..." Harold Feldman to Shirley Martin, June 6, 1965."Whoever wrote the letters..." "Oswald and the FBI," *The Nation*, January 27, 1964, p. 88.

32. Harold Feldman to Shirley Martin, June 6, 1965.

33. Memorandum, "Lee Harvey Oswald/Internal Security – Russia – Cuba," William Branigan to William Sullivan, January 25, 1964. Assassination Records Review Board Record Number 124-10021-10429.

34. *Ibid.*

35. *Ibid.*

36. Harold Weisberg to David Starks, videotaped interview, May 1997.

37. See *The Nation*, Vol. 197, No. 20, December 14, 1963.

38. "A prompt reading..." Carey McWilliams to Harold Feldman, December 23, 1963; "I have decided..." Carey McWilliams to Harold Feldman, January 6, 1964.

39. *Maverick: Fifty Years of Investigative Reporting*, by Fred J. Cook, p. 272.

40. *Ibid.*

41. "...quite willing to test..." *The Education of Carey McWilliams*, by Carey McWilliams, p. 259. "We have made some cuts..." Carey McWilliams to Harold Feldman, January 14, 1964.

42. *The Nation*, January 27, 1964, p. 81.

43. "A Few Lines," by Kenneth Burke, *The Nation*, "Letters," February 17, 1964, Vol. 198, No. 8.

44. Mark Lane interview, February 10, 2004, and *A Citizen's Dissent*, by Mark Lane, pp. 6-7.

45. Mark Lane interview, February 10, 2004, and *A Citizen's Dissent*, by Mark Lane, p. 7.

46. "Seeds of Doubt," by Jack Minnis and Staughton Lynd, *The New Republic*, December 21, 1963, p. 14. Collaboration on article: Staughton Lynd to author, October 8, 2002. Some of the other reporters included Fred Cook and Richard Dudman of *The Saint Louis Post-Dispatch*.

47. Radio contest: Harold Weisberg interview, November 30, 2000. "His prize was a small transistor radio..." Harold Weisberg interview, November 30, 2000; Weisberg to David Starks, videotaped interview, May 1997. "Like everyone else..." Weisberg, *Case Open*, pp. vii-viii.

48. See, for example, *The New York Times*, November 25, 1963, p. 1, and *The Dallas Morning News*, November 23, 1963, p. 1.

49. Harold Weisberg to David Starks, videotaped interview, 1997.

50. *Case Open*, by Harold Weisberg, p. viii.

Chapter Four – Promises to Keep

1. U.S. citizenship accident of birth: Harold Weisberg to David Starks, videotaped interview, May 1997. Quote: Harold Weisberg interview, November 30, 2000. Parents: Weisberg interview, November 30, 2000, and autobiographical sketch by Harold Weisberg, Weisberg archives, Hood College.

2. Sense of duty on investigating JFK's assassination: See *Whitewash II: The FBI-Secret Service Coverup*, by Harold Weisberg, p. iii. "It cannot be consigned..." Harold Weisberg to David Starks, videotaped interview, September 1993.

3. Harold Weisberg interview, December 14, 2000.

4. Harold Weisberg interview, December 14, 2000; January 30, 2001; *Never Again!* by Harold Weisberg, pp. viii-x, and pp. 20-26.

5. Moved to Delaware: Harold Weisberg interview, January 30, 2001, and untitled autobiographical sketch, approximately 1976, Weisberg archive, Hood College. High school newspaper: Harold Weisberg to David Starks, videotaped interview, May 1997, and author's interview, March 8, 2001.

6. Harold Weisberg interview, January 30, 2001; February 13, 2001.

7. *Turbulent Years: A History of the American Worker, 1933-1941*, by Irving Bernstein, pp. 348-9. *Labor in a Changing America*, Chapter 8, "The History of the American Labor Movement with Special Reference to Developments in the 1930s," by Sidney Fine, pp. 110-15.

8. *Turbulent Years: A History of the American Worker, 1933-1941*, by Irving Bernstein, p. 451. *Labor in a Changing America,* Chapter 8, "The History of the American Labor Movement with Special Reference to Developments in the 1930s," by Sidney Fine, pp. 114-5.

9. Harold Weisberg interview, February 13, 2001.

10. "Scotch taping ripped up pieces of paper..." Harold Weisberg interview, February 27, 2001. See also *"Young Bob" La Follette: A Biography of Robert M. La Follette, Jr., 1895-1953*, by Patrick J. Maney, pp. 174-75. Additional information on early Committee hearings: *Turbulent Years: A History of the American Worker, 1933-1941,* by Irving Bernstein, p. 451; *Labor in a Changing America,* Chapter 8, "The History of the American Labor Movement with Special Reference to Developments in the 1930s," by Sidney Fine, p. 115.

11. *Labor and Liberty: The La Follette Committee and the New Deal,* by Jerold S. Auerbach, Chapter V; *Advocate and Activist,* by John J. Abt, pp. 63-66.

12. La Follette Committee investigates Harlan: *Bloody Ground,* by John F. Day, Chapter XIX; *Labor and Liberty: The La Follette Committee and the New Deal,* by Jerold S. Auberbach, Chapter V. "We can't do business if..." Unidentified coal operator, quoted in *The Lean Years,* by Irving Bernstein, p. 378.

13. Harlan County as toughest place to unionize: *Harlan Miners Speak,* by members of the National Committee for the Defense of Political Prisoners, p. 38, and *The Wobblies: The Story of Syndicalism in the United States,* by Patrick Renshaw, p. 264. Spies infiltrate unions: "War in the Kentucky Mountains," by Sterling D. Spero and Jacob Broches Aronoff, *The American Mercury,* February 1932, pp. 226-233.

14. Dreiser Committee: *Harlan Miners Speak.* Quote: *The Best Times: An Informal Memoir,* by John Dos Passos, p. 206.

15. Harold Weisberg interview, February 13, 2001.

16. Harold Weisberg interview, November 30, 2000, and February 13, 2001. *Bloody Ground,* by John F. Day, Chapter XX.

17. Harold Weisberg interview, February 28, 2001.

18. *Ibid.*

19. "He didn't believe it..." Harold Weisberg interview, March 8, 2001. Return to Washington: Harold Weisberg interview, February 27, 2001.

20. Harold Weisberg interview, January 17, 2001.

21. Memorandum from Alexander Rosen to Cartha DeLoach, June 1, 1966.

22. "All of that's false..." Harold Weisberg to David Starks, videotaped interview, May 1997. "I never leaked a thing..." Harold Weisberg interview, February 27, 2001.

23. *"Young Bob" La Follette,* pp. 215-19. "La Follette wanted to get me..." Harold Weisberg interview, February 27, 2001.

24. Weisberg still on Agriculture Dept. payroll, resigns, becomes freelance writer: Harold Weisberg interview, February 13, 2001. Nazi cartels: Weisberg interview, January 17, 2001, February 13, 2001, and untitled autobiographical sketch, approximately 1976, Weisberg archive, Hood College. Uncredited articles: Harold Weisberg interview, March 8, 2001.

25. "Japan's Mein Kampf Lists U.S. as Next Victim," by "Jefferson Hale," *Click Magazine,* November 1941, Vol. 4, No. 11. Weisberg is Jefferson Hale: Weisberg interview, March 29, 2001.

26. Harold Weisberg interview, February 13 and February 27, 2001.

27. Induction to Army, mumps, and re-assignment: Harold Weisberg interview, November 17, 2000, and autobiographical sketch by Harold Weisberg, Weisberg archives, Hood College. "I was not a spook..." Harold Weisberg to David Starks, videotaped interview, September 1993. OSS disbanded: Harold Weisberg interview, February 13, 2001. See also *The Man Who Kept the Secrets: Richard Helms and the CIA,* by Thomas Powers, Pocket Books edition, p. 31, and *Red Scare,* by Griffin Fariello, p. 153.

28. "These post-war years..." *The Great Fear,* by David Caute, p. 18. *Red Scare: A Study in National Hysteria, 1919-1920,* by Robert K. Murray. Special Committee on Un-American Activities, and quote re: "hundreds of left-wingers": *The Great Fear,* pp. 88-89. Quote re: "...paralyze the left wing element": *The Yahoos,* by Mike Newberry, p. 109.

29. "The Press: 98% Biased," *In Fact,* Vol. 1, No. 3, June 17, 1940, p. 4.

30. Truman Doctrine: *War, Peace, and International Politics,* by David W. Ziegler, pp. 48-50. Loyalty Program: *Red Scare,* by Griffin Fariello, pp. 36-8.

31. Dies Committee/HUAC: *Red Scare,* p. 17. Weisberg and State Department firings: Harold Weisberg interview, February 13, 2001; *Washington Witch Hunt,* by Bert Andrews, pp. 10-11; *Better Red than Dead,* by Michael Barson; *Red-Listed,* by Selma R. Williams, p. 180; *Fortas: The Rise and Ruin of a Supreme Court Justice,* by Bruce Allen Murphy, pp. 81-2.

32. "...nothing less than a blueprint..." *Advocate and Activist,* by John J. Abt, p. 184; *"Young Bob" La Follette,* by Patrick J. Maney, p. 174.

33. "There were no charges filed against me..." Harold Weisberg to David Starks, video-taped interview, May 1997. "Hearings...what the hell for?..." *Red Scare,* by Griffin Fariello, p. 124.

34. Anti-semitism: Harold Weisberg interview, February 27, 2001. Harold Weisberg to David Starks, videotaped interview, May 1997; Harold Weisberg intvw, February 13, 2001.

35. Three allowed to resign: *The New York Times,* November 3, 1947. Written statements: Harold Weisberg to David Starks, videotaped interview, May 1997, and letter, Arnold, Fortas and Porter, to Assistant Secretary of State John E. Peurifoy, July 9, 1947, quoted in *Washington Witch Hunt,* by Bert Andrews, p. 18.

36. "...in all its grim detail": *Washington Witch Hunt,* by Bert Andrews, p. 20; Pulitzer Prize: *The Pulitzer Prizes,* by John Hohenberg, p. 191.

37. *Washington Witch Hunt,* by Bert Andrews, p. 73; "I beat the sons of bitches," Harold Weisberg interview, February 13, 2001.

38. No background in farming: Harold Weisberg interview, July 12, 2001. "The peaceful clucking..." *Case Open,* by Harold Weisberg, p. x.

39. Harold Weisberg interview, November 17, 2000.

40. Harold Weisberg interview, December 14, 2000.

41. *Case Open,* by Harold Weisberg, p. x. Harold Weisberg interview, January 17, 2001.

42. Harold Weisberg interview, November 30, 2000, and January 17, 2001.

43. *Case Open,* by Harold Weisberg, p. viii.

44. *Case Open,* by Harold Weisberg, p. viii. "Can you understand...?" Harold Weisberg to David Starks, videotaped interview, May 1997.

45. Katzenbach memo to Bill Moyers, reproduced in *Addendum B,* by Raymond Marcus, p. 20a, and *Hearings before the Select Committee On Assassinations of the U.S. House of Representatives, Ninety-Fifth Congress, Second Session,* Vol. III, pp. 567-568, and Vol. XI, pp. 411-412. *Hearings before the Select Committee* cited hereafter as HSCA with appropriate volume number, *e.g.* HSCA Vol. III.

46. Harold Weisberg interview, December 14, 2000.

47. Katzenbach memo to Bill Moyers: HSCA Vol. III, pp. 567-568, and Vol. XI, pp. 411-412.

48. "Proof that the government sought to prevent..." See *Never Again!* by Harold Weisberg, Preface, pp. vii-xxix. "They're talking about what they're doing..." Harold Weisberg to David Starks, videotaped interview, May 1997.

49. Weisberg believes assassination is a political crime: *Whitewash*, "Introduction," p. ix. Quote: Harold Weisberg interview, December 14, 2000.
50. Harold Weisberg to David Starks, videotaped interview, May 1997.

Chapter Five – "I Guess You're On Your Own"

1. "At least eighty civil rights workers..." *Like a Holy Crusade*, by Nicolaus Mills, p. 22; "Communiqué From the Mississippi Front," *The New York Times* magazine, Nov. 8, 1964.
2. "There's no state with a record..." June 1963. Quoted in *Eyes on the Prize*, Episode 5: "Mississippi: Is This America?", © Blackside, Inc., 1986.
3. "Primed for violence" – *I've Got the Light of Freedom: The Organizing Tradition and the Mississippi Freedom Struggle*, by Charles M. Payne, p. 301, and *The Struggle for Black Equality*, by Harvard Sitkoff, pp. 159-160. Additional background: *My Soul Is Rested*, by Howell Raines.
4. Local custom taking precedence over Supreme Court rulings: See, for example, *We Are Not Afraid*, p. 23. Brown decision and White Citizens' Councils: see *I've Got the Light of Freedom*, pp. 34-35. A thorough discussion of the Citizens' Councils is in *The South Strikes Back*, by Hodding Carter III, and *The Citizens' Council*, by Neil R. McMillen.
5. Till case: *Eyes On the Prize: America's Civil Rights Years*, Episode 1, Awakenings; *Eyes On the Prize Civil Rights Reader*, pp. 37-39; *My Soul Is Rested*, by Howell Raines, p.133; *Voices of Freedom*, edited by Henry Hampton and Steve Fayer, pp. 3-4.
6. Supreme Court ruling: Boynton v. Virginia, 1960; *The New York Times*, "Bus Terminal Segregation Curbed by Supreme Court," December 6, 1960, and *The Struggle for Black Equality*, by Harvard Sitkoff, pp. 88-89. *Freedom Riders: The Eyes On the Prize Civil Rights Reader*, edited by Clayborne Carson *et al*, p. 124. "We felt that we could then count on..." *Voices of Freedom*, edited by Henry Hampton and Steve Fayer, p. 75.
7. Freedom Rides: *Freedom Bound*, pp. 55-63, *My Soul Is Rested*, pp. 109-129. Everyone on his bus prepared to die: *My Soul Is Rested*, quoting Dave Dennis, p. 277, fn. No police protection, promise to KKK: *Freedom Bound*, pp. 57-58, *My Soul Is Rested*, p. 116.
8. Kennedy administration agreement with Mississippi: *Freedom Bound*, p. 61, and *Eyes On the Prize: America's Civil Rights Years*, Episode 3, "Ain't Scared of Your Jails." Mark Lane arrested: details from *The New York Times*, June 9, 1961, and Mark Lane interview, February 10, 2004. Quote: *NYT*, June 9, 1961. Charges dismissed: *A Citizen's Dissent*, by Mark Lane, p. 181, and *NYT*, March 30, 1962.
9. Meredith details: *Freedom Bound*, pp. 66-68, and *The New York Times*, all editions between September 20 and October 2, 1962.
10. *The New York Times*, September 29, 1962.
11. *The Civil Rights Movement*, by William T. Martin Riches, pp. 67-69. *The New York Times*, September 30, October 1, October 2, 1962. *Freedom Bound*, pp. 66-68. Walker psychiatric test: *The Assassination of John F. Kennedy: The Reasons Why*, by Albert H. Newman, pp. 255-56, citing *The Fort Worth Star-Telegram*, October 7, 1962.
12. *Freedom Bound*, p. 67.
13. Jeannine Herron to Vincent J. Salandria, March 14, 1964.
14. Information on Herrons: *The Voyage of the Aquarius*, by Matt, Jeannine, Matthew, and Melissa Herron, Saturday Review Press/Dutton, 1974. "It was undergoing..." Matt Herron interview, May 22, 2000. Beckwith trial: "Notes on the Beckwith Trial," by Jeannine Herron, *The Nation*, February 24, 1964.
15. Matt Herron interview, May 10 and May 22, 2000.
16. Matt Herron interview, May 2000.

17. *Ibid.*

18. Vincent J. Salandria to Jeannine Herron, April 18, 1964.

19. *Faces of Freedom Summer,* p. 9; *Ibid.* (McAdam), p. 66. *River of No Return,* pp. 94-110.

20. John Doar and Staughton Lynd quotations: *Freedom Summer* (Belfrage), pp. 22-23.

21. "The Road to Mississippi," by Louis Lomax, included in *Mississippi Eyewitness.*

22. *Weary Feet, Rested Soul,* p. 286.

23. "The Klan had targeted Schwerner..." *Three Lives for Mississippi,* by William Bradford Huie, pp. 44-45, et al. Goodman, Schwerner and Chaney pulled over and jailed: *The New York Times,* June 23, 1964, *et al.*

24. *The New York Times,* June 23, 1964; *Witness in Philadelphia,* by Florence Mars, pp. 86-87.

25. *Freedom Bound,* by Robert Weisbrot, pp. 92-114; *Like A Holy Crusade,* by Nicolaus Mills, Chapter 6. Moses knew the three were dead: *Freedom Summer,* by Sally Belfrage, p. 26.

26. FBI inquiry: *The New York Times,* June 23, 1964. Walter Cronkite and "Bloody Neshoba": *Witness in Philadelphia,* by Florence Mars, p. 95. Discovery of car: *The New York Times,* June 24, 1964, *et al.* "...some sort of publicity stunt," *Witness in Philadelphia,* by Florence Mars, Chapter Three. Dulles to Mississippi: *The New York Times,* June 24, 1964, et al.

27. Dialogue recounted by Lawrence Guyot in *My Soul is Rested,* by Howell Raines, p. 289.

28. *We Are Not Afraid,* by Seth Cagin and Philip Dray, p. 357, and *Freedom Summer* (Belfrage), p. 30.

29. Bodies found and first autopsy: *The New York Times,* August 5, 1964.

30. Independent autopsy and quote: "Mississippi Autopsy," by David Spain, M.D., in *Mississippi Eyewitness: The Three Civil Rights Workers – How They were Murdered,* a special issue of *Ramparts* magazine, 1964. See also *The New York Times,* August 8, 1964.

31. JFK calls for civil rights legislation: *The New York Times,* June 12, 1963. LBJ signs Civil Rights Act: *Eyes on the Prize,* Ep. 5: "Mississippi: Is This America?"; *We Are Not Afraid,* p. 318.

32. LBJ signs Civil Rights Act: *The New York Times,* July 3, 1964; *We Are Not Afraid,* p. 318. MFDP and Democratic National Convention: *The New York Times,* August 24, 26, 27, *We Are Not Afraid,* Chapter 12, and *Eyes on the Prize,* Episode 5: "Mississippi: Is This America?"

33. Vincent J. Salandria to Jeannine Herron, April 18, 1964. William L. Moore was an idealistic mail carrier and CORE member who attempted what was perhaps the quirkiest protest of the Civil Rights era. In April 1963 he left Chattanooga, Tennessee, alone and on foot, bound for Jackson. He intended to personally deliver a letter against segregation to Mississippi Governor Ross Barnett. Moore had made similar journeys before, delivering letters to the governor of Maryland and to President Kennedy. For this march, he wore sandwich boards reading "End Segregation in America. Eat At Joe's, both Black and White," on one side, and on the other, "Equal Rights for All. Mississippi Or Bust." His letter to Governor Barnett said, in part, "The end of Mississippi colonialism is fast approaching. Be gracious." On the third day of his walk, Moore was shot to death alongside an Alabama highway. Moore's death was reported in *The New York Times,* April 24, 1963. Further details: *The Struggle for Black Equality,* pp. 125-6, *Powerful Days: The Civil Rights Photography of Charles Moore,* text by Michael S. Durham, pp. 72-86, *Weary Feet, Rested Souls,* by Townsend Davis, pp. 66-67.

34. Vincent J. Salandria cover letter to correspondence group, April 8, 1994, and to author, spring 2000.

35. *A Citizen's Dissent,* by Mark Lane, Holt, Rinehart and Winston, 1968, p. 9.

36. Salandria interview.

37. Mark Lane to Vincent J. Salandria, April 1, 1964.

38. Vincent J. Salandria to Mark Lane, April 2, 1964.

39. Vincent J. Salandria to Jeannine Herron, April 18, 1964.

40. "Mighty close to Texas...you and Matt are invited" – Vincent J. Salandria to Jeannine Herron, June 10, 1964. "Get Jeannine and the kids out" – Matt Herron interview, May 2000. "Bowels of fascism" – Jeannine Herron to Vincent J. Salandria, March 14, 1964.

41. Deirdre Griswold to Vincent J. Salandria, June 23, 1964.

42. "A couple doing graduate work..." Deirdre Griswold to Vincent J. Salandria, June 9, 1964.

43. George Nash to Vincent J. Salandria, June 16, 1964.

44. Vincent J. Salandria to Jeannine Herron, June 10, 1964.

45. Trip details: Vincent J. Salandria letter to family, June 25, 1964; Salandria interview, spring 2000. "Mrs. M." – Deirdre Griswold to Vincent J. Salandria, June 23, 1964.

46. Vincent J. Salandria letter to family, June 25, 1964.

Chapter Six – "We All Loved Kennedy"

1. Shirley Martin interview, April 19, 2000.

2. Climate of fear: see "The Legacy of Penn Jones, Jr.," by David Welsh, *Ramparts* magazine, November 1966, Vol. 5, No. 5; *Citizen's Arrest,* p. 111; Shirley Martin interview, May 14, 2001. Adlai Stevenson assault: *The New York Times*, October 25, 1963. General Walker: *Who's Who in the JFK Assassination,* by Michael Benson, p. 468.

3. "Very, very wrong" – Shirley Martin to Vincent J. Salandria, undated letter, probably October or November 1964. "I started early..." Shirley Martin, "Assassination and the Truth" (book review), *Latitudes* magazine, Vol. I, No. 2, Summer 1967. "She would never have taken her kids"...Shirley Martin interview, May 14, 2001. Home schooling her children: Shirley Martin interview, October 17, 2000.

4. Shirley Martin interview, April 2000.

5. Earle Cabell quote: "Don't Blame Dallas," by Earle Cabell, *Coronet*, March 1964, p. 21.

6. "It took the Martin family..." and subscribing to *The New York Times*: Shirley Martin interview, spring 2000. Subscription to *Dallas Morning News*: Shirley Martin interview, October 16, 2001. "...Shirley wanted to talk to some of the witnesses..." Shirley Martin interview, spring 2000, and May 14, 2001. E-mail from Steven M. Martin to author on October 9, 2005, helped clarify several points.

7. Shirley Martin interview, spring 2000.

8. Dialog with Johnson: Shirley Martin email, spring 2000, quoting contemporaneous notes.

9. Shirley Martin interview, March 12, 2004.

10. Shirley Martin interviews, June 2, 2000, and March 12, 2004.

11. Shirley Martin interview, spring 2000.

12. Steven M. Martin to author, October 9, 2005. Quote: Shirley Martin to Vincent J. Salandria, undated letter, probably 1965.

13. Steven M. Martin to author, October 9, 2005. Shirley Martin interview, June 4, 2000.

14. "I began researching him..." Shirley Martin interview, April 28, 2000. 1960 election, and "We were not popular..." Shirley Martin interview, April 2000. Victoria's age: Shirley Martin interview, June 14, 2000. Election night 1960: Shirley Martin to Vince Salandria, November 1964. Repeated to author, April 2000.

15. Shirley Martin interview, spring 2000.

16. Shirley Martin to Livy Salandria, December 24, 1964.

17. Shirley Martin interview, May 17, 2000.

18. Shirley Martin interview, June 3, 2000. The Oswald quote has been widely reproduced in print, movies, and TV. See, for example, *The Men Who Killed Kennedy*, pt. 1.

19. Shirley Martin interview, June 3, 2000.

20. "But she had told authorities on the day of the assassination..." Decker Exhibit No. 5323, WC Vol. 19, p. 479.

21. Undated letter, Shirley Martin to unnamed recipient. Copies sent to Vincent J. Salandria and David S. Lifton. Shirley Martin to Thomas G. Buchanan, June 18, 1965. "...and at that time did not positively identify Oswald..." CE 2523, WC Vol. 25, p. 731. Date of Reynolds shooting: The Warren Report, p. 663.

22. Undated letter, Shirley Martin to unnamed recipient. Copies sent to Vincent J. Salandria and David S. Lifton. "...may have been Jack Ruby..." Shirley Martin to Thomas G. Buchanan, June 18, 1965. "...an opinion she repeated to the Warren Commission..." WC Vol. 6, p. 212.

23. February 1964 visit: Shirley Martin interview, spring 2000. Martin phone call to Paines: Ruth Paine testimony, WC vol. IX, p. 349.

24. Oswalds and Paines meet, and living arrangements: The Warren Report, pp. 13-15. "I've been expecting you..." from the sworn testimony of Dallas Police Detective Gus Rose, WC Vol. VII, p. 229. In his 2002 book, *Mrs. Paine's Garage,* author Thomas Mallon refers to Mrs. Paine's greeting to Det. Rose as an "assassination legend," which, he goes on, Mrs. Paine firmly denies: "I was not expecting them, and I did not say that" *(Mrs. Paine's Garage,* footnote, p. 57). Oswald, Ruth Paine, and Abt: WC Vol. 3, pp. 85-89.

25. Teresa Martin interview, June 16, 2000. FBI report, Ruth Paine to Special Agents Bardwell D. Odum and James P. Hosty, February 29, 1964. Shirley Martin interview, October 17, 2000.

26. WC Vol. IX, pp. 349-350.

27. Report by Bardwell D. Odum and James P. Hosty, February 29, 1964. ARRB Record Number 179-10002-10244.

28. Report by Bardwell D. Odum and James P. Hosty, February 29, 1964. ARRB Record Number 179-10002-10244.

29. Hoover says "bright nut" – ARRB Record Number 124-10026-10357. "Possible mental case" – FBI radiogram, February 27, 1964, ARRB Record Number 1801005110369.

30. Intercepted telephone call described in *Conspiracy,* by Anthony Summers, Paragon House edition, p. 103, citing Commission Document 206, p. 66.

31. Shirley Martin interview, October 16, 2001.

Chapter Seven – Mrs. Oswald and Mrs. Markham

1. *McCall's,* October 1965, Vol. XCIII, No. 1.

2. *Jean Stafford: A Biography,* by David Roberts, p. 355.

3. *The Interior Castle,* by Ann Hulbert, p.338.

4. *A Mother In History,* p. 32.

5. "...evidence is inconclusive..." The Warren Report, p. 256.

6. *A Mother In History,* p. 33.

7. *Ibid.*

8. *Jean Stafford: A Biography,* p. 356.

9. *A Mother in History,* p. 12.

10. *The Interior Castle*, p. 341.

11. *Jean Stafford*, by Mary Ellen Williams Walsh, pp. 82-4.

12. Number of readers who saw "The Unsinkable": Paul Krassner to author, October 23, 2000. Mr. Krassner estimates the 1964 circulation of *The Realist* at "at least" 40,000. In contrast, *McCall's* 1965 circulation, when Stafford's article appeared, was "over 8,400,000," according to the masthead of *McCall's,* October 1965.

13. Vincent J. Salandria interview, April 25, 2000.

14. "The Unsinkable Marguerite Oswald," by Harold Feldman, *The Realist,* September 1964. Except where otherwise indicated, this section is derived from this article.

15. The Warren Report, p. 167.

16. Feldman.

17. On March 26, 1964, Helen Markham told Warren Commission attorney Joseph Ball that she was no longer married (WC Vol. III, p. 305). Yet she seems to have led Feldman and Salandria to believe they were still married. Presumably the Mr. Markham they encountered in June was the former husband.

18. Markham terror: Vincent J. Salandria to David Starks, videotaped interview, 1993.

19. Vincent J. Salandria interview.

20. CE 3122, WC, Vol. 26, pp. 786-88.

21. Vincent J. Salandria interview, spring 2000.

22. Feldman.

23. *The New York Times*, December 20, 1963.

24. Vincent J. Salandria interview, spring 2000.

25. *Ibid.*

26. Feldman.

27. Author's collection.

28. Vincent J. Salandria interview, spring 2000.

29. WC Vol. XXV, p. 727, and *A Citizen's Dissent,* p. 22.

30. Rankin-Lane letters: WC Vol. XXV, pp. 719-728. (For some reason, the first letter of this series appears last, on p. 728 of Vol. XXV. Otherwise the letters are in proper sequence.) Lane won't reveal source: WC Vol. II, p. 60.

31. WC Vol. XXV, pp. 725-726; *A Citizen's Dissent,* p. 21; "smacked of police state tactics:" *The New York Times*, April 30, 1964, p. 21.

32. WC Vol. V, p. 547.

33. *Ibid.*

34. *Ibid.*

35. *Rush to Judgment*, pp. 180-189.

36. WC Vol. V, p. 550.

37. WC Vol. V, pp. 550-551.

38. WC Vol. V, p. 553.

39. WC Vol. V, p. 555-556.

40. Transcription: Markham Exhibit No. 1, WC Vol. XX, pp. 571-599. Lane sends tape, gets no reply: *Rush to Judgment*, p. 182, including second footnote (†).

41. CE 3122, WC, Vol. 26, pp. 786-88. This report, to which the agents did not affix their names, is dated July 31, exactly one week after the interview with Helen Markham.

42. Vincent J. Salandria interview, June 2, 2000.

43. CE 3122, WC, Vol. 26, pp. 786-88.

44. CE 3122, WC, Vol. 26, pp. 786-88. The tape recording referenced here appears to be lost.

45. Vincent J. Salandria to Jeannine Herron, July 6, 1964.

Chapter Eight – Mrs. Markham and Mrs. Clemons

1.   Time of Tippit shooting: The Warren Report, pp. 156-157.
2.   The Warren Report, pp. 156-160.
3.   The Warren Report, pp. 161-163.
4.   The Warren Report, p. 162.
5.   The Warren Report, pp. 163-165.
6.   The Warren Report, p. 165.
7.   WC Vol. VI, p. 443.
8.   Ball-Roberts dialog: WC Vol. VI, p. 443. "It was never determined..." *Accessories After the Fact*, by Sylvia Meagher, p. 264.
9.   Details of Tippit shooting: The Warren Report, p. 165.
10.   The Warren Report, p. 166.
11.   The Warren Report, p. 166.
12.   WC Vol. XXIV, p. 202.
13.   The Warren Report, p. 166.
14.   *Ibid.*, p. 168.
15.   *Ibid.*, p. 169.
16.   *Ibid.*, pp. 169-171.
17.   Markham tells Lane warned not to talk: Markham Exhibit No. 1, WC Vol. XX, pp. 571-599. Ex-husband tells Salandria and Feldman about threats: "The Unsinkable Marguerite Oswald," by Harold Feldman, *The Realist,* September 1964.
18.   The Warren Report, p. 167.
19.   *Ibid.*, pp. 176-9.
20.   Markham and amonia: testimony of Police Capt. Will Fritz, WC Vol. IV, p. 212. Picks Oswald from lineup: The Warren Report, p. 167. "When I saw this man I wasn't sure..." WC Vol. III, p. 311.
21.   *Document Addendum to the Warren Report,* David Lifton, Ed., Sightext Pub., 1968, p. 359 (warning re: selective use of evidence) and 361 (quote re: Tippit shooting and Markham).
22.   Opinions about Helen Markham: *Inquest,* by Edward J. Epstein, pp. 134-136.
23.   The dialogue in this section comes from Helen Markham's Warren Commission testimony of July 23, 1964, WC Vol. VII, pp. 499-506.
24.   The Warren Report, p. 168.
25.   "Hot but otherwise OK", Nashes to Vincent J. Salandria, July 1964. "Division of labor", Deirdre Griswold to Vincent J. Salandria, June 9, 1964.
26.   "The Other Witnesses," *The New Leader*, October 12, 1964.
27.   Markham-Nash dialog: "The Other Witnesses," *The New Leader*, October 12, 1964.
28.   "The Other Witnesses," *The New Leader*, October 12, 1964.
29.   *Ibid.*
30.   *Ibid.*
31.   *Ibid.*
32.   *Ibid.*
33.   *Ibid.*
34.   *Ibid.*
35.   *Ibid.*
36.   *Ibid.*
37.   *Ibid.*
38.   Vincent J. Salandria interview, April 25, 2000.

39. The Warren Report, p. 652. "The Other Witnesses," by George and Patricia Nash, *The New Leader*, October 12, 1964.

40. The dialogue in this section comes from a transcript of the interview by Shirley Martin of Acquilla Clemons, August 1964. Transcript prepared by Vickie Martin and provided to the author by Shirley Martin. Details supplemented by interviews with Mrs. Martin, spring and summer, 2000, and June 2001.

41. The Warren Report, pp. 5-6; p. 165.

42. The amount of money was not recorded. In July 2000 Mrs. Martin remembered it only as "a small gratuity."

43. The Warren Report, pp. 166-169.

44. The Warren Report, p. 663.

45. WC Vol. 11, pp. 434-442.

46. *Ibid.*

47. Domingo Benavides tells police he can't ID gunman: The Warren Report, p. 166. "The purpose of a lineup..." *Rush to Judgment*, by Mark Lane, p. 178.

48. Edward Benavides: *Accessories After the Fact*, by Sylvia Meagher, pp. 299-300. Domingo Benavides on CBS: CBS New Inquiry: The Warren Report, Part III, June 27, 1967.

49. *Forgive My Grief*, Vol. II, by Penn Jones, Jr., p. 1.

Chapter Nine – Texas

1.   *Citizen's Arrest,* by H.C. Nash, p. 41, and *The Lomax Show,* October 1, 1966.

2.   Quote from *Citizen's Arrest,* p. 41. Jones also told this anecdote on *The Lomax Show,* October 1, 1966.

3.   Just past 49th birthday: *Citizen's Arrest,* p. 17. Salad: "The Death of Democracy," by Wendy Govier, *The Journal of the Society of Newspaper Design,* October/November/December, 1990, p. 14. Transistor radio: "Editor Jones Story of the Dallas Killing," *The Midlothian Mirror,* November 25, 1963. "I rushed over to where these other..." *Citizen's Arrest,* pp. 41-2.

4.   *The Midlothian Mirror,* November 25, 1963, and *Citizen's Arrest,* p. 42; *Forgive My Grief,* Vol. IV, by Penn Jones, Jr., p. 120.

5.   *Midlothian Mirror,* November 25, 1963, and *Citizen's Arrest,* p. 42.

6.   *Midlothian Mirror,* November 25, 1963.

7.   *Forgive My Grief,* Vol. 1, by Penn Jones, Jr., p. 184.

8.   Bought paper for 4K in 1945: *Forgive My Grief,* Vol. 4, Preface, third page (unnumbered in book) and *The Windmill Fighter,* p. 23. Quote: *Citizen's Arrest,* p. 24.

9.   "A tuckered out little weekly..." *Citizen's Arrest,* p. 24. Louise and Penn: *Citizen's Arrest,* pp. 22-23. Editorial "we": *The Windmill Fighter,* p. 8.

10. *Citizen's Arrest,* p. 24.

11. First issue of *Mirror* under Jones a day late, and a "pitiful effort": *The Windmill Fighter,* p. 23. No business buying the paper: "One Man's Grief," by Robert Bonazzi, *The Texas Observer,* September 29, 1967. The rest of this paragraph: *Citizen's Arrest,* p. 25, and *The Midlothian Mirror,* December 14, 1945.

12. *Citizen's Arrest,* pp. 25-26.

13. *Citizen's Arrest,* p. 17. Unpainted shack, single fireplace: *The Windmill Fighter,* p. 45-a. "When I was growing up..." *Forgive My Grief,* by Penn Jones, Jr., Vol. III, p. 77.

14. *Citizen's Arrest,* pp. 18-19.

15. Jones five feet three inches: Louise Jones to Sylvia Meagher, January 12, 1966. Rest of this paragraph: *Citizen's Arrest,* p. 20.

16. *Citizen's Arrest*, p. 20.

17. *Citizen's Arrest*, pp. 20-21. Captain: *Citizen's Arrest*, p. 24.

18. Letter quoted in *The Windmill Fighter*, pp. 22-23. Savings bond: *Citizen's Arrest*, pp. 23-24.

19. *The Windmill Fighter*, pp. 4-5.

20. *Citizen's Arrest*, pp. 96-97. Background on Mansfield incident: "Mansfield, Texas: A Report of the Crisis Situation Resulting from Efforts to Desegregate the School System," by John Howard Griffin; *The Establishment in Texas Politics*, p. 189; and *Man in the Mirror: John Howard Griffin and the Story of Black Like Me*, by Robert Bonazzi, pp. 25-27.

21. *Citizen's Arrest*, pp. 96-97, and *Man in the Mirror*, pp. 25-27.

22. "Stranger in Town," by Robert Bonazzi, *Latitudes* magazine, Summer 1967, Vol. I, No. 2.

23. Quote: *The Windmill Fighter*, p. 36.

24. *Citizen's Arrest*, p. 33, and *The Windmill Fighter*, pp. 27-28.

25. *Citizen's Arrest*, p. 35; "Stranger in Town," *Latitudes* magazine, Summer 1967, Vol. I, No. 2; and *The Windmill Fighter*, pp. 35-36.

26. *Citizen's Arrest*, p. 35, and "Stranger in Town," *Latitudes* magazine, Summer 1967, Vol. I, No. 2. (The two accounts differ slightly and I have synthesized them – jk.)

27. *Citizen's Arrest*, p. 35, and "Stranger in Town," *Latitudes* magazine, Summer 1967, Vol. I, No. 2.

28. "The hell it isn't!" and "You son of a bitch!" "Stranger in Town," *Latitudes* magazine, Summer 1967, Vol. I, No. 2.

29. "He put some pretty good knots..." *Citizen's Arrest*, pp. 35-36.

30. Fight, and allusion to Seay's alleged homosexuality: *The Midlothian Mirror*, May 3, 1962. "How long have you been a homosexual?" *The Windmill Fighter*, p. 39.

31. Fight details: *Citizen's Arrest*, p. 36. "A police officer broke up the fight..." and "I will admit..." "Stranger in Town," *Latitudes* magazine, Summer 1967, Vol. I, No. 2.

32. *Citizen's Arrest*, p. 35, "Stranger in Town," *Latitudes* magazine, Summer 1967, Vol. I, No. 2, and *The Windmill Fighter*, by Penn Jones, Jr., pp. 1-2. "My lungs got full of smoke..." "One Man's Grief," *The Texas Observer*, September 29, 1967. Watchman armed with Jones' shotgun: *The Windmill Fighter*, p. 12.

33. Estimate of fire damage: "One Man's Grief," by Robert Bonazzi, *The Texas Observer*, September 29, 1967. Investigators say arson: *The Windmill Fighter*, p. 2. Reward: *Citizen's Arrest*, p. 37, and *The Midlothian Mirror*, multiple editions following incident.

34. Seay clears polygraph: *The Windmill Fighter*, p. 211, and *Citizen's Arrest*, p. 37. "There were too many inconsistencies..." *Citizen's Arrest*, p. 37. Reward never claimed: *Citizen's Arrest*, and author's inspection of *Midlothian Mirror* issues.

35. "Some mighty bad things have happened..." and "Gonna get out a paper...?" plus reply: "Stranger in Town," *Latitudes* magazine, Summer 1967, Vol. I, No. 2.

36. "Why, hell yes..." : "Stranger in Town," *Latitudes* magazine, Summer 1967. Headline: *The Midlothian Mirror*, May 3, 1962.

37. *Citizen's Arrest*, p. 39. Congratulations from JFK: *The Midlothian Mirror*, July 18, 1963.

38. *Citizen's Arrest*, p. 39.

39. Mary Ferrell interview, November 18, 2000.

40. Lunch at Chaparral Club, and "I didn't even care enough..." "Woman on a Mission," *Fort Worth Star-Telegram*, September 3, 2000. Lifelong Republican, and "And I heard the first description..." Mary Ferrell interview, November 18, 2000.

41. Mary Ferrell interview, November 18, 2000.

42. *Ibid.*

43. *Ibid.*

44. *Ibid.*

45. "Assassin Crouched and Took Deadly Aim," reproduced in facsimile in *The Assassination Story.* "Tip to FBI Warned of Oswald Death," reproduced in facsimile in *Forgive My Grief*, Vol. III, pp. 108-109. "There were very few copies of that..." Mary Ferrell interview, Nov. 18, 2000.

46. Mary Ferrell interview, November 18, 2000.

47. French TV interview: *Forgive My Grief*, Vol. I, preface by John Howard Griffin.

48. *Black Like Me*, by John Howard Griffin.

49. *Forgive My Grief*, Vol. I, preface by John Howard Griffin.

50. *Ibid.*

51. Penn Jones to Louis Lomax, *The Lomax Show*, October 1, 1966.

52. Jones conducts a few early interviews: "Transcript of Interview with Penn Jones, Jr., by Pamela Mason, Los Angeles radio, September 1966," by Sylvia Meagher. "We didn't see him for a month..." *Citizen's Arrest*, pp. 42-43. Fifteen sets of Hearings and Exhibits: "One Man's Grief," by Robert Bonazzi, *The Texas Observer*, September 29, 1967.

53. Search for Earlene Roberts: *Forgive My Grief*, Vol. I, p. 171. "We found 'Earlene Roberts'..." *Citizen's Arrest*, p. 42. Roberts testimony "astounding": *The Continuing Inquiry*, October 22, 1978, p. 5. Roberts death: *The Dallas Morning News*, January 10, 1966, p. D-3, and *Ramparts* magazine, November 1966, p. 43. Both reports omit Roberts' age. *Time* magazine gave it as 60 in its November 11, 1966, issue, p. 34.

54. "Third degree": WC Vol. VI, p. 444. Cheek and Ruby: WC Vol. XIII, pp. 383-390.

55. *Forgive My Grief*, Vol. I, Chapter 1.

56. *The Midlothian Mirror*, June 3, 1965, "The Assassination No. 1, Reopen the Warren Commission."

57. *The Midlothian Mirror*, June 3, 1965, p. 2, "An Explanation."

58. Jarnigan FBI statement: CE 2821, WC Wol. 26, pp. 254-259. Jones on Jarnigan: *Forgive My Grief*, Vol. I.

59. *The Midlothian Mirror*, June 3, 1965, "The Assassination No. 1, Reopen the Warren Commission."

60. *Forgive My Grief*, Vol. I, foreword.

Chapter Ten – Loyalty

1. McCarran and UN: *The Great Fear*, by David Caute, p. 325; Right-wing views on UN: *The Far Right*, by Donald Janson and Bernard Eismann, pp. 8-9.

2. United Nations purge: *The Great Fear*, by David Caute, Chapter 16. Witness No. 8: *The New York Times*, July 24, 1949. UN Staff committee resolution and Byron Price quote: *The New York Times*, July 25, 1949.

3. Immigration and Nationality Act of 1952, and Internal Security Act of 1950: *Red Scare*, by Griffin Fariello, p. 18. See also "Patrick McCarran," The Biographical Resource Group, Galenet.

4. *The Great Fear*, by David Caute, p. 330.

5. "There was nothing to spy on..." *United Nations: The First Fifty Years*, by Stanley Meisler, p. 82. "While publicly Lie protested..." *The Great Fear*, by David Caute, pp. 325-6, and *United Nations: The First Fifty Years*, p. 82.

6. "Thirty American employees of the United Nations..." *The Great Fear*, by David Caute, pp. 326-7. Use of Fifth Amendment: *The Great Fear*, by David Caute, pp. 150-52, and *The Communist Controversy in Washington*, by Earl Latham, pp. 12-13. "From the

Inquisition to the Salem witch trials..." *Advocate and Activist,* by John J. Abt, p. 152.

7. Ruth Elizabeth Crawford background: *The New York Times*, January 22, 1953.

8. "I know that I might have invoked..." from "I Have a Thing to Tell You," by Ruth Elizabeth Crawford, *The Nation*, January 24, 1953.

9. Progressive Party and Communism: *Henry Wallace, Harry Truman, and the Cold War,* by Richard J. Walton, p. 249. "What I did as an employee..." from "I Have a Thing to Tell You," by Ruth Elizabeth Crawford, *The Nation*, January 24, 1953. Crawford fired: *The New York Times*, January 22, 1953. UN Article 19 quoted in Crawford's *Nation* article.

10. UN Administrative Tribunal, firings illegal: *The New York Times*, September 2, 1953. *Washington Post* editorial: September 3, 1953. Hammarskhöld's ruling against Crawford, and quote: *The New York Times*, September 3, 1953. Crawford quote: letter to supporters, October 3, 1953, in Sylvia Meagher Collection, Special Collections and Archives of the Beneficial-Hodson Library, Hood College, Frederick, Maryland. Material from this collection cited in the present work identified hereafter as "Meagher Collection, Hood College."

11. *The New York Times*, July 14, 1954, and December 4, 1954.

12. Ruth E. Crawford, letter to supporters, Oct. 3, 1953, Meagher Collection, Hood College.

13. *Ibid.*

14. Information Circular No. 8, January 28, 1953, World Health Organization, Meagher Collection, Hood College.

15. Sylvia Meagher to Dr. Brock Chisolm, Feb. 5, 1953. Meagher Collection, Hood College.

16. Sylvia Meagher to Dr. Brock Chisolm, undated letter, probably April 1953. Meagher Collection, Hood College.

17. Sylvia Meagher to Albert F. Bender, Jr., April 16, 1953. Meagher Collection, Hood College.

18. Pierce J. Gerety to Sylvia Meagher, February 5, 1954. Received by Meagher on February 10: Meagher to Gerety, February 17, 1954. Meagher Collection, Hood College.

19. International Organizations Employees Loyalty Board, "Interrogatory, Sylvia Orenstein Meagher," Meagher Collection, Hood College.

20. "When Sylvia was angry..." Harold Weisberg to David Starks, videotaped interview, May 1997. "She told Gerety that her views..." etc., Sylvia Meagher to Pierce J. Gerety, February 17, 1954. Meagher Collection, Hood College.

21. Prepared statement for IOELB hearing by Sylvia Meagher. Meagher Collection, Hood College.

22. Gerety resigns: *The New York Times*, December 20, 1954. "...contributed to the suicide...": *The Great Fear,* by David Caute, p. 328.

23. Pierce J. Gerety, Chairman, International Organizations Employees Loyalty Board, August 26, 1954. Meagher Collection, Hood College.

24. 10422 declared unconstitutional: *Secretariat News,* May 30, 1986. Meagher Collection, Hood College.

Chapter Eleven – Friends in LA

1. "I wish others more qualified..." Raymond Marcus to Orleans Parish Grand Jury, May 11, 1967. Transcript privately published as *Orleans Parish Grand Jury Proceedings of May 10, 1967,* p. 2.

2. *Addendum B,* by Raymond Marcus, p. 20.

3.   "We are talking about..." and "I was told, 'Well, don't use...'" *Orleans Parish Grand Jury Proceedings of May 10, 1967,* p. 1.

4.   "He had always been interested..." Ray Marcus interview, July 12, 2000. "When the government put out the word..." Ray Marcus interview, June 27, 2000.

5.   *Life* magazine: November 29, 1963. "...they were first published in black and white due to..." *The Zapruder Film: Reframing JFK's Assassination,* by David R. Wrone, p. 35, and *Pictures of the Pain,* by Richard B. Trask, pp. 93-95.

6.   Marcus bought two copies: Ray Marcus interview, July 12, 2001. "In one of those pictures..." and "I wasn't sure of it..." *Orleans Parish Grand Jury Proceedings of May 10, 1967,* p. 4.

7.   "The Assassination of President Kennedy," *Life* magazine, November 29, 1963, p. 24; "End To Nagging Rumors: The Six Critical Seconds," *Life* magazine, December 6, 1963, p. 52F. Copy in author's collection.

8.   *Orleans Parish Grand Jury Proceedings of May 10, 1967,* p. 4.

9.   Ray Marcus interview, June 27, 2000.

10.   Ray Marcus interview, May 17, 2001.

11.   Ray Marcus interview, July 25, 2001.

12.   Albert Einstein to Ray Marcus, May 16, 1951.

13.   Ray Marcus to Earl Warren, December 29, 1963.

14.   Ray Marcus interview, July 12, 2000.

15.   Ray Marcus to Mark Lane, January 8, 1964.

16.   Maggie Field to Sylvia Meagher, July 13, 1965.

17.   Gwen Field interview, July 9, 2001.

18.   "The Buffs," by Calvin Trillin, *The New Yorker* magazine, June 1967.

19.   "...a seamstress who regularly came..." and three sets of WC volumes: Gwen Field interview, July 9, 2001.

20.   Gwen Field interview, July 9, 2001.

21.   *Ibid.*

22.   *Ibid.*

23.   *Ibid.*

24.   *Ibid.*

25.   *Ibid.*

26.   *Ibid.*

27.   "The assassination gave them an instant common ground..." Ray Marcus interview, July 25, 2001, and Ray Marcus to Ayda Field, August 15, 1997. "For Maggie as for me..." Ray Marcus to Ayda Field, August 15, 1997.

Chapter Twelve – The Report Goes Public

1.   *New York Times,* "Johnson Gets Assassination Report," September 25, 1964.

2.   *Ibid.*

3.   *Ibid.*

4.   *Ibid.*

5.   *Ibid.*

6.   *Ibid.*

7.   *Ibid.*

8.   *Ibid.*

9.   Ray Marcus interview, June 27, 2000.

10.   Vincent J. Salandria interview, April 24, 2000.

11.   Harold Weisberg interview, November 30, 2000.

12. *A Citizen's Dissent,* by Mark Lane, p. 57.

13. "The evidence of Oswald's single-handed guilt…" Warren Report, Bantam Books (NYT) paperback edition, p. xxix. "…amazing in its detail…" *Time*, October 2, 1964, p. 45.

14. "Within minutes…" Warren Report, p. 144.

15. "Stuff that leaped off the pages…" Ray Marcus interview, June 27, 2000. "Pace yourself…" Vincent J. Salandria to Shirley Martin, November 15, 1964.

16. Shirley Martin to Make Lane's "whole office," undated, probably Oct. or Nov., 1964.

17. Vincent J. Salandria to Shirley Martin, November 14, 1964.

18. Vincent J. Salandria to Shirley Martin, October 12, 1964.

19. Vincent J. Salandria to Shirley Martin, October 8, 1964.

20. *Philadelphia Evening Bulletin*, October 23, 1964, by way of *The Legal Intelligencer,* November 2, 1964.

21. Vincent J. Salandria to Shirley Martin, October 8, 1964.

22. Vincent J. Salandria interview, May 31, 2000.

23. "It surprised me to see…" Vincent J. Salandria to Shirley Martin, November 9, 1964. *The Legal Intelligencer,* Philadelphia, Pennsylvania, November 2, 1964, Vol. 151.

24. "It took about three hours…" Vincent J. Salandria, cover letter to correspondence group, August 25, 1994.

25. "The illustrious Mr. Specter…" – "The Warren Report's Analysis of Shots, Trajectories and Wounds – A Dissenting View," unpublished first draft, author's collection. "I volunteered to a second…" Vincent J. Salandria to Shirley Martin, November 9, 1964.

26. "The Warren Report Analysis of Shots, Trajectories and Wounds: A Lawyer's Dissenting View," by Vincent J. Salandria, *Legal Intelligencer,* November 2, 1964.

27. *Ibid.*

28. "If the smell of gunpowder…" "The Warren Report Analysis of Shots, Trajectories and Wounds: A Lawyer's Dissenting View," by Vincent J. Salandria, *The Legal Intelligencer,* Nov. 2, 1964. Republished in *History Will Not Absolve Us* by E. Martin Schotz, 1996, and *False Mystery: Essays on the Assassination of JFK,* by Vincent J. Salandria, privately published, 1999.

29. "The Warren Report Analysis of Shots, Trajectories and Wounds: A Lawyer's Dissenting View," by Vincent J. Salandria, *The Legal Intelligencer,* November 2, 1964.

30. Bullet hits cement: Warren Report, p. 116. "The obvious deduction…" – "The Warren Report Analysis of Shots, Trajectories and Wounds: A Lawyer's Dissenting View," by Vincent J. Salandria, *The Legal Intelligencer,* November 2, 1964.

31. "The Warren Report Analysis of Shots, Trajectories and Wounds: A Lawyer's Dissenting View," by Vincent J. Salandria, *The Legal Intelligencer*, November 2, 1964, citing The Warren Report, p. 111.

32. "The Warren Report Analysis of Shots, Trajectories and Wounds: A Lawyer's Dissenting View," by Vincent J. Salandria, *The Legal Intelligencer*, November 2, 1964.

33. Specifics on the President's clothing: all cited in "The Warren Report Analysis of Shots, Trajectories and Wounds: A Lawyer's Dissenting View," by Vincent J. Salandria, *The Legal Intelligencer*, November 2, 1964, citing in turn the Warren Report, p. 92.

34. "The Warren Report Analysis of Shots, Trajectories and Wounds: A Lawyer's Dissenting View," by Vincent J. Salandria, *The Legal Intelligencer*, November 2, 1964, citing Warren Report, pp. 92-3.

35. Shirley Martin to Vincent J. Salandria, November 5, 1964.

36. *Ibid.*

37. FBI memorandum, "The President's Commission on the Assassination of President

Kennedy," SAC, Philadelphia (157-016) to Director, FBI, November 5, 1964. Assassination Records Review Board Record Number 124-10265-10326.

38. Vincent J. Salandria to Earl Warren, November 4, 1964.

39. *The Legal Intelligencer*, November 23, 1964.

40. "In my other copy of the same..." *The Legal Intelligencer*, November 23, 1964.

41. Vincent J. Salandria to Shirley Martin, December 15, 1964.

42. "Salandria said wasn't much different..." Vincent J. Salandria to Shirley Martin, December 23, 1964. "Staughton Lynd of Yale..." Vincent J. Salandria to Shirley Martin, December 15, 1964.

Chapter Thirteen – The First Anniversary

1. Shirley Martin to Vincent J. Salandria, undated letter, probably mid-November 1964.

2. Shirley Martin to "the whole office" of Mark Lane, undated letter, probably late 1964 or early 1965.

3. Shirley Martin to Vincent J. Salandria, undated letter, probably mid-November 1964.

4. Vincent J. Salandria to Shirley Martin, November 19, 1964.

5. *Evening Bulletin* article quoted in letter, Salandria to Shirley Martin, Nov. 19, 1964.

6. Vincent J. Salandria to Shirley Martin, November 19, 1964.

7. *The Dallas Morning News*, Nov. 23, 1964, and *The Dallas Times Herald*, Nov. 23, 1964.

8. *The New York Times*, November 23, 1964.

9. *Ibid.*

10. Shirley Martin to Vincent J. Salandria, November 24, 1964.

11. *Ibid.*

12. "A Philadelphia Lawyer Analyzes the President's Back and Neck Wounds," *Liberation*, March 1965.

13. *Dallas Times-Herald,* November 22, 1964.

14. Warren Report goes on sale at GPO retail store: *The New York Times*, September 28, 1964. Weisberg purchases multiple copies of Warren Report and 26 volumes, and donates them in 1992: *Case Open*, by Harold Weisberg, p. xi.

15. "I had a Concord voice activated..." Harold Weisberg interview, November 30, 2000. Weisberg also said, rather specifically, that he used a crayon to mark up the 26 volumes. Unfortunately I did not ask him, "Why a crayon?" Manuscript completed February 1965: *Post Mortem*, by Harold Weisberg, jacket blurb. Book contract: Harold Weisberg to David Starks, May 1997. "Industan" subtitle: facsimile copy from Harold Weisberg Collection, Special Collections and Archives of the Beneficial-Hodson Library, Hood College, Frederick, Maryland. Hereafter cited as "Weisberg archive."

16. Shirley Martin to Harold Feldman, December 5, 1964.

17. 20,000 pages and ten million words: Sylvia Meagher, *Accessories After the Fact*, p. xxvii. Dental records: See WC Vol. XXII, p. 395. Lane on dental records: Lane made this quip on more than one occasion, one of them during a debate on January 25, 1967, with former Commission attorney Wesley Liebeler.

18. "Organized chaos..." *Whitewash II*, by Harold Weisberg, p. 86. "It would be tantamount...": Sylvia Meagher, *Accessories After the Fact*, p. xxvii.

19. Sylvia Meagher to Vincent J. Salandria, September 3, 1965.

20. Sylvia Meagher to Maggie Field, July 15, 1965; Meagher Collection, Hood College.

21. Sylvia Meagher to Maggie Field, August 26, 1965; Meagher Collection, Hood College.

22. Meagher at the UN building: *Accessories After the Fact*, by Sylvia Meagher, p. xxi. "I said with irony that a leftist..." Sylvia Meagher to Lillian Castellano, March 26, 1965. Meagher Collection, Hood College.

23. Meagher's early suspicions: *The Scavengers and Critics of the Warren Report*, by Richard Warren Lewis and Lawrence Schiller, pp. 72-73. "Bitter Thoughts After the 22nd of November," written "about 30 Nov. 1963," and Sylvia Meagher to Earl Warren, December 26, 1963 – Assassination Collection, Hood College. Meagher at Town Hall lecture, and CCI contributions: Sylvia Meagher to Maggie Field, August 7, 1965. August 1964 Europe trip: Sylvia Meagher to Mark Lane, September 11, 1964.

24. *The Scavengers and Critics of the Warren Report*, by Richard Warren Lewis, p. 72.

25. "The Warren Commission Report: A Critique," by "Isabel Meagher Davis," Meagher Collection, Hood College. Also re: employment concerns: see Meagher to Mark Lane, September 11, 1964.

26. "The Warren Commission Report: A Critique," by Sylvia Meagher, p. 1. Meagher Collection, Hood College.

27. Parallel development – *e.g.* Sylvia Meagher to Maggie Field, July 15, 1965.

28. "The Warren Commission Report: A Critique," by Sylvia Meagher. Meagher Collection, Hood College.

29. Marital status: Sylvia Meagher to Maggie Field, August 9, 1965. "Some years ago, I suddenly began to feel..." Sylvia Meagher to Shirley Martin, April 9, 1966.

30. Maiden name and year of birth: "Identification and Personnel Data for Employment of United States Citizen," dated April 6, 1953. Document among Loyalty Board papers in Meagher Archive, Hood College. Grew up in Brooklyn: "Identification and Personnel Data for Employment of United States Citizen," dated April 6, 1953. The rest of this paragraph, including quote: Sylvia Meagher to Shirley Martin, December 12, 1966.

31. Sylvia Meagher to Maggie Field, August 9, 1965.

32. 1953 document: "Identification and Personnel Data for Employment of United States Citizen," dated April 6, 1953. Filed with Loyalty Board papers in Meagher Archive, Hood College. Comments on James Meagher's alcoholism: Sylvia Meagher to Maggie Field, August 9, 1965.

33. Release date of Hearings and Exhibits: *The New York Times*, November 24, 1964. "I was wildly excited..." *The Scavengers and Critics of the Warren Report*, by Richard Warren Lewis, p. 72.

34. Warren Report critique withdrawn: Sylvia Meagher to Lillian Castellano, March 26, 1965. A collection of rejection slips for this piece is among the papers in the Meagher Archive, Hood College.

35. "Each day, she took one of the volumes to work..." *The Scavengers and Critics of the Warren Report*, by Richard Warren Lewis, p. 73. "It was appalling to find how many..." and "she hoped to develop her discoveries..." Sylvia Meagher to Lillian Castellano, March 26, 1965. Meagher Collection, Hood College.

36. "I am trying to exclude everything..." Sylvia Meagher to Maggie Field, July 20, 1965. Magnifying glass, and "I just couldn't bear it any more...": *The Scavengers and Critics of the Warren Report*, by Richard Warren Lewis, p. 73.

37. *New School Bulletin*, Spring Semester, 1965.

38. Sylvia Meagher to Lillian Castellano, March 26, 1965. Meagher Collection, Hood College.

39. "I suspected I'd get fanatics and buffs..." and class description, Joseph S. Lobenthal,

Jr., interview, October 15, 2001. Approaches Dean, and quote: Joseph S. Lobenthal, Jr., interview, November 19, 2001.

40. Joseph S. Lobenthal, Jr,. interview, November 19, 2001.

41. *Ibid.*

42. "Seminar of equals:" Joseph S. Lobenthal, Jr., interview, October 15, 2001. Other class participants: from the papers of Joseph S. Lobenthal, Jr.

43. *Newsweek*, Feb. 1, 1965, p. 47.

44. Duration of class: letter from Joseph S. Lobenthal, Jr., to Warren Report Class, May 27, 1965, from the papers of Joseph S. Lobenthal, Jr. The rest of this paragraph, including quote: Joseph S. Lobenthal, Jr., to Maggie Field, May 17, 1965.

45. Macdonald and Sauvage in Warren Report class: Joseph S. Lobenthal, Jr., to Maggie Field, May 17, 1965. Macdonald considers forming private committee: *A Moral Temper: The Letters of Dwight Macdonald*, edited by Michael Wreszin, p. 359.

46. Lobenthal list: letter from Joseph S. Lobenthal, Jr., to Warren Report Class, May 27, 1965, from the papers of Joseph S. Lobenthal, Jr.

47. Sylvia Meagher to Maggie Field, undated letter, probably late June or early July 1965.

Chapter Fourteen – A Middle-Aged Lochinvar

1. Evidence not made available, and Warren quote: *The New York Times*, February 5, 1964. 357 cubic feet of evidence: *Reasonable Doubt*, by Henry Hurt, p. 433, citing interview with Marion Johnson of the National Archives. Conviction against Oswald in two days: *The New York Times*, November 22, 1966. Critics derided as charlatans: *The Memoirs of Earl Warren*, by Chief Justice Earl Warren, editor's note, p. 363.

2. Dulles episode: "Notes and Comments on Interview with Allen Dulles, 12/7/65," by David Lifton. Lifton referred to this as a "confrontation and/or interview" in a letter to Vincent J. Salandria dated December 10, 1965. Also described in *Best Evidence*, by David Lifton, pp. 33-37.

3. "Piecing Together the Evidence," by Gerald R. Ford, *Life*, October 2, 1964, p. 51.

4. "The Commission Report is filled with distortions..." CCI Press Release, Dec. 1, 1964. "Were Oswald permitted to live..." and paraphrasing: "The Doubts Remain," *The National Guardian*, October 3, 1964, reprinted in *Critical Reactions to the Warren Report*, pp. 34-48.

5. *TMO* usually produced about 26,000 copies of each issue, according to "Statement of Ownership, Management and Circulation," *The Minority of One*, November 1964, p. 24.

6. Arnoni background: International Institute of Social History web site. Death camp tattoo: Sylvia Meagher to Maggie Field, August 6, 1967. Prisoner uniform at speaking engagements: Vincent J. Salandria interview, February 28, 2002, and *The Electric Kool-Aid Acid Test,* by Tom Wolfe, Bantam paperback edition, p. 195. "It is hard to believe that a human being..." Sylvia Meagher to Maggie Field, June 30, 1966.

7. "Who Killed Whom and Why?" *The Minority of One*, January 1964, p. 1.

8. *The New York Times*, March 20, 1964, and *The Minority of One*, April 1964.

9. *The Minority of One*, April 1964.

10. "...that there had been an appalling miscarriage..." *The Life of Bertrand Russell,* by Ronald W. Clark, p. 616.

11. Who Killed Kennedy? committee details and quote: Ralph Schoenman interview, August 14, 2000.

12. Ralph Schoenman interview, August 14, 2000.

13. "16 Questions On the Assassination" – only the questions are presented here; they are taken from a Citizens' Committee of Inquiry pamphlet reprinting the original article in the September 1964 issue of *The Minority of One*.

14. Marcus admires Lane, considers him "point man" – Ray Marcus interview, July 25, 2001. "Since the obvious purpose..." Ray Marcus to Mark Lane, April 1, 1964. Lane in Budapest: ARRB Record Number 11910002110487.

15. "No fewer than thirty FBI informants..." FBI memorandum, October 30, 1964, ARRB Record Number 1801003410479. Lane not unaware of monitoring: public statements made December 4, 1964, Beverly Hills, CA. See Chapter 16, "Dueling Attorneys."

16. FBI memorandum, October 30, 1964, ARRB Record Number 1801003410479.

17. Cost of admission: FBI memorandum, October 30, 1964, ARRB Record Number 1801003410479. CCI bank account: FBI memorandum, November 17, 1964, ARRB Record Number 1801004710101.

18. FBI memorandum, October 30, 1964, ARRB Record Number 1801003410479.

19. FBI memorandum, October 30, 1964, ARRB Record Number 1801003410479. No prepared remarks: Mark Lane interview, February 10, 2004.

20. *The New York World Telegram,* September 3, 1964, ARRB Record Number 180-10082-10319.

21. *Ibid.*

22. September 28 lecture: FBI memorandum, October 30, 1964, ARRB Record Number 1801003410479.

23. October 3 lecture: FBI memorandum, October 30, 1964, ARRB Record Number 1801003410479.

24. Information on Belli debates: ARRB Record Number 1801003410470, ARRB Record Number 1801004710102; *The Village Voice,* October 22, 1964; *A Citizen's Dissent,* pp. 32-36; and tape recording of October 9, 1964, San Francisco debate, Ray Marcus Collection, Special Collections and Archives of the Beneficial-Hodson Library, Hood College, Frederick, Maryland, cited hereafter as Ray Marcus Archive.

25. *A Citizen's Dissent,* p. 32.

26. Melvin M. Belli letter to Earl Warren: ARRB Record Number 180-10083-10408.

27. "The Bellicose Mr. Belli," *Fact* magazine, July-August 1964.

28. Telegram: ARRB Record Number 124-10081-10124. Olsen: WC Vol. XIV, pp. 624-640.

29. WC Vol. XIV, pp. 624-640. Quotation, p. 631.

30. "They should cut [Oswald] inch by inch..." and "if he was in England..." WC Vol. V, p. 191, and Warren Report, p. 343. Coleman denies statement and Olsen can't remember: The Warren Report, p. 344, and WC Vol. XIV, p. 648.

31. WC Vol. XIV, p. 637. Olsen's long pause was actually noted in the published testimony.

32. "It wouldn't have been any problem..." *The Ruby Cover-Up,* by Seth Kantor, p. 103.

33. Debates a "breakthrough": Deirdre Griswold to Raymond Marcus, August 19, 1964. Four thousand people in attendance: ARRB document 1801004810247. Debate details: Lane-Belli debate, Oct. 9, 1964, tape recording from Ray Marcus Archive, Hood College; ARRB document 1801003410470. Tuxedos: *A Citizen's Dissent,* p. 33.

34. Lane-Belli debate, Oct. 9, 1964, tape recording from Ray Marcus Archive, Hood College. Unless otherwise noted, all quotations, paraphrasings, and information in this section are derived from this tape recording.

35. Weitzman affidavit: WC Vol. XXIV, p. 228 [CE 2003, p. 63].

36. Brennan unable to make a positive identification, and seeing Oswald's picture on TV: Warren Report, p. 145.

37. "…no tape recordings, notes, or stenographic records of this questioning…" The Warren Report, p. 180.

38. At least three FBI informants: ARRB Record # 1801004710102, p. 2. See also ARRB Record # 1801004810247 and 124-10256-10022. Kunstler as moderator: *A Citizen's Dissent*, p. 35.

39. Oswald requests Abt: WC Vol. X, pp. 116-117. "I agreed to represent Oswald…" and handling Ruby's appeal: *My Life as a Radical Lawyer*, by William Kunstler, p. 153. Ruby dies: *The New York Times*, January 4, 1967.

40. Lane goes first: ARRB record numbers 124-10256-10022 and 1801004710102. "…a brief resume of his usual talk": ARRB record numbers 124-10256-10022. Other details: "Lane & Audience TKO Middle-Aged Lochinvar," by Stephanie Harrington, *The Village Voice*, October 22, 1964.

41. "Lane & Audience TKO Middle-Aged Lochinvar," *The Village Voice*, October 22, 1964.

42. *Ibid.*

43. "…was bright and he had…" and "A disorderly crowd of New York liberals…" *Melvin Belli: My Life On Trial*, by Melvin Belli with Robert Blair Kaiser, p. 281. Belli cancels third debate: *A Citizen's Dissent*, p. 35.

Chapter Fifteen – The Oswald Affair

1. Contemporary Authors Online. The Gale Group, 2000. Fascism and emigration to US: *Education of a Reluctant Radical*, Vol. I, pp. 121-153. (Hereafter cited as *Education…*) Williams College and Oxford University: *Education…* Vols. II and III. International Brigade, *Education…* Vol. III, Chapter One. A copy of *Deadline for Action* was generously provided to the author by Tony Marzani.

2. Marzani imprisoned, OSS and Donovan: *Red Scare*, pp. 152-154; *Education…* Vol. V, "Reconstruction." Weisberg on Donovan: Harold Weisberg to David Starks, May 1997.

3. Marzani certain his film led to incarceration: *Education…* Vol. V, Appendix, "Prison Notebooks," pp. 107-108, p. 182. Quote: ibid, p. 182.

4. Police spy witness: "A New Weapon for Witch-Hunters," by I.F. Stone, *The Nation*, July 12, 1947. Quotation: *We Can Be Friends*, by Carl Marzani, Introduction, p. 11. Pleas for leniency: Red Scare, p. 157.

5. "A New Weapon for Witch-Hunters," by I.F. Stone, *The Nation*, July 12, 1947.

6. *Education of a Reluctant Radical*, Vol. 5, "Reconstruction," Chapters Three and Five. Books that upset status quo: *Education of…* Vol. 5, p. 29. Marzani on assassination: *Education…* Vol. 5, "Reconstruction," p. 85, and Tony Marzani to author, September 24, 2002.

7. Joesten book speculative but worthwhile: *Education of a Reluctant Radical*, Vol. 5, "Reconstruction," p. 85. Quote: *Time*, June 12, 1964, p. 47.

8. "Put his whole heart and soul…" and book published within five weeks: *Oswald: Assassin or Fall Guy?* by Joachim Joesten, Acknowledgments.

9. Joesten in Dallas: CE 2709, WC Vol. 26, pp. 79-84. *Oswald: Assassin or Fall Guy?* by Joachim Joesten. Quotation: p. 11.

10. *Oswald: Assassin or Fall Guy?* Preface, pp. 8-14. Rankin letter reproduced in facsimile in the Joesten book.

11. *Oswald: Assassin or Fall Guy?*, p. 9.

12. *Ibid.*

13. "Since I had been located…" *Oswald: Assassin or Fall Guy?* p.10. "He kept rambling on all day…" CE 2708, WC Vol. 26, p. 79.

14. "...the assassination of the President was a..." and Joesten allegations re: Walker and Weissman: CE 2709, WC Vol. 26, p. 82. Weissman asked about Walker: WC Vol. 5, p. 494.

15. Background information from jacket blurb, *Oswald: Assassin or Fall Guy?* Joesten's name appears on *Newsweek* mastheads during early 1940s, *e.g.* issue of June 29, 1942, Vol. XIX No. 26, p. 8. Communist Party of Germany membership: ARRB Record Number 180-10092-10397.

16. Mark Lane during debate with Wesley Liebeler, January 21, 1967, University of California, Los Angeles. Tape recording in Ray Marcus archive, Hood College.

17. ARRB Record Number 180-10092-10397.

18. Information and quotations from ARRB Record Number 180-10092-10397. This document is quoted here verbatim, including the parenthetical remarks.

19. Shirley Martin to Vince Salandria, October 10, 1964.

20. *New Times,* September 23, 1964.

21. "Assassin or Fall Guy?" by Victor Perlo, *New Times,* September 1964.

22. "Oswald Book Filled With Inaccuracies," by Hugh Aynesworth, *Editor and Publisher,* August 1, 1964.

23. Attributed to Joesten but written by Marzani: Tony Marzani to author, Sept. 3, 2002.

24. ARRB Record Number 180-10092-10352.

25. Publicity over Buchanan's firing: see, for example, *Time*, June 12, 1964, "JFK: The Murder and the Myths," p. 44. *TMO* review: "Four Assassinations, One Pattern," by Cedric Belfrage, *The Minority of One*, October 1964, p. 18.

26. *Who Killed Kennedy?*, by Thomas Buchanan, European edition. Quote: p. 11.

27. *Ibid.*, pp. 142-152.

28. *Ibid.*

29. "If Lee Harvey Oswald were alive today..." *Who Killed Kennedy?*, European edition, p. 75.

30. "It has become a truism that..." See, for example, *The Expanding Vista: American Television in the Kennedy Years,* by Mary Ann Watson, "Epilogue," pp. 213-229. Paradox, and quote: "Television: A Transformation," by John Horn, *Columbia Journalism Review*, Winter 1964, p. 18.

31. "Assassination and its Aftermath," Part One, by Martin Dies, *American Opinion*, March 1964, p. 5. Reproduced in WC Vol. XX, p. 698.

32. "Marxmanship in Dallas," Pt. One, by Revilo P. Oliver, *American Opinion*, February 1964. Reproduced in WC Vol. XX, pp. 720-735.

33. *American Opinion*, February 1964, p. 25. Reproduced in WC Vol. XX, p. 732.

34. WC Vol. XV, pp. 730-731.

35. "The Warren Commission: An Editorial." *Commentary*, January 1964, p. 24.

36. *Ibid.*

37. *Commentary* article a summary, and "My father just became..." Pierre Sauvage interview, February 22, 2002.

38. "The Oswald Affair," by Léo Sauvage, *Commentary*, March 1964. See also *The New York Times*, December 4, 1963, and December 10, 1963.

39. *The Oswald Affair*, by Léo Sauvage, pp. 17-18.

40. Pierre Sauvage interview, February 22, 2002.

41. Sauvage as freelance journalist: Pierre Sauvage interview, November 11, 2003. Other background details: "Americans Who Cared," by Pierre Sauvage, speech on Holocaust Memorial Day, Temple Israel of Hollywood, April 19, 1996, and Pierre Sauvage interview, February 22, 2002. Exit visas: *Surrender On Demand,* by Varian Fry, pp. 16 and 86, and

Vichy France and the Jews, by Michael R. Marrus and Robert O. Paxton, pp. 161-162. Relatively few attempting to alert the world: See *The Abandonment of the Jews,* by David S. Wyman, pp. 19-41.

42. "The Massacre of the Jews," by Varian Fry, *The New Republic*, December 21, 1942.

43. Sauvage to Le Chambon: Pierre Sauvage interview, February 22, 2002. No one turned away or betrayed: "The American Experience of the Holocaust," Yom Hashoah (Holocaust Memorial Day) 1993 and 1996 addresses by Pierre Sauvage.

44. Pierre Sauvage interviews, February 22, 2002, and November 11, 2003, and "Léo Sauvage is Dead," press release by Pierre Sauvage, 1988.

45. Sauvage move to the United States and early employment there: Pierre Sauvage interview, February 22, 2002. Latin America and Guevara book: *The New York Times,* November 5, 1988; and "Léo Sauvage is Dead," by Pierre Sauvage, November 1988.

46. "The Oswald Affair," *Commentary*, March 1964, p. 56.

47. *Ibid.*, p. 57.

48. *Ibid.*

49. *Ibid.*, p. 65.

50. *The Oswald Affair*, p. 399.

51. "...an attempt to keep alive..." *I.F. Stone's Weekly*, Jan. 17, 1953, Vol. I, No. 1, p. 3. *In Fact* information: *Izzy: A Biography of I.F. Stone*, p. 175. Marcus an *In Fact* subscriber: *Addendum B*, p. 31.

52. *Izzy: A Biography of I.F. Stone,* p. 176. "I had fought the loyalty purge..." *In a Time of Torment,* by I.F. Stone, p. xvii.

53. Marcus quotes: *Addendum B*, p. 31. "It is always dangerous..." *I.F. Stone's Weekly*, December 9, 1963, "Oswald's Mexican Trip May Prove The Key to The Assassination," p. 2.

54. *I. F. Stone's Weekly*, "The Left and the Warren Commission Report," October 5, 1964, p. 1.

55. "I want to start with..." *I.F. Stone's Weekly,* "The Left and the Warren Commission Report," October 5, 1964, p. 1. Russell sees advance copy of Warren Report: Ralph Schoenman interview, August 14, 2000.

56. *I. F. Stone's Weekly*, "The Left and the Warren Commission Report," October 5, 1964, p. 2.

57. *Ibid.*, p. 3.

58. "What was totally lacking..." *Addendum B*, p. 32.

59. Ray Marcus to I.F. Stone, October 8, 1964.

60. *Ibid.*

61. *Addendum B*, p. 32.

Chapter Sixteen – Dueling Attorneys

1. "Unlike the majority of Commission members..." *A Citizen's Dissent*, by Mark Lane, p. 124.

2. Joseph Ball appearance: *A Citizen's Dissent*, by Mark Lane, p. 124; *Addendum B*, by Raymond Marcus, p. 34, and Raymond Marcus interview, June 16, 2000. "These lectures were very well attended..." *Addendum B*, p. 34.

3. *A Citizen's Dissent*, p. 124.

4. Ray Marcus interview, June 27, 2000

5. Meetings at Field home, and quote: Ray Marcus to author, June 27, 2000. Lane briefed: Ray Marcus interview, September 3, 2002.

6. Ray Marcus interview, July 12, 2000.

7. Handbill for event, author's collection.

8.   Ray Marcus interview, March 11, 2002, and September 3, 2002. Lane's appearance on the UC-Santa Barbara campus is described in UCSB's student paper, *El Gaucho,* December 4, 1964, "Lane charges Warren Commission published 'cover-to-cover fraud.'"

9.   Auditorium filled early, others turned away: *Addendum B*, p. 34. "I do not think it ought to be…" Tape recording of event. Unless otherwise noted, quotations and information in this section come from the tape recording, and from the *Los Angeles Free Press,* Dec. 18, 1964.

10.   "The Commission Report is filled with…" Citizens' Committee of Inquiry press release, December 1 1964.

11.   FBI simulations: Lane cited *The New York Times*, December 6, 1963, p. 18, "Kennedy Slaying Is Reconstructed."

12.   Humes forbidden to talk: *The New York Times*, December 6, 1963, p. 18, "Kennedy Slaying Is Reconstructed."

13.   Markham picks Oswald from lineup: The Warren Report, p. 167. Confirms identification, March 26, 1964: WC Vol. III, p. 311.

14.   "…clearly indicated he knew virtually nothing…" *Addendum B*, p. 34.

15.   Ball a partner in Ball, Hunt and Hart: The Warren Report, p. 477.

16.   *Addendum B*, p. 35.

17.   *The Nation*'s article in support of the Report: "A Measure of the Achievement," by Herbert L. Packer, *The Nation*, November 2, 1964.

18.   "I believe the Commission has done a first-rate job…" *I.F. Stone's Weekly*, October 5, 1964.

19.   Philbrick: *Red Scare*, p. 68, fn. 10, and *The Great Fear*, pp. 117-118.

20.   Post-debate audience reaction: tape recording, Ray Marcus Archive.

21.   Lane post-debate interview: tape recording, Ray Marcus Archive

22.   Los Angeles branch formed: Deirdre Griswold to Vincent J. Salandria, January 5, 1965.

23.   "I have a very good tape (broadcast quality)…" Ray Marcus to Deirdre Griswold, January 10, 1965.

24.   Deirdre Griswold to Vincent J. Salandria, January 12, 1965.

25.   Vincent J. Salandria to Deirdre Griswold, January 18, 1965.

26.   Vincent J. Salandria to Deirdre Griswold, January 7, 1965.

Chapter Seventeen – Some Contacts

1.   "Zapruder Film of JFK Assassination Added to Registry," Associated Press. Screenings of bootleg copies: *The Zapruder Film: Reframing JFK's Assassination*, pp. 59-61.

2.   *Life* purchases Z-film: *Pictures of the Pain*, pp. 83-85. "In motion, the dramatic thing…" Ray Marcus interview, September 20, 2000. No comment on *Life*'s control of Z-film: *The Zapruder Film: Reframing JFK's Assassination*, p. 51.

3.   JFK first hit: Warren Report, p. 98 and p. 105. 1,772 fps, Connally wounds: Warren Report, p. 105. Missed shot: Warren Report, p. 111. Head shot at Z-313: Warren Report, p. 108.

4.   WC Vol. 18, pp. 1-80. Frame 212: see Vol. 18, p. 19. Weisberg quote: *Whitewash*, p. 45.

5.   Camera, film, and weapon data: Warren Report, p. 97.

6.   "A Philadelphia Lawyer Analyzes the Shots, Trajectories, and Wounds," *Liberation*, January 1965, citing The Warren Report p. 112 (JFK hit in neck region at Z-225), p. 103 (Connally shows no reaction at Z-225), and p. 112 (Connally insists he was not hit by first shot to hit JFK).

7.   "A Philadelphia Lawyer Analyzes the Shots, Trajectories, and Wounds," *Liberation*, January 1965.

8. *Ibid.*

9. *Ibid.*

10. Orleans Parish Grand Jury Proceedings of May 10, 1967, p. 4.

11. Razor blade details, and quote: Ray Marcus interview, September 5, 2000.

12. "...it is not necessary..." The Warren Report, p. 19. Marcus believes it is necessary: Hypothesis A, "Hypotheses re: the Zapruder Film," by Raymond J. Marcus, March 1965.

13. Hypothesis A, "Hypotheses re: the Zapruder Film."

14. "Hypotheses re: the Zapruder Film," by Raymond J. Marcus, March 1965. Marcus later determined that Connally's right hand was not on a hand-hold: "Connally's right hand and wrist were elevated in a position which would preclude its having been struck by that point [Z-232], while JFK was clearly reacting to a hit (I mistakenly believed Connally was gripping a hold bar, instead of his hat)." Ray Marcus to Josiah Thompson, December 15, 1967.

15. Working paper to be shared: Ray Marcus interview, September 5, 2000. Maggie Field types manuscript: Ray Marcus interview, September 3, 2002. Copy sent to Mark Lane: Ray Marcus to Josiah Thompson, December 15, 1967 (p. 8). Field sends Meagher copy: "Comments on the Seven Hypotheses" (Manuscript from Mrs. Field, Beverly Hills), July 8, 1965, by Sylvia Meagher.

16. "Comments on the Seven Hypotheses," July 8, 1965, by Sylvia Meagher.

17. "Hypotheses re: Zapruder film; Comments on the Seven Hypotheses" (Manuscript from Mrs. Field, Beverly Hills), July 8, 1965, by Sylvia Meagher.

18. "Hypotheses re: Zapruder film; Comments on the Seven Hypotheses," July 8, 1965, by Sylvia Meagher.

19. "Report on Visit to National Archives, Washington, D.C., to View the Zapruder Color Slides, 22 July 1965," by Sylvia Meagher. Meagher archive.

20. *Ibid.* The probable Marion Johnson is identified in this Meagher report only as "Mr. Johnson."

21. *Ibid.*

22. *Ibid.*

23. *Ibid.*

24. "Telephone Call to Mr. Herbert Orth, Assistant Chief, *Life* Photo Lab, Thursday 4 November 1965 at 7:30 p.m.," by Sylvia Meagher, ARRB document number 180-10089-10247.

25. *Accessories After the Fact*, p. 22.

26. "Report on Visit to National Archives, Washington, D.C., to View the Zapruder Color Slides, 22 July 1965," by Sylvia Meagher. Meagher archive.

27. *Ibid.*

28. "One of the most reprehensible..." *Accessories After the Fact*, p. xxiv.

29. Sylvia Meagher to Earl Warren, June 15, 1965. Margaret McHugh [Warren's executive secretary] to Sylvia Meagher, June 25, 1965. Sylvia Meagher to Gerald R. Ford, June 17, 1965. Gerald R. Ford to Sylvia Meagher, July 8, 1965. Sylvia Meagher to Albert E. Jenner, June 22, 1965.

30. Sylvia Meagher to Joseph A. Ball, September 24, 1965. Joseph A. Ball to Sylvia Meagher, October 6, 1965.

31. Sylvia Meagher to Joseph A. Ball, October 12, 1966.

32. Sylvia Meagher to Melvin Eisenberg, June 8, 1965.

33. *Ibid.*

34. Sylvia Meagher to Melvin Eisenberg, June 25, 1965.

35. "Notes on a telephone conversation with Melvin Eisenberg, July 1, 1965, 10-11:15

p.m.," by Sylvia Meagher. Meagher suspects Crehan: Sylvia Meagher to Shirley Martin, January 19, 1966.

36. "Notes on a telephone conversation with Melvin Eisenberg, July 1, 1965, 10-11:15 p.m.," by Sylvia Meagher, unnotarized certification by William Crehan, July 6, 1965.

37. "Notes on a telephone conversation with Melvin Eisenberg, July 1, 1965, 10-11:15 p.m.," by Sylvia Meagher.

38. *Ibid.*

39. *Ibid.*

40. *Ibid.*

41. *Ibid.*

42. *Ibid.*

43. Conversation goes until 11:15: "Notes on a telephone conversation with Melvin Eisenberg, July 1, 1965, 10-11:15 p.m.," by Sylvia Meagher. Copy of ad mailed eight days later: Sylvia Meagher to Melvin Eisenberg, July 10, 1965.

44. Sylvia Meagher, July 3, 1965.

45. Albert E. Jenner, Jr., to Sylvia Meagher, July 8, 1965. "Will wonders never cease?" Sylvia Meagher to Maggie Field, July 11, 1965.

46. Sylvia Meagher to Albert E. Jenner, Jr., July 10, 1965. Sylvia Meagher to Albert E. Jenner, Jr., August 20, 1965.

47. Sylvia Meagher to Alfred Goldberg, July 2, 1965.

48. "Telephone call from Thomas Stamm, Sunday 9 p.m., 1 August 1965." Memo by Sylvia Meagher

49. *Ibid.*

50. *Ibid.*

51. *Ibid.*

52. *Ibid.*

53. "Fifty-one Witnesses: The Grassy Knoll," by Harold Feldman, *The Minority of One*, March 1965.

54. Shirley Martin to Vincent J. Salandria, undated letter, probably spring 1965.

55. "Fifty-one Witnesses: The Grassy Knoll"

56. *Ibid.*

57. *Ibid.*

58. O'Donnell-O'Neill dialogue: *Man of the House,* by Thomas "Tip" O'Neill, p. 211.

59. "Fifty-one Witnesses: The Grassy Knoll." *The Minority of One*, March 1965.

60. "Fifty-one Witnesses: The Grassy Knoll." Quotation from the testimony of Bonnie Ray Williams, WC Vol. III, p. 175. *The Minority of One*, March 1965.

61. "No credible evidence suggests..." The Warren Report, p. 61. Article excerpt: "Fifty-one Witnesses: The Grassy Knoll." *The Minority of One*, March 1965.

62. "The Kennedy Body Snatchers," by Harold Feldman. *The Realist,* March 1965.

63. "Psychoanalysis and Lee Oswald," by Harold Feldman, incomplete draft, author's collection. Silvano Arieti quote: United Press International dispatch, which appeared in *The Dallas Morning News*, November 24, 1963, reprinted in facsimile in *The Assassination Story.*

64. Harold Weisberg interview, November 30, 2000. "Preface," *Whitewash*, pp. v.-viii. Limited edition: *Whitewash*, p. viii, and "Application for Registration of a Claim to Copyright," Weisberg archive, Hood College. Quote: *Post-Mortem*, by Harold Weisberg, p. 370.

65. *Whitewash*, Preface, p. v.

66. *Ibid.*

67. Random House as Sauvage's would-be publisher: Pierre Sauvage interview, February 22, 2002; also Mark Lane, *A Citizen's Dissent*, p. 39. Sauvage's contract broken: *The Oswald Affair* [book], "American Postscript," p. 399.

68. *The Oswald Affair*, p. 399.

69. Jason Epstein to Léo Sauvage, November 4, 1964, quoted in *The Oswald Affair*, p. 400. In his "American Postscript," Sauvage does not identify Epstein. He was identified to the author by Pierre Sauvage.

70. *The Oswald Affair*, p. 400.

71. Lane's cancelled contract: *A Citizen's Dissent*, p. 38, and Deirdre Griswold to Ray Marcus, February 16, 1964. "Omissions and distortions"...a phrase popular among some critics. See *The Oswald Affair*, p. 401, and *Accessories After the Fact*. Also letter, Harold Weisberg to David Welsh of *Ramparts*, February 17, 1966.

Chapter Eighteen – Films and Photographs

1. "Hypotheses re: the Zapruder Film."

2. Lifton contacts Marcus: *#5 Man, November 22, 1963*, by Ray Marcus, pp. 1-2, and *Best Evidence*, by David Lifton, p. 6. Lifton contacts Field and Solomon, and Field's opinion of Lifton: Maggie Field to Sylvia Meagher, August 4, 1965.

3. *#5 Man, November 22, 1963*, pp. 1-2. "I had been a physics major..." *Best Evidence*, p. 6.

4. *Best Evidence*, p. 8.

5. *Best Evidence*, p. 9; *Four Dark Days in History*.

6. "The Moorman photograph, and attempting to analyze it..." David Lifton interview, January 13, 2000. Examines picture, obtains negative: *Best Evidence*, p. 9. "That negative then produced..." David Lifton interview, January 13, 2000.

7. Additional prints: David Lifton interview, January 13, 2000. "He was definitely there..." *Best Evidence*, p. 10.

8. "We were both very excited..." David Lifton interview, January 13, 2000. "After having enlargements made..." *#5 Man, November 22, 1963*, p. 2.

9. Maggie Field to Sylvia Meagher, August 4, 1965.

10. Joseph Ball on "News Conference," KNBC, Saturday, February 27, 1965. Transcript reproduced in facsimile in *#5 Man, November 22, 1963*.

11. *#5 Man, November 22, 1963*, p. 11.

12. Ray Marcus (as "Irving J. Rosenthal") to Joseph Ball, May 19, 1965. Letter reproduced in facsimile in *Addendum B*.

13. Joseph Ball to Ray Marcus (as "Irving J. Rosenthal"), May 25, 1965. Letter reproduced in facsimile in *Addendum B*.

14. Lillian Castellano to *TMO*, March 1965, p. 30. Mrs. Castellano's letter had its origins in a "Statement" she wrote dated December 15, 1964. This statement is nearly identical in wording and may have been edited by M.S. Arnoni for publication in *TMO*. A copy is in the Castellano-Meagher correspondence in the Meagher Archive at Hood College.

15. *Ibid.*

16. Jack Ruby in police basement: The Warren Report, p. 208. Lillian Castellano to *TMO*, March 1965, p. 30.

17. "My questioning began..." Lillian Castellano to Vincent. J. Salandria, November 19, 1965. "Nobody pays any attention to my words..." Lillian Castellano to H.D. Corson, December 29, 1964. Mr. Corson was an employee of *The New York Times* who supervised mail distribution. While *The Times* did not use any of the material Mrs. Castellano sent, Corson saw it and wrote her back. "Mr. Corson seemed so genuinely interested that I sent

him copies of my complete former communications with the Warren Commission beginning in the early part of April, 1964," Mrs. Castellano wrote Sylvia Meagher on March
23, 1965. "I told him to show it to anybody he pleased." Corson had dropped out of the
picture by early 1965.

18. Lillian Castellano to H.D. Corson, December 29, 1964.

19. Sylvia Meagher to *TMO*, May 1965.

20. Lillian Castellano to Sylvia Meagher, March 23, 1965

21. Sylvia Meagher to Maggie Field, July 9, 1965.

22. *Ibid.*

23. *Ibid.*

24. *Ibid.*

25. "Telephone conversation with Mrs. F. Beverly Hills Friday 9 July 1965 1 p.m.," Sylvia
Meagher.

26. *Ibid.*

27. Sylvia Meagher to Maggie Field, July 11, 1965. Crawford background and speech:
Critical Reactions to the Warren Report anthology.

28. Sylvia Meagher to Maggie Field, July 11, 1965.

29. Maggie Field to Sylvia Meagher, July 13, 1965.

30. Maggie Field to Sylvia Meagher, undated letter, probably mid-July 1965, p. 4.

31. Maggie Field to Sylvia Meagher, July 13, 1965.

32. *Ibid.*

33. Quote: WC Vol. VII, p. 517.

34. Photograph the fifth in Altgens sequence: *Pictures of the Pain*, pp. 310-312. Quote:
Whitewash II – The FBI-Secret Service Coverup, by Harold Weisberg, p. 250.

35. *Photographic Whitewash*, by Harold Weisberg, pp. 188-189. Quote*: The New York
Herald Tribune* magazine, May 24, 1954, "The Picture With a Life of its Own," p. 10.

36. Commission says Lovelady is man in doorway: Warren Report, pp. 147-149. Oswald
places self on first floor: Warren Report, p. 600. Commission notes Lovelady-Oswald
resemblance: Warren Report, p. 644. Meagher quote: *Accessories After the Fact*, p. 362.

37. Ray Marcus interview, September 5, 2000. Mr. Marcus also supplied photocopies of
his comparison data to the author.

38. *The New York Herald Tribune* magazine, May 24, 1954, "The Picture With a Life of
its Own."

39. *The New York Herald Tribune* magazine, May 24, 1954, "The Picture With a Life of
its Own," and ARRB Document # 180-10014-10041 (re: photographer).

40. Shirley Martin hires private investigator: *Rush to Judgment*, p. 355. Martin children
attempt to photograph Lovelady: Steve Martin to author, May 28, 2000, and Teresa
Martin to author, June 16, 2000.

41. *The New York Herald Tribune* magazine, May 24, 1954, "The Picture With a Life of
its Own."

42. Lovelady in striped shirt: *Whitewash II*, inside back flap. Quote: *Whitewash II*, p. 191.

43. "She insists it is 'my Billy...'" *Photographic Whitewash*, by Harold Weisberg, p. 294. For
photographs of "the man in the doorway," Oswald, and Lovelady in striped and checked
shirts, see *The Killing of a President*, by Robert J. Groden, pp. 186-187.

44. Marcus concludes it was Lovelady: Ray Marcus interview, September 5, 2000.
Weisberg quote: Harold Weisberg interview, April 26, 2001.

45. Quote: Lillian Castellano to H.D. Corson, March 13, 1965.

46. Receives 26 volumes in January that year (1965): "Statement," by Lillian Castellano,
dated December 15, 1964, with undated "Epilogue" written no earlier than February

1965. "Frame 212 has obviously..." Notes and documents prepared by Lillian Castellano, undated but probably early 1965.

47. Notes and documents prepared by Lillian Castellano, undated but probably early 1965.

48. This dialogue is from WC Vol. 7, p. 495. Willis's photograph was the fifth in a sequence he took. Because it was entered into the official evidence several times, this photograph has at least three different designations: Hudson Exhibit #1 (WC Vol. 20, p. 183), Willis Exhibit #1 slide #5, and Shaneyfelt Exhibit #25 (both WC Vol. 21, pp. 770 and 471 respectively). The exchange between Liebeler and Willis was edited slightly for this book. Unedited, it goes: "And you heard it just about the time you took the picture that has been marked?" Liebeler asked. "That's right," Willis replied. "Prior to the time you took the picture, which is marked Hudson Exhibit No. 1?" "Absolutely."

49. Notes and documents prepared by Lillian Castellano, undated but probably early 1965.

50. "You have done an excellent..." Sylvia Meagher to Lillian Castellano, November 3, 1965.

51. Surveyor's map device: Marcus sent the author a photocopy of the map. The original is now at Hood College. He called it a "study device" and described it in an interview on July 25, 2001. Plastic triangles were attached to the map by pins, "a moveable triangle representing the camera view, as it moved around at various frames. And I had a little cut-out of the limousine that I could move down Elm Street." The device is also described in *The New Yorker*, June 10, 1967, "The Buffs," by Calvin Trillin. "She absolutely proved..." Ray Marcus interview, September 5, 2000.

52. Lifton obtains negatives, first one the best: David Lifton interview, January 13, 2000.

53. *#5 Man, November 22, 1963*, p. 2.

54. Ray Marcus interview, September 7, 2002.

55. Quotation and expert opinion: Ray Marcus to David Walsh, June 10, 1966. Time period for double head-hit conclusion: "Foreword to Hypotheses re: Zapruder Film," by Ray Marcus, April 25, 1975. Double head-hit described in detail in *The HSCA, The Zapruder Film, and the Single Bullet Theory*, by Raymond Marcus, "Sources and Notes," Note 17, pp. 26-27.

56. JFK Photo Panel #1, by Raymond Marcus. Ray Marcus to Josiah Thompson, December 15, 1967, p. 16. *Best Evidence*, by David Lifton, Chapter 1, "Entering the Labyrinth," p. 7, Carroll and Graf edition, 1988. Ray Marcus interview, September 5, 2000. Weisberg quote: *Photographic Whitewash*, by Harold Weisberg, p. 24. Weisberg discusses this issue on pp. 24-25. Marcus discussed the frame reversal in his testimony to the Orleans Parish Grand Jury, Orleans Parish Grand Jury Proceedings of May 11, 1967, pp. 8-9. See The Garrison Transcripts CD-ROM, 2002, Assassination Archives and Research Center, and History Matters.

57. JFK Photo Panel #1, by Raymond Marcus. Lifton describes his December 6, 1965, letter to the FBI in *Best Evidence*, Chapter 12, "An Oral Utterance." At the time of his letter Lifton worked at North American Aviation, a position requiring a security clearance. Because he believed his assassination work might cause him some problems with the clearance, his letter to the FBI was signed by a friend, Judith R. Schmidt. See ARRB document #1801004810438. Text of Hoover letter, dated December 14, 1965, published in *Photographic Whitewash*, by Harold Weisberg, p. 145, and included in ARRB document #1801004810438.

58. "Printing errors" indecent and obscene, plus quote: *Photographic Whitewash*, p. 25.

59. Press kits mailed out: *#5 Man, November 22, 1963*, p. 2. Marcus letter to RFK reproduced in facsimile in *Addendum B*, p. 28.

60. Robert F. Kennedy to Ray Marcus, September 16, 1965. Letter reproduced in facsimile in *Addendum B*, p. 28-a.
61. *Addendum B*, p. 28.
62. Sylvia Meagher to Maggie Field, July 15, 1965.
63. Concerns about Sauvage, and "So I continue to hesitate" quote: Sylvia Meagher to Maggie Field, July 15, 1965. Sauvage surprised Meagher preoccupied, but impressed with her contacts: "Telephone Call from Léo Sauvage, Thursday night 29 July 1965," by Sylvia Meagher. Buchanan-Sauvage back-and-forth: see *The New Leader*, November 9, 1964, p. 8. See also *Critical Reactions to the Warren Report*, p. 56.
64. "Telephone Call from Léo Sauvage, Thursday night 29 July 1965," by Sylvia Meagher.
65. Sylvia Meagher to Maggie Field, July 15, 1965.
66. Panoplies: author's inspection, December 7 and 8, 2001. Quotations: the *Los Angeles Free Press*, "FP Interviews Mrs. Field on Warren Report 'Errors,'" December 8, 1967.
67. Maggie Field to Sylvia Meagher, undated letter, approximately mid-July 1965.
68. Warren Commission's first conclusion: Warren Report, p. 18. 3x5 cards from Sylvia Meagher Archives, Hood College.
69. Maggie Field to Sylvia Meagher, August 4, 1965.
70. *Ibid.*

Chapter Nineteen – More Contacts

1. "Visit from Vincent Salandria, Wednesday 7 p.m.-midnight 4 August 1965," memo by Sylvia Meagher.
2. *Ibid.*
3. *Ibid.*
4. *Ibid.*
5. John Sherman Cooper to Griscom Morgan, April 8, 1965.
6. "Visit from Vincent Salandria, Wednesday 7 p.m.-midnight 4 August 1965." Index nearing completion: Sylvia Meagher to Vince Salandria, September 3, 1965. Maggie Field sees *AAF* drafts: Sylvia Meagher to Maggie Field, July 20, 1965 (p.2) and memo of phone call from Field by Meagher, July 26, 1965. Meagher gratified by response: Meagher to Field, August 4, 1965.
7. "Visit from Vincent Salandria, Wednesday 7 p.m.-midnight 4 August 1965." No Secret Service agents stay in Dealey Plaza: The Warren Report, p. 52. Joe Marshall Smith encounters man with Secret Service credentials: WC Vol. VII, p. 535. "Where Did the Shots Come From?" *Accessories After the Fact*, pp. 9-27.
8. *Accessories After the Fact*, p. 26.
9. "Visit from Vincent Salandria, Wednesday 7 p.m.-midnight 4 August 1965."
10. *Ibid.*
11. *Ibid.*
12. *Ibid.*
13. *Ibid.*
14. *Ibid.*
15. Untitled notes on viewing the Nix, Muchmore, and Zapruder films, August 9, 1965, tape recording transcript by Vincent J. Salandria.
16. *Pictures of the Pain*, by Richard Trask, p. 194.
17. Indoor film: *Pictures of the Pain*, p. 184. Quote: Untitled notes on viewing the Nix, Muchmore, and Zapruder films, August 9, 1965.

18. Nix on direction of shots: Nix to Mark Lane, filmed interview, in movie *Rush to Judgment*. Salandria observations: Untitled notes on viewing the Nix, Muchmore, and Zapruder films, August 9, 1965.

19. Untitled notes on viewing the Nix, Muchmore, and Zapruder films, August 9, 1965.

20. *Ibid.*

21. *Ibid.*

22. *Ibid.*

23. *Ibid.*

24. "On Viewing the Zapruder Film and Slides and the Nix and Muchmore Films of the Assassination of President Kennedy," by Thomas Stamm.

25. *Ibid.*

26. *Ibid.*

27. *Ibid.*

28. *Ibid.*

29. Fruitcake: Shirley Martin to Livy Salandria, December 24, 1964. "Oswald is the most..." Livy Salandria to Shirley Martin, January 7, 1965.

30. Shirley Martin quotes: Shirley Martin to Vince Salandria, undated letter, probably late 1964 or early 1965. Ruark article: "Puzzled by Warren Report," by Robert C. Ruark, *The New York World Telegram,* October 9, 1964, and *Critical Reactions to the Warren Report.*

31. Martin quote: Shirley Martin to Vince Salandria, May 29, 1965. Salandria quote: Vince Salandria to Shirley Martin, June 1, 1965.

32. "Mama O. called..." Shirley Martin to Vince Salandria, undated letter, probably May 1965. Marguerite surveillance, and quote: *The Fort Worth Star Telegram*, May 17, 1965. "Please allow me to feel ashamed..." Vince Salandria to Marguerite Oswald, May 20, 1965.

33. "The Dallas idea en masse..." Shirley Martin to Vince Salandria, probably late May or early June 1965. "Mother says to tell you..." Vickie Martin to Vince Salandria, May 13, 1965. This section supplemented by interviews with Salandria and Martin, 2000 and 2001.

34. Trip details and quote: Vince Salandria interview, October 25, 2000, and Vince Salandria cover letter to correspondence group, June 16, 1995.

35. *Ibid.*

36. "Telephone conversation with Vincent Salandria, Monday night 13 September 1965," memorandum by Sylvia Meagher.

37. Vincent J. Salandria interview, October 25, 2000, and Vincent J. Salandria cover letter to correspondence group, June 16, 1995.

38. "Michael Paine advised us..." Vincent J. Salandria to Sylvia Meagher, September 2, 1965. Salandria concludes Michael Paine knew Oswald well: "Telephone conversation with Vincent Salandria, Monday night 13 September 1965," memorandum by Sylvia Meagher.

39. Vincent J. Salandria interview, October 25, 2000, and Vincent J. Salandria cover letter to correspondence group, June 16, 1995.

40. Shirley Martin interview, October 17, 2000.

41. Vincent J. Salandria interview, October 25, 2000, and Vincent J. Salandria cover letter to correspondence group, June 16, 1995. Shirley Martin interview, October 17, 2000.

42. Vincent J. Salandria interview, October 25, 2000, and Vincent J. Salandria cover letter to correspondence group, June 16, 1995.

43. Vincent J. Salandria interview, October 25, 2000.

44. ARRB Record Number 124-10041-10137.

45. Vincent J. Salandria to Sylvia Meagher, September 2, 1965. Salandria made a strong

case: "Telephone conversation with Vincent Salandria, Monday night 13 September 1965," memorandum by Sylvia Meagher.

46. "Telephone conversation with Vincent Salandria, Monday night 13 September 1965," memorandum by Sylvia Meagher.

47. Maggie Field might attend meeting: Field to Sylvia Meagher, August 4, 1965, p. 8. Salandria delighted: "Telephone conversation with Vincent Salandria, Monday night 13 September 1965," memorandum by Sylvia Meagher.

48. Original guest list: "Telephone Call from Maggie Field, Saturday night, 11 September 1965." "I should warn you..." Sylvia Meagher to Maggie Field, August 26, 1965.

49. Sylvia Meagher to Maggie Field, August 26, 1965.

Chapter Twenty – The Meeting

1. "I did not even go out to the incinerator..." Sylvia Meagher to Maggie Field, August 9, 1965. Trip to Miami painful: Sylvia Meagher to Maggie Field, July 26, 1965.

2. Sylvia Meagher to Maggie Field, July 26, 1965.

3. Maggie Field supportive: Field to Sylvia Meagher, August 4, 1965, p. 8. Toll on Meagher's health: Sylvia Meagher to Maggie Field, August 26, 1965. *Life* article: "'Cursed Gun' – The Track of C2766," by Keith Wheeler, *Life*, August 27, 1965. "Cheap old weapon" – WC Vol. 4, p. 29. Other evidence of rifle's inferiority: WC Vol. 24, p. 2 (CE 1977 p. 1); Vol. 26, p. 22 (CE 2694, p. 11); WC Vol. 11, p. 203; WC Vol. 26, p. 771 (CE 3119, p. 19).

4. Sylvia Meagher to Maggie Field, August 26, 1965.

5. *Ibid.*

6. Sylvia Meagher to Maggie Field, August 7, 1965.

7. *Ibid.*

8. "Telephone Call from Maggie Field, Saturday night, 11 September 1965."

9. *Ibid.*

10. Salandria invites Harris: Sylvia Meagher to Maggie Field, September 26, 1965. Meagher invited Epstein earlier: "Telephone conversation with Ed Epstein, Monday night 13 September 1965." Memo by Sylvia Meagher.

11. "Telephone Call from Jones Harris 3-6 p.m. Saturday 25-9-65," memo by Sylvia Meagher. Sylvia Meagher to Maggie Field, September 26, 1965.

12. Sylvia Meagher to Maggie Field, September 26, 1965.

13. Meagher calls Cook: "Telephone Conversation with Fred Cook, Interlocken, New Jersey, Friday Night, 24-9-65," memo by Sylvia Meagher. *Maverick: Fifty Years of Investigative Reporting*, p. 276.

14. *Maverick: Fifty Years of Investigative Reporting*, pp. 277-278.

15. *Ibid.*, p. 277.

16. *Ibid.*, p. 278.

17. *Ibid.*, pp. 280-281.

18. *Ibid.*, p. 278, and "Telephone Conversation with Fred Cook, Interlocken, New Jersey, Friday Night, 24-9-65."

19. *Addendum B*, p. 44. Undeterred by Stone experience: Ray Marcus to author, November 13, 2002.

20. Fred Cook to Ray Marcus, September 10, 1965.

21. "Telephone Conversation with Fred Cook, Interlocken, New Jersey, Friday Night, 24-9-65."

22. Maggie Field to Sylvia Meagher, October 18, 1965.

23. "Notes on Meeting of Warrenologists – Sunday 3 October 1965," memo by Sylvia Meagher.

24. Vincent J. Salandria to Shirley Martin, July 22, 1964.

25. "On Viewing the Zapruder Film and Slides and the Nix and Muchmore Films of the Assassination of President Kennedy." Lobenthal play: *Commission*, by Joseph S. Lobenthal, Jr., author's collection, and Joseph Lobenthal interview, October 19, 2001.

26. "Notes on phone call from Lillian Castellano, Sunday, October 3, 1965 about 2 p.m.." Memo by Sylvia Meagher.

27. "It was quite a coincidence..." Sylvia Meagher to Lillian Castellano, October 6, 1965. Details on phone call: "Notes on phone call from Lillian Castellano, Sunday, October 3, 1965 about 2 p.m.." Memo by Sylvia Meagher. "I wish someone would give me..." Lillian Castellano to *Newsweek*, December 15, 1964.

28. "The Separate Connally Shot," by Vincent J. Salandria, *The Minority of One*, April 1966. (Second of two articles.)

29. Sylvia Meagher to Lillian Castellano, October 6, 1965.

30. "Notes on Meeting of Warrenologists – Sunday 3 October 1965," by Sylvia Meagher.

31. "Notes on Meeting of Warrenologists – Sunday 3 October 1965, Additional Epstein items," by Sylvia Meagher.

32. "Notes on Meeting of Warrenologists – Sunday 3 October 1965," by Sylvia Meagher.

33. *Ibid.*

34. *Ibid.*

35. "Notes on Meeting of Warrenologists – Sunday 3 October 1965, Additional Epstein items," by Sylvia Meagher.

36. *Ibid.*

37. "Notes on Meeting of Warrenologists – Sunday 3 October 1965," by Sylvia Meagher.

38. *Ibid.*

39. *Ibid.*

40. "Notes on Meeting of Warrenologists – Sunday 3 October 1965," by Sylvia Meagher. Sniper's nest discovered "around 1 p.m." – Warren Report, p. 79.

41. "Notes on Meeting of Warrenologists – Sunday 3 October 1965," by Sylvia Meagher.

42. *Ibid.*

43. *Ibid.*

44. Sylvia Meagher to Edward Jay Epstein, October 4, 1965.

45. Edward Jay Epstein to Sylvia Meagher, October 16, 1965. Sylvia Meagher to Edward Jay Epstein, October 18, 1965.

46. Thomas Stamm to Edward Jay Epstein, November 3, 1965.

47. "Notes on Meeting of Warrenologists – Sunday 3 October 1965, Maggie Field on Ed Epstein," by Sylvia Meagher.

48. "Telephone conversation with Ed Epstein, Monday night 13 September 1965." Notes by Sylvia Meagher.

49. Meagher asks will book please Commissioners: "Telephone conversation with Ed Epstein, Monday night 13 September 1965." Several guests wonder whether revelations will be in book: "Notes on Meeting of Warrenologists – Sunday 3 October 1965, 'Additional Epstein Items,'" by Sylvia Meagher.

50. "Telephone conversation with Melvin Eisenberg, 26 October 1965," by Sylvia Meagher.

51. *Ibid.*

52. *Ibid.*

53. *Ibid.*

54. "Telephone Call from Léo Sauvage 28 October 1965," by Sylvia Meagher.
55. *Ibid.*
56. *Ibid.*
57. Doubts the Warren Report, and quote: *A Rebel In Defense of Tradition: The Life and Politics of Dwight Macdonald*, p. 547, note 3.
58. "Telephone Call from Jones Harris 28 October 1965," by Sylvia Meagher.
59. Sylvia Meagher to Maggie Field, October 21, 1965.
60. Sauvage sees Fox book: "Telephone Call from Léo Sauvage 28 October 1965," by Sylvia Meagher. Harris sees book: "Telephone Call from Jones Harris 28 October 1965," by Sylvia Meagher.
61. "Telephone Call from Jones Harris 28 October 1965," by Sylvia Meagher.
62. *Ibid.*
63. Sylvia Meagher to Maggie Field, October 21, 1965.
64. Sylvia Meagher to Maggie Field, October 21, 1965. *The Doorbell Rang*, by Rex Stout.
65. *Rex Stout: A Biography*, pp. 456-457.
66. "The whole book revolves about the FBI..." Sylvia Meagher to Maggie Field, October 21, 1965. Stout as ACLU Board member, FBI encounter, Hoover comment: *Rex Stout: A Biography*, pp. 457-459.
67. Sylvia Meagher to Maggie Field, October 21, 1965.

Chapter Twenty-One – No Exit

1. "The Warren Commission's Case Against Oswald," by Léo Sauvage, *The New Leader*, November 22, 1965.
2. "We prefer not to be confronted..." from "Between Issues," *The New Leader*, November. 22, 1965.
3. "The Warren Commission's Case Against Oswald," by Léo Sauvage, *The New Leader*, November 22, 1965, p. 16, summarizing The Warren Report, p. 195, "Conclusion."
4. "The New York publisher broke the contract..." "The Warren Commission's Case Against Oswald," *The New Leader*, November 22, 1965.
5. Letter to editor by Harold Weisberg, *The New Leader*, January 31, 1966.
6. Sylvia Meagher to Harold Weisberg, January 31, 1966.
7. *Ibid.*
8. Harold Weisberg to Sylvia Meagher, February 9, 1966.
9. Quotation, possibility of private printing: Harold Weisberg to Sylvia Meagher, February 9, 1966. Copyright registration: Harold Weisberg interview, July 12, 2001.
10. Harold Weisberg to Sylvia Meagher, February 9, 1966.
11. Harold Weisberg to Sylvia Meagher, February 12, 1966. Sylvia Meagher to Harold Weisberg, February 15, 1966. re: "must have pleased him..." see Weisberg letter to David Welsh, 2-17-66, in which he quotes passages of her comments on *Whitewash.*
12. Sylvia Meagher to Harold Weisberg, February 15, 1965.
13. *Ibid.*
14. Sylvia Meagher to Harold Weisberg, February 17, 1965.
15. Sylvia Meagher to Shirley Martin, December 26, 1965.
16. Sylvia Meagher to Shirley Martin, December 26, 1965.
17. "Witnesses Tell Fear of Death," by Dorothy Kilgallen, *The New York Journal-American*, September 25, 1964.
18. Shirley Martin to Sylvia Meagher, December 28, 1965.

19. Sylvia Meagher to Shirley Martin, December 30, 1965. Shirley Martin to Sylvia Meagher, January 2, 1966.

20. "...a *terrific* new development..." Sylvia Meagher to Shirley Martin, January 14, 1966. "We plan to devote..." David Welsh to Sylvia Meagher, January 12, 1966.

21. Meagher thrilled by *Ramparts'* interest, and quotes: Sylvia Meagher to David Welsh, January 15, 1966. Sends entire manuscript: Sylvia Meagher to David Welsh, January 17, 1966.

22. Harold Weisberg to David Welsh, February 17, 1966.

23. Ray Marcus to Vincent J. Salandria, March 4, 1966.

24. *Ramparts* recruits Maggie Field, she gives them panoply: Maggie Field to Sylvia Meagher, undated letter, probably early January 1966. Lifton writes dialogue: *Best Evidence*, p. 39. A copy is in the Sylvia Meagher archive at Hood College. Cook's article completed at 20,000 words: Fred J. Cook to Ray Marcus, September 23, 1965. "...a bottleneck at *Ramparts*..." Fred J. Cook to Ray Marcus, March 10, 1966.

25. *Maverick*, p. 281.

26. Sylvia Meagher to Penn Jones, Jr., November 21, 1965.

27. *Ibid.*

28. "The next six weeks..." Penn Jones, Jr., to Sylvia Meagher, November 26, 1965. Jones investigation: "One Man's Grief," *The Texas Observer*, September 29, 1967, and *Citizen's Arrest*, p. 42. Advocates re-opening JFK probe: "Reopen the Warren Commission," *The Midlothian Mirror*, June 3, 1965.

29. Wanda Joyce Killam and Ruby: The Warren Report, p. 363, and *Forgive My Grief*, Vol. I, pp. 7-8.

30. *Forgive My Grief*, Vol. I, p. 7.

31. *Forgive My Grief*, Vol. I, p. 8, citing CE 2882 and CE 2993, WC Vol. XXVI, pp. 338-339.

32. *Forgive My Grief*, Vol. I, p. 8.

33. *Ibid.*

34. Penn Jones, Jr. to Sylvia Meagher, November 26, 1965.

35. Sylvia Meagher to Penn Jones, Jr., November 29, 1965.

36. *Ibid.*

37. *Kilgallen: An Intimate Biography of Dorothy Kilgallen*, by Lee Israel, pp. 357-358, and pp. 395-427.

38. *Forgive My Grief*, Vol. I, p. 24.

39. Penn Jones, Jr., to Sylvia Meagher, December 16, 1965.

40. *Ibid.*

41. "The Impossible Tasks of One Assassination Bullet," by "Victor" J. Salandria, *The Minority of One*, March 1966, and "The Separate Connally Shot," by Vincent J. Salandria, *The Minority of One*, April 1966.

42. Quote: "The Impossible Tasks of One Assassination Bullet," *The Minority of One*, March 1966, p. 18.

43. Quote: "The Separate Connally Shot," by Vincent J. Salandria, *The Minority of One*, April 1966, p. 9.

44. "The Separate Connally Shot," *The Minority of One*, April 1966, p. 12.

45. *Ibid.*, April 1966, p. 13.

46. *Ibid.*, p. 13. Article cites Investigation of Assassination of President John F. Kennedy, November 22, 1963, p. 18.

47. FBI Supplemental Report supports no-exit conclusion: Investigation of Assassination of President John F. Kennedy, November 22, 1963, Supplemental Report, Federal Bureau of Investigation, John Edgar Hoover, Director, January 14, 1964, p. 2. This report states "that the bullet which entered [JFK's] back had penetrated to a distance of less than a finger length." Warren Report reference to FBI Summary Report: Foreword, p. xi.

48. CE 399: WC Vol. XVII, p. 49. No trace of blood or tissue: WC Vol. III, p. 428. CE 856: WC Vol. XVII, p. 850.

49. Ray Marcus interview, July 12, 2000.

50. Ray Marcus interview, September 5, 2000.

51. Marcus tries to interest publishers: rejection letters in author's files. *The Bastard Bullet* was submitted to Fawcett World Library, Grove Press, Award Books, and Bantam Books, among others. *Philadelphia* magazine also considered it. Arnoni expresses interest, and quote: Ray Marcus interview, July 12, 2000. Penn Jones briefly considered publishing it, which Marcus mentioned in a letter to Salandria dated November 7 or 8, 1966 (the original typed letter has a strikeover on the date). That same letter has a comment on its length: "I felt I had to list all plausible alternate hypotheses, and note all contrary evidence to each, before concluding that 399 was planted. I knew this would make for damned tedious reading, but felt it was the heart of the study, and the proper approach for a research piece – without which the article added little to previous material. I still feel that way, and would like to proceed with its limited publication as it is."

52. *The Bastard Bullet*, pp. 3-5; quote, p. 4.

53. Humes: *The Bastard Bullet*, p. 7, citing WC Vol. II, p. 375. Finck: *The Bastard Bullet*, p. 7, citing WC Vol. II, p. 382.

54. Quote: *The Bastard Bullet*, p. 14. Comparison photos: *The Bastard Bullet*, p. 15. CE 399 printed in WC Vol. 17, p. 49; CE 856 printed in WC Vol. 17, p. 850.

55. Warren Commission account of discovery: Warren Report, pp. 79-81.

56. *The Bastard Bullet*, p. 74, footnote.

57. Warren Commission account of discovery: Warren Report, pp. 79-81. Marcus on stretcher: *The Bastard Bullet*, pp. 16-18. Tomlinson says corridor stretcher: WC Vol. 6, p. 130.

58. Quote: WC Vol. 6, p. 133.

59. *The Bastard Bullet*, p. 22.

60. Specter questioning: *The Bastard Bullet*, pp. 20-24, citing WC Vol. 6, pp. 130-135. Tomlinson quote: *The Bastard Bullet*, p. 24, citing WC Vol. 6, p. 134.

61. This dialogue from *The Bastard Bullet*, Appendix A, "Transcript of Interview, R. Marcus and Darrell Tomlinson, July 25, 1966," p. 85. This appendix did not appear in the first edition of *The Bastard Bullet* but was added in subsequent printings. A recording of this conversation is in the author's collection.

62. Bullet "pretty clean": *The Bastard Bullet*, p. 82. Marcus traces bullet possession: *The Bastard Bullet*, pp. 37-41. Chain of possession inconsistencies: *The Bastard Bullet*, pp. 31-34; quote: *The Bastard Bullet*, p. 34. Marcus cites CE 2011, WC Vol. 24, p. 412.

63. "...but also had done nothing..." *The Bastard Bullet*, p. 54.

64. *The Bastard Bullet*, p. 77.

65. "None should exist..." *Whitewash*, p. 181.

66. *Whitewash*, p. 181.

67. Autopsy photos and X-rays not entered into record: HSCA Vol. 7, p. 2, and HSCA Vol. 1, p. 143. (The HSCA asserts in Vol. 1, p. 143 that Earl Warren was "reported" to have seen them, but does not elaborate.) Sketches by illustrator under supervision of Humes and Boswell: WC Vol. 2, p. 349. "The doctors almost begged...": Harold Weisberg to George Herman, *Mike Wallace At Large,* CBS radio, broadcast July 26, 1966. Weisberg statement re: Humes asked if visual record would change testimony: see WC Volume 2, p. 371.

68. See Meagher's analysis in *Accessories After the Fact*, Chapter 5, "The Autopsy and Medical Findings." For the changing wound reports Meagher cites the following: *The New York Post*, November 24, 1963, p. 2, col. 3; *The New York Herald-Tribune*, November 24, 1963, pp. 1 and 9; *The New York Times*, December 17, 1963, p. 31, cols. 7-8, "2D Shot Reported Fatal to Kennedy," *The New York Times*, December 18, 1963, "Officials Silent on Kennedy Shots," *The New York Times*, December 19, 1963, and "12 Perplexing Questions About Kennedy Assassination," *The New York Times*, January 26, 1964. Humes burns autopsy notes: WC Volume 17, p. 48. Humes says forbidden to talk: "Kennedy Slaying is Reconstructed," *The New York Times*, December 6, 1963, p. 23.

69. *Accessories After the Fact*, p. 138, n. 20.

70. Sylvia Meagher to Ray Marcus, March 1, 1966. The brief *New York Times* article, "Experts Find Gaps in Warren Report," was published February 26, 1966. A four page outline of the American Academy of Forensic Sciences annual meeting is among the ARRB material, as Record Number 205-10001-10003. #10 on this itemized report summarizes Dr. Wecht's remarks.

71. *Cause of Death*, by Cyril H. Wecht, and "A Critique of the Medical Aspects of the Investigation into the Assassination of President Kennedy," by Cyril H. Wecht, published in the *Journal of Forensic Sciences*, Vol. 11 No. 3, July 1966, and presented at the Eighteenth Annual Meeting of the American Academy of Forensic Sciences, Chicago, Illinois, February 24, 1966.

72. "A Critique of the Medical Aspects of the Investigation into the Assassination of President Kennedy," pp. 310 (two of three autopsy doctors not forensic pathologists). See also Wecht's comments in *Cause of Death*, paperback edition, p. 23: "...it was a botched autopsy, a terrible piece of medicolegal investigation."

73. *Ibid.*, p. 309 (pathologists did not contact Parkland doctors), pp. 311-313 (adrenal glands), 313 (autopsy X-rays and photographs), and 313-314 (Wecht agrees with Warren Report's basic findings).

74. Index finished, bound, due March 21: Sylvia Meagher to Maggie Field, March 13, 1966. Meagher had accepted offer previous fall: Sylvia Meagher to Fred J. Cook, October 14, 1965.

75. Scarecrow Press material attached to FBI data, ARRB Record Number 1801005110092.

76. ARRB Record Number 1801005110092.

77. Sylvia Meagher to Maggie Field, "Written on 16 April 1966, to be mailed in June."

78. *Ibid.*

79. *Ibid.*

80. *Ibid.*

81. *Ramparts* delays: Sylvia Meagher to Maggie Field, "Written on 16 April 1966, to be mailed in June," *et al. Ramparts* and FBI Summary Report: Sylvia Meagher to Vincent J. Salandria, April 29, 1966. Telegram to Welsh: April 29, 1966, copy in author's collection and in Meagher Archive, Hood College.

82. Sylvia Meagher to Maggie Field, "Written on 16 April 1966, to be mailed in June."

83. "The dramatic transition..." from "Four Books on the Warren Report: The Summer of Discontent," by Sylvia Meagher, *Studies on the Left*, September-October 1966. Also *The New Yorker*, June 10, 1967.

84. Sylvia Meagher to Maggie Field, May 18, 1965 (typed version).

85. Getting book before public, "I had to improvise," booksellers convention: Harold Weisberg interview, November 30, 2000. Contacts bookstores: Harold Weisberg to Sylvia Meagher, May 21, 1966.

86. *Whitewash*, by Harold Weisberg, preface, pp. v-viii.
87. Sylvia Meagher to Maggie Field, May 18, 1966 (handwritten draft).
88. Sylvia Meagher to Maggie Field, May 18, 1966 (handwritten draft). Meagher also discussed the question of FBI Summary Report credit in a letter to Ray Marcus, May 15, 1966. In comments about the newly-published *Whitewash*, she told Marcus that Weisberg "has tacked on a 'postscript,' a new chapter on the FBI report which was the subject of Salandria's article in the April *TMO*, without a single word of credit or acknowledgement that Salandria had found and published that crucial excerpt long before Weisberg even knew about it. As a matter of fact, he found out about the article from me, when he called me as he was about to end a brief visit to New York. When I told him about the article, he went to the Archives instead of going directly to his home, consulted the document, and then wrote his new chapter as if he was the first and only researcher to uncover that new evidence. All this saddens me greatly, since we need to work on the basis of mutual trust and co-operation, not to be constantly on guard against back-knifing and rivalry, with all the consequent dissipation of effort and emotion."
89. Sylvia Meagher to Maggie Field, June 12, 1966.

Chapter Twenty-Two – Strange Authors

1. *The New York Times*, June 6, 1966.
2. *Ibid.*
3. "Hurry up, nigger..." *The Nation*, June 27, 1966. Media: *Eyes on the Prize II: America At the Crossroads – 1965 to 1985*. Part Two: "The Time Has Come (1964-1965)." "The tension is high..." *The New York Times*, June 7, 1966.
4. "Nonviolence is not..." *The Nation*, June 27, 1966.
5. *The New York Times*, June 7, 1966.
6. *Ibid.*
7. *Ibid.*
8. *Los Angeles Times*, June 7, 1966. #5 *Man, November 22, 1963*, p. 28.
9. *The New York Times*, June 7, 1966.
10. *Maverick*, p. 282.
11. *Ibid.*
12. "Some Unanswered Questions," by Fred J. Cook, *The Nation*, June 13, 1966, p. 706.
13. *Ibid.*, p. 710. Emphasis in original.
14. *Ibid.*, p. 712.
15. Spectators and number of shots: "Some Unanswered Questions," by Fred J. Cook, *The Nation*, June 13, 1966, p. 737. Wound location and drawings: *Ibid.*, p. 740-741.
16. CE 397: WC Vol. XVII, p. 48.
17. "Testimony of the Eyewitnesses," by Fred J. Cook, *The Nation*, June 20, 1966, p. 746.
18. "The Vital Documents," by Jacob Cohen, *The Nation*, July 11, 1966, p. 43. *Honest Verdict:* "Background Survey of Books Concerning the Assassination of President Kennedy (CIA document), ARRB Record Number 180-10098-10177.
19. "The Vital Documents," by Jacob Cohen, *The Nation*, July 11, 1966, p. 43.
20. *Ibid.*
21. *Ibid.*
22. *Ibid.*, p. 45.
23. *Ibid.*, p. 46.
24. *Maverick*, p. 286.
25. "Cook on Cohen," *The Nation*, August 22, 1966, p. 138.

26. "Reader's Choice," by Oscar Handlin, *The Atlantic*, August 1966.

27. "*Inquest*: How Many Assassins?" *Newsweek*, June 13, 1966.

28. "What Did Happen in Dallas?" by Alex Campbell, *The New Republic*, June 25, 1966.

29. "The Duality of the Warren Report," by Léo Sauvage, *The New Leader*, June 20, 1966.

30. "On 'Closing Doors, Not Opening Them,' or, The Limits of the Warren Investigation," by Sylvia Meagher, *The Minority of One*, July-August 1966.

31. "A New Wave of Doubt," by Fletcher Knebel, *Look*, July 12, 1966.

32. Weisberg bothered: Harold Weisberg to Vincent J. Salandria, June 25, 1966.

33. Vincent J. Salandria interview, February 28, 2002.

34. Ira Einhorn: *The Unicorn's Secret*, by Steven Levy, and *The Philadelphia Daily News*, Online Edition, July 20, 2001. Einhorn's fortunes changed dramatically in the years to come. In 1981 he fled the United States before the start of his trial for the 1977 murder of his girlfriend. In 1993 he was convicted *in absentia*. Finally, in 2001, he was captured in France and returned to the U.S., where he began serving a life sentence.

35. Einhorn says review too strident, Karpowitz introduced Einhorn and Salandria: Vincent J. Salandria interview, January 2, 2001.

36. "A Move Toward the Center," *Liberation*, August 1966, pp. 52-54.

37. "A Move Toward the Center," *Liberation*, August 1966.

38. *Ibid.*

39. Gaeton Fonzi interview, January 28, 2002.

40. "Who Killed JFK?" by Gaeton Fonzi, *The Washingtonian*, November 1980.

41. "The President's Been Shot!" by Gaeton Fonzi, as told to Mike Mallowe, *Philadelphia* magazine, November 1988.

42. Salandria impresses Fonzi: *The Last Investigation*, pp. 14-15, and Gaeton Fonzi interview, January 28, 2002. Quote: "The President's Been Shot!" by Gaeton Fonzi, as told to Mike Mallowe, *Philadelphia* magazine, November 1988.

43. *The Last Investigation*, Gaeton Fonzi, pp. 14-15.

44. "*Inquest:* How Many Assassins?" *Newsweek*, June 13, 1966. Salandria helps Fonzi prepare: Gaeton Fonzi interview, January 28, 2002, and Vincent J. Salandria interview. Eleven pages of questions: author's collection.

45. *The Last Investigation*, p. 18.

46. Specter assigned Area I: *Inquest*, p. 28. Specter 34: The Warren Report, p. 478. Adams leaves, does not resign: *Inquest*, p. 79.

47. Unless otherwise indicated, the dialogue and data in this section comes from a transcript of the Fonzi-Specter interview supplied to the author by Fonzi.

48. Fonzi careful not to mention Salandria: Gaeton Fonzi interview, January 28, 2002. Salandria on father: speech to the National Conference of the Coalition on Political Assassinations (COPA), November 20, 1998, and Salandria interview, May 31, 2001.

49. Specter stands and paces: "The Warren Commission, the Truth, and Arlen Specter," by Gaeton Fonzi, *Greater Philadelphia* magazine, August 1966.

50. *The Last Investigation*, p. 27. "I got the feeling..." Fonzi interview, January 28, 2002.

51. "Phone call from Vince Salandria, Thurs. p.m. 6/30/66 7:30 p.m.," by Sylvia Meagher. Vincent J. Salandria interview, November 25, 2002.

52. Maggie Field to Sylvia Meagher, May 16, 1966.

53. "I, too, am on needles..." and clipping service: Sylvia Meagher to Maggie Field, May 18, 1966. Lerner column: Sylvia Meagher to Maggie Field, June 30, 1966.

54. Arnoni has comparative study chapters, may start publishing regularly on assassination: Sylvia Meagher to Maggie Field, June 30, 1966. Meagher knew Freeman slightly:

Sylvia Meagher to Shirley Martin, April 9, 1966.

55. Meagher private comments on *The Two Assassins*: Sylvia Meagher to Shirley Martin, April 9, 1966. Quotes from review, including anagrams: "A Psychiatrist's Retroactive Clairvoyance," by Sylvia Meagher, *The Minority of One*, June 1966. Deleted anagram: Sylvia Meagher to Maggie Field, May 11, 1966. "Jekyll-Hyde": *The Two Assassins*, p. 147. Warren Report on Hartogs: Warren Report, p. 379, which says "...[Hartogs'] psychiatric examination did not indicate that Lee Oswald was a potential assassin [or] potentially dangerous..."

56. Sylvia Meagher to Maggie Field, June 30, 1966.

57. Inscription: *Subject Index*, author's collection. "With the help of three co-authors..." Sylvia Meagher to Maggie Field, June 30, 1966. Field and *Inquest*: Maggie Field to Sylvia Meagher, September 24, 1966.

58. Not sharing documents: Sylvia Meagher to Vincent J. Salandria, draft of note that may never have been mailed.

59. Jones purchased numerous Index copies: Sylvia Meagher to Maggie Field, May 18, 1966. Jones and multiple sets, and quotation: "One Man's Grief," *The Texas Observer*, September 29, 1967. Louise Jones wrote to Meagher: "Why did Penn get such a stack of copies on the *Subject Index*? Because he wanted them, that's why. True, he possibly need-ed only one – but when several of us are working – then we need more." Louise Jones to Sylvia Meagher, May 21, 1966.

60. Edwin A. Walker to Sylvia Meagher, July 13, 1966.

61. Sylvia Meagher to Edwin A. Walker, draft reply, July 18, 1966.

62. Walker and Beckwith: *The Wounded Land,* p. 301.

63. Meredith reluctant: *The River of No Return*, p. 160. *The New York Times*, June 7, 1966. *Witness in Philadelphia*, p. 206.

64. *The New York Times*, June 9 and 10, 1966. *Eyes on the Prize II: America At the Crossroads – 1965 to 1985*. Part Two: "The Time Has Come (1964-1965)."

65. King and others head for Philadelphia: *Witness in Philadelphia*, pp. 206-207. Church rebuilt, plaque: *Witness in Philadelphia*, pp. 180-181.

66. *Witness in Philadelphia*, pp. 206-207, and *The New York Times*, June 22, 1966.

67. *Ibid.*

68. *The New York Times*, June 22, 1966. *Witness in Philadelphia*, pp. 142-144. Convictions and acquittals of conspirators: *We Are Not Afraid*, 445-456.

69. *Witness in Philadelphia*, pp. 207-209, and *The New York Times*, June 22, 1966.

70. *Witness in Philadelphia*, p. 210, and *The New York Times*, June 22, 1966.

71. *Witness in Philadelphia*, p. 210.

72. *Ibid.*

73. *Ibid.*, pp. 211-212.

74. *Ibid.*

75. *The New York Times*, June 27, 1966. King and Carmichael quotations: *Eyes on the Prize II: America At the Crossroads – 1965 to 1985*. Part Two: "The Time Has Come (1964-1965)." (Same quotations given incorrectly in *The New York Times*)

76. *The New York Times*, June 27, 1966.

77. Last great march of the era: *Eyes on the Prize II: America At the Crossroads – 1965 to 1985*. Part Two: "The Time Has Come (1964-1965)." *The New York Times*, June 12, 1966. Number of those to register: *Eyes on the Prize II: America At the Crossroads – 1965 to 1985*. Part Two: "The Time Has Come (1964-1965)." Film clips of El Fondren are included in this segment. He is also described in the *Times* article.

Chapter Twenty-Three – Developments Thick and Fast

1.   *Rush to Judgment* tops best seller list: See *New York Times Review of Books*, Jan. 1, 1967.

2.   Ralph Schoenman interview, August 14, 2000. In Denmark: *A Citizen's Dissent*, p. 37. "I was possessed of neither..." *A Citizen's Dissent*, p. 39.

3.   Ray Marcus to Deirdre Griswold, January 10, 1965, and Deirdre Griswold to Ray Marcus, February 16, 1965.

4.   Dallas trips: see *Rush to Judgment*, p. 455, note 205.

5.   "It is indeed a sad fact..." *The Oswald Affair* (English edition), p. 407.

6.   *The Oswald Affair* (English edition), p. 418.

7.   French not very good: Sylvia Meagher to Léo Sauvage, July 30, 1966. Meagher reaction to tribute: Sylvia Meagher to Maggie Field, July 25, 1966.

8.   Quote: Vincent J. Salandria to Sylvia Meagher, September 16, 1966.

9.   "Background Survey of Books Concerning the Assassination of President Kennedy," January 4, 1967. ARRB Number 180-10098-10177. [Emphasis in original.]

10.   "Background Survey of Books Concerning the Assassination of President Kennedy," January 4, 1967. ARRB Number 180-10098-10177.

11.   Longest article to appear: "Off the Cuff," *Greater Philadelphia*, August 1966. Excerpt: "The Warren Commission, the Truth, and Arlen Specter," by Gaeton Fonzi, *Greater Philadelphia* magazine, August 1966.

12.   Specter never answers article: Gaeton Fonzi interview, January 28, 2002.

13.   "SOS" note: Sylvia Meagher to Vincent J. Salandria, July 30, 1966. "...the most serious establishment organ..." Vincent J. Salandria to Tom Bethell, December 31, 1966.

14.   Sylvia Meagher to Vincent J. Salandria and Gaeton Fonzi, August 3, 1966.

15.   Sylvia Meagher to Vincent J. Salandria and Gaeton Fonzi, August 3, 1966, and *Greater Philadelphia* magazine, September 1966. Letter meant for Fonzi but Meagher pleased it was printed: Sylvia Meagher to Vincent J. Salandria, September 17, 1966.

16.   *Forgive My Grief* printed at Jones' expense: *Citizen's Arrest*, p. 44. Michael Jones studies poem, suggests title: Michael Jones interview, August 29, 2002.

17.   *Forgive My Grief*, Vol. 1, preface, by John Howard Griffin.

18.   Criticisms of *Forgive My Grief*: See *Citizen's Arrest*, p. 118-119. Jones acknowledges "unpolished journalist:" *The Windmill Fighter*, p. 79. His statement was in the context of the *Mirror's* appearance. "And we might insert here that *The Midlothian Mirror* certainly has never won any prizes for make-up. *The Mirror* has gone in for more of what was said than how it was placed on the page. We are not bragging about it, but since we are not trained journalists we haven't made an effort to be very style conscious and the *Mirror's* make-up certainly shows it." Also Louise Jones to Sylvia Meagher, May 21, 1966: "Neither Penn nor I ever had a course in journalism...My only qualification is that I read so much: Seven daily papers, possibly 30 weeklies, and maybe 5 books a week." [Ellipsis in original.] Weisberg quote: *Oswald in New Orleans*, "Introduction," p. 22.

19.   Decker Exhibit 5323, WC Vol. 19, pp. 483-484.

20.   *Forgive My Grief*, Vol. 1, p. 25.

21.   *Ibid.*, Vol. 1, pp. 30-34. Craig statements: Decker Exhibit, WC Vol. 19, p. 524 (11-23-63); CE 1967, WC Vol. 23 (mentions Rambler), p. 817 (11-23-63); and CE 1993, WC Vol. 24, p. 23 (11-25-63). Craig testimony appears in WC Vol. 6, pp. 260-273.

22.   This dialogue from Craig testimony, WC Vol. 6, p. 270.

23.   *Forgive My Grief*, Vol. 1, p. 33, quoting WC Vol. 4, p. 245.

24.   *Ibid.*, Vol. 1, p. 34.

25. *Ibid.*, Vol. 1. Chapter 1, "Meeting at Ruby's Apartment," and Chapter 23, "Earlene Roberts" (includes William Whaley and stripper references).

26. Sylvia Meagher to Vincent J. Salandria, August 16, 1966.

27. Circumstances of death: *Forgive My Grief*, Vol. II, p. 27. Jones considers death sinister: Sylvia Meagher to Maggie Field, Aug. 25, 1966. Death threats: *Forgive My Grief*, Vol. II, p. 27.

28. Bowers reticent by nature, and quote: ARRB Record Number 180-10113-10264. Bowers' observations: CE 2003 p. 10, WC Vol. 24, p. 201.

29. ARRB Record Number 124-10041-10137.

30. *Ibid.*

31. "More killings are going to be necessary..." *Forgive My Grief*, Vol. I, p. 185.

32. "The Relevance of an Inquest," *The Minority of One*, July-August, 1966.

33. "Research on the Assassination," *The Minority of One*, September 1966.

34. "Moved to the very bones," Sylvia Meagher (quoting Arnoni) to Maggie Field, July 25, 1966.

35. Harold Weisberg to George Herman, *Mike Wallace at Large*, broadcast July 24, 1966. Audio tape from Ray Marcus archive, Hood College.

36. See *Whitewash*, p. 19, and testimony of Jack Dougherty, WC Vol. 6, p. 377.

37. Harold Weisberg to George Herman, *Mike Wallace at Large*, broadcast July 24, 1966. Audio tape from Ray Marcus archive, Hood College.

38. Attacked during radio appearance: Harold Weisberg interview, November 30, 2000. "Congratulations for performing with dignity..." Sylvia Meagher to Harold Weisberg, June 26, 1966. "Everything any one of us says..." Harold Weisberg to Sylvia Meagher, June 29, 1966.

39. Epstein on *Mike Wallace at Large*: undated audio recording, probably early July 1966. (Wallace says on 7-24-66 Weisberg broadcast that Epstein appeared "two weeks ago.") "He was pressured into accepting..." Sylvia Meagher to Harold Weisberg, June 19, 1966. "He'll get clobbered..." Harold Weisberg to Sylvia Meagher, June 29, 1966.

40. Sylvia Meagher to Maggie Field, August 25, 1966.

41. *Ibid.*

42. Comparative study completed: "Chronology of writing *Accessories After the Fact*," by Sylvia Meagher. Meagher contacted by Random House: Sylvia Meagher to Maggie Field, August 25, 1966.

43. Sylvia Meagher to Maggie Field, August 25, 1966.

44. Contacted by *Esquire* and *Studies on the Left*: Sylvia Meagher to Maggie Field, August 25, 1966. Rejects *Book Week* offer: Sylvia Meagher to Maggie Field, August 16, 1966.

45. Sylvia Meagher to Maggie Field, August 25, 1966.

46. *Ibid.*

47. "Round Two," by Fred Graham, *The New York Review of Books*, August 28, 1966.

48. *Ibid.*

49. Dialog in this section from *The Barry Farber Show*, August 31, 1966. Audio tape in author's collection.

50. *Ibid.*

51. Penn Jones quote: *The CBS Evening News*, October 27, 1966.

52. "Pamela knows little about the case..." Maggie Field to Sylvia Meagher, September 24, 1966. Details of Mason show, and quote: "Transcript of Interview with Penn Jones, Jr., by Pamela Mason, Los Angeles radio, September 1966," by Sylvia Meagher. (This is an unofficial transcript. A tape of this program is in the Ray Marcus archive at Hood

College.) Additional background: Gwen Field interview, October 26, 2001.

53. Penn Jones to Louis Lomax, *The Lomax Show,* October 2, 1966.

54. Maggie Field to Sylvia Meagher, September 24, 1966.

55. *The Lomax Show,* October 2, 1966.

56. "Who is Popkin?" Harold Weisberg to Sylvia Meagher, July 19, 1966. Popkin data: *The Second Oswald.*

57. "The Second Oswald," by Richard Popkin, *New York Review of Books*, July 28, 1966.

58. *Ibid.*

59. *Ibid.*

60. Harold Weisberg to Sylvia Meagher, July 19, 1966.

61. Weisberg alleges plagiarism, and Crawford: Harold Weisberg to Sylvia Meagher, July 29 and August 2, 1966.

62. Sylvia Meagher to Harold Weisberg, July 30, 1966.

63. Vincent J. Salandria to Dave Dellinger (*Liberation*), May 26, 1966. M.S. Arnoni to Harold Weisberg, May 16 and May 20, 1966.

64. Salandria quote: Vincent J. Salandria to Shirley Martin, November 15, 1964. Weisberg quote: *Whitewash*, p. 138.

65. Ray Marcus interview, July 12, 2000, and letter to author, March 11, 2002.

66. "I contacted his office..." Ray Marcus interview, July 25, 2001. Further background, shows two books on camera: Ray Marcus to Sylvia Meagher, August 28, 1966.

67. Sylvia Meagher to Ray Marcus, December 20, 1966.

68. Ray Marcus to Sylvia Meagher, December 30, 1966.

69. *The Mort Sahl Show*, September 4, 1966. Audio tape in author's collection. Unless otherwise noted, this section with its description of Lane's appearance on the Sahl show comes from the audio tape.

70. Survey data: Gallup Poll, January 1967. Kupferman: *The New York Times*, September 29, 1966, p. 26, and Congressional Record, 89th Congress, 2d Session, Sept. 28, 1966, pp. 24157-24161.

71. Sylvia Meagher to Shirley Martin, October 3, 1966.

72. Maggie Field's letters to elected officials were sent to Sen. Thomas Kuchel, Sen. George Murphy, Sen. William Fulbright, Rep. Theodore Kupferman, and Rep. Thomas Rees, all dated October 16, 1966. Letters to the media: Marshall Lumsden, Editor of *West* magazine, November 30, 1966, and Osborn Elliot of *Newsweek*, December 11, 1966. "The urgency of this request..." Maggie Field to Sen. Murphy.

Sen. Kuchel sent a token reply dated October 21, 1966: "The [Warren Commission] members were outstanding, knowledgeable, conscientious American citizens...I am in no position to judge the competence or qualifications of various less-known authors of the several critical commentaries which have appeared lately..." Sen. Murphy's reply dated October 24, 1966.

Sylvia Meagher received copies of all this correspondence. On December 14, 1966, she told Maggie, "Your letters to *West* and *Newsweek* flame with truth, conviction, and the sense of justice which has all but disappeared from American life."

73. *The New York Times*, October 23, 1966.

74. Quote: *Accessories After the Fact*, p. xxxii.

75. "In The Shadow of Dallas," *Ramparts*, November 1966, Vol. 5, No. 5.

76. Bogus book review: *Ramparts*, November 1966, pp. 59-61. Bookseller orders: *If You Have a Lemon, Make Lemonade*, p. 243.

77. *Ramparts* magazine, January 1967, "Marginalia" (Meagher and Marcus comments) and "Apologia" (Hinckle apology).

78. "Who Killed President Kennedy?" by Harrison Salisbury, *The Progressive*, November 1966.

79. "A Matter of Reasonable Doubt," *Life*, November 25, 1966. Sylvia Meagher to Maggie Field, November 21, 1966.

80. Sylvia Meagher to Maggie Field, November 1, 1966. Editor's opinion: memo, "Telephone conversations with Bob Ockene, Bobbs-Merrill," October 28, 1966. *Supreme Injustice* title: manuscript in Meagher Archive.

81. "Much excitement since *Life*..." Sylvia Meagher to Shirley Martin, November 24, 1966.

82. "Defenders of the Gospel According to Warren," by Sylvia Meagher. Unpublished poem, placed in Sylvia Meagher archive, Hood College.

Chapter Twenty-Four – An Ugly Question

1. Shirley Martin to Vincent J. Salandria, June 12, 1965.

2. Speech to the Coalition on Political Assassinations, "The JFK Assassination: A False Mystery Concealing State Crimes," delivered in Dallas, November 20, 1998; reprinted in *False Mystery: An Anthology of Essays on the Kennedy Assassination*, by Vincent J. Salandria, privately published, 1999, p. 111.

3. Sylvia Meagher to Vincent J. Salandria, December 17, 1968.

4. "How do I prove...?" Sylvia Meagher to Vincent J. Salandria, April 4, 1967.

5. "CIA Subsidy Probe to Include Refugee Aid," by Robert S. Allen and Paul Scott, *The Oakland Tribune*, February 24, 1967.

6. "I am flabbergasted..." Sylvia Meagher to Harold Weisberg, April 4, 1967. "A completely independent project..." Sylvia Meagher to the Editor, *The Oakland Tribune*, April 5, 1967.

7. Advertisement in author's collection: "Seven Judges, No Jury..." Meagher couldn't make it, suggests Salandria: Sylvia Meagher to Ray Marcus, November 27, 1966. Epstein declines: Sylvia Meagher to Maggie Field, December 1, 1966 (Marcus collection).

8. *Honest Verdict* still mentioned: See author blurb in *Frontier* article, November 1966.

9. *The Scavengers and Critics of the Warren Report*, p. 139.

10. *History Will Not Absolve Us*, p. 177.

11. "Notes from Boston – Prepared December 1, 1966," by Vincent J. Salandria.

12. *Ibid*. Epstein-Salandria exchange also recounted in Sylvia Meagher to Maggie Field, December 1, 1966 (Marcus collection).

13. This section is derived from "Notes from Boston – Prepared December 1, 1966," by Vincent J. Salandria.

14. *Maverick: Fifty Years of Investigative Reporting*, by Fred J. Cook, pp. 287-88.

15. Sylvia Meagher to Vince Salandria, December 5, 1966.

16. *Ibid*.

17. "The Fine Edge of Believability," by Joe McGinniss, *The Philadelphia Inquirer*, Jan. 6, 1967.

18. "The Fine Edge of Believability," *The Philadelphia Inquirer*, January 6, 1967.

19. *Ibid*.

20. *Ibid*.

21. *Ibid*.

22. *Ibid*.

23. *Ibid*.

24. *Ibid*.

25. Josiah Thompson interview, October 12, 2004.

26. Quote: Josiah Thompson interview, October 12, 2004. Also consulted: Thompson COPA remarks, October 21, 1995, and *The New Yorker*, June 10, 1967.

27. Josiah Thompson interview, October 12, 2004, and *The New Yorker*, June 10, 1967.

28. "I immediately quit when..." and reason for quitting: Vincent J. Salandria to author, April 7, 2000. "I was unwilling to say..." Josiah Thompson interview, October 12, 2004.

29. *Six Seconds in Dallas*, "A Note from the Publisher," pp. xv-xviii. "The two projects..." Josiah Thompson interview, October 12, 2004.

30. "Memo re: Thompson," by Ray Marcus, November 1990.

31. Marcus hears about Thompson, plus quote: "Memo re Thompson." Marcus business trip: Ray Marcus interview, July 25, 2001.

32. *Addendum B*, p. 32.

33. *Ibid.*

34. "Memo re: Thompson," November 1990.

35. Marcus in *Life* offices: "Memo re: Thompson," November 1990. "It was stunning to me..." Marcus interview, September 20, 2000.

36. Marcus shows Kern and Wainwright his interpretations: "Memo re: Thompson," November 1990. Connally: "A Matter of Reasonable Doubt," *Life*, November 25, 1966.

37. "Memo re: Thompson," November 1990.

38. Thompson at *Life*: Josiah Thompson interview, October 12, 2004. Zapruder film screening: *Six Seconds in Dallas*, pp. 6-10, and Josiah Thompson e-mail to author, April 19, 2005. Film "shockingly clear": Thompson interview, October 12, 2004, and *Six Seconds*, pp. 8-9.

39. "Memo re: Thompson."

40. *Ibid.*

41. Thompson has no recollection of meeting but concedes it probably took place: Josiah Thompson interview, October 12, 2004. Marcus quote: "Memo re: Thompson," November 1990.

42. Quote: Sylvia Meagher to Harold Weisberg, February 2, 1967.

43. Sylvia Meagher to Shirley Martin, February 7, 1967.

44. "I was leery of him..." Shirley Martin to Sylvia Meagher, February 10, 1967. Striso in China, and "We are a very sick nation..." Jules Striso to Shirley Martin, February 4, 1967. Warnings that critics might be in danger: Sylvia Meagher to Shirley Martin, February 7, 1967.

45. Sylvia Meagher to Shirley Martin, February 7, 1967.

46. *Ibid.*

47. Untitled notes on Rollins-Salandria visit, January 31, 1967, by Vincent J. Salandria.

48. *Ibid.*

49. *Ibid.*

50. Sylvia Meagher to Maggie Field, February 2, 1967.

51. *Ibid.*

52. *Ibid.*

53. "Despite my strong predisposition..." Sylvia Meagher to Maggie Field, February 2, 1967. Rollins interview by Salandria, Meagher, Arnoni, *et al:* Untitled notes on Rollins-Salandria visit, January 31, 1967, by Vincent J. Salandria.

54. Sylvia Meagher to Maggie Field, February 2, 1967.

55. Dialogue from untitled notes on Rollins-Salandria visit, January 31, 1967, by Vincent J. Salandria.

56. Sylvia Meagher to Maggie Field, February 2, 1967.

57. *Ibid.*

58. *Ibid.*

59. Sylvia Meagher to Maggie Field, February 2, 1967. Rollins and nursing: *Destiny Betrayed,* p. 363, note 66. This description similar, but not identical, to description in untitled notes on Rollins-Salandria visit, January 31, 1967, by Vincent J. Salandria.

60. Sylvia Meagher to Maggie Field, February 2, 1967.

61. Untitled notes on Rollins-Salandria visit, January 31, 1967, by Vincent J. Salandria, and Salandria interview, January 9, 2003.

62. Untitled notes on Rollins-Salandria visit, January 31, 1967, by Vincent J. Salandria.

63. *Ibid.*

64. "If They've Found Another Assassin, Let Them Name Names and Produce New Evidence," by John Berendt, *Esquire* magazine, August 1967. Hereafter cited as "If They've Found Another Assassin..."

65. *Ibid.*

66. *Ibid.*

67. *Ibid.*

68. "If They've Found Another Assassin..." Vincent J. Salandria interview, January 13, 2003.

69. *Ibid.* Red Ford: WC Vol.6, p. 453.

70. *Ibid.*

71. *Ibid.*

72. *Ibid.*

73. *Ibid.*

74. *Ibid.*

75. "On the Police Beat," by Jack Dempsey, *The New Orleans States-Item*, January 23, 1967. Quoted in *Let Justice Be Done,* by Bill Davy, p. 64.

76. *Let Justice Be Done,* and *The New York Times*, February 18, 1967.

77. Garrison wanted probe secret: *The New York Times*, February 21, 1967. Garrison quote: February 1967, included in *He Must Have Something,* a video documentary by Steven Tyler.

78. Lane says he'll cooperate: *The New York Times*, February 21, 1967. Telegram: Meagher to Jim Garrison, February 22, 1967. Copy in Sylvia Meagher Collection, Hood College.

Chapter Twenty-Five – Counterattack

1. "He even coaxed..." Sylvia Meagher to Maggie Field, November 14, 1966.

2. Sale of *Accessories After the Fact* [hereafter *AAF*]: Sylvia Meagher notes on phone call from Bob Ockene, December 28, 1966. Léo Sauvage peer review: Meagher notes on phone call from Ockene, "Friday afternoon 10/28/66." Meagher grows antsy, "I talked to our Eminent Reader..." Sylvia Meagher to Bob Ockene, November 23, 1966.

3. Ockene asks Sauvage how review is coming: Bob Ockene to Léo Sauvage, December 8, 1966. Sauvage assessment: "Sylvia Meagher: *Accessories After the Fact*," by Léo Sauvage. Sauvage calls *AAF* reference book: cover letter to Ockene dated December 10, 1966.

4. Phrase "reference book" and "If I were Bobbs..." Sylvia Meagher to Bob Ockene, December 14, 1966. *AAF* accepted, and terms of sale: Meagher notes, phone call from Ockene, Wednesday, December 28, 1966. Publication date: Sylvia Meagher to Sales Division, World Wide Photo, March 8, 1967. Dazed and happy: Sylvia Meagher to Penn Jones and Shirley Martin, December 29, 1966.

5. Mark Lane, *The Mort Sahl Show*, September 4, 1966.

6. *Ibid.,* October 9, 1966.

7. *The New York Times*, November 23, 1966.

8. *Ibid.*, November 24, 1966.

9. *Ibid.*

10. *Forgive My Grief*, Vol. III, p. 13.

11. "La Verita e Vicina," by Livio Caputo, *Epoca* magazine, November 1966. Copy in author's collection.

12. Schiller calls Meagher on November 23, 1966: Notes on call from "Lawrence Schiller, Capitol Records, 11/23/66, 8 p.m.," by Sylvia Meagher.

13. Sylvia Meagher to Lawrence Schiller and Richard Warren Lewis, December 4, 1966.

14. Meagher's reasons for not signing release: Sylvia Meagher to Lawrence Schiller and Richard Warren Lewis, December 4, 1966. Schiller and Lewis telephone for follow-up interview, Meagher reads letter over the phone, and "These scavengers are not worth..." Sylvia Meagher to Maggie Field, December 4, 1966.

15. "I am more and more..." Harold Weisberg to Sylvia Meagher, January 26, 1967. Schiller and Lewis say work scholarly, and "What you did..." Harold Weisberg to Lawrence Schiller, January 7, 1967. Mark Lane on Schiller and Lewis: *A Citizen's Dissent*, pp. 178-179.

16. "A keening pack of speculators..." "The Scavengers," *The World Journal Tribune*, January 22, 1967. Critic descriptions: *The Scavengers and Critics of the Warren Report*.

17. "A drawling backwoods prophet," troubled teen, "macabre doctrine," and implication Jones was a drunk: *The Scavengers and Critics of the Warren Report*. Schiller or Lewis asking for a drink, and quote: "One Man's Grief," *The Texas Observer*, September 29, 1967.

18. *The Controversy*, Capitol Records, 1967.

19. *The Scavengers and Critics of the Warren Report*, p. 21. Traffic tickets: *The New York Times*, April 3, 1962.

20. "Where Lane likes to float around..." *The Scavengers and Critics*, p. 65. House guarded by a "vicious" german shepard: *The World Journal Tribune*, January 22, 1967. Lane was never in pool: *A Citizen's Dissent*, pp. 181-182. Details of Brondo attack: *A Citizen's Dissent;* Ray Marcus to Ayda Field, August 15, 1997; Gwen Field interview, July 9, 2001.

21. "Lawrence Schiller was the only person..." Gwen Field interview, July 9, 2001. "Memory of Brondo's attack..." Ray Marcus to Ayda Field, August 15, 1997.

22. Shirley Martin picks up at airport, they ask about dogs: *A Citizen's Dissent*, p. 182. "Schiller called himself 'James Bond'" and "Lewis made me promise..." Shirley Martin to Sylvia Meagher, undated letter, probably January 1967.

23. *The World Journal Tribune*, January 22, 1967.

24. Shirley Martin interview, June 23, 2000.

25. Teresa Martin interview, June 16, 2000.

26. Teresa Martin to author, via email, June 16, 2000.

27. Shirley Martin to author, via email, June 23, 2000.

28. *The New York Times*, January 4, 1967.

29. Gray had other critics on: Lane – *A Citizen's Dissent*, p. 147, and Sauvage – *The Barry Gray Show*, August 29, 1966. Audio tape in author's collection. Meagher contacted, other guests on show: Sylvia Meagher to Ray Marcus, January 4, 1967.

30. Description of program: Sylvia Meagher to Ray Marcus, January 4, 1967. "A researcher who closeted herself..." *The Controversy*, side two.

31. "Transcript of tape recording of the Barry Gray programme WMCA radio 3 January 1967 from 11 p.m. to 1am. Excerpt."

32. Sylvia Meagher to Ray Marcus, January 4, 1967.

33. Second broadcast: Sylvia Meagher to Ray Marcus, January 4, 1967. Sylvia accompanied by Crehan and Sprague: Sylvia Meagher to Maggie Field, Ray Marcus, and Harold Weisberg, January 5, 1967. Sprague and photographic evidence: *AAF*, p. 22, n. 13.

34. Sylvia Meagher to Maggie Field, Ray Marcus, and Harold Weisberg, January 5, 1967.

35. Sylvia Meagher to New York State Attorney General, January 26, 1967. Alfred J. Scotti, chief assistant district attorney, to Sylvia Meagher, January 30, 1967.

36. WC Vol. 14, pp. 474-475. See also p. 402.

37. *A Citizen's Dissent*, p. 181.

38. Sylvia Meagher to Maggie Field, February 1, 1967.

39. Meagher helps Lane, thinks he didn't need help, sits with niece: Sylvia Meagher to Maggie Field, February 1, 1967.

40. Details of program, and "Lane responded that, leaving himself aside..." Sylvia Meagher to Maggie Field, February 1, 1967. "He in no way showed..." Sylvia Meagher to Maggie Field, February 6, 1967.

41. Lane quotes Jenner re: autopsy photos: Sylvia Meagher to Maggie Field, February 1, 1967, and *A Citizen's Dissent*, p. 129. Jenner quote: Lane cites "Broadcast on WNYC-TV, New York City, December 23, 1966" (Lane citaton: *A Citizen's Dissent*, endnotes for Chapter 23, p. 272, note 1).

42. Meagher and niece see Jenner's daughter, and quotes: Sylvia Meagher to Maggie Field, February 1, 1967. The conversation between Jenner and his daughter is also recounted in *A Citizen's Dissent*, pp. 129-130, footnote.

43. Lane says he might sue Liebeler: *The Mort Sahl Show*, October 9, 1966. Liebeler on *Rush to Judgment* and *Inquest*: *The New York Times*, October 23, 1966. Additional background in *A Citizen's Dissent*, pp. 132-134.

44. This anecdote described in unpublished letter, Ray Marcus to Ayda Field, August 15, 1997.

45. Lane on defense books: *A Citizen's Dissent*, p. 178.

46. Manchester commissioned: *The New York Times*, March 27, 1964.

47. Legal battle: See, for example, *The Manchester Affair*, by John Corry. Quips about deleted material: *e.g.* Mark Lane on *The Mort Sahl Show*, October 9, 1966.

48. "After the Battle, the Book," by Sylvia Meagher, *The Minority of One*, June 1967.

49. Letter from Richter to Marcus dated February 10, 1967, reproduced in facsimile form in *#5 Man, November 22, 1963*, p. 33.

50. "I shall be happy to assist..." Ray Marcus to Robert Richter, February 14, 1966. Letter reproduced in facsimile form in *#5 Man, November 22, 1963*, p. 34.

51. *Esquire* image, *#5 Man, November 22, 1963*, pp. 112-115. Meagher's opinion: Sylvia Meagher to Ray Marcus, December 12 and 20, 1966. Marcus certainty: Ray Marcus to Sylvia Meagher, December 18, 1966. "The fact that on close inspection..." *#5 Man*, p. 112. "I can state without question..." Jacques de Langre to Ray Marcus, December 15, 1966. Letter reproduced in facsimile form, *#5 Man*, p. 115.

52. *Boston Herald Traveler* item: April 19, 1967. Article reproduced in facsimile form in *#5 Man, November 22, 1963*, p. 36.

53. *#5 Man, November 22, 1963*, p. 27.

54. *Ibid.*

55. *#5 Man, November 22, 1963*, p. 27-28.

56. *#5 Man, November 22, 1963*, p. 28.

57. Midgley reaction: *#5 Man, November 22, 1963*, p. 31.

58. *#5 Man, November 22, 1963*, p. 29, and Ray Marcus to author, March 3, 2002.

59. Maggie travels to New York in March 1967 to find publisher: Sylvia Meagher to Harold Weisberg, March 3, 1967. Sylvia and Maggie visit, grow closer, Sylvia's insights: Sylvia Meagher to Maggie Field, March 6, 1967.
60. Panoplies: author's inspection, December 7-8, 2001. "I've taken the actual testimony..." *Los Angeles Free Press,* December 8, 1967.
61. "She has had phenomenal success..." Sylvia Meagher to Harold Weisberg, March 3, 1967. "The immediate enthusiasm..." Sylvia Meagher to Maggie Field, March 6, 1967.
62. *The Oswald Affair* and *AAF: passim. Rush to Judgment: A Citizen's Dissent,* p. 39.
63. "If They've Found Another Assassin...," Vincent J. Salandria interview, January 13, 2003.
64. *Ibid.*
65. *Ibid.*
66. *Ibid.* (Salandria concludes Vaganov a red herring.)
67. *The Great Fear,* p. 297. Smith Act quoted in *Red Scare,* p. 18.
68. Holmes testifies against Lightfoot, speaks for Birch Society: *The Great Fear,* p. 547. Supports Wallace: *Time,* July 5, 1968, p. 48.
69. Untitled notes on Rollins-Salandria visit, January 31, 1967, by Vincent J. Salandria.
70. *Ibid.*

Chapter Twenty-Six – Garrison

1. *The New York Times,* February 18 and 19, 1967.
2. Survey data: The Gallup Report, "Doubts that Oswald Acted Alone as Widespread as Ever," January 11, 1967.
3. Not-too-closely-guarded secret: Salandria email, February 11, 2003. Salandria said Tom Bethell did not request he keep the matter of the Garrison probe in confidence. Louise Jones called the probe "hush-hush." Louise Jones to Sylvia Meagher, January 27, 1967. There is other material relative to this. Investigation "routine," and "We were making good progress..." *The New York Times,* February 19, 1967. Arrests months away, not weeks: *The New York Times,* February 21, 1967. "Let justice be done..." Garrison on CBS News, February 18, 1967, quoted in *Accessories After the Fact,* p. 456, note 1.
4. Life of witness in danger: *The New York Times,* February 21, 1967. "David Ferry" named early: *The New York Times,* February 19, 1967. Ferrie knew Oswald: Investigation of the Assassination of President John F. Kennedy. Appendix to Hearings Before the Select Committee on Assassinations of the U.S. House of Representatives, Ninety-fifth Congress, Second Session. Volume IX, pp. 114-115. Former Civil Air Patrol recruit instructor Jerry Paradis told the HSCA that Oswald had attended many CAP meetings at which Ferrie had been the instructor. "I know they were there because I was there," Paradis said. "Supposedly, I have been pegged..." and "big joke": *The New York Times,* February 23, 1967, citing *The New Orleans States-Item,* February 18, 1967. This quote praraphrased in *The New Orleans Times-Picayune,* February 19, 1967.
5. *The New York Times,* February 23, 1967.
6. *Ibid.*
7. Warren and Dulles have no comment: *The Boulder Daily Camera,* February 19, 1967, Associated Press dispatch. McCloy quote: *The San Francisco Examiner,* February 19, 1967, Associated Press dispatch.
8. Oswald spends summer 1963 in New Orleans: Warren Report, pp. 403-404. Garrison investigator in November 1963: *On The Trail of the Assassins,* by Jim Garrison, pp. 5-7. Hereafter cited as *On the Trail.* See also HSCA Vol. 10, p. 105.

9. *On the Trail*, pp. 7-11. In a story published just before his death, Ferrie said of his sudden Texas trip, "We drove by car to Vincton, Louisiana, then to Houston and Galveston, where we hunted geese. Our route brought us back by Alexandria on the Sunday after; and it was there I learned that thirteen law officers, including Garrison and former assistant district attorney Frank Klein, had broken into my home and carted off books, photographs and some other personal belongings...we were all thrown in jail and booked with being fugitives from Texas." *The New Orleans Times-Picayune*, February 19, 1967.

10. Gives little thought to case, "The conclusion of these two..." *On the Trail*, p. 13.

11. Garrison and Hale Boggs: *A Farewell to Justice*, by Joan Mellen, p. 2. For the rest of his life, Garrison maintained it was the doubts of Louisiana Senator Russell Long that sparked his interest in the JFK case. Mellen, whose book gives the fullest account of the Garrison investigation to date, states that Garrison was protecting former Commissioner Boggs by crediting Senator Long. Memory of Ferrie nags Garrison: *Playboy* interview, Oct. 1967.

12. Garrison reads critical literature, and quote: *Playboy* interview, October 1967.

13. Background: *The Electric Windmill*, by Tom Bethell, p. 7. Quote: "Interview with Tom Bethell," by Karen Minto and David Oyerly, Full Context, Vol. 11, No. 3 (January/February 1999), online version, http://www.fullcontext.org/people/bethell_intx.html. "Most of these contacts appear to have been made by...Tom Bethell." See note 15.

14. Bethell to Baton Rouge: *The Electric Windmill*, pp. 60-61.

15. Bethell sent to Dallas: *The Electric Windmill*, p. 61. Mary Ferrell recalled meeting Bethell before he was hired by Garrison: Mary Ferrell interview, November 17, 2000. First contacts, then visits Salandria: Tom Bethell to Vincent J. Salandria, October 19, 1966, and Salandria interview, February 4, 2003. Visits Meagher: Sylvia Meagher to Shirley Martin, February 27, 1967. Meagher made a veiled reference to Bethell in a letter to Maggie Field dated January 31, 1967: "[Bethell] is the man who was staying with Penn...[he] brought the electrifying information that an official (not federal) agency is quietly pursuing the events, because they are not satisfied with the WR at all but they feel, as we do, that it was a bigger thing, and they incline toward the very same groups that we have felt were exiled in their cloaks and daggers." Bethell and Weisberg: *Oswald in New Orleans*, by Harold Weisberg, pp. 21-24. Bethell visits Mary Ferrell: Ferrell interview, November 17, 2000.

16. Investigations discreet: *e.g.* Salandria interview, and Louise Jones to Sylvia Meagher, January 27, 1967. "It is difficult for me to tell you..." and *AAF* chapters: Sylvia Meagher to Jim Garrison, February 23, 1967.

17. "What wonderful news..." Shirley Martin to Sylvia Meagher, February 23, 1967. "Light at the end..." Shirley Martin to Sylvia Meagher, February 25, 1967.

18. "Telephone call from Philippe Labro (New Orleans) Saturday 2 p.m. 2/25/67," by Sylvia Meagher.

19. Vincent J. Salandria to Sylvia Meagher, February 20, 1967.

20. Details on Shaw's arrest: *The New York Times*, March 2, 1967. Shaw interviewed in December 1966: *Let Justice Be Done*, p. 63, citing "NODA interview with Clay Shaw, December 23, 1966."

21. Quote: *The New York Times*, March 3, 1967, p. 22.

22. Bertrand telephones Andrews: CE 1931 (WC vol. 23, p. 726).

23. Oswald comes to Andrews' office: WC Vol. 11, p. 326. Andrews sees Oswald handing out leaflets: WC Vol. 11, p. 328.

24. Andrews hospitalized: WC vol. 23, p. 726 (CE 1931), and WC Vol. 11, pp. 331-334.

25. This exchange from WC Vol. 11, p. 334.

26. Richter asks for index: Sylvia Meagher to Jim Garrison, February 23, 1967. CBS promotes documentary as unprecedented: *A Citizen's Dissent*, p. 75. Advertisement re: "the most valuable four hours": *The New York Times*, June 25, 1967, p. 16D.

27. Text of letter to Midgley included in facsimile form in *#5 Man, November 22, 1963*, pp. 38-48.

28. Additional copies of #2 and #5 enclosed: *#5 Man, November 22, 1963*. Details on phone call to Richter: tape recording, Marcus to Richter, June 20, 1967 (Marcus archive).

29. Castro, Batista: HSCA Vol. 10, p. 6. Eisenhower authorizes CIA: HSCA Vol. 10, p. 7. CIA recruits organized crime: HSCA Vol. 10, pp. 151-152.

30. HSCA Vol. 10, pp. 8-9 (p. 8 re: CIA organized, directed, funded anti-Castroites).

31. Newman Building: HSCA Vol. 10, pp. 123-125.

32. Newman Building, Lafayette and Camp Street entrances and occupants: HSCA Vol. 10, pp. 123-125.

33. Cuban exile thought Oswald was anti-Castro: WC Vol. 10, pp. 35-36 (Carlos Bringuier testimony). See also HSCA Vol. 10, p. 123, and WC Vol. 26, p. 783 (Camp Street address).

34. The Warren Report, p. 407.

35. Newman Building owner and other tenants don't recall Oswald: HSCA Vol. 10, p. 123. Banister phone interview: HSCA Vol. 10, p. 126. Commission states no link: Warren Report, p. 408.

36. *On the Trail*, pp. 29-32, and HSCA Vol. 10, p. 130 (details and quote).

37. Garrison's view of Jack Martin: *On the Trail*, p. 31, and pp. 38-43. Martin's appearance: *A Farewell to Justice*, pp. 34-35. Joan Mellen also reports that Jack Martin was a former CIA employee who maintained connections with the Agency through the period Martin was in contact with Garrison.

38. *On the Trail*, pp. 36-37, and HSCA Vol. 10, pp. 130-131.

39. "From this index list..." *On the Trail*, p. 39. Index list also discussed in *A Heritage of Stone*, pp. 98-99.

40. *A Heritage of Stone*, p. 99.

Chapter Twenty-Seven – The Proof of a Plot

1. *On the Trail*, pp. 150-151. *Let Justice Be Done*, p. 123. *The New York Times*, March 3, 1967, p. 22. *Oswald in New Orleans*, p. 233.

2. Testimony of Perry Raymond Russo, Clay Shaw preliminary hearing, March 14 and 15, 1967. Transcript from *The Garrison Transcripts* CD-ROM.

3. Testimony of Vernon Bundy, Clay Shaw preliminary hearing, March 17, 1967. Transcript from *The Garrison Transcripts* CD-ROM.

4. *The New York Times*, March 18, 1967, p. 1, and *Let Justice Be Done*, p. 129.

5. Meagher sends list of Commission Exhibits: Sylvia Meagher to Jim Garrison, March 5, 1967. Garrison says Meagher's index useful: Jim Garrison to Sylvia Meagher, April 18, 1967. Meagher resists impulse to go to New Orleans, cautions Garrison about CIA sponsored index: Sylvia Meagher to Jim Garrison, April 22, 1967.

6. *Heartland*, by Mort Sahl, p. 116.

7. Transcript, "Mark Lane on KLAC Radio, Los Angeles (by phone from New Orleans) (Mort Sahl program) 3/29/67," by Sylvia Meagher.

8. *The Mort Sahl Show*, April 3, 1967.

9. Quote: "The JFK 'Conspiracy,'" *Newsweek*, May 15, 1967, p. 36.

10. Quote: *Playboy* interview, October 1967.

11. Oswald to Mexico City: The Warren Report, pp. 412-413.

12. Odio active in JURE, parents imprisoned: WC Vol. 26, pp. 835-838 (CE 3147). Details of visit: The Warren Report, pp. 321-324. Security chain: WC Vol. 11, p. 370.

13. Sister gets a good look at visitors: WC Vol. 11, p. 371. The visitors' appearance: *Conspiracy,* p. 387. About to leave on trip: Warren Report, p. 322.

14. Warren Report, p. 322.

15. *Ibid.* "At first, I thought he was just..." WC Vol. 11. p. 373.

16. Odio faints: WC Vol. 11, p. 381. No doubt about identity: WC Vol. 11, p. 382, and The Warren Report, p. 322.

17. Quote: The Warren Report, p. 324.

18. Slawson and Liebeler: *Inquest,* pp. 104-105. "At this stage, we are supposed to be..." *Inquest,* p. 105.

19. Loran Hall, and "The Commission has concluded..." The Warren Report, p. 324.

20. From "The Proof of the Plot," *Accessories After the Fact,* p. 379.

21. *Whitewash,* p. 154.

22. *Whitewash II,* p. 55.

23. Transcript, Orleans Parish Grand Jury Proceedings of April 28, 1967; *Oswald in New Orleans,* p. 26.

24. Weisberg, Oswald, Leopoldo, and Angelo: *Oswald in New Orleans,* pp. 251-299; *Whitewash II,* pp. 51-70.

25. Transcript, Orleans Parish Grand Jury Proceedings of April 28, 1967, p. 48-49.

26. This exchange: Transcript, Orleans Parish Grand Jury Proceedings of April 28, 1967, p. 52.

27. *Accessories After the Fact,* p. 387.

28. Transcript, Orleans Parish Grand Jury Proceedings of April 28, 1967, p. 9.

29. Transcript, Orleans Parish Grand Jury Proceedings of April 28, 1967, pp. 63-64.

30. Transcript, Orleans Parish Grand Jury Proceedings of April 28, 1967, pp. 5-6. Weisberg convinced Oswald was "man in doorway": Harold Weisberg interview, April 26, 2001.

31. Connection to CIA: Transcript, Orleans Parish Grand Jury Proceedings of April 28, 1967, p. 47. Oswald "all right" – Transcript, Orleans Parish Grand Jury Proceedings of April 28, 1967, p. 45, and *Whitewash II,* p. 46. Security clearance: Transcript, Orleans Parish Grand Jury Proceedings of April 28, 1967, p. 46, and *Oswald in New Orleans,* pp. 85-87. Delgado: Transcript, Orleans Parish Grand Jury Proceedings of April 28, 1967, p. 47, and *Oswald in New Orleans,* p. 94, citing WC Vol. 8, pp. 232 and 259.

32. This exchange: Transcript, Orleans Parish Grand Jury Proceedings of April 28, 1967, p. 82.

33. Harold Weisberg to Sylvia Meagher, May 3, 1967.

34. *Ibid.*

35. Orleans Parish Grand Jury Proceedings of May 10, 1967. Lane's testimony transcript from *The Garrison Transcripts* CD-ROM, © 2002, Assassination Archives and Research Center and History Matters.

36. Orleans Parish Grand Jury Proceedings of May 10, 1967, pp. 38-39. Lane cites Warren Report re: Andrews' sedation, WR p. 325.

37. Orleans Parish Grand Jury Proceedings of May 10, 1967, pp. 34-35.

38. Orleans Parish Grand Jury Proceedings of May 11, 1967, p. 1. It is worth noting the reaction of Mr. Marcus on first seeing his testimony in 1998, thirty-one years after he had given it. "Taken as a whole, the transcript is an accurate representation of my testimony," he said. "However, it contains numerous stenographic and/or transcribing errors...some of

these errors result in puzzling formations and garbled syntax, conveying in a few cases impressions different from those intended." (From note in front matter of the transcript, which Marcus self-published.)

39. Orleans Parish Grand Jury Proceedings of May 11, 1967, pp. 1-3.

40. Marcus and *Life*: Orleans Parish Grand Jury Proceedings of May 11, 1967, pp. 3-4. Double head hit and Thompson: p. 9. Marcus describes JFK head hits: pp. 12-13. Marcus on Connally wounds: p. 55.

41. Orleans Parish Grand Jury Proceedings of May 11, 1967, pp. 50-51.

42. *Ibid.*, pp. 52-54.

43. *Ibid.*, pp. 100-102.

44. *Ibid.*, pp 72-73.

45. *Ibid.*, pp 73-74.

46. *Ibid.*, p. 74.

47. *Ibid.*, pp. 74-75.

48. *Ibid.*, pp. 75-76.

49. *Ibid.*, p. 77.

50. "A Philadelphia Lawyer Analyzes the Shots, Trajectories and Wounds," by Vincent J. Salandria, *Liberation*, January 1965.

51. *Ibid.*, citing *Life* magazine, October 2, 1964 (version #1).

52. *Ibid.*, October 2, 1964 (version #2).

53. Salandria quote: Vince Salandria interview, September 18, 2000.

54. Quote: Salandria to Ed Kern, November 25, 1966. Salandria interview, Sept. 18, 2000.

55. Ed Kern to Vince Salandria, November 28, 1966.

56. Speech before the National Coalition on Political Assassinations, Nov. 20, 1998.

57. *The Making of the President – 1964*, by Theodore H. White, p. 33.

58. Vincent J. Salandria to Theodore H. White, November 11, 1966. Theodore White to Salandria, undated note written on Salandria's letter to White.

59. Recordings: *The Making of the President – 1964*, by Theodore H. White, pp. 9-10. Salandria to Dr. Robert Bahmer, November 11, 1967.

60. Dr. Robert Bahmer to Vincent J. Salandria, November 20, 1967.

61. *With Kennedy*, by Pierre Salinger, pp. 3-10.

62. Vincent J. Salandria to Pierre Salinger, December 3, 1967.

63. Pierre Salinger to Vincent J. Salandria, December 26, 1967.

64. Dr. Robert Bahmer to Vincent J. Salandria, January 9, 1968. Col. James U. Cross to Vincent J. Salandria, January 2, 1968.

65. Quote: Speech at the National Coalition on Political Assassinations, November 20, 1998.

66. Search of Shaw's home, address book with Odom entry: *Destiny Betrayed*, p. 154.

67. Oswald's notebook: WC Vol. 16, p. 58. Photos of Oswald entry and Shaw entry both appear in *Destiny Betrayed*, p. 154 (Note: the identifying captions in *Destiny Betrayed* are mistakenly reversed).

68. *The New York Times*, May 18, 1967, p. 32.

69. *Ibid. On the Trail*, pp. 146-147.

70. Sylvia Meagher to Jim Garrison, May 16, 1967.

71. *Ibid.*

72. Sylvia Meagher to Ray Marcus, May 17, 1967.

73. *Ibid.*

74. *Ibid.*

Chapter Twenty-Eight – Fatal Ruptures

1. Sylvia Meagher to Maggie Field, June 8, 1967. "The Buffs," by Calvin Trillin, *The New Yorker*, June 10, 1967.

2. *The New Yorker*, June 10, 1967.

3. *Ibid.*

4. Sylvia Meagher to Maggie Field, March 6, 1967.

5. Sylvia Meagher to Vince Salandria, May 30, 1967.

6. Sylvia Meagher to Harold Weisberg, June 1, 1967.

7. *The New York Times*, June 25, 1967.

8. *Should We Now Believe the Warren Report?* by Stephen White, "Preface," by Walter Cronkite, pp. vii-viii.

9. "I decided to watch..." "Who Killed Kennedy? CBS Is Wrong," by Mark Lane, *True* magazine, December 1967. Lane meets with Richter, and "What had evidently been...": *A Citizen's Dissent*, pp. 80-84.

10. *Who Killed Kennedy?* (U.S. Ed.) p. 77.

11. *CBS New Inquiry: The Warren Report*, June 25-28, 1967.

12. *CBS New Inquiry: The Warren Report*, Part One, June 25, 1967.

13. Schiller quote: *CBS New Inquiry: The Warren Report*, Part One, June 25, 1967. See also *Should We Now Believe the Warren Report?* by Stephen White, p. 213. The book includes a transcript of the four part CBS special.

14. Negative not recovered: The Warren Report, p. 127. The picture was marked CE 133-A by the Warren Commission. The Commission reported that the negative for a similar photograph marked 133-B was in fact taken by a camera belonging to Oswald. FBI expert Lyndal Shaneyfelt "could not test Exhibit No. 133-A in the same way because the negative was never recovered." Lane quote: *A Citizen's Dissent*, p. 85.

15. *CBS New Inquiry: The Warren Report*, Part Two, June 26, 1967.

16. Sylvia Meagher to Richard Salant, July 3, 1967.

17. *CBS New Inquiry: The Warren Report*, Part Three, June 27, 1967.

18. *Ibid.*

19. This Garrison-Wallace exchange, *CBS New Inquiry: The Warren Report*, Part Three, June 27, 1967.

20. Wallace holds up smallest version of picture: *#5 Man, November 22, 1963*, p. 31. Wallace quote: *CBS New Inquiry: The Warren Report*, Part Three, June 27, 1967.

21. "Who Killed Kennedy? The Warren Report was Right," *True*, December. 1967, p. 32.

22. Richter note: Bob Richter to Ray Marcus, June 28, 1967, published in facsimile form in *#5 Man, November 22, 1963*, p. 51. Dialog in this section: Ray Marcus and Robert Richter phone conversation, tape recording in Marcus archive, Hood College.

23. "Misconduct and malfeasance:" Transcript, Orleans Parish Grand Jury Proceedings of June 28, 1967. Gurvich comments to reporters: *The New York Times*, June 29, 1967, p. 18.

24. *The New York Times*, June 29, 1967, p. 18.

25. *Playboy* interview, October 1967.

26. *Ibid.*

27. *CBS New Inquiry: The Warren Report*, Part Four, June 28, 1967. Unless otherwise noted, the data and quotations in this section come from this same source.

28. *CBS New Inquiry: The Warren Report*, Part Four, June 28, 1967, and *The New York Times*, June 29, 1967, p. 18.

29. *The New York Times*, July 5, 1967.

30. *The New York Times*, November 22, 1966.

31. Maggie and Joe Field social life: Gwen Field interview, July 13, 2001. "Maggie told us..." Ray Marcus to Ayda Field, August 15, 1997.

32. "FP interviews Mrs. Field on Warren Report 'Errors,'" *Los Angeles Free Press,* Dec.8,1967.

33. Sylvia Meagher to Maggie Field, June 11, 1967.

34. Meagher quotes: Sylvia Meagher to Maggie Field, June 11, 1967. Marcus quotes: Ray Marcus to Ayda Field, August 15, 1997.

35. Sylvia Meagher to Ray Marcus, July 19, 1967.

36. Meagher commits views to writing, reiterates position on postal code, states Bundy and Russo have no credibility: Sylvia Meagher to Vincent J. Salandria, July 8, 1967. Adds she is bitterly unhappy over split, won't yield on matter of principle, "On the day that I accept..." Sylvia Meagher to Vincent J. Salandria, August 9, 1967.

37. Vincent J. Salandria to Sylvia Meagher, August 19, 1967.

38. This dialogue derived from "Telephone call from Penn Jones, Friday 11:45 p.m. 7/28/67," by Sylvia Meagher.

39. Sylvia Meagher to Penn Jones, Jr., July 29, 1967.

40. Ray Marcus interview, September 5, 2000.

41. Itek study: *The New York Times,* May 19, 1967. Marcus reaction: *#5 Man, November 22, 1963,* by Raymond Marcus, Chapter 5. In his book Marcus describes the Itek incident in far greater detail.

42. "Blow-up!! November 22, 1963. New Facts About the Mary Moorman Photo," by Raymond Marcus, *Los Angeles Free Press,* November 24, 1967.

43. "Blow-up!! November 22, 1963." The *Los Angeles Free Press,* November 24, 1967.

44. Roger Aldi interview with Joseph Ball, KHJ Radio, November 27, 1967. Recording in Raymond Marcus archive, Hood College.

45. Quote: Sylvia Meagher to Maggie Field, July 17, 1967. Meagher comment on Salandria/Garrison: Sylvia Meagher to Maggie Field, August 6, 1967. Meagher overriding concern that WR criticism continue: Sylvia Meagher to Maggie Field, August 18, 1967.

46. Maggie Field agrees to go to New Orleans for KPFK: Maggie Field to Sylvia Meagher, September 7, 1967. MF uneasiness re: Garrison: Maggie Field to Vince Salandria, October 2, 1967. Salandria on Garrison having no case: Vince Salandria interview, February 28, 2002.

47. Maggie Field to Sylvia Meagher, August 15, 1967.

48. *Ibid.*

49. Field quote: Maggie Field to Sylvia Meagher, September 7, 1967. Meagher quotes: Sylvia Meagher to Maggie Field, September 10, 1967.

50. Dialog from "Notes on phone conversation with Maggie Field, Wednesday 7 p.m. 20 September 1967," by Sylvia Meagher.

51. Sylvia Meagher to Maggie Field, September 21, 1967.

52. Meagher quotes: Sylvia Meagher to Harold Weisberg, September 23, 1967. Harold Weisberg to Sylvia Meagher, September 27, 1967.

53. Sylvia Meagher to Harold Weisberg, September 30, 1967.

54. Quote: Sylvia Meagher to Ray Marcus, October 31, 1967.

55. Sylvia Meagher to Shirley Martin, October 3, 1967.

56. Shirley Martin to Sylvia Meagher, undated note, October 1967.

57. Shirley Martin interview, October 17, 2000.

58. Sylvia Meagher to Penn Jones, Jr., October 8, 1967.

Chapter Twenty-Nine – Single-Spaced Letters

1. Ray Marcus to Sylvia Meagher, October 18, 1967.

2. "I would be less apprehensive..." Sylvia Meagher to Shirley Martin, October 3, 1967. Revised ending months earlier: Sylvia Meagher to Penn Jones, Jr., October 31, 1967. Two epilogues: *Accessories After the Fact*, draft manuscript, Meagher Archive. Footnote re: unanswered letters: *Accessories After the Fact*, p. xxv.

3. "A New Investigation," by Sylvia Meagher, draft copy, Meagher Archive.

4. *Accessories After the Fact*, p. 457. Opinion on Garrison written in June 1967: Sylvia Meagher to Penn Jones, Jr., October 31, 1967.

5. Harold Weisberg to Sylvia Meagher, September 27, 1967, and Sylvia Meagher to Harold Weisberg, September 30, 1967.

6. Foreword an excellent piece of writing: Harold Weisberg interview, August 30, 2001, and Harold Weisberg to Jim Garrison, October 17, 1967.

7. Sylvia Meagher to Harold Weisberg, November 1, 1967.

8. Harold Weisberg to Sylvia Meagher, November 3, 1967.

9. "Garrison and Warren: Anything in Common?" by M.S. Arnoni, *The Minority of One*, October 1967.

10. *Ibid.*

11. "Jim Garrison Knows Himself to be Right," letter to the editor by Jim Garrison, *The Minority of One*, November 1967.

12. *Ibid.*

13. All letters quoted here are from the December, 1967 issue of *The Minority of One*, pp. 29-30.

14. O'Brien asked for dust jacket quote: Connor Cruise O'Brien to Robert Ockene, June 27, 1967. O'Brien tells Meagher he's impressed by what he read: Connor Cruise O'Brien to Sylvia Meagher, September 1, 1967. Review: "Veto by Assassination?" by Conor Cruise O'Brien, *The Minority of One*, December 1967, pp. 16-18.

15. Draft of dedication in Meagher archive, Hood College.

16. *Accessories After the Fact*, "Introduction," by Léo Sauvage, pp. viii-xvi.

17. Advanced copies received: Untitled and undated list compiled by Sylvia Meagher, Meagher archive, "Letters re: AAF." Ray Marcus to Sylvia Meagher, November 3, 1967.

18. Vincent J. Salandria to Sylvia Meagher, November 2, 1967. Louise Jones to Meagher, November 22, 1967. Other messages referenced: Meagher archive, Hood College.

19. Maggie Field to Sylvia Meagher, November 7, 1967.

20. "Despite the fact that embarrassing gaffes..." "Studies in Disbelief," by Fred Graham, *The New York Times Book Review*, February 18, 1966. Sauvage response: *The Barry Gray Show*, August 29, 1966. Meagher response: *Accessories After the Fact*, p. xxiv.

21. "Studies in Disbelief," by Fred Graham, *The New York Times Book Review*, February 18, 1968.

22. "Studies in Disbelief," *The New York Times Book Review*, February 18, 1968.

23. *Ibid.*

24. "From the Editor," by William A. Emerson Jr., *Saturday Evening Post*, December 2, 1967, p. 3.

25. "The Crossfire that Killed President Kennedy," by Josiah Thompson, *Saturday Evening Post*, December 2, 1967.

26. *Ibid.*

27. Vince Salandria to Ray Marcus, December 3, 1967; Marcus memos re: Salandria phone calls, December 16, 1967, December 24, 1967, January 22, 1968.

28. Ray Marcus to Josiah Thompson, November 20, 1967.

29. Flurry of letters: copies in author's collection. Quote: Ray Marcus to Josiah Thompson, December 15, 1967, p. 13.

30. Meagher involved, heavy workload, father ill, quotation: Sylvia Meagher to Ray Marcus, December 26, 1967. Sylvia Meagher to Josiah Thompson, January 10, 1968.

31. Sylvia Meagher to Ray Marcus, January 11, 1968.

32. Ray Marcus memo of phone call from Vince Salandria, December 16, 1967.

33. Thompson-Meagher meeting at Salandria home: Sylvia Meagher to Ray Marcus, December 1, 1967, and Ray Marcus to Josiah Thompson, January 12, 1968. Marcus on meeting: Marcus to Thompson, January 12, 1968.

34. Salandria inclined to agree with Marcus: Ray Marcus memo of phone call from Vince Salandria, December 16, 1967. Marcus disagrees: M.S. Arnoni to Ray Marcus, Decmeber 18, 1967.

35. Quotes from readers: *Saturday Evening Post,* January 13, 1968, p. 4.

36. "I cannot take seriously..." Sylvia Meagher to Ray Marcus, January 11, 1968. "You have been had..." Ray Marcus to Sylvia Meagher, January 18, 1968.

37. Ray Marcus to Sylvia Meagher, January 20, 1968 (telegram).

38. Josiah Thompson, speech to Coalition on Political Assassinations, Washington, D.C., October 21, 1995. Tape recorded by author.

39. Vincent J. Salandria to Josiah Thompson, March 22, 1968.

40. Josiah Thompson to Vincent J. Salandria, undated note.

Chapter Thirty – The Trial

1. "A Reporter At Large: Garrison," by Edward J. Epstein, *The New Yorker*, July 13, 1968.

2. *Mirror* article: July 25, 1968, reprinted in *Forgive My Grief*, Vol. III. Dean Andrews perjury conviction: *On the Trail*, pp. 170, 243, and *The New York Times,* August 14, 1967, p. 15.

3. Ray Marcus to William Shawn, July 11, 1968. Reprinted in facsimile form in *#5 Man, November 22, 1963*, pp. 105-106.

4. Milton Greenstein to Ray Marcus, July 23, 1968. Reprinted in facsimile form in *#5 Man, November 22, 1963*, p. 107.

5. Garrison, NBC and equal time; Garrison on *The Tonight Show: On the Trail*, pp. 208-213, and *Heartland*, pp. 117-119.

6. Lane and Sahl rehearse Garrison, and Lane quote: *The JFK Assassination: The Jim Garrison Tapes,* a film by John Barbour, 1992, and *Heartland*, p. 118.

7. *The Tonight Show,* January 31, 1968. Audio tape from the Ray Marcus Archive, Hood College. Unless otherwise specified, all quotations in this section come from the audio tape of the program.

8. Sylvia Meagher to Clay Shaw, June 1, 1968. Letter from Meagher archive, Hood College.

9. Clay Shaw to Sylvia Meagher, July 8, 1968. Letter from the private papers of Léo Sauvage.

10. "Speech made by Vincent J. Salandria on June 9, 1968 in Central Park, New York City."

11. "Speech made by Vincent J. Salandria on June 9, 1968 in Central Park, New York City." Quotation from Fay book: *The Pleasure of His Company*, by Paul B. Fay, pp. 174-175.

12. "Speech made by Vincent J. Salandria on June 9, 1968 in Central Park, New York City."

13. Dialogue from "Telephone call from Vince Salandria, Friday night, 6:45 p.m., 9 March 1968," by Sylvia Meagher.
14. *On the Trail*, p. 182.
15. Vincent J. Salandria to Sylvia Meagher, November 17, 1968.
16. Vincent J. Salandria to Sylvia Meagher, December 14, 1968.
17. Sylvia Meagher to Vincent J. Salandria, December 17, 1968.
18. Vincent J. Salandria to Sylvia Meagher, January 29, 1969.
19. Sylvia Meagher to Vincent J. Salandria, February 1, 1969.
20. *The New York Times*, February 6, 1969.
21. *The New York Times*, February 6, 1969.
22. *The New York Times*, January 11, 1969. Access restrictions by Kennedy family: *The New York Times*, January 6, 1968.
23. Kupferman efforts: ARRB Record Number 186-10006-10193, a group of letters among Kupferman, Archivist Robert Bahmer, and Kennedy family representative Burke Marshall. See also *Six Seconds in Dallas*, Appendix E, "Official Correspondence of Representative Theodore R. Kupferman."
24. *The New York Times*, January 17, 1969, and "Chronology and Summary of Attempts to Obtain Photos and X-Rays of Autopsy of President Kennedy," undated and unsigned document of Orleans Parish District Attorney's office, in facsimile on *The Garrison Transcripts* CD-ROM. Quote: *Post Mortem*, by Harold Weisberg, p. 133. Additional background: *The New York Times*, January 17, 1969.
25. Weisberg due to testify, "Have you studied...?" and "Which one?..." from *Post Mortem*, p. 134.
26. *Post Mortem*, p. 135.
27. Harold Weisberg to Vince Salandria, February 3, 1969.
28. Salandria denial: Vince Salandria to Sylvia Meagher, February 8, 1969. The matter further discussed in Vince Salandria interview, February 28, 2002.
29. Transcript, State of Louisiana v. Clay Shaw, February 6, 1969, p. 3, from *The Garrison Transcripts* CD-ROM.
30. Transcript, State of Louisiana v. Clay Shaw, February 6, 1969, pp. 16-17, from *The Garrison Transcripts* CD-ROM, and *The New York Times*, February 7, 1969.
31. Transcript, State of Louisiana v. Clay Shaw, February 6 (c), 1969, pp. 5-6, from *The Garrison Transcripts* CD-ROM.
32. *Let Justice Be Done*, pp. 101-117. (There are numerous sources for Clinton story.)
33. *On the Trail*, pp. 182-186. The Nagell case is given its fullest treatment in *The Man Who Knew Too Much,* by Dick Russell.
34. Nagell meets Garrison in May 1968: *The Man Who Knew Too Much*, p. 727. Nagell prepared to testify, Garrison decides against it: *On the Trail*, p. 229.
35. "The bomb that shattered..." *On the Trail of the Assassins*, p. 236. Spiesel testimony: *On the Trail*, pp. 236-237, and *The New York Times*, February 8, 1969.
36. *The New York Times*, February 9, 1969.
37. *Let Justice Be Done*, p. 174.
38. Transcript, State of Louisiana v. Clay Shaw, February 10 and 11, 1969, from *The Garrison Transcripts* CD-ROM. Russo quote from Feb. 11 trial transcript, pp. 201-202. Additional source: *The New York Times*, February 15, 1969.
39. Garrison subpoenas Zapruder film: *On the Trail of the Assassins*, p. 239. Quote: *The New York Times*, February 14, 1969.
40. *Forgive My Grief*, Vol. III, pp. v-vi.
41. Garrison warned by *Life* not to copy, and quote: *The Zapruder Film: Reframing JFK's*

Assassination. Warning: p. 60. Quote: p. 307, note 64. Garrison and Lane make Zapruder film copies: *On the Trail of the Assassins*, p. 239, footnote. Jones has bootleg copies of Zapruder film made: *Citizen's Arrest*, p. 92. Order form included in *Forgive My Grief*, Vol. IV, author's collection.

42. *Life* announces it will release missing frames: *The New York Times*, January 30, 1967. Frames in *Six Seconds in Dallas*: SSID, p. 217. *Life* denies permission, sues: Josiah Thompson interview, October 12, 2004. *Life* loses suit: *The New York Times*, October 1, 1968.

43. Transcript, State of Louisiana v. Clay Shaw, February 14(b), 1969, pp. 83-84, from *The Garrison Transcripts* CD-ROM, and *The New York Times*, February 15, 1969.

44. "Chronology and Summary of Attempts to Obtain Photos and X-Rays of Autopsy of President Kennedy," undated and unsigned document of Orleans Parish District Attorney's office, in facsimile on *The Garrison Transcripts* CD-ROM, and *Post Mortem*, by Harold Weisberg, p. 133. Judge rules Wecht can see photos and X-rays: *The New York Times*, February 15, 1969, and "Chronology and Summary of Attempts to Obtain Photos and X-Rays of Autopsy of President Kennedy." See also *Cause of Death*, by Cyril Wecht, paperback edition, p. 32.

45. "Chronology and Summary of Attempts to Obtain Photos and X-Rays of Autopsy of President Kennedy," and *The New York Times*, February 21, 1969.

46. *The New York Times*, August 27, 1972, "Mystery Cloaks Fate of Brain of Kennedy."

47. Transcript, State of Louisiana v. Clay Shaw, February 19(b), 1969, from *The Garrison Transcripts* CD-ROM, and *The New York Times*, February 15, 1969.

48. Transcript, State of Louisiana v. Clay Shaw, February 19(b), 1969, pp. 185-186, from *The Garrison Transcripts* CD-ROM, and *The New York Times*, February 15, 1969.

49. Defense says might have been conviction without Spiesel background: *Let Justice Be Done*, p. 185, citing letter from Edward Wegmann to Elmer Gertz, March 12, 1969. Garrison on sabotage: *On the Trail*, p. 237. Haggerty says Shaw lied under oath: *He Must Have Something*, a video documentary by Steve Tyler.

50. *On the Trail*, p. 251, and *The New York Times*, March 2, 1969.

51. "Not with a Roar but a Whimper: The Shaw Trial, the Garrison Wreck," by Sylvia Meagher.

52. *Ibid.*

53. Penn Jones quote: *Citizen's Arrest*, p. 92.

54. *Forgive My Grief*, Vol. III, revised edition, from the Foreword, unnumbered page.

55. Jones, Garrison, and Boxley: *Forgive My Grief*, Vol. III, pp. 38-42. Garrison and Boxley: *On the Trail*, pp. 174-175. Additional data: ARRB Record #180-10070-10309, "Memorandum, William Wood AKA Bill Boxley," September 1977 (HSCA document).

56. Robert Perrin a gun runner, commits suicide: WC Vol. XIV, p. 334-335. Garrison and Boxley: *Forgive My Grief*, pp. 38-42. Weisberg says Boxley loyal to JG: Harold Weisberg to David Starks, May 1997. Garrison credits Salandria: *On the Trail*, pp. 190-191.

57. Weeping confession: *A Farewell to Justice*, by Joan Mellen, p. 293, citing May 6, 1969, memorandum from Lou Ivon to Jim Garrison. Bethell quote: "Was Sirhan Sirhan on the Grassy Knoll?" by Tom Bethell, *The Washington Monthly*, March 1975.

58. Vincent J. Salandria in cover letter to correspondence group, June 16, 1995.

59. Ray Marcus to Jim Garrison, March 1, 1969.

60. Truman article: "US Should Hold CIA to Intelligence Role," *The Washington Post*, December 22, 1963. At the urging of Marcus, the article was reprinted in the January 24, 1975 edition of the *Los Angeles Times*, and in facsimile form in *Addendum B*, by Raymond Marcus. Marcus considers it important policy statement: *Addendum B*, p. 74. "I'm amazed it has..." Ray Marcus to Vincent J. Salandria, January 20, 1969.

61. "US Should Hold CIA to Intelligence Role," *The Washington Post,* December 22, 1963, reprinted in facsimile form in *Addendum B.*
62. "I can't read it any other way..." Ray Marcus to Vincent J. Salandria, January 20, 1969. See also *Addendum B*, pp. 74-76a. Early in 2006, Marcus received a copy of the typescript of the article from the Truman Library. This typescript was dated December 11, 1963 – eleven days earlier than it was published. "To me," Marcus observed, "this further strengthens the already high probability that in warning of the Agency's excesses he had the assassination in mind." Ray Marcus to author, January 2006.
63. Ray Marcus interview, July 2001.
64. *Addendum B*, p. 28.
65. *Ibid.*
66. *Addendum B*, p. 29.
67. *Ibid.*
68. *Addendum B*, p. 65, and *Best Evidence*, pp. 30-31.
69. *Addendum B*, p. 65.
70. *Addendum B*, pp. 65-66.

Epilogue

1. "One Man's Grief," by Robert Bonazzi, *The Texas Observer*, September 29, 1967.
2. HSCA conclusion: Report of the Select Committee on Assassinations, U.S. House of Representatives, Ninety-fifth Congress, Second Session, p. 1.
3. Fonzi and HSCA and Church Committee: *The Last Investigation*, pp. 30-34.
4. *Ibid.*, pp. 28-29.
5. *Ibid.*, p. 113.
6. *Ibid.*, pp. 117-145; HSCA Report, pp. 135-136; HSCA Vol. 10, pp. 37-56.
7. *The Last Investigation*, pp. 141-142; HSCA Vol. 10, pp. 37-56.
8. *Ibid.*, p. 142.
9. *Ibid.*, pp. 153-160.
10. Phillips as chief of Cuban operations: *The Last Investigation*, p. 266. Balance of paragraph and ensuing dialogue, pp. 161-170.
11. HSCA Vol. 10, pp. 47-52. Blakey declines perjury charges: *The Last Investigation*, p. 423.
12. *The Last Investigation*, p. 396.
13. Quote: Sylvia Meagher to Bill O'Connell, April 9, 1969.
14. "The Assassination of President John F. Kennedy: A Model for Explanation," speech at the conference of the New England Branch of the Women's International League for Peace and Freedom, Cambridge, Mass., October 23, 1971. Published in *Computers and Automation*, December 1971, Vol. 20, No. 12.
15. *Ibid.*, October 1971.
16. Thomas Stamm to Vincent J. Salandria, February 1972 (copy typed by Sylvia Meagher). Meagher quote: Sylvia Meagher to Thomas Stamm, February 14, 1972.
17. Sylvia Meagher to Ray Marcus, November 26, 1975.
18. "We could mention..." Ray Marcus interview, January 14, 2002.
19. Patricia Orr, Special Assistant to the Chief Counsel and Director of the House Select Committee on Assassinations, to Ray Marcus, January 17, 1977; Ray Marcus to Patricia Orr, February 12, 1977; Patricia Orr to Ray Marcus, March 15, 1977. These letters reproduced in facsimile form in *#5 Man, November 22, 1963.*
20. Sylvia Meagher to Ray Marcus, April 29, 1977.

21. HSCA learns of recording: HSCA Vol. II, p. 17. Acoustic Analysis results: HSCA Report, p. 1. Sylvia Meagher to Ray Marcus, June 9, 1979.

22. Moorman analysis: HSCA Vol. VI, pp. 124-125.

23. *Ibid.*

24. Quote: Shirley Martin to Sylvia Meagher, February 25, 1967. Shirley Martin's views on Garrison: Shirley Martin interview, October 17, 2000.

25. "Sometimes she 'quits'..." Sylvia Meagher to Maggie Field, September 28, 1966. "I really dropped out of almost everything..." Shirley Martin interview, October 16, 2001.

26. Vincent J. Salandria to Shirley Martin, July 26, 1969.

27. "We have means of getting this information..." *Let Justice Be Done*, pp. 178-179, citing CIA memo from Office of General Counsel to New Orleans, November 30, 1967. Marchetti quote: *Let Justice Be Done*, p. 130, citing interview with Marchetti by Bud Fensterwald, published in *True* magazine, April 1975.

28. DeLoach memo quote: *Let Justice Be Done*, p. 192, citing FBI memo from DeLoach to Clyde Tolson, March 2, 1967, FBI Document # 62-109060-4635. Schiller quote: ARRB Record Number 124-10043-10277, p. 3. "Bertrand" as code name: ARRB document 179-20002-10329.

29. Memorandum from Blackmer to Blakey, *et al.,* September 1, 1977. ARRB Record Number 180-10105-10199.

30. Vincent J. Salandria to Shirley Martin, September 20, 1969.

31. Maggie Field to Ray Marcus, December 24, 1967.

32. *Ibid.*

33. Gwen Field interviews, February 4, 2002, and June 18, 2003.

34. Gwen Field interviews, July 9 and July 13, 2001.

35. Gwen Field interview, July 9, 2001.

36. Poster boards: author's inspection, December 7-8, 2001.

37. "FP Interviews Mrs. Field on Warren Report 'Errors,'" *Los Angeles Free Press,* December 8, 1967.

38. Immie Feldman interview, February 16, 2001.

39. "Eulogy for Harold Feldman," by Vincent J. Salandria, undated, reconstructed from extemporaneous talk.

40. Harold Feldman to Shirley Martin, June 29, 1965.

41. Pierre Sauvage interview, November 14, 2003; *The New York Times,* November 5, 1988; and "Léo Sauvage is Dead," by Pierre Sauvage, November 1988.

42. "America's Nazis and their Defenders," by Léo Sauvage, *The New Leader,* August 14, 1978.

43. *The New York Times,* November 5, 1988; *Los Angeles Times,* November 6, 1988; and "Léo Sauvage is Dead," by Pierre Sauvage, November 1988.

44. Interest in baseball after 1969 Mets: Sylvia Meagher to Josiah Thompson, October 17, 1969, and Jerry Policoff to author, April 22, 2001. 1987 Engagement Calendar among personal effects in Meagher archive, Hood College. Mets-Pirates game: *The New York Times,* April 8, 1987.

45. Sylvia Meagher 1987 Engagement Calendar.

46. Sylvia Meagher 1987 Engagement Calendar. Request from Prentice-Hall: Memorandum re: phone call from Kathy Kiernan, "April 10, 1987, Friday 3 p.m.," by Sylvia Meagher. Evaluation: Sylvia Meagher to Mark Jaffee, November 19, 1987.

47. Meagher asked to review JG manuscript: Philip Pochoda to Sylvia Meagher, November 24, 1986. Meagher evaluation: Sylvia Meagher to Philip Pochoda, December 18, 1996, with chapter-by-chapter commentary enclosed.

48. Sylvia Meagher to Philip Pochoda, December 18, 1986.

49. Quotations: Sylvia Meagher to Philip Pochoda, December 27, 1986. Manuscript rejected: Philip Pochoda to Jim Garrison, January 14, 1987. Sorrels' testimony on route: WC Vol. VII, p. 337.

50. Garrison telephones Meagher, and "She described him to me...": Roger Feinman to author, April 22, 2001. Garrison and Meagher plan to meet: Jerry Policoff to author, April 22, 2001.

51. Death: *The New York Times*, January 15 and 16, 1989.

52. "Her work on the case..." Roger Feinman to author, April 22, 2001.

53. "I wish I could say..." *The JFK Assassination: The Jim Garrison Tapes*, A film by John Barbour. 1992. "He simply helps illuminate..." Jim Garrison to Jonathan Blackmer, September 14, 1977, ARRB Record Number 180-10076-10032.

54. "Why We Still Care," *Life*, December 1991.

55. *The Legal-Intelligencer*, January 15, 1992.

56. *Ibid.*

57. "When Oliver Stone's movie JFK came out..." Gwen Field interview, July 13, 2001. Meagher: Roger Feinman to author, April 21, 2001. Weisberg: Harold Weisberg to David Starks, videotaped interview, 1993.

58. Marcus, JFK film and *#5 man*: Ray Marcus interview, July 25, 2001. It is worth noting that in *JFK: The Documented Screenplay*, published in 1992, the non-shooting draft of the screenplay contains a reference to "a potential shooter" in a Moorman-photo blowup. It is referred to as the "Badgeman" image in a note on p. 122 of the book. This detail appears to be the same as #2 man as identified by Ray Marcus and David Lifton. In any case, these references were deleted from the screenplay and were not in the film, including the director's cut released on DVD. "I have just seen the film *JFK...*" Ray Marcus to Jim Garrison, January 1, 1992.

59. *He Must Have Something*, a video documentary by Steve Tyler.

60. *The San Francisco Chronicle, et al*, October 22, 1992.

61. Harold Weisberg interview, August 30, 2001.

62. "That's a legitimate question..." Harold Weisberg interview, August 30, 2001. Garrison had no one to blame but himself: Harold Weisberg to David Starks, videotaped interview, May 1997.

63. "What I am writing..." *Photographic Whitewash*, by Harold Weisberg, p. 11. Weisberg's books a record for history: Harold Weisberg to David Starks, May 1997, videotaped interview.

64. Use of FOIA in 1966: *Post Mortem*, by Harold Weisberg, p. 247. Weisberg basement: in 1993, following a videotaped interview, Weisberg gave David Starks and his videocamera a tour of his basement, thus creating a visual record of Weisberg's archive. The archive has since been transferred to Hood College in Frederick, Md.

65. Harold Weisberg to David Starks, videotaped interview, 1993.

66. "I think very often..." Harold Weisberg interview, July 12, 2001.

67. Marguerite Oswald death: *The New York Times*, January 18, 1981, and *Newsweek*, January 26, 1981. "When she died, and I read..." Shirley Martin to author, spring 2000. "Who's the mother here?" Shirley Martin to author, May 16, 2000.

68. This paragraph drawn from a series of interviews and informal conversations with Shirley Martin, 2000-2004.

69. Shirley Martin interview, March 12, 2004.

70. Ford opinion, and quote: *Let Us Begin Anew*, pp. 461-462.

71. Belin quote: "The Warren Commission was Right," *The New York Times*, November 22, 1971. Reprinted in *The Assassinations: Dallas and Beyond*, pp. 259-261.

72. *Passion for Truth,* by Arlen Specter (with Charles Robbins), pp. 1-3.

73. "He was satisfied..." *Whitewash IV: JFK Assassination Transcript,* p. 21. Weisberg and Russell: *Whitewash IV,* pp. 20-22, and *Never Again!,* pp. 221-233.

74. "Senator Russell Dissents," unpublished paper by Harold Weisberg, undated but approximately 1994.

75. *Forgive My Grief,* Vol. IV, p. 120. The expression was apparently a favorite of Jones's. In his unpublished 1962 memoir *The Windmill Fighter,* Jones related how an editor from another small paper asked him why he never gave up. "I quoted," Jones wrote, "When someone picks me up as a hunk of dirt to chink a crack against the wind 20,000 years from now, I hope he will pause, feel the mud tenderly between his fingers and comment – 'Man, that is good clay.' But it fazed my friend not at all. 'Hell,' he muttered, 'he will probably say – "Too much sand in that to use.""'

76. Penn Jones sells *Mirror: Forgive My Grief,* Vol. IV. Military as culprit: *Forgive My Grief,* Vol. III, foreword.

77. Jones to author, December 7, 1993. When Penn Jones wrote this, I was just trying to buy copies of *Forgive My Grief* and not yet planning the present work. I would like to acknowledge here that Jones was also kind enough to send me copies of *The Continuing Inquiry,* an assassination poster, and a Super-8 mm copy of the Zapruder film.

Penn's meeting with JFK is described in Chapter 9, "Texas." He described meeting RFK in an article written in 1978. He did not date the meeting, but it was probably in 1964, "while Robert Kennedy was still the attorney general under Lyndon Johnson." Writing that "I could no longer contain myself" about the assassination, he called former JFK speechwriter Theodore Sorensen, who was then in Boston working on his JFK memoir *A Thousand Days.* Jones flew there and the two discussed evidence of conspiracy. Afterward Sorensen asked what Jones wanted him to do. "Hell, I don't know," Jones replied. "I guess just pat me on the back and tell me to go on back home."

But Sorensen surprised Jones by arranging a meeting with RFK. "Kennedy shook hands warmly," Jones wrote. "He wanted me to talk to his top assistant, Mr. Nicholas Katzenbach. Kennedy told an assistant to take me downstairs to Mr. Katzenbach, then told the man 'I want to see Mr. Jones before he leaves.'" Jones told Katzenbach everything he had told Sorensen, but Katzenbach "did not take a single note."

Jones did see RFK after meeting with Katzenbach, but it was clear, he recalled, that the Attorney General "did not want to talk about the assassination of his brother." Kennedy arranged for a car to take Penn to JFK's grave at Arlington National Cemetery, and then to the airport where he caught a flight home. "I do not know if Mr. Katzenbach ever reported to Attorney General Kennedy, but I feel quite certain that he never told Lyndon Johnson what I told him that day." (Summarized from "My Visit to Robert Kennedy," by Penn Jones, Jr., *The Continuing Inquiry,* November 22, 1978.)

78. Penn Jones, Jr., November 22, 1993, from videotape in author's collection.

79. Death reported in the *Midlothian Mirror,* Thursday, January 29, 1998, and *The Waxahachie Daily Light,* January 27, 1998. By the time of his death, Penn and L.A. Jones were divorced. L.A. died on January 12, 2000. Chris Pike to author, citing Michael Jones, October 21, 2005.

80. Ray Marcus interview, November 6, 2001.

81. 2001 study: "Study Backs Theory of 'Grassy Knoll,'" by George Lardner, Jr., *The Washington Post,* March 26, 2001, and "Echo correlation analysis and the acoustic evidence in the Kennedy assassination revisited," by D.B. Thomas, *Science and Justice,* 2001, 41(1): 21-32.

82. The case for Zapruder-film alteration can be found in several books, including *Bloody Treason* by Noel Twyman, and *Assassination Science,* edited by Jim Fetzer. Quote: Ray

Marcus interview, September 20, 2000.

83. Ray Marcus interview, July 12, 2000.

84. Public Law 102-526 passes, Bush signs and Clinton appoints: *Final Report of the Assassination Records Review Board,* p. 7. JFK Act printed as Appendix C of ARRB's *Final Report,* pp. 183-195.

85. *Final Report of the Assassination Records Review Board.* Quote re: government secrecy: p. 1. Recommendations: pp. 169-176. Quote re: full disclosure: p. 7.

86. The FBI report, ARRB Document Number 124-10145-10036, was discovered by independent researcher Chris Courtwright, and describes the observations of one Roy Cooper. Cooper's account was nearly identical to that of Marvin Robinson, whose observations were recorded in an FBI report that later became ARRB Document Number 180-10111-10337. Cooper had driven behind Robinson, his boss, through Dealey Plaza shortly after the assassination. Both observed a man leave the TSBD, go to a waiting car driven by another man, and leave the area. Neither report was included in the Warren Commission's 26 volumes, and neither Cooper nor Robinson was called to testify before the Warren Commission.

87. COPA info: from COPA pamphlet, "A National Conference, October 20-22, 1995, Omni Shoreham Hotel, Washington, D.C."

88. Survey data obtained from Assassination Archives and Research Center. See also *USA Today,* November 22, 1993.

89. Doug Horne on Air Force One tapes: Speech to JFK Lancer conference, November 19, 1999, attended by author. Horne, a military records analyst on the Assassination Records Review Board, said he and other Board staff members tried, among other sources, the Air Force and the White House Communications Agency. "We didn't get anywhere," he said. "We even tried the paper trail at the LBJ Library. We thought, Well, if we can go to the LBJ Library, and see how they got their edited copy of the tape, we might be able to track down the originals." But it was a dead end. Horne later stated his belief that the original unedited tapes no longer exist.

90. Speech to Coalition on Political Assassinations, November 21, 1998. See also *False Mystery: an Anthology of Essays on the Assassination of President Kennedy*, by Vincent J. Salandria, p. 119, privately published, 1999.

91. Speech at American University, June 10, 1963, by John F. Kennedy. Complete text published in *The New York Times*, June 11, 1963, p. 16, and in *History Will Not Absolve Us*, pp. 41-49.

92. Speech to Coalition on Political Assassinations, November 21, 1998. See also *False Mystery: an Anthology of Essays on the Assassination of President Kennedy,* by Vincent J. Salandria, p. 119, privately published, 1999.

93. Speech to Coalition on Political Assassinations, November 21, 1998. See also *False Mystery: an Anthology of Essays on the Assassination of President Kennedy,* by Vincent J. Salandria, p. 119, privately published, 1999.

94. Mark Lane speech on grassy knoll, November 22, 1998, videotaped by author.

Appendix A – New Developments

1. Sixth Floor Museum at Dealey Plaza press release, February 19, 2007. The museum web site is at http://www.jfk.org.

2. Gary Mack to author, March 7, 2007.

3. *Ibid.*

4.   "We were very surprised…" Gary Mack to author, March 7, 2007. "The clearest, best film…" Associated Press, February 19, 2007.

5.   Ron Rosenbaum's assassination writing: see, for example, "Oswald's Ghost," in *Travels with Dr. Death and Other Unusual Investigations* (Viking, 1991). Bowers-Rosenbaum interview archived: http://link.brightcove.com/services/link/bcpid494808731/bctid525685864.

6.   Salandria wrote about Bennett in his early article "A Philadelphia Lawyer…" citing the Warren Report, p. 111. Clint Hill: WC Vol. II, p. 143.

7.   From a transcript of the Fonzi-Specter interview supplied to the author by Fonzi.

8.   "Specter made a fool…" Vince Salandria to author, March 6, 2007.

9.   Salandria quote: *The Philadelphia Inquirer,* January 6, 1967. Penn Jones quote: *Forgive My Grief,* Vol. III, pp. v-vi. Stamm quote: "On Viewing the Zapruder Film and Slides and the Nix and Muchmore Films of the Assassination of President Kennedy," by Stamm.

10. *The Camera Never Blinks,* by Dan Rather with Mickey Herskowitz (Ballantine, pp. 132-133).

11. A transcript and discussion of Rather's description may be found in *Pictures of the Pain,* by Richard B. Trask, pp. 85-90.

12. "Zapruder film of Kennedy shown at Shaw Trial," by Martin Waldron, *The New York Times,* February 14, 1969, p. 20.

13. Forgive My Grief, Vol. IV, p. 119.

14. "Honest error:" *Forgive My Grief,* Vol. IV, p. 175. "I challenge anyone..." *The Camera Never Blinks,* by Dan Rather with Mickey Herskowitz (Ballantine, p. 134).

15. Jones quote: *Forgive My Grief,* Vol. IV, p. 118. Rather quote: *The Camera Never Blinks,* p. 134.

16. Jones quote: *The Continuing Inquiry,* "Dan Rather Blinked," July 22, 1977.

17. This description of the Cooper film is based on a copy in the author's possession. Due to the film's curious history this description should not be considered definitive.

18. Associated Press dispatch, February 19, 2007.

19. Estimate of motorcade route spectators: AP dispatch, February 19, 2007.

20. *Pictures of the Pain,* by Richard Trask, Chapter 23, "Dallas Cinema Associates." Later, a much longer film entitled *Four Days in November,* was produced by Wolper Productions. Among its contributors was "Dallas Cinema Association." A relationship between this film and the DCA film seems obvious enough, but has not been confirmed.

21. Death of Shirley Martin: Steven Martin to author, October 15, 2006, and *The Tulsa World,* October 4, 2006.

22. Shirley Martin to author, October 17, 2000.

23. *Ibid.*

Bibliography

1.   Abt, John J., with Michael Myerson. *Advocate and Activist: Memoirs of an American Communist Lawyer.* Urbana and Chicago: University of Illinois Press, 1993.
2.   Abt, John J. *The People vs. McCarthyism: The Case Against the McCarran Act.* New York: Civil Rights Congress, 1953.
3.   Andrews, Bert. *Washington Witch Hunt.* New York: Random House, 1948.
4.   Assassination Records Review Board. *Final Report of the Assassination Records Review Board.* Washington, D.C.: Government Printing Office, 1998.
5.   Auerbach, Jerold S. *Labor and Liberty: The La Follette Committee and the New Deal.* Indianapolis and New York: Bobbs-Merrill, 1966.
6.   Barson, Michael. *Better Dead Than Red! A Nostalgic Look at the Golden Years of Russiaphobia, Red-Baiting, and Other Commie Madness.* New York: Hyperion, 1992.
7.   Belfrage, Sally. *Freedom Summer.* New York: Viking, 1965.
8.   Belli, Melvin M., with Maurice C. Carroll. *Dallas Justice: The Real Story of Jack Ruby and His Trial.* New York: David McKay, 1964.
9.   Belli, Melvin M., with Robert Blair Kaiser. *Melvin Belli: My Life On Trial.* New York: William Morrow, 1976.
10.   Benson, Michael. *Who's Who in the JFK Assassination.* New York: Citadel Press, 1993.
11.   Bernstein, Irving. *The Lean Years: A History of the American Worker, 1920-1933.* Boston: Hougton Mifflin, 1960.
12.   _____. *Turbulent Years. A History of the American Worker, 1933-1941.* Boston: Hougton Mifflin, 1969.
13.   _____. *A Caring Society. The New Deal, the Worker, and the Great Depression.* Boston: Hougton Mifflin, 1985.
14.   Bernstein, Walter. *Inside Out: A Memoir of the Blacklist.* New York: Knopf, 1996.
15.   Bethell, Tom. *The Electric Windmill: An Inadvertent Autobiography.* Washington, D.C.: Regnery Gateway, 1988.
16.   Bishop, Jim. *The Day Kennedy was Shot.* New York: Funk and Wagnall's, 1968.
17.   Bonazzi, Robert. *Man in the Mirror: John Howard Griffin and the Story of Black Like Me.* Maryknoll, New York: Orbis Books, 1997.
18.   Buchanan, Thomas G. *Who Killed Kennedy?* Two editions: 1) London: Secker & Warburg, 1964, and 2) New York: G.P. Putnam's Sons, 1964.
19.   Burner, Eric. *And Gently He Shall Lead Them: Robert Parris Moses and Civil Rights in Mississippi.* New York and London: New York University Press, 1994.
20.   Cagin, Seth, and Dray, Phillip. *We Are Not Afraid: The Story of Goodman, Schwerner, and Chaney and the Civil Rights Campaign for Mississippi.* New York: Macmillan, 1988.
21.   Carson, Clayborne; Garrow, David J. (eds). *Eyes on the Prize Civil Rights Reader: Documents, Speeches, and Firsthand Accounts from the Black Freedom Struggle.* New York: Penguin, 1991.
22.   Carter, III, Hodding. *The South Strikes Back.* Garden City, New York: Doubleday, 1959.
23.   Caute, David. *The Great Fear: The Anti-Communist Purge Under Truman and Eisenhower.* New York: Simon and Schuster, 1978.
24.   Clark, Ronald W. *The Life of Bertrand Russell.* New York: Knopf, 1976.
25.   Clausen, Henry C. and Lee, Bruce. Pearl Harbor: *Final Judgement.* Crown, 1992.

26. Clifford, Clark, with Richard Holbrooke. *Counsel to the President: A Memoir.* New York: Random House, 1991.

27. Colodny, Len and Gettlin, Robert. *Silent Coup: The Removal of a President.* New York: St. Martin's Press, 1991.

28. Cook, Fred J. *The FBI Nobody Knows.* New York: The Macmillan Company, 1964.

29. _____. *Maverick: Fifty Years of Investigative Reporting.* New York: G.P. Putnam's Sons, 1984.

30. Corry, John. *The Manchester Affair.* New York: G.P. Putnam's Sons, 1967.

31. Cottrell, Robert C. *Izzy: A Biography of I.F. Stone.* New Brunswick, New Jersey: Rutgers University Press, 1992.

32. Crawford, Curtis, *et al. Critical Reactions to the Warren Report* (anthology). New York: Marzani & Munsell. No publication date listed, probably 1964 or 1965.

33. Cray, Ed. *Chief Justice: A Biography of Earl Warren.* New York: Simon and Schuster, 1997.

34. Daniel, Bradford (ed). *The John Howard Griffin Reader.* Boston: Houghton Mifflin, 1968.

35. David, Jay (pseudonymous editor). *The Weight of the Evidence: The Warren Report and its Critics.* New York: Meredith Press, 1968.

36. Davis, Townsend. *Weary Feet, Rested Souls: A Guided History of the Civil Rights Movement.* New York: W.W. Norton, 1998.

37. Davy, William. *Let Justice Be Done: New Light on the Jim Garrison Investigation.* Reston, Virginia: Jordon Publishing, 1999.

38. Day, John F. *Bloody Ground.* Lexington, Kentucky: University Press of Kentucky, 1981. Originally published by Doubleday, Doran, 1941.

39. DiEugenio, James. *Destiny Betrayed: JFK, Cuba, and the Garrison Case.* New York: Sheridan Square Press, 1992.

40. Dos Passos, John. *The Best Times: An Informal Memoir.* New York: New American Library, 1966.

41. Durham, Michael S. *Powerful Days: The Civil Rights Photography of Charles Moore.* New York: Stewart, Tabori & Chang, 1991.

42. Elias, Robert H. *Theodore Dreiser: Apostle of Nature.* New York: Knopf, 1949.

43. *Encyclopedia Americana, International Edition,* Vol. 26. Danbury, Connecticut: Grolier, 1995.

44. Epstein, Edward Jay. *Inquest: The Warren Commission and the Establishment of Truth.* New York: Viking, 1966.

45. Fariello, Griffin. *Red Scare: Memories of the American Inquisition, an Oral History.* New York: W.W. Norton, 1995.

46. Fast, Howard. *Being Red: A Memoir.* Boston: Houghton Mifflin, 1990.

47. Fay, Jr., Paul B. *The Pleasure Of His Company.* New York, Evanston, and London: Harper and Row, 1966.

48. Fischel, Jack R. *Historical Dictionary of the Holocaust.* Lanham, Maryland, and London: Scarecrow Press, 1999.

49. Flammonde, Paris. *The Garrison Conspiracy: An Uncommissioned Report on the Jim Garrison Investigation.* New York: Meredith Press, 1969.

50. Flynn, Elizabeth Gurley. *The McCarran Act: Fact and Fancy.* (Pamphlet). New York: Gus Hall-Benjamin Davis Defense Committee. Exact publication date unknown; *ca.* 1961.

51. Foerstel, Herbert N. *Freedom of Information and the Right to Know: The Origins and Applications of the Freedom of Information Act.* Westport, Connecticut; London: Greenwood Press, 1999.

52. Fonzi, Gaeton. *The Last Investigation.* New York: Thunder's Mouth Press, 1993.

53. Ford, Gerald, with Stiles, John. *Portrait of the Assassin.* New York: Ballantine, 1966.

54. Fry, Varian. *Surrender On Demand.* Boulder, CO: Johnson Books, 1997. Originally published by Random House in 1945.

55. Garrison, Jim. *On the Trail of the Assassins: My Investigation and Prosecution of the Murder of President Kennedy.* New York: Sheridan Square Press, 1988.

56. Goodhart, Arthur L., *et al.* "Symposium on the Warren Commission Report." *New York University Law Review,* Vol. 40, No. 3. May 1965.

57. Green, George Norris. *The Establishment in Texas Politics: The Primitive Years, 1938-1957.* Westport, Connecticut and London, England: Greenwood Press, 1979.

58. Griffin, John Howard. *Black Like Me.* New York: Signet, 35th Anniversary Edition, 1996; and San Antonio: Wings Press (definitive edition), 2004.

59. Griffin, John Howard, and Freedman, Theodore. *Mansfield, Texas: Report of the Crisis Situation Resulting from Efforts to Desegregate the School System.* New York: Anti-Defamation League of B'nai Brith, 1956.

60. Groden, Robert J. *The Killing of a President.* New York: Penguin, 1993.

61. _____. *The Search for Lee Harvey Oswald.* New York: Penguin, 1995.

62. Gun, Nerin E. *Red Roses from Texas.* London: Frederick Muller Limited, 1964.

63. Haber, William (ed). *Labor in a Changing America.* New York: Basic Books, 1966.

64. Habe, Hans. *The Wounded Land: Journey Through a Divided America.* New York: Coward-McCann, 1964.

65. Hane, Mikiso. *Modern Japan: A Historical Survey.* Boulder, CO: Westview Press, 1992. (Earlier version published by Charles Scribner's Sons, 1972.)

66. Harman, Willis and Rheingold, Howard. *Higher Creativity: Liberating the Unconscious for Breakthrough Insights.* New York: Jeremy P. Tarcher/Putnam, 1984.

67. Hampton, Henry and Fayer, Steve, eds. *Voice of Freedom: An Oral History of the Civil Rights Movement from the 1950s through the 1980s.* New York: Bantam, 1990.

68. Hevener, John W. *Which Side Are You On? The Harlan County Coal Miners, 1931-39.* Urbana: University of Illinois Press, 1978.

69. Hinckle, Warren. *If You Have a Lemon, Make Lemonade.* New York: Bantam, 1973.

70. Hohenberg, John. *The Pulitzer Prizes: A History of the Awards in Books, Drama, Music, and Journalism, Based on the Private Files over Six Decades.* New York and London: Columbia University Press, 1974.

71. Herron, Matt, *et al. The Voyage of the Aquarius.* New York: Saturday Review Press/Dutton, 1974.

72. Hoover, John Edgar. *Federal Bureau of Investigation, United States Department of Justice. Investigation of Assassination of President John F. Kennedy.* Uncredited facsimile version.

73. _____. *Investigation of Assassination of President John F. Kennedy.* Supplemental Report. January 13, 1964. Uncredited facsimile version.

74. Huie, William Bradford. *Three Lives for Mississippi.* New York: WCC Books, 1965.

75. Hulbert, Ann. *The Interior Castle.* New York: Knopf, 1992.

76. Hurt, Henry. *Reasonable Doubt: An Investigation into the Assassination of John F. Kennedy.* New York: Henry Holt, 1985.

77. Israel, Lee. *Kilgallen: An Intimate Biography of Dorothy Kilgallen.* New York: Dell, 1980.

78. James, Rosemary, and Wardlaw, Jack. *Plot or Politics? The Garrison Case and its Cast.* New Orleans: Pelican, 1967.

79. Jansen, Donald, and Eismann, Bernard. *The Far Right.* New York: McGraw Hill, 1963.

80. Joesten, Joachim. *Oswald: Assassin or Fall Guy?* New York: Marzani & Munsell, 1964.

81. _____. *The Gaps in the Warren Report.* New York: Marzani & Munsell, 1964.

82. Jones, Penn. *Forgive My Grief,* Vols. I-IV. Midlothian, TX: *Midlothian Mirror,* 1966, 1967, 1969, 1974.

83. _____. *The Windmill Fighter.* Unpublished manuscript, 1962.

84. Jones, Ernest. *The Life and Work of Sigmund Freud,* Vol. III. New York: Basic Books, 1957.

85. Kantor, Seth. *The Ruby Cover-Up.* Originally titled *Who Was Jack Ruby?* New York: Zebra Books, Kensington Publishing, 1978.

86. Kennedy, Robert F. *Thirteen Days: A Memoir of the Cuban Missile Crisis.* New York and London: W.W. Norton, 1968.

87. Kirkwood, James. *American Grotesque: An Account of the Clay Shaw-Jim Garrison affair in the city of New Orleans.* New York: Simon and Schuster, 1970.

88. Krock, Arthur. *Memoirs: Sixty Years on the Firing Line.* New York: Funk & Wagnalls, 1968.

89. Kunstler, William M. *My Life as a Radical Lawyer.* New York: Birch Lane Press, 1994.

90. La Follette, Robert M., *et al. Oppressive Labor Practices Act. Hearings before a Subcommittee of the Committee on Education and Labor, United States Senate,* Seventy Sixth Congress, First Session on S. 1970. Washington, D.C.: Government Printing Office, 1939. (Microfische copy, University of Colorado, Norlin Library, Boulder, CO.)

91. Lane, Mark. *A Citizen's Dissent.* New York: Holt, Rinehart and Winston, 1968.

92. _____. *Plausible Denial.* New York: Thunder's Mouth Press, 1991.

93. _____. *Rush to Judgment.* New York: Holt, Rinehart and Winston, 1966.

94. Latham, Earl. *The Communist Controversy in Washington: From the New Deal to McCarthy.* Cambridge: Harvard University Press, 1966.

95. Levine, Ellen. *Freedom's Children: Young Civil Rights Activists Tell Their Own Stories.* New York: G.P. Putnam's Sons, 1993.

96. Levy, Steven. *The Unicorn's Secret. Murder in the Age of Aquarius.* New York: Prentice Hall, 1988.

97. Lewis, Richard Warren, and Schiller, Lawrence. *The Scavengers and Critics of the Warren Report.* New York: Delacorte Press, 1967.

98. Lifton, David. *Best Evidence.* New York: Carroll & Graf, 1988.

99. _____, ed. *Document Addendum to the Warren Report.* El Segundo, CA: Sightext Publications, 1968.

100. Lingeman, Richard. *Theodore Dreiser: An American Journey, 1908-1945.* New York: G.P. Putnam's Sons, 1990.

101. Lomax, Louis, *et al. Mississippi Eyewitness: The Three Civil Rights Workers – How They were Murdered.* A special issue of *Ramparts* magazine. San Francisco: Layman's Press, 1964.

102. Ludington, Townsend. *John Dos Passos: A Twentieth Century Odyssey.* New York: E.P. Dutton, 1980.

103. Lynd, Staughton. *Living Inside Our Hope: A Steadfast Radical's Thoughts on Rebuilding the Movement.* Ithaca and London: ILR Press, 1997.

104. Malcolm, Janet. *The Journalist and the Murderer.* New York: Knopf, 1990.

105. Maney, Patrick J. *"Young Bob" La Follette: A Biography of Robert M. La Follette, Jr., 1895-1953.* Columbia and London: University of Missouri Press, 1978.

106. Marcus, Raymond. *Addendum B: Addendum to The HSCA, The Zapruder Film, and the Single Bullet Theory.* Privately published, 1995.

107. _____. *The Bastard Bullet: A Search for Legitimacy for Commission Exhibit 399.* Privately published, 1966.

108. _____. *The HSCA, The Zapruder Film, and the Single Bullet Theory.* Privately published, 1992.

109. _____. *Orleans Parish Grand Jury Special Investigation.* Privately published, 1998.

110. _____. *#5 Man, November 22, 1963.* Privately published, 1997.

111. Marrus, Michael R., and Paxton, Robert O. *Vichy France and the Jews.* New York: Schocken Books, 1983.

112. Mars, Florence, with Lynn Eden. *Witness in Philadelphia.* Baton Rouge and London: Louisiana State University Press, 1977.

113. Marzani, Carl. *Education of a Reluctant Radical,* Book One, "Roman Childhood." New York: Topical Books, 1992.

114. _____. *Education of a Reluctant Radical,* Book Two, "Growing Up American." New York: Topical Books, 1993.

115. _____. *Education of a Reluctant Radical,* Book Three, "Spain, Munich, and Dying Empires." New York: Topical Books, 1994.

116. _____. *Education of a Reluctant Radical,* Book Four, "From Pentagon to Penitentiary." New York: Topical Books, 1995.

117. _____. *Education of a Reluctant Radical,* Book Five, "Reconstruction." New York: Topical Books, 2001.

118. _____. *We Can Be Friends.* New York: Topical Books, 1952.

119. Matthiessen, F.O. *Theodore Dreiser.* William Sloane, 1951.

120. McAdam, Doug. *Freedom Summer.* New York, Oxford: Oxford University Press, 1988.

121. McAleer, John. *Rex Stout: A Biography.* Boston-Toronto: Little, Brown, 1977.

122. McMillen, Neil R. *The Citizens' Council: Organized Resistance to the Second Reconstruction, 1954-64.* Urbana: University of Illinois Press, 1971.

123. McWilliams, Carey. *The Education of Carey McWilliams.* New York: Simon and Schuster, 1978.

124. Meagher, Sylvia. *Accessories After the Fact.* New York: Vintage Books, 1992. Originally published by Bobbs-Merrill, 1967.

125. _____. *Subject Index to the Warren Report and Hearings & Exhibits.* New York and London: Scarecrow Press, 1966.

126. Meisler, Stanley. *United Nations: The First Fifty Years.* New York: Atlantic Monthly Press, 1995.

127. Mellen, Joan. *A Farewell to Justice: Jim Garrison, JFK's Assassination, and the Case That Should Have Changed History.* Washington, D.C.: Potomac Books, 2005.

128. Mills, Nicolaus. *Like a Holy Crusade: Mississippi 1964 – The Turning of the Civil Rights Movement in America.* Chicago: Ivan R. Dee, 1992.

129. Murphy, Bruce Allen. *Fortas: The Rise and Ruin of a Supreme Court Justice.* New York: William Morrow, 1988.

130. Murray, Robert K. *Red Scare: A Study in National Hysteria, 1919-1920.* Minneapolis: University of Minnesota Press, 1955.

131. Nachman, Gerald. *Seriously Funny: The Rebel Comedians of the 1950s and 1960s.* New York: Pantheon, 2003.

132. Nash, H.C. *Citizen's Arrest: The Dissent of Penn Jones, Jr., in the Assassination of JFK.* Austin: Latitudes Press, 1977.

133. National Committee for the Defense of Political Prisoners (Theodore Dreiser, *et al*). *Harlan Miners Speak: Report on Terrorism in the Kentucky Coal Fields.* New York: Harcourt, Brace, 1932.

134. National Committee for the Repeal of the McCarran Act. *What You Need to Know About the McCarran Act.* Chicago: National Committee for the Repeal of the McCarran Act, *ca.* 1963.

135. *New American Desktop Encyclopedia,* 4th ed. New York: Signet, 1997.

136. *New Encyclopædia Britannica,* Vol. 11. Chicago, et al: Encyclopædia Britannica, 1998.

137. Newman, Albert H. *The Assassination of John F. Kennedy: The Reasons Why.* New York: Clarkson N. Potter, 1970.

138. O'Neill, Thomas ("Tip") with Novak, William. *Man of the House: The Life and Political Memoirs of Speaker Tip O'Neill.* New York: St. Martin's Press, 1987.

139. Payne, Charles M. *I've Got the Light of Freedom: The Organizing Tradition and the Mississippi Freedom Struggle.* Berkeley and Los Angeles: University of California Press, 1995.

140. Pelling, Henry. *American Labor.* Chicago: University of Chicago Press, 1960.

141. Pollock, Jack Harrison. *Earl Warren: The Judge Who Changed America.* Englewood Cliffs: Prentice-Hall, 1979.

142. Popkin, Richard H. *The Second Oswald: A Startling Alternative to the Single Assassin Theory of the Warren Commission Report.* New York: Avon, 1966.

143. Posell, Elsa Z. *Russian Composers.* Boston: Houghton Mifflin, 1967.

144. Powers, Thomas. *The Man Who Kept the Secrets: Richard Helms and the CIA.* New York: Pocket Books, 1979.

145. Prange, Gordon W., with Goldstein, Donald M., and Dillon, Katherine V. *Pearl Harbor: The Verdict of History.* New York: Penguin, 1986.

146. Randall, Herbert (Photography). *Faces of Freedom Summer.* Text by Bobs M. Tusa. Tuscaloosa and London: University of Alabama Press, 2001.

147. Raines, Howell. *My Soul is Rested: Movement Days in the Deep South Remembered.* New York: Penguin, 1983. First published (minus index) by G.P. Putnam's Sons, 1977.

148. Rather, Dan. With Herskowitz, Mickey. *The Camera Never Blinks: Adventures of a TV Journalist.* New York: Ballantine, 1977.

149. Reeves, Thomas C. *The Life and Times of Joe McCarthy.* New York: Stein and Day, 1982.

150. Renshaw, Patrick. *The Wobblies: The Story of Syndicalism in the United States.* New York: Doubleday, 1967.

151. Riches, William T. Martin. *The Civil Rights Movement: Struggle and Resistance.* New York: St. Martin's Press, 1997.

152. Roberts, David. *Jean Stafford: A Biography.* Little, Brown, 1988.

153. Russell, Dick. *The Man Who Knew Too Much.* New York: Carroll and Graf, 1992.

154. Rutkoff, Peter M., and Scott, William B. *New School: A History of the New School for Social Research.* New York: The Free Press; London: Collier-Macmillan, 1986.

155. Sahl, Mort. *Heartland.* New York and London: Harcourt Brace Jovanovich, 1976.

156. Salandria, Vincent J. *False Mystery: An Anthology of Essays on the Assassination of President Kennedy.* Boulder, CO: privately published, 1999.

157. Salinger, Pierre. *With Kennedy.* New York: Doubleday, 1966.

158. Sauvage, Léo. *The Oswald Affair: An Examination of the Contradictions and Omissions of the Warren Report.* Cleveland and New York: World Publishing, 1966. Originally published in France by Les Editions de Minuit, Paris, 1965.

159. Schlesinger, Arthur M. Jr. *Robert Kennedy And His Times.* New York: Ballantine, 1978, 1985.

160. _____. *A Thousand Days: John F. Kennedy in the White House,* 2 vols. Boston:

Houghton Mifflin; Cambridge: The Riverside Press, 1965.

161. Schotz, E. Martin. *History Will Not Absolve Us.* Brookline, MA: Kurtz, Ulmer, & DeLucia, 1996.

162. Scott, Peter Dale, Hoch, Paul L., and Stetler, Russell (eds). *The Assassinations: Dallas and Beyond. A Guide to Cover-Ups and Investigations.* New York: Vintage, 1976.

163. Scott, William E. *November 22, 1963. A Reference Guide to the JFK Assassination.* Lanham, New York, Oxford: University Press of America, 1999.

164. Seldes, George. *Never Tire of Protesting.* New York: Lyle Stuart, 1968.

165. _____. *Witness To a Century. Encounters with the Noted, the Notorious, and Three SOBs.* New York: Ballantine, 1978.

166. Sellers, Cleveland, with Robert Terrell. *The River of No Return: The Autobiography of a Black Militant and the Life and Death of SNCC.* New York: William Morrow, 1973.

167. Seymour-Smith, Martin. *Who's Who in Twentieth Century Literature.* New York: Holt, Rinehart and Winston, 1976.

168. Sitkoff, Harvard. *The Struggle for Black Equality.* New York: Hill and Wang/Noonday Press, 1993.

169. Specter, Arlen. With Charles Robbins. *Passion for Truth: From Finding JFK's Single Bullet to Questioning Anita Hill to Impeaching Bill Clinton.* New York: HarperCollins, 2000.

170. Stafford, Jean. *A Mother in History.* New York: Farrar, Straus and Giroux, 1966.

171. Steinberg, Peter L. *The Great "Red Menace."* Westport, CT, and London: Greenwood Press, 1984.

172. Stinnet, Robert B. *Day of Deceit.* New York: The Free Press, 2000.

173. Stone, I.F. *In A Time of Torment, 1961-1967: A Nonconformist History Of Our Times.* Boston, Toronto, London: Little, Brown, 1989.

174. Stout, Rex. *The Doorbell Rang.* New York: Viking, 1965.

175. Strober, Gerald S. and Deborah H. *Let Us Begin Anew.* New York: HarperCollins, 1993.

176. Summers, Anthony. *Conspiracy.* New York: Paragon House. First published by McGraw-Hill, 1980.

177. Thompson, Josiah. *Six Seconds in Dallas: A Microstudy of the Kennedy Assassination.* New York: Bernard Geis Associates, 1967.

178. Toland, John. *Infamy: Pearl Harbor and its Aftermath.* New York: Berkley Books, 1983.

179. Trask, Richard B. *Pictures of the Pain: Photography and the Assassination of President Kennedy.* Danford, MA: Yeoman Press, 1994.

180. Uncredited anthology. *The Assassination Story: Newspaper clippings from the two Dallas dailies, The Dallas Morning News, November 23-December 11, 1963, The Dallas Times-Herald, November 22-December 10, 1963*, privately published.

181. Untermeyer, Louis (ed). *A Concise Treasury of Great Poems, English and American.* New York: Simon and Schuster, 1942.

182. House of Representatives. *Investigation of the Assassination of President John F. Kennedy.* Appendix to Hearings Before the Select Committee on Assassinations of the U.S. House of Representatives, Ninety-fifth Congress, Second Session. Twelve volumes. U.S. Government Printing Office, 1979.

183. _____. *Report of the Select Committee on Assassinations*, U.S. House of Representatives, Ninety-fifth Congress, Second Session. U.S. Government Printing Office, 1979.

184. Wallechinsky, David. *The Complete Book of the Olympics.* New York: Viking, 1984.

185. Walsh, Mary Ellen Williams. *Jean Stafford.* Boston: Twayne Publishing, 1985.

186. Walton, Richard J. *Henry Wallace, Harry Truman, and the Cold War.* New York: Viking, 1976.

187. Warren, Earl. *The Memoirs of Earl Warren.* Garden City, New York: Doubleday, 1977.

188. Warren, Earl, *et al. Hearings Before the President's Commission on the Assassination of President Kennedy.* 26 Volumes. Washington, D.C.: Government Printing Office, 1964.

189. _____. *Report of the President's Commission on the Assassination of President Kennedy.* Washington, D.C.: Government Printing Office, 1964.

190. Watson, Mary Ann. *The Expanding Vista: American Television in the Kennedy Years.* New York, Oxford: Oxford University Press, 1990.

191. Wecht, Cyril, with Mark Curriden and Benjamin Wecht. *Cause of Death: The Shocking True Stories Behind the Headlines – A Medical Expert Speaks Out on JFK, RFK, Elvis, Chappaquiddick, and other Controversial Cases.* New York: Penguin, 1993, 1994.

192. Weisberg, Harold. *Case Open: The Omissions, Distortions and Falsifications of Case Closed.* New York: Carroll & Graff, 1994.

193. _____. *Never Again!* New York: Carroll and Graff, 1995.

194. _____. *Oswald in New Orleans: Case for Conspiracy with the CIA.* New York: Canyon Books, 1967.

195. _____. *Photographic Whitewash: Suppressed Kennedy Assassination Pictures.* Frederick, MD: Harold Weisberg, publisher, 1967.

196. _____. *Post Mortem. JFK Coverup Smashed.* Frederick, MD: Harold Weisberg, publisher, 1975.

197. _____. *Whitewash: The Report on the Warren Report.* New York: Dell, 1966. Originally published in 1965.

198. _____. *Whitewash II: The FBI-Secret Service Coverup.* Frederick, MD: Harold Weisberg, publisher, 1966.

199. _____. *Whitewash IV: JFK Assassination Transcript.* Frederick, MD: Harold Weisberg, publisher, 1974.

200. Weisbrot, Robert. *Freedom Bound: A History of America's Civil Rights Movement.* New York: W.W. Norton, 1990.

201. White, G. Edward. *Earl Warren: A Public Life.* New York and Oxford: Oxford University Press, 1982.

202. White, Stephen. *Should We Now Believe the Warren Report?* New York: Macmillan, 1968.

203. White, Theodore. *The Making of the President, 1960.* New York: Atheneum, 1964.

204. _____. *The Making of the President, 1964.* New York: Atheneum, 1965.

205. Williams, Selma R. *Red-Listed: Haunted by the Washington Witch Hunt.* Reading, MA, Menlo Park, CA, etc.: Addison-Wesley, 1993.

206. Wrone, David R. *The Zapruder Film: Reframing JFK's Assassination.* Lawrence, KS: University Press of Kansas, 2003.

207. Wyman, David S. *The Abandonment of the Jews: America and the Holocaust, 1941-1945.* New York: Pantheon, 1984.

208. *World Almanac and Book of Facts,* 1999. Mahwah, NJ: World Almanac Books, 1998.

209. Wreszin, Michael (ed). *A Moral Temper: The Letters of Dwight Macdonald.* Chicago: Ivan R. Dee, 2001.

210. _____. *A Rebel in Defense of Tradition: The Life and Politics of Dwight Macdonald.* New York: Basic Books, 1994.

211. Zelizer, Barbie. *Covering the Body: The Kennedy Assassination, the Media, and the Shaping of Collective Memory.* Chicago and London: University of Chicago Press, 1992.

212. Ziegler, David W. *War, Peace, and International Politics*, 2nd ed. Boston and Toronto: Little, Brown, 1977.

Sources

The following individuals granted the author one or more interviews.

1. Robert Bonazzi
2. Roger Feinman
3. Fred Feldman
4. Irma (Immie) Feldman
5. Mary Ferrell
6. Gwen Field
7. Gaeton Fonzi
8. Matt Herron
9. Michael Jones
10. The Hon. Theodore R. Kupferman
11. Mark Lane
12. David Lifton
13. Joseph Lobenthal
14. Staughton Lynd
15. Raymond Marcus
16. Shirley Martin
17. Steve Martin
18. Teresa Martin
19. Tony Marzani
20. H.C. Nash
21. Jerry Policoff
22. Vincent J. Salandria
23. Gary Schoener
24. Ralph Schoenman
25. Pierre Sauvage
26. Josiah Thompson
27. Harold Weisberg

Archives

The following archives were accessed by the author.

1. Special Collections and Archives of the Beneficial-Hodson Library, Hood College, Frederick, Maryland. The papers of Harold Weisberg, Sylvia Meagher, and Raymond J. Marcus are housed here.
2. The papers of Vincent J. Salandria.
3. The papers of Léo Sauvage.
4. The papers of Harold Feldman.
5. The papers of Marjorie C. (Maggie) Field.
6. The papers of Joseph Lobenthal.
7. The Texas/Dallas History and Archives at the Dallas Public Library, Dallas, Texas.
8. *The Midlothian Mirror.*
9. The National Archives and Records Administration, College Park, Maryland.

Additionally, the author made extensive use of the Norlin Library at the University of Colorado in Boulder; the Boulder, Colorado Public Library; and the Donald C. Davidson Library at the University of California, Santa Barbara.

Index

About the Author

Born in Rockford, Illinois, John Kelin grew up mostly in Michigan. He worked for several years in public radio at WEMU-FM in Ypsilanti, then moved to the news department at WXYZ-TV in Detroit. In 1991, Kelin began working as a technical writer at Sun Microsystems in San Francisco. Shortly thereafter, Kelin and his family moved to Colorado, where they remain.

John Kelin was seven years old when President Kennedy was assassinated, and that event remains his earliest clear memory in life. His present interest in the assassination and the first-generation critics dates to 1976 when he attended a lecture by Mark Lane, now one of the subjects of *Praise from a Future Generation*. Kelin co-founded *Fair Play* magazine in 1994 on the then-fledgling World Wide Web. *Fair Play* was the first of what by now are many JFK-oriented sites. As the magazine's publisher and editor, he presented the work of many Kennedy assassination researchers and writers, including Christopher Sharrett, James W. Douglass, and Joan Mellen, as well as his own work, including a 1999 interview with Kerry McCarthy, a cousin of John F. Kennedy.

In 1998 Kelin met Vince Salandria at a JFK conference in Dallas. Salandria gave Kelin complete access to his assassination-related correspondence from the 1960s, which began the research that led to *Praise from a Future Generation*. Kelin's assassination writing has also appeared in *The Kennedy Assassination Chronicles*. In 1999 he edited *False Mystery*, a collection of Salandria's early Warren Commission criticism. That same year Kelin was a recipient of JFK Lancer's "New Frontier" award. He has been listed in several editions of the *Master Researcher Directory*.

Wings Press was founded in 1975 by Joanie Whitebird and Joseph F. Lomax, both deceased, as "an informal association of artists and cultural mythologists dedicated to the preservation of the literature of the nation of Texas." The publisher/editor since 1995, Bryce Milligan is honored to carry on and expand that mission to include the finest in American writing, without commercial considerations clouding the choice to publish or not to publish. Technically a "for profit" press, Wings receives only occasional underwriting from individuals and institutions who wish to support our vision. For this we are very grateful.

Wings Press attempts to produce multicultural books, chapbooks, CDs, DVDs and broadsides that, we hope, enlighten the human spirit and enliven the mind. Everyone ever associated with Wings has been or is a writer, and we know well that writing is a transformational art form capable of changing the world, primarily by allowing us to glimpse something of each other's souls. Good writing is innovative, insightful, and interesting. But most of all it is honest.

Likewise, Wings Press is committed to treating the planet itself as a partner. Thus the press uses as much recycled material as possible, from the paper on which the books are printed to the boxes in which they are shipped.

Associate editor Robert Bonazzi is also an old hand in the small press world. Bonazzi was the editor / publisher of Latitudes Press (1966-2000). Bonazzi and Milligan share a commitment to independent publishing and have collaborated on numerous projects over the past 25 years. As Robert Dana wrote in *Against the Grain*, "Small press publishing is personal publishing. In essence, it is a matter of personal vision, personal taste and courage, and personal friendships."

Welcome to our world.

Colophon

This first edition of *Praise from a Future Generation*, by John Kelin, has been printed on 60 pound non-acidic paper containing fifty percent recycled fiber. Titles have been set using Cochin type; the text in Caslon. Wings Press books are designed by Bryce Milligan.

Wings Press
www.wingspress.com
All Wings Press titles are distributed to the trade by
Independent Publishers Group
www.ipgbook.com